HELL TO PAY

HELL TO PAY

Operation Downfall and the
Invasion of Japan, 1945–1947

D. M. Giangreco

NAVAL INSTITUTE PRESS
Annapolis, Maryland

This book has been brought to publication with the generous assistance of Edward S. and Joyce I. Miller.

Naval Institute Press
291 Wood Road
Annapolis, MD 21402

Library of Congress Cataloging-in-Publication Data

Giangreco, D. M., 1952-
  Hell to pay: Operation Downfall and the invasion of Japan, 1945–1947 / D.M. Giangreco.
      p. cm.
  Includes bibliographical references and index.
  ISBN 978-1-59114-316-1 (alk. paper)
  1. Operation Downfall, 1945-1946. 2. World War, 1939-1945–Campaigns–Japan.
  3. United States–Armed Forces–History–World War, 1939-1945. I. Title.
D767.2.G53 2009
940.54'252--dc22

                                                                                    2009027766

Printed in the United States of America on acid-free paper ∞

14 13 12 11 10 09   9 8 7 6 5 4 3 2

Contents

List of Illustrations   vii
Foreword: "Three Colonels" by Stanley Weintraub   ix
Preface and Acknowledgments   xiii

Chapter 1   The Maximum "Bloodletting and Delay"   1
Chapter 2   Spinning the Casualties   8
Chapter 3   The First Army and Kwantung Redeployments   18
Chapter 4   The Pacific Build-up and Berlin Decision   28
Chapter 5   "Not a Recipe for Victory"   37
Chapter 6   The Decision   49
Chapter 7   Japanese Defense Plans   61
Chapter 8   "Victory Might Be Salvaged"   76
Chapter 9   The "Manpower Box"   92
Chapter 10   Mistakes and Misperceptions   102
Chapter 11   What Is Defeat?   114
Chapter 12   The Amphibious Operation   125
Chapter 13   On the Ground   141
Chapter 14   Unexamined Factors   156
Chapter 15   A "Target-Rich Environment"   167
Chapter 16   Half a Million Purple Hearts   187
Chapter 17   "Punishment from Heaven"   194

Appendix A   G-2 Estimate of Enemy Situation on Kyushu, U.S. Sixth Army,
              August 1, 1945   205
Appendix B   G-2 Analysis of Japanese Plans for the Defense of Kyushu, U.S.
              Sixth Army, December 31, 1945   246
Appendix C   Proclamation Defining Terms for Japanese Surrender Issued at
              Potsdam, July 26, 1945 (Potsdam Declaration)   276
Appendix D   Extract from a Letter Written by James Michener,
              October 20, 1995   278
Notes   280
Index   349

Illustrations

PHOTOGRAPHS

The SS *Queen Elizabeth* arrives in the Port of New York on June 29, 1945. 29

A wing of the Takatsuki Dump near Osaka. 66

The king-sized USS *Midway*. 81

Combat experience in the Pacific. 103

Postwar U.S. Army Signal Corps photo of Japanese nationals praying over the charred remains of their countrymen. 122

Japanese midget submarines at the Kure naval base. 130

The Yokosuka K4Y1 Training Seaplane; the Kawanishi E7K "Alf" Reconnaissance Seaplane. 136

The skeletal remains of a Filipino or American soldier. 142

Coastal terrain typical of southern Kyushu. 144

Highly defensible terraced rice fields. 152

Sugar Loaf on Okinawa, an unimposing little hill. 152

Japanese illustration of a "flanking gun emplacement" overlooking Sagami Bay. 170

Even when rice paddies are as ostensibly dry as this one is, they present formidable barriers. 172

Some rice fields stretched almost unbroken for dozens of miles up Kyushu's valleys. 172

The Mark 97 20-mm rapid-fire antitank rifle. 180

A mountain village in central Honshu. 183

American ships ride peacefully at anchor below Mount Fuji. 184

War Department pamphlet distributed to Army and Army Air Force personnel in May and June 1945. 198

MAPS

The component operations of Operation Downfall.   39
The disposition of forces on Kyushu, August 1945.   46
Defense plan of Japan's 12th Area Army, August 1945.   68
The defense plan of Japan's 16th Area Army, August 1945.   72
Provisional landing force fighter defense for Operation Olympic.   84
The assault plan for Operation Olympic.   129
Japanese dispositions in southeast Kyushu and landing beaches.   146
Japanese dispositions in southwest Kyushu and landing beaches.   148
The assault plan for Operation Coronet.   168
Effect of rice land, natural, and artificial flooding on cross-country movement
    on the Kanto Plain.   173
The schematic layout for the Ironhorse artificial harbor, Operation Coronet.   178

Foreword: "Three Colonels"

BY STANLEY WEINTRAUB

From what we learned in the last days and the aftermath of the two-hemisphere world war that closed with the collapse of Nazi Germany and Imperial Japan, we know what the world would have been like had we been unwilling to pay the price to defeat them. Yet as the war dragged on beyond Europe and the casualties escalated, and as some combat veterans began returning while others now never would, the home front was becoming less willing. The public began to lean toward militarily unthinkable negotiation, while encouraging Japan's submission by air and sea power, avoiding the heavy costs of invasion.

In 1945, during the intense final months of World War II, the price of victory was being calculated and its extent determined by three men who, in 1918, had been in uniform in France. One was a Missouri National Guard captain whose 35th Division, in the six days of the culminating Meuse-Argonne offensive, had suffered nearly 7,300 casualties, half its front-line strength. In the interwar years, even before he went to Washington as a senator, Harry Truman rose to Reserve colonel. In wartime he made a sterling reputation heading the U.S. Senate investigating committee on military spending effectiveness. Truman was now president, succeeding Franklin D. Roosevelt, who had died suddenly in mid-April.

Another in the leadership trio who once bore the "bird" on his shoulders was the now-elderly Secretary of War Henry Stimson, who was once an artillery officer and twice a Cabinet member, with War and State Department portfolios under earlier, Republican administrations, and who still preferred being called "Colonel." The third had been a colonel and on the General Staff of the American Expeditionary Forces (during World War I). On his return to the States after the war he was meanly reduced to his prewar permanent rank of captain. On September 1, 1939, as war again broke out in Europe, George Marshall moved up, as Roosevelt's appointee, from the one star he had finally earned seventeen frustrating years after the army was drastically downsized, to an instant four stars as Army chief of staff.

Some of the major decisions closing the war with Germany and accelerating the down-fall of Imperial Japan were inherited by Truman. The feisty accidental president, who took pride in his Oval Office motto, "The buck stops here," had to make sweeping decisions advised and backed by Marshall and Stimson. Ironically the civilian-suited war secretary was more militarily tough-minded than his seemingly austere top general, who now wore his congressionally mandated super rank of five stars, but always, realistically, kept in mind public attitudes, industrial capacity, and logistical limitations. Winston Churchill, who called George Marshall "the architect of victory," was not being overly theatrical when he recalled that the British government, its fading imperial sway at stake, was pragmatically "resolved to share the agony . . . [of] the final and perhaps protracted slaughter."

D. M. Giangreco's striking title, *Hell to Pay*, represents the closing wartime dilemmas and the likely repercussions to their solutions. After ten years of violent aggrandizing in China, Japan had, in 1941, simultaneously and shockingly, attacked four nations over a seventh of the earth's surface. Defeating the sprawling Japanese empire had required fiscal fortitude, technological breakthroughs, immense transfers of men and materiel across two oceans, and continuing evaluation of the terrible human cost of the two stage invasion of Japan building up on the Pacific Rim—Operation Downfall. To pacify a fickle electorate believing that a war half-won only required half-mobilization the rest of the way, the American military establishment, at odds with its needs, began sending some seasoned veterans home even as Nazi Germany imploded into chaos.

The complex conditions perceived by both Japanese and American decision makers, and the difficult assessments made at the time, require, in *Hell to Pay*, the portrayal of vast arrays of numbers. In few books about any subject other than astrophysics are figures more provocative—and more persuasive. Giangreco turns number crunching into high drama. The clouds of supporting aircraft assembled, from the Marianas and the Philippines to Iwo Jima, Okinawa, and dozens of fleet carriers, ran into five figures, so many that they hazarded getting in each other's flight paths. The assault shipping (four thousand oceangoing vessels alone) being gathered, and troops committed for the Kyushu landings planned for late October 1945, far exceeded D-day in Normandy (to face a Japanese buildup that by the time of their surrender totaled nearly 917,000 troops on the island). The coordination of landings in predawn darkness and in the fog of smoke screens risked a nightmare of swampings, collisions, objectives gone awry, and deadly friendly fire. The Japanese intended— conceding extraordinary losses—to inflict 20 percent casualties before any GI set foot on the beaches and further carnage thereafter during "the inexorable grind of daily close-in battle conducted at the distance that a man can throw a grenade."

The long-lived and much-quoted canard that estimates of horrific casualties during an invasion of Japan were postwar apologetics for the Bomb is set aside here by Giangreco, an indefatigable and precise military historian, in clubs, diamonds, hearts, and spades. The "frightful dimensions" of putting Allied boots on the ground on Kyushu and Honshu are spelled out from both Japanese and American planning documents and the recollections of participants on both sides. The consequences could be projected. On and adjacent to Okinawa, an island only sixty miles long and a third as wide, 13,000 Americans died and 37,000 were wounded. Japanese deaths, including hapless Okinawan civilians, exceeded 142,000. The seas were crimson with corpses. Harry Truman told his assembled planners in a momentous White House conference, as the enormous casualty figures were still coming in, that he hoped to avoid the intolerable cost of another Okinawa, grotesquely magnified, "from one end of Japan to the other."

The Japanese military culture had, historically, long rejected surrender. Okinawa was not a worst-case scenario, it was a reality. The far more extensive killing ground of Japan was waiting to happen.

Although Japan's colonial empire was shrinking and its internal resources were dwindling, so was the American war enthusiasm generated by Pearl Harbor. A negotiated peace rather than overwhelming victory might, however, merely postpone, rather than preclude, another and more horrible war. The three former colonels all understood that likelihood from their experience in France in 1918 and beyond. That war had been won; only the peace was lost. Not an inch of German soil had been occupied when the Armistice was concluded, and the German flag continued to fly over an unoccupied Berlin. That anomaly had not happened again in Germany in May 1945 and could not be permitted by default in Japan.

But lengthy attrition was not in the American playbook. What Operation Downfall would cost was projected in the planning documents but only became concrete after the surrender. Here Giangreco lays it out by the numbers. After the war, for example, the Japanese in the Home Islands surrendered 28,428 "knee mortar" grenade launchers with 51,000,000 of their ballistic grenades. And contrary to popular belief, they had aviation fuel stockpiled for thousands of suicide planes and thousands of manned torpedoes and suicide craft in hiding. The Japanese could persevere under harsh conditions alien to Americans, as troops had already discovered in New Guinea and on Iwo Jima. The Japanese even counted on, as in their past history, punishing typhoons (or *kamikaze,* literally "divine wind") and torrential rain to disrupt and scatter the enemy, as actually would occur off Okinawa, in early September, the first full month of peace.

Throughout East Asia and the western Pacific, roughly 400,000 people, civilian and soldier, from their conquered territories in the Dutch East Indies to China and Manchuria and the Home Islands, died in *each* of the last months of the war, several times the terrible human cost of the two atomic strikes that shocked Emperor Hirohito into warning of the imminent nuclear destruction of the Japanese people. Nearly every Japanese city over 40,000 in population had already been laid waste by conventional bombing alone. Scorning Hirohito's unwillingness to intervene until catastrophe had come, one of his formerly respectful subjects composed a bitter *tanka*:

> While I read the Emperor's rescript that came too late,
> Atomic bomb victims writhe on the scorched ground.

The Japanese already knew about hell to pay, and relentlessly prepared to pay it, but the concept of surrender was new, and nuclear. And now overwhelming.

Stanley Weintraub is author of *Long Day's Journey into War: Pearl Harbor and a World at War, The Last Great Victory: The End of World War II,* and *15 Stars: Eisenhower, MacArthur, Marshall: Three Generals Who Saved the American Century.*

Preface and Acknowledgments

In the spring and summer of 1945, the United States and Imperial Japan were rushing pell-mell toward a confrontation of catastrophic proportions. World War II's sudden and unexpected conclusion after atom bombs were dropped on Hiroshima and Nagasaki masked the fact that the United States had already commenced the opening stages of Operation Downfall, a series of land invasions on the Japanese Home Islands that U.S. Army planners and senior leaders calculated would cost anywhere from 250,000 to 1 million American casualties during just the initial fighting.

The United States had entered the war "late," and because of its sheer distance from Europe and the western Pacific it did not begin to experience casualties comparable to those of the other belligerents until the conflict's final year. By then the U.S. Army alone was losing soldiers at a rate that Americans today would find astounding, suffering an average of 65,000 killed, wounded, and missing each and every month during the "casualty surge" of 1944–45, with the November, December, and January figures standing at 72,000, 88,000, and 79,000 respectively in postwar tabulations.

Most of these young men were lost battling the Nazis, but Secretary of War Henry Stimson warned the newly sworn-in president, Harry S. Truman, that because of the nature of the Japanese soldier and the terrain in the Home Islands, Americans would "have to go through a more bitter finish fight than in Germany." Gen. George C. Marshall, the Army chief of staff, agreed and told Truman, "It is a grim fact that there is not an easy, bloodless way to victory." By the time these words were spoken in June 1945, the United States was already several months into the steep increase in draft calls implemented under President Franklin D. Roosevelt to produce a 100,000-men-per-month "replacement stream" for Downfall's casualties.

Although details of the operation had been a closely guarded secret, the near doubling of Selective Service inductions was hardly something that could escape the notice of a war-weary citizenry and their representatives in Washington. In mid-January 1945, as part of the Roosevelt administration's effort to prepare the public for the ratcheting up of the draft that year, Marshall and Adm. Ernest J. King, the chief of naval operations, spelled out in a joint letter to Congress what must be done to meet the needs for what was now a one-front war against Imperial Japan: "The Army must provide 600,000 replacements for overseas theaters by June 30, and, together with the Navy, will require a total of 900,000 inductions."

Despite its publication in many newspapers, including a page-one article in the January 18 *New York Times* ("Roosevelt Urges Work-or-Fight Bill to Back Offensives"), the Marshall-King letter remained completely invisible decades later during the controversy over the *Enola Gay* exhibit at the Smithsonian Institution's National Air And Space Museum (NASM). Not so the World War II veterans, who generated plenty of visibility when they firmly maintained that they had been told to expect half a million casualties. Said Robert P. Newman, one of the few academics to defend veterans' claims publicly, "Any account of this argument should acknowledge the basic accuracy of what veterans 'knew.'"

Newman's words, however, fell on deaf ears, for while the veterans had indeed made their presence felt politically, they had no evidence beyond Truman and Stimson's writings and their own memories of troop briefings conducted for the men during the partial demobilization that occurred after the victory over Nazi Germany. Displaying a marked inconsideration for the busy schedules of future historians, some yet to be born, the young soldiers of 1945 inexplicably failed to take detailed notes for the benefit of those scholars. The briefings, carried out worldwide—specifically at such diverse locations as the Pacific-bound U.S. First Army Headquarters in Weimar, Germany, the B-29 training bases in the southwestern United States, and the Pentagon itself—all utilized a uniform figure of 500,000 for expected casualties, somewhat lower than the figure that had been released to the press.

But while this "low" figure originated as purely an Army "public information" tool divorced from actual military planning, it nevertheless was widely disseminated to the troops themselves, and as anyone who followed the *Enola Gay* controversy can attest, its effect was pronounced and long term. Readers of this volume will gain an appreciation of how the casualty projections, created by a variety of different Army and War Department staffs for their own purposes and chains of command, were formed, connected, and used. They will see the scale of the estimates and what was briefed to the president before his meetings with British prime minister Winston Churchill and Soviet premier Joseph Stalin at the Potsdam Conference. And yet, while these numbers were indeed huge, they were not the end of the story.

As the war drew closer and closer to the Home Islands, the U.S. military's ability to "island hop" and bypass Japanese garrisons steadily decreased. Even though American assault and amphibious techniques were honed to near perfection, casualties were nevertheless rising at alarming rates, and losses during prolonged battles at Okinawa and Iwo Jima far exceeded earlier estimates. It was clear that the Japanese were riding their own learning curve. As early as the summer of 1944, Pentagon planners had produced a worst-case scenario of "half a million American lives and many times that number wounded," and the Imperial Army's increased efficiency at killing Americans, particularly on Okinawa, demonstrated to Secretary Stimson and many Pentagon planners that the worst case was a real possibility.

This begged a question. If the situation could already be seen—fully half a year before the initial assault on the southernmost Home Island of Kyushu—to be moving in the direction of what originally had been projected to be the worst case scenario, was there an *even worse case* that had not been anticipated? Would the Selective Service draft calls, nearly doubled just a few months before, be adequate for the task ahead? Or would they have to be ramped up again and deferments further tightened on protected categories such as agricultural workers? To answer these questions Stimson instituted a multistudy reexamination of the Army's manpower and training requirements for the duration of the war as well as the possible casualties the Japanese might be able to inflict on the invasion force.

The conclusion delivered to the War Department in July 1945, shortly before Potsdam, was that the United States could squeak by with the current six-figure level of inductions, but a new "worst case" had now been created: "We shall probably have to kill at least 5 to 10 million Japanese [and] this might cost us between 1.7 and 4 million casualties including 400,000 and 800,000 killed."

The Japanese leadership had come to a similar conclusion. Nearly 178,000 Japanese civilians had lost their lives in recent months—most burned to death or asphyxiated by American incendiary bombs—and 8 million had been made homeless even before the atomic bombs were dropped. Imperial General Headquarters in Tokyo made its own clear-eyed assessments. Based largely on the recent fighting on Okinawa, where nearly 130,000 combatants and perhaps as many as a quarter of the island's 400,000 men, women, and children were dead by July, a remarkable 20 million (representing total casualties in some records and deaths in others) became the figure discussed in Imperial circles.

Yet even such terrible numbers as these only served to strengthen the militarists' conviction that they could still salvage a victory of sorts over a decadent America less concerned with winning than with the lives of its sons. For the militarists, the bloodletting among the Okinawan population was of little consequence. What they beheld was that a force amounting to the equivalent of three infantry divisions plus locally raised auxiliaries had held out for one hundred days against a lavishly equipped American army more than five times as large. Within Japan, the Okinawa battle was regularly trumpeted as an example of Imperial troops stretching out a campaign in the face of a vastly superior enemy. A senior staff officer (and son-in-law to the war minister) later explained to U.S. interrogators:

> We did not believe that the entire people would be completely annihilated through fighting to the finish. Even if a crucial battle were fought in the homeland and the Imperial Forces were confined to the mountainous regions, the number of Japanese killed by enemy forces would be small. Despite the constant victories of Japanese troops in the China Incident, relatively few Chinese were killed. Almost all the strategic points in China were occupied, but the Chungking Government could not be defeated. [But] even if the whole [Japanese] race were all but wiped out, its determination to preserve the national polity would be forever recorded in the annals of history.

The idea that the 10 to 25 million Chinese who had died since the Marco Polo Bridge incident was seen as "relatively few," and that just tens of millions of dead Japanese would still offer the bright side that "the entire people [had not been] complete annihilation," is so alien to Americans, then and now, as to practically defy comprehension. Shortly before the radically increased Selective Service calls were announced to the public, Stimson told President Roosevelt in January 1945 that "a so-called negotiated peace was impossible in this kind of war where one side was fighting for civilization and the other side represented barbarism; there was no common meeting ground and there therefore necessarily had to be a fight to the finish; that a fight to the finish meant a long horrible contest where we needed all the manpower that we could summon."

The Treaty of Versailles, the resurgence of Germany after the "War to End All Wars," the weak-kneed response by the League of Nations to growing aggression, France and Britain's appeasement of Nazi Germany, and the subsequent plunge into an even bloodier conflagration than the previous war—these matters were so deeply imbedded in the American psyche that they were seldom directly mentioned in the press by the later war years, but all hung like a cloud over the American consciousness as the fighting in the Pacific reached its climax.

The result of the country's general consensus on the events of the previous thirty years girded a grim determination, both inside and outside of Washington, to see the war through to the bitter end of "unconditional surrender" lest an inconclusive finish, such as in World War I, lead the next generation into an even bigger, bloodier conflict twenty years hence (with, unlike in Vietnam, no college deferments for that one). Despite a growing war weariness and worry among some that stiff terms might prolong the fighting, the understanding that the war must be prosecuted until Japan either gave up or was pummeled into submission was so fundamental that it did not warrant much discussion beyond the sticky matter of how to accomplish victory and bring the boys home at the earliest possible date.

Some civilian elements within Japan's ruling circle were determined to try to find a way to end the war before the U.S. invasion was launched. Unfortunately, the militarists were in firm control of the government, and Japanese moderates had to tread gingerly for fear of arrest or assassination. In the summer of 1945, Emperor Hirohito requested that the Soviets accept Prince Konoye as a special envoy to discuss ways in which the war might be "quickly terminated." But far from a coherent plea to the Soviets to help negotiate a surrender, the proposals were hopelessly vague and viewed by both Washington and Moscow as little more than a stalling tactic ahead of the Potsdam Conference to prevent Soviet military intervention, an intervention that Japanese leaders had known was coming ever since the Soviets' recent cancellation of their Neutrality Pact with Japan.

The subsequent exchange of diplomatic communications between Japan's foreign minister and its ambassador to the Soviet Union has been characterized by some as evidence that the country was on the brink of calling it quits. American officials reading the secretly intercepted messages between Moscow and Tokyo, however, could clearly see that the "defeatist" ideas of the ambassador received nothing more than stinging rebukes from his superiors. The fanatical Japanese militarists retained their grip on the decision-making process until the simultaneous shocks of the atom bombs and Soviet entry into the war in August 1945 stampeded Japan's leaders into an early capitulation.

Today the Japanese military's own estimates of casualties from starvation, disease, and battle are just as invisible on the other side of the Pacific as Marshall and King's warning in the *New York Times*. This is hardly a new phenomenon. As early as 1981 Pacific veteran Paul Fussell wrote in the *New Republic* that the "degree to which Americans register shock and extraordinary shame about the Hiroshima bomb correlates closely with lack of information about the war." Nearly three decades after Fussell's comments, World War II is not even a dim memory for most Americans, and the numbers killed versus the numbers saved are just abstract figures with long strings of zeroes. But the fact remains, albeit uncomfortable or inconvenient for some, that President Harry S. Truman's much-derided accounts of massive casualties projected for the two-phase invasion of Japan is richly supported by U.S. Army, White House, Selective Service, and War Department documents produced prior to the use of nuclear weapons against Japan and stretching all the way back through the last nine months of the Roosevelt administration.

Some scholars have for years—indeed, decades—picked over the bones of every decision relating to the use of nuclear weapons against Imperial Japan. Every nuance of Truman's most casual asides has been examined, parsed, and psychoanalyzed as critics of the decision have tried to prove that the president lied when he stated that the atom bombs were dropped in the hope that they would induce a defeated Japan to surrender before U.S. forces—being gathered in the Pacific from as far away as the battlefields of Germany—were forced into a prolonged, bloody ground invasion.

In 1945, however, Truman and his senior military and civilian advisors had no such luxury. The clock was ticking on the invasion countdown, and George M. Elsey, who worked closely with Truman throughout his presidency, later remarked, "You don't sit down and take time to think through and debate ad nauseam all the points. You don't have time. Later somebody can sit around for days and weeks and figure out how things might have been done differently. This is all very well and very interesting and quite irrelevant."

The later examination of Truman's decisions was further complicated because his critics had little knowledge of military historiography and even less of the language and assumptions that are standard features of what is produced by planning staffs. For example, some have promoted the idea that General Marshall's staff believed an invasion of Japan essentially would have been a walk-over. To bolster their argument, they point to highly qualified—and limited—casualty projections in a variety of briefing documents produced in May and June 1945, roughly half a year before Downfall's initial invasion operation, Olympic, was to commence. The numbers in these documents, however, were not recognized for what they are: estimates of only the *first thirty days* of fighting. Consequently, they were grossly misrepresented by individuals with little understanding of how the estimates were made and exactly what they represented.

In effect, it is as if someone during World War II had come across casualty estimates for the invasion of Sicily and then declared that the numbers would represent losses from the entire Italian campaign—and then, having gone that far, announced with complete certitude that the numbers actually would represent likely casualties for the balance of the war with Germany. Of course, back then such a notion would be dismissed as laughably absurd, and the flow of battle would speedily move beyond the single event the original estimates—be they good or bad—were for. That, however, was more than six decades ago. Today, historians doing much the same thing have won the plaudits of their peers, received copious grants, affected the decisions of major institutions, and misled a young man who would become president.

★　　★　　★

Operation Downfall, the onrushing event driving both American and Japanese decision making, has received far less examination than the political side of the process, which was utterly subordinate to it in 1945. With some notable, fine exceptions, the tendency has been for historians to regurgitate the same limited selection of planning and briefing documents or go to the other extreme and print everything that one can get his hands on while displaying little ability to separate the wheat from the chaff. This is also true for Olympic, while of the second invasion operation, Coronet, against the Tokyo area in 1946, the lack of examination is explained away by the supposed lack of documentation.

Readers of this volume will find that misconceptions abound as to the state of Japanese readiness to meet the invasion. This principally is due to the uncritical acceptance of assumptions and incomplete intelligence in the relatively few presurrender documents that have formed the core of many scholars' opinions. The state of Japanese air power is an excellent case in point. The often-repeated common wisdom holds that there were only 5,500, or at most 7,000, aircraft available and that all of Japan's best pilots had been killed in earlier battles. What the U.S. occupation forces found after the war, however, was that the number of aircraft exceeded 12,700, and thanks to the wholesale conversion of training units into kamikaze formations, there were some 18,600 pilots available. Most were admittedly poor flyers, but due to the massive influx of instructors into combat units, more than 4,200 were rated high enough for either twilight or night missions. A deadly turn of events.

Based on intelligence reports during the summer of 1945, U.S. commanders also believed that the Imperial air forces were "out of gas" both figuratively and literally. But while it was true that fuel for training units was being severely rationed both before and after the units were given combat status, it did not become clear until after the war that the Japanese had succeeded in building up a large strategic reserve of aviation fuel separate and distinct from stocks used for training and day-to-day activities, reserves which would only be tapped for the final battles in the Home Islands. The idea that there was a dearth of fuel was further reinforced in American eyes by the manifestly weak reaction of the Imperial air forces to the B-29 raids against Japanese cities and virtually no response at all to a series of shore bombardments by American and British battleships that it was hoped would lure large numbers of aircraft to their destruction by waiting carrier aircraft. Despite the best efforts of the U.S. Navy and Army Air Force, the Japanese displayed a fanatical adherence to their plan to not launch air attacks until it was confirmed that the invasion was actually taking place.

One matter that set off urgent alarm bells within the U.S. Navy in the war's very last days was that the Japanese had begun to launch kamikaze attacks of a type for which there was no effective defense. Japan's naval air arm had inadvertently stumbled upon the fact that the thousands of largely wooden trainers that they had redesignated as combat aircraft were functionally invisible to radar, and now that they had the night-qualified pilots to fly them, the Japanese had the ability to stealthily attack U.S. warships before few, if any, guns could be brought to bear on the aircraft. Moreover, the normally deadly "proximity fuze" fired by the U.S. Navy's antiaircraft guns had to pass extremely close to a wooden aircraft before it would be influenced by its presence and explode. That the antiquated "sticks 'n' string kamikazes" went three for three in attacks against U.S. destroyers immediately before Japan surrendered has rarely been mentioned beyond a brief reference in the official Navy history of the Pacific war, or been examined outside of long-declassified documents, in spite of the intolerable situation they foreshadowed if the war had continued.

As for operations on land, the perception has grown that the Imperial Army intended to expend itself in division-sized banzai charges into the face of American artillery and naval guns. In this respect, some modern historians have fallen just as prey to the militarists' call for "a decisive battle" on Kyushu as the targets of their exhortations in 1945, the Imperial foot soldiers and civilian levies. The plentiful, and dead earnest, propaganda to relentlessly storm the beachheads has tended to obscure the fact that the highly choreographed attacks against the correctly determined American beachheads were anything but mindless mass charges in which Imperial infantry would offer themselves up for annihilation. Likewise, the "coastal defense divisions" tasked with delaying the establishment of American lodgments and movement inland only placed one-fifth to one-third of their men (depending on the nature of the terrain) in the well-sheltered positions along the beaches with the balance ensconced in all-around battalions and company positions in the craggy hills to their rear. Indeed, the bulk of Japanese positions, as at Okinawa, were well away from the targeted beachheads.

The tactical and operational details of Imperial Japan's counterpart to Downfall, Ketsu-Go, generally have seen far less misrepresentation and misinformation than other aspects of this subject for the simple reason that Ketsu-Go generally has been ignored. Beyond the goundbreaking studies by Edward J. Drea and the late Alvin D. Coox, tactical and operational matters have been of little interest to Eurocentric historians who, at most, take whatever fragments of Coox and Drea's work that best suits them. Not so in this volume. Moving further down into the weeds, Ketsu-Go No. 6 and Ketsu-Go No. 3, the Japanese counterparts, respectively, for Olympic and Coronet, are examined in detail. From the weeds, we burrow into the mud, covering the Mutsu Operation No. 1, the defense plan for southern Kyushu, as well as its three defense zones in the very areas of Kyushu where U.S. forces planned to come ashore. This material was garnered from postwar interrogations and reports produced by the relevant Japanese staffs from field units on Kyushu through Imperial General Headquarters in Tokyo, and readers will find that there is no basis for the often-repeated notion that Japan's military lacked the capacity to effectively resist an invasion.

Juxtaposed against Japanese efforts are the tactical intelligence analyses produced by the U.S. Sixth Army targeting Kyushu—both immediately before the dropping of the atom bombs and several months later, when, with American "boots on the ground," direct examination was possible of Japanese defense preparations. U.S. personnel were stunned at the scale and depth of the defenses. The Japanese had, to put it bluntly, "figured us out," said one officer. Chillingly, a highly placed member of the Imperial Army staff told the Sixth Army's Intelligence chief not only that they expected the initial invasion to be launched on Kyushu in October 1945 but also that they knew the precise locations of the landings.

Instead of a grinding war of attrition, the U.S. military had hoped for a less costly battle of maneuver, but both the interrogations and the layout of the Japanese defenses indicated that this had not been in the cards. Moreover, the Japanese had expanded their forces on Kyushu far beyond anything imagined by U.S. planners. While neither the highly perceptive positioning of the Japanese defenses nor the increase in forces were apparent before Truman, Stimson, and Marshall left for the Potsdam Conference, by the third week in July it finally became alarmingly clear that a Japanese buildup of stunning proportions had been accomplished right under the noses of U.S. intelligence and was continuing at a rapid pace with "the end not in sight." Meanwhile, American preparations for use of atom bombs against four specially chosen cities continued apace and the Japanese leadership chose to ignore warnings issued by the Allies at the conclusion of the conference.

General Marshall, who by now had returned to Washington and been made fully aware of activities on Kyushu, could not assume that the fanatical Japanese would surrender even when atom bombs were raining down on their cities and the Soviet entry into the war dashed their hopes of a negotiated settlement. An examination of alternative invasion sites for Kyushu had been launched when the scale of the Japanese troop buildup had become evident, but both the chief of staff and his commander in the Pacific, Gen. Douglas MacArthur, agreed that none of the sites were adequate substitutes. U.S. leaders were encouraged by the official Japanese government inquiries initiated after the dropping of the first two bombs and Soviet invasion of Manchuria, but optimism that the war might soon be over vanished. Communications had suddenly stopped, and it appeared that Japanese intransigence or indecision was about to scuttle peace efforts.

After a tense weekend with no word from Tokyo, Marshall informed his Pacific commanders, "The President directs that we go ahead with everything we've got." Conventional air strikes were resumed and components for the third atom bomb were released for use. But the Army chief and his senior staff had something else in mind now that it was beginning to look like the "shock" of atom bombs had failed in its strategic purpose of loosening the iron grip the country's militarists had on Japanese decision making.

Marshall had long been a proponent of the tactical use of the developing atomic arsenal and poison gas in support of ground operations. Strategic use of atom bombs against cities had certainly been worth a try, but the militarists appeared to be completely unmoved, and to Marshall, atom bombs were too precious an asset to waste in an apparently futile strategic campaign. With the invasion still very much "on" and forces gathering for it from as far afield as Europe, he now threw his staff into planning for the use of the full range of weapons in the United States' arsenal, today referred to as weapons of mass destruction or WMDs, to trump the human tide welling up on Kyushu. Marshall's plans called for most—and if he could convince Stimson and Truman, *all*—of the bomb production through December 1945 to be dropped on Japanese defense concentrations along or near the beaches.

A more complete appreciation of the dangers posed by nuclear radiation was still in the future, and millions of Japanese, and Americans, on Kyushu and close by at sea would have been affected by the tightly packed set of perhaps nine detonations in a triangle-shaped zone roughly analogous to the area bounded by Newport, Rhode Island, Worcester, Massachusetts, and Boston. The emperor's surrender broadcast on August 15, 1945, effectively ended any need for Marshall and his staff to pursue the initiative, and like so many aspects of Downfall, the hideous consequences of the imminent switch from strategic to tactical use of nuclear weapons if the Japanese has not surrendered has not been closely examined before.

★   ★   ★

Although I didn't know it at the time, work on *Hell to Pay* began when I was engaged in military government studies at the Harry S. Truman Library and Museum in Independence, Missouri, in the early 1980s. Many years later, *Military Review* editor in chief Lt. Col. George L. Humphries and Dr. Michael E. DeBakey, colonel, USA (Ret.), encouraged me to do a book on the invasion planning, but it wasn't until the back-to-back publication on matters relating to the U.S. Army's casualty projections for Downfall in the June 1997 *Journal of American History* and the following month in the *Journal of Military History* that Larry Bland, coeditor of *The Papers of George Catlett Marshall*, said that I "*must*" finally get down to work. I saluted and said, "Yes, sir!"

Larry was particularly interested that I should document such things as the massive production of Purple Hearts in anticipation of the invasion, and the relationship of the Pacific-bound redeployment of forces from Europe to General Marshall's firm determination to not allow the Army to get bogged down in a prolonged battle for Berlin. These and other matters in which we shared a deep interest were beyond the scope of his then-current project, volume 5 of the *Papers*, spanning 1945 and 1946, and both are covered in this book. Friends and colleagues of Larry will recognize his hand throughout *Hell to Pay*.

Both Michael DeBakey and John Correll, during their tenures, respectively, at the Baylor College of Medicine in Houston, Texas, and the Air Force Association in Arlington, Virginia, were of great assistance personally, and DeBakey also assigned students to help locate certain documents produced during his time with the Army's Surgical Consultants' Division in 1944–46. Similarly, Correll arranged for the association's Juliette Kelsey to twice do important preliminary work at the National Archives before my research there on Purple Heart production. George Elsey made later work at the archives much less of a financial strain by graciously putting me up at his club, and he provided valuable insights into President Truman's thinking and the flow of intelligence information to Truman and his senior advisors. His friend, Maj. Gen. Donald S. Dawson, USAF (Ret.), also from Truman's staff, made similar beneficial arrangements during yet another research siege.

Throughout this project, my lovely wife (and frequent coauthor) Kathryn Moore pitched in at the drop of a hat, as did my daughter Andrea Giangreco during the indexing and document transcriptions. Three individuals of inestimable help with this book were Alvin D. Coox and Edward J. Drea on all matters relating to the Japanese military, and Sadao Asada on the decisions of the Japanese cabinet. (Asada also shared his experiences as a young boy during the late war years and U.S. occupation.) These scholars answered my questions promptly, fully, and with far more patience than I deserved. The U.S. Naval Institute Press crew, particularly Karin Kaufman and Elizabeth Bauman, were a delight to work with, and the Press' cartographer, Christopher Robinson, spent nearly fifty hours producing the superb set of maps on these pages. Edward S. Miller provided varied and valuable contributions, and Richard Russell on the "business" end of the Press also found himself doing a little double duty on this book since, having written extensively on U.S.-Soviet cooperation in the Pacific, he was a ready and willing resource.

The list is long of others who generously lent their time, knowledge, and encouragement to this project and includes Lefteris Lavrakas, George McColm, Tim McGarey, Werner Gruhl, Eric Berguid, Stephen J. Waszak, Terry Griswold, Gary R. Hovatter, Thomas E.

Conrad, Dennis Bilger, Von Hardesty, Dean Allard, Robert Aquilina, Bill Maulden, Maurice Matlof, Andrew J. Goodpaster, Robert W. Coakley, Stanley L. Falk, Shelby L. Stanton, Roger Pineau, Norman Polmar, Thomas B. Allen, Ken Werrell, Denis Warner, Trevor N. Dupuy, Elliot Richardson, Ike Skelton, Clarence M. Kelley, Vince Shartino, Morey Amsterdam, William F. Buckley Jr., Selwyn Pepper, Alexander Herd, William G. P. Rawling, Jon Parshall, Joao Paulo Matsuura, Sarandis (Randy) Papadopoulos, Jeffrey Barlow, Fred L. Schultz, Wade G. Dudley, Michael D. Pearlman, Geoff Babb, Graham H. Turbiville, Jacob Kipp, Lester Grau, Samuel Loring Morison, Arthur G. Volz, Michael Kort, Josh Reynolds, Kevin Ullrich, Martin Allday, Andrew A. Rooney, William A. Rooney, Ben Nicks, James Pattillo, Burr Bennett, Jack Moore, Samuel J. Giangreco, John J. Maginnis, John E. Greenwood, Victor Krulac, Edwin Simmons, Bernard J. Humes, Strom Thurman, Victor Fic, Robert A. Silano, Marc Gallicchio, Jeffery J. Roberts, Richard F. Snow, Frederick E. Allen, Fritz Heinzen, Robert P. Newman, Stanley Weintraub, Robert James Maddox, John Bonnett, Hal Wert, Ian V. Hogg, Earl F. Ziemke, Mackenzie Gregory, Dwight M. Miller, Robert H. Ferrell, Erwin Muller, Dennis Bilger, Patrick Connelly, Pauline Festerman, Liz Safly, Randy Sowett, JoAnne Knight, and, finally, Barton J. Bernstein, whose phone calls and 102 letters were instructive in many unexpected ways.

I have been playfully teased by former and forthcoming coauthors of mine, John T. Kuehn, commander, USN (Ret.), and Donald L. Gilmore—colleagues from my years at Fort Leavenworth, Kansas—over how I have approached American and Japanese planning for the invasion. Both have remarked that, unlike in previous works, Olympic and Ketsu-Go are given the somewhat dense "Staff College treatment" in *Hell to Pay*. I can only plead guilty. This level of examination had to be done, however, because there are so many deep-rooted misconceptions attached to this subject, particularly regarding the true state of the Imperial Army and well as the Army and Navy's air elements, and the basic realities "on the ground" in the Olympic and Coronet invasion areas.

Larry Bland, seconded by others, also cautioned, "You are dumping so much genuinely new material on people that you should consider recapping some of the key points somewhere in the middle," and he suggested that readers be allowed to "take a breath before going on." Wise advice, and I have followed it in the first half of chapter 9. As for the matter of expected casualties, Japanese as well as American, DeBakey got right to the heart of the matter. After fretting over the deterioration in America's institutional knowledge of the environment in which all life-and-death decisions had to be made in 1945, he stated that having to demonstrate that the invasion of Japan would produce "catastrophic casualties" was ridiculous. Said DeBakey, "It's like having to prove that slamming someone's head with a meat ax will kill him."

Larry Bland and Michael DeBakey both passed away as this book was entering its final stages, and it is a sad fact of life that many of the gentlemen in these acknowledgments are no longer with us. From Newt Tritico to Paul Tibbits, it was an honor to have met them, and to still learn from the old soldiers, sailors, airmen, and Marines who, as one of their number put it, are still "alive and kickin'." With the sole exception of Elliot Richardson, then a decorated and twice-wounded medic with the 4th Infantry Division, who said that he was looking forward to the invasion, the veterans to a man stated that they dreaded what was to come. And even Richardson admitted that his outlook in 1945 was out of the ordinary, explaining that he was "young, gung-ho, and foolish."

During the *Enola Gay* affair at NASM, Veterans groups were frequently dismissed as being overly sensitive to supposedly "inconsequential" points in the exhibit that focused almost entirely on Japanese civilian casualties in the closing days of the war. Yet it's like Kissinger used to say, "Even paranoids have real enemies." Martin Allday, wounded on Okinawa and headed for Tokyo in Operation Coronet, related how his persistent efforts to get friend and fellow vet, author James Michener, to weigh in publicly with his knowledge of what the men faced was one battle that he could not win. Although Michener would take part in several local events in Texas, his well-founded fear of the reaction from the literary and Hollywood circles he moved in was so strong that he made Allday promise not to release one eloquent letter he'd written until after his death. An excerpt from Michener's letter is reproduced in the epilogue to this volume.

That Michener preferred to keep his opinions to himself, though disappointing, is not particularly surprising when one remembers the derision veterans were receiving at the time from some historians and major institutions. NASM director Martin Harwit wrote after his dismissal that the *Enola Gay* controversy was a battle between a "largely fictitious, comforting story" presented by the veterans and the "event [Hiroshima] as revealed in trustworthy documents now at hand in the nation's archives," which the veterans "feared . . . could cast into doubt a hallowed, patriotic story." Many in the academy support this contention. Laura Hein, for example, praised the "contemporary historical scholarship" displayed in the original, disputed exhibit script and maintained that "a great many U.S. soldiers in the Pacific in 1945 believed the bombs brought the war to a speedy end, but they were not in a position to know." This presumed, however, that assumptions based on these "trustworthy" documents were themselves correct and derived from a comprehensive understanding of the material. They weren't.

The type of characterization made by Truman critics that "the exhibit might be interpreted as celebrating the deaths of 150,000 to 200,000 Japanese civilians, mostly old men, women and children" only served to confirm the veterans' suspicions that scholarly discussion of this subject is dominated by those who, for whatever reason, do not acknowledge that even excluding mounting deaths along the Asian littoral—and according to the Japanese government's own estimates—anywhere from 50 to nearly 150 times the number of Japanese who died at Hiroshima and Nagasaki would be killed during the invasion, taking a significant number of Americans with them. For veterans, the "celebration" was not in the deaths of innocents, but that their own lives, and those of their buddies, were spared.

Hopefully this book will allow Americans to get a glimpse of what many of these men would have confronted during Operation Downfall.

A Note on Japanese Names and American Ranks: With the exception of Japanese authors cited in the notes, all names of Japanese nationals in *Hell to Pay* are rendered in English according to Japanese usage, surname first. Readers will also find that some U.S. officers make their appearance with different ranks. In each case, the officers' ranks are appropriate to the time frames of the events portrayed.

CHAPTER 1

The Maximum "Bloodletting and Delay"

Victory was never in doubt. Its cost was. . . . What was in doubt, in all our minds, was whether there would be any of us left to dedicate our cemetery at the end, or whether the last Marine would die knocking out the last Japanese gun and gunner.

—MAJ. GEN. GRAVES B. ERSKINE, commanding general, 3d Marine Division [1]

The United States . . . is confronted with numerous problems; such as, mounting casualties, the death of Roosevelt, and a growing war weariness among the people. . . . Should Japan resolutely continue the war and force heavy enemy attrition until the latter part of this year, it may be possible to diminish considerably the enemy's will to continue the war.

—"Basic General Outline on Future War Direction Policy,"
adopted at the June 6, 1945, Imperial Conference [2]

The old artilleryman thoroughly enjoyed the fireworks. In rapid succession, the USS *Augusta*'s eight 5-inch guns blasted out round after round of antiaircraft shells as dual 40-mm "pom-poms" let loose streams of fire at nonexistent targets.[3] The racket raised by the "test firing," performed for his benefit, was not new to the *Augusta*'s guest. Nearly three decades earlier he had captained a battery of four French-made 75-mm guns that hurled some 2,009 rounds at a series of German positions in the space of three hours and twenty-one minutes during the opening of the Meuse-Argonne offensive. At specific points during the captain's dawn fire mission in 1918, his sweating gunners were firing so fast that they had to place water-soaked gunny sacks on their guns' long barrels to cool them down.[4]

The artilleryman, now President of the United States Harry S. Truman, was returning from the Potsdam Conference, where he had been happy to report, "I've gotten what I came for—Stalin goes to war August 15."[5] The Soviet Union's imminent entry into the war meant that the struggle with Imperial Japan would certainly be brought to a conclusion with far fewer dead and maimed Americans than if the United States would have had to fight on almost alone or even with assistance from Britain's empire. The icing on the cake had come just the previous day, when on August 6, 1945, Truman was brought word that the secretly developed atomic bomb had been successfully detonated at the port city of Hiroshima.

It seemed certain that the Japanese must finally admit defeat, but there had been little thought that the giant war machine channeling men and material toward Imperial Japan in staggering numbers might suddenly shut down. Even the USS *Augusta*, in expectation of facing kamikaze attacks, was slated to augment the impressive antiaircraft defenses witnessed by Truman and receive an updated radar suite. Now, however, there was a very real chance that the whole blessed thing would soon be over and the millions of young men converging on Japan could go home.

On Monday, the sixth of August, roughly 5,400 of those men, soldiers of the 20th Armored Division aboard the SS *John Ericsson*, were nearing New York while the *Augusta*, almost six hundred nautical miles due east, was making its own approach to Chesapeake Bay and the naval base at Norfolk. After carefully navigating through the minefields protecting the harbor, the *Ericsson* continued west then turned northwest toward the narrows and its Hudson River pier when the ship was greeted by a yacht with a Women's Army Corps (WAC) band and a bevy of beautiful babes who waved and threw kisses. This was not a time for any fears of what the future might hold, and the soldiers eagerly looked forward to thirty-day furloughs before they had to report in at their Camp Cook, California, staging area for the Japan invasion. They knew nothing yet of the strange new weapon that was saving many of their lives or, for that matter, that they had been sharing a piece of ocean with the president.[6]

In fact, nearly 100,000 westbound soldiers earmarked for the invasion—in addition to the first few thousand heading home permanently because they were lucky enough to be "out on points"—had passed Truman on the high seas in July as the *Augusta* raced east at an average speed of twenty-six-plus knots to deliver him to the Potsdam Conference.[7] Little more than a day after Truman's departure, he crossed paths with both the 4th Infantry Division heading for New York and the 8th Infantry Division, which would retrace his route through Chesapeake Bay while heading for Hampton Roads. Troops from both divisions disembarked on July 10 and were immediately hustled into trains that brought them to camps, where they received new uniforms, huge dinners with all the trimmings, and entertainment from USO troupes before leaving on furlough.[8]

The process repeated itself near the mid-Atlantic with the 87th Infantry Division, sailing for a New York arrival of July 11, and again with the 2d Infantry Division, which, moving in a convoy of three slow transports, would not dock in New York until the twentieth. Numerous ships with mixed passenger complements of smaller units and individual soldiers were passed during the *Augusta*'s approach to the English Channel and as it and its escorts picked their way through the Channel minefield and scores of wreck buoys marking the graves of Allied and Axis vessels. By the time the *Augusta* prepared to sail up the Wester Schelde Estuary for the final run to Antwerp, the *Queen Elizabeth* had already pulled into the Clyde with the 44th Infantry Division and, to the south at Le Havre, advance elements of the 5th Infantry Division had begun boarding for their voyage to Boston.[9] The objective of this vast movement of men and material was nothing less than Tokyo itself.

On August 6, 1945, the United States had been at war for almost exactly three years and eight months. Entering World War II "late," and with no invading armies rampaging across its soil, it had not even begun to suffer the huge day-in, day-out losses common to the other antagonists until just the previous summer. Operation Overlord, the invasion of France, and Operation Forager, the invasion of the Mariana Islands, marked the beginning of what the U.S. Army termed "the casualty surge" in postwar analyses, a year-long bloodletting that saw an average of 65,000 battle casualties among young American soldiers and Army airmen each and every month from June 1944 to May 1945. And these figures did not include the considerable Army losses due to sickness and disease or the appalling Marine and Navy casualties in the Pacific.[10]

The number of dead, wounded, injured, and missing reached its peak during the months of November, December, and January at 72,000, 88,000, and 79,000 respectively, even as the War Department, in conjunction with the Office of War Mobilization, hammered out both the details of how to handle the nation's manpower shortage and what needed to be done to ensure that the public's support for the war with Japan did not waver during 1945 and 1946. The result was a partial demobilization in what was then believed to be the *middle* of the conflict. Through use of a "points system," the longest-serving troops were allowed to return home for good, even as Selective Service inductions were nearly doubled in March 1945 to 100,000 men per month in preparation for the grim losses expected from the upcoming series of operations on the Japanese Home Islands.[11]

Official figures for American casualties during the war, repeated in countless books and articles, vary only slightly depending on such things as whether or not the early phases of the postwar occupations of Germany and Japan are included, or the loss of the U.S. Army's Philippine Scouts are factored in, and usually stand at 291,577 dead and 671,846 wounded. Occasionally, when "other deaths" from accidents and disease are added, the mortality figure is presented as 405,399, and totals are often rounded.[12] These figures are perfectly sufficient for most uses, such as general comparisons with the losses suffered by other nations or of America's previous wars, but it is important to understand that they represent only a fraction of what the nation's military and civilian leaders at that time recognized as the war's true cost.

Excluding the Merchant Marine, a civilian body whose 243,000 sailors actually suffered the highest American combat mortality rate of the war,[13] some 16,425,000 men and 150,000 women (including 17,000 who served in combat theaters) put on uniforms between 1941 and 1946. The U.S. Army saw 12,435,500 soldiers and airmen pass through its ranks as it struggled to maintain an authorized strength of 7,700,000.[14] And maintaining that troop level often seemed an impossible task. While the frequently quoted number of Army and Army Air Force casualties stands at 936,259, this figure does not include a wide array of administrative separations as well as 9,256 nonbattle deaths or other categories that continually drained the Army of manpower and were closely monitored by senior leaders.[15] These included 50,520 disability discharges due to nonbattle injuries in combat zones (such as loading accidents), combat-related psychiatric breakdowns accounting for 312,354 discharges, and medical discharges totaling a stunning 862,356 from illnesses contracted in disease-ridden overseas theaters—and none of these figures account for soldiers who were hospitalized and then returned to their units after recovery.[16]

Navy and Marine Corps battle casualties at first appear small by comparison, only 159,495 to 162,668 men (depending on how one constructs the totals), but these figures were more than eight times the number of killed and wounded among our seaborne forces in all the other wars of the United States combined. They also do not include stateside administrative and medical attrition of military personnel; the Merchant Marine and Coast Guard's 10,095 dead and 12,000 other battle casualties, primarily from German submarines; nor the Navy and Marines' 30,442 nonbattle deaths. There were also 111,426 Army and Army Air Force prisoners of war in Europe and missing in action in the Pacific who survived their captivities and were counted as casualties *during* the war.[17] In all the United States' armed services had to contend with losses amounting to no fewer than 2,580,000 men in overseas theaters, with the monthly totals running generally in tandem with the rapid growth of forces overseas and leaping upward when the tempo of operations intensified during the last year of fighting. And this was before a single soldier or Marine set foot on a Japanese beach.

★   ★   ★

Although the precise details of Selective Service conscription statistics remained a closely guarded secret until after the war, Truman, his military and civilian advisors, and senior members of Congress were painfully aware that there was a yawning gap between the draft "calls"—essentially targets—and the number of men actually inducted. Subsequent to a spate of successful months in early 1943, when the number inducted exceeded the calls, the rest of the year and 1944 saw few occasions when quotas were met. The armed services absorbed 4,915,912 draftees during that period, an impressive figure by any standards. However, the calls, in order to fulfill the insatiable demands of global war, had actually totaled 5,815,275.[18]

This shortfall of nearly a million men fell heaviest on the draft's biggest customer, the Army, and had an immediate impact on the ground force element that engages in the heaviest, most prolonged fighting—the infantry. And although the effort to generate a large pool of potential inductees to choose from resulted in the calls exceeding the armed services' actual needs, the dearth of young men being sent forward was painfully real and contributed to a deficit of up to 400,000 soldiers during the countdown to the invasion of France.[19] Without either an upswing in the number of new men wearing khaki, or a serious revamping of its force structure, the Army would not be able to conduct a two-front war without risking serious reverses and possibly even local defeats that would prolong the fighting and ramp up the nation's cost in "blood and treasure."

Seeing the writing on the wall, the Army embarked on myriad initiatives to minimize losses, such as imposing the highest practical hygiene standards on units in the field, while simultaneously fine tuning and downsizing the composition of combat divisions themselves. For example, the table of organization strength of the Army's eighty-nine active divisions in April 1945 was only 70,000 men higher than the seventy-three and a half largely paper divisions in December 1942.[20] Still, the huge shortfalls made the formulation of a stable replacement pool virtually impossible, and stateside divisions were gutted, sometimes repeatedly, to supply new men for the ones already deployed. It was not unusual to find a formation in the midst of training losing nearly the equivalent of its stated strength in a series of "division drafts." One standard-sized, 14,253-man division, the 69th, was forced to give up 22,235 enlisted personnel and 1,336 officers before it was finally shipped to France.[21]

Administrative manipulations and gyrations of this sort were largely, but not completely, beyond the eyes and ears of both Japanese intelligence and diplomatic corps, and the structure of the U.S. division cut off in the Philippines in 1941, and eventually lost, was only generally representative of what such formations looked like by 1943. Fighting against complete U.S. combat divisions in New Guinea generated some idea of their weight and structure through use of signals (radio) intelligence, but the fact that Japanese units took few American prisoners and were, in any event, either cut off or functionally annihilated meant that the Imperial General Staff in Tokyo operated largely in the dark and had to depend on the Germans for detailed intelligence on the U.S. Army's force structure. What the Japanese could and did get, however, was a look at the overall U.S. war effort and public opinion from the American press. And it was quite an eyeful.

Foreign agents, often working in the embassies and consulates of neutral or nominally allied nations, harvested newspapers and magazines of all kinds, including official publications such as *Yank* and *Air Force,* which could be obtained for the price of a subscription.[22] Despite military censorship and the great care taken by domestic newspapers to follow the Office of Censorship's "voluntary" guidelines, articles designed to buck up home-front morale or run-of-the-mill news stories often carried nuggets of hard information that could be combined to form at least some understanding of what the Arsenal of Democracy was capable of producing in terms of the war's basic hardware, such as ships and planes, as well as the manpower available to prosecute the war.[23] Yet it was the robust criticism of the lengthening war and growing casualty lists—all gleaned from editorials, letters, and opinion pieces—that supplied much of the rationale behind the strategic decisions of Imperial Japan and Nazi Germany alike when it came to deciding how to handle the United States.

The leaders of both nations had entered the war convinced that there was little to fear from America, and Adolf Hitler voiced the prevailing wisdom one month after Pearl Harbor when he said, "It's a decayed country. And they have their racial problem, and the problem of social inequalities. . . . Everything about the behavior of American society reveals that it is half Judaized and the other half Negrified. How can one expect a State like that to hold together—a country where everything is built on the dollar?"[24] The Japanese were confident that their devastating attack on the U.S. Pacific Fleet, quick string of Asian and Pacific conquests, and the decision by an ascendant Germany to honor its alliance by immediately declaring war on the United States would cow the feckless Americans into accepting the reality that they simply could not win. One of their number, however, was less certain.

Admiral Yamamoto Isoroku had conceived and planned the strike on Pearl Harbor, yet he warned that Japan would likely lose the war if it could not be wrapped up quickly. As a young man, he had studied at Harvard and later served as Japan's naval attaché in Washington.[25] Yamamoto's nearly six years in the United States gave him insights into an America that was incomprehensible to his warrior colleagues raised in a homogeneous, and in many ways still closed, society. As with the Nazis, they had little real understanding of how the American press worked, let alone how it fit into a society that somehow managed to be both skeptical and optimistic at the same time. What they beheld was a chaotic, mongrel nation suffering under the weight of a weak, inefficient democratic process; what Yamamoto saw was vitality and inner strength.

In the space of just a few years, Yamamoto was dead, the victim of broken Japanese codes and long-range American fighter aircraft. Hitler and his regime were clearly reaching their end, too, as massive armies pummeled their way toward the German borders from east and west. Articles in the American press of victories and armies moving ever forward were familiar to the totalitarians in Tokyo and what was left of the Third Reich, which exercised an iron control over their own newspapers and state-controlled radio. But to the Japanese in particular, much hope was derived from what must have appeared to them to be a shocking amount of publicly allowed and reported negativity.

Editorial after editorial forcefully complaining about America's allies, the conduct of generals, and even of specific pieces of military equipment; fathers and mothers bemoaning in letters that their sons were pulled from the colleges they attended under the once much-ballyhooed Army Specialized Training Program (ASTP) to fill the critical need for soldiers with engineering, language, mathematics, and other demanding skills; readers appalled at the rapidly escalating casualties and demanding that eighteen-year-old draftees be given more training before being shipped overseas; church groups and individual citizens expressing outrage that the U.S. House of Representatives had passed a bill authorizing the drafting of women nurses; wives demanding to know why husbands with small children who had been drafted a year before Pearl Harbor could not be sent home now that there were "so many men in uniform"—it could all be found on the pages of daily newspapers as well as in the periodic lists of local dead and wounded.[26] Moreover, the rallies and marches by the gaggle of organizations making up the isolationist America First movement, some huge by standards of the day, were hardly a distant memory.[27]

The "weakening will" that Japanese leaders perceived from the American press offered them a degree of hope at a time when they had lost battle after battle and finally the key Marianas chain in the summer of 1944, a calamitous event that put U.S. heavy bombers in range of the Home Islands. While this came as a shock to Japanese from all walks of life, including Emperor Hirohito himself, the country's military leaders firmly maintained that America's victories were built on her industrial might and that it was they, not their own people, purportedly infused with the "Yamato spirit," who were "suffering and desperately trying to bring the war to a decisive end as early as possible."[28] Optimism and firm assurances, however, don't win battles, and by the time the American juggernaut reached the Philippines in the fall, Japan's increasingly desperate military failed again, even though it authorized the first use of kamikaze planes and offered up a significant part of their remaining fleet for destruction as a decoy.

Yet in spite of America's successes, there seemed to be almost as much bad news as good for the U.S. press to report. Just weeks after optimistic stories of a collapsing German army, predictions that the war in Europe might be over by Christmas, and reports of the destruction of the Japanese navy in the Leyte Gulf battles, the papers were filled with demands for finding who was to blame for the Germans' early successes during their Ardennes counteroffensive and why so many ships were falling prey to kamikazes in Philippine waters. There were also ominous warnings from Washington that monthly draft calls were going to have to be increased (they, in fact, were nearly doubled between December 1944 and March 1945) and that "the number of returned sick and wounded is now so large that the Medical Department can no longer make it a policy to send patients to hospitals nearest their hometowns."[29]

Yes, battle after battle had been lost and the fleet was gone, but Japan still had millions of men under arms and it appeared that there was good reason to believe that they could still salvage a victory of sorts over a decadent United States less concerned with winning than with the lives of its sons. Victory was redefined as achieving a military stalemate that left, at minimum, the core empire intact (the Home Islands, Manchuria, Korea, and Formosa) and guaranteed the continuance of the imperial structure. A decision was made to stretch out the fighting through "vigorous, protracted operations" designed to inflict the maximum "bloodletting and delay" (*shukketsu* and *jikyu senjutsu*) on U.S. forces. The Japanese military confidently maintained that attrition warfare or "bloodletting operations" (*shukketsu sakusens*) would simply prove too much for Americans to bear.[30]

Whether or not the country's military leaders actually believed this or were, as some Japanese officials and midlevel officers suspected, simply engaged in posturing to brazen their way through a deteriorating situation, it was the Japanese militarists that were in firm control of the government and their view was summed up in a 1945 Imperial General Headquarters (IGHQ) strategic assessment: "The fighting morale of the United States is being weakened by fear of large casualty tolls, there has been an increase in labor strife, criticism of the military, and agitation from the ranks to engage in a precipitous demobilization. Should the USA be defeated in the battle for Japan itself, public confidence in the President and military leaders will decline abruptly, fighting spirit will deteriorate in the flurry of recriminations, and Japan will find herself in a much more favorable political position."[31]

Yet behind the mysticism and "Yankees are crybabies" wishful thinking, were the simple mathematics of scale and distance that would surely come into play as the fighting drew nearer to Japan and eventually on the Home Islands themselves. Gen. Jonathan Wainwright, held by the Japanese since the U.S. defeat in the Philippines, was told by a confident Japanese colonel that "there are a hundred million people in the Japanese empire. It will take ten times one hundred million to defeat Japan. To move such a force against Japan even if you had that many warriors, would be impossible." Said one field army staff officer to his interrogators after the war, "I thought that the war would continue three or four [more] years because, although Japanese national power was far below standard, it was considered that [the United States' power] would be insufficient. . . . It was thought that the battle for the homeland would be difficult, would require years and, with the help of Manchuria, would be fought to a draw."[32]

CHAPTER 2

Spinning the Casualties

The Army must provide 600,000 replacements for overseas theaters before June 30, and, together with the Navy, will require a total of 900,000 inductions by June 30.

—GEN. GEORGE C. MARSHALL and ADM. ERNEST J. KING in the January 17, 1945, *New York Times*[1]

What it must have been like for some old-timer buck sergeant . . . who had been through Guadalcanal and Bougainville and the Philippines, to stand on some beach and watch this huge war machine beginning to move and stir all around him and know that he very likely had survived this far only to fall dead in the dirt of Japan's Home Islands.

—JAMES JONES, author and 25th Division infantryman on Guadalcanal[2]

Americans' concern over casualties was very real and hard to miss. The Army, already struggling with a dangerous deficit in replacements, knew that this concern would only grow and was painfully aware that a casualty surge of indefinite duration would accompany the June 1944 invasions of the Marianas and Normandy. A series of heated disagreements between Army Chief of Staff George C. Marshall and Secretary of War Henry Stimson over the structure and deployment to Europe, then redeployment to the Pacific (discussed in chapter 4), were, like the Army's administrative manipulations and gyrations, invisible to the Japanese—and even President Roosevelt. However, demonstrating to our long-suffering Allies the depth of our commitment while preparing the American public for the grueling struggle ahead was a delicate balancing act that, by its very nature, was a highly public affair.

The rapid increase in losses during the long-expected casualty surge, though slightly lower than anticipated,[3] was so politically sensitive that the War Department changed how it reported Army losses not only through the civilian press but also to its own troops, principally through the Army publication *Yank,* which distributed up to 2.6 million copies weekly to soldiers and airmen starved for reading material. The remarkable thing about these changes in the methodologies used to produce its publicly released figures was that they resulted first in a pronounced inflation, and then deflation, of cumulative casualty figures all within the space of little more than half a year.[4]

From the commencement of offensive operations in 1942 through the summer of 1943, the Office of War Information and the War Department's own Bureau of Public Relations, seldom released cumulative casualty data for the Army, preferring instead to present such information at the conclusion of individual campaigns or operations such as those at Guadalcanal or in North Africa, the Gilbert Islands, and Aleutians. A fairly comprehensive account of casualties through the third week of June 1943 was published in mid-July and listed four principal loss categories—killed, wounded, missing, and prisoners—and their totals by theater of operation. Army casualties from all these categories totaled 63,958. That number included 12,506 Philippine Scouts, who were among the nearly 32,000 personnel lost when the islands fell. Navy, Coast Guard, and Marine casualties in these four categories increased the total number by nearly a third to 90,860.[5]

Not included in the tally were other categories that were even then draining the Army of manpower. "Nonbattle" losses among troops in the field were omitted, as were losses from administrative attrition such as separations from the service due to age or infirmity. Most apparent to commanders overseas were the destructive effects on unit combat strength of nonbattle losses from disease and, to a lesser degree, the psychiatric breakdowns popularly known as "battle fatigue." For example, the destruction of Merrill's Marauders in Burma by disease and exhaustion is recounted in a number of works,[6] and in New Guinea, the 32d Infantry Division attained a rate of 5,358 cases of malaria, dengue fever, and fevers of undetermined origin *per one thousand troops* from October 1942 to February 1943.[7]

Naturally the war's other belligerents also lost great numbers of men from "noncombat" factors. Japanese forces cut off in the New Guinea–New Britain area were already suffering terribly, and even the Germans, with relatively stable supplies of food and medicine, were by now intimately familiar with the debilitating effects of disease on the successful prosecution of combat operations in both Russia and the Mediterranean. Sickness among German forces in North Africa regularly halved their combat power by sapping a stunning 40 to 50 percent of their front-line strength in 1942 and 1943,[8] and U.S. forces in that theater later found that approximately nine of every ten admissions to field hospitals were *not* the result of combat.[9]

Excluding soldiers who recovered enough to return to duty, the U.S. Army would ultimately discharge some 1,225,230 men for nonbattle injuries in combat zones, diseases contracted overseas, and combat-related psychiatric breakdowns.[10] There was little public interest in this either during or after the close of hostilities, and the mounting losses they represented went essentially unreported during the war except for a brief period in 1944 (when they were released somewhat obliquely) because there were two very good reasons for never releasing such figures. First, unlike the periodic accountings by the Army Medical Corps of personnel discharged in the United States because of ailments such as heart defects or mental disabilities, these numbers came principally from *deployed* forces and thus would provide the enemy with a much fuller picture of the Army's effective fighting strength. Just prior to the invasion of France, totals for wounded troops were omitted as well, undoubtedly for the same reason.[11] Second, the American public was understandably focused on the cost of *combat* operations. There was no crying demand for collateral information—no squeaking wheel.

The exclusion of figures for both the sick and wounded, however, created other problems, not the least of which was that smaller, more selective loss figures were reported to the public at a point in the war when many Americans already believed, to varying degrees, that their country was making less of a contribution to the war effort than the Allies. This was a very sensitive subject, often raised by the media and the government itself. The Roosevelt administration's energetic efforts to manage this perception affected everything from congressional elections to global war planning with Great Britain and the Soviet Union, and even what the public was told about the Army's "losses."

The last-released U.S. Army casualty figures before the 1944 casualty surge were published at the beginning of June and totaled 156,676 from the categories killed, missing, prisoners, and wounded through April of that year.[12] *Yank*, which was published by Brig. Gen. Frederick H. Osborn's Special Services Division of the Army Service, contrasted this number with the nearly 670,000 men lost by the British Empire and had earlier editorialized on the Soviet loss of some 6 million troops in battles against the Nazis.[13] Other Special Services products, such as Frank Capra's movie *The Battle of Britain* (1943) and his Oscar-nominated movie *The Battle of Russia* (1943), reinforced this contrast. Moreover, stories of the huge sacrifices made by the Allies were not limited to mass-distribution military publications and films but were common in civilian newspapers, radio, newsreels, and feature-length Hollywood films as well.

As noted, the cumulative figures for wounded through April 1944 were dropped from casualty totals released just before the invasions of France and the Marianas. This should have resulted in an even greater disparity between U.S. and Allied casualty figures. However, the Army now established a policy to disseminate virtually the entire administrative flux and flow of manpower not periodically, but on a monthly basis through public relations channels to the press and through its own organs to its troops. By adding the categories "honorable discharges" and "other separations" to the totals for April 1944, released in late June, published Army losses almost immediately leaped from 156,000 to 1,163,000 even *before* the casualty surge began to show up in the figures.[14] For those who did not look too closely at how the number was constructed, the clear implication was that most or all of these losses were combat related.

This new accounting method produced figures that seemed to be much more in tune with the combat losses of the British and Soviets and ostensibly demonstrated to the public and to both allies and enemies alike that America's commitment to the war was unequivocal and its resources were enormous. They also implied that America was already pulling its share of the load against the Axis powers. Releasing the artificially large monthly totals, which lumped together losses through purely administrative matters with battle and nonbattle deaths, prisoners, and missing while still withholding figures for the sick and wounded, would also prove useful for the Roosevelt administration because doing so inadvertently provided a way to soften the potential blow to America's war resolve when the sudden upsurge of major ground operations beginning in the summer of 1944 caused *real* casualties to skyrocket.

Through this month-by-month dissemination of figures combining administrative separations with selected combat-related categories, soldiers, airmen, and the public at large became at least partially conditioned to seeing steadily growing million-plus loss figures months before it became apparent that American troops were now experiencing the frightening attrition of manpower that had been commonplace among the other antagonists for several years. For example, in August 1944, after the standard seventy-five days it took to collect, collate, vet, and publish the data, the War Department released an inflated "total Army losses" figure of 1,234,000 for December 7, 1941, through May 1944.[15] As noted earlier, however, it was department policy not to indicate how many of these were casualties directly related to combat. By this time combat-related casualties numbered no less than 194,000 men, and that figure did not include the appalling losses to sickness in the overseas theaters.[16]

The June 1944 reporting period, which covered the first three weeks in Normandy and two from the Marianas, was added to the total made public in September and was handled in the same manner as the other recent releases. The 1944–45 casualty surge had begun that month and was clearly visible in the marked jump in the number of "total losses" reported. That figure, still minus the sick and wounded, suddenly spurted well beyond the roughly 1,250,000 mark to 1,279,000 in the space of just one month. If the War Department had not taken certain measures, such as putting an almost complete halt to the Army's administrative separations, the figure released for the August 1944 reporting period would have soared to approximately 1,407,000.[17]

The total-losses formula had certainly produced much larger numbers that were seemingly more in sync with the casualties suffered by the United States' principal allies, but the problem now had to be considered from a different perspective. At what point did the numbers become too big and start to become a hindrance to the war effort? The Army was on track to release the August figures in November, and one can only speculate as to whether or not there was now, after only six months of using the uniform new system, an apprehension that the upcoming tally would constitute a psychological crossroads for the American people. It was clear that attrition alone could push "total Army losses" past the million-and-a-half mark in the December release.

The American public, already uneasy over the lengthening name-by-name casualty lists appearing in nearly every hometown newspaper, would be sure to take notice of such huge numbers. The release of loss figures in the million-and-a-half range would not only provide a long string of zeros guaranteed to command the attention of editorial writers and pundits but also coincide with fresh combat along Germany's western frontier and in the western Pacific. Additionally, the release of these loss figures and the intensified fighting would occur at precisely the time that the Army was formulating both the following year's steep increase in draft quotas for the planned 1945 and 1946 invasions of Japan's Home Islands, as well as the Points Discharge System, which would allow some soldiers to be released after a specified amount of time in combat combined with length of service.[18]

In full view of the German and Japanese intelligence gatherers, Army Chief of Staff Marshall, Secretary of War Stimson, and President Roosevelt were already contending with the political fallout from their decision to withdraw 110,000 men from college under the ASTP and transfer them and others from the Army Air Forces to the Army Ground Forces (AGF).[19] Later, during the uproar over the transfer of Army Service Forces troops—and even more Army Air Forces personnel—to the AGF, principally to compensate for severe losses among the infantry, an exasperated General Marshall told a gathering of historians, "I think I heard from the mothers of most of these men who were taken from the other branches, and from every father whose son I was forced to take out of college."[20] The artificially high casualty listings would serve only to aggravate a worsening situation.

Of course, the War Department had put itself onto this path the previous summer by releasing total-loss figures that included the full range of the Army's administrative separations. But the department could minimize or delay this fast-approaching public relations bombshell (which was likely to explode at the worst possible time, immediately before Selective Service inductions were scheduled to be nearly doubled in preparation for the Japan invasions) by returning to some form of narrowed criteria for publicly released casualty figures. The War Department did not publish figures in October, but in November, it publicly experimented with various formulas that distinguished casualties from total losses. One listed a narrow range of specific combat-related casualty categories, a complete reversal of the policy of presenting total losses. This format restarted the base-line numbers at a far lower level and resulted in a figure of 384,395 "Army battle casualties" through October 6, 1944. The category "wounded" (208,392 men) was displayed for the first time since April, but those incapacitated by disease were still not included.

Once reinstated, however, the listing of wounded could not easily be made to "go away." When the monthly total-losses figure was released two weeks later, it glaringly excluded "wounded in action" from the total of 1,357,000 through August 31, 1944.[21] Although the respective figures represented end points five weeks apart, the number of wounded was a subject of intense interest to soldiers and civilians alike and all could do the math. Adding wounded to the equation pushed total Army losses to far beyond one and a half million.

Members of the relevant Congressional committees from both parties would have been aware of, or had access to, this data, but the methods by which casualty information was released to the public were of no particular interest to them. As for the press, radio copy was (with a few notable exceptions) basically lifted from the newspaper headlines and a newspaper's world began and ended on the day it was produced. These kinds of changes in methodology, compressed here but at the time spread far apart in a saturated news environment, were essentially invisible—certainly less pressing than a troop ship being torpedoed or a train derailment. And even if a particularly observant columnist noticed what was going on and wrote a piece about changes in how casualty data was released, it is difficult to see how his newspaper, operating under wartime censorship guidelines, would publish it.

Figure 1. Cumulative U.S. Army Loss/Casualties Totals in *Yank*

(Excludes published totals for individual battles or campaigns which were run separately)

Army Killed	23 July 1943 (thru 24 June)	63,958	(all-services, 90,860)
Wounded	24 Dec 1943 (thru 15 Nov)	94,918	(all-services, 126,919)
Missing and	11 Feb 1944 (thru 23 Dec)	105,229	(no figure published)
Prisoners	3 Mar 1944 (not given)	112,030	(all-services, 150,478)
	2 June 1944 (thru 28 Apr)	156,676	(all-services, 201,454)
Screened areas:	23 June 1944 (thru 31 Mar)	1,163,000	(no figure published)
Army Deaths	28 July 1944 (thru 30 Apr)	1,200,000	"
Honorable Discharges	25 Aug 1944 (thru 31 May)	1,234,000	"
Prisoners and Missing	29 Sept 1944 (thru 30 June)	1,279,000	"
Other Separations			
	17 Nov 1944 (thru 6 Oct)	384,895*	"
	1 Dec 1944 (thru 31 Aug)	1,357,000	"
	12 Jan 1945 (thru 28 Nov)	483,957	(all-services, 562,368)
	2 Feb 1945 (thru 21 Dec)	556,352	(all-services, 638,139)
	2 Mar 1945 (thru 28 Jan)	676,796	(all-services, 764,584)
	9 Mar 1945 (thru 7 Feb)	693,342	(all-services, 782,180)

*The casualties total published in the 17 November 1944 edition of *Yank* did not include prisoners.

It was the numbers themselves, not how they were crafted, that were key to public perceptions, and the casualty surge had rendered the policy of releasing total losses politically unacceptable only seven months after it had been initiated. Yet the battle casualties formula was not completely satisfactory either, particularly in how it was presented. The War Department's January 1945 release of figures, which stopped short of Germany's December counterattack in the Ardennes, used the same formula as the revamped November listing and displayed a cumulative Army casualty figure of 483,957. The department also stated that "some 55,000 enlisted men from the Air Forces and 25,000 men from the Service Forces are being transferred to the Ground Forces" by the end of January.[22]

When figures next appeared in the February 2, 1945, edition of *Yank*, it was apparent that total-losses listings had finally been completely abandoned, but the narrowly constructed Army battle casualty listing, which incorporated the first week of the German counteroffensive, had nevertheless climbed to a whopping 556,352 through December 21, 1944. Moreover, instead of continuing to list the numbers in easy-to-read column form, they were now buried within a lengthy paragraph that included Navy casualties, limited comparative analyses for weeks in mid-December, estimates of German losses for the same period, and a warning that "the number of returned sick and wounded is now so large that the Medical Department can no longer make it a policy to send patients to hospitals nearest their home towns." Further down the column was also a reminder that the United States still had not experienced the grievous human cost incurred by its stalwart British ally. Under the headline "British Losses" was a breakdown by country of the 1,043,554 casualties within the British

Empire. It stated that "the United Kingdom suffered most heavily with 635,107 military casualties," a figure far larger than the U.S. total to date.[23]

Manipulating the way casualties were reported, however, could only go so far to mask the fact—sensed more than specifically known to most Americans—that roughly 65,000 of their young men were now being killed, wounded, injured, or declared missing in combat theaters each and every month during the casualty surge, and this did not include the sick and psychological casualties.[24] From afar the Japanese militarists took careful note.

The Roosevelt administration and military chain of command tried to soften the psychological impact of these losses through efforts ranging from the nonsensical to the well-considered and straightforward. European theater commander Gen. Dwight D. Eisenhower sent out a directive to use the term "reinforcement" for individual soldiers sent to units at the front instead of "replacement," which had a cannon-fodder ring to it.[25] This order went essentially unnoticed and unenforced at lower command levels since a young rifleman sent forward from what was now called a *reinforcement* depot was nevertheless understood by all concerned to be a *replacement* for another soldier killed, sick, missing, or wounded. Dr. Arthur G. Volz later recalled, "I clearly remember [the] introduction of the British term 'reinforcement' for 'replacement.' It was a useless exercise. . . . People in the replacement stream in the ETO were well aware of what faced them. When I crossed the Channel with a replacement package in early September 1944 one of the lieutenants in another package aboard the ship was returning to the Continent for the second time, following his third wound. He didn't have any illusions."[26]

General Marshall, however, took a very different tack. Shortly before Germany's Ardennes counteroffensive and the announcement of increased Selective Service inductions, he stated in a public address at New York's Waldorf-Astoria Hotel that

> we are daily confronted with the bitter human cost of this great struggle. We do not have the destroyed homes of England or daily casualties among our peaceful civil population as they do; but because of our expanding battlefront our military casualties are steadily increasing. . . . The great battles now in progress must be kept going, every front must be kept blazing until we break the Nazi control of the German Army and people. . . . [It is] far better to accept heavy casualties for a brief period than the much greater total which inevitably accumulates from the daily attrition of prolonged periods of inactivity on the battlefield.[27]

Passions ran high during the winter of 1944–45. Almost midway through the bloody fighting for Iwo Jima and with Allied forces in Germany stalling on the "wrong" bank of the Rhine (the invasion of Okinawa was still weeks away), Marshall assured Congressman William E. Hess in a March 5 letter, "I, and others in responsible places in the War Department, are keenly sensitive to the daily casualties we are suffering."[28] The next day he wrote to General Eisenhower in Europe that there was "a terrific drive on against the use of 18-year-old men in combat which has been fulminated by a speech by Senator [Robert A.] Taft on the floor of the Senate."[29] Although casualty information was made available to members of Congress by Marshall and Stimson in numerous closed sessions at both the Pentagon and on Capital Hill,[30] the War Department felt that continued publication of the cumulative totals was inflammatory, and during its intense negotiations with Congress over the sensitive manpower issue, the Army abruptly went from running monthly listings to running no listings at all.

The last U.S. casualty figures ever displayed in *Yank* were in its March 9, 1945, edition. Published losses through February 7 totaled 782,180, including 693,342 for the Army alone, and were displayed next to a tongue-in-cheek cartoon depicting a lone pup tent flanked by a campfire and swaying palm trees under a starry, starry sky. From inside the tent in this idyllic scene comes a voice: "So I says to the captain, 'Where are all these guys to send overseas?'"[31]

A Japanese intelligence specialist may well have wondered what this cartoonist was getting at. An American soldier certainly wouldn't have known either if *Yank* was his sole source of information. The last time that publication had run anything on the draft was nearly a year before, when it printed comments from Selective Service director Brig. Gen. Lewis B. Hershey and informed readers about the War Department's announcement that the Army had reached its planned strength of 7.7 million.[32] Beyond the pages of *Yank*, however, the Roosevelt administration and commanders of both the Navy and Army were putting the publication's *future* readers—young men who had yet to enter the armed services—as well as the rest of America on notice that the war was far from over and that additional sacrifices were necessary.

Months before public demand peaked in May 1945 for what was essentially a partial demobilization in the middle of the war through the Point Discharge Plan, the Roosevelt administration and the Army struggled with how to juggle the nation's rapidly dwindling reserves of eligible manpower. Secretary Stimson continually pressed for better legislation to support manpower needs and stressed to Congress that "Selective Service calls are now confined almost entirely to combat replacements."[33] Fortunately, a short-term personnel crisis caused by unexpected and extensive troop losses during Germany's December counterattack in the Ardennes was solved, although less by the arrival in Europe of Army replacements already in the pipeline than by the draconian culling of excess support personnel in the European theater's rear areas.

Germany's action had also opened up an interesting opportunity. With the invasion of Japan now less than a year away, Stimson hoped there might be some benefit to be derived from Hitler's last throw of the dice. He believed the Battle of the Bulge would help soften congressional resistance to a variety of manpower proposals to tighten draft deferments on such groups as agricultural workers. He also wished to expand the categories of those to be inducted, although one proposal in particular made no headway since the Senate, with soon-to-be-president Harry S. Truman as its presiding officer, balked at the House bill to draft women nurses.[34] On January 4, 1945, Stimson was pleased to write in his diary about "the general excitement in Congress over the German attacks making it possible for us to get legislation which would give us more individuals from the draft."[35]

A classified telegram sent the day before from Director Hershey to the state Selective Service directors got to the heart of the matter. Although Congress and the public were understandably focused on the Ardennes fighting, this January 3 message tied proposed or directed changes in various draft deferments to the long-term needs of the coming one-front fight against Japan rather than to a passing crisis precipitated by the German counteroffensive. In his message he quoted a letter from the director of the Office of War Mobilization, Truman's future secretary of state, James F. "Jimmy" Byrnes: "The Secretaries of War and Navy have advised me jointly that the calls from the Army and Navy to be met in the coming year will exhaust the eligibles in the 18 through 25 age group at an early date. The Army and Navy believe it is essential to the effective prosecution of the war to induct more men in this age group."[36]

The following week, on January 11, Secretary Stimson held a press conference to announce that the Army's monthly Selective Service call-up, which had already been increased from 60,000 to 80,000 in January, was to be ratcheted up again in March to 100,000 per month.[37] The total draft calls actually climbed to over 140,000 when the Navy and Marine calls were added.[38] One week later President Roosevelt, Chief of Staff Marshall, and Adm. Ernest J. King, the chief of naval operations, sent letters outlining the military's critical manpower needs to House Military Affairs Committee chairman Andrew J. May. Those letters were released to the *New York Times* on January 17, 1945. The public, and by default the Japanese, were informed in front-page articles that "the Army must provide 600,000 replacements for overseas theaters before June 30, and, together with the Navy, will require a total of 900,000 inductions by June 30."[39]

In the winter and spring of 1945 the administration had thus moved from discussing official published cumulative casualty numbers in the past tense to discussing them in the future tense. Interestingly, briefings and motivational addresses held by the Army at such diverse locations as the Pacific-bound U.S. First Army Headquarters, still in Weimar, Germany, B-29 training bases in the southwestern United States, and the Pentagon all utilized a uniform figure for expected casualties that was somewhat lower than the ones released to the *New York Times*—just 500,000.[40] Frank McNaughton, an early Truman biographer who had worked on Truman's Senate Investigating Committee, also noted that interservice politics of the day led to the Navy *leaking* casualty figures that were somewhat larger.[41] Those figures showed up in some very public places.

Kyle Palmer, the longtime political editor of the *Los Angeles Times,* had traded in his editorial desk for a position as the paper's war correspondent in the Pacific. Attached to the central Pacific headquarters of Adm. Chester A. Nimitz, commander in chief, Pacific Fleet (CINCPAC), he covered the first aircraft carrier strikes against Japan and the costly U.S. invasions of Iwo Jima and Okinawa, then made a brief return to Los Angeles for a medical checkup. Before he shipped out again, Palmer hammered away at the need for additional manpower in both articles and appearances before civic groups. "It will take plenty of murderous combat before our soldiers, sailors and marines polish off the fanatical enemy," he declared.[42] Under the headline "Palmer Warns No Easy Way Open to Beat Japs," the *Los Angeles Times* quoted one of his speeches: "We are yet to meet the major portion of the ground forces of the Jap empire." And the next line must have been particularly gratifying for senior Japanese generals and admirals to read in their intelligence summaries: "They have 5,000,000 or 6,000,000 under arms and it will cost 500,000 to 750,000, perhaps 1,000,000 lives of American boys to end this war."[43]

At this point it is worthwhile to mention that veterans of World War II have been roundly dismissed when claiming that they "remembered" that they had been told that the invasion of Japan might cost half a million casualties. In fact these reading-starved troops had been regularly exposed to such numbers from the fighting against Germany in both Army organs and hometown newspapers. Similar figures were now appearing for the upcoming fighting in Japan, and the Army was making it a priority to warn soldiers and the home front alike of prolonged fighting ahead through all means at its disposal. A year and a half was given as the minimum time to "get it over unless there is a sudden collapse."[44]

CHAPTER 3

The First Army and Kwantung Redeployments

We dreaded and we feared the specter of the Kwantung Army. We pleaded with the Russians, since the very day of Pearl Harbor, to pin down the Kwantung Army, relieve pressure upon our hard-pressed forces in the Philippines, and thereby "save the Pacific" from the Japanese, as General MacArthur put it. At the same time we (and the Soviets) worried lest the Japanese assault the USSR first, like the jackal Mussolini had jumped the reeling French in 1940. . . . When, for example, the American Military Mission proposed to the Russians, in December 1943, that a U.S.-supplied logistical base be set up east of Lake Baikal in Siberia, the Soviet Army authorities were shocked by the idea and "literally turned white."

—ALVIN D. COOX, "The Myth of the Kwantung Army," 1958[1]

Both the United States and Imperial Japan engaged in massive redeployments of their forces before the expected invasion of the Home Islands. The number of formations were involved, twenty American divisions from Europe and ironically, an almost equal number of Japanese divisions of the Kwantung Army in Manchuria together with a host of independent brigades and four more divisions from China and Korea. But while the U.S. formations flowed as one continuous river of men beginning in June 1945, the Japanese movement started in early 1943 and occurred in fits and starts as the Imperial Army desperately tried to shore up the empire's deteriorating situation.

The American counter to Japan's attempted cutting of the sea lanes to Australia in the summer of 1942 was both bigger and faster than the Japanese expected. When the Imperial divisions rushed forward to New Guinea and Guadalcanal from Java and Sumatra failed to right the situation, the dearth of a meaningful reserve in the Home Islands meant that combat forces had to be pulled from the empire's relatively quiet western frontiers.[2]

The movement of the 20th and 41st Divisions from Korea and northern China to New Guinea in February 1943 went smoothly but, setting a pattern that was soon too become all to familiar, the in-theater reinforcement of the island was stopped cold when, in March, U.S. aircraft sent nearly the entire convoy carrying the 51st Division to the bottom of the Bismarck Sea. Next, the 32d and 35th Divisions, redeploying from China, were largely destroyed while en route by U.S. submarines in April and early May.[3]

Belatedly Japan was now raising new divisions which freed up the 52d to be sent to Truk in November 1943 (where it sat out the war in the bypassed garrison amid conditions of increasing deprivation) and the 43d in a pair of convoys to Saipan in May 1944. Though the second convoy was terribly mauled by nearly continuous submarine attacks that sank five of its transports, most of its troops were rescued only to be landed as disorganized, weaponless survivors just days before the U.S. invasion. However, the garrison at nearby Guam, another Marianas island and U.S. possession slated for recapture, was defended by the crack 29th Division, which arrived from Manchuria in February. It and the 14th Division sent to the Palau Islands were the first two Imperial divisions weaned away from the Kwantung Army guarding Japan's richest prize on the Asian mainland.[4]

Al Coox has described this "self-contained, autonomous" army as "the cream of the entire Japanese armed forces and the master of the greatest industrial potential on the Asiatic Continent."[5] Naturally the Imperial General Headquarters in Tokyo was reluctant to withdraw any units at all from Manchuria in spite of the fact that the Red Army in Asia was no longer capable of conducting large-scale mechanized operations. Soviet premier Joseph Stalin had pulled significant forces from the border for the defense of Moscow in the winter of 1941 and quickly siphoned off the rest, replacing them with less capable formations (designed principally to train soldiers for combat against Germany) as well as relatively immobile garrison divisions.[6] Yet it was only with the greatest trepidation that these first two of the Kwantung's then nineteen divisions were withdrawn in February 1944.[7] They would not be the last.

In June the empire's "absolute zone of national defense" burst wide open when the Americans bypassed the fortress atoll of Truk in favor of a direct thrust at the Marianas island chain six hundred miles to the northwest, then utterly crushed a long-planned Japanese counterstroke in the Battle of the Philippine Sea. Immediate action was needed to bolster key defensive positions on Japan's doorstep before the United States' next move. Having still made no serious effort to increase the Army's strategic reserves, IGHQ could only count on the Kwantung as a pool of ready soldiers.[8]

Great profit—in terms of both time and lives saved—had been obtained by the twin U.S. drives through the southwest and central Pacific, ignoring certain Japanese garrisons other than using them for periodic target practice. As American forces drew closer to the Home Islands, though, the ability to simply "isolate and move on" became a diminishing option. And both sides knew it. A vanguard of seven Kwantung divisions was rapidly dispersed to threatened points in the Pacific in June and July 1944 even as fighting still raged on Saipan, Guam, and Tinian. The 1st, 8th, 10th, and 24th would battle until extinction in the service of the emperor within the next year in the Philippines and Okinawa, as would the Kwantung 14th Division elements sent to Peleliu earlier that year.[9] Another formation, the 109th Division formed in June 1944 specifically for the defense of the key bastion of Iwo Jima and under the direct control of IGHQ in Tokyo,[10] would meet the same proud end, while the Kwantung's 23d and 2d Armored Divisions, though beaten down to mere skeletons, continued organized resistance in the mountains of northern Luzon until ordered to surrender in August 1945.[11] Only two of the above Kwantung formations bypassed the 28th on Miyako Jima, near Okinawa, and 9th on Formosa, were denied the honor of battle.[12]

The previously mentioned Kwantung 23d Division was shipped to Luzon later than the others in October 1944, after Gen. Douglas MacArthur's "return" to the Philippines. By a strange twist of fate, this division, which had been badly mauled and surrounded by Soviet tank columns during a bloody border clash in 1939, survived its eight months of combat with the Americans as well, surrendering as a decimated but still functioning formation in the mountains of northern Luzon on August 15, 1945.[13] But that was still many months away in an unknown future. And although comparatively free movement of Imperial units within the Philippine archipelago was maintained during those first months of the American invasion, the 23d Division's unscathed arrival had as much to do with pure luck as it did with the fact that U.S. carrier operations were being seriously disrupted by the opening round of kamikaze strikes.[14] IGHQ decided against attempting to send more forces to the Philippines from Manchuria in the face of growing U.S. land-based air power.

The attrition-by-decree of the Kwantung continued in December and again in January 1945, with, respectively, the 12th and 71st Divisions sailing into the East China Sea to what the Japanese believed to be the next likely American target, the island of Formosa.[15] IGHQ in Tokyo fully agreed with the U.S. Navy's assessment that Formosa was "ideally situated to block the flow to Japan of the oil, tin, rubber, quinine, and other vital areas of the East Indies area,"[16] and U.S. code breakers duly watched as the original two-division garrison climbed to five plus,[17] none of whom would ever confront an American invasion. The third former Kwantung formation reinforcing Formosa, the 9th Division, did not come directly from Manchuria but was withdrawn from Okinawa, where it had earlier been sent to form the keystone of the island's defense. The removal of nearly one-third of Okinawa's combat troops in December 1944 ultimately saved many thousands of American lives there and was seen by its garrison commander as nothing less than a body blow. "If the 9th Division is detached and transferred," he said, "I cannot fulfill my duty of defending this island."[18]

Not counting the considerable number of air and service units that had been sucked out of Manchuria, the Kwantung Army—in terms of its veteran formations—was now twelve-plus divisions thinner in January 1945 than it had been just eleven month before. The Kwantung also held few illusions about the state of affairs, and its own "exhaustive studies" led it to "conclude that its strength had been weakened far beyond estimation" and that even though "new divisions were rapidly formed, they had only a fraction of the fighting effectiveness of the transferred divisions."[19] Senior Japanese military leaders initially rationalized this pronounced reduction in combat power as being of little consequence because the Soviets had earlier done the exact same thing, and former premier General Hideki Tojo characterized the strength of the Soviet Far Eastern armies and the Kwantung as being "in balance" during a private audience with Emperor Hirohito on February 26.[20]

Although generally correct in terms of pure manpower and for the correlation of forces at that moment, this analysis left much to be desired and the emperor asked if the Soviets were likely to attack Japan. Tojo replied that his "most recent information was inconclusive" but hastened to add that "the Soviets were committed fully against Germany" and that "only if the latter collapsed would the USSR possess sufficient reserves to fight Japan."[21] With both Soviet and Allied armies now fighting on German soil, such an answer could not have been completely reassuring. The Soviets, in fact, were already preparing to fulfill secret agreements made with the British and Americans at the recently concluded Yalta Conference. Campaign planning for the invasion of Manchuria would begin in earnest within weeks, and the first east-bound shipments of men and material along the Trans-Siberian Railroad were already scheduled to start in April.[22]

The suddenness of the U.S. recovery after Pearl Harbor, plus the shocking speed and power of its twin drives across the Pacific—particularly while engaged in massive operations against the Germans—amazed the Japanese, who despite the seemingly relentless character of the American advance always seemed confident that the juggernauts must *surely* run out of steam or be defeated in just one more "decisive battle" before Japan's sacred soil was truly threatened. It wasn't until January 1945, after their spectacular failure in the Battle of Leyte Gulf, that various concrete structural and organizational steps started to be taken to prepare the nation for the grim series of battles that were certain to take place within Japan itself. Steep increases in conscription were instituted concurrent with the activation in March, April, and May of forty-five divisions, sixteen of them strong mobile formations with the balance to be used for coastal defense (see chapter 7).[23] When completed, this rapid build-up would far exceed what MacArthur's headquarters estimated in March 1945 as the maximum increase in the Japanese force structure, with *the new divisions alone* equaling the total number of such formations that his headquarters believed would be available in the Home Islands by the end of the year.[24]

By mid-June, Emperor Hirohito would preside at eight palace ceremonies in full-dress army uniform, complete with sword and medals, as 103 regimental flags were bestowed upon newly formed units.[25] Training and equipping these formations was going to be a difficult, but not insurmountable, task in view of the fact that the Japanese had correctly deduced that the principal invasion operations would come in the late fall of 1945 on the southern island of Kyushu and the early spring of 1946 near Tokyo.[26] But IGHQ, which had always underestimated the speed at which the Americans could act, now flew to the other extreme, believing the Americans capable of striking anywhere, at any time, including the Home Islands themselves, as early as June if the Americans were willing to risk a smaller, ad hoc operation.

With virtually none of the new formations expected to be fully combat ready before summer, IGHQ drew down the Kwantung yet again in March as the 11th, 25th, 57th, and 1st Armored Divisions were ordered back to Japan and the 111th, 120th, and 121st Divisions were sent to defend Korea against possible incursions by the Americans (followed shortly by four experienced divisions in the Chinese hinterland that were pulled back to protect threatened coastal areas like Shanghai).[27] In addition, IGHQ's army component reasoned that an American invasion of Kyushu would also free at least two of the three

Kwantung divisions that had been moved to southern Korea since Olympic would not leave enough U.S. troops available for a similar operation in Korea prior to the main invasion on Honshu's Kanto Plain. Although American submarines and aircraft rendered Japanese movement in the East China Sea nearly impossible (as would future Soviet operations in the northern Sea of Japan), Imperial forces would have still retained considerable freedom of action in the Sea of Japan's critical southern reaches between Korea and the Home Islands to make this moment of two additional divisions possible.[28] The hemorrhage of men and equipment from Manchuria only stopped when the Soviet Union, on April 5, 1945, announced that it would not renew its 1941 neutrality pact with Japan. Naturally, this immediately precipitated yet another scramble, this time to send understrength and second-rate divisions in China north to rebuild the Kwantung, as well as raise new units locally, a process begun only half-heartedly the year before.[29]

The IGHQ's—indeed, the entire Japanese government's—propensity to bounce like a pinball from one crisis situation to the next with seemingly little realistic strategic planning is a subject that has been thrashed over for more than half a century. Failures in battle, however, did lead IGHQ to institute two projects that would have had a profound impact on Japanese defense planning. First, their inability to defeat the Americans in the Marianas prompted an immense building project in central Honshu's Nagano province involving complex layers of tunnels within three mountains as a refuge for the emperor, as well as both the center for the government and IGHQ's headquarters, in the event of an invasion of Honshu (see chapter 14, with additional references in 7 and 8). Second, when it became clear that victory could not be obtained in the Philippines, a dozen tankers at the Sumatra oil fields were ordered to be topped off with all the refined fuel they could carry in March 1945, then rushed north before U.S. air power choked off the shipping routes to the Home Islands. This refined fuel formed a secret strategic reserve, held back from training and ongoing tactical needs, that was to be used solely for kamikaze operations defending Japan itself (see chapter 8).

★   ★   ★

In addition to the Americans and Japanese, a third force redeploying for the invasion of the Home Islands was the lion's share of Britain's Royal Navy as well as comparatively small slices of His Majesty's army and air services; all operating not as independent, self-sustaining forces acting in unanimity with the Americans through a "combined" headquarters, but completely within the operational structures of CINCPAC, U.S. Army Forces, Pacific (AFPAC), and USAFTAC.

In the beginning the prospect of working with the British services in the Pacific was not looked upon favorably by the U.S. Joint Chiefs of Staff, or virtually any senior American commanders, because of the well-founded fear that the British simply did not have the ability to adequately support even modest operations so far from Europe. Consequently, when agreement was reached for the employment of air and naval forces—over the "vehement protests" of Admiral King—it was stressed that the British contingents "must be balanced and self-supporting" so that they would not create a drain on strained U.S. resources.[30] As envisioned in the summer of 1945, the ground and air elements, in combination with the full-bore Royal Navy commitment, would ultimately entail that nearly a million British and empire servicemen be gathered for Operation Coronet, the invasion of Honshu near Tokyo.

The Royal Navy began shifting warships large and small to the Indian Ocean after the Normandy invasion, and the tempo picked up sharply after arrangements were made in the fall of 1944 for the new British Pacific Fleet to operate with the Americans. Ships from the Atlantic and Indian oceans joined the U.S. task forces in time to take part in strikes launched up and down the Japanese coast plus Formosa, and they aggressively defended the invasion shipping off Okinawa. Although dwarfed by the U.S. Navy's Pacific Fleet, the British naval commitment to the western Pacific was already the largest *sustained* concentration of their sea power in history in terms of both tonnage and manpower, and it was destined to grow still larger. Plans formulated in the spring of 1944 called for maintaining a Pacific deployment centered around five fleet carriers, five light fleet carriers, six battleships, and twenty-five cruisers before the spring 1946 invasion of the Tokyo area on Honshu. Moreover, much of the smaller but still potent British East Indies Fleet supporting operations in southeast Asia was to be folded into their Pacific Fleet by December 1945,[31] at which point a remarkable 90 percent of the 866,000-man Royal Navy—and essentially all of the available Commonwealth naval forces afloat—were scheduled to take part in Coronet and other operations against the Japanese, either directly or along the vast supply lines and facilities in their respective countries.[32]

Getting the RAF's heavy bombers up and running in the Pacific was a much harder proposition. The British had originally envisioned a deployment of twenty Lancaster bomber squadrons called Tiger Force at a base built from the ground up in northern Luzon. The canceled Cagayan Valley airfield complex, however, also had required its own small port to be built to support a projected peak strength of 96,000 RAF, Royal Engineers, and other personnel, plus it was so far from Japan that combat missions would have suffered badly from the poor trade-off between bombs and the required aviation fuel. Next the Americans volunteered to turn over Miyako Jima's airfields, some 450 miles closer to Japan, after what undoubtedly would have been a costly campaign to annihilate its sizable, dug-in garrison centered around the Japanese 28th Division from Manchuria.[33]

The lengthening struggle for Okinawa and critical lack of Army service troops for airfield and base development forced the Miyako invasion to be canceled and threw Tiger Force planning into confusion.[34] Fortunately the Americans offered to shoehorn a smaller contingent into the extensive but already overcommitted airfield complex being rushed to completion on Okinawa. Agreement was reached to co-locate an initial ten British and Canadian squadrons (220 aircraft, including some Mosquito light bombers) with their old Eighth Air Force comrades. This vastly simplified the RAF's manpower requirements particularly regarding its engineer commitment which, for the time being, shrunk to just 34,890. At war's end the first convoy of Royal Engineers was closing on Okinawa, and a second with ground crew and more engineers had cleared the Panama Canal.[35]

Although the Chiefs of Staff in London had actively promoted the commitment of the RAF and Royal Navy in the Pacific since 1943, they realized early in the process that their Washington counterparts desired absolutely no British army participation during the invasion of Japan, and early estimates of what they might contribute after the defeat of Germany went into a black hole in the Pentagon.[36] Consequently, while there was a vague intention to have ground troops involved in the fighting on Japanese soil, British proposals put forth as late as April 1945 called only for units from Europe to reinforce the South East Asia Command (SEAC) fighting in Burma, and soon, Malaysia. It wasn't until early July 1945 that a concrete proposal for a British-led land combat component was put forth. By now, however, the British found that the American's attitude had made an abrupt and unexpected about-face.

On the heels of the Okinawa campaign, the Americans were having to face the fact that the invasion was going to be even more costly than anticipated. After a meeting of the Combined Chiefs of Staff at Potsdam, a pleasantly surprised Field Marshall Lord Alanbrooke wrote that things had "turned out more successful than I had hoped for." While he also admitted that the British chiefs, because of the limited nature of their proposed commitment, were treading on "thin ice" in their efforts to gain a meaningful role in deciding Pacific strategy, General Marshall had even assured them that their views would be considered.[37]

This was no small matter to the British since they could now claim to have an ability to influence the course of the campaign on Honshu, and Britain would enhance its postwar role in the Far East by taking part in the climactic battles half a world away from Europe. Moreover, the commitment of all three services to combat in Japan would help to slow the steady decrease in Lend-Lease shipments that began in earnest with the defeat of Germany.[38] And then there was the determination of the British and Commonwealth governments to see the war through to the bitter end. After a private meeting with President Truman at Potsdam, British prime minister Winston Churchill wrote in a memorandum that the president was weighted down by the "terrible responsibilities that rested upon him in regard to the *unlimited* effusion of American blood" (emphasis added).[39] Churchill later spoke for both his outgoing Coalition government and the new Labor government when he said, "We were resolved to share the agony . . . [of] the final and perhaps protracted slaughter."[40]

The "we" in this case was the Commonwealth Corps, three to five divisions created from what even a U.S. official history derisively called "the so-called increment forces."[41] Initially it included the British 3d Infantry Division from Europe and volunteers from the armies of Australia and Canada who would be organized into their own national formations, most of whom would have to be retrained on U.S. equipment. New Zealand was doggedly attacking the systemic roadblocks to adding their own 2d Division when the war ended, but a proposal to field a British-Indian division from SEAC was nixed by MacArthur because of "logistic and linguistic complications."[42] It was planned that the passage of the British 3d Infantry Division and air units of Tiger Force across Canada and the United States be accompanied by the maximum possible press coverage, and a lead element of the cross-continent trek, the 20th Anti-Tank Regiment, was preparing for its Atlantic crossing when the war ended.[43]

Prime Minister Churchill clearly had in mind that this commitment would grow considerably beyond what was promised at Potsdam if the war became prolonged. Moreover both domestic and international political considerations dictated that senior U.S. commanders would just have to swallow hard and accept additional British troops if higher than expected casualties during the earlier, all-American invasion operation, Olympic, indicated that a larger force structure would be needed for Coronet.

Unlike the grudging acceptance of British land forces, the prospect of Canadian participation in the Pacific was viewed favorably by General Marshall and General MacArthur.[44] Canada's soldiers had taken part in Pacific ground operations with the Americans in August 1943 in the Aleutians, and looking ahead to the ultimate invasion of the Home Islands, the General Staff in Ottawa came to the conclusion as early as January 1944 that "it is desirable that Canada should participate in the war with Japan by sea, land and air."[45] The two North American governments agreed that army elements would be organized and equipped along American, rather than British, lines but that the individual units would still retain regimental affiliations and their current uniforms. The Canadian Army Pacific Force (CAPF) was to be centered around the newly reconfigured 6th Infantry Division and fully integrated into the U.S. order of battle under an American corps headquarters.[46]

Some Canadian soldiers moved south in the fall of 1944 to begin specialized training at U.S. facilities, and by the time of the Potsdam Conference, when Churchill volunteered Commonwealth divisions to the invasion, roughly 1,200 "instructors" were already undergoing training at bases and camps spread across the States, with more on the way.[47] All planning and preliminaries had been conducted under the government-to-government agreement that the CAPF would serve with American forces since part of the objective was to forge closer ties between the United States and Canada.[48] Thus Churchill's proposal, if accepted by the government in Ottawa, would not only be at odds with the existing arrangement but also would insert a British layer of command between the Americans and Canadians and raise the disturbing possibility that Canada's full-blood entry into the Pacific war would be seriously delayed if its forces had to now wait for a separate "British" corps structure to be formed and trained for fighting the Japanese.

The war's sudden termination postponed the public unpleasantness that was sure to come between Ottawa and London, but the dissatisfaction of Canadian prime minister Mackenzie King and his War Cabinet finally boiled to the surface after yet another unilateral British proposal was made, this time involving the British Commonwealth Occupation Force (BCOF) for the occupation of Japan.[49] There was no delay at all, however, in what could only be termed a "forceful" response from Down Under.

Aside from the Canadian division, the most acceptable—and ready—Allied formation was the powerful Australian 1st Corps, which MacArthur, on April 19, 1945, had requested for Coronet. In the face of loud political pressure at home to just sit tight and let the war run its course with diminished Australian involvement, the Aussie high command already had started the process of freeing up its forces–and options–by eliminating or heavily attriting organized Japanese resistance in captured Australian and British territories to the north, which in effect were holding down roughly half of Australia's combat elements.[50] The surprise announcement of Churchill's proposed Commonwealth Corps came in the midst of these operations and the 1st Corps cleaning up the last Japanese resistance to its invasion of oil-rich Borneo. And even more galling was the British assumption that one of their generals with no experience fighting the Japanese, a corps commander from the Italian campaign, would lead the force and that British officers would make up his staff.

Australian war leaders, civilian and military, were determined that their army not be "submerged" in an organization that, in any event, might not even be ready in time to take part in the fighting.[51] On the question of command, their official history of the period stated, "It is unlikely that the Australian Government would have concurred in the appointment of an army commander who had no experience of fighting against the Japanese."[52] Indeed the sarcasm was dry and pointed when the new Australian prime minister, Joseph B. Chifley, fired off a cable to Churchill's equally new successor, Clement Attlee: "It is noted that you refer to 'British Commanders.' This expression is taken to mean officers of the United Kingdom Forces and not officers of Commonwealth Forces. . . . There are, of course, in the Australian Forces, officers who have distinguished themselves in the campaigns in the Middle East and the Pacific who have claims for consideration in the appointment of Commanders and Staffs."[53]

Events soon to play out in the formation of the BCOF provide a sure indication of how the command struggle for the Commonwealth Corps would have been resolved had the war continued. In this instance the government in London was dragged kicking and screaming into conceding the occupation's top spot to a succession of Australian commanders.[54] In the meantime, though, the Australian invasion force itself was, at least temporarily, cut back to one reinforced division. The announced downsizing of the U.S. and British armies after the victory in Europe made retention of six deployed Australian divisions a political impossibility, and plans were formed to cut this number in half. This in turn forced the Australian commitment to Coronet down to a reinforced division amalgamated from the 1st Corps' formations while the other two divisions continued to deal with the very sizable Japanese forces still fighting from the northern New Guinea coast through New Britain (Rabaul), to Bougainville.[55]

Sustained efforts to further degrade or completely eliminate these garrisons would free up numerous Aussie brigades, but the fielding of a full-up pure-Australian corps of more than two divisions was now highly unlikely. The Australians, nevertheless, were ready to give it their all and planned to keep a watchful eye for any signs that other Commonwealth elements—specifically the British—were slipping behind schedule.[56] In such an eventuality they were fully prepared to make their own arrangements with the other Commonwealth governments—specifically the New Zealanders[57]—and MacArthur maintained that it was "unthinkable that the AIF [Australian Imperial Force] should be separated from the U.S. Forces after they had been fighting together for three and a half years."[58]

One thing is certain, the Commonwealth Corps' late organization and retraining with American equipment, plus no reasonable expectation that time and resources would be available to train the Canadians in the specialized procedures for storming an enemy beach, would have all conspired to guarantee that no British Empire ground units would take part in the initial landings near Tokyo.[59] The corps would, however, be part of the "assault reserve afloat" to come ashore with other American elements relatively early in the Coronet battle, and before the massive pile-on of forces that included the U.S. Tenth Army. It is also reasonable to suggest that, with the Canadians very unlikely to take part, and the British just as likely to be depending on the Australians to round out the 3d Infantry Division's support elements, the Commonwealth Corps was going to be principally an Australian and New Zealand (ANZAC) formation commanded by an Australian three-star general. In any event, MacArthur made no secret of the fact that he planned to establish his invasion headquarters aboard an Aussie cruiser during the actual assault landings, and was emphatic that he would "hoist his flag on an RAN [Royal Australian Navy] ship."[60]

★   ★   ★

Lastly there were the Soviets, who planned to invade the northernmost Home Island of Hokkaido little more than two weeks after their armies stormed into Manchuria. It must be noted, however, that both the Soviet army's intent and capabilities are regularly blown well out of proportion by breathless individuals who have not bothered to closely read the works of the principal Western scholar to have intimately examined this subject.[61] At one point the Soviets had looked at the possibility of conducting an amphibious operation to seize the relatively populous southern half of the island.[62] But between their essentially nonexistent assault shipping, some transportable artillery but no armor, woefully inadequate naval gunfire support, and no ability to provide air support for the operation, plus the fact that the Japanese Fifth Area Army's defenses in southern Hokkaido, although undermanned, were well developed and recently upgraded, the Soviets wisely changed course. U.S. planners looking at the same territory estimated that four U.S. infantry divisions and one armored division, with the customary lavish support, were required for much the same task.[63]

Instead the Soviets switched to an operation calling for landings at a small, isolated port on the northwest coast. When the war ended, plans were on hold for the piecemeal insertion of two 87th Rifle Corps infantry divisions supported by a naval infantry battalion and as many as two construction battalions, while a third division continued mopping up the Kuril Islands and could eventually be made available for the lodgment. It was intended that air elements sufficient to support the invasion be hastily deployed forward to captured Japanese airfields on the southern half of Sakhalin Island, and the Soviets would have been able to do this with not an excessive amount of difficulty.

The Soviet navy's support was another matter, and the operation's naval component was so ludicrously small that the second rifle division to land would have had to wait until the six Lend-Lease LCIs (landing craft infantry) and a variety of slow-moving vessels used in place of assault shipping (trawlers, torpedo cutters, subchasers, and American-made minesweepers), returned more than two hundred miles to a recently secured Sakhalin port to pick them up.[64] Soviet warships had conducted no exercises, either combined or on their own initiative, in naval gunfire support of troops ashore, and all ships' antiaircraft protection and training were dangerously inadequate.

Despite the obvious deficiencies in Soviet amphibious capabilities, limitations in both manpower and materiel for this operation, and likelihood that the understrength 87th Rifle Corps would have been easily contained by minimal Japanese forces in this heavily mountainous region, a successful lodgment would nevertheless have served the wider political purposes of the Soviet government by its simple presence on Japanese soil if Washington had given a green light to the escapade.

CHAPTER 4

The Pacific Build-up and Berlin Decision

I told [President Roosevelt] that a so-called negotiated peace was impossible in this kind of war where one side was fighting for civilization and the other side represented barbarism; there was no common meeting ground and there therefore necessarily had to be a fight to the finish; that a fight to the finish meant a long horrible contest where we needed all the manpower that we could summon.

—HENRY L. STIMSON, diary entry, January 11, 1945[1]

As the last of the Kwantung's crack divisions disembarked unscathed from their transit across the Yellow Sea and surviving tankers from the southern oil fields reached Japan, U.S. Army planners completed what they hoped would be the final iteration of the redeployment plan they had been laboring over since early 1944. They had originally, and optimistically, believed that 2,442,000 men could be shipped to the Pacific from Europe and the United States (concurrent with 1,600,000 to the United States), all on the transport ships projected to be available after the defeat of Germany. Unfortunately the plan assumed that the Nazis would surrender by January 1945 and that nine months would be available for the overseas movements. There was also no way that the Pentagon planners could anticipate that in little more than a year—and unlike the Navy and Marines—the Army would find itself having to demobilize much of its manpower for political reasons. These and other matters forced the number of Pacific-bound men down, and down again, to 1,694,000 in December 1944, then 1,074,000 in March 1945 before the reality of increasingly casualty-intensive combat against the Japanese began to push the numbers back up.[2]

U.S. Army Forces, Pacific, under Gen. Douglas MacArthur, planned to absorb a myriad of new units during the last six months of 1945. The table of organization and equipment (TOE) strength of these formations totaled 1,039,000 men, who would swell AFPAC to

The SS *Queen Elizabeth*, carrying principally Army Medical Corps personnel, arrives in the Port of New York on June 29, 1945, the first of four transits that would cycle 70,000 redeploying troops to the United States by mid- August. Later that year, the *Queen Elizabeth, Queen Mary, Aquitania, Maureta- nia, Nieuw Amsterdam,* and *Ile de France* (collectively known as the "Monsters") were to begin the movement of redeployed formations from West Coast ports to Manila Bay as well as a British division to the Far East for Downfall. (U.S. Army)

some 2,440,000 by 1946, a figure that does not include either attrition replacements or the Navy, Marine, and, yes, even some Army elements that were being added to the forces oper- ating under the CINCPAC headquarters of Adm. Chester Nimitz in the central Pacific.[3] Excluding ground forces that would pass into the control of field commanders after the assault landings, planners estimated that the Navy in the Pacific would steadily swell to more than 1,150,000 men plus approximately 270,000 Marines, most of whom would pass into AFPAC's control.[4] Nor did it include the Army elements flooding into the Marianas and Okinawa to join the new U.S. Army Strategic Air Forces (USASTAF) led by Gen. Carl A. Spaatz. Between June 1945 and March 1946, Spaatz's command would increase by 166,000 men to 313,700, with more than two-thirds coming from the Army Air Forces and the balance split between the ground and service forces.[5] Secretary of War Stimson would later report that the number of American military personnel involved in operations to subjugate Japan "was of the order of 5,000,000 men; if all those indirectly concerned are included, it was larger still."[6]

Figure 2. Divisional Redeployment for the Invasion of Japan, 1945

Divisions	Arrives / United States	Arrives / Training Base	Arrives / Staging Base	Departs / United States	Arrives / Far East
86th Infantry* /Third Army	June 17 / New York	June 21 / Camp Gruber, Ok	August 14 / Camp Stoneman, Oakland, Calif.	August 21 / San Francisco	September 7 / Philippines (assigned garrison duty)
97th Infantry* /Third Army	June 26 / New York	June 28 / Fort Bragg, N.C.	August 22 / Fort Lawton, Wash.	September 1 / Seattle, Wa	September 24 / Japan (assigned occupation duty)
95th Infantry / Ninth Army	June 29 / Boston	July 3 / Camp Shelby, Miss.			
104th Infantry / First Army	July 3 / New York	July 9 / Camp San Luis Obispo, Calif. (both training and staging base)			
4th Infantry /Third Army	July 10 / New York	July 13 / Camp Butner, N.C.			
8th Infantry / First Army	July 10 / Hampton Roads, Va.	July 13 / Ft. Leonard Wood, Mo.			
87th Infantry /Third Army	July 11 / New York	July 14 / Fort Benning, Ga.			
5th Infantry /Third Army	July 19 / Boston	July 22 / Camp Campbell, Ky.			
2d Infantry /Third Army	July 20 / New York	July 22 / Camp Swift, Tex.			
44th Infantry /Third Army	July 20 / New York	July 24 / Camp Chaffee, Ark.			
13th Armored /Third Army	July 23 / Newport News, Va.	July 30 / Camp Cooke, Calif. (both training and staging base)			
28th Infantry** / Fifteenth Army	August 2 / Boston	August 7 / Camp Shelby, Miss.			
20th Armored / Seventh Army	August 6 / New York	August 13 / Camp Cooke, Calif. (both training and staging base)			
10th Mountain / Fifth Army	August 11 / Newport News, Va.	August 16 / Camp Carson, Colo.			
35th Infantry /Third Army	September 10 / New York	September 13 / Camp Breckenridge, Ky.			
91st Infantry / Fifth Army	September 10 / Hampton Roads, Va.	September 14 / Camp Rucker, Ala.			

Note: Alerted for movement to the United States and Pacific in August 1945: 69th, 78th, 91st, and 100th Infantry Divisions.

*Received amphibious training at Camp San Luis Obispo, Calif., in 1944.

**Earliest withdrawal from combat operations in preparation for redeployment, March 7, 1945.

After the defeat of Germany, all combat divisions in Europe were placed into one of four categories. Category I units were to stay as part of the occupations of Germany, Austria, and northeast Italy, while Category II units were to redeploy for the invasion as part of the Eighth Army and Tenth Army, already in the Pacific, and the "odd-number" U.S. First Army from the European theater. Category III units were slated for extinction and subject to a huge reshuffling that sent their "low-point" men to replace "high-point" men lost from the Pacific-bound and occupation divisions. Meanwhile their own high-point soldiers (those with scores totaling up to the magic number 85 or more) were transferred to Category IV divisions to be sent home for discharge. The Category IVs, however, would first have to cool their heels at camps in France while the Category IIs shipped out for the United States, where they would take on additional replacements while the cadre from Europe was on thirty-day leave.[7] To ensure that the base infrastructure to support these men was ready to receive them, 400,000 soldiers from nondivisional support service and construction troops were to be sent directly to the Pacific via the Panama Canal because of the Army Engineers' "exasperating shortage of units" and "failure to receive enough replacements" for the ones already in the Pacific theaters. More than 155,350 of these urgently needed service support and engineer soldiers left port from May through late August.[8]

By the time that representatives of Imperial Japan signed surrender documents aboard the USS *Missouri* on September 2, 1945, all but two of the initial sixteen divisions bound for the Pacific had arrived in the United States, and at least four more in Europe had received alerts for commitment to the following year's battles in Japan. Earlier, in March, the replacement stream for the war against Germany was for all practical purposes shut down. Correspondingly, ground replacements arriving in Europe, which had already dropped from 58,555 in March to 46,302 in April, now plummeted to only 737 in May.[9] The principal beneficiary of a replacement pipeline directed solely toward the Pacific was AFPAC, which was delighted to report that their perpetual "understrength" was reduced to less than 5,000 men thanks to the arrival of 46,420 replacements in May. By the end of the following month, MacArthur's command found itself with its first "overstrength" in the three and a half years since Pearl Harbor—23,029 men—in spite of a larger than anticipated number of soldiers having to be shifted to replacement depots on Okinawa, where the much-bloodied Tenth Army was fighting under CINCPAC.[10]

As far as the Army's senior leaders in Washington and Supreme Allied Headquarters, Europe (SHAFE) were concerned, the balance of fighting against Germany was simply going to be a giant mop-up stretching from the Adriatic to the North Sea. Not that mopping up, even in the strategic sense, is a painless affair. On the ground it still involves the lone platoon clearing a small wood, or the regiment-sized combat command forcing a river crossing in the face of heavy small arms and even artillery fire. Men are killed and wounded every day through what the British euphemistically refer to as "normal wastage" until the last scattered resistance is finally snuffed out, and American casualties in the European theater amounted to 41,058 and 2,028 in April and May respectively.[11] Yet even if the Germans did manage to form some semblance of an organized defense in a "National Redoubt" centered in the Bavarian Alps and western Austria,[12] such a concentration could be isolated, dissected into smaller and smaller pieces, and thoroughly pummeled by tactical air elements. Operations to reduce or force the surrender of diehard Nazis might persist into the summer, but with manageable casualties unaffected by any movement of forces to the Pacific because they would be spread over a period of time and replaced by troops already on hand from the demobilized Category III divisions. The planned redeployment and shift to a single, Pacific-oriented replacement stream did, however, have an unavoidable impact on one long-anticipated operation in Europe—the final Allied drive on Berlin.

If you had asked an American soldier trudging down a dusty French road where the fighting against Hitler's Nazis would finally end, "Berlin" would have been the answer, whether the GI wore stripes on his sleeve or stars on his collar. On April 4, 1945, Gen. Omar N. Bradley's Twelfth Army Group issued formal orders for the drive into the heart of Germany. The Ninth Army, under Lt. Gen. William H. Simpson, was instructed to seize a bridgehead over the Elbe River and "be prepared to continue the advance on Berlin or to the northeast," the latter move being one that would put the First Army on its right into the capital instead. By April 13 Simpson's army had its bridgehead and orders were issued to expand it "to include Potsdam," when he was told two days later by Bradley to halt on the river.[13] The question of what to do about Berlin had been boiling for weeks among the SHAFE commander Gen. Dwight D. Eisenhower, London, and Washington, with the British prime minister and Chiefs of Staff stressing the political and psychological importance of seizing Berlin while Eisenhower, with the decisive backing of President Roosevelt and General Marshall, firmly maintained that the focus must remain on the German army itself.[14]

But why this almost single-minded determination to seemingly throw out the window the fundamental Clausewitzian dictum that war is "dominated by the political object" on the part of Eisenhower?[15] The SHAFE commander had stated several times that he would take advantage of "an opportunity to capture Berlin cheaply" and even "cheerfully adjust" his plans if so ordered. But Eisenhower's bosses in Washington, although under heavy and persistent pressure from Churchill and others to do so, pointedly refrained from issuing such orders, and the British were wise enough to not press for a formal decision by the Combined Chiefs of Staff because of the simple fact that all concerned knew the United States had another dangerous foe to conquer in addition to the Nazis.[16]

Time was tight. Shipping was tight. And while most of the Category II divisions destined for 1946 operations in the Pacific were *not* part of the Ninth and redeploying First Armies eyeing Berlin but belonged instead to Third Army (much to the chagrin of its commander who would soon find this out), there was little muscle behind the spearheads on the Elbe River.[17] Eisenhower reminded Marshall that his center of gravity was far to the rear,[18] and both commanders knew well that a soldier-intensive battle in Berlin would force the bulk of U.S. forces east and commit them to a fight of unknown duration at the exact time that many European theater divisions had to prepare for an about-face that would send them west.[19]

Hundreds of Eisenhower's smaller nondivisional engineer and support elements were critically needed in the Pacific, and the invasion schedule—with "little margin of error"—required that many of them begin the process of leaving directly for the Pacific, where they would be immediately absorbed into MacArthur's AFPAC, not for Operation Coronet in

1946 but for Olympic, a scant six months in the future.[20] Moreover, the replacement spigot, in anticipation of no significant fighting, had been shut off and divisions were already beginning to be pulled from combat operations in preparation for the movement west. One of them, the Ninth Army's 95th, received its marching orders on the very day that Simpson was ordered to sit tight at the Elbe.[21]

The War Department had begun as early as February to press Eisenhower for his redeployment plans and his intelligence chief, Maj. Gen. Kenneth Strong, who "had great respect for the Germans' resilience, [also] cautioned Eisenhower right up to the very end to take no chances." The supreme allied commander had "frequently mentioned to [Strong] the worries he had about readying troops for movement to the Pacific"[22] but was willing to consider making a run at Berlin if it could be done on the cheap—perhaps 10,000 casualties—and asked Bradley what would be the cost. Bradley's answer that it might be as high as 100,000 casualties slammed the door on any further discussion, for although Army Group Commander Bradley thought in terms of this as being a "pretty stiff price to pay for a prestige objective,"[23] the strategic complications presented by this quantity of losses was crystal clear at Eisenhower's level of command.[24]

Eisenhower had not yet been fully briefed on Olympic and Marshall was allowing him great latitude in deciding on the closing offensive actions, but even though the SHAFE commander was not anxious to send his divisions east, Marshall was also keeping a close eye on the situation lest the British senior commanders and Churchill somehow succeed in maneuvering Eisenhower into an ill-considered attempt to seize the city.[25] He had little to worry about. For both soldiers there was no question at all that a full-scale battle east of the Elbe must be avoided, because if it did occur, precisely how would Eisenhower manage to reconstitute the units from which the approximately 100,000 men were "deducted"?

The answer is, Eisenhower couldn't. To do so would either gut his occupation forces or require potentially severe dislocations for Coronet by throwing some Category II divisions into the cauldron, outcomes that would have put at risk national war aims. Subjecting Category II divisions to potentially heavy and prolonged combat was not a risk that anyone in the U.S. chain of command would even suggest. The nine Third Army divisions earmarked for the Pacific, and five more in the European theater scattered from Bavaria to the Rhineland (two more were in Italy), simply could not be a part of any battle for Berlin, nor would it have been likely that the Category IIs from the First and Ninth Armies be tasked with anything more than flank protection. With the British having their own troubles pushing units toward Denmark, and other American armies rushing south to head off any German consolidation in the Alps,[26] the grim task of wading into the 321 square mile urban area would have fallen on the still-dispersed First and Ninth Armies. Eisenhower, meanwhile, would be in the uncomfortable position of having to explain to Joseph Stalin, to whom he had outlined his closing moves in central Germany, why he was now sending his forces in a different direction than where he told the Soviets to expect them.

U.S. divisions racing forward to be committed in ones and twos, instead of a clenched fist, invited very severe losses once they got inside the city. The replacement stream to the European theater was shut down for good, yet units savaged in house-to-house fighting *must* be at least partially reconstituted for reasons of morale and politics. There are some very uncomfortable ways to do this in-theater through a draconian culling of service and support units, but that would have been highly disruptive and carried out practically on the heels of the same situation during the Germans' recent Ardennes offensive.[27] To make matters worse, many of those potential replacements were scheduled to ship out for the Pacific. And would it be a separate shuffling of personnel or one attempted as part of the planned redeployment musical chairs? Put simply, the U.S. Army in Europe did not have the manpower where it needed it to adequately support a brutal street fight in Berlin generating casualties that were neither anticipated nor prepared for in one lump during April and early May. Nor would replacements be readily available afterward to reconstitute the infantry's depleted ranks. Eisenhower could, however, cover several months of stiff but incremental fighting in the "Redoubt" with what was on hand. The Soviets, meanwhile, were already massed within striking distance of the capital and anxious to crush the "Nazi beast" in one final, titanic blow. Eisenhower's forces were more dispersed than is commonly realized, had accomplished their part in the defeat of Germany, and had other things to do.

That requirements for the invasion of Japan were a factor in the American resolve to not get bogged down in Berlin has remained off the radar screens of historians because constraints on the U.S. Army from the dispersal of it forces and general lack of troops was so fundamental, so elementary, that it need not be outlined and reiterated in communications among the senior commanders in Washington and Europe. There was the occasional cryptic comment or shorthand reference to the unfavorable disposition of American forces or prohibitive casualties but that, frankly, was all the generals really had to say among themselves because all concerned understood that a costly, open-ended battle this late in the campaign would throw carefully laid redeployment and occupation plans into turmoil. And for what gain? No one but Churchill envisioned that a half-century-long struggle for control of Europe was about to begin and that the struggle would have Berlin at its apex. What they did know was that wherever the American field armies came to a stop—and at least a dozen U.S. divisions were already conducting combat operations in the future East Germany— they would soon move yet again to the "temporary" national occupation zones agreed upon at the Yalta Conference.[28]

Thus while this gigantic movement of men to the Pacific would, in the end, have no effect on the outcome of the war with Japan because of the war's early termination, it did influence what many consider to be one of the most important decisions of World War II, a decision that would have a pivotal impact on Germany and East-West relations during the Cold War. And unlike the final death throes of the Nazis, which saw Soviet troops engage the bulk of German strength and suffer 352,475 casualties, including 78,291 dead, during their final, twenty-three-day assault on Berlin and central Germany, American casualties for essentially the same period would be 43,086 with 8,351 killed in action.[29] Many of these soldiers were hastily buried in battlegrounds that would soon be turned over to the Red Army as part of the Soviet-administered territory. Over the next two years, some 2,334 Americans, including many Army Air Forces personnel lost earlier, were reinterred in U.S. military cemeteries after the military government authorities of both nations made arrangements for their painstaking recovery from what would later become East Germany.[30]

It is not surprising that most of the focus on the U.S. Army's redeployment has centered on the large, 14,000-man combat divisions. Because of their "all-arms" makeup of a wide variety of fighting and support elements, plus their degree of independence during battle, they have been of great interest to historians and military professionals alike. Divisional veterans associations' ranks were also swelled after the war by the surprisingly large numbers of soldiers cycled through the longest-serving divisions whose exploits were featured in the Movie Tone newsreels and newspapers around the country. Other, less-famous divisions still garnered much national interest, and even more attention locally in the case of National Guard units, the ranks of which retained a strong regional flavor long after their front-line infantry battalions had been "nationalized" through the daily grind of combat. Unlike these formations, however, the 400,000 European and Mediterranean theater nondivisional service and construction troops destined for the Pacific are rarely given a second thought.

By the spring of 1946, when the last of these men were to finally reach the Far East, there would be 236,000 Army Engineers fielded on just the Kanto Plain near Tokyo during Coronet, almost as many as existed in MacArthur's entire command in October of the previous year, some 253,400 Army Engineers.[31] On top of this there were another 59,000 naval construction battalion personnel and 25,000 Australian engineers under AFPAC when Japan surrendered in September 1945.[32] In the summer of 1945, however, Navy, Army Air Corps, the Army Transportation Corps (with its own fleet of allocated Liberty ships and chartered transports), plus MacArthur's private navy of more than 130 transports and cargo ships,[33] were struggling to deliver the redeploying Service Forces and "roll up" the Southwest Pacific bases that were now far to the rear and irrelevant to the coming invasion.[34]

Filling out the U.S. Sixth Army's TOE with the men and equipment required for the grim fighting on Kyushu was a daunting task, but one that was likely to be adequately addressed because the functions and interchangeability of service and support units make them relatively easy to plug into the scheme of operations and because of the sheer effort behind the movement. Unfortunately, "adequate" was as good as could be hoped for Olympic since the redeployment and roll-up of these elements, following the sad pattern of earlier Pacific efforts,[35] was grinding along at a painfully slow pace and inhibiting the ability of many such units to engage in the planned *support* of the buildup of which they were a part. The situation would have largely rectified itself during the run-up to next year's Operation Coronet because of the Herculean efforts of military engineers in the Philippines and Okinawa, but that was then and this was now.[36]

A July 28, 1945, accounting of units controlled by, or in transit to, the Sixth Army shows that 221 of them at the now-useless Pacific bases in New Guinea, the Solomon Islands, and even New Caledonia were yet to depart for the Olympic staging areas on Luzon or Okinawa. Fully 355 more of this truly eclectic collection of combat-power multipliers—the 1527th Engineer Dump Truck Company, 239th Quartermaster Laundry Detachment, 443d MP POW Processing Company, 3073 Quartermaster Refrigeration Company, 3083d Ordnance Motor Vehicle Distribution Company, 30th Traffic Regulation Group, 814th Signals Service Company (Port), 671st Medical Collection Company, 1018th Engineer Treadway Bridge Company, 24th Signals Heavy Construction Battalion, 2855th Engineer Well Drilling Detachment, and so on—were somewhere along the pipeline between

Europe and the western Pacific. Not counting sixteen general hospitals that were going to stage directly from the United States during the invasion, there were thirty-two other units known to be deploying from the States, but the very large number of military government units were excluded from the tally so the number from the States is even larger.[37]

The going was also slow for the Army Air Forces where "the problems of demobilization threatened to swamp the machinery established for redeployment."[38] And while this would, like so many of the redeployment's teething problems, work itself out over time, as of war's end only the 319th Bombardment Group (an A-26 Invader medium bomber outfit) plus the 369th and 514th Air Service Groups had reached the Far East intact and initiated operations. Eighth Air Force headquarters was officially transferred to the Pacific on July 16, 1945, but aside from a few "key figures" from the European theater, its personnel at that time all came from the Pacific or United States.[39] The initial combat elements of the Eighth were going to be hastily declared operational in order to get them into the air on what would turn out to be the last day of the war, but Okinawa's still very limited runways were tied up by previously scheduled Fifth Air Force missions and it did not achieve operational status until after the close of hostilities.[40]

The Air Force later conceded that "when Japan surrendered in mid-August 1945, the units redeployed from Europe to the Asiatic-Pacific theaters were still insignificant in number." But this certainly wasn't anticipated as late as the March 1945 time frame when it was believed that most of these elements would deploy nonstop to the Far East. Early Army Air Forces redeployment plans seem to have been formed by staff who were either unaware of just how tight the shipping situation was or operated under the assumption that ample vessels would simply become available. This, however, is only a guess, and one official Air Force historian found the situation so murky that he was driven to speculation: "Perhaps the setback AAF planners had suffered when Germany failed to collapse on schedule, in the fall of 1944, caused them to be caught off balance when V-E Day did come, despite the fact that it had been so long in sight; perhaps it was merely the magnitude of the operation that made the redeployment machine so slow in getting under way."[41]

Estimates for the number of direct transits hit rock bottom when the May 15, 1945, "Revised Redeployment Forecast" announced that the Army Air Force units set to sail for the Pacific had been slashed to only a service command headquarters, a fighter wing headquarters, and two complete air service groups before some relief to shipping bottlenecks elsewhere freed up more assets for AAF use. A small number of elements were put back on the list, and units culled from the Ninth, Twelfth, Fifteenth, and "old" Eighth Air Forces received orders to pack up and be ready for a long sea voyage when the assigned vessels became available. Two Twelfth Air Force units destined for the "new" Eighth on Okinawa, the 35th Fighter Group and the 547th Air Service Group, eventually "got as far on their way to the Pacific as the Panama Canal on V-J Day; [but] with the announcement of the Japanese surrender, orders were changed, and the transport headed for New York."[42]

CHAPTER 5

"Not a Recipe for Victory"

I am sure people do not realize how close we came to catastrophe. Shortages of personnel forced us to strip division after division that we had trained. This drove the division commanders to strenuous protests. Just as those new units were reaching an excellent standard of efficiency, we would rip them to pieces in order to provide men as replacements for the growing battles overseas. We lacked sufficient replacements because deliveries from Selective Service were short in terms of a hundred thousand or more. We were confronted with a terrible problem for which the armies in the field paid the price. . . . We had just enough and no more, and it all went in.

—GEN. GEORGE C. MARSHALL, June 11, 1945[1]

Implementing the November 1945 invasion of Kyushu, Operation Olympic, was going to require fully half of the U.S. Army's divisions in the Pacific and half of the Marine divisions as well. These thirteen picked formations—really fourteen "division equivalents" because of the addition of two heavily augmented regimental combat teams—belonged to the U.S. Sixth Army under Lt. Gen. Walter Krueger. Although a few had not yet been severely bloodied, all were veteran units with the exception of the 98th Infantry Division fresh from Hawaii, while four, the Americal, 25th, 77th, and the 2d Marine, had seen so much fighting that their most experienced soldiers had been scooped up wholesale and whisked away to staging locations for the trip home during the "midwar" demobilization. Three of Sixth Army's divisions, the 1st Cavalry, 43d, and 77th (formerly with Tenth Army), had fought well into the summer on central Luzon and Okinawa but would nevertheless have an amount of time to refit and take on replacements that would have made division staffs in the European theater green with envy.[2]

The relatively new U.S. Eighth Army of Lt. Gen. Robert L. Eichelberger had landed on Luzon in late January 1945, then initiated wide-ranging amphibious operations throughout the central and southern Philippines in February with five divisions, some culled from the overweight Sixth. By summer an extensive reshuffling resulted in three divisions being sent to the Sixth in exchange for five others as the Eighth absorbed all divisions not retained by Krueger's command for Olympic. The Eighth and Tenth Armies were also in the process of receiving their shares of the European theater divisions when the war ended, as was the newly arrived First Army of Lt. Gen. Courtney Hicks Hodges, the only "odd number" European theater army given the job of also fighting the Japanese. Interestingly the First was assigned three divisions from the U.S. Tenth Army on Okinawa and three from the Marines, thus giving it far more major combat elements from the Pacific than from Europe. As for Lt. Gen. Joseph "Vinegar Joe" Stilwell's Tenth Army, it was quickly stripped of nearly every Army and Marine division in its order of battle after the Okinawa campaign—and would likely lose all of them—but was just as speedily going to be repopulated with redeployed formations.

The apportionment of European theater divisions to Operation Coronet's three American field armies was roughly a month from finalization when the war ended, and the order of battle on the accompanying AFPAC chart was purely notional, produced only to give commanders and staffs an overview of what was going to be available for the desperate fighting on Honshu. An example of this is the 96th Infantry Division in XXIV Corps under the First Army. While the corps' other divisions and headquarters had still not been shifted out of the Tenth Army by war's end, the 96th was reassigned, not to the First Army, but to the Eighth. And of the five "lettered" corps which would command the actions of three divisions apiece in battle, only "A" was confirmed to be the XIII Corps' headquarters and staff of Maj. Gen. Alvin C. Gillem—but even this was subject to change.[3] The other corps commanders and staffs that had yet to be matched up were Maj. Gen. James A. Van Fleet's III Corps, Maj. Gen. Clarence R. Huebner's V Corps, Lt. Gen. J. Lawton Collins's VII Corps, and Maj. Gen. Matthew B. Ridgway's XVIII Airborne Corps.[4] And while this list includes some of the Army's foremost combat leaders, General Marshall in Washington suggested that this "who's who" should be further expanded.

Much has been made about the mythical "black book" of George C. Marshall,[5] in which he was reputed to have listed the strengths and weaknesses of officers that he had met earlier in his career, but Marshall may have had something very real in mind relating to Pastel deception operations (see chapter 14) when he initially put forward the names of four specific divisional commanders from Europe for MacArthur's consideration: Maj. Gen. Maxwell D. Taylor, Maj. Gen. Anthony C. McAuliffe, Maj. Gen. James M. Gavin, and Maj. Gen. Robert T. Frederick.[6] Aside from their reputations as well-rounded—and aggressive—officers, each man, coincidentally, belonged to the exceedingly small circle of general officers with extensive airborne experience, and the latter two carried the additional distinction of being regularly mistaken for battalion, or even company, commanders when in the field with their paratroopers. The "baby-faced" Gavin, of the 82d Airborne Division, was widely touted in the press as being the youngest general since George Armstrong Custer, while Frederick, who was only eight days his senior and wore a thin mustache in a failed

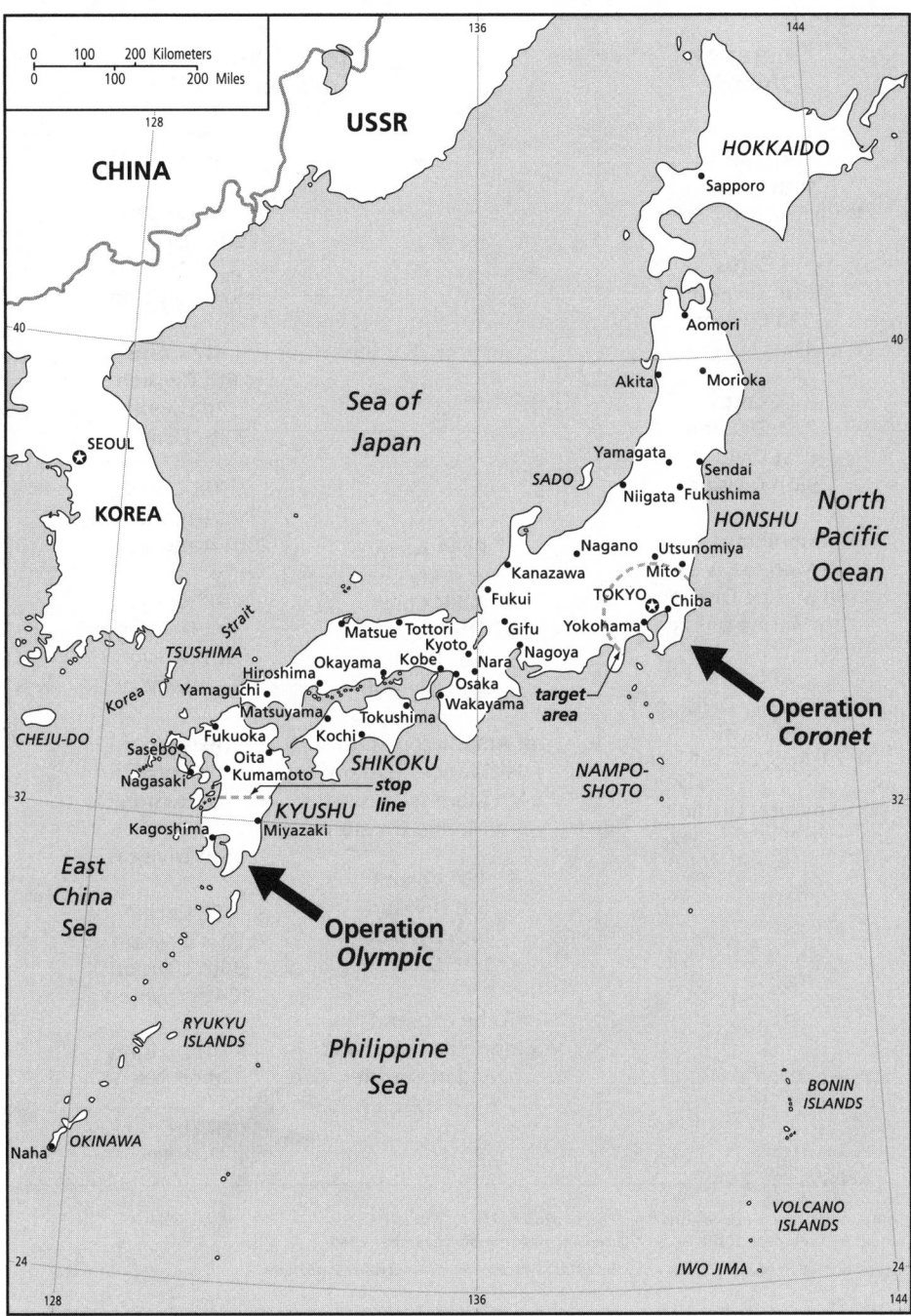

Map derived from D. M. Giangreco, "Operation Downfall: The Devil Was In The Details," Joint Force Quarterly (Autumn, 1995), 88.

The component operations of Operation Downfall.

attempt to hide his youth, commanded the Seventh Army Airborne Division (Provisional), then 45th Infantry Division.[7]

MacArthur, however, was having none of it. He replied that his divisions were already "magnificently officered" and diplomatically threw the suggestion back at Marshall: "I

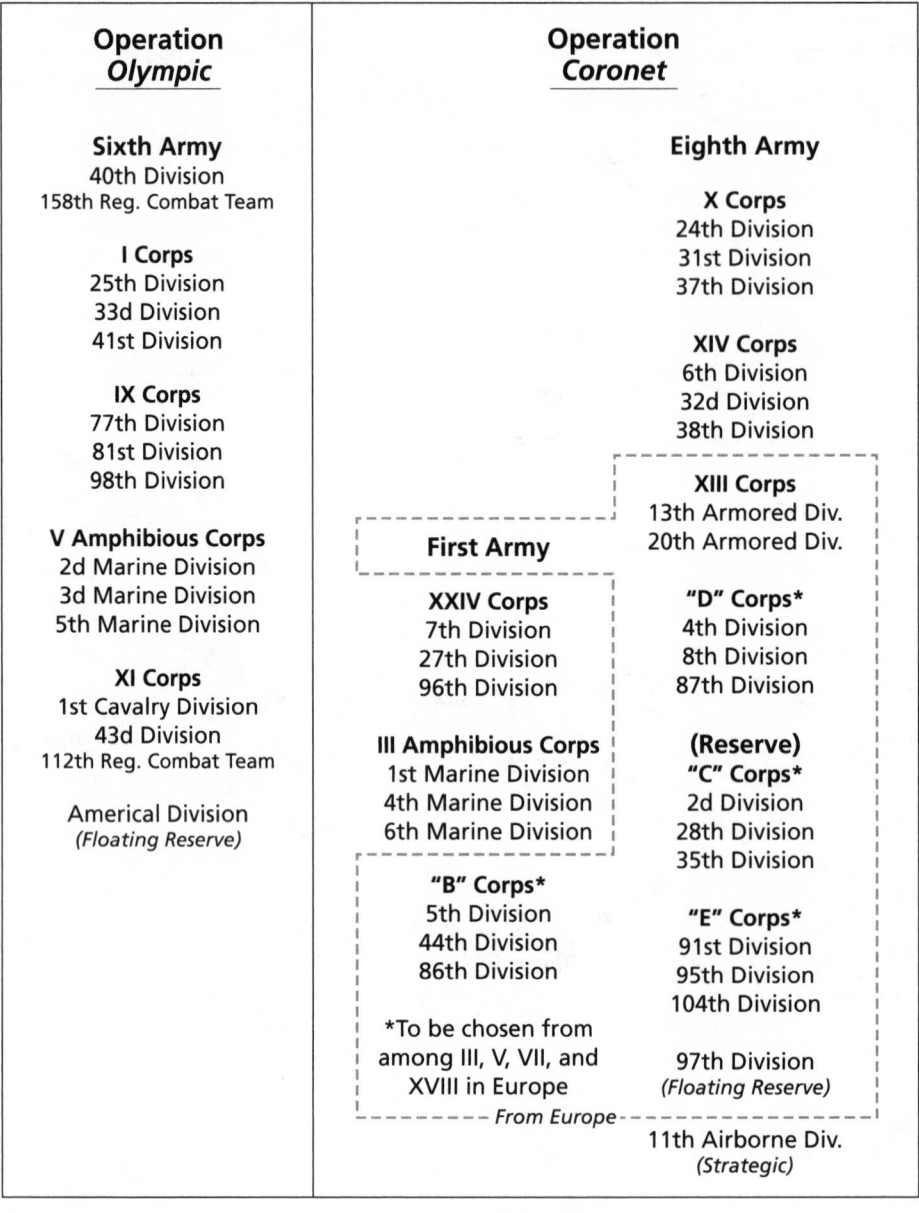

Operation Olympic

Sixth Army
40th Division
158th Reg. Combat Team

I Corps
25th Division
33d Division
41st Division

IX Corps
77th Division
81st Division
98th Division

V Amphibious Corps
2d Marine Division
3d Marine Division
5th Marine Division

XI Corps
1st Cavalry Division
43d Division
112th Reg. Combat Team

American Division
(Floating Reserve)

Operation Coronet

Eighth Army

X Corps
24th Division
31st Division
37th Division

XIV Corps
6th Division
32d Division
38th Division

First Army

XXIV Corps
7th Division
27th Division
96th Division

III Amphibious Corps
1st Marine Division
4th Marine Division
6th Marine Division

"B" Corps*
5th Division
44th Division
86th Division

*To be chosen from among III, V, VII, and XVIII in Europe
— — — — — — From Europe

XIII Corps
13th Armored Div.
20th Armored Div.

"D" Corps*
4th Division
8th Division
87th Division

(Reserve)
"C" Corps*
2d Division
28th Division
35th Division

"E" Corps*
91st Division
95th Division
104th Division

97th Division
(Floating Reserve)

11th Airborne Div.
(Strategic)

Some combination of divisions from the provisional B, C, D, and E Corps would become part of the reconstituted Tenth Army by November 1945.

Source: General Headquarters, U.S. Army Forces in the Pacific, Operation Coronet Staff Study.

believe, moreover, that in view of the splendid record of the four general officers you named that careful consideration should be given to their appropriate assignment to redeployed divisions."[8] This was a disappointing, and rather disingenuous, answer in light of the fact that the new 98th Infantry Division had as yet seen no combat. And undoubtedly there were some European commanders who hoped to replace Maj. Gen. Robert S. Beightler at the helm of the 37th Infantry Division, for although he was an excellent fighting general,

Beightler had risen to his position through the National Guard, a practically scandalous state of affairs to some officers in the regular Army. Lieutenant General Krueger, Beightler's commander throughout most of the war, would later comment that "Beightler's only trouble was he was a damn National Guardsman."[9]

MacArthur had earlier ignored the chief of staff's "intent" when Marshall said in an April 6 message that those who had "not demonstrated a high standard" of battlefield prowess should be replaced by European theater soldiers who had. Marshall specifically mentioned that Lt. Gen. George S. Patton (who was about to have most of his Third Army divisions redeployed out from under him) as well as Omar Bradley both desired to fight in the Pacific.[10]

Before D-day, in fact, Patton had directed his intelligence section to maintain a situation map of Pacific operations (as well as the Soviet's eastern front) and perform regular briefings on the theater. Then on March 24, 1945, the day after his Third Army forced a crossing over the Rhine, he ordered that terrain maps for Japan be obtained with a special emphasis placed on its rivers.[11]

Another helpful hint by Marshall in June that Patton and various other generals were available to replace the Tenth Army commander, recently killed on Okinawa by Japanese artillery fire, was also disregarded by MacArthur. The Army chief of staff finally put his boot down when MacArthur stated that he planned to move one of his corps commanders into the Tenth Army top spot, and Marshall curtly informed him that he had directed General Stilwell to take the job.[12] Stilwell, who had been fighting Japanese field armies—and an inept, duplicitous Chinese leadership—since 1942 in the China-Burma-India theater, was an excellent choice for the job and most recently had been placed in command of Army Ground Forces, where he brought his experience to bear in training forces for the upcoming invasions of Kyushu and Honshu.

Even as late as mid-August 1945, when the Japanese announced their surrender, and months after Stilwell took command on Okinawa, the Tenth Army was still a mighty nebulous entity, and the only two redeploying divisions that would actually make it to the Far East, the 86th and 97th, had not yet left the United States. The victims of an unforeseen German offensive, War Department politics, and the Army's perpetual manpower shortage, these two formations had originally not been envisioned to be part of the redeployment at all.

The 97th Infantry Division, followed by the 86th, completed amphibious training specifically for the invasion of Japan at Camp San Luis Obispo, California, the year before, and both were briefly co-located at nearby Camp Cooke before the Germans' December 1944 strike in the Ardennes. Throughout the period that they trained for fighting the Japanese, Secretary of War Henry L. Stimson in Washington was pushing to have more of the Army's manpower allotted to the formation of additional combat divisions like them, but General Marshall was just as adamant that the lack of soldiers, and especially officers, made it impossible to efficiently support more divisions.[13] The Germans' Ardennes offensive brought renewed pressure from Stimson to create such formations, but Marshall was just as firm that this could not be done without creating immense manpower disruptions. Marshall had successfully rebuffed Stimson for almost a year on this issue, but in the crisis atmosphere of the current emergency, "head-on fight[s]" (Stimson's description) erupted between Stimson, Marshall, and Marshall's deputy chief of staff, Maj. Gen. Thomas T. Handy.[14] "Mr. Stimson gave orders to start work on ten new divisions," said Marshall. "I told Mr. Stimson that I opposed this to the point of resigning, and asked him to tell the president this. . . . Then he dropped it."[15]

The only way to keep peace in the War Department family was for Marshall to send the uncommitted 86th and 97th Infantry Divisions to Europe in spite of the fact that they would have absolutely no impact on either the current emergency or the defeat of Germany. Stimson disliked this option almost as much as Marshall because the units were functionally the nation's total strategic reserve since the other uncommitted divisions in the United States were already slated for the European theater.[16] The ostensibly small amount of forces available to reinforce Eisenhower was the stated reason for having these divisions pull up stakes in California, but the impression among their officers and men alike was that they were really being sent to Europe because their leaders in Washington had "panicked" over the temporary German resurgence. This was only reinforced when it became clear to the men that more than a half dozen other fresh divisions were sailing to Europe ahead of them.[17]

The 86th and 97th crossed the Atlantic together between February 14 and March 1, 1945, in a sixty-ship convoy to Le Havre, France. Elements of both divisions were involved in combat operations by early April as the German army, having expended nearly all of its reserves in the Ardennes offensive and elsewhere, neared its final collapse. By the end of the war they had suffered 1,714 casualties fighting their way into Czechoslovakia and Austria, respectively, and then "revisited" Le Havre, from which they were shipped home in June. Because they were the first redeployed units to return and had already undergone amphibious training, both divisions were sent back to the West Coast again and speedily readied for movement to the Pacific after their soldiers received the mandatory thirty-day leave due Pacific-bound veterans. With few demobilization points accrued by VE-day, they became a ready asset for freeing up long-serving troops in the Far East, and both shipped out across the Pacific just before VJ-day, the 86th for garrison duty in the Philippines and the 97th for the occupation of Japan—not an insignificant amount of travel since their February boarding of east-bound troop trains in California.[18]

★   ★   ★

What did the Japanese know about this enormous movement of men and materiel all aimed directly at *them*? As noted earlier the fact that Japanese units took few American prisoners and were, in any event, functionally annihilated or cut off shortly after they entered combat meant that they had few opportunities to obtain, let alone communicate, meaningful and comprehensive battlefield intelligence to higher headquarters.[19] Consequently IGHQ in Tokyo operated largely in the dark on such fundamental matters as the U.S. order of battle except for what they could obtain from their German allies until that avenue was finally eliminated as well. Communications intelligence directed principally at U.S. Navy message traffic (aided all too often by weak American signals discipline) and long-range aerial reconnaissance (sometimes selectively allowed for deception purposes) provided glimpses of the frightful build-up, but as they had done throughout the war, the Japanese leaned heavily on American press reports.

The IGHQ planning documents and reports from 1945, as well as postwar inter-rogations and recollections of both formal and informal meetings of senior officers and other civilian officials, frequently display an almost touching faith in the accuracy of the American media and the veracity of official U.S. military pronouncements. Comments such as "the partial demobilization and reconversion following the end of hostilities in EUROPE aroused optimism" and "re[j]ection of the National Conscription Law, increases in labor strife, criticism of strategy, et cetera are obstacles to success of the government's war measures"[20] can only have been derived from a close monitoring of the press. Moreover, in addition to "unconfirmed reports," changes to IGHQ's interpretation of the U.S. Army's order of battle in 1945 cited published press releases from the "Allied Expeditionary Headquarters on 22 May," "Supreme Headquarters of the Allied Powers made on the first of June," "an announcement made by the United States,"[21] and an "early June announce-ment by Headquarters, Allied Expeditionary Forces."[22] This is not to say, however, that the conclusions of Japanese analysts were correct, and there is even some evidence that mistakes in the German army's interpretation of the U.S. Army's strength, prompted by the Allies' extensive deception campaign ahead of the Normandy invasion, eventually crept into Japanese estimates as well.

Although the U.S. Army's fielded infantry divisions were numbered 1 through 106, there were numerous gaps in the sequence where units simply did not exist. Widespread press reports throughout 1942 that the Army planned to raise roughly two hundred divi-sions of all types did not go unnoticed by the Germans and Japanese, who were able to closely follow the sometimes raucous deliberations of one House and *five* Senate investiga-tions of the manpower question.[23] It took a while for the realities of industrial-agricultural production and Army Air Force needs, plus the snowball effect of severe monthly shortfalls in the number of men inducted,[24] to be fully appreciated, but by 1943 the number of such formations was scaled back considerably and eventually shrank to a planned "troop basis" of one hundred divisions.

It was soon apparent, however, that even this could not be properly maintained, and on the heals of a public announcement that an expansion of the force by at least twelve divi-sions was going to be "deferred until 1944," the Army found that it instead had to cut the one-hundred-division goal still further to a barely adequate force of ninety divisions. This removal of ten divisions (essentially one field army) already scheduled for activation was kept a closely guarded secret "lest this news lead the American public to overconfidence and a relaxation of the war effort" and because it could lead "the enemy [to] conclude that the reduction signified that the United States was unable to fulfill its mobilization schedule."[25]

The Germans and Japanese knew nothing of the removal of these formations, infor-mally referred to within the U.S. Army as "ghost divisions," the unorganized component regiments and artillery battalions of which may also have been known to them. In addi-tion nineteen more completely fictitious "Phantom" divisions with corresponding support elements and even fake corps and field army headquarters were created for a wide-ranging deception operation designed to support the invasion of France in 1944. And unlike the unorganized ghost divisions, which were quietly dropped, the Army—with the full and energetic cooperation of the British—went to great lengths to make the apparent existence of the Phantom formations seem as real as possible by allowing tantalizing glimpses of their simulated troop movements, radio nets, encampments, and interaction with Phantom corps headquarters as well as real units.[26]

The deception included vehicle markings for nonexistent units and even shoulder patches worn by some of the skeletal engineer and intelligence elements making up the Phantom divisions in Britain as well as ports of embarkation in the United States. The patches, in fact, were commercially produced, along with legitimate insignia under standard Army contracts, and allowed to enter the militaria collectors market through one or more firms in Manhattan and a "Shoulder Patch Exchange" administered by *Yank*.[27] These patches were designed and produced under the direction of Arthur Du Bois, chief of the Heraldic Section of the Office of the U.S. Army Quartermaster General, who supplied them and fabricated heraldic data, along with authentic patches, insignia, and data, to *National Geographic* Magazine for open publication in a special edition.[28] The Germans believed completely in the existence of the Phantom divisions, and their patch designs—conveniently supplied by double agents in Great Britain—ultimately ended up on a U.S. order-of-battle wall chart in the German army's theater headquarters, OB West, in Paris.

But why not just use some of the announced but unactivated ghost divisions for the deception? On one hand, considerable work had already taken place on the mechanics of how these units would be organized and trained, plus there were elements within both the Army and War Department running as high as the secretary of war himself advocating that at least a portion of these formations be activated.[29] In addition the Phantom divisions were created to enhance certain perceptions that the Germans already had formed about the U.S. mobilization: First, that we could—and according to the deception, did—field a large number of airborne divisions in order to conduct significant operations almost anywhere along their "Atlantic Wall," and second, the perception that the United States could raise an army numbering in the hundreds of divisions. Consequently more than half of the Phantom divisions were either airborne formations (the 6th, 9th, 18th, and 21st), ones with very high numbers (the 108th, 119th, 130th, 141st, and 157th), or both (the 135th Airborne Division).[30]

This and other faulty intelligence was duly passed along to the Japanese by the German High Command, which was held captive by the deception operation until it finally unraveled in early August 1944 after some of the real divisions, which were also part of the ruse, appeared in Normandy, and their supposed commander, Patton, was found to be leading the American breakout from the invasion area.[31]

In the spring and summer of 1945, Japanese intelligence produced U.S. order of battle analyses based on (1) definitively known American units they or the Germans had faced in combat, (2) a range of strategic intelligence sources that were both constricted and problematical, (3) Allied disinformation passed on by the Germans, and (4) faulty assumptions that had much in common with those of medieval map makers who drew mythical islands where they supposed land might be. The Japanese believed that the U.S. Army contained a minimum of ninety-six infantry divisions (including the airborne divisions and single mountain division), far more than the true total of seventy-two such formations. An examination of the order of battle charts from mid-June and July 1, 1945, readily reveals that Japanese intelligence analysts had simply filled in a string of numbered divisions that only sporadically corresponded with the "ghost" divisions that the U.S. Army pulled back from activating in 1943.[32] The Phantom divisions created for the Normandy invasion are another matter.

The bogus airborne and high-number Phantom divisions do not appear in the IGHQ forecasts of what America might hurl at them, but nearly all of the remaining Phantom divisions do, and they generally carry "Germany" as a geographical designation while most of the other imaginary divisions are listed as being in the United States. Although it may simply be a coincidence that nine Phantom divisions are present in the later order of battle chart (up from eight in the spring), it appears more likely that this reflects the influence of German intelligence.[33]

In spite of Japanese intelligence being wrong on the specifics of the U.S. order of battle and their overestimating of the number of divisions likely to take part in the invasion, document after document demonstrates that they were uncannily accurate on the more pressing questions of precisely where and when the divisions would be committed.[34] To put it bluntly they had figured us out. Colonel Hattori Takushiro (twice chief of the Army General Staff's Operations Section and secretary to the war minister, General Anami Korechita) not only told U.S. Army interrogators in 1945 that they expected the initial invasion to be launched on Kyushu in October 1945 but also named the precise locations of the landings. Instead of a grinding war of attrition, the American military hoped for a less-costly battle of maneuver, but what Hattori told the Sixth Army's Intelligence chief Col. Horton V. White just after the surrender indicated that this had not been in the cards, and it must have made the intel officer's hair stand on end:

> They expected [the invasion] to be made during or after October 1945, they expected it to be made in southern Kyushu, and that our landing would be made on the beaches of Miyazaki, Ariake Wan, and Satsuma Peninsula. Their available combat forces had been deployed according to these expectations, with reserves being strengthened when hostilities ceased. . . . The Japanese forces planned to make a final stand near the beaches and units were instructed to remain in place until annihilated. Heavy counter-offensives in the beach areas were planned and little preparation was made for defense in depth.[35]

★   ★   ★

U.S. Army campaign planners envisioned the opening U.S. assault on southern Kyushu as one where overwhelming American strength would be directed against only a portion of Japan's forces cut off from reinforcement, and MacArthur had originally expected the Sixth Army to face from six to ten enemy divisions on Kyushu by the time the invasion was launched near the end of 1945. Unfortunately, as demonstrated above and confirmed by Edward J. Drea and Alvin D. Coox in separate studies, after three years of island hopping and end runs, the Japanese had gained a clear understanding of the methods and logistic

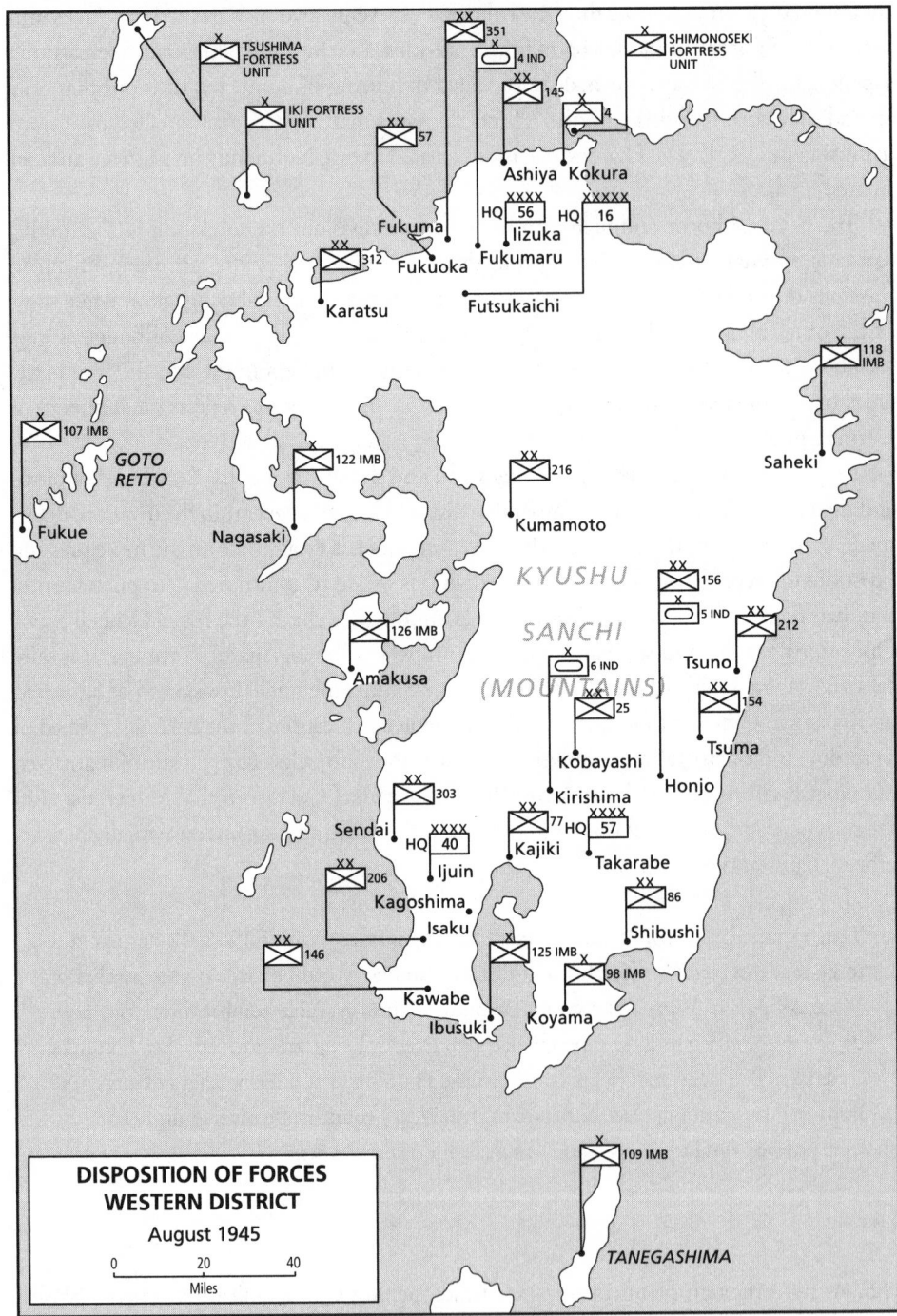

Map derived from "Homeland Operations Record" (Tokyo: U.S. Army Forces Far East, Military History Section, 1959; distributed by the Office of the Chief of Military History Washington, D.C.), 123.

The disposition of forces on Kyushu, August 1945.

requirements of America's rigidly set-piece amphibious operations and correctly deduced that southern Kyushu would be the next stepping-stone on the drive toward the heart of their empire.[36]

When interrogated after the war, Major Hori Eizo, a general staff officer charged with divining American intentions, simply noted that an invasion of Kyushu made "strategic common sense."[37] U.S. decryptions of intercepted radio transmissions, largely confirmed or supported by air reconnaissance, began to display an alarming buildup to intelligence staffs in Washington and Manila even as the Joint Chiefs confidently assured the new American president, Harry Truman, in mid-June that Kyushu could be cut off from significant reinforcements from Honshu once U.S. air power on Okinawa could be built up.[38] The Japanese feared this as well and had moved quickly to transfer troops and supplies to the threatened area *before* the bases on Okinawa could be brought fully into play. By combining reinforcements with the existing garrison and indigenously raised units, troop strength on the island climbed from four-plus division equivalents at the end of April to six one month later. By the end of June it was up to MacArthur's projected maximum of ten and soon reached thirteen-plus division equivalents. And while this was not immediately apparent, it had become alarmingly clear by the third week in July that a Japanese buildup was occurring at a swift, steady pace with "the end not in sight."[39]

MacArthur's intelligence chief, Maj. Gen. Charles A. Willoughby, warned:

> If this deployment is not checked it may grow to a point where we attack on a ratio of one (1) to one (1) which is not the recipe for victory. . . . The rate and probable continuity of Japanese reinforcements into the Kyushu area are changing the tactical and strategical situation sharply. . . . Massing in present attack sectors is evident. Unless the use of these [communications] routes is restricted by air and/or naval action . . . enemy forces in Southern Kyushu may be still further augmented until our planned local superiority is overcome, and the Japanese will enjoy complete freedom of action in organizing the area and in completing their preparations for defense.[40]

Willoughby applied a standard military analysis based on force ratios, terrain, recent experience, and other factors to the number of known Japanese troops on Kyushu that produced a range of possible U.S. battle casualties running from approximately 210,000 to 280,000 during the push to a stop line almost half way up the island. The intelligence chief then rounded this down to a conservative estimate of 200,000 battle casualties inflicted by the thirteen to fourteen Japanese divisions then accounted for on Kyushu.[41] This figure implies nearly 500,000 losses to *all causes* during Operation Olympic, although perhaps 50,000 of these men would return to duty after light to moderate care.

Unfortunately Japanese troop strength continued to soar. Several months later, when Willoughby wrote an appreciation for field grade and general officers, he referred to these Japanese divisions accounted for in his July 29, 1945, intelligence analysis but did not note that an *additional* two divisions and a division equivalent (two armored brigades) had appeared by the time Japan surrendered. This was not an oversight, for although the July 29 intelligence report, though classified, was nonetheless widely disseminated and known, the existence of the new divisions had not been released beyond the top secret summaries of decoded Japanese radio traffic and thus could not be included in Willoughby's unclassified assessment.[42] In any event the number of stated Japanese divisions was "sinister" enough as it was, and Willoughby said so to his military audience. Interestingly, this same analysis by MacArthur's intelligence chief could be, and eventually was, breezily dismissed by critics of Truman's decision to use nuclear weapons as simply a "postwar creation" since it was not committed to paper until several months after the fighting was over. And naturally this begs a question. Just what did President Truman and his senior military and civilian advisors know about potential casualties during the invasion?

CHAPTER 6

The Decision

We knew that [the Japanese] had been making these ploys and they'd been suggesting some prince [Konoye Fumimaro] to see the Russians. We knew that these ploys were being made. . . . There must have been a party which—on some terms—would talk about quitting. But we weren't at all sure that that party would succeed.

—HARVEY H. BUNDY, special assistant to Secretary of War Stimson[1]

The situation in the Pacific involves countless American lives and it seems clear to us that every type of weapon should be utilized.

—WILLIAM J. DONOVAN, director, Office of Strategic Services, July 18, 1945[2]

The Japanese defenders of Okinawa were inflicting casualties on U.S. combat units at a rate that was both faster and higher than in previous campaigns. The ratios of only 4.6 and 5 Japanese casualties (usually deaths) for every 1 American battle casualty during the recent fighting on Leyte and Luzon respectively were far closer than what had been experienced during earlier Southwest Pacific operations. By Okinawa the ratio had shrunk to 2 to 1 and an even more appalling 1.25 to 1 during the brutal fighting that had finally sputtered to an end on Iwo Jima.[3]

How did the terribly costly Okinawa and Iwo Jima campaigns affect the thinking of President Truman and senior members of his administration? First, it is important to understand that all of these men had long been in positions that enabled them to absorb ongoing military intelligence and were deeply involved in the never-ending struggle to get enough American men into the war. Moreover, the long-expected "casualty surge" that they had all known was coming finally arrived in the summer of 1944 with D-day in France and the invasion of the Mariana Islands in the Pacific. Of America's roughly 1,250,000 combat and combat-related casualties in World War II, nearly 1 million of this number would be suffered from June 1944 to June 1945, a degree of losses that people today would understandably find astounding.[4]

For almost a year before the invasion of Okinawa, a Joint Chiefs of Staff (JCS) planning group in the Pentagon had been working on a document outlining its concept of the final stages of the Pacific war. This document was released for comment by other groups on June 6, 1944, and approved for submission to the Joint Chiefs as JCS 924, "Operations Against Japan Subsequent to Formosa," midway through the month-long battle for Saipan in the Marianas. It was regularly updated well into the Truman presidency.[5]

At Saipan the cost of 3,426 American dead plus more than 13,000 wounded to kill 22,000 Japanese defenders had a sobering effect on the JCS's Joint Strategic Survey Committee, which presided over the refinements made to "Operations against Japan Subsequent to Formosa."[6] Through the spring of 1945, long after its name was rendered obsolete by the rush of events, JCS 924 was used as the primary outline for planning the series of campaigns to culminate on Japan's soil—Operation Olympic against the southernmost island of Kyushu in late 1945 and Operation Coronet against Tokyo itself in spring 1946.[7] In the document's August 30, 1944, annex, the planners estimated the number of Japanese troops that could be made available to defend the Home Islands at 3.5 million. An extrapolation of that number against a not yet complete count of the destroyed Japanese garrison on Saipan led planners to conclude that "in our Saipan operation, it cost approximately one American killed and several wounded to exterminate seven Japanese soldiers. On this basis it might cost us half a million American lives and many times that number wounded . . . in the home islands."[8]

This "Saipan ratio" suggested that defeating Imperial Japan would be at least as costly as the defeat of Nazi Germany, and the ratio set the standard for strategic-level casualty projections in the Pacific. Perhaps the most telling example of this is the fact that the chairman of the Joint Chiefs of Staff, George C. Marshall, personally used this ratio to estimate casualties in upcoming operations at precisely the time when the Army's manpower requirements for the coming year, 1945, were being formulated and before Truman became vice president.[9] The Army would not move beyond preliminary studies for continuing operations in 1946 until the spring of 1945.[10]

Together with the experience of combat attrition of line infantry units in Europe, the Saipan ratio provided the basis for the U.S. Army and War Department manpower policy for 1945 and became a critical factor in both (1) the ratcheting up of Selective Service inductions from 60,000 to 100,000 men per month in order to feed the "replacement stream" for what would be a "one-front" war against Japan then projected to last almost into 1947, and (2) the corresponding expansions of the training, supply, and medical infrastructures to support increased manpower needs. All of this took place as the war in Europe was winding down and, indeed, "the capacity of Army Ground Force replacement training centers reached a wartime peak of 400,000 in June 1945," nearly two months after U.S. Army divisions pulled to a halt along Germany's Elbe River.[11]

Later in the summer of 1945, General MacArthur's intelligence chief, Major General Willoughby, would develop a formula dubbed the "sinister ratio" based principally on the Okinawa fighting.[12] But the practical side of the August 1944 Saipan ratio was that, whether or not a very general formulation of that type would hold up in the final analysis—at least two and a half years in the future—it indicated that very high troop strengths would have to be maintained in the face of an increasing public demand that the longest-serving troops be returned home after the defeat of Germany. The War Department and Army's solution was to tighten draft deferments on such groups as agricultural workers and expand the categories of those to be inducted while simultaneously initiating a "points system" that allowed some soldiers to be released after a specified amount of time in combat combined with length of service.[13]

Yet even before public demands peaked during May 1945 for what was essentially a partial demobilization in what was then viewed to be the *middle* of the war, the Roosevelt administration and the Army struggled with how to juggle America's dwindling reserves of eligible manpower. In January 1945 directives from Selective Service director Brigadier General Hershey and director of the Office of War Mobilization Jimmy Byrnes, as well as letters to Congress from President Roosevelt, Marshall, and King, which were subsequently released to the press, all pointed up America's urgent manpower needs. The near doubling of draft calls and corresponding increases in the training infrastructure all occurred as the daily press recounted the bloody fighting on Iwo Jima and Okinawa. Meanwhile, in Congress, both houses passed legislation that eighteen year olds could not be sent into combat unless they had finished a minimum of six months of training, and the Senate—with Vice President Harry Truman engaged each and every day as its presiding officer—balked on a House bill to draft women nurses.[14]

This raises an interesting point. Truman is frequently referred to as having been a "former battery commander during World War I" but in reality he had only recently left the active Reserves as a highly respected colonel in the Reserve Officer Corps. After serving with distinction as a battery commander during the Meuse-Argonne offensive in World War I, the former Missouri "dirt farmer" had renewed his commission and rose through the ranks to become the commander of the 381st Artillery Regiment in 1932 and then was offered command of the 379th Artillery Regiment in 1935—*very* senior positions in a *very* diminutive between-wars club called the U.S. Army.[15]

Truman took his commission seriously and immersed himself in soldiering in spite of his increasing duties in a series of political positions. He was a familiar figure at the Fort Sill and Fort Riley artillery ranges, and after arriving in Washington as a newly elected U.S. senator, he admitted in a letter to his wife that he "played hooky" from a meeting of the Senate Appropriations Committee to attend a lecture on Gen. Robert E. Lee by Douglas Southall Freeman at the Army War College.[16] On another occasion, when an Army friend, future treasury secretary John Snyder, paid a visit to him in Washington, the two artillerymen drove over to the Gettysburg battlefield to perform what the Army today calls a "terrain walk" in order to examine the military aspects of the ground that Union and Confederate forces fought over in 1863.[17]

Truman had been a member of three key armed services committees: the Military Affairs Committee, the Military Subcommittee of the Appropriations Committee, and the Senate Special Committee to Investigate the National Defense Program (as its chairman). The Transportation Act of 1940, known as the Wheeler-Truman Act, was formulated by Truman and greatly increased America's preparedness for war.[18] When hostilities finally broke out, Truman went to General Marshall offering to rejoin the regular Army but was rebuffed by the chief of staff, who said it was more important for him to stay where he was because: "You've got a big job to do right up there at the Capitol with your Investigating Committee."[19]

In spite of all this, however, Truman is regularly characterized by historians, who tend to study the Roosevelt and Truman presidencies independent of what was happening in Congress, as being completely out of the loop during this period when brutal legislative fights were taking place—right in front of him on the Senate floor—over the politically explosive questions involving the lives of virtually millions of young Americans. It is as if Truman supposedly went brain-dead during the several months he was vice president. In fact, after the 1944 presidential election, Truman personally petitioned Marshall to assign an officer to the tiny vice presidential staff so that he could better monitor military affairs. Vice presidents did not have military liaison officers until Truman, as they say, "made it happen."[20]

As we have seen, there was plenty to "monitor" such as the politically painful ramping up of the Selective Service calls. And what the radically increased draft quotas meant in terms of the planned invasions of Japan was essentially this: Starting in March 1945, when levies were increased to 100,000 per month for the U.S. Army alone—the Navy and Marine Corps counted separately and brought the total March call-up to more than 141,000—nearly every man inducted would enter the "replacement stream" now oriented for a one-front war against Japan. The Army did not sugarcoat the prospect of a long, bloody war for the soldiers in the field and new inductees; in June 1945 it warned that various "major factors—none of them predictable at this stage of the game—will decide whether it will take 1 year, 2 years or longer to win the Far East war."[21]

Not everyone in the Pentagon believed the war would last that long. With the end of the war in Europe in sight and Japan's Imperial Army soon to bear the full weight of American might, some strategic planners were clearly more optimistic about how potential losses against the Japanese might play out than were other strategic planners whose thinking paralleled that of the Pentagon's manpower and medical planners crunching the numbers generated by the Pacific fighting.

The estimate from the Saipan ratio that subjugating Japan "might cost us half a million American lives and many times that many wounded" appeared, in the long run, to be unrealistically high to a cross-section of strategic planners and senior leaders in Washington. After all, it seemed reasonable to assume that U.S. forces would learn how to better cope with Japanese defensive techniques through hard-learned battle experience.[22] For briefing purposes the implied top-end figure of approximately 2 million battle casualties, built from the Saipan ratio, was slashed to a best-case scenario figure of 500,000, in spite of the casualty figures from Okinawa. This number was not so huge as to make the task ahead appear insurmountable, and it was far lower than the already publicly released figure of 600,000 men needed to be inducted through June, which would carry the Army through Operation Olympic and other worldwide needs during that period (much of the Navy-Marine Selective Service target of 300,000 had to do with the manning of the rapidly expanding fleet and not casualty replacement).[23]

The battle casualty figure of 500,000 became "the operative one at the working level" among strategic planners during the spring of 1945.[24] Future four-star general and West Point superintendent Andrew J. Goodpaster, then a staff officer working for the JCS, noted that "Secretary Stimson used the number regularly" and the figure, now representing total casualties and not just deaths, was given in briefings at such diverse locations as the U.S. First Army Headquarters in Weimar, Germany, B-29 training bases in the southwestern United States, and to newly assigned planning personnel at the Pentagon.[25] This smaller figure was not constructed from either previous or ongoing combat operations, and appears to have been based purely on the assumption that the U.S. military would certainly learn to better counter Japanese tactics. Whether bravado or racism figured most heavily in its creation is unknown, but the assumption nonetheless neglected the fact that, as evidenced by the casualty ratios then emerging from Iwo Jima and Okinawa, the Imperial Japanese Army was riding its own learning curve.

The low 500,000 number for total battle casualties, used widely in briefings, was not, however, used for ongoing operational purposes, and it had no effect on the nearly doubled Selective Service call-up, the expansion of the Army's training base, or the plans of the Transportation Corps, Medical Corps, and other U.S. Army organizations. For example, at the same time that the lower figure was appearing in briefings, the Army Service Forces under Lt. Gen. Brehon B. Somervell was working with estimates of "approximately" 720,000 for the projected number of replacements needed for "dead and evacuated wounded" through December 31, 1946, numbers that included only U.S. Army and Army Air Force personnel and did not include Navy and Marine Corps losses.[26] (And neither the briefing nor planning figures factored in the feared mass executions of captured U.S. and other Allied personnel when Japan was invaded because the personnel in question were already removed from the U.S. force structure.)[27] Yet while the low 500,000 figure originated as simply a "public information" tool divorced from actual planning, as anyone who followed the *Enola Gay* controversy can attest, its effect was nevertheless pronounced and long-term. Pentagon planner Samuel Halpern said forty-five years later that the figure "made a deep, indelible impression on a young man, 23 years old. It is something I have never forgotten."[28]

★   ★   ★

As if out of the blue, a seemingly unlikely character now entered the discussion of projected losses for the invasion of Japan, former president Herbert Hoover. Condemned to a political wilderness by his own party and the Roosevelt administration, Hoover was well outside of the Washington mainstream in spite of his frequent, but low-key assistance to congressional committees. Even this limited activity, however, brought him to the attention of what the editor of Truman's private papers, Robert H. Ferrell, has described as "a Pentagon cabal of smart colonels," a group of men who, according to one of its members, believed it their duty to ensure that "vital facts" and "intelligence reports" from a wide variety of different agencies were "acted upon rather than ignored."[29] Their method, quite simply, was to get the material into the hands of a "certain few senators [and congressmen] who were both totally trustworthy as intelligence receivers, and highly able to get actions—without letting the sources of their facts become known."[30]

Papers discovered by the Herbert Hoover Presidential Library's senior archivist, Dwight M. Miller, reveal that this revolving group contained both European and "Asiatic" intelligence specialists; coalesced as early as 1942; was known to or utilized by a number of senior Pentagon officials, such as the assistant chief of staff for intelligence, Maj. Gen. Clayton L. Bissell; and had at least four military intelligence officers at its core: Col. Peter Vischer, Col. Joseph A. Michela, Col. Percy G. Black, and Col. Truman Smith, the latter an intimate of General Marshall who had only recently retired but was very much "plugged in." Col. Ivan D. Yeaton may have been actively involved as well, and the colonels worked closely with William LaVarre, who held numerous senior positions during the war including chief of the Commerce Department's American Republics Unit combating Axis and Communist activities in South America.[31]

The recipients of their highly classified offerings included Howard Smith, who was chairman of the House Rules Committee and powerful Special Committee to Investigate Executive Agencies, as well as Republican senators Styles Bridges, George Malone, John W. Bricker (Thomas E. Dewey's running mate in 1944), and one lone Democrat—the chairman of the Senate Special Committee to Investigate the National Defense Program, Harry S. Truman. In addition to these legislative officials, said LaVarre, "one of our very best 'transmission patriots' was not in Washington. That was, of course, Herbert Hoover." LaVarre had apparently met Hoover in the early 1920s and an extensive correspondence exists between the two. But while LaVarre may have been the one who opened a dialogue between Hoover and the colonels, several of the group were soon making the periodic trips to the former president's "high lair atop the Waldorf Towers in Manhattan to discuss selected items." The briefings and materials received by Hoover were all classified, and the colonels found that Hoover, in spite of his outsider position, "was always able to securely use them for the Republic's good."[32]

A close examination of Hoover's papers makes it clear that he had a very comprehensive understanding not only of ongoing military matters unknown to the general public but also of developing high-level policy considerations. Indeed, it was his knowledge and insight which placed the incurable number cruncher Hoover in such demand by members of Congress.[33] Although he regularly received richly detailed reports from *Army and Navy Journal* publisher John Callan O'Laughlin, who obtained his information—nearly all of which was top secret—from a wide variety of senior officers up to and including Chief of Staff Marshall, both Dwight Miller and Robert Ferrell had long believed that the nature of the information in the former president's hands indicated that "Hoover had a pipe line into the Pentagon for intelligence information."[34] Discovery of the colonels' connection to Hoover certainly verifies their contentions. Ferrell also points out that this discovery virtually guarantees that JCS 924, outlining the end game in the Pacific, would have been made available to the former president. "This is a basic document," said Ferrell, "and it is inconceivable that they would not show Hoover the plans for the invasion of Japan which included the Saipan ratio suggesting up to 500,000 American dead."[35]

After Truman became president, Stimson, who had formerly served as Hoover's secretary of state, attempted to get the two statesmen together but Hoover would not insert himself into the process. He would not go to the White House without an invitation. On May 15, two days after a lunch and afternoon meeting at Stimson's Long Island estate, Hoover provided him with a memorandum outlining his views on ending the war with Japan. In this document and another prepared for Truman later that month, Hoover suggested that the invasion could cost "500,000 to 1,000,000 lives," an estimate that pointedly warned of as many as twice as many deaths then postulated by the Army in JCS 924. Stimson sent the paper to Marshall's staff for comment and hid its origins by stating only that it had been authored by "an economist." Had Hoover come up with this larger top-end number himself or had it come via the "cabal of smart colonels"? An important clue comes from yet another source: Kyle Palmer, the *Los Angeles Times'* longtime political editor.

Palmer had traded in his editorial desk for a position as the paper's war correspondent in the Pacific. Attached to the headquarters of Adm. Chester A. Nimitz, central Pacific commander, he covered the first aircraft carrier strikes against Japan and the costly U.S. invasions of Iwo Jima and Okinawa, then made a brief return to Los Angeles for a medical checkup. Before he shipped out again, Palmer hammered away at the theme that "it will take plenty of murderous combat before our soldiers, sailors and marines polish off the fanatical enemy" in both articles and appearances before civic groups. Under the headline "Palmer Warns No Easy Way Open to Beat Japs," the *Los Angeles Times* quoted from one of his speeches: "We are yet to meet the major portion of the ground forces of the Jap empire. They have 5,000,000 or 6,000,000 under arms and it will cost 500,000 to 750,000, perhaps 1,000,000 lives of American boys to end this war."[36]

What is interesting about this statement is not that Palmer's top-end figure matched what Hoover had put in the memo to Stimson just two days earlier, because while "it is true," noted Ferrell, "that possible high casualty figures were appearing in newspapers, planted by Nimitz's press organization, one must assume that Hoover would not have written Truman about a figure taken from a newspaper."[37] The real value of Palmer's figures lies in the fact that Palmer's statement on Japan's potential troop strength also matched the revised estimates then being pushed upward from the mid-1944 estimate of approximately 3.5 million by intelligence officers in the Pentagon. This information was not yet widely disseminated, even within higher headquarters' organizations, and almost certainly was leaked to Palmer through Nimitz's command which, like the rest of the Navy leadership, was still angling, sometimes buttressed by selective leaks to the press,[38] to swing future operations away from a direct assault on Japan's Home Islands to a campaign of encirclement and blockade designed to starve the Japanese into surrender.

As noted earlier, the U.S. Army's initial planning for the twin invasions of Japan, Operation Olympic against the southernmost island of Kyushu in late 1945 and Operation Coronet against the Tokyo area in 1946, had begun in earnest in the summer of 1944. JCS 924's Saipan ratio was based on the early assumption that U.S. forces would have to face approximately 3.5 million combatants. But as further analysis of Japan's manpower and training capabilities was conducted, the realization began to slowly dawn within the Army bureaucracy that their opponent's two-tiered mobilization system was on its way to producing at least 5 million trained and properly equipped soldiers, a force far surpassing what U.S. specialists originally believed probable.[39] Greater Japanese troop strength invariably changed the projections of how many American casualties they might be able to inflict,[40] and this became an even more critical issue as the fighting raged on Okinawa, where U.S. ground force casualties had averaged nearly seven thousand *per week* during the first half of April and had dropped back to a still appalling three thousand–plus each and every week that the campaign ground on.[41] As Japan invasion planner George McColm succinctly put it, "Every time" Japanese troop strength increased in the Home Islands "they had to revise the casualty numbers up."[42] Military intelligence analysts would have been the very first personnel working the revised figures against the Saipan ratio—plus other ratios developed from more recent operations—and it was members of this same close-knit community that made up Hoover's Pentagon pipeline.

Two days after their meeting, Secretary Stimson again failed to persuade Hoover to visit Truman without a specific invitation but finally succeeded in convincing Truman of the need for a meeting. Against the pointed advice of some of his political staff from the Roosevelt administration, on May 24 Truman invited Hoover to the White House, writing out the invitation in his own hand, placing a 3 cent stamp on the envelope, and mailing it himself.[43] (This was apparently his staff's first—and far from the last—experience with Truman's propensity to use the U.S. Postal Service to circumvent their better judgment.)[44] The two presidents finally met on the twenty-eighth. Before they parted Truman requested that Hoover prepare memorandums on the issues discussed.

Upon his return to his home at the Waldorf in New York, Hoover prepared extensive notes on the meeting which had apparently started early and lasted far longer than expected. He then produced four memoranda on "(1) The European Food Organization; (2) The Domestic Food Organization; (3) The Creation of a War Economic Council; [and] (4) The Japanese Situation." In memo 4, a brief work less than 700 words in length, Hoover stated twice that the cost to America from an invasion of Japan could run from "500,000 to 1,000,000 lives." It and the other memos were sent to Truman via the president's longtime friend, Press Secretary Charley Ross, in order to avoid possible mischief from the Roosevelt holdovers. Hoover's letter left New York on either Wednesday, May 30 or Thursday, May 31.[45]

Truman, like his congressional colleagues (and anyone who read the *New York Times* closely), knew that the Army was in the midst of trying to induct 600,000 men as replacements through June of that year. This, however, only covered the Army's needs through Olympic, and what Hoover had done in his memo 4, "The Japanese Situation," and the earlier memorandum to Stimson was to cut to the bottom-line cost, as represented by the Saipan ratio, of a U.S. victory in the war through the defeat of the Imperial Japanese Army on the Home Islands (with the Chinese, British, and presumably, the Soviets, taking on a roughly equal number of Imperial troops on the Asian mainland).

The existence of these memos, as well as the two subsequent Pentagon analyses of the memos requested by Stimson, are widely known, and all have been noted in a variety of venues.[46] What remained unknown, however, was the *president's reaction* to the memos, and one scholar of the Truman era, speaking specifically of memo 4 with the casualty estimates, even maintained that "there is no proof that Truman ever saw the Hoover memo."[47] Recently discovered documents at the Harry S. Truman Library and Museum tell a different story.

The discovery of the post-Hoover memo "Truman-Grew-Hull-Stimson-Vinson exchange" sheds new light on the importance of Hoover's memo 4 by demonstrating not only that the president saw the memos, but that he had singled out memo 4 for extensive, high-level scrutiny. "What we now know," said Ferrell, "is that Truman seized upon this memo and sent memoranda to Secretary Stimson, Undersecretary [of State] Joseph C. Grew, Director of the Office of War Mobilization and Reconversion, Fred M. Vinson and former secretary of state Cordell Hull, asking for written judgments from each." Moreover, adds Ferrell, the "discovery [of this exchange] not merely shows that Truman knew about such a high casualty figure" far in advance of the decision to use atom bombs against Japan but also that "Truman was exercised about the half-million figure, no doubt about that."[48]

Truman received the material from Ross, and after writing "From Herbert Hoover" across the top he forwarded the original copy of memo 4, "Memorandum on Ending the Japanese War," to his manpower czar, Vinson, on or about Monday, June 4. The War Mobilization and Reconversion director did not bat an eye over the casualty estimate when he responded on Thursday, June 7. He returned both the original memorandum and Truman's directive to examine it as well as his own memo suggesting that Hoover's paper be sent to Stimson and Grew, as well as Hull, who was currently in Bethesda Naval Medical Center. Truman agreed and had his staff type up additional copies of memo 4 on Saturday, June 9 (carbon copies were also made) and sent them to Stimson, Grew, and Hull. Truman asked each for a written analysis of memo 4 and told Grew and Stimson that he wished to discuss their individual analyses personally, *eye to eye,* after they submitted their papers.[49] Grew immediately initiated an oral and written exchange on the memo with longtime Roosevelt advisor and speech writer Judge Samuel L. Rosenman, who was then serving as Truman's special counsel.[50] Stimson subsequently sent his copy to the deputy chief of staff, Maj. Gen. Thomas J. Handy, because he wanted to get "the reaction of the Operations Division Staff to it" and mentioned in his diary that he "had a talk both with Handy and with Marshall on the subject."[51]

Hull was the first to respond. He branded memo 4 as Hoover's "appeasement proposal" in his June 12 letter because it suggested that the Japanese be offered lenient terms to entice them to a negotiating table. Hull did not take issue with the casualty estimate. Grew also did not take issue with the casualty estimate in his June 13 memorandum and confirmed that the Japanese "are prepared for prolonged resistance" and that "prolongation of the war will cost a large number of human lives."[52] It should also be noted that Grew's opinion would not have come as any surprise to the president since he had told Truman, ironically just hours after the meeting with Hoover, that the "Japanese are a fanatical people capable of fighting to the last man. If they do this, the cost in American lives will be unpredictable."[53]

One can readily surmise that Hoover and Grew's statements, hitting virtually back to back in the midst of America's costliest campaign of the Pacific war, were not of much comfort to the new commander in chief.

Grew's memorandum, messengered by government courier, and Hull's letter both arrived on Wednesday, June 13, and Truman subsequently met with Adm. William D. Leahy on the matter.[54] In addition to serving as the president's White House chief of staff, the admiral was also his personal representative on the Joint Chiefs and acted as unofficial chairman at their meetings. The day after the Hull and Grew messages arrived on Truman's desk, Leahy sent a memorandum, stamped "URGENT" in capital letters, to the other JCS members as well as Secretary of War Stimson and Secretary of the Navy James Forrestal. The president wanted a meeting the following Monday afternoon, June 18, 1945, to discuss "the losses in dead and wounded that will result from an invasion of Japan proper" and stated unequivocally that "it is his intention to make his decision on the campaign with the purpose of economizing to the maximum extent possible in the loss of American lives. Economy in the use of time and in money cost is comparatively unimportant."[55] The night before the momentous meeting, Truman wrote in his diary that the decision whether to "invade Japan [or] bomb and blockade" would be his "hardest decision to date."[56]

★   ★   ★

The president's meeting with the JCS and service secretaries took place before one of the recipients of Truman's directive, Stimson, had submitted a written response. It was not until after the meeting and several drafts that Stimson wrote, "The terrain, much of which I have visited several times, has left the impression on my memory of being one which would be susceptible to a last ditch defense such as has been made on Iwo Jima and Okinawa and which of course is very much larger than either of those two areas. . . . We shall in my opinion have to go through a more bitter finish fight than in Germany [and] we shall incur the losses incident to such a war."[57]

At the Monday meeting all the participants agreed that an invasion of the Home Islands would be extremely costly but that it was essential for the defeat of Imperial Japan. Said Marshall, "It is a grim fact that there is not an easy, bloodless way to victory." There was also considerable discussion of the tactical and operational aspects surrounding the opening invasion of Kyushu, the southernmost of Japan's Home Islands, with the emphasis on their effects on U.S. casualties. One portion of that discussion would have a great impact on the *Enola Gay* debate five decades later. The meeting transcript states that "Admiral Leahy recalled that the President had been interested in knowing what the price in casualties for Kyushu would be and whether or not that price could be paid. He pointed out that the troops on Okinawa had lost 35 percent in casualties." Leahy noted, "If this percentage were applied to the number of troops to be employed in Kyushu, he thought from the similarity of the fighting to be expected, that this would give a good estimate of the casualties to be expected. He was interested therefore in finding out how many troops are to be used in Kyushu."[58]

Leahy did not believe that the narrow, presented figure of 34,000 ground force battle casualties in a ratio table accompanying General Marshal's opening presentation offered a true picture of losses on Okinawa, which, depending on the accounting method used, actually ran from 65,631 to 72,000, largely because of combat fatigue and psychiatric breakdowns. He used the total number of casualties to formulate the 35 percent figure.[59] Since Leahy, as well as the other participants, including Truman, already knew that ground force casualties on Okinawa were far higher than 34,000 and approximately how many men were to be committed to the Kyushu fight, he was obviously making an effort—commonly done in such meetings—to focus the participants' attention on the statistical consequences of the disparity. Fifty years later, Leahy's use of the 35 percent figure from Okinawa as a way to gain a better understanding of potential casualties during Olympic was to be controversial.[60]

The table of organization and equipment strength of strictly ground force combat units at the commencement of Operation Olympic was 190,000 troops. Applying the 35 percent to this TOE results in a thumbnail casualty estimate of approximately 63,000 for the first month, and indeed Leahy noted in both his diary and autobiography his impression that Marshall was "of the opinion" that this number represented likely casualties from some undefined portion of the invasion.[61] However, even though 63,000 is in line with a one-month estimate derived from the TOE, one can only guess at what the number truly represents. Because it is not in evidence in the meeting transcript, and Leahy attached no parameters to the estimate, it has been discarded by military historians who instead used more properly documented estimates.[62]

The number is mentioned here because, according to Martin Harwit, former director of the National Air and Space Museum, it is the figure ultimately adopted by that institution at the insistence of Stanford professor Barton J. Bernstein, as the total number of casualties expected by the U.S. military during the invasion of Japan. Use of the artificially low figure further enflamed veterans' passions during the *Enola Gay* controversy and contributed to Harwit's dismissal.[63] In any case none of the meeting's participants found Leahy's approach in the least unusual or took issue with his statement that 35 percent "would give a good estimate of the casualties to be expected." Instead Marshall presented the most recent figure for the troop commitment, 766,700, and allowed those around the table, including Leahy, to draw their own conclusions as to long-term implications.[64]

A discussion then ensued on the sizes of the opposing Japanese and American forces which was fundamental to understanding how Leahy's 35 percent might play out. Finally, Truman, who had been monitoring the rising casualty figures from Okinawa on a daily basis, frequently with Leahy at his side,[65] cut to the bottom line since Operation Olympic was only the first of two invasions: "The President expressed the view that it was practically creating another Okinawa closer to Japan [Tokyo] to which the Chiefs of Staff agreed."

More discussion ensued and Truman asked "if the invasion of Japan by white men would not have the effect of more closely uniting the Japanese?" Stimson stated that "there was every prospect of this." He added that he "agreed with the plan proposed by the Joint Chiefs of Staff as being the best thing to do, but he still hoped for some fruitful accomplishment through other means." The other means included a range of measures from increased political pressure brought to bear through a display of Allied unanimity at the upcoming conference in Potsdam to the as yet untested atomic weapons that it was hoped would "shock" the Japanese into surrender.

Continued discussion touched on military considerations and the merits of unconditional surrender, and the president moved to wrap up the meeting: "The President reiterated that his main reason for this conference with the Chiefs of Staff was his desire to know definitely how far we could afford to go in the Japanese campaign. He was clear on the situation now and was quite sure that the Joint Chiefs of Staff should proceed with the Kyushu operation" and expressed the hope that "there was a possibility of preventing an Okinawa from one end of Japan to the other."[66]

CHAPTER 7

Japanese Defense Plans

The capture of Okinawa cost the United States Navy . . . over 4,900 sailors killed or missing in action, and over 4,800 wounded. Tenth Army lost 7,613 killed or missing in action and 31,800 wounded. Sobering as it is to record such losses, the sacrifice of these men is brightened by our knowledge that the capture of Okinawa helped to bring Japanese leaders to face the inevitable surrender.

—SAMUEL ELIOT MORISON, *The Two-Ocean War*[1]

The Okinawa Operation . . . achieved its objective, which was more important than the aforementioned figures of war results. This strenuous fighting provided us with valuable time to complete the general preparations for the homeland decisive operation and to delay the enemy's attack. . . . Moreover, the brave resistance of soldiers and civilians struck the enemy with horror and made him more cautious about attacking the homeland.

—HATTORI TAKUSHIRO, *The Complete History of the Greater East Asia War*[2]

What do the Japanese know—or think they know—about the invasion plans? This became the central question faced by key intelligence personnel in the Pacific and Washington. By late July 1945 it was clear that the Japanese were rapidly building up their forces at the exact spots targeted by Operation Olympic, but the communications intercepts that revealed this activity could only go so far in providing a window to the assumptions by IGHQ that led to the massing in Kyushu. While off the mark in numerous particulars and some of the data which led to these assumptions, the Japanese were ultimately correct not only in the sequence, timing, and areas to be assaulted but also in the specific invasion beaches and the approximate number of U.S. combat divisions slated to plunge over them.

Throughout the summer the Army staff group within IGHQ struggled to come to grips with the likely size of the U.S. invasion operations. Estimates fluctuated, but based on a comprehensive analysis of distances between U.S. ports and forward bases, available shipping, and other logistic factors, the Japanese believed that the opening invasion on Kyushu would be conducted by fifteen divisions in the late fall with a potential follow-up of up to twenty-five divisions (U.S. plans called for fourteen divisions and no follow-up as only one field army was to be committed). For the Kanto Plain on which Tokyo is situated, a force of some twenty-five divisions was expected in the spring of 1946 with an additional twenty-five more possible. Actual U.S. plans entailed a slightly larger initial force, twenty-eight divisions, followed by at least ten to twelve American and British Commonwealth formations.[3]

Paralleling strategic discussions within the U.S. military, questions were raised at different times throughout the spring and summer over whether the United States might not decide instead to wait out Japan by imposing a lengthy blockade or take an opposite approach by launching a ground invasion immediately at the Tokyo area. For this latter tack the Imperial Army staff group believed that if—and it was an extremely big if—the U.S. felt that it had attained a large enough "preparatory concentration" in the Philippines and Marianas, a strike directly at the Tokyo area might be attempted with as few as thirty divisions. The Japanese military thought that they could deal with such an eventuality, but only with the greatest difficulty since the staggered development of the Home Islands defenses necessitated that preparations on the Kanto Plain not be completed until early 1946, and that this buildup was surely to be adversely affected by American air power.[4]

For similar reasons the possibility of a lengthy blockade before a ground invasion was even more worrisome than an early assault on Tokyo since Japanese supplies were clearly finite. But the prospect of Kyushu being bypassed was thought to be extremely unlikely because an operation directly against Tokyo would then have to be carried out beyond the range of ground-based aircraft, and a delayed invasion was also unlikely because "the enemy's objective . . . will be the early termination of the war."[5] The Army staff group explained that "President Truman's message to Congress [on June 3, 1945] made clear the elements of strategy in the war with Japan: A. To envelope the Japanese army in various places and destroy it piecemeal. B. To increase pressure on the Japanese forces by ground, naval, and air attack so they will become static. C. To achieve operational objectives with a minimum of loss."[6]

Beyond Truman's domestic considerations was the assessment that manpower requirements of a blockade and bombardment would impose very real constraints on the United States' strategic options because such a course could entail the maintaining of massive, and largely inactive, forces in the Pacific while waiting for the blockade to finally strangle Japan (U.S. planners generally believed that this could take as long as two years).[7] The IGHQ's army staff group maintained that the U.S. landings necessary to truly close a ring around the Home Islands were the Korea Straits and the "Central CHINA coast" at Shanghai, in addition to Kyushu, but that such moves would mean that there "will not be enough [American] troops to use in the decisive battle in the KANTO area the following spring."

The staff group believed that U.S. troops would still have to land at Kyushu to form an effective blockade. The result of the multiple assaults, they argued, was that U.S. forces would have to "be deployed from the KYUSHU area" to make an invasion of the Tokyo area possible, and that if the initial invasion force could not be destroyed, Kyushu's defenders should prevent these troops from being used against Tokyo by prolonging aggressive action on Kyushu.[8]

Okinawa, where fewer than three full divisions held out for one hundred days against a U.S. force more than five times as large, was regularly trumpeted as an example of Imperial Army troops stretching out a campaign in the face of a vastly superior enemy.[9]

Throughout all the agonizing formulation of assessments and reassessments, the High Command remained steadfast in its April decision to give the first perceived target, Kyushu, top priority in men and supplies, with build-up in the ultimate—but later—target, the Kanto Plain on which Tokyo is situated, not going into high gear until the defensive preparations on Kyushu were completed in September. All other areas in the Home Islands were far down the priorities list except the southern tip of Shikoku across the Bungo Strait from Kyushu.[10] IGHQ was confident that America could be forced to sue for peace not only because the Japanese army was intact and still relatively unbloodied but also because the large and growing number of airfields had made it "possible to preserve planes from severe bombing" prior to the invasion, and the American landing operations . . . would require more than three times the number of transports used in the war against Germany; hence, there would be more chances to attack the U.S. supply lines."[11] Their defense plans were both comprehensive and chillingly prescient.

The following account of Japanese defense preparations, "Homeland Operations Record," originated as four studies prepared immediately after the war by the Japanese government's First (Army) and Second (Navy) Demobilization Bureaus under orders from General MacArthur's headquarters.[12] Members of the Allied Translator-Interpreter Service, a component of the Intelligence Section (G-2) of Headquarters, Far East Command, quickly translated and released the manuscripts in October 1945, and they are frequently cited in the 1950 *Reports of General MacArthur*. In the mid-1950s, the War Histories Room staff at the Japanese Ground Defense Force Key Personnel School began work on a combined volume at the request of the Foreign Histories Division of Headquarters, United States Army, Japan. The resulting 255-page 1959 monograph, "Homeland Operations Record," "correct[ed] many errors and fill[ed] many gaps in the earlier manuscripts," after which a "re-translation of ambiguous portions" was undertaken.[13] Nevertheless the following excerpt, the first of three in this narrative, had to be heavily abridged and edited for clarity. This also entailed the shifting of numerous paragraphs into a more coherent order (and author's notes have been added).

To better understand the following, readers should take note that the Japanese formation referred to as an "army" or "field army" is, like its Soviet counterpart, generally analogous to an American or British "corps" of approximately three combat divisions. A Japanese "area army" equates to an Anglo-American "army" of as few as two, and sometimes as many as four, "corps" formations. A Japanese "general army" is functionally the same as a Soviet "front" and Anglo-American "army group." An independent mixed brigade is made up of three to six infantry battalions, in addition to artillery and engineer elements of one company to one battalion each. Most of the material in the "Homeland Operations Record" describes a series of Japanese defense plans released in April 1945 and covers many of the subsequent changes that were made as the situation evolved and plans were modified throughout the summer.

HOMELAND OPERATIONS RECORD

Reorganization of the Army Commands. Recognizing that defeat in the Philippines was only a question of time and with the knowledge that an invasion of Japan proper was now a definite probability, IGHQ moved to strengthen the homeland's defensive forces on February 6, 1945, by reorganizing three military districts, Eastern, Central and Western, and adding two more, Northeastern and East Coast. The Army commands within the new military districts were likewise increased to five and redesignated as area armies.

Aside from a reshuffling of areas, the addition of two additional districts and corresponding area armies, and the redesignation of the commands, there was little change in the command organization and the commanders of the area armies continued to act as commanders of the military districts. As had been the case prior to the reorganization, the commanders reported to the Commander in Chief of Defense, General Prince Naruhiko Higashikuni, heading up the General Defense Command (GDC) on matters concerning the area armies and to the War Ministry, under General Anami Korechita, on all military district affairs which included any necessary civilian administration or coordination as well as lines of communications activities such as ordnance, medical, and signals operations.[14]

The GDC and the five area armies received orders from IGHQ outlining the duties and missions of the reorganized command, instructions which differed from previous directives in that defense against air attack was no longer the primary consideration. Now, the strengthening of land defenses at the most logical invasion points was emphasized and the protection of land transportation and harbor facilities was also stressed. As was customary in IGHQ orders of this type, the GDC was instructed to cooperate with the Navy and, "by aggressive use of the air arm, destroy any invasion fleet while it is still at sea."[15]

Reorganization of Japan's Defense Forces. On April 8, 1945, with invasion imminent and inevitable, it was realized that the defense of Japan was too great a task for the one defense headquarters. Accordingly, it was decided to divide the country into Eastern and Western defensive areas, and to establish separate general army [army group] headquarters in each to control the ground defense forces in the two areas. The First General Army, incorporating the Kanto Plain and Tokyo, extended from the Nagoya area through northern Honshu, while the Second General Army was responsible for the Osaka-Kyoto area south through Kyushu.

At the same time the Air General Army was established to assume the task of directing air defense. The 1st Air Army [eastern Japan], which previously had been concerned primarily with training missions, and the 6th Air Army [western Japan], already a tactical force, were brought under the operational control of the Air General Army.[16]

Note: The division of the country into two defensive areas and reorganization of the army's ground commands were put into effect because the increase in the number of combat formations on Honshu and Kyushu necessitated a corresponding increase in command organizations to both train and field them in combat. The April 8, 1945, directive establishing army groups in eastern and western Japan further stated, "In order to meet the expected gradual increase in pressure upon land and sea transportation services, self-sufficiency in each district and area army will be emphasized, particularly as regards food, material repair, and certain classes of arms and equipment procurement."[17] In addition the newly appointed divisional district chiefs were "veteran generals hailing from their own birthplaces" and were picked through a "selective procedure intended somewhat to cement local relationships."[18] Thus while the government recognized that a unified national structure was "absolutely essential to the prosecution of the war, . . . a realistic view of what Japan would inevitably face" drove the moves to "strengthen local self reliance,"[19] a move made extremely difficult not only by the ongoing deterioration of industrial capacity but also by the lack of trained army staff and logistics officers.[20]

The Ketsu-Go Operations. Simultaneously with the activation of the First, Second, and Air general armies, and the initial phase of the *Sho-Go* [Victory Operation] against American forces at Okinawa, IGHQ issued orders for the implementation of the *Ketsu-Go* [Decisive Operation]. This operation was designed as an all-out joint defense effort to be conducted by the entire strengths of the army, navy and air forces. Entirely defensive in nature, the operation divided the Japanese home territory—including the Kuriles, Karafuto [southern Sakhalin], and Korea—into seven zones in which might be fought the final decisive battles to determine the fate of the nation.

Ketsu-Go, No. 1—Northern Military District (Fifth Area Army)
Ketsu-Go, No. 2—Northeastern Military District (Eleventh Area Army)
　　　　　　　　　First General Army
Ketsu-Go, No. 3—Eastern Military District (Twelfth Area Army)
Ketsu-Go, No. 4—East Coast Military District (Thirteenth Area Army)
Ketsu-Go, No. 5—Central Military District (Fifteenth Area Army) Second General Army
Ketsu-Go, No. 6—Western Military District (Sixteenth Area Army)
Ketsu-Go, No. 7—Korea (Seventeenth Area Army)[21]

Ketsu-Go, No. 3. provided for the defense of the Eastern Military District, including the Kanto Plain, by the Twelfth Area Army under the direction of the First General Army. This Kanto Plain area was considered the most vital part of the nation, containing the Imperial Palace, the nation's capital, centers of government administration, many military facilities including the highest military headquarters, and the great Tokyo-Kawasaki-Yokohama industrial complex. In addition, the Kanto Plain was one of the important rice producing

A wing of the Takatsuki Dump near Osaka. The underground stockpiling of munitions, gasoline, and other war supplies was well advanced at the time of the surrender, roughly four months before the opening invasion of Kyushu and perhaps as much as eight months before the assault on Honshu. From a purely technical standpoint, eight months is practically an eternity to prepare for an invasion. American planners assumed the war could last at least to the end of 1946. (U.S. Army)

centers upon which the populace of the area and the military forces of the Eastern Military District were dependent.

For this reason the Twelfth Area Army initially had more material and greater strength at its disposal than did the other area armies. Unfortunately, progress in fortification construction was hampered by real estate difficulties and political interference. Defensive positions had been planned on the assumption that the most logical points for landings of invasion forces were Kujukuri-hama located north of the Bose Peninsula and east of Tokyo, Sagami Bay to the south, or the shore of the Kashima Sea northeast of Tokyo. By April only the defense positions at Kujukuri-hama had made significant progress. The others were still in the initial stages of construction and had to await their full allotment of resources until after the defenses on Kyushu were nearly complete. The best prepared defensive works by August were located in the Sagami Bay and Kujukuri-hama areas as these offered the most advantageous landing sites for an invasion force, and it was estimated that decisive battles would undoubtedly be fought in those areas.[22]

Ketsu-Go, No. 6. was concerned with the defense of Kyushu by the Sixteenth Area Army under the direction of the Second General Army. That the enemy would direct its initial attack at Kyushu was regarded as a virtual certainty and, as a consequence, the island's fortification was of the greatest urgency. Kyushu's defense was also the most difficult of all the Home Island districts as it had the greatest length of vulnerable sea coast to defend. Preparations for *Ketsu-Go, No. 6*, had an almost equal priority with those for *Ketsu-Go, No. 3*, and had an earlier, October 1945, completion date designated by IGHQ. By dint of strenuous efforts, positions on the Osumi and Satsuma Peninsulas and on the Miyazaki Plains were roughly 50-percent completed in April, and preparations in the Ryukyus [Okinawa, Miyako Jima, and O Shima] to the south were also well advanced. In addition, communication facilities had been vastly improved and stockpiling of supplies and ammunition was proceeding satisfactorily.[23]

Defenses in Other Areas. Although the Kanto Plain–Tokyo area was considered the most important parts of the country to be protected, defenses in the other areas could not be neglected. The Shimokita Peninsula and Tsugaru Strait, in the northern part of Honshu, and the entrance to Ise Bay and the Nagoya area were also of great importance. The First General Army, utilizing the Twelfth Area Army, would concentrate on building up the defenses of the Eastern Military District but would also render all possible assistance to the Eleventh and Thirteenth Area Armies in their defense preparations.

ESTIMATE OF U.S. INVASION PLANS[24]

Note: Ketsu Operation Nos. 1, 2, 4, 5, and 7, outlined in the "Homeland Operations Record," received a substantially lower priority than Nos. 3 and 6 of the Twelfth and Sixteenth Area Armies and are not repeated here beyond this one-paragraph summary above. The document's outline of plans to defend Kyushu, however, will be recounted in detail.

Inter-service Agreements. In the various orders and directives issued by IGHQ regarding *Ketsu-Go*, inter-service cooperation was stressed. The basic plan for the operation called for the Navy to defend the coasts by attacking invasion fleets with its combined surface, submarine and air forces. The Air General Army would cooperate with the Navy in the accomplishment of this first phase of the defense. Should the enemy succeed in making a landing, the area army concerned would assume command of all naval ground forces in its area and would exercise operational control of air forces in support of ground operations.

Although no specific agreement was ever reached regarding the operational control of land based naval aircraft, it is assumed that the First and Second General Armies and their subordinate area armies would have been given operational control of naval air units in the event of an invasion. The details and actual implementation of the inter-service cooperative agreements would be worked out by mutual agreement between the commanders of the First and Second General Armies, the Air General Army, and the Navy General Command. Below this level, commanders of the area armies would also cooperate with, and could expect cooperation from, naval and air units in their areas.[25]

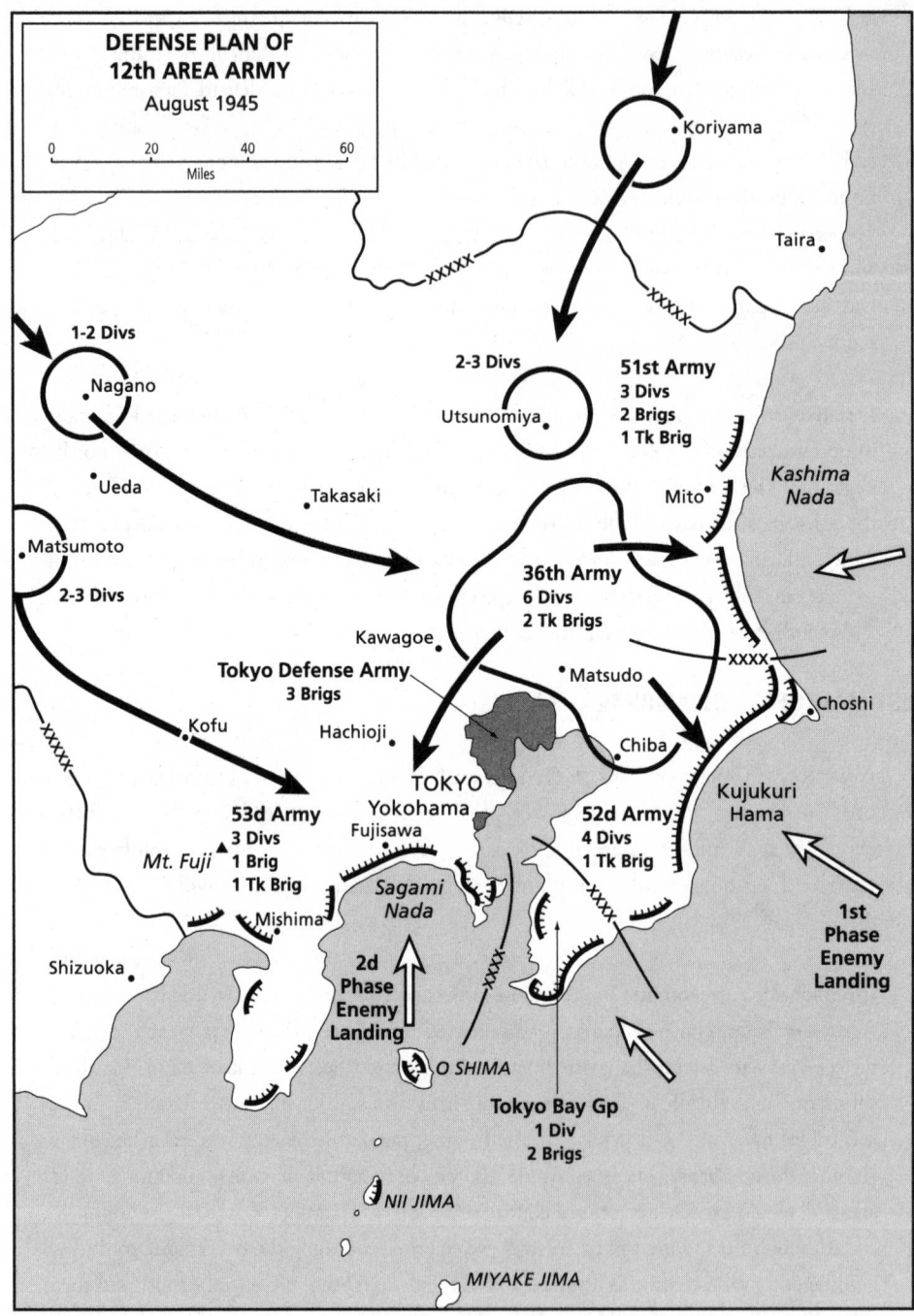

DEFENSE PLAN OF 12th AREA ARMY
August 1945

0   20   40   60
Miles

Koriyama

Taira

1-2 Divs

Nagano

2-3 Divs

Utsunomiya

51st Army
3 Divs
2 Brigs
1 Tk Brig

Kashima Nada

Ueda

Takasaki

Mito

Matsumoto

2-3 Divs

36th Army
6 Divs
2 Tk Brigs

Kawagoe

Tokyo Defense Army
3 Brigs

Matsudo

Choshi

Kofu

Hachioji

Chiba

Kujukuri Hama

TOKYO

53d Army
3 Divs
1 Brig
1 Tk Brig

Yokohama
Fujisawa

52d Army
4 Divs
1 Tk Brig

Mt. Fuji

Sagami Nada

1st Phase Enemy Landing

Mishima

2d Phase Enemy Landing

Shizuoka

O SHIMA

Tokyo Bay Gp
1 Div
2 Brigs

NII JIMA

MIYAKE JIMA

Map derived from "Homeland Operations Record" (Tokyo: U.S. Army Forces Far East, Military History Section, 1959; distributed by the Office of the Chief of Military History Washington, D.C.), 85.

Defense plan of Japan's 12th Area Army, August 1945.

Note: Agreements principally centered on infantry combat training for naval personnel, the limited use of each services' air bases by its sister service, clarification for the command chain of army personnel at naval bases, and other matters such as the command of "special attack" (suicide) forces.[26] The army's operation section chief at IGHQ later wrote, "The

Army wanted very much to assume the unified command of the entire ground operations even during operational preparations, but owing to the Navy's opposition, the Army's wishes were not realized. Finally, an agreement was reached providing that the First and Second General Army commanders may issue orders [to Navy elements] during operational preparations only in matters regarding ground defense plans and necessary training."[27] The military secretary to General Anami blamed the lack of a unified command on the "strong opposition, mainly on the part of the Navy Minister Yonai [Mitsumasa]," and stated that "the reason for his resistance was not very clear" beyond both services' "own time-honored traditions," which were "difficult to reconcile."[28]

> **Mutual Support.** An integral part of the *Ketsu-Go* operational planning included reinforcement of sectors under attack by troops transferred from other districts. Since enemy air raids had already seriously disrupted the transportation system and it was known that every effort would be made to completely neutralize the entire system, time schedules were planned to provide for all troop movements to be made on foot. This, in turn, would require the defending force in contact with the enemy to conduct successful holding actions for long periods. The Air General Army also recognized the need for mutual support, both in defending against enemy air raids and in combatting an invasion. Accordingly, on July 1, 1945, the principles of the *Sei-Go* unified air defense plan were published and the air forces of both the Army and Navy organized to send the maximum support to any area under air or ground attack.[29]

Note: The assumption that U.S. air power would force all marches to be performed at night and along secondary roads, which offered better opportunities for concealment than primary roads, resulted in transit estimates of up to sixty-five days for two divisions moving from Kyushu in the event that an invasion was launched at Kanto without a preliminary operation against Kyushu.[30] However, this was largely due to the fact that the divisions would first have to move surreptitiously and in small packets from Kyushu to the southern tip of Honshu. Up to eight divisions reinforcing the Kanto area from points all across Honshu would begin arriving in staging areas centering around Nagano north of Tokyo and other points, within ten days of receiving their marching orders, and another five would follow from as far away as Hokkaido within thirty days. A variety of employment options were examined by IGHQ, and the stockpiling of food and munitions at key points was stepped up at all command levels.[31] Reinforcement options for Kyushu will be examined below.

> **Estimate of U.S. Invasion Plans.** On 19 April, senior staff officers of the area armies were called to a meeting at the First General Army's new headquarters. The battle for Okinawa was at its height and although the defense was stubborn, it appeared that the U.S. would be successful in taking the island because of the massive forces assigned to the task. It was certain that Allied Forces would immediately begin preparations for the invasion of Japan after the capture of Okinawa. Intelligence estimates indicated that while the invasion might come as early as July, it was not believed that the U.S. would be prepared to launch an invasion until the fall of 1945, probably some time after the 1st of October. It was believed, however,

that the assault on Japan would be made as soon as possible after that date. All defense preparations, therefore, were to be completed by the end of September.[32]

Note: Prioritization of the First General Army's efforts naturally occurred, and as summarized in Ketsu-Go No. 3 above, "the best prepared defensive works by August were located in the Sagami Bay and Kujukuri-hama areas."

Struggle for Equipment and Supplies. With the First General Army limited in what logistic support it could provide, the individual area armies made efforts to obtain weapons, ammunition, and construction materials through their own channels. Since much of the shortage of supply at the troop level was attributable to lack of transportation, the area armies used their nonorganic transportation and were successful in obtaining much of the material required, particularly that which was needed for construction of coastal fortifications.

As a result of the observations of the commander and staff of the First General Army, new operational and logistical plans were made and on 7 May, at a meeting with the senior staff officers of the area armies, the new plans were outlined. Once more it was emphasized that an invasion could be expected in the fall and that operational preparations must be complete by that time.[33]

Mobilization. A mass mobilization, resulting in a tremendous increase in the strength of Japan's armed forces, particularly the ground forces, was one of the most important facets of defense planning. A series of three mobilizations were to be completed by late summer 1945. Although the order of battle published for the First General Army in April showed a large number of division sized units, many of them were not operational at the time of activation and some of them were, in fact, still in the planning stage.

Although manpower aspects of the mobilization plans were proceeding according to schedule, firepower had not increased in the same ratio, as production of weapons had not kept pace with the induction of men. Thus, while the First General Army had almost doubled in numerical strength, many of the recently added divisions were virtually unarmed when organized.[34]

Two types of divisions were formed during the mobilization period: Coastal Defense and Assault Groups. In general, the divisions in the 100 and 300 series were largely immobile and earmarked for coastal defense while those in the 200 series had assault missions. The Coastal Defense Divisions were strongly reinforced with artillery which increased their firepower but had decreased mobility. The Assault Divisions also had firepower superior to that of the average division but were highly mobile. These latter divisions were to be used as shock troops to hit the enemy after the invader had been contained by the Coastal Defense Divisions.[35]

Note: In addition to numerous independence brigades, and excluding the last four Kwantung divisions redeployed from Manchuria, IGHQ ordered the activation of eighteen First Stage Mobilization "100-series" coastal defense divisions on February 28, 1945. Eight very high quality "200-series" assault divisions were activated during the Second Stage Mobilization on April 2, and nineteen more as part of the Third Stage Mobilization on

May 23. Of this third group, eleven were organized as coastal defense "300-series" formations, with the balance made up of 200-series assault divisions.[36] Some of the first divisions activated in the First and Second Mobilization stages also experienced delays in becoming combat ready due to incomplete mobilization plans. Seven divisions were formally assigned to the First General Army and five to the Second General Army by early May. Within a few weeks seven more divisions were added to the First General Army and four divisions to the Second.[37]

Third Stage Mobilization. The final mobilization exhausted practically all the reserve manpower of Japan and the majority of those called up were either untrained or old. If Japan had been attacked at in May or June it would have been impossible to conduct an adequate defense. However, the strong defense by the troops on Okinawa was buying time for preparations on the homeland.

Because the organization of the Second General Army was steadily improving and liaison with IGHQ and the area armies was further advanced, employment of units organized under the final mobilization was carried out smoothly in the most vulnerable area, Kyushu. The divisional size units were completely organized by early July (and the smaller units by early August). Both the newly formed coastal defense and assault divisions were, however, inferior in quality of personnel and equipment to those previously organized. This was partially offset by the final mobilization coastal defense divisions being strongly reinforced with artillery.[38]

Note: While augmenting these formation's firepower was IGHQ's intent, the trio of 300-series divisions intended for Ketsu-Go No. 6 were deployed ahead of schedule and, at least initially, with a heavy mortar section substituting for artillery because there was a chance that Kyushu might be invaded early. Japanese planners also reasoned that a quick deployment would allow the divisions "more time to familiarize themselves with their operational areas."[39]

Second General Army. It was obvious that if the enemy invasion operation should achieve any appreciable degree of success, communications and liaison between the Second General Army's area armies and their sub-ordinate units might well be impossible, and that Kyushu, Shikoku and Chugoku (the western portion of Honshu) would be completely cut off from each other. The establishment of at least one army command within each of these areas appeared, therefore, to be a vital necessity. Since an acute shortage of headquarters and staff-personnel made the establishment of additional headquarters extremely difficult, it was determined to re-organize existing installations. The headquarters of the Zentsuji military Sub-district [Shikoku] was reorganized as the 55th Army Headquarters and the sub-district was redesignated as the Shikoku Military District. As in the area armies and military districts, the commander and some of the staff served in dual capacities as members of the army headquarters and military district headquarters staffs. In the same manner, the Hiroshima Military Sub-district was reorganized as the 59th Army and the sub-district redesignated as the Chugoku Military District.

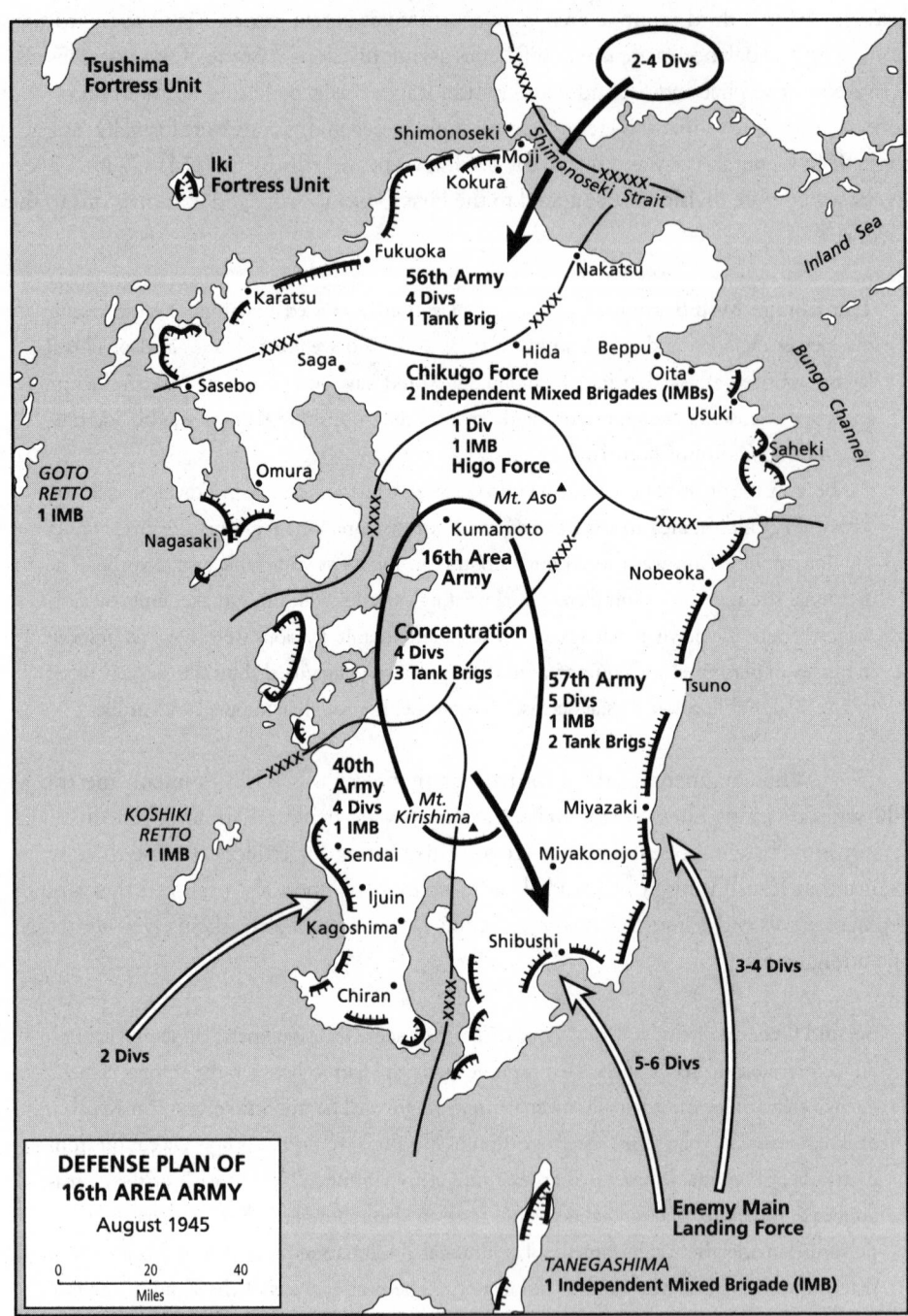

Map derived from "Homeland Operations Record" (Tokyo: U.S. Army Forces Far East, Military History Section, 1959; distributed by the Office of the Chief of Military History Washington, D.C.), 128.

The defense plan of Japan's 16th Area Army, August 1945.

In Kyushu, the Sixteenth Area Army had two subordinate army commands; the Fifty-Sixth, with the mission of defending the northern Kyushu area from Nagasaki east to the Bungo Strait and southern Honshu, and the Fifty-Seventh which would defend Miyazaki Prefecture and the Osumi Peninsula in the southeast. Since it had been determined that

Kyushu would undoubtedly be the scene of the initial invasion attempt, it was believed that two additional army headquarters would be required; one to take command of the units on the Satsuma Peninsula in the southwest, and a second to command the highly mobile reserve force. Here, again, the shortage of personnel with command and staff experience posed a problem. To establish the army headquarters for the defense of the Satsuma Peninsula, the Fortieth Army headquarters had to be redeployed from Formosa with the commanding general and staff officers arriving by air on 10 June and assuming command on the 15th. The army headquarters for the mobile reserve was still not organized by mid-August and the war ended with the assault divisions still assigned to the Fortieth and Fifty-Seventh Armies for administrative purposes.[40]

Defense of Kyushu. Since it was generally conceded that the enemy would make his initial landings in Kyushu, the Sixteenth Area Army had been given priority in the receipt of supplies and in the build-up of troop strength. Fortification construction had also been emphasized and, in general, preparations were further advanced in Kyushu than in other areas of Japan.

Ketsu-Go, No. 6 was the over-all guide for the defense of Kyushu but the Sixteenth Area Army prepared its own detailed defense plan. Known as the *Mutsu* Operation, the Army's plan divided Kyushu into three principal sectors which were, in turn, broken down into seven area subdivisions:

Mutsu Operation, No. 1—Southern Kyushu
Part A Miyazaki Plain
Part B Ariake Bay
Part C Satsuma Peninsula

Mutsu Operation, No. 2—Northern Kyushu
Part D Moji to Maebara
Part E Karatsu to Sasebo

Mutsu Operation, No. 3—Central Kyushu
Part F Amakusa Area
Part G Bongo [Hoyo] Channel[41]

Deployed throughout Kyushu and adjacent islands, the Sixteenth Area Army had three armies totaling 15 divisions [including one antiaircraft division], two special attack forces, seven independent mixed brigades, three independent tank brigades, and two fortress units. The defense concept under the *Mutsu* Operation Plan called for each army to hold one division in reserve. In the event of an invasion, the Sixteenth Area Army would concentrate a force composed principally of the armies' reserve divisions and the three tank brigades which would be utilized as an assault group to be rushed to the areas where the main enemy effort was being directed. During the period in which the assault force was being concentrated, the coastal defense units would contain the enemy as had been done on Iwo Jima and Okinawa.[42]

Note: IGHQ directed that no reserves were to be held back: "As soon as the location of the enemy main effort has been determined, all reserves available in the Area Army will be redeployed to the decisive battle front, leaving the coastal combat units to wage holding actions on the secondary fronts."[43] As will be seen from the Sixteenth Area Army plans below, the three divisions to be used as the initial in Mutsu Operation counterattack force varied according to the locations of the American landings, and it was envisioned to occur as early as a week after the initial landings. Only Mutsu No. 1 is outlined because Operation Olympic would not have activated the other plans.

Mutsu Operation, No. 1. covered the defense of southern Kyushu by the Fortieth and Fifty-Seventh Armies. This part of Kyushu was considered the most probable area to be invaded. *Mutsu No. 2*, provided for the defense of the northwest coast between Moji and Sasebo by the 56th Army and the naval forces in the Sasebo area of northwest Kyushu. *Mutsu No. 3*, was the operational plan for the defense of the central belt extending from Shimabara Bay, on the west coast, northeast across Kyushu to the shores of the Bungo Channel. To further protect the coasts of Kyushu, the Gate Archipelago, or Goto Islands, west of Sasebo and Nagasaki were defended by the Goto Group (107th Independent Mixed Brigade), while the 109th Independent Mixed Brigade defended Tanegashima Island, south of the Shibushi Peninsula.[44]

Mutsu No. 1, Part A. was the defense of the east coast, particularly the plains area of Miyazaki Prefecture, by the 154th, 156th and 212th Divisions of the Fifty-Seventh Army. In the event of an invasion in this area, those units would hold the attackers until the mobile reserve could be assembled and moved from their inland locations. The counterattack phase would be carried out by a mobile reserve composed of the 25th, 77th and 216th Divisions together with the 4th, 5th and 6th Independent Tank Brigades which would move initially to Honjo and Tsuma. As an additional reserve to bolster the counterattack or launch a third phase attack, two divisions would be sent from the Fifteenth Area Army on Honshu and, if possible, one additional division from the Fortieth Army.

Mutsu No. 1, Part B. would be activated if the enemy invaded the Ariake Bay region. Initial defense would be conducted by the 86th and 156th Divisions plus the 98th Independent Mixed Brigade of the Fifty-Seventh Army. The mobile reserve for execution of the second phase would be composed of the 25th, 57th and 216th Divisions as well as the 4th, 5th, and 6th Independent Tank Brigades. These units would advance to Iwakawa to contain the invading force on the Shibushi Peninsula on the east side of Kagoshima Bay and counterattack when conditions warranted. The two divisions from the Fifteenth Area Army would be used as additional reinforcements to support the counterattack phase.

Mutsu No. 1, Part C. provided for the defense of the Satsuma Peninsula region west side of Kagoshima Bay by the 146th and 303d Divisions and the 125th Independent Mixed Brigade of the Fortieth Army. In the second, or counterattack, phase the 25th M, 57th, 77th, 212th and 216th Divisions together with the three tank brigades would advance to the vicinity of Ijuin to hold the invaders on the peninsula and be prepared to execute the counterattack. Here again, two divisions from the Fifteenth Area Army would be moved south to activate a third phase of the operation.[45]

Note: Of the four assault divisions, the 25th from Manchuria and 216th were expected to take part in the opening counterattack against a U.S. invasion force on any invasion beach. However, it was not originally envisioned that the 77th Division would be sent deep into the Shibushi Peninsula if Mutsu No. 1, Part B was activated. Likewise the 57th, another crack Kwantung division, was not slated to take part in the opening phase of Mutsu No. 1's Part A contingency, and was, in fact, more than three hundred miles to the north since it was originally part of the Mutsu No. 2 counterattack force. It was only later that plan were made to move the 57th as well as the 4th Independent Tank Brigade, which was also based in the north, to locations in central Kyushu so that they could more quickly respond to a strike in the south. Although plans, originally called for two divisions on Honshu to be prepared to reinforce the Sixteenth Area Army, this was later expanded to three divisions, and will be discussed in chapter 14.

With the U.S. Sixth Army landing almost simultaneously at each of the possible invasion sights, the Sixteenth Area Army of Lieutenant General Yokoyama Isamu would be confronted with the terrible choice of which part of the Mutsu Operation to implement. And it was clear that Imperial forces would be under enormous pressure.

The IGHQ staff studies confidently predicted that naval and air special attack forces targeting largely stationary invasion shipping might succeed in sinking as much as 30 to 40 percent of the vessels during landing operations. Reports of success during ongoing kamikaze operations at Okinawa prompted the estimates to balloon to as much as 50 percent, thus costing the Americans the equivalent of five combat divisions lost at sea. But while this level of success was accepted by IGHQ, "commanders responsible for the conduct of ground operations within the scope of *Ketsu No. 6* recognized that these estimates were excessively high." Their own figures "indicated a possible maximum loss to the enemy of 20 percent of the invasion fleet transports or about three divisions."[46] But were even these "conservative" figures at all realistic?

CHAPTER 8

"Victory Might Be Salvaged"

Myron Lieberman, G-2, U.S. Army Air Forces, Far East: "What percentage of success was necessary to make it worthwhile for the Japanese to continue the Kamikaze tactics?"

Captain Inoguchi Rikibei, Imperial Japanese Navy: "Inasmuch as the Kamikaze attacks were the last means of any favorable results in the war and the only chance for breaking down American resistance a little, we did not care how many planes were lost. Poor planes and poor pilots were used, and there was no ceiling on the number of either available for use. . . . If enough damage could be done to American ships and enough American casualties resulted, perhaps there would be a 'new deal' later in which some form of victory might be salvaged from the war."

—Interrogation of CAPTAIN INOGUCHI RIKIBEI, March 7, 1947 [1]

In early 1943 the growing supremacy of U.S. warships and aircraft prompted some Japanese military leaders to contemplate the systematic use of suicide aircraft. But not until late the following year, after they had lost many of their best pilots at Midway, the Solomons, New Guinea, and the Marianas, was the kamikaze—the "divine wind"—examined seriously as a last-ditch alternative to conventional bombing attacks.[2] A novice pilot willing to die for his emperor could fly an obsolescent aircraft into a warship infinitely more easily than he could aim a bomb at it, and sheer momentum would frequently carry a damaged, burning aircraft to its target even after its pilot had been killed. More experienced pilots, deemed too valuable to sacrifice, were to provide fighter cover or fly conventional strikes.[3]

At first suicide attacks were organized on an ad hoc basis from Nichols Field in the Philippines, and on October 13, 1944, the aircraft carrier USS *Franklin* (CV-13) was apparently the first target of a kamikaze one week prior to official authorization of the thirteen-aircraft Shimpu Tokubetsu Kogekitiai (Divine Wind Special Attack Corps) unit of volunteer suicide pilots.[4] First blood was drawn on October 25–26, when a five-plane raid sank the escort carrier *St. Lo* (CVE-63) and damaged three similar carriers. This prompted many more young fliers to volunteer, and on October 30, a kamikaze attack damaged three large fleet carriers so severely that they had to be pulled back to the Ulithi anchorage for repairs. Within days another large flattop fell victim, as did three more toward the end of November. This stunning disruption of carrier air power spelled the loss of ten Liberty ships and tank landing ships (LSTs) as well as six destroyer-type vessels during the opening days of the Philippines campaign and had a pronounced effect on the conduct of the ground campaign.[5]

Buoyed by reports of both real and imagined U.S. losses in this and earlier battles, IGHQ decided to conduct its main battle for the Philippines on Leyte instead of Luzon and transferred four infantry divisions to the island along with various independent brigades and regiments. Although roughly 80 percent of Japan's ships taking part in the reinforcement effort were eventually sunk during the course of their round trips, most troops and supplies arrived intact, and several Japanese units were successfully evacuated when ordered off in January 1945.[6] The conquest of Leyte eventually involved more than 100,000 additional U.S. ground troops than anticipated and took so long to accomplish that the island never became the major staging base for the invasion of Luzon as was intended.[7]

Prior to the October–November battles, 20-mm Oerlikon antiaircraft guns had been the greatest killers of Japanese aircraft. After the kamikaze's appearance, however, their lack of hitting power rendered them little more than psychological weapons against plunging aircraft. Commanders relied increasingly on the larger 40-mm Bofors guns, because they could blast apart a closing aircraft. As more became available, additional mounts of the twin and quad Bofors jammed already overcrowded deck spaces on everything from minesweepers and LSTs to battleships and carriers.[8] Destroying enemy aircraft on the ground, always an important part of carrier operations, was given increased emphasis, but the Japanese did not need extensive airfields to operate essentially one-way kamikazes, and planners worried that the Japanese would simply disperse and camouflage the thousands of planes remaining in the Home Islands and Formosa. It was also clear that radar picket destroyers would play a critical role in warning the fleet of approaching aircraft. The ring of such ships around Okinawa was to be beefed up considerably with combat air patrols (CAPs) assigned to the most dangerous picket stations since the highly vulnerable "tin cans" were likely to be the first targets seen, and dived on, by inexperienced kamikaze pilots.[9]

The resulting ordeal endured by the radar pickets and the U.S. carrier fleet off Okinawa and Japan has been documented extensively. Exactly four hundred warships and large landing craft were struck by kamikazes or bombs, including thirty-two that were sunk outright with more than forty so heavily damaged that they had to be scrapped, plus more than sixty others knocked out for extensive repairs.[10] Yet unlike Leyte, Okinawa was far removed from sources of Japanese ground troops. And the kamikazes, while deadly, had no practical effect on efforts to conquer the island stronghold. Upcoming operations on the Japanese Home Islands were shaping up to be another matter entirely.

Japanese plans in mid-July 1945 called for the Imperial Army and Navy air arms to convert all obsolescent and obsolete aircraft into kamikazes. This amounted to 10,440 aircraft,[11] including 3,230 fighters and reconnaissance planes, 1,810 bombers, and a whopping 5,400 trainers, thus leaving approximately 2,300 of the most modern combat aircraft for conventional operations to be carried out by the air regiments as well as a miscellany of planes for administrative and training purposes.[12] Not included in these figures were roughly 600 planes capable of being staged against American targets through Formosa, or the production of conventional aircraft, simple, purpose-built kamikazes,[13] and even a small number of advanced jets.[14] But despite the fact that production began to accelerate after the initial slow-downs caused by the dispersal of manufacturing plants, only a portion of this new construction would be ready for combat by Operation Ketsu-Go No. 6 in October, when the Japanese believed that the invasion of Kyushu would be launched.

The Japanese assumed that of the 5,500 aircraft earmarked to destroy the Olympic invasion force, roughly 10 percent would not take part because of either mechanical difficulties or their destruction while still on the ground during U.S. fighter sweeps. They estimated that this would leave as many as 4,300 kamikazes and 700 conventional aircraft for strikes,[15] and, upon further analysis, the new joint air staff believed that the number of escorting fighters could be brought up to some two thousand conventional aircraft during Ketsu-Go No. 6 by staging aircraft in central and southern Honshu through fields closer to the battle.[16]

The Japanese devised a simple method for the immediate organization of fully equipped and completely staffed Special Attack formations—the mass conversion of existing training units to the new mission by decree. At least some Japanese flight instructors, not sufficiently infused with the *bushido* spirit, were in despair over the lack of training being given to the novice kamikaze pilots, but airmen such as Captain Inoguchi Rikibei, commanding the 10th Air Fleet's "special attack" pilot training, enthusiastically enforced the new orders.[17] Said Inoguchi: "Inasmuch as the kamikaze attacks were the last means of any favorable results in the war and the only chance for breaking down American resistance a little, we did not care how many planes were lost. Poor planes and poor pilots were used, and there was no ceiling on the number of either available for use."[18]

According to Captain Fuchida Mitsuo of the Combined Fleet's Air Operations Staff, members of the first Shimpu Tokubetsu Kogekitai (usually referred to as Tokko-Tai, or simply Tokko units) were some of the very best pilots in the Philippines with an average of three hundred flight hours apiece.[19] By Okinawa the average flight hours had dropped to roughly half among kamikaze pilots, and with the decision to launch massive, smothering attacks concentrated over little more than a week came the conclusion that while thirty to fifty flying hours was desirable, a bare-bones fifteen would have to do.[20] However, the all-or-nothing death struggle ahead necessitated that the flight instructors themselves be designated as combat pilots—and well-trained ones at that—for the conventional aircraft. In addition fully nine hundred pilots in Southeast Asia and the East Indies were to be transported back to the Home Islands by the end of August over safe air routes across occupied China and the Yellow Sea,[21] although it is unclear whether the sixty pilots shifted to Formosa to bolster the effort to interdict invasion shipping from the Philippines were included in this figure.[22] The postwar United States Strategic Bombing Survey (USSBS) in Japan found that including the now-former instructors, the Imperial Navy had 10,600 pilots at the end of hostilities and the Imperial Army another 8,000. And while 5,950 navy pilots were low skilled, 2,450 were rated high enough for night missions and 1,750 for dawn and dusk missions. Fully 2,000 fliers in the smaller Army force had at least seventy air hours under their samurai headbands.[23]

Ordnance to be supplied to the Special Attack Force units by the end of July were three thousand each of 100- and 500-kilogram bombs, seven thousand 250-kilogram bombs, and an additional three hundred bombs of 800 kilograms (1,764 lbs.) to be used against heavily armored warships engaged in shore bombardments.[24] Having correctly deduced both the location and approximate times of both Operations Olympic and Coronet, the Japanese decided to expend the bulk of the kamikazes allotted to Ketsu-Go 6 during the pivotal first ten days of the invasion of Kyushu, and were likely to repeat the tactic during Ketsu-Go 3 when U.S. forces arrived off Honshu in 1946. In both cases the landing forces themselves were to be the main focus of Japanese efforts, with additional aircraft allotted to the keep the carrier task forces occupied.[25]

But where, precisely, was the aviation fuel to come from for such massive and wide-ranging operations? There was ample communications intelligence late in the war that the Japanese were suffering badly from a lack of fuel in both the civil and military spheres, including the fact that the aviation fuel allotment for training purposes had been severely curtailed. This was further reinforced in American eyes by the lack of fleet activity and manifestly weak reaction of the Japanese air forces to the strategic bombing raids conducted from the Marianas, and virtually no response at all to a series of shore bombardments by American and British battleships that it was hoped would lure large numbers of aircraft to their destruction (see chapter 10).

The incoming intelligence data couldn't have been clearer. The Home Islands were completely cut off from their oil sources in the captured Dutch East Indies, and domestic oil facilities and storage was believed to have been destroyed by the B-29s.[26] In addition to the ratcheting down of flight hours in their pilot training, reports obtained from neutral embassies also indicated that the civilian population had not only been deprived of liquid fuel, but that badly needed foodstuffs, such as potatoes, corn, and rice, were also being requisitioned for synthetic fuel production.[27] So while American commanders in the Pacific were aware that some large number of aircraft and fuel stocks had been successfully hidden to await the invasion, the recurring weakness of Japan's response to attacks seemingly confirmed the idea that those aircraft were no longer able to maintain combat operations.

To the most optimistic analysts, all the signs pointed to a "slam dunk" for American pilots who would end Olympic with considerably more aces among their ranks. Many Navy men, however, were less optimistic since combat operations had clearly demonstrated that, no matter how many "Nips" were shot out of the sky, if a "bogey" managed to elude the CAPs, it stood a very good chance of actually crashing a ship. Nearly all took heart, however, in that the Japanese had apparently "run out of gas," not just figuratively, but literally. But what no one knew at the time—and failed to understand later even though all the relevant data was discovered after the war and scattered throughout the USSBS—was that the Japanese had made a conscious decision early in 1945 to build up decentralized fuel reserves in the Home Islands separate from stocks used for training and day-to-day activities, reserves which would only be tapped for the final battles.[28]

The IGHQ had seen the writing on the wall when U.S. forces reestablished themselves in the Philippines and succeeded in rushing shipments of refined fuel from the East Indies past the newly established Philippine bases in February and March before the sea lanes were completely choked off. The annihilation of a nine-tanker convoy and their escorts off Qui Nhon, French Indochina, in January prompted the Japanese to switch to small convoys with dispersed escorts during the "breakthrough transportation operation," a tactic which met with some success.[29] U.S. aircraft and submarines sank roughly two-thirds of the tankers running north, but four or five got through with 40,000 tons of refined fuel. These precious cargoes, along with some domestic production, formed the core of what became Japan's strategic reserve.[30]

Although communications intercepts (1) revealed the build-up of tankers and cargo ships plus land-based air power to protect them, (2) quoted communications stating why the surge of tankers was being undertaken, (3) described transit routings to make American interception more difficult, and (4) chronicled the sinking of Japanese ships during the two-phase operation,[31] it was not understood by either those crafting, or reading, the Magic summaries that the Japanese now had enough refined aviation fuel on hand in ready, but jealously guarded, depots and in the strategic reserves for Imperial Army and Navy air elements to carry out their assigned missions against the U.S. invasion fleets.

Excluding fuel under the control of individual combat, training, and support units, or available in depots, the strategic reserve included 190,000 barrels of aviation gas in hidden Army stockpiles and a further 126,000 barrels held by the Navy, much of it stored underground in the Nagano area of central Honshu.[32] By July 1945 military stocks in the Home Islands were made up of the Japanese army's 704,000 barrels and the navy's 452,000, for a total inventory of 1,156,000 barrels of aviation fuel.[33] It is instructive to compare this figure with the 604,000 barrels consumed from April to June 1945 within Japan's Inner Zone (incorporating Formosa to the south, west through Korea, and the former Russian territory far to the north). In spite of the fact that this period included 1,809 Navy and 848 Army combat sorties during the Okinawa fighting,[34] along with an unknown number of administrative, training, and reconnaissance flights, the amount of aviation fuel used by the two air services actually decreased more than 132,000 barrels from the previous quarter and 201,000 barrels from the one before that.[35]

How could this be, in light of the brutal and costly struggle between the U.S. Fleet and the kamikazes? Economies in pilot training were enforced with such a rigid (one might even say fanatical) determination that overall consumption plummeted even as intensive air strikes were launched from Kyushu and Formosa.[36] This data paints an even more ominous picture of the true amount of aviation fuel available to Imperial air forces during the invasion of Japan when one realizes that aircraft targeting U.S. fleet elements around Okinawa had to fly at great distances—roughly double to triple the miles they would have to fly during Olympic—and thus used up correspondingly more fuel per sortie. The many anguished accounts of Japanese flight instructors and unit commanders about their lack of fuel have served hand-in-glove with the completely accurate, if misleading, reports by U.S. pilots of

The king-sized USS *Midway*, with its armored flight deck, unique port-side elevator, and truly pro-digious amount of firepower ringing the hull, underway in Hampton Roads on October 20, 1945. President Truman was informed that two behemoths of this class would be ready for combat opera-tions in March 1946, but construction times of the USS *Roosevelt,* and numerous *Essex*-class carriers that also were to be ready for Operation Coronet, were lengthened to varying degrees after the early end of hostilities. (U.S. Army)

the lack of Japanese air activity to give an utterly false impression of the amount of gas that the Imperial air forces had hoarded to repel the invasion.

★   ★   ★

The one bright spot in this grim equation was U.S., and British, carrier strength. *Essex*-class carriers *Bon Homme Richard* and *Shangri-La* had joined the fleet during the prolonged Okinawa campaign, with the *Boxer, Antietam* (whose captain, James R. Tague, was born in Japan), and possibly *Lake Champlain* arriving forward by January 1946.[37] The U.S. Navy in the Pacific would have had as many as twenty-five American fleet and light fleet carriers (designated respectively CVs and CVLs) with roughly 1,912 aircraft available to conduct Olympic as well as ten of the operational Royal Navy equivalent classes launching from 550 to 560 aircraft from two task groups.[38]

One ship, however, would not be part of the "murderers row" of carriers at the huge Ulithi Atoll anchorage and forward staging base. Although crewed by valiant, battle-hard-ened sailors, the *Saratoga* had been forced to leave the western Pacific after being repeatedly struck by suicide aircraft during the Okinawa campaign. It would serve the rest of the war training air crews off Hawaii after extensive repairs, but the elderly *Saratoga*'s relegation to the backwater of training operations was actually due not to combat damage but to structural inefficiencies that hampered flight operations. With carriers of the *Essex, Independence, Saipan,* and *Midway* classes newly commissioned, or following wartime schedules that amounted to a stunning average of one carrier per month joining the Pacific Fleet from August 1944 through the spring of 1946, the grand old lady was no longer needed for front-line service.[39]

Unlike the *Saratoga,* the *Enterprise, Bunker Hill,* and *Intrepid*—all so heavily damaged by kamikazes that they had to be sent stateside for extensive repairs—would be back by the invasion of Kyushu, as would the *Hornet* and *Wasp,* which both lost great lengths of their flight decks during summer 1945 typhoons. The light carrier *Langley,* sent home for a badly needed refit, would also have returned.[40] In all the U.S. Fifth Fleet of Adm. Raymond A. Spruance (handling operations to the west of a north-south coordination line east of Hiroshima and the Kure naval base at the thirty-third meridian) and the Third Fleet under Adm. William F. "Bull" Halsey (ranging far up the coast beyond Tokyo) would have approximately thirty-five American and British fleet carriers and more than 2,500 aircraft to hurl against Japan during Olympic.[41] Moreover, accelerated replacement of torpedo squadrons by fighters in the carrier air groups guaranteed that nearly all these aircraft could be employed with great flexibility during the critical opening days of the ground invasions, and new night-fighter squadrons were proving their worth daily.[42]

Even more carriers were on the way for Coronet. There was also a serious effort to make the *Franklin* combat ready again after it was gutted by internal fires during the Okinawa fighting, and, on paper it was scheduled to take part in the invasion of the Kanto Plain. Obviously, however, the early end of the war made the determined effort on the *Franklin*'s rebuilding unnecessary and significantly stretched out the construction of many other carriers.[43] In the summer of 1945, however, the U.S. Navy had no clue that the war would soon be over and naval aviation's prospects for 1946 looked bright indeed as the *Lake Champlain*—plus the king-sized *Midway* and *Roosevelt,* designated CVBs (fleet carrier big), with their armored flight decks—would have all joined the fleet by Coronet or in time to support subsequent operations. Additional *Essex*-class ships, the *Kearsarge, Princeton,* and *Tarawa,* as well as the *Saipan,* the lead ship of a new class of light carriers, would come available in the summer of 1946, a fact masked by the dates of their commissionings and shakedown cruises, which occurred at a much more relaxed and economical pace during an unanticipated postwar environment.[44]

Interestingly, the projected surge of shipyard-fresh carriers into the western Pacific during the first half of 1946 would not represent a significant change in available flattops since the first carriers would have arrived in the winter and early spring of that year when perhaps as many as half a dozen of their sisters would be sent back across the Pacific for badly needed refits or damage repairs. Indeed the Joint Chiefs of Staff's deployment schedule produced for President Truman's use at the Potsdam Conference—22 CVs, 9 CVLs, and 2 CVBs in the Pacific by March 1, 1946—was tempered by the warning that "three months after the

Kyushu operation it is estimated that approximately 10 percent will either have been lost or still undergoing repairs to damage received in this operation."[45]

Irrespective of additional losses during Coronet, however, refits based solely on the normal wear and tear of sea service would have likely taken place after Coronet's initial surge and as more ships arrived in the summer of 1946 to largely trade places with their sisters that had been commissioned in the latter half of 1944. Yet with the Fifth Air Force firmly emplaced on the Home Islands and Imperial air power largely a thing of the past by summer 1946, it would have been unlikely for more than a handful of the new carrier pilots to have even seen a Japanese plane in the air as they performed their daily grind of close air support for Army, Marine, and Commonwealth ground-pounders.

That delightful prospect, however, seemed still an eternity away in the summer of 1945, and the Navy looked to yet another source of naval air power to provide valuable support—the extremely large number of escort carriers available for combat operations. Excluding the nearly three dozen escorts engaged principally in the transportation of replacement aircraft and setting up of advance air bases, at least thirty-six American and six British "baby flat-tops" were originally envisioned to take part in some facet of Olympic, but the demands on these ships were extremely heavy with many siphoned off to protect the far-flung elements of the invasion force. For example, four escort carriers were assigned to provide cover for slow-moving convoys plying the waters between the Philippines and Kyushu against more than 600 Japanese aircraft known to be operating out of, or capable of being staged through, Formosa.[46] Just sixteen of these ships with approximately 450 aircraft (minus the large number of planes required to protect the vulnerable assault shipping) were scheduled to support the soldiers and Marines of the landing force directly. Recently commissioned escort carriers sailing to the war zone, plus the arrival of the British escort squadron that had fought in the Mediterranean, freed up more American decks for this task, eventually bringing the estimated number of ships to twenty-four handling approximately 670 aircraft. It should be noted, though, that in terms of CAPs and close air support, this number would functionally be reduced by six decks as an escort carrier in each of the three amphibious groups would be solely dedicated to naval gunfire spotting and another for antisubmarine duties.[47]

Plans called for 136 aircraft from the escort carriers to be on station from dawn to dusk to provide a last-ditch defense of the landing areas and with whatever aircraft available over this number tasked with providing close air support for the ground forces.[48] Of course, virtually every one of the escorts' aircraft would be required to maintain this continuous presence plus supply robust CAPs over the carriers themselves, and the assistance of ground troops would have suffered since many of those aircraft would inevitably have been siphoned off as they were at Okinawa. During Operation Iceberg, close air support sorties amounted to a paltry 704 of the 4,841 launched between April 7 and May 3, as protection of the Fifth Fleet and the landing/support areas from kamikazes remained the top priority.[49] Some help would come from the Fifth Air Force, which planned to maintain thirty-two fighters over the invasion beaches at all times. This meager presence would be achieved by sending aloft hundreds of aircraft in a virtually continuous stream of squadrons on the long haul from Okinawa and a small number from nearby Kikai Jima, which was to be seized for construc-

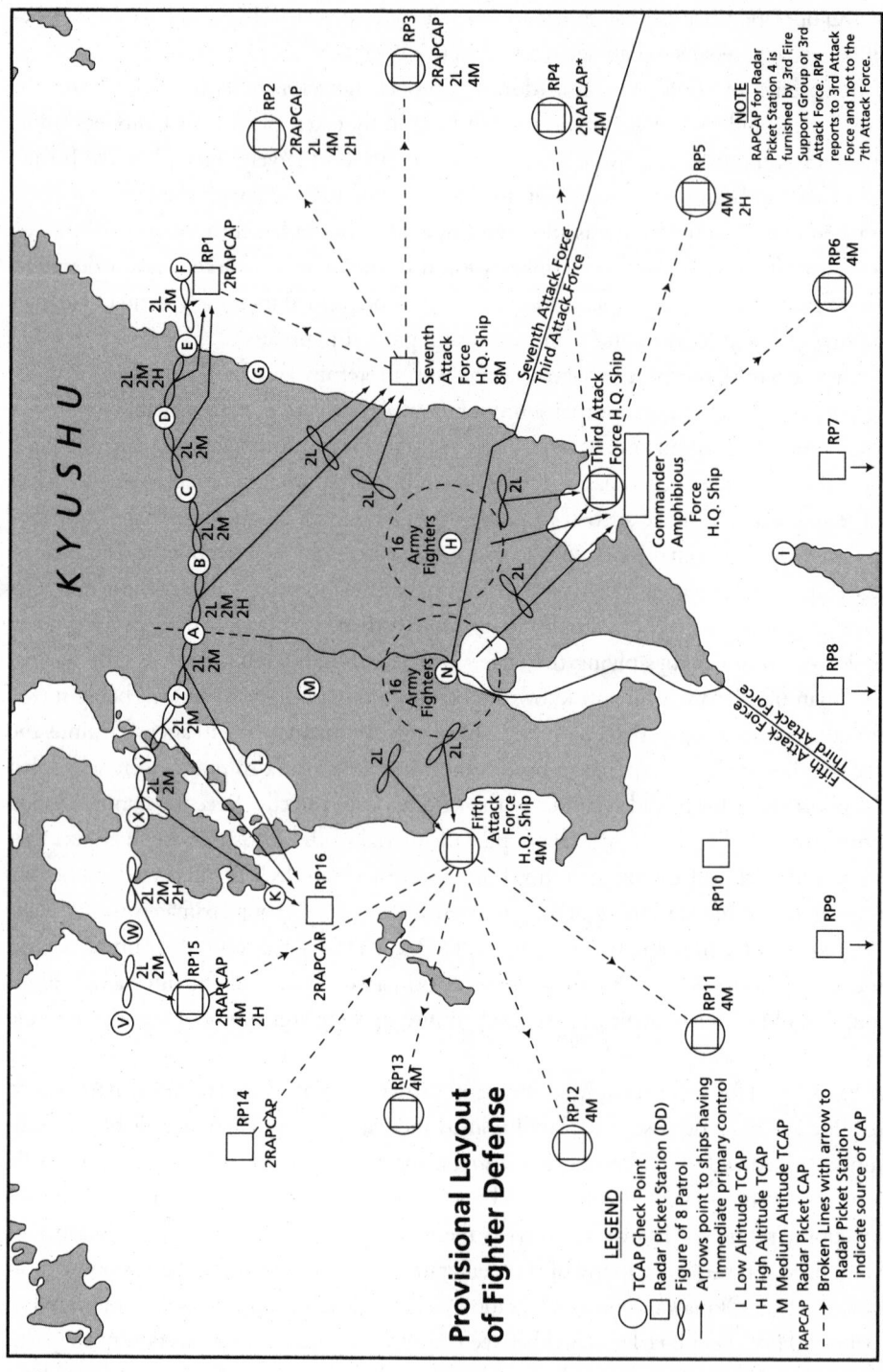

Provisional Layout of Fighter Defense

LEGEND

- ◯ TCAP Check Point
- ▢ Radar Picket Station (DD)
- ∞ Figure of 8 Patrol
- → Arrows point to ships having immediate primary control
- L Low Altitude TCAP
- H High Altitude TCAP
- M Medium Altitude TCAP
- RAPCAP Radar Picket CAP
- --→ Broken Lines with arrow to Radar Picket Station indicate source of CAP

KYUSHU

RP1 2RAPCAP

RP2 2RAPCAP 2L 4M 2H

RP3 2RAPCAP 2L 4M

RP4 2RAPCAP* 4M

RP5 4M 2H

RP6 4M

RP7

RP8

RP9

RP10

RP11 4M

RP12 4M

RP13 4M

RP14 2RAPCAP

RP15 2RAPCAP 4M 2H

RP16 2RAPCAR

Seventh Attack Force H.Q. Ship 8M

Third Attack Force H.Q. Ship

Commander Amphibious Force H.Q. Ship

Fifth Attack Force H.Q. Ship 4M

Seventh Attack Force / Third Attack Force

Fifth Attack Force / Third Attack Force

16 Army Fighters

16 Army Fighters

NOTE
RAPCAP for Radar Picket Station 4 is furnished by 3rd Fire Support Group or 3rd Attack Force. RP4 reports to 3rd Attack Force and not to the 7th Attack Force.

Map derived from "Report on Operation 'Olympic' and Japanese Counter-Measures, Part 4, Appendices" British Combined Operations Observers (Pacific), (London: Combined Operations Headquarters, August 1, 1946), app. 35.

Provisional landing force fighter defense for Operation Olympic.

tion as an emergency/forward strip in August. Upon reaching the invasion area, the Army aircraft would pass into the control of a Navy commander in chief operating directly under the commander, Amphibious Force, near Ariake Bay.[50]

Beyond the beachhead fighters from one of the two fast carrier groups operating off Kyushu would attempt to form a barrier against Japanese aircraft halfway up the island, but the ability of the CAPs to actually maintain coverage of this area once battle was joined (the CAP check points averaged fifteen miles apart over a clutter of cloud covered peaks) was going to be extraordinarily difficult, even if a semblance of airborne control was initiated.[51] Because of the heavy fuel consumption and ammunition expenditure during periods of intense combat, there would be a conveyor belt of nearly 250 aircraft in the air just to ensure that the 104 needed for the mid-island barrier and radar picket CAPs were maintained. Together with CAPs over the fleet and raids against known airfields, the southernmost task group of fleet carriers off Kyushu would be stretched to the limit. The second task group, immediately to its northeast, would be principally involved in protecting the eastern-most picket stations plus aggressive raiding from northern Kyushu through Shikoku and southern Honshu.

No one could guess what kind of losses these carriers would suffer off Kyushu. Even with assault shipping bearing the brunt of Japan's wrath, a portion of both the fleet and escort carriers would also be knocked out of the fight and possibly sunk, and as noted earlier, the Navy had hung its hat on losses of approximately 10 percent when making an estimate for President Truman.[52] Vice Adm. Marc Mitscher had himself experienced such occurrences months earlier at Okinawa. Japanese attacks had forced him to transfer his flag to the *Enterprise* (CV-6) after suicide and conventional strikes severely pummeled the *Bunker Hill* (CV-17), flagship of Task Force 58. When the *Enterprise* suffered a similar fate, he had to move yet again, this time to the *Randolph* (CV-15), which earlier had been grievously damaged by a kamikaze while it was anchored in the comparative safety of Ulithi.[53]

★   ★   ★

Okinawa represented the first coordinated effort by Japanese pilots to use cliffs and hills to foil U.S. radar. The size of the island and the distances to be flown from Japanese air bases, together with the fact that the Japanese had only just begun to experiment in this area, initially limited the usefulness of such tactics, but successes were nonetheless numerous.[54] The literature is replete with references by sailors, in ships that were close ashore, to kamikazes appearing so suddenly that even fully alert crews had little time to respond. Jack Moore, who later served as a radar man in the *Fletcher*-class destroyer *Wadleigh* (DD-689), noted that had the Japanese used such tactics during operations off Leyte, a tactical setting disturbingly similar to that of Operations Coronet and Olympic, the *Wadleigh* and many other ships might well have been sunk: "When one had altitude, you could pick it up without much trouble. If they'd come out of those hills—coming in low rather than flying up here around 10,000 feet and diving down, frankly, they could have massacred us in the Philippines."[55]

Innovations were made to increase point defense capabilities by shortening antiaircraft weapons' response times during engagements that seldom lasted more than fifty seconds between when firing commenced on an incoming aircraft, and it was either shot down or crashed into its target. By summer 1945 slewing sights for the 5-inch gun mount officer's station were helping to ensure quick, non-radar-directed action, and many U.S. vessels had begun to rig cross connections between their 5-inch guns' slow Mark 37 directors and the 40-mm guns' more nimble Mark 51 directors. These innovations (and a projectile in the loading tray) enabled the long-range 5-inch guns to come on line more quickly to counter sudden attacks but switch back to the longer-range Mark 37 director if radar found additional targets at a more conventional range. The new Mark 32 radar, which allowed early and accurate identification of incoming aircraft, also would have been widely distributed by the time of Operation Olympic.[56]

Although 20-mm Oerlikon guns had proved vastly less effective against a plunging kamikaze than the 40-mm Bofors, that did not mean crews were eager to do away with them in order to free up deck space because these weapons at least had the advantage of not being operated electrically. Even if a vessel's power was knocked out, the "door knockers" could still supply defensive fire. And while production of the Oerlikon was discontinued, the advent of the kamikaze threat prompted the extensive remaining stocks to be reconfigured in twin mounts for replacement of single-gun mounts in order to beef up the firepower from ships' spaces already established for the weapon. By June 30, 1945, 2,381 twin mounts had been installed on Navy ships in the Pacific, and 10,180 singles remained throughout the fleet. The numbers of quad, double, and single 40-mm mounts stood at 1,585, 3,045, and 510 respectively.[57]

If the war had continued into the winter of 1945–46, the appearance of the 3-inch/50 rapid-fire gun would have generated great excitement within the Pacific Fleet. Early production models were slightly delicate, but the 3-inch/50 was nevertheless a marvelous new weapon that postwar single-mount test firings against "Nakajima-type fighter planes" demonstrated was as effective as two—that's *two*—quad 40s against conventional planes. The Navy's Bureau of Ordnance reported that against the Baka piloted rocket bomb, the advantage over the redoubtable Bofors was even more pronounced as it took fully five quad 40s (twenty guns) to equal the performance of a single 3-inch/50.[58] A few hundred of these rapid-fire guns would have been installed on a first-come, first-served basis before Coronet as warships received overhauls or weapons upgrades at Pearl Harbor, West Coast yards, and even Ulithi, with intensive crew training taking place in-theater or as they headed west across the Pacific. And they would need the 3-inch/50—badly.

Reviewing the outcome of the extended radar picket operations off Okinawa, an August 1945 report from Admiral King's staff came to the grim conclusion that "one destroyer cannot be expected to defend itself successfully against more than one attacking enemy aircraft at a time" (many did, in fact, but were eventually overwhelmed) and noted that in the future a full destroyer division should be assigned to each picket station if the tactical situation allowed such a commitment of resources.[59] Another tactical innovation under consideration by Admiral King's staff may also have been at least partially offset by corresponding changes in Japanese tactics had the war continued. For example, it was noted that, while large warships' antiaircraft gunnery was not affected greatly by evasive maneuvers, violent turns by a diminutive destroyer to disturb the aim of the kamikaze, or to bring more guns to bear during a surprise attack, caused extreme pitches and rolls that degraded accuracy.[60]

Gunnery improved dramatically when the small ships performed less strident maneuvers, even if fewer guns could be brought into play quickly. Unfortunately, by summer 1945, would-be suicide pilots were being told that because they did not need the big, broadside targets normally required when aiming bombs, the best results in their type of operation would come from bow- or stern-on attacks that enabled them to be targeted by the least amount of defensive fires—a sort of divine wind "crossing the T" perhaps made much easier by less radical destroyer maneuvers under consideration.[61]

How evolving U.S. and Japanese tactics actually would have played out during the invasions of Japan is anybody's guess (and most novice pilots would likely have continued to aim for the wide expanse of a ship's side), but an example of this new Japanese tactic's effectiveness, when properly executed, can be seen in the attack on the destroyer USS *Kimberly*. Spotting an incoming Aichi D3A "Val" on March 29, 1945, the ship immediately maneuvered to bring the maximum number of guns to bear. The pilot, however, was able to line-up low on the stern in spite of the fact that the Kimberly was on hard right rudder, and he threw off the aim of the few guns that could be brought to bear by "performing continuous right and left skids" while "always remain[ing] in the ship's wake." The Val began to smoke but "only the after guns could bear and each 5-in salvo blasted the 20-mm crews off their feet." In seconds the plane came in over the stern, aiming for the bridge, and crashed aft of the rear stack between two five-inch mounts killing four men and wounding fifty-seven.[62]

★　★　★

Some historians and air-power enthusiasts have tended to discount the potential destructiveness of the kamikaze and have noted that many would certainly have been destroyed by preinvasion fighter sweeps. To destroy them on the ground, however, U.S. forces would have first had to know where they were. U.S. air operations as recent as the 1991 Gulf War's "Scud hunt" and 1998 combat operations against Serbian forces in the Balkans illustrate that this is generally not as easy as some presume it to be.[63]

Throughout World War II increasingly effective sweeps by U.S. fighters and medium bombers played havoc with Japanese air bases. Anticipating that attacks would only grow worse as the U.S. Navy and Army Air Forces neared the Home Islands, the Japanese stepped up the dispersion of their units and spread aircraft throughout more than 125 bases and airfields known to U.S. intelligence and literally hundreds more that remained hidden.[64] This effort intensified after the U.S. Navy caught hundreds of aircraft on the ground at Kyushu bases preparing for suicide runs at Okinawa.[65] As for the planes slated for use as kamikazes, they did not require extensive facilities, and many were in the process of being hidden away to take off from roads and fields around central billeting areas.[66] In addition to the secret dispersal fields being constructed by the dozen, use of camouflage, dummy aircraft, and propped-up derelicts performed as desired during U.S. strikes against known facilities.[67]

After some initial sparring with carrier aircraft and Far East Air Force elements flying out of Okinawa, the Japanese essentially glued their aircraft to the ground in order to preserve them for use during the invasions. The few available high-performance Ki-61 Hein "Tony" and J2M Raiden "Jack" fighters were used against the B-29s, and the juggling of the limited assets available to the conventional air regiments (which had no access to strategic fuel supplies) was a separate and distinct matter from the acquisition and readying of special attack units.[68] In fact, the Japanese planned no significant employment of either conventional or kamikaze aircraft, even during the approach of the American fleets, since Imperial Headquarters believed that being drawn out early would cause needless losses and correctly anticipated that U.S. forces would attempt to lure their aircraft into premature battle through elaborate feints and other deception measures. The massive Japanese response would occur only when they could confirm U.S. landing operations had commenced,[69] and the one coordinated effort to entice the Japanese into the air before the end of the war—a series of mid-July coastal bombardments by U.S. and British warships while swarms of fighters waited in vain to pounce—reinforced the notion within the U.S. command that the Imperial air forces were impotent.[70]

The Japanese had seven interrelated advantages during the defense of the Home Islands that they did not have at Okinawa:

- Their aircraft could approach the invaders from anywhere along a wide arc, thus negating any more U.S. victories along the line of the 1944 Marianas Turkey Shoot or the spring 1945 Kikai Jima air battles, where long distances required Japanese aircraft to travel relatively predictable flight paths. Moreover, the perceived inability of the Japanese to send up large numbers of aircraft encouraged the U.S. Navy to believe that the landing area's immediate defense could be left to escort carriers and Army fighters from Okinawa while the 1,900 aircraft of Task Force 58's fleet carriers were assigned missions as far north as six hundred miles from Kyushu, well beyond Tokyo. Aircraft from only two of Spruance's task groups were dedicated to suppression efforts north and east of the screen thrown up by Adm. Clifton A. F. Sprague's escorts.[71]

- The high mountains of Japan would have masked low-flying kamikazes from search radars, thus limiting ships' response times to incoming enemy aircraft. Plans were made to establish radar sites within U.S. lines and on the outlying islands as quickly as the tactical situation allowed, but this would have only a minor effect on the central problem—the mountains. In addition most shore-based radar units during Olympic were not slated to be operational until after X+10, when the kamikaze attacks would be drawing to a close (assuming, of course, that a portion of the ships carrying them had not already been sunk).[72] The radar picture would be further complicated by use of the now-plentiful legion of night-qualified pilots due to the wholesale transfer of flight instructors to combat operations along with some 5,400 wood-and-fabric training aircraft that were largely radar resistant (see chapter 12).[73]

- The Japanese were suffering from a severe shortage of radios, and some writers have discounted their ability to coordinate attacks from dispersed air fields and hiding places through telephone lines. At this point in the war, however, Japanese reliance on telephones was more a strength than a weakness. No Ultra or Magic intercepts here.[74] U.S. forces could neither monitor nor jam the land lines, and like the Japanese electrical system, it presented few good targets for air attack.[75]

- Related to the second advantage, the fourth had to do with the virtually static nature of the assault vessels while conducting the invasions. Because the ships disembarking the landing force would be operating at a known location, kamikazes would not have to approach from a high altitude, which allowed them the visibility needed to search for far-flung carrier groups yet also made them visible to radar. Instead they would be able to approach the mass of slow-moving transports, cargo ships, and defending destroyer-type vessels from the mountains and then drop to very low altitudes. The final low-level run on the ships would offer no radar and little visual warning as well as limit the number of antiaircraft guns that could be brought to bear against them. During operations against U.S. ships at Okinawa, a much larger percentage of kamikazes got through to targets when flying under radar coverage to fixed locations (such as assembly and bombardment areas and the Kerama Retto anchorage) than those approaching the roving task groups at sea from higher altitudes. But despite the advantages offered by radar picking up the high-flyers, operating at any fixed location invited concentrated attack, and the radar pickets near certain Japanese approach routes to Okinawa suffered far more than those on the move with fast carrier task forces.

- The U.S. Navy had begun extensive use of destroyers as radar pickets as early as the Kwajalein operation in January 1944, and by the end of that year comparatively sophisticated combat information centers were effectively providing tactical situation plotting and fighter direction from select destroyers. Unfortunately, coordination within, and timely communications from, the radar pickets' newly installed CICs presented a problem, with the centers frequently becoming overwhelmed by the speed of events and sheer quantity of bogies,[76] which, according to Capt. Lefteris Lavrakas, "rendered the CICs only partially effective in getting the job done—reporting all planes in sufficient time to shoot them down."[77] Add a nearby landmass to the equation as at Kyushu, and things get dicey in a hurry.

- As previously noted, radar coverage of the countless mountain passes would have been virtually nil during the Kyushu operation, and the Fifth Fleet CAPs attempting to form a barrier halfway up the island would have been on their own. In any event they would have been frequently out of direct contact with the pickets controlling their checkpoints. The barrier patrol over the 120-mile-wide midsection of Kyushu and Amakusa-Shoto, an island close to the west, would be able only to find and bounce a comparatively small percentage of attackers coming through the mountains, and this number would shrink even further with a modest amount of cloud cover. As it turned out both Olympic and Coronet would have been launched during times when the weather would be ideal for Japanese purposes. Not only would the moderate to heavy cloud cover, ranging from three thousand to seven thousand feet, tend to mask the low-level approach of aircraft to the landing beaches, but the inexperienced Japanese pilots searching for carriers out to sea from a high altitude would also find that these clouds provided good cover from radar-vectored CAPs while being no great hindrance to navigation.

• Perhaps most important of all, a proportionately small number of suicide aircraft got through to the vulnerable transports off Okinawa because of the natural tendency of inexperienced pilots to dive on the first target they saw. As a result the radar pickets had, in effect, soaked up the bulk of the kamikazes before they reached the landing area, but accomplishing this entailed terrible losses even though the destroyers frequently had their own CAPs and were supported by landing craft acting as gunboats. At Kyushu and Honshu, however, there would be no radar pickets on the landward side of the assault shipping to absorb the blows meant for the slow-moving troop transports and supply vessels, which would have had to lock themselves into relatively static positions offshore during landing operations. These were the ships that kamikaze pilots were specifically to target, and circumstance and terrain were going to go a long way toward helping them achieve their goal of killing the largest amount of Americans possible.

These same troop transports and cargo vessels that were highly vulnerable while they lay off the invasion beaches—and that were indeed the prime targets—were the very ships in most critically short supply. World War II production figures for such vessels as Liberty ships, Victory ships, and LSTs are impressively huge, but worldwide commitments, intra-theater needs, and a persistent lack of discharge facilities had created a potentially dangerous lack of redundancy, especially for the second invasion, Coronet.[78] Unexpectedly heavy losses in assault shipping at Kyushu not only would have meant the deaths of many thousands of sailors and their human cargoes, but as we will see in chapter 15, it also could have seriously disrupted the U.S. military's ability to conduct the invasion of Honshu early enough to give ground operations and airfield construction a good start before the increasingly heavy rains of the spring and summer of 1946 weighed in on Japan's side.[79]

Another element worth emphasizing is that U.S. intelligence turned out to be dead wrong on the sheer quantity of Japanese aircraft available for defense of the Home Islands. Early estimates that approximately 6,700 planes could be made available in a piecemeal fashion to throw against the invasions grew to only 7,200 at the time of the surrender and turned out to be short by some 5,500 of the 12,700 aircraft that the Japanese planned to use in the opening ten-day phases of both operations. Moreover, production continued in hidden, decentralized factories in spite of material shortages and the U.S. bombing campaign. And that did not include aircraft available from the Asian mainland and Formosa.[80]

This difference would have had little practical effect on the Kyushu operation because of the restricted nature of Japan's Ketsu-Go 6 response to Olympic. But it would have been an unpleasant surprise during the invasion on Honshu, making that operation even more costly than anticipated. This was an obvious and highly significant intelligence failure that became clear once U.S. troops were "on the ground" in occupied Japan, and MacArthur's G-2 chief, Major General Willoughby, adopted the attitude that the less said about it the better.[81] The disparity became even more ominous in light of the fact that the postwar examination of Japanese records revealed that Japanese aircraft losses at Okinawa were far below often-repeated U.S. estimates for the campaign.

Many Japanese aircraft were not destroyed on the ground, in flight, or in suicidal attacks. For example, of the 1,809 sorties logged by the Imperial Navy's 3d, 5th, and 10th Air Fleets, (which flew the bulk of the Okinawa missions), fully 879 kamikazes and escorts successfully returned to base after not finding a target or completing conventional missions.[82] The number of kamikaze and conventional aircraft actually lost or expended by these units, combined with approximately 500 lost or expended by the Imperial Army at Okinawa,[83] was roughly 1,430, or little more than a quarter the number of the 5,500 aircraft *missed* by U.S. intelligence on the Home Islands—1,430 aircraft, which killed 4,900 U.S. sailors in Okinawan waters and severely wounded 4,800 more.[84]

CHAPTER 9

The "Manpower Box"

If the study shows that the behavior of nations in all historical cases comparable to Japan's has in fact been invariably consistent with the behavior of the troops in battle, then it means that the Japanese dead and ineffectives at the time of the defeat will exceed the corresponding number for the Germans. In other words, we shall probably have to kill at least 5 to 10 million Japanese. This might cost us between 1.7 and 4 million casualties including 400,000 and 800,000 killed.

—WILLIAM B. SHOCKLEY, "Proposal for Increasing the Scope of Casualties Studies," July 21, 1945 [1]

Long before U.S. intelligence discovered the dangerous buildup in Kyushu and realized the true significance of Japan's wholesale conversion of pilot-training units into kamikaze formations, it was clear that the massive scope of the Japanese mobilization was on the way to producing an Imperial Army far larger than what U.S. Army planners had anticipated. [2] On the heels of Iwo Jima, and with the bloody fighting on Okinawa grinding on day by day, it was already becoming apparent to some that the Saipan ratio, currently at the top end of the casualty estimate spectrum with up to half a million American dead, was being outpaced by events as the fighting drew closer to the Home Islands. [3]

As noted in chapter 6, Herbert Hoover's maximum figure of up to 1 million American dead was fully double the mortality figure used in JCS 924 and far beyond the cumulative total of the Army's replacement stream of 100,000 men per month that was, by now, several months into its implementation. Consequently it is not surprising that when Secretary of War Henry Stimson solicited a "staff opinion" on the figures presented in Hoover's May 30 memorandums to President Truman, General Marshall endorsed the comments by the Operations Division planner, who said that the estimate "appears to deserve little consideration." The previous week Marshall similarly endorsed an apparently different planning officer's comments on the same estimate in Hoover's earlier memorandum submitted directly to Stimson on May 15 after their Long Island meeting. Even though the two commentaries offered different interpretations, they were both sound appreciations completely in line with Army doctrine, and the chief of staff signed off on both.[4]

The May 15 memorandum traveled the same path as the May 30 memorandum requested by Truman: Marshall's deputy chief of staff, Maj. Gen. Thomas T. Handy, down to Brig. Gen. George A. Lincoln's Strategy and Policy Group, then back up the chain with its accompanying commentary to Stimson, who forwarded neither set of documents to Truman. The staff officer responding to the May 15 memorandum agreed that Hoover's casualty estimate was "entirely too high," yet the pointed disclaimer that immediately follows—"under the present plan of campaign"—is regularly deleted from accounts of the analyses by critics of Truman's atomic bomb decision, even though, excluding headlines, it is literally the only portion of the 550-word response with a typed underline.[5] This emphatic qualifier would soon turn out to be highly perceptive.

Hoover's estimate of 500,000 to 1 million dead implied, as the author of the later staff assessment correctly noted, total all-causes casualties running in the area of 2 million to as many as 5 million. These numbers were in line with casualties suffered by World War II's other major combatants, who had entered hostilities much earlier than the United States, and in themselves were not unimaginable if the intent had been to conquer virtually all resisting Japanese on the Home Islands by force of arms. Such, however, had never been the intent or desire of planners who firmly believed that "under the present plan of campaign" effective "military control" of all Japan could be "obtained by the securing of a relatively few vital coastal areas" on Honshu[6] and that the opening invasion of Kyushu would only entail seizing enough land to serve as a base to launch the Honshu invasion against the Tokyo area in 1946.

Military and civilian leaders, and most strategic planners, believed that the Japanese, isolated and without allies, would surrender after their capital was taken and their cities destroyed, thus rendering unnecessary a bloody mop-up of the mountainous, California-sized nation. The Army's 100,000-men-per-month replacement stream to the Pacific was believed to be fully sufficient to supply manpower for these limited but still daunting objectives, and it was envisioned that major offensive operations would be concluded by 1947.

But would operations play out as expected? The "present plan of campaign" upon which literally all of the Army's Pacific-related actions for the previous eleven months had been based, envisioned the opening U.S. invasion on southern Kyushu as one in which overwhelming American strength would be directed against only a portion of Japan's forces cut off from reinforcement. Unfortunately, after three years of fighting, the Japanese had "figured us out" and gained a clear understanding of the U.S. methods and logistic requirements that were key factors in the selection of targets.[7] IGHQ correctly inferred that southern Kyushu would likely be the next target and were already moving quickly and decisively to reinforce Kyushu with a massive number of troops before it could be cut off by U.S. air and sea power, and 916,828 military personnel were either in position or in various stages of deployment on the island at the time of the surrender.[8]

At this point, however, the piling-on of Imperial forces at the invasion sites was not yet apparent, though the massive Japanese mobilization, in combination with the ominous upsurge of American casualties, was. And while Secretary Stimson was willing to expose others' thoughts to the president unfiltered by his own analysis, as when he personally forwarded the letter of Manhattan Project engineer Oswald C. Brewster to Truman,[9] he either saw nothing in the staff comments that warranted the commander in chief's direct examination or was leery about the Pentagon staff's confident assertions that, in spite of the casualties from Okinawa and Iwo Jima, the U.S. was not moving into the realm of the worst-case scenario outlined in JCS 924. Yet to Stimson and many Pentagon planners, the worst-case scenario now seemed a real possibility.[10] And this begged a question, if the situation could be seen to be moving in that direction—fully half a year before Olympic—was there an *even worse case* that had not been anticipated?

★   ★   ★

As early as May 1944, Secretary of War Stimson repeatedly fretted over the lack of troops being committed to the upcoming invasion of France. He pushed hard for a greater share of the Army's limited manpower to be allotted to the formation of additional combat divisions, but the Army's senior leadership was just as adamant that the lack of soldiers, and especially officers, made it impossible to efficiently support more divisions. They argued that the greatest asset the United States brought to the Allied coalition was its immense production capacity.[11]

Stimson, fearing a possible stalemate on the western front, complained in his diary and to aides that the Army's chief of staff, George C. Marshall, "takes quite a different view—a more optimistic view on some things that I think are rather dangerous," yet he did not raise his concerns with President Roosevelt because he did not want "to make an appearance of an issue with Marshall," with whom he was in fundamental agreement on so many matters.[12]

Events during the German's December 1944 Ardennes offensive proved that Stimson had been at least partially correct, and by May 1945 he was again concerned with the casualties question, this time for the invasion of Japan. And instead of grudgingly deferring to Marshall and the Army leadership as he had the previous year, he specifically wanted civilian personnel not connected to Army Ground Forces to be called in for a reexamination of manpower "requirements"[13] for what he and Marshall both agreed would be a more brutal slugfest than the war in Europe largely because of the terrain and the character of the Japanese soldier.[14]

It is instructive to briefly revisit the casualties suffered by the U.S. Army between Stimson's combative memos to Marshall on May 10 and 16, 1944, and his June 9, 1945, initiation of a top-level review of the replacement system, as well as the manpower situation as it was seen at that time. As outlined in chapter 5, the "casualty surge" that U.S. military and civilian leaders had long expected finally arrived in the summer of 1944 with D-day in France and the invasion of the Mariana Islands in the Pacific. Of America's roughly 1,250,000 combat and combat-related casualties in World War II, nearly 1 million of this number would be suffered from June 1944 to June 1945, a number that people today understandably find almost incomprehensible.[15]

America was suffering an average of 65,000 combat casualties each and every month during the casualty surge, with November, December, and January figures for the Army and Army Air Force standing at 72,000, 88,000 and 79,000 respectively in postwar tabulations.[16] The heavy American losses during the Ardennes offensive and lack of U.S. combat divisions to add weight behind General Patton's strike into the base of the "Bulge" spurred Stimson to press more forcefully to create additional combat formations in the European theater—and Marshall remained just as firm that this could not be done without creating immense manpower disruptions.[17]

Marshall had successfully rebuffed Stimson for almost a year on this, but in the crisis atmosphere of the current emergency, "head-on fight[s]" (Stimson's description) erupted among Stimson, Marshall, and Handy, Marshall's deputy chief of staff.[18] The compromise solution was to send the last nine uncommitted divisions, some of which were already scheduled for deployment to Europe, across the Atlantic by mid-February, including the 86th and 97th Infantry Divisions, which had been training specifically for the invasion of Japan. Meanwhile, manpower requirements for that very operation were moving to the front burner as Stimson called a press conference on January 11, 1945, in which he announced that the Army's monthly Selective Service call-up, which had already been increased from 60,000 to 80,000 in January 1945, was going to be ratcheted up yet again in March to 100,000 men per month in anticipation of the invasion of Japan.[19]

One week later, letters outlining the military's critical manpower needs were sent from Roosevelt, Marshall, and Chief of Naval Operations Ernest J. King to the House Military Affairs Committee and released to the *New York Times* and other newspapers on January 17, 1945. The public was informed in front-page articles that the "Army must provide 600,000 replacements for overseas theaters by June 30, and, together with the Navy, will require a total of 900,000 inductions."[20] To handle the influx of draftees, the Army also planned to increase the number of training regiments to thirty-four in order to form a ready pool of replacements, and AGF replacement training centers were expanded to a wartime peak of 400,000 in June, long after U.S. divisions had pulled to a halt along the Elbe River.[21]

What this near-doubling of draft quotas meant in terms of the planned invasions of Japan was essentially this: Starting in March 1945, when levies were increased to 100,000 per month for the U.S. Army and 40,000 for the Navy and Marines, nearly every man inducted would enter the "replacement stream" now oriented for a one-front war against Japan. The Army did not sugarcoat the prospect of a long, bloody war for the soldiers in the field and new inductees, and warned that various "major factors—none of them predictable at this stage of the game—will decide whether it will take 1 year, 2 years or longer to win the Far East war."[22]

May 1945 saw the United States already several months along a Selective Service track to support roughly the same quantity of casualties over the one-year period starting with the initial invasion operation, Olympic, in the fall of that year, as it had during the one-year "casualty surge" that began in June 1944. At this point, however, two disturbing things happened: (1) the discovery that the Imperial Army, on Japan itself, was gearing up to be nearly twice as large as the estimated 3.5 million the Army's original manpower require-ments were based on,[23] and (2) Okinawa—that the Japanese were capable of inflicting casu-alties at a much higher rate than anticipated.

The clock was ticking. And the crux of the problem facing Stimson and the rest of the senior leadership had to do with the casualty ratios emerging from Okinawa, which if duplicated in Japan's Home Islands threatened to outstrip the carefully constructed replace-ment stream for troop losses projected through the end of 1946. This was both a military and political problem.

Early in 1945 Stimson, in conjunction with Marshall and then Jimmy Byrnes, director of the Office of War Mobilization and Truman's future secretary of state, had worked out the huge increase in Selective Service call-ups and other manpower issues at the exact time that numbers were being crunched within the Army to ensure that the criteria for a partial demobilization of the longest-serving troops through the "Points System" would not be so drastic as to harm further operations against Japan. The politically painful Selective Service increase had been under way for several months by May, and the administration was now publicly committed to the partial, yet still huge, midwar demobilization. However, when the emerging casualty ratio from Okinawa was extrapolated against the projected troop strength resulting from the increased call-ups and concurrent demobilization, it was apparent that the Army was in danger of finding itself in a "manpower box" in which its 100,000-man-per-month replacement stream, originally believed to be more than adequate for both Olympic in 1945 and Operation Coronet on the Tokyo Plain in 1946, would fall far short of combat needs during Coronet, which involved two, then eventually three, field armies.

As military intelligence officers in the Pentagon were beginning the process of crunching the new Japanese force structure figures and coming up with decidedly unsettling results, Stimson reached outside the administration of the newly sworn-in Truman for support of his manpower views. In secret from the cabinet and all but perhaps one or two members of the White House staff, Stimson was working to arrange a meeting between Truman and Stimson's old boss when he was secretary of state, that incurable number-cruncher, Herbert Hoover, who had been testifying before congressional committees on some of the trouble-some aspects of America's mobilization.[24]

Truman and Hoover met in the Oval Office on May 24 (see chapter 6), and Hoover followed up by, at Truman's request, producing a memorandum which, in the middle of the bloody fighting on Okinawa, predicted up to 1 million American dead during the invasion of the Japanese Home Islands,[25] a mortality figure double what the Army staff had used as the maximum for the manpower policy it was already intricately involved in carrying out. Two criticisms of Hoover's figures were supplied by Marshall's staff,[26] and Stimson, who by now was highly skeptical of the Army's official estimates relating to manpower issues, forwarded neither to Truman.

As for Hoover and his memorandum, it is well known to students of the era, but until recently it was generally assumed by the president's many critics that Hoover had likely pulled his casualty numbers out of thin air. What we now know, thanks to the recently retired senior archivist at the Herbert Hoover Presidential Library, Dwight Miller, is that the estimate almost certainly originated during Hoover's regular, and unofficial, briefings by Pentagon intelligence officers, a group working under assistant chief of staff for intelligence, Maj. Gen. Clayton Bissell, that Robert Ferrell wryly refers to as "a cabal of smart colonels."[27] Interestingly, individuals high up within the Navy, apparently still angling in support of the Navy's advocacy of a strategy of blockade and bombardment instead of invasion, also took it upon themselves at this time to leak both the revised Japanese troop strength and the markedly higher U.S. casualty estimates that they generated.[28]

Truman forwarded Hoover's memorandum to the director of the Office of War Mobilization and Reconversion, Fred M. Vinson, who had no quarrel with the casualty estimate and suggested that Hoover's paper be shown to Acting Secretary of State Joseph Grew, former secretary of state Cordell Hull, and Stimson (who was already completely familiar with Hoover's views). On June 9 Truman sent copies of the memo to all three men, asking each for a written analysis and summoning Grew and Stimson to a subsequent meeting to discuss their analysis with him.[29]

None of Truman's senior advisor's batted an eye at the estimate. Grew confirmed that the "Japanese are a fanatical people capable of fighting to the last man, [and] if they do this, the cost in American lives will be unpredictable." Stimson wrote Truman, "We shall in my opinion have to go through a more bitter finish fight than in Germany."[30]

Truman's reaction to the responses that arrived by June 13 was to call a meeting of the JCS, Stimson, and Navy Secretary James Forrestal for the following Monday afternoon, June 18, to discuss "the losses in dead and wounded that will result from an invasion of Japan proper."[31]

At the meeting all the participants agreed that an invasion of the Home Islands would he extremely costly, but that it was essential for the defeat of Imperial Japan. Stimson said he "agreed with the plan proposed by the Joint Chiefs as being the best thing to do, but he still hoped for some fruitful accomplishment through other means."[32] Those other means ranged from increased political pressure brought to bear through a display of Allied unanimity at the imminent Potsdam Conference to the as-yet-untested atomic weapons that might "shock" the Japanese into surrender. As for Truman, he said at the meeting that he "was clear on the situation now and was quite sure that the Joint Chiefs should proceed" but expressed the hope "that there was a possibility of preventing an Okinawa from one end of Japan to the other."[33]

Stimson, meanwhile, had been far from idle. Returning to the never-ending manpower issue that had been severely complicated by the increases in the size of the Imperial Army, Stimson instituted a multifaceted examination of the Army's replacement system as well as the underlying assumptions concerning the ultimate cost in killed and wounded that America could expect to suffer. But having been burned—in his opinion—on multiple occasions by the Army's firm assurances that it had a better understanding of all the factors involved, Stimson specifically wanted, as noted earlier, civilian personnel not connected to AGF or the Operations Division Staff to be called in to scrutinize manpower needs.

On the same day that Truman sent Hoover's memorandum to Grew, Hull, and Stimson, June 9, 1945, Stimson began his own initiative by directing Edmund P. Learned and Dan T. Smith, Harvard Business School economists on Gen. Hap Arnold's Army Air Forces staff, to take an independent look at AGF manpower and training requirements for the duration of the war against Japan.[34] Marshall, who shared an adjoining office with Stimson, knew that it was time to take a step back and he kept completely out of the way of what quickly became known as the Learned-Smith Committee.

Another facet of Stimson's effort was handled by his special assistant, Edward Bowles. Bowles initiated a study on possible casualties that the Japanese as a nation might be able to inflict on an invasion force. The study team included Quincy Wright from the University of Chicago and was headed up by future Nobel laureate William B. Shockley, who was placed "on loan" to the effort from the Navy, where he served as director of research for the Antisubmarine Warfare Operations Research Group. They were given full access to key intelligence and planning personnel, including Col. James McCormack and Col. Dean Rusk (intelligence officers and former Rhodes Scholars on the Operations Division's small but influential Strategic Policy Section), as well as highly classified Pentagon manpower and casualties data, including the top-secret analyses of escalating U.S. troop losses produced by Dr. Michael DeBakey and Gilbert W. Beebe.[35]

This was quite a line-up. DeBakey, then an Army Medical Corps colonel, would become the principal proponent behind development of MASH (Mobile Army Surgical Hospital) units and be well known to the public for his work in the field of heart surgery. Beebe, after the war, played a central role in the organization and operations of the Atomic Bomb Casualty Commission and later became chief of research, then director, of the Radiation Effects Research Foundation. Shockley? He was still a decade away from being awarded a Nobel Prize for his part in the development of the transistor. Wright, a highly respected historian who had recently written the two-volume *A Study of War*, was not a spring chicken in 1945, having received his degree at the University of Illinois in 1915. But very shortly after taking part in Stimson's initiative he entered the Army, was given the rank of colonel, and served as a technical advisor to the Nuremberg tribunal. Learned and Smith were likewise well known in the economics field, and Learned's case-study method is still used today as an instructional process. McCormack was soon appointed director of the Atomic Energy Commission's Military Application Division and later transferred to the Air Force, where he rose to major general. As for Rusk, he would have a long and distinguished career in government service.

But getting back to Stimson's initiative, beyond the officially stated reason for its formation, the low-visibility Learned-Smith Committee was created as a backstop to answer anticipated public—meaning congressional—inquiries into the need for continued high Selective Service call-up rates and the possibility that deferments, already generating loud protests from their tightening during the run-up to the invasion of Japan, might be squeezed even further. Other efforts, such as that of the Shockley-Wright report, were geared to helping frame further discussion.

The Shockley-Wright effort "to determine to what extent the behavior of a nation in war can be predicted from the behavior of her troops in individual battles" concluded: "If the study shows that the behavior of nations in all historical cases comparable to Japan's has in fact been invariably consistent with the behavior of the troops in battle, then it means that the Japanese dead and ineffectives at the time of the defeat will exceed the corresponding number for the Germans. In other words, we shall probably have to kill at least 5 to 10 million Japanese. This might cost us between 1.7 and 4 million casualties including 400,000 and 800,000 killed."[36]

As for the Learned-Smith Committee, it was naturally given full cooperation by the AGF. When its report was made available in late June, AGF generally concurred with the committee's findings and was greatly relieved to find that the committee agreed with the current Army policy of producing replacements "against maximum requirements rather than against continually revised estimates of minimum needs."[37] This conclusion also has relevance for today since it can be argued that some revisionist historians (safely removed nearly six decades from events) as well as a significant number of serving politicians are "minimum needs" advocates.

So what came of all this? Essentially nothing. Secretary Stimson would have received the Learned-Smith Committee's report prior to leaving for the Potsdam Conference, but *might* not have seen the Shockley-Wright report in the brief period between his return from Germany and the atomic bombing of Hiroshima. But while the sudden and unexpected end of the war eliminated the need for these taskings, it is important to remember that Stimson himself initiated them.[38]

The irony of this is that for many years, critics of Truman's bomb decision[39] regularly maintained that estimates of massive casualties during an invasion of Japan were a postwar creation, and when the copious documentation that they were wrong began to come to light in the late 1990s, they then switched to the line that the estimates must certainly have been developed and seen only by lowly subordinates,[40] when in fact, far from being considered by obscure officers tucked away in the recesses of the Pentagon, this vital—and highly secret—matter was being examined by some of the finest minds this country has produced from Quincy Wright and Dean Rusk to Michael DeBakey and William Shockley, and examined by the government's most senior military and civilian leaders. Moreover, Truman had not only monitored the appalling casualties in the Pacific on a daily basis, often with Admiral Leahy at his side,[41] but reacted decisively to them and the dire warnings of Grew, Hoover, and, likely, Stimson, by calling the June 18, 1945, White House meeting in which the invasion of Japan was given the green light in spite of their frightful dimensions (see chapter 6).

Truman's multiple references to Okinawa at the close of the meeting, and most pointedly his comment of the invasion operations representing "an Okinawa from one end of Japan to the other," indicate clearly what he believed would be the magnitude of the fighting. The Japanese navy was essentially destroyed, but U.S. intelligence was already indicating that Japanese air power was being expanded and preserved for a massive surge of kamikaze attacks during the invasions. More important, intelligence estimates clearly demonstrated that Japan's field armies in the Home Islands were swelling rapidly, and there was ample time to train and arm recruits not only for the defense of the Tokyo area in 1946 but for the defense of Kyushu in the coming winter. Future wars along the Asian littoral would demonstrate the limitations of America's industrial dominance when applied against enemies fighting an infantry-intensive war on rugged home ground, but the situation facing the armed forces in 1945 was already painfully evident to the secretary of war. Stimson summed up his view of the June 18 meeting and the casualties question in his July 2, 1945, memo to the president:

> There is reason to believe that the operation for the occupation of Japan following the landing may be a very long, costly and arduous struggle on our part. The terrain, much of which I have visited several times, has left the impression on my memory of being one which would be susceptible to a last ditch defense such as has been made on Iwo Jima and Okinawa and which of course is very much larger than either of those two areas. According to my recollection it will be much more unfavorable with regard to tank maneuvering than either the Philippines or Germany [because of the extensive network of dikes, canals, and rice paddies].
>
> If we once land on one of the main islands and begin a forceful occupation of Japan, we shall probably have cast the die of last ditch resistance. The Japanese are highly patriotic and certainly susceptible to calls for fanatical resistance to repel an invasion. Once started in actual invasion, we shall in my opinion have to go through with an even more bitter finish fight than in Germany. We shall incur the losses incident to such a war and we shall have to leave the Japanese islands even more thoroughly destroyed than was the case with Germany. This would be due both to the difference in the Japanese and German personal character and the differences in the size and character of the terrain through which the operations will take place.[42]

Stimson had been a colonel of artillery during the brutal fighting of World War I, and Truman would not take lightly his appraisal of the targeted Japanese terrain gained from direct examination on multiple occasions between the wars. On the subject of casualties, the president did not need to have it explained to him what Stimson meant by "an even more bitter finish fight than Germany" since he and everyone else who had taken part in the June 18 meeting knew that it had cost roughly a million American all-causes casualties to defeat the Nazis and that American casualties were actually small when compared to those of its major allies. Moreover, Marshall told the president the same thing at the meeting when he stated that because of Japan's mountainous terrain, "the problem would be much more difficult than it had been in Germany." Stimson's warning that "we shall incur the losses incident to such a war" was equally clear. For anyone not understanding the reference, Stimson spelled it out in his high-profile *Harper's* article after the defeat of Japan: "We estimated that if we should be forced to carry this plan to its conclusion, the major fighting would not end until the latter part of 1946, at the earliest. I was informed that such operations might be expected to cost over a million casualties."[43]

As for the man who ordered the invasion of Japan in the face of massive casualty estimates, Harry S. Truman, he knew exactly what he was asking of his soldiers, sailors, and Marines, and he understood it at a level that most Americans today cannot conceive. Across a span of six days during the Meuse-Argonne offensive—although the heaviest carnage was compressed into just four days—the 35th Division, to which the future president belonged, suffered nearly 7,300 casualties, or 50 percent of its front-line strength. Virtually all of these losses occurred within two to three miles of Truman's artillery battery, as it, at some points, literally dragged its guns forward through the shredded battlefield. He and his men ultimately went into position within what one artilleryman described as "a cemetery of unburied dead" approximately one hundred yards forward of where then-colonel George S. Patton was shot down. The U.S. 1st Division, which replaced the 35th, would suffer a further six thousand–plus casualties in this very same killing field, although at not so nearly rapid a pace.[44]

Truman understood "casualties" as only one who had lived and fought under such circumstances could, yet his experience was far from unique. The Treaty of Versailles, the resurgence of Germany after the "War to End All Wars," the weak-kneed response by the League of Nations to growing aggression, France and Britain's appeasement of Nazi Germany, and the subsequent plunge into an even bloodier conflagration than World War I—these matters were so deeply imbedded into the American psyche by 1945 that they were seldom directly mentioned in the press by the later war years, but all hung like a cloud over the American consciousness as the fighting in the Pacific reached its climax. The result of the country's general consensus on the events of the previous thirty years girded a grim determination, both in and out of Washington, to see the war through to the bitter end of "unconditional surrender," lest an inconclusive finish, as in World War I, lead the next generation into an even bigger, bloodier conflict. Despite a growing war weariness and worry among some that stiff terms would prolong the fighting, the understanding that the fight must be prosecuted until Japan either gave up or was pummeled into submission was so fundamental that it actually did not warrant much discussion beyond the sticky matter of "how to" accomplish this at the earliest possible date.[45]

CHAPTER 10

Mistakes and Misperceptions

[Diplomacy will have a better chance] after the United States has sustained heavy losses. We cannot pretend to claim that victory is certain, but it is far too early to say that the war is lost. That we will inflict severe losses on the enemy when he invades Japan is certain, and it is by no means impossible that we may be able to reverse the situation in our favor, pulling victory out of defeat.[1]

—Minister of War GENERAL ANAMI KORECHITA

Japan's situation, as revealed through Ultra sources, suggests her unwillingness to surrender stems primarily from the failure of her otherwise capable and all-powerful Army leaders to perceive that the defenses they are so assiduously fashioning actually are utterly inadequate. . . . Until the Japanese leaders realize that the invasion cannot be repelled, there is little likelihood that they will accept any peace terms satisfactory to the Allies.

—Naval Intelligence analysis in "'Magic'—Diplomatic Summary," 1945[2]

Army Ground Forces, and indeed the Army hierarchy as a whole, was greatly relieved that the Learned-Smith Committee was in general agreement with how its manpower and training system was going about business during the run-up to the Japan invasions. Stimson's snoopers and the AGF quibbled over relatively minor points that would have no practical effect on the war's prosecution, but the Army "regarded as the most important recommendation of the committee," the one seconding the ongoing effort "to secure flexibility, namely, the production of replacements against maximum requirements rather than against continually revised estimates of minimum needs."[3]

Combat experience in the Pacific demonstrated that the small-unit, decentralized nature of the fighting, combined with the "all-around" nature of the threat and lengthy periods at the front, as on Okinawa, would tend to psychologically exhaust U.S. combat elements. (U.S. Army)

By the end of June, the number of replacements in the United States (1) standing ready for deployment, (2) still in some phase of their basic training, or (3) attending either Army schools or part of the now truncated ASTP, stood at 717,945, with 209,226 more replacements spread overseas from the Pacific all the way back to France, and another 44,736 in U.S. iduction stations or reception centers.[4] Each of these ment, even the most fresh-faced 18-year-old draftees set to receive the mandated six months basic training, would be available for the assault on Honshu. Yet the Army was strained to the maximum making this work because of not only the scale of the redeployment, but also both the new Congressional restrictions and the mid-war demobalization.

Army logistics instructors in the mid-1980s regularly remarked in classes attended by field grade officers that the relief at the Learned-Smith Committee findings was quite profound within the AGF and Pentagon because of their concurrence that the Army *could squeak by* on the 100,000-men-per-month replacement stream that it was already deeply involved in implementing. If the committee had reported otherwise, they explained, the entire training and replacement structure might have had to have been turned on its head during the midst of the invasion countdown.[5]

The assumption of the AGF and Army Service Forces (ASF) in the summer of 1945 was that even though the massive invasion of the Tokyo area in 1946 could produce casualties at a far higher rate than the Kyushu operation, this would nevertheless be maintainable because (1) a casualty rate during Olympic lower than the 100,000-men-per-month replacement stream would produce an excess that could be drawn upon during Coronet, (2) there would be many lightly wounded soldiers returned to duty so replacements for Olympic might be able to be further reduced, and (3) other undefined economies could be made.[6] However, Sixth Army planners looking ahead to Olympic arrived at a figure of 394,859 for the full range of battle and nonbattle casualties serious enough to be permanently removed from unit rolls during the four-month push to, and consolidation of, its "stop line" in the mountains of central Kyushu—functionally 100,000 men per month, which did not include soldiers returned to their units and thus would further pump up the number of those absent, at least temporarily, from combat operations.[7]

Obviously, however, figures produced above the Sixth Army assumed that there would be an "excess" available from Olympic, and one month to the day after the Learned-Smith Committee published its report came the July 29 assessment of MacArthur's intelligence chief, Willoughby, outlining in clear, unambiguous terms that the Japanese were ratcheting up their troop commitment in the exact invasions areas at an alarming rate.[8] Unknown to AGF and Stimson's snoopers, the assumptions upon which the committee had based its findings were rendered moot even before they were presented because the Japanese had their own reinforcement plans for Kyushu and had largely completed troop movements to the island while U.S. air and naval elements were still focused on the Okinawa battle (see chapters 5 and 9).[9]

Indications that this was happening had been building since June and become painfully obvious to intelligence gatherers in the Pacific and Washington by mid-July. In hindsight one could argue that the trend of the buildup should have been clear by the time of President Truman's June 18 meeting with the JCS and service secretaries. But allowing for the lag time in the decryption, analysis, and distribution of the intelligence data (plus the prioritization that took place at each of these steps), the troop-strength figures available to the individual JCS members would have been anywhere from about five days to as much as two weeks old at the time of the meeting. Once the matter of Japanese reinforcements had been flagged as an area of great concern, as it almost certainly was by mid-July, dissemination of the information could be accomplished within a two-day cycle or even less.[10]

Marshall flew into Washington from the Potsdam Conference on July 31 as Pentagon planners struggled to come to grips with the growing concentration of Imperial forces on Kyushu.[11] However, Stimson, who returned on the 28th, was not made aware of the ominous development and tried to recuperate from the trip as best he could while devoting himself to the complex issues relating to the imminent use of the atom bomb.[12] With the future still very much unknown, Marshall pursued two tracks, continuing with preparations for a long, bitter war while ensuring that Pacific commanders were ready for a swift entry into the Home Islands in case the Potsdam Declaration, buttressed by the impending use of nuclear weapons and Soviet declaration of war, finally shocked Japan's leaders into admitting defeat.[13]

The War Department estimated that the size of the Army after continued Selective Service inductions—offset by the partial demobilization, other administrative separations, plus combat losses from Olympic and the first four months of Coronet—would result in a projected strength of approximately 6,968,000 men by June 30, 1946. Marshall distributed this information to reporters in a one-page memorandum at his August 7 press conference as "background-only" information in order to help shape press accounts in the wake of the atomic bombing of Hiroshima, which had splashed across evening newspapers the day before.[14] Marshall's hand-out warned: "Whether this figure can be decreased will depend upon the success of our operations, the Japanese reaction, the action of the Soviets, etc."[15] Similarly, the estimate that American casualties could reach 1 million was stated to reporters shortly before the release of Marshall's memorandum during the off-the-record portion of a briefing at U.S. Army Forces, Pacific, headquarters in Manila. Although the estimate and the looming battle in Japan had figured in discussions among MacArthur's midlevel staff and the press corps, this was the first—and perhaps only—time it was noted officially by the command.[16]

Marshall and the Pentagon planners had been monitoring the intelligence on the Kyushu build-up garnered from Ultra and Magic communications intercepts before, during, and after the Potsdam Conference. He was also familiar with the tendency of his superb planning staff—on the other side of the world from the developing situation—to sometimes come to conclusions that made more sense on paper than in fact. Marshall's frequent way of dealing with this throughout the war, and likely going well before that in his military career, was not to argue a matter with subordinates or issue a command directive to "forget it" (either of which would tend to stifle discussion) but to present the staff with the views of the commander in charge of actual operations in the field in order to sharpen the planners' focus on the specifics of the situation in which the theater commander was embroiled. As we shall soon see, Marshall requested just such an appreciation from MacArthur on August 7, but for more than simply keeping his planning staff's eyes on the ball.

★   ★   ★

As staffs are want to do in situations where they are required to present options on little or no notice, they simply reached into their files to recycle previously-produced studies.[17] Elements of Marshall's staff, most notably Brig. Gen. William W. Bessell Jr.'s Joint War Plans Committee (JWPC), presented the risky alternatives of either a direct strike at Tokyo or an intermediate operation against either southern Shikoku or Sendai north of Tokyo, both of which offered terrain adequate for large-scale airbase development but meager anchorage capacity. They were also very badly off track in offering up northern Honshu as an invasion site.

The nonsensical nature of the northern-most proposed target is an indication of how little seriousness was attached to locating an alternate invasion site so close to X-day, and the internal memos between Marshall's assistant chief of staff, Lt. Gen. John E. Hull, and Bessell's boss, Strategy and Policy Group chief Brig. Gen. George A. Lincoln, bear this out.[18] Northern Honshu was along an undeveloped axis of advance that had been rejected on multiple occasions for a host of good reasons, and its acceptance would have entailed launching the invasion from staging areas located far to the south.[19] This in turn would have necessitated roundabout sea voyages of some 2,000 and 2,800 miles respectively from Okinawa and Luzon (versus relatively direct transits of 450 and 1,400 to southern Kyushu)[20] to set up a staging base and airfield complex in time to support the invasion of the Tokyo area in March—at a time when northern Honshu was still held fast in winter's grip.

An initial JWPC paper discussing operations against Shikoku and the Kanto Plain, "Alternatives to Olympic," reached the Joint Planning Staff (JPS), where it was tabled.[21] Although the Shikoku option carried a series of liabilities running from a lack of appropriate loiter time for attacking U.S. aircraft flying the long haul from their Okinawan bases to insufficient anchorage space once a hard-won lodgement had been obtained, it had at least some potential for fitting usefully into the scheme of maneuver. Not so the Kanto Plain option. An almost ad hoc assault directly toward Tokyo in the November–December 1945 period was obviously an extremely high-risk proposition. While such an operation presents a tempting subject for speculation more than a half century later, it could not have been adequately supported by either air power or assault shipping and thus risked a costly stalemate on the ground and the failure of stated war aims. For similar reasons, the various plans for Operation Roundup, an early invasion of France in 1943, were also cast aside in favor of the more meticulously planned Overlord the following year.[22]

Kyushu, for better or worse, was indeed the best of a poor set of options. Aside from the myriad logistical problems ranging from the minor to the impossible, none of the four alternate invasion sites being examined at this time, in addition to Tokyo and Kyushu, offered an easy victory over the Imperial Army. Said Willoughby: "Each one of these areas had the potentiality of another Okinawa," and estimates for initial American battle casualties ranged from 30,000 at Sendai to 80,000 on Shikoku when examining only the Japanese units stationed in these possible target areas during the summer of 1945.[23] What the troop strength at these sites would be by November–December, particularly Sendai, which could be very easily strengthened, was anyone's guess given that the Japanese were more adept at reinforcing threatened areas than was originally anticipated; a disturbing precursor to what U.S. forces would find in future wars on the Asian mainland. Moreover, the time available for Japan's mobilization of manpower would give them adequate troops at all but the northernmost option to slow the movement of an invasion force to a crawl as they had on Okinawa and Iwo Jima.[24]

A message stressing the perceived vulnerability of northern Honshu in the Ominato–Mutsu Bay region was drafted by the JWPC for transmittal to MacArthur. This was done in spite of the fact that such a proposal at this stage of the invasion countdown would have been akin to the Pentagon suggesting to General Eisenhower in the spring of 1944 that, instead of crossing the English Channel, he should consider moving the D-day invasion from Normandy to the Barritz-Bayonne area, some four hundred miles due south, because there were fewer Germans near the Spanish border. The message received some editing by Lincoln, was forwarded to Marshall for his approval, then dispatched shortly after his August 7 press conference with a copy going to Admiral King's office for transmittal to Nimitz:

OPD WAR (MARSHALL) to MACARTHUR passed by COMINCH to CINCPAC ADV HQ TOP SECRET. FOR ADMIRAL NIMITZ EYES ONLY. MARSHALL TO MacARTHUR EYES ONLY. WAR 45369.

Intelligence reports on Jap dispositions which have been presented to me and which I understand have been sent to your staff are that the Japanese have undertaken a large buildup both of divisions and of air forces in KYUSHU and southern HONSHU. The air buildup is reported as including a large component of suicide planes which the intelligence estimates here consider are readily available for employment only in the vicinity of their present bases. Concurrently with the reported reinforcement of KYUSHU, the Japanese are reported to have reduced forces north of the TOKYO PLAIN to a point where the defensive capabilities in northern HONSHU and HOKKAIDO appear to be extraordinarily weak viewed from the standpoint of the Japanese General Staff. The question has arisen in my mind as to whether the Japanese may not be including some deception in the sources from which our intelligence is being drawn.

Para. In order to assist in discussions likely to arise here on the meaning of reported dispositions on JAPAN proper and possible alternate objectives to OLYMPIC, such as TOKYO, SENDAI and OMINATO [northern Honshu], I would appreciate your personal estimate of the Japanese intentions and capabilities as related to your current directive and available resources.[25]

The clock was running down. If the war was to have a reasonable chance of being concluded by the end of 1946, a powerful invasion force had to be landed within immediate reach of Tokyo before the spring rains, then summer monsoons, set in, and that lodgement could not be made until substantial ground-based air power was established within range of the target area because air operations from carriers, while impressive on paper, would not be nearly enough to support one, let alone two, American field armies in contact with a determined enemy. MacArthur replied on August 9, with a copy to Nimitz via King,[26] that the buildup was likely to be a "deception" (it was not),[27] noted that there were indications (which actually were part of a deception) that Japanese air power was no longer a threat, and reminded Marshall that the factors weighing against the alternative sites in the Home Islands had not changed since their original rejection in 1944:

CINCAFPAC to WARCOS passed by COMINCH to CINCPAC ADV HQ (ADMIRAL NIMITZ EYES ONLY)

TOP SECRET. C 31897 EYE ONLY for GENERAL MARSHALL from MacARTHUR.

Reference WAR 45369 (0715352). I am certain that the Japanese air potential reported to you as accumulating to counter our OLYMPIC operation is greatly exaggerated. We have recently seen the 3rd Fleet approach the northern and central shorelines of JAPAN close enough for gunfire bombardment and yet no reaction from the Japanese air has taken place. Our air forces are daily flying throughout JAPAN and provoke no reaction. The situation repeats that of the PHILIPPINE campaigns. Prior to the invasion of LUZON, reports were received of the concentration of air both on LUZON and on FORMOSA. An erroneous estimate of widely dispersed planes being held back for the eventuality of landings was repeatedly made. I further doubt the often repeated reports that large numbers of aircraft are still being manufactured in JAPAN. As to the movement of ground forces, the Japanese are reported to be trying to concentrate in the few areas in which landings can be effected from TOKYO southward, and it is possible that some strength may have been drawn from the areas of northern HONSHU. I do not credit, however, the heavy strengths reported to you in southern KYUSHU. The limited capacity of railroads and the continued shipping losses discourage belief that large forces can be concentrated or supported effectively in southern KYUSHU. Kenny's air forces are only now becoming effective from OKINAWA and it is anticipated that there will be a rapid buildup to an effective strength in early September of approximately 2000 combat planes, and prior to OLYMPIC of approximately 3000 planes. These are in addition to the VLR [B-29 bombers] and escorting fighters in the MARIANAS. It is anticipated that this great weight of air will quickly seek out and destroy in the southern Japanese islands all enemy air potential and will practically immobilize ground forces in their present positions. The maintenance of such forces in southern KYUSHU cannot fail to become increasingly difficult and it is anticipated that they will be greatly weakened prior to OLYMPIC.

Para. In my opinion, there should not be the slightest thought of changing the OLYMPIC operation. Its fundamental purpose is to obtain air bases under cover of which we can deploy our forces to the northward into the industrial heart of JAPAN. The plan is sound and will be successful. An attack directly into TOKYO or to the northward thereof would have to be made without the benefit of land based aviation other than VLR and for that reason alone would be fraught with greatest danger. I seriously doubt the advisability of a direct attack into TOKYO without the installation of heavy air forces closer than OKINAWA. Only a limited study has been made of the SENDAI and OMINATO areas. Insofar as OMINATO is concerned, weather alone would seem to indicate the impracticability for an attack during 1945 or early 1946, especially for the installation of air forces which would prepare the way into the industrial heart of JAPAN. SENDAI has somewhat greater potentialities although some difficulty in establishing satisfactory bases might be experienced. This area is very close to the TOKYO area and would be subjected to heavy infiltration of ground troops there from. Throughout the Southwest Pacific Area campaigns, as we have neared and operation intelligence has invariably pointed to greatly increased enemy forces. Without exception, this build-up has been found to be erroneous. In this particular case, the destruction that is going on in JAPAN would seem to indicate that it is very probable that the enemy is resorting to deception.

The copy of the above cable forwarded to Nimitz was accompanied on August 9 by a further brief message to the central Pacific chief that would prompt much speculation five decades later:

COMINCH AND CNO to CINCPAC ADV HQ.
KING to NIMITZ EYES ONLY.

Desire your comments on WAR 45369 (071535) and MacARTHURS 31897 (090443) passed to you EYES ONLY. Send your reply info MacARTHUR.[28]

As outlined in chapters 7 and 8, the reinforcement of Kyushu was largely completed when MacArthur provided this response. And while King, when referring to the same naval operation as MacArthur, also noted that "no attempt was made to conceal the location of the fleet but, in spite of this, little enemy air opposition was encountered," he was apparently unaware that the manifest lack of Japanese air activity was, in fact, part of IGHQ's long-established plan to not allow U.S. forces the luxury of destroying their aircraft before the invasion was underway.[29] In this respect the Japanese were just as disciplined, in the face of far greater devastation, as the British were widely reputed to have been during the Battle of Britain when various German attacks were supposedly allowed to transpire relatively unmolested so that the secret that German codes were being broken would not be revealed.[30]

General Marshall and senior members of his planning staff suspected—and General MacArthur was at least outwardly convinced—that the Japanese air threat was overstated. The Army hierarchy in Washington and the Pacific was unwilling to believe the signals intelligence.[31] The Navy's concurrence was articulated by Rear Adm. Forrest Sherman as late as July in its principal planning document for the invasion which stated that attacks by U.S. forces "will have served to reduce the enemy air force to a relatively low state" by the projected November 1 invasion.[32] As for Admiral King, he reiterated that it was the intent of the Navy's "huge armada" to "complete the destruction of the Japanese fleet, conduct a preinvasion campaign of destruction against every industry and resource contributing to Japan's ability to wage war, and maintain maximum pressure on the Japanese in order to lower their will to fight." The lack of a Japanese response to the coastal raids had also convinced him that Imperial air power had descended into impotence. Said King, "The strong protective screen around the fleet was too much for the fading enemy air strength."[33]

As noted earlier, the day after Marshall's August 7 message to MacArthur and before the Pacific chief's response, the JPS (which included both Lincoln and Bessell among its members) received and tabled "Alternatives to Olympic," and there it still lay a week later when the Japanese announced that they were finally throwing in the towel. Likewise Admiral King's query to Nimitz on August 9 was not answered before war's end, as neither King nor Nimitz offered opinions on the alternate invasion sites being discussed. Meanwhile the JWPC formalized their thoughts on the Ominato–Mutsu Bay operation to the far north in "Plan for the Invasion of Northern Honshu (Alternative to Invasion of Southern Kyushu)."[34]

This turned out to be yet another rushed and inadequately staffed plan that, like the many others about which MacArthur once mused, was destined "to be filed in the dusty pigeon holes of the War Department" because the proposed operation, fundamentally different from the invasion of Kyushu in terms of support required, called for far more than just reworking the shipping tables.[35] Most critically the vessels to maintain the radically lengthened movements between the target and staging areas, plus increased tonnages from expanded construction requirements of the air base complex, could not be assembled before 1946. Moreover, wholly inadequate time was allotted to air base construction before the worst of the winter weather intervened. The officers writing and vetting the paper were also oblivious to the weather itself, which included not only annual snowfalls averaging twenty-five feet[36] but also a high mean temperature hovering at the freezing mark from December through February, which results in a continual process of partial melting and refreezing.[37]

These were all rather key matters when one considers that the whole point of the initial invasion was to establish air bases supporting the subsequent Kanto Plain operation, Coronet, in 1946. The lack of time and serious consideration put into the various alternatives indicates that either Marshall's staff (1) had suddenly gone brain-dead, (2) they had produced the papers largely as an academic exercise because they had been instructed to, or (3) they were produced purely as an effort to demonstrate that alternatives were examined. What Marshall really wanted, and received, was MacArthur's August 9 appreciation rejecting the alternatives out of hand. And with this tucked safely in his back pocket, Marshall began to formulate plans to ramp up the destruction of Imperial forces on Kyushu to unprecedented levels.

★   ★   ★

President Truman had ordered a moratorium on use of nuclear weapons after the August 9 Nagasaki blast. Early the next morning, uncoded Japanese radio transmissions were received stating that Imperial Japan would accept the surrender terms announced at the Potsdam Conference as long as the Allied powers explicitly agreed to allow Emperor Hirohito to remain the country's "Sovereign Ruler." Marshall quickly called a halt to the Pacific shipment of bomb components and suspended B-29 raids but left in play the tactical, preinvasion air operations conducted from Okinawa. Carrier strikes were also temporarily postponed, not due to orders from Washington but from a scheduled refueling followed by bad weather. The Allies announced their receipt of the Japanese message and accepted the stipulation regarding Emperor Hirohito's retention yet pointedly added that the divine descendant of the sun goddess Amaterasu-ō-mi-kami would be subject to Allied authority.[38]

No Japanese answer came that day—or the next. Initial elation among the U.S. military and civilian leadership turned into apprehension as they waited throughout a tense weekend for a response. By the morning of Monday, August 13, it was beginning to look like the "shock" of atom bombs obliterating two of Japan's major industrial cities, even when combined with the Soviet declaration of war, had failed in its strategic purpose of loosening the iron grip that the country's militarists had on Japanese decision making.[39] At this point Truman and his senior advisors had had enough, and just after 9:00 am Marshall cabled MacArthur and the strategic bombing chief in the Pacific, General Spaatz: "The President directs that we go ahead with everything we've got."[40] The hold on B-29 operations was now lifted, and orders were issued to drop over Japanese population centers the 5 million leaflets containing the Potsdam Declaration—and, most important, the Japanese government acceptance—that Office of War Information personnel on Saipan had begun printing two days earlier as a contingency.[41]

The rapid and massive reinforcement of southern Kyushu by Imperial forces had still not been briefed to Secretary Stimson, or Truman, nor would it before the Army came up with a concrete plan of action.[42] Marshall's staff, however, was already in the midst of producing the boiler plate to demonstrate that the Pentagon had examined various alternatives. These papers would be made available to Stimson (if he wanted to examine them) at the same time as theater commander MacArthur's assessment and Marshal's concurrence that none of the alternatives were appropriate vehicles for attaining America's national objective of defeating Japan and wrapping up the war at the earliest possible date.[43] The swift appearance of the initial Japanese surrender message on August 11 could well have precipitated a delay among the planning staffs, but the very real possibility that the Japanese intransigence or indecision was about to scuttle peace efforts now galvanized Marshall to prepare for Stimson's consideration a plan for the use of the full range of weapons in America's arsenal, today referred to as weapons of mass destruction (WMDs), to trump the human tide welling up on Kyushu.[44]

★   ★   ★

Immediately after the Nagasaki blast, numerous senior military commanders (and undoubtedly most rank-and-file servicemen) had believed that Tokyo itself would become a nuclear target.[45] Marshall, a strong proponent for the tactical use of atom bombs, feared that this could indeed come to pass and was quoted as saying that if the Japanese did not capitulate soon, "it was only a question of days for Tokyo to suffer the effects of the new weapon."[46] However, the apparent unwillingness of the Japanese leadership to capitulate even after the destruction of two cities was tragically in line with their lack of reaction after 72,000 men, women, and children had perished in the capital during a single night's firebombing earlier that year, an attack that had actually made Tokyo a poor target for a nuclear weapon because so much of the city was already destroyed. Moreover, an atomic strike somewhere in the sprawling Tokyo area presented an intolerable risk that Hirohito might be killed, thus removing the one authority capable of ordering the surrender of all Imperial forces from one end of the empire to the other.[47]

Strategic use of atom bombs against cities had certainly been worth a try, but the militarists appeared to be completely unmoved, and to Marshall atom bombs were too precious an asset to waste in a continued strategic, rather than tactical, campaign. As early as the daily Pentagon briefing of April 18, Marshall had stunned Anthony Eden, the British secretary of state for foreign affairs, and Ambassador Lord Edward Halifax with his assessment of how the war was likely to play out. "Marshall's stern report forecast a prolonged struggle in the Far East, if conventional weapons only were used," Eden said. "The sober reserve with which he recited his appraisal made it all the more disturbing. He was, I knew, no alarmist."[48]

Now, four months later, the response to Japanese intransigence was obvious, and concurrent with President Truman's August 13 directive to resume the strategic bombing campaign, Marshall that morning had General Hull personally check into the precise status of current and future atom bomb production. Although only two of the four Japanese cities in the approved atom bomb target set and had yet been struck,[49] Marshall desired to retain all future bombs, perhaps as many as eight completed by November, for tactical use on Kyushu. This would have cut short the bombing of cities which was central to Stimson's strategy of using the bombs principally as a psychological weapon that might stampede the Japanese government into an early surrender.[50]

In a lengthy telephone call to Col. Lyle E. Seeman, Targeting Committee chief on the Manhattan Project, Hull prefaced their exchange with the comment that "General Marshall feels we should consider now whether or not dropping them as originally planned, or [if] these we have should be held back for use in direct support of major operations." Much later in the exchange, General Hull voiced what was likely being thought by many on Marshall's staff regarding the current policy to "shock" the Japanese into surrendering: "Within the next ten days, the Japanese will make up their minds one way or the other, so the psychological effect is lost so far as the next one is concerned in my opinion. Should we not hold off a while and group them one-two-three?"[51] Meanwhile Stimson, who was still thinking in terms of nuclear strikes against cities, requested that shipment of atom bomb components to the Pacific be resumed and Marshall ordered the resumption before noon.[52]

Marshall also moved ahead that morning on another weapon, which was "readily available and which assuredly can greatly decrease the cost in American lives"—poison gas.[53] Marshall had long been an advocate for the use of gas against the Japanese and firmly maintained that "the character of the weapon was no less humane than phosphorous and flame throwers."[54] Just before he left for the Potsdam Conference in the company of General Arnold, Marshall received confirmation from MacArthur that the training of chemical weapons personnel was being stepped up and that stocks of chemical munitions, principally agents CK (cyanogen chloride), H (mustard), and CN (tear gas), were being moved forward to Luzon from facilities in Australia and New Guinea. Now, on August 13, he had a memorandum prepared for the other Joint Chiefs declaring that adequate stocks of nonpersistent gas bombs, CG (phosgene) and CK, would be available by the Olympic invasion date, November 1, 1945.[55]

Thus Marshall was following common practice by assembling data that outlined (1) the growing problem on Kyushu, (2) alternative invasion sites (be they appropriate or inappropriate), (3) the theater commander's conviction that Olympic go forward as planned, and (4) his own data demonstrating that a quantum leap in applied destructive force was a solution to the problem of Japanese reinforcements on Kyushu. With this material in hand, Marshall and his senior staff could suggest to Stimson, as a prerequisite to moving the proposal along to the Truman and the JCS, that the remaining cities on the approved target set be spared *atomic* attack in favor of using the allotted bombs and the projected nuclear stockpile tactically instead of strategically, and that they be used in combination with poison gas. Thankfully, plans went no further since Japanese capitulation came the following day, August 14, 1945, when a special broadcast was made of the emperor's surrender statement.

★   ★   ★

American planners monitoring Japanese military and diplomatic communications beheld a fanatical determination to fight to the death,[56] and although it is well known that Imperial forces were gearing up for a "decisive battle" on Kyushu that they believed could well decide the war, Ketsu-Go No. 6 was to be fought principally with the national supplies gathered by

September, at which point the Tokyo area was to become the focus of supply efforts. Once this occurred, Kyushu's heavily populated, industrialized north was to become the principal supplier for both the buildup in the invasion area and the source of supplies and manpower once the battle was joined so as to not weaken Imperial forces preparing for Ketsu-Go No. 3.[57] Thus IGHQ envisioned and was preparing for multiple "decisive battles" (emphasis added) stretching throughout 1946 and beyond as enormous resources were spent building up defenses not only in the Tokyo area but also in the mountains beyond.[58]

CHAPTER 11

What Is Defeat?

Should the enemy invade our mainland, 100 million of us, as the Special Attacking Forces, must exterminate them to protect our native soil and maintain our everlasting empire. . . . The safety pin must be removed from Molotov cocktails, which should be hurled so that the side of the bottle impacts against vehicles. In aiming against descending enemy parachutists, allow two-and-a-half lengths. When engaging tall Yankees, do not swing swords or spears sideways or straight down; thrust straight into their guts. Attack from behind employing hatchets, sickles, hooks, or cleavers. In karate or judo assaults, smash the Yankee in the pit of his stomach or kick him in the testicles.

—People's Handbook of Resistance Combat[1]

The intelligence officer of the U.S. Fifth Air Force declared on July 21, 1945, that "the entire population of Japan is a proper military target," and he added emphatically, "There are no civilians in Japan."

—PAUL FUSSELL, *Thank God for the Atom Bomb and Other Essays*[2]

Japan was a defeated nation long before the *Enola Gay* lifted off from Tinian Island with its cargo of a single bomb that would kill tens of thousands instantly and as many as 80,000 later from residual blast and radiation deaths.[3] Just exactly when it was defeated is up to the whims of hindsight. After the war many Japanese leaders, both civilian and military, claimed to have known that this end was inevitable after either the fall of the Marianas or the Philippines. Others said that the insight—shocking to those steeped in the *bushido* tradition—struck them after Iwo Jima, or Okinawa, or when the first American fighter planes appeared over Tokyo. An American might argue that defeat for the resource-poor Japanese could clearly be seen when they failed to dislodge the Marines on Guadalcanal or when they expended most of their best pilots in a failed effort to stem the American tide in the Solomons. Or was it at the Battle of Midway? Even before Japanese aircraft failed to find and destroy the U.S. Pacific Fleet's carriers at Pearl Harbor, Admiral Yamamoto famously remarked, "I shall run wild for six months or a year, but I have utterly no confidence for the second or third year. . . . I hope you will endeavor to avoid a Japanese-American War."[4]

An enemy facing what appears to be certain defeat doesn't necessarily *surrender*. It is often forgotten that Germany, as well, was arguably just as much a "defeated" nation in 1944 as was Japan in 1945. Failure to prevent the D-day invasion of France allowed the establishment of a "Second Front" of British and American armies to grind down the German forces between themselves and the Soviets in the East and marked the end of any chance that the Nazi regime might survive the war. The blow to its army in the summer of 1944 was nearly unimaginable. The captured and the dead in Normandy alone totaled at least 530,000 men. To this must be added the 103,000 German dead and prisoners lost to the U.S. and French forces invading southern France, plus 700,000 more men lost during the Soviet offensive timed to coincide with Operation Overlord. Another 100,000 Germans were bottled up in half a dozen French ports that, with the exception of Brest, the Allies did not believe were worth taking. Thus, *excluding* wounded, the Wehrmacht lost an average of half a million men a month from June through August yet fought on for almost a year, forcing the Allied armies to destroy it piece, by piece, by piece in one costly campaign after another.[5]

Between the Atlantic and the post-1939 Soviet border in Eastern Europe, at least 10.3 million civilians died from the ravages of war, more than 9 million of them during *Die Götterdämmerung* of Nazi Germany's collapse in 1944 and 1945, with German military and civilian dead for the entire war exceeding 5.5 million.[6] Japan was spared this fate. However, with no knowledge of the impending use of WMDs during the planned invasion—or knowledge that one component of them, nuclear weapons, even existed—the Shockley-Wright War Department report of July 1945 stated that "Japanese dead and ineffectives . . . will exceed the corresponding number for the Germans. In other words, we shall probably have to kill at least 5 to 10 million Japanese."[7]

The U.S. Army also flirted with a third category of WMDs, biological agents.[8] A variety of deadly diseases were studied by the Chemical Warfare Service's Special Projects Division to assess their suitability against personnel. Chemical munitions were developed to spread anthrax and botulism, but there was no desire to use such weapons except as retaliation in the event that the Japanese, who were known to have used germ warfare in China, employed them first. There was, however, keen interest by General Marshall and many senior officers within Army Service Forces in the use of a variety of chemical compounds against Japanese crops in the Home Islands and bypassed garrisons attempting to sustain themselves through local food production.

Although cleared as being perfectly legal by the Army's judge advocate general as long as there was no "poisonous effects" on people or animals from ingestion or contact with treated crops, interest came to a screeching halt in May 1945.[9] It dawned on planners that any near-term success with the plant killers would ultimately necessitate that the Army be forced to ship in staggering amounts of food to prevent the starvation of Japanese civilians in areas it had seized.[10] Fundamental tenants of the "U.S. Basic Policy for Invasion and Occupation of Japan" included warnings that food storage and food processing plants must not be targeted and that invasion operations not be launched while crops were in the field, but this latter proviso was already known to be a moot point.[11] Agricultural specialists working under the JCS confirmed that the principal cereal crop in the target area, rice, would be harvested and the fields largely drained of water for the planting of barley (a less-important winter crop) by October 30, just before Olympic was to be launched.[12]

While this was encouraging news, it obviously could not be counted on that any *significant* food stocks would be available in southern Kyushu, and the official U.S. policy was that the Army should "use all available and lawful means to prevent enemy civilians from coming within U.S. control."[13] Having made that point, however, ASF planners nevertheless expected that about a third of the estimated 3.3 million civilians living within the Olympic target area would flee north or be killed, leaving roughly 2.2 million persons under U.S. jurisdiction when the Sixth Army bellied up to the stop-line roughly three to four months after the landings. As noted earlier approximately 180,000 would have to be removed to refugee or internee camps from areas near the front, land slated for base development, or security zones. All would have to be fed. For planning purposes it was assumed that captured military supplies might be able to feed 200,000 people for sixty days, and while available stocks would be consumed during this period, local production might perhaps be able to support 1.7 million persons starting roughly sixty days into the operation. It was also estimated that the number of sick or wounded to be cared for by Army medical personnel would average 150,000 per month with many requiring hospitalization. Although still in its preliminary stages, the ASF planning for Coronet concluded that of the 14.5 million Japanese in the minimum target area, 5.1 million Japanese evacuations and deaths due to combat would leave approximately 9.4 civillians behind American lines by D+90. Planners warned that "Preliminary aerial and naval bombardment, and artillery support will result in wounded or ill aggregating about 700,000 from the remaining population (9,400,000) who will require medical treatment and some portion (to be estimated by the Surgeon General) will require hospitalization.[14]

The potential problems relating to keeping the population of occupied Kyushu fed and relatively healthy during an invasion, however, paled in comparison with those faced elsewhere in Japan after the surrender, and began as early as the winter of 1945–46. Agricultural experts within the U.S. Military calculated in 1944 that there would be enough food available to sustain the population on a subsistence level but had correctly foreseen that "the possibility of localized famines beginning within the first few months of 1946 was a very real possibility."[15] Some factors, such as the willingness, or unwillingness, of Tokyo and the prefectoral governments to feed millions of "excess mouths" not directly contributing to the war effort, could not be known. U.S. military and civilian officials privy to Magic intercepts duly took note, however, that the anguished warnings by the Japanese ambassador to Moscow, Sato Naotake—including that if the fall 1945 harvest failed the nation would face "absolute famine"—were disdainfully rejected by his superiors.[16] It was also clear that a disruption of the rail system by U.S. air power plus the growing number of refugees would likely collapse the system and that "we'd eventually have to pick up the pieces."[17]

Some today assert, in effect, that it would have been more humane to have just continued the conventional B-29 bombing of Japan, which in six months had killed nearly 178,000 people and displaced or rendered homeless more than 8 million, than to have dropped the atom bombs or launched an invasion.[18] They also imply that the growing U.S. naval blockade would have soon forced a surrender because the Japanese faced imminent starvation. U.S. planners at the time, however, weren't nearly so bold, and the whole reason why advocates of tightening the noose around the Home Islands came up with so many different estimates of when blockade and bombardment *might* force Japan to surrender was because the situation wasn't nearly as cut and dried as it appears today, even when that nation's ocean supply lines were severed.[19]

Japan would indeed have become "a nation without cities," as urban populations suffered grievously under the weight of Allied bombing, but over half the population during the war lived and worked on farms.[20] Back then the system of price supports that has encouraged Japanese farmers today to convert practically every square foot of their land to rice cultivation *did not exist.* There was more food available in rural areas than is generally understood as wheat was widely grown, and large vegetable gardens were a standard feature of a family's land.[21]

Food reserves existed that were largely unaccounted for immediately after the war because responsibility for the storage and distribution of strategic stocks had been moved from national to principally prefectoral control in April due to the anticipated destruction of the transportation system (see chapter 7), and farmers had begun to hoard their crops in contravention of government directives. The idea that the Japanese were about to run out of food any time soon was largely derived from exaggerated interpretations of the "Summary Report," to the 104 reports in the United States Strategic Bombing Survey for the Pacific war, and the well-documented fear among some Japanese leaders that shortages could lead to severe unrest.[22] The idea that the Japanese were on the brink of starvation is usually (and rather loosely) attributed to the USSBS and the official Army Air Force history. However, using survey findings, what editors James Lea Cate and James C. Olson did in the multivolume history *The Army Air Forces in World War II,* was to detail the successful U.S. mine-laying efforts against Japanese shipping, which essentially cut Japanese oil and food *imports,* and they stated only that by mid-August "the calorie count of the average man's fare had shrunk dangerously."[23]

Obviously some historians enthusiasm for the point they are trying to make has gotten the better of them since the reduced nutritional value of meals is somewhat different than imminent starvation. But the life-and-death question for a family that might well find itself in one of the areas of "localized famine" within as few as six months was how would the militarists in charge of their prefecture or district, who essentially believed that the population was expendable, allot the dwindling food supplies in the midst of an invasion? One indication of what likely would have transpired came from future prime minister Yoshida Shigeru, who before war-surplus food stocks from across the Pacific were rushed to Japan stated in January 1946 that as many as 10 million might die of starvation and malnutrition in "spot famines" that were forecast to begin by the summer of that year.[24]

★   ★   ★

Data from the first campaign to present high-level planners with a convincing model for combat against Japanese field armies in Japan itself, the invasion of the Mariana Islands,[25] weighed heavily on the ASF's conclusions as to what they might face when dealing with the civilian population on Kyushu. The three phases of Operation Forager, which coincided with the operations Overlord and Cobra in France, involved 125,000 ground troops and massive naval elements seizing the islands of Guam, Saipan, and Tinian. Planners found the combat on Saipan particularly relevant to future campaigns in that the joint Army-Marine force conducted both an opposed landing and ground offensive on a corps (multidivision) frontage against sizable enemy forces defending terrain similar to that on Japan—and all on an island which contained large numbers of enemy civilians.[26] And more disturbing than the fact that many noncombatants died during Forager was both the greater numbers than expected and the unanticipated, macabre nature of the deaths which happened right before the eyes of American troops.

By the middle of the initial invasion operation on Saipan, considerable evidence existed of Imperial soldiers killing civilians with grenades when they committed ritual *hara kiri*, and as the major fighting came to an end in early July, Marines witnessed even mothers with children being shot down when they tried to reach American lines. Several hundred frightened Japanese civilians also committed suicide by leaping to their deaths from the heights above Marpi Point at the island's extreme northern tip. Before the area was secured, 4th Division Marines had observed numerous instances of armed Japanese soldiers forcing people over the cliffs to the jagged rocks below.[27] "At times," said the Army history of the campaign, "the waters below the Point were so thick with floating bodies of men, women, and children that naval small craft were unable to steer a course without running over them."[28] Nor were civilian deaths confined to Saipan, as a captured Japanese warrant officer from the 56th Naval Guard Force (who, himself, had obviously not committed *hara kiri*) boasted that about one thousand "loyal citizens" in nearby Tinian allowed the military to blow them up in caves.[29]

Such atrocities were undoubtedly factored in when ASF planners examined what the Army might expect on Kyushu and were used for wholly different purposes by Japanese propagandists, who translated a *Time* magazine account of the tragedy and had it published in numerous newspapers as proof that even civilians possessed the "Yomato spirit."[30] But while ASF's grim, and extremely rough, estimates were formulated in the wake of these forced suicides and murders by Japanese troops of as many as eight hundred Japanese and Okinawan colonists on Saipan (islanders and Korean laborers largely avoided becoming victims by keeping well away from the troops), civilian death tolls from the month-long battle for Manila and the invasion of Okinawa were not yet part of the equation.[31]

More than 100,000 Manilenos were killed, many in the closing days of the battle when the restrictions on the use of American artillery were lifted, but most lost their lives at the

hands of the sixteen-thousand-man Imperial Navy garrison made up principally by the
31st Naval Special Base Force troops who routinely slaughtered civilians trapped behind
their lines singly and in groups of up to several hundred at a time throughout February
1945.[32] A like number of Okinawans may have perished from starvation or as the fighting
rolled over them during the prolonged fight for the island in April, May, and June, but the
figure of actual counted bodies (which missed civilians sealed up in caves during the battle)
amounted to a still-horrific 40,000.[33] The number of deaths could have been even higher
but was held down by a variety of factors:

- A certain amount of stockpiling of food was done beforehand by families.
- Each Tenth Army division entered the battle with 70,000 civilian rations of rice,
  soybeans, and canned fish.
- Roughly one thousand Navy medical personnel were tasked solely to meet civilian
  needs at a five-hundred-bed mobile hospital and multiple twenty-four-bed dispen-
  saries.[34]

And perhaps of greatest benefit:
- Army psychological warfare teams incorporating U.S. soldiers with some Japanese
  language training as well as those of Japanese decent (Nisei) had honed their skills in
  convincing frightened civilians that they would not be harmed.
- Imperial soldiers were frequently not co-located with civilians and thus could neither
  kill them nor force them to commit suicide.[35]

Still, between a tenth and a quarter of the island's 400,000 men, women, and children
were dead by July as the 144,311 civilians who had passed into American control at the end
of May swelled by 80,000 (at least one-third of whom were wounded) during the last bitter
fighting in the XXIV Corps zone alone.[36] Army and Navy military government personnel
were encouraged by the large number of survivors and found that, after recovering from the
astonishment that they weren't going to be killed by the Americans and receiving enough
food and medical assistance to stabilize their individual situations, the Okinawan's worked
industriously to get their small farms back in order as quickly as possible.[37]

But Okinawans had always been second-class citizens of the empire, and the millions
of American leaflets showering Japanese-held territory instructing them to wear white
clothing whenever possible and keep away from Japanese soldiers,[38] largely adhered to
either by happenstance or design, were apparently read by enough receptive eyes to help
prevent many civilian casualties. Would the Japanese of Kyushu and Honshu receiving the
full brunt of Tokyo's virulent propaganda barrage about the murderous, bestial Americans,
also *allow* themselves to survive?[39]

Up to this point the American ground-pounders had manifestly treated Japanese civilians as something apart from the "savage" Imperial troops who fought until they were exterminated. Thus deaths and woundings among Okinawans by American action had occurred
either in the immediate proximity of Imperial troops or from artillery and long-range naval
guns that were only intermittently monitored by forward or aerial observers. But what

would be the reaction by individual American soldiers and Marines on the Home Islands once it became obvious that they were being attacked by "civilians," not sporadically as in the Vietnam War, or rarely as more recently in Iraq, but on a consistent, systematic basis?

It was the militarists who controlled the Japanese government until loyalty to the Chrysanthemum Throne, coupled with the ability to save face and their own skins that the atom bomb offered, finally compelled them to lay down their arms.[40] Before, some among Japan's military had worried that the United States might drag out the war and thus force them to use up precious supplies just by maintaining their armies in readiness.[41] That this fear appeared to be unfounded was supported by the plain evidence of both the Pacific build-up and monitored Western press reports that the Americans desired to end the war quickly through an invasion, and held open the hope that massive U.S. casualties would prompt a negotiated settlement.[42]

After Hiroshima and Nagasaki, however, the militarists were presented with the frightful possibility that the Americans might well deny them battle on ground of their choosing—Japan itself—and just simply drop atom bombs as the military stood helplessly by.[43] They had no way of knowing that General Marshall now advocated that the nuclear bombing of one city after another be abandoned in favor of tactical use during an invasion that the Japanese bitter-enders now feared would not happen. Up until the atomic bombings (and for some militarists, even after) they were deadly earnest in their belief that every man, woman, and child in Japan were "human explosives who would throw themselves beneath the enemy's tanks."[44] And the Japanese people knew that these were not empty words to imbue the *bushido* spirit into the populace. Said one Japanese scholar after the war, "The brave talk about holding off the enemy with bamboo spears turned out not to be just rhetoric. It was to be a martial virtue born of necessity."[45]

Concurrent with the massive mobilization of new combat formations and transfer of the last veteran Kwantung divisions from Manchuria (see chapter 3) had come a series of laws, official decrees, guidance manuals, and public announcements under the National Resistance Program, the motto of which was "Every citizen a soldier." The duties and objectives of this force were outlined in the Ketsu-Go plan and made it clear that the better trained and equipped Internal Resistance (guerrilla) formations were to draw on Home Guard units not only for logistic and other support but also as human cannon fodder when push came to shove with the invasion forces:

THE INTERNAL RESISTANCE AND HOME GUARD

The main purpose of Internal Resistance [guerrilla operations] and the Home Guard (referring mainly to the guarding of everything in the country) is to annihilate the enemy, to remove various obstacles in the execution of the war, to help in the operations, and at the same time to preserve the national sovereignty by uniting the government and the people and by completing the general arming of the nation with the Army as the nucleus.

Internal Resistance: The main purpose of Internal Resistance, in the event of invasion by landing (airborne) units, is to hinder the movements of the enemy by raiding and spying, by hindering, concealment and bivouacking, by cutting off supplies, and at the same time, by dissipating the enemy's strength. As a rule, Internal Resistance will be used to meet the following circumstances, moreover, it will conform to the direction of the operation and plan and prepare the disposition of all the necessary items.

- When our operational force cannot distribute any troops or when our troops are few.
- When leading the internal activity against small operations.
- When changing over to internal resistance after failing to win a quick victory at the front.

The Internal Resistance force will not only utilize the various [Home] Guard units but also will use the civilian defense organizations with a portion of the field army as the nucleus and with the leadership of the Army [divisional] area commander.

The Home Guard: The main purpose of the Home Guard, in the event of a rebellious movement or internal disorder following air raids, bombardments, enemy invasion, or disaster or due to enemy propaganda, is to protect and cover military movements, vital material and transportation, to preserve military secrets, and to maintain peace and order should the need arise. Although the force used for Home Guard will also be used in the event of Internal Resistance, effort should be made to assign beforehand units to this task, and . . . employing the Kempei [military police] plan for the conserving of the military strength.[46]

Even before the Ketsu-Go operation's initial draft was released on March 20, 1945, the government was moving on plans to fully integrate every citizen into the struggle against the Yankee peril. On March 6 the National Labor Mobilization Ordinance was enacted, and less than two weeks later, on March 18, the cabinet adopted Decisive Battle Educational Measures Guidelines suspending all school classes above grade six from April 1 to March 31, 1946. The cabinet then ordered the formation of the Patriotic Citizen's Fighting Corps on March 23, which emerged in mid-April as the National Volunteer Corps and was principally aimed at strengthening internal defense and increasing production. The organization's elements operated under the nominal civilian control of prefectorial governors, down the line through mayors and the Japanese equivalent of ward bosses in the cities, and village elders in rural areas. Units were also formed within government offices, corporations, industrial plants, and other establishments employing large numbers of workers. The following day IGHQ ordered that Area Special Policing Units, operating under military commanders, be ready to conduct internal security operations as well.[47]

A variety of incremental measures were taken to prepare the population for what was to come, and on June 23, some five months before Olympic, the Japanese Diet (legislature) supplemented the conscription already in effect for the regular armed forces by enacting the Volunteer Military Service Law establishing the National Volunteer Combat Force, commonly referred to as the People's Volunteer Corps. Hardly "volunteer," the law essentially expanded the Volunteer Corps and turned it into a paramilitary force by mandating military service for all males ages fifteen to sixty and all females aged seventeen to forty. Plus the conscripted civilians were under complete military jurisdiction and organized along the

Postwar U.S. Army Signal Corps photo of Japanese nationals praying over the charred remains of their countrymen. Below the image area is food left as an offering to the dead. The figure of 20 million—sometimes for "casualties" and sometimes for "dead"—was regularly used by senior Japanese military and civilian authorities when discussing the ultimate price that Japan would pay during a prolonged land invasion by U.S. and Allied forces. (U.S. Army)

lines of standard combat battalions and companies directed by assigned cadres of Army and Navy personnel. These militia units would receive regular combat training with whatever weapons could be scrounged while continuing to perform their agricultural and industrial duties unless directed to other tasks, such as building defensive works, by area commanders. Some 28 million Japanese fell under the provisions of the law in addition to the 1.3 million civilians already working for the Navy and 2.25 million for the Army.[48]

As would be expected, the dearth of experienced Japanese officers, which slowed the training of the newly formed combat divisions, was more pronounced for the units slated for guerrilla operations and even worse for the militias. Although specialized training cadre were being produced by the Rikugun Nakano Gakko (Army Nakano School) for intelligence gathering and covert action in Tokyo,[49] it frequently fell to long-retired soldiers to train the haphazardly armed local units which were on the bottom of the supply list and expected to largely use their own initiative when arming themselves, especially if they were located outside southern Kyushu and Tokyo's Kanto Plain. The result was predictable and had been foreseen as early as 1943 by the government's Greater East Asia Ministry, which warned that "continuation of this *modern war* will become almost impossible" (emphasis added).[50]

But "modern war" was not what the Army wanted from the People's Volunteer Corps. They wanted an enraged populace willing to sell their lives while bleeding, and distracting, the invaders much as the armies of revolutionary France used its peasant *levées* and skir-mishers against their far better trained and equipped foes in the eighteenth century. Thus while the stoic prime minister, Admiral Suzuki Kantaro, was appalled at the bizarre assort-ment of weapons displayed for him at a July inspection near Tokyo (which included single-shot muzzle-loading muskets, longbows and arrows, pitchforks, and the ever-present bamboo spears), the officers who invited him were delighted at the presentation and the militia's "fighting spirit."[51]

Training, though, was uneven at best and only in its beginning stages when the war ended less than two months later, and Edward Drea echoed Al Coox when he noted that many of the regional and local units had yet to even be formed. Both scholars knew many Japanese who had lived through those times, and Drea once related:

> A few months ago, I contacted my professor in Tokyo, who was sixteen years old in 1945 and well remembered the People's Volunteer Corps—he was in it. His "equipment" consisted of a bamboo spear and a backpack filled with two large stones. He practiced huddling in a dank, stinking foxhole, waiting for the Americans. If the enemy approached, he would exchange his stones for a land mine. His mission was to destroy an enemy tank, and himself, with it. Reflecting back, the training, indeed the whole notion, was similar to something out of a demented cartoon. But, he emphasized, the military was serious. And if the Americans landed, he is certain he would have perished. My point is the nation was facing disaster, but the idea of surrender remained inconceivable.[52]

The practical reality of these activities and unceasing drumbeat of noxious propaganda was that the Japanese militarists were well on their way to succeeding in their effort to erase the line between civilians and soldiers among the population. In terms of aerial bombing, this distinction had begun its inexorable erosion half a world away in Rotterdam and Warsaw at the dawn of World War II, long before Pearl Harbor, and even before that in China, Spain, and Ethiopia. This blurring of civilian and military had not, however, extended to Western ground forces, who avoided killing civilians unless their own men were directly at risk. Once the invasion was underway, however, the consequences of repeated attacks by un-uniformed combatants would be profound, and it would take very little for the alien concept of civilian-as-soldier to be accepted by American infantrymen who already viewed Imperial troops as utterly fanatical in their suicidal willingness to welcome death as a "shield for the emperor."

Was the fantastic cost that this would generate in civilian lives irrelevant to Japan's leaders? It certainly was to the militarists, and to varying degrees among the "peace faction" within the ruling circle as well. Not surprisingly, the Shockley-Wright report theorizing that "we shall probably have to kill at least 5 to 10 million Japanese" apparently had a counter-part among the emperor's closest advisors.[53] Said the vice chief of the Naval General Staff,

Admiral Onishi Tikijiro, *after* the nuclear bombings and Soviet entry into the war, "If we are prepared to sacrifice 20,000,000 Japanese lives in a special attack effort, victory shall be ours!"[54]

Whether this figure was extrapolated from American press reports of the number of surviving civilians under U.S. military government control on Okinawa or was simply a rough guess that more than one in every four Japanese in the Home Islands would die is unknown. Nor has it been examined how "the invasion of Japan by white men," as President Truman put it, might well have played out during operations Olympic and Coronet.[55]

CHAPTER 12

The Amphibious Operation

Suicide speed boats. *Target: transports, [large] landing craft. It shall be the general rule to use concentrated great numbers in the initial movements. In a delaying action, they will be used in in-depth raids by small forces.*

Suicide torpedo boats. *Target: transports. At first they will attack the enemy convoy in the vicinity of the anchorage, and later, when it becomes difficult to attack the anchorage, they will attack in the outer areas. . . . After all the torpedoes have been fired, they will crash into the enemy ships with explosives attached to the bow.*

Human torpedoes. *Target: Battleships, aircraft carriers, carriers, transports. When the enemy approaches within their sphere of action (about 25 miles) they will sally forth and attack.*

—"Essentials for the Directing of Surface and Submarine Special Attack Operations," 1945[1]

The midgets [suicide speed boats] approached from astern, and when nearly alongside heaved a depth charge with a shallow setting over the stern and attempted a quick getaway. These simple tactics were effective, because if a boat succeeded in approaching undetected it was so close to its intended victim that no guns could be brought to bear.

—SAMUEL ELIOT MORISON, *The Liberation of the Philippines*[2]

Operation Olympic in 1945 would have been the largest amphibious assault in history. Twelve days into the June 1944 invasion at Normandy, some 314,514 American combat and support troops had come ashore in the U.S. sector, and a nearly identical number of personnel, 314,547, had flowed across the British beaches.[3] Although these totals add up to 200,000 more troops than the 432,198 men projected to have landed on Kyushu by two weeks after X-day,[4] the initial surge of Sixth Army forces during the critical first three days of the campaign might have exceeded a quarter million men if Admiral Richmond Kelly Turner's Pacific Fleet Amphibious Force, Task Force 51, could get them ashore intact and on schedule in the face of ferocious opposition. And while D-day at Normandy was a "shore to shore" operation mounted by 2,727 ships and craft from Jutland-era battleships to diminutive LBVMs crossing the English Channel "on [their] own bottoms," it was an oceangoing force of more than four thousand ships and craft that would appear off the Home Islands in the fall of 1945 for X-day at Kyushu.[5]

Leaving aside for a moment the Pacific Fleet's nearly two dozen battleships, 100-plus carriers of all types, 70-plus cruisers, more than 670 destroyers and destroyer escorts, nearly 200 submarines, 160 minesweepers, and hundreds of support and replenishment ships, the assault shipping alone for Olympic—projected at 2,700 ships and craft—was to be as large as the entire Normandy force and far heavier in tonnage.[6] A snapshot of the forces under Turner's command circa July 1945 is instructive:

- 3 amphibious forces (3rd, 5th, 7th) each structured to protect and land a corps-sized ground force
- 14 amphibious groups structured to land a division-sized ground force, each incorporating an amphibious force command ship (AGC) and transport squadron of approximately 14 attack transports (APAs) and 6 attack cargo ships (AKAs) (approximately 294 ships in total)
- 1 air support control unit
- 27 landing ship, tank (LST) flotillas of 36 LSTs each (total 972)
- 16 landing craft mechanized (LCM) flotillas of 12 LCMs each (192)
- 18 landing craft, infantry (LCI) flotillas of 36 LCIs each (648)
- 3 landing craft, support (LCS) flotillas of 36 LCSs each (108)
- 30 landing craft, tank (LCT) flotillas of 36 LCTs each (1080)
- 12 high speed transports (APD) divisions of 9 APDs each (108)
- 140 attack transports (APAs) unassigned to squadrons
- 20 attack cargo ships (AKAs) unassigned to squadrons
- 11 landing ships, docks (LSDs)
- 6 landing ships, vehicles (LSVs)
- 1 administrative command with 5 subordinate bases and units
- 1 training command with 12 subordinate bases or schools
- 1 underwater demolition team (UDT) with 2 squadrons[7]

This force, more than 3,570 vessels larger than individual landing boats such as the LCVP (landing craft vehicle personnel) and the legendary DUKW (pronounced "duck") amphibious truck and Amtrac-types, had been growing exponentially ever since the landings at Guadalcanal and Tulagi, where a paltry 51 ships and craft were all that could be scraped together. The number had surged to 435 during the Marianas fighting, and to 1,213 at Okinawa, even as nearly 2,000 more were engaged in refits, shakedowns, training, and innumerable other duties stretching all the way back across the central Pacific to Hawaii and north to the Aleutians. In addition a nearly mirror image of this assault shipping at Okinawa, albeit organized somewhat differently and supplemented by a wide, and truly strange, assortment of coastal craft, was serving within MacArthur's Southwest Pacific theater under either direct Army control or the U.S. Seventh Fleet of Adm. Thomas C. Kinkaid.[8] And for Olympic, a fourth assault group, Reserve Amphibious Force (often referred to as the Reserve Afloat), would join the 3d, 5th, and 7th, with the number eventually growing to an astounding seven such organizations to handle the two field armies storming ashore in Coronet.

As noted in chapter 8, IGHQ staff officers in Tokyo, elated over the losses believed to have been inflicted by kamikazes off Okinawa, maintained that naval and air special attack forces might succeed in sinking as much as 50 percent of this assault shipping. And the Japanese were not far off when they determined that this portion of the vessels would carry the equivalent of approximately five combat divisions. Even the comparatively conservative estimates from Japanese commanders on Kyushu appeared to demonstrate that they expected to inflict approximately 20 percent losses on U.S. amphibious ships,[9] their human cargoes either drowned or turned into stunned, and largely weaponless, refugees on the fire-swept invasion beaches.

The JCS guess of 10 percent shipping losses presented to Truman before the Potsdam Conference was actually much lower than it initially appears when matched up against the Japanese figures because while Imperial Army planners characterized the expected American losses as ships actually sunk, the JCS figure represented those forced out of the fight because of severe damage as well as those that went down.[10] And as outlined earlier, a far higher amount of this pummeling was going to be experienced by the relatively stationary targets at Ariake Bay, the Satsuma Peninsula, and Miyazaki Beach than on the task forces at sea.

No matter whose estimate would have turned out to be closest to the painful reality off Kyushu, the U.S. Navy, which had experienced a costly campaign in the Philippines followed by the bloodiest battle in its history at Okinawa, was now gearing up for an even more savage confrontation, all within the space of essentially just one year. Several troubling aspects of this amphibious operation deserve a close examination: naval gunfire support, Shinyo suicide speed boats, obsolete but radar-resistant wood-and-fabric training aircraft used as kamikazes, and the critical vulnerability of the blood supply for wounded soldiers and Marines ashore during the opening phase of Olympic.

★   ★   ★

Fully twenty-five American battleships and "big-gun" cruisers would be arrayed against Japan when the Pacific Fleet bellied up against the Home Islands in November 1945. The power of this force was unquestionably immense and prompted one awed author to state, "That the coast defense units could have survived the greatest preinvasion bombardment in history to fight a tenacious, organized beach defense was highly doubtful."[11] As with so many aspects of the planned invasion, however, perceived force ratios were not always what they seemed.

Similar confident assertions have been made before many battles throughout history (including before the Somme in 1916), and it is worthwhile noting that *every* square inch of Iwo Jima and Okinawa was well within the range of the Navy's 8-, 14-, and 16-inch guns during those campaigns in which 67,928 soldiers and Marines were killed or wounded by outnumbered Japanese garrisons.[12] Moreover, the twelve new "fast" battleships and battle cruisers were never going to come within sight of Kyushu, although some had earlier been siphoned away from their normal duty screening the carrier task forces during failed efforts to lure out Japanese aircraft by bombarding steel mills along the Honshu coast. Likewise the four modern *King George V*–class battleships of the British Pacific Fleet would be largely confined to providing antiaircraft support for Britain's two (by that time) carrier task groups.[13]

Running clockwise from the northern-most invasion beach a trio of pre–Pearl Harbor battleships were the centerpiece of the 7th Fire Support Group, 7th Amphibious Force, supporting the Miyazaki landings; six more belonging to the 3d Fire Support Group, 3d Amphibious Force, were to take on the formidable Japanese defenses at Ariake Bay; and four of the old battle wagons were assigned to the 5th Fire Support Group, 5th Amphibious Force, assaulting the Satsuma Peninsula and Koshiki Retto.[14] Added to this lineup but as yet unassigned would be a pair of similar prewar-vintage battleships (one of them French) sent north from the British East Indies Fleet after the conclusion of Operation Zipper, the planned August 1945 invasion of Malaya.[15]

The diverse and widely spread assault zones on Kyushu ensured that virtually none of the targeted beaches would receive the going-over that Iwo Jima or Okinawa had. For example, while the 5th Fire Support Group was slated to be made up of four battleships, three heavy cruisers, and four light cruisers during Olympic, at Iwo Jima it employed six of the old battleships and five heavy cruisers during a "very gratifying" two-day preliminary bombardment that was principally conducted as direct fire from only 2,500 to 3,000 yards off shore.[16] Two "fast" battleships (bringing the total to eight), a heavy and two light cruisers joined for the third day's shooting, and all were supplemented by an array of destroyers, plus gun and rocket boats.[17]

The statement by Samuel Eliot Morison, the U.S. Navy's World War II historian, that "in no previous operation in the Pacific had naval gunfire support been so effective" as at Iwo Jima[18] is not diminished by the fact that the Marines suffered 25,851 casualties, including 5,931 dead,[19] in taking the sulfurous island. The three days of concentrated bombardment and continuing gunfire support undoubtedly saved hundreds, perhaps thousands, of American lives, but the human cost in spite of the pounding demonstrates the inexorable grind of daily close-in battle conducted at the distance that a man can throw a grenade. On Kyushu, with the principal exception of night movements by reserve divisions streaming to the front and the nocturnal reinforcement/resupply of tactical positions, it was the intent of Imperial forces to not have troops in the open where they could be readily seen and targeted by air and ground observers. The weakened gunfire support available to cover likely Japanese approach routes would only make these movements easier to achieve and allow reserve elements to arrive at the U.S. beachheads in greater strength.

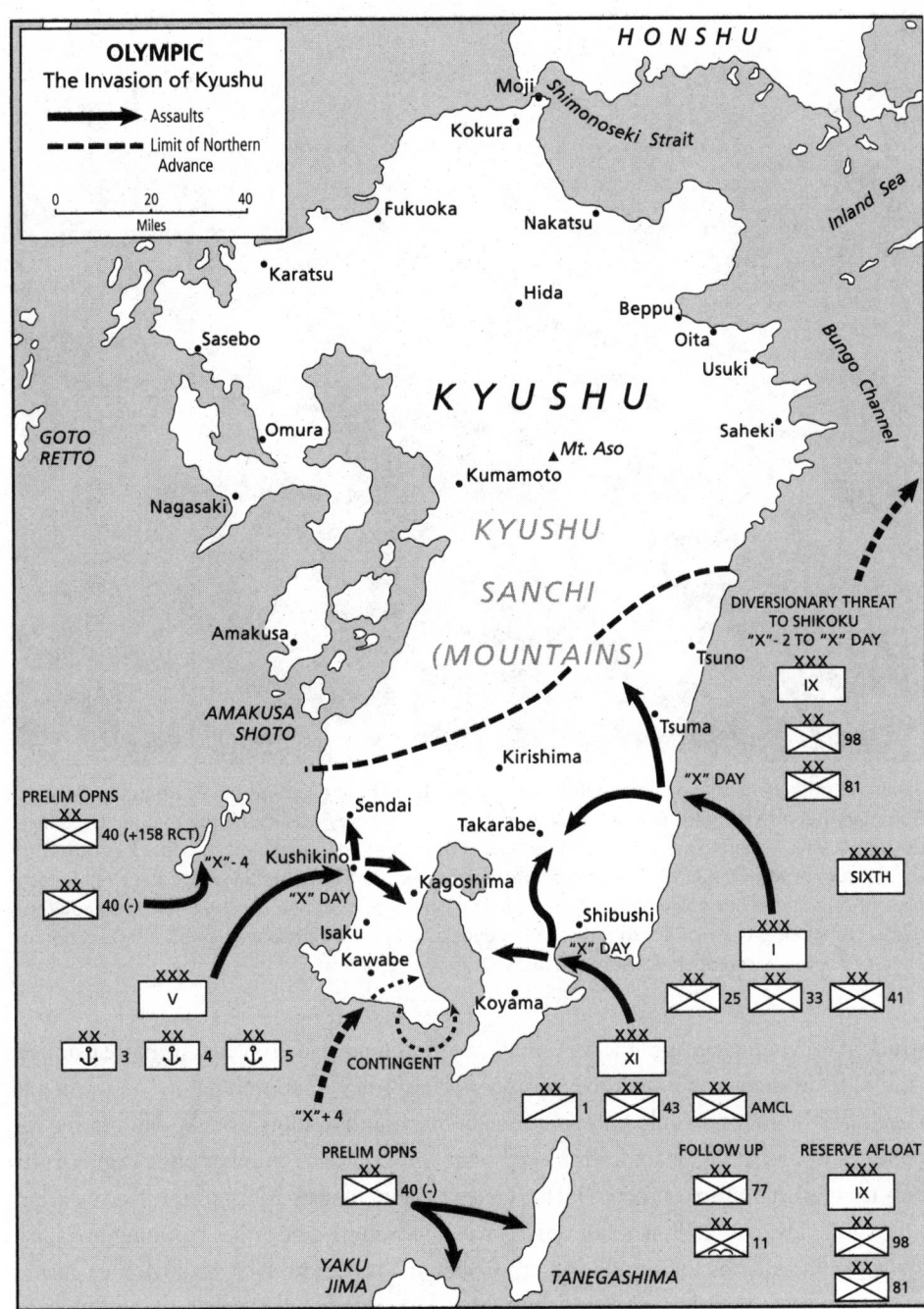

Map derived from Reports of General MacArthur (Tokyo: General Headquarters, Supreme Allied Command, Pacific, 1950), vol. 1, bk. 1, p. 413.

The assault plan for Operation Olympic.

One bright spot did exist in this grim scenario, however. By June 1945, B-29 incendiary raids had burnt out all the major Japanese cities and the Superfortresses had begun to inexorably work their way through every medium-sized urban area except Kyoto and the cities slated for atomic attack. Even those with populations as small as 38,000 and 40,000 were

Japanese midget submarines at the Kure naval base. Reading the U.S. Strategic Bombing Survey's Summary Report one gets the impression that Japanese industry was kaput. But the highly political document was written to advance the objectives of air power advocates and presented a somewhat rosy picture of what the Army Air Force had accomplished. As this photo demonstrates, highly technical priority items not only could still be produced in quantity by the Japanese but also could be missed or successfully hidden from the prying eyes of U.S. reconnaissance aircraft fully six months after they commenced operations from nearby Okinawa. (U.S. Army)

struck in the closing weeks of the war, and it was becoming plain to Army Air Force planners that, as far as strategic bombardment was concerned, they were running out of "profitable targets."[20] This process would only accelerate in the months leading up to X-day, but the big bombers would hardly be underemployed since the dwindling number of strategic targets only meant that more resources could be directed to softening up Kyushu and adjacent areas. During the invasion itself, it is not unreasonable to assume that carpet bombing missions, along the lines of those during Operations Cobra in Normandy, Avenger at Monte Cassino in Italy, and Arc Light in Vietnam, would be commonplace during Olympic, and perhaps go some way toward making up for the pronounced deficiencies in naval gunfire support.

★   ★   ★

The many bases for Japanese navy Shinyo (Sea Quake) and army Renraku-tei (liaison boat) special attack craft[21] dotting the southern coast and offshore islands were high-priority targets for the U.S. Navy's surface and air elements. By August 1945 hundreds of these deadly craft were known to be hidden within easy reach of the assault ships' crowded assembly areas.[22] And unlike the Imperial Navy's midget submarines and Kaiten (Those Who Shake the Heavens) manned torpedoes, which by their nature were more difficult to produce and required a fairly high degree of proficiency to operate effectively, the much smaller, explosive-packed motor boats were manufactured in great quantity. Japan's surrender froze the production of these suicide craft at 2,412 for Operation Ketsu-Go,[23] but measuring an average of only eighteen feet long and powered by inefficient, but readily available, automobile engines, the Japanese were on their way to easily tripling this number by the time Olympic was launched.

Approximately half of the suicide craft would be based on Kyushu or have accessibility to the invasion sites from nearby Shikoku, and fully 1,074 were located in these areas at the time of the Japanese surrender.[24] Navy Shinyo boats contained 551 pounds (250 kg) of explosives packed into their bows, while the army's Renraku-tei, which was originally not thought of as a suicide craft, usually carried a stern-mounted depth charge to rupture a ship's hull by exploding four seconds after release. Experience in the Philippines and Okinawa had taught the Japanese to keep the boats well hidden during the day, and there are very few recorded instances of U.S. fighter aircraft locating and destroying any of the burgeoning force which, because of the extremely small size of the craft (half the length and less than one-fifth the weight of an LCVP landing craft), were easily concealed in natural or man-made caves near the water's edge within the countless coves, inlets, and streams along the coast and offshore islands.[25]

Areas known to contain the boats were to be the subject of area bombardments by gunfire support ships leading up to X-day, but the best shield against the suicide craft was thought to be a tightly woven defense of the invasion areas by PT boats and large landing craft converted to gunboats, backed up by destroyer escorts or subchasers, and all employing a shoot-on-sight policy for anything beyond their defensive perimeter. High hopes were also pinned on "Flycatcher" operations involving similarly organized flotillas operating astride areas where U.S. intelligence suspected that "suiciders" were hidden.[26] Since the Japanese crafts' low freeboard and wooden construction rendered them extremely difficult to detect by radar, both the close-in defenders and Flycatchers would depend on lookouts, searchlights, and starshells to detect their presence.

Unfortunately, with ocean swells commonly running far higher than the boat's two or less feet of freeboard, and little wake left by a slow-speed initial approach, suicide craft operating at night in the Philippines had frequently gotten right on top of American amphibious forces before being seen. All too often an overly generous use of starshells (in the absence of surface radar's dependability against such craft) resulted in degraded night vision among lookouts. Capt. Lefteris Lavrakas, who served as the illumination officer aboard the USS *Eberle* when an ensign, also notes that "[Starshell] use was by-guess and by-God. You were expected to use one of the 5″ guns as a starshell gun, placing the stars behind the target so that it could be seen optically from the gun director. A most difficult—impossible—task, especially when the target was a fast-mover. We also had a 36″ searchlight which threw out a powerful beam—seldom towards a target."[27]

Japan's ability to conduct surface suicide strikes during the Okinawa invasion was effectively gutted by the capture of more than 250 Renraku-tei when the outlying Kerama Retto island group was seized immediately before Iceberg's main landings,[28] and only a few gunboats and destroyers were sunk or irreparably damaged. Suicide strikes at Kyushu, however, were more likely to resemble the wild mêlées that developed throughout the months of January and February in Philippine waters.

The official tally of U.S. losses to suicide boats during operations along the Luzon coast include the sinking of LST-1028, PC-1129, LCI(M)-974, LCI(G)-365, LCS(L)-7, LCS(L)-26, and LCS(L)-49, while LSTs 610 and 925 were seriously damaged and the *LaSalle*-class transport AP-168 *War Hawk* was holed below the waterline killing sixty-one men. Less well known is the collateral damage of the attacks: PT-77 and PT-79 sunk by "friendly fire" from destroyers, two transports and an LST badly damaged from collisions while performing evasive maneuvers in a crowded anchorage under attack, a captured suicide craft sunk and PT boats strafed by "trigger-happy" U.S. fighter aircraft, and later, at Okinawa, DD-682, the USS *Porterfield*, shot up by fire intended for the suiciders.[29]

Suspected bases would be attacked, and attacked again (with the destruction of decoy craft duly reported as genuine kills by aircrew), but very few suicide boats would be caught in these raids. Interception by the Flycatchers, as the Shinyo and Renraku-tei emerged at night for their attempts at the assembly areas, was recognized as the most sure way to locate and engage the threat, and most suiciders would certainly be destroyed by PT boats and the queer assortment of gunboats assigned to the task. However, through a combination of feints and ruses, ambiguity in the dark of night, and sheer quantity of suicide craft, some number of the diminutive attackers would get among the transports. For example, at the same time that some suiciders at Luzon became the focus of attention when making high speed runs at the nearest targets, others maneuvered casually through the relative cover of American LCVPs and other craft to approach bigger game from the stern or bow, and then drop a depth charge along the hull.[30] Once a suicide craft started to get close aboard an American ship or large landing craft, the targets' guns became essentially useless since they could not be depressed enough to hit the boat, the crew's personal weapons becoming a rather weak last line of defense.[31]

Ultimately, though, the principal benefit for the Japanese from motor boat attacks during Ketsu-Go/Olympic might be less the damage they *directly* inflicted on U.S. shipping than the general disruption of assembly areas that required assault shipping to be very carefully stationed if finely choreographed landing and resupply operations were to be carried out effectively. And even more ominously, that the suiciders would divide the attention of fatigued sailors aboard the ships—get them "looking down" when, perhaps, they should be "looking up" for hostile aircraft, just as surely as the futile attacks by low-level American torpedo bombers at Midway had opened up the Japanese carrier fleet to strikes from above. Complicating matters further was that the invasion shipping locked into landing and resupply operations would purposely reduce the effectiveness of their own lookouts because of the discharge of smoke screens whenever Japanese aircraft approached, a practice which would further mask the movements of small craft that had managed to penetrate the outer defenses.[32]

As noted in chapter 8, the Imperial Navy, principally through the planned use of instructors as combat pilots, now had 2,450 flyers who were rated to be highly enough skilled for night missions and another 1,750 for dawn and dusk operations.[33] Throughout the war, aerial attacks at night had been extremely infrequent, and sailors looked forward to the hours of darkness—even more so after the advent of the kamikaze—as a time of relative freedom from the fear of "death from above" as they repaired damage, took on supplies, and grabbed some sleep. This would change at Kyushu as the threat from both surface and air night attacks springing upon bone-tired sailors with little or no warning would now close off even temporary respites from the oppressive fear of violent death. That these attacks were not likely to be coordinated in any meaningful way was largely irrelevant to the synergistic effect that they were going to have on degrading the fleet's antiaircraft performance, resupply, and reinforcement of the beachhead, and, thus, the very ground forces the Navy was to support. And if all of this was not bad enough, the Japanese had stumbled upon the perfect weapon to deliver these nighttime attacks.

★   ★   ★

The Pacific Fleet was beginning to develop a degree of confidence that it could handle the developing threat from suicide pilots when, on two nights in a row, the Japanese succeeded in trading a single, antiquated, twin-float biplane for a U.S. Navy destroyer. First the USS *Callaghan* was sunk with the loss of forty-seven dead and seventy-three wounded on the night of July 28–29. The *Cassin Young* was struck the following night and knocked out of the war as twenty-two sailors were killed and another forty-five wounded. With little radar warning, and no visual fix on the solitary attackers until they were practically upon the ships (even with a bright, third-quarter moon), the slow-moving biplanes were the functional equivalents of today's stealth aircraft.[34] A third destroyer, the USS *Prichett,* was similarly struck while assisting the *Callaghan,* but although a sailor was killed and the ship suffered extensive hull and superstructure damage, the *Prichett* continued its radar picket mission until relieved.[35]

Ironically, although the Japanese were well aware that wood absorbed radar waves instead of bouncing them back to a receiver, this aspect of the material was purely a secondary factor, and a distant one at that, to why they had for years been keen to lessen the amount of radar-reflective metals in their aircraft. The Japanese recognized the acute vulnerability of their supply lines to the resource-rich southern conquests, and even with the region solidly in their possession, shortages of various strategic minerals were a disturbingly common occurrence.[36] Bauxite scoured from the open-pit mine on Bintan Island, across the Singapore Strait from the former British bastion, was the critical component in the construction of light-weight aluminum used in their aircrafts' frames and skins, and a preliminary examination of wood as a possible replacement for some components in their most modern models was begun as early as 1943. That year, Germany provided plans and drawings of high-performance British and Soviet aircraft that utilized wood, but a subsequent shipment of British Mosquito bomber components was lost when the submarine *I-29* was sunk in July 1944 as it neared the Home Islands.

As bauxite stockpiles began to shrink dangerously in the last months of 1944, the search for aluminum substitutes became desperate. A final surge of imports from the Southern Resource Area in February and March would allow the use of aluminum in the most vital parts during fiscal year 1945 production (extending through March 1946), but the end was clearly in sight. Wood was the most obvious replacement material, but although Japan had built literally thousands of trainers as well as obsolete and obsolescent combat aircraft that utilized wooden frames, the level of craftsmanship in their construction was far below that needed for high-performance aircraft. Even with detailed information supplied by the Germans on adhesives, plywood skins, and special processes for joining highly stressed parts, so little progress was made that the Japanese experimented with tin, and even steel, as possible replacements for aluminum.

The mass conversion of training units into combat units in July 1945 added not only thousands of experienced pilots but also 5,400 wood-and-fabric trainers as well as a dizzying variety of other elderly aircraft types containing varying amounts of wooden construction (see chapter 8).[37] American intelligence analysts monitoring the upheaval within the Imperial air forces speculated on what the Japanese were up to, and perhaps because they had seen the Japanese interest in wood as something related to their perpetual aluminum crisis, made absolutely no connection to the fact that the sputtering antiques were almost impervious to some of America's most advanced technologies—radar and the VT "proximity" or "influence" fuze.

At first the Japanese (who, frankly, had always been slow to realize both the potentials and weaknesses of radar) did not understand just how dynamic was the wooden windfall that they now had at their disposal. But someone in the Imperial Navy's air command structure on Formosa apparently had by the end of July, as evidenced by the brilliant successes scored against the *Callaghan* and *Cassin Young*. Interestingly, even if the intent to use the biplanes at night had been based solely on the expectation that darkness would help mask their lumbering approach—with only passing appreciation of the benefits of their wooden construction—the fact that these aircraft had a low radar cross-section would have prompted few, if any, practical differences in how the Japanese actually employed them tactically. For the American soldiers, sailors, and Marines at sea, just the appearance of these antique "new" weapons made a world of difference.

Even though the mass conversion of training units into combat units wasn't well understood at the time by American commanders and intelligence analysts, the successful night attacks by largely wooden trainers immediately brought the threat into focus.[38] First of all it was observed that even though the aircrafts' construction lessened warning times considerably, standard ship-borne radars could still manage to "see" the approaching planes at a far enough distance for the long-range, 5-inch antiaircraft guns utilizing VT fuzes to come into play, even if only briefly, due to the radar returns from their engines and other peripherals such as the bombs they carried.[39] And this same general situation would have also carried over to the radar-equipped or -directed night fighters coming into increasing use by both the Pacific Fleet and Fifth Air Force. Yet it was also brutally clear that, as historian Samuel Eliot Morison plainly stated, "proximity fuzes were not effective [against] biplanes of fabric and wood."[40]

The development of the proximity fuze had been a long and tedious affair, marked by many frustrations. The segment of its development relevant to this discussion centers around the discovery through a combination of detailed calculation plus trial and error that, in essence, if the amount of "ripple" from a projectile's transmitter was too strong, the shell would detonate early, leaving its target undamaged. The U.S. Navy's Bureau of Ordnance ultimately decided that a blast approximately sixty to seventy feet from a target achieved the best compromise of a variety of combat factors.[41] However, Japan's sudden use of aircraft with less material to reflect radio waves would have required transmitters with a boosted ripple otherwise a projectile could pass fairly close without detonating at all.

Originally concern had been so great that the Germans might be able to develop a jamming system to counter the proximity fuze, that the first two years of its use was confined to U.S. and Royal Navy ships so that the extremely high percentage of duds, approximately 30 percent of the rounds fired, would fall harmlessly into the sea thus rendering their recovery extremely difficult if not impossible. After the war the Bureau of Ordnance proudly maintained in its official history that "the Axis was never able to countermeasure the weapon." Certainly not in terms of *active* countermeasures, but as the earlier statement by Morison demonstrates, the views on the subject within the Pacific Fleet were somewhat at odds regarding the *passive* countermeasures that the Japanese had stumbled upon.[42]

The war ended before the Navy was forced to come to grips with this threat, but the prominent coverage within the *"Magic"—Far East Summary* demonstrates that the appearance of what might be referred to as Japan's "stealth" biplanes was already on the "front burner" as a topic whose urgency would demand action. Said Morison, writing of the kamikaze menace as a whole and not just the biplanes, "The prospect of thousands of them being used against our invasion forces in the autumn was disquieting. The Navy, far from satisfied with the situation, detached from Task Force 58 Vice Admiral Willis A. Lee, one of the best brains in the service, to set up a research and experiment unit to devise a remedy for the kamikaze disease."[43]

In addition to whatever recommendations emerged from this group, the increasing and decreasing of the amount of signal transmitted from a proximity fuze to affect the range in which it detonated from a target was a well-trod path which the Bureau of Ordinance would be able to take advantage of to order subtle changes in a portion of the fuzes which, by this stage of the war, were being manufactured at some twenty-three plants by Sylvania Electric Products and its subcontractors.[44] There is every likelihood that a modified fuze would have been produced both in quantity and with enough lead time that the initial production could be distributed to key fleet elements by the November landings. And although this daunting challenge could reasonably be expected to be met, it was actually the easiest part of the equation as the ability to use them effectively in combat was going to prove to be extraordinarily difficult.

Some number of the 5-inch shells with the special fuzes would be kept among the ready ammunition within gun turrets, perhaps only a few rounds during the day and a much larger quantity at night when wooden biplanes could take advantage of a combination of their relative stealthiness and flying low to get close before being detected. During daylight hours such an aircraft stood even less chance of getting near a ship than the American TBD

The Yokosuka K4Y1 Training Seaplane (*top*) was one of several Japanese wood-and-fabric aircraft that defied radar detection at militarily useful distances and were largely immune to proximity-fuzed shells. Use of such aircraft at night in the last days of the war cost the U.S. Navy three destroyers sunk or heavily damaged–at the cost of just three antique planes. Aircraft which contained more metal in their construction, such as the Kawanishi E7K "Alf" Reconnaissance Seaplane (*bottom*), were marginally more detectable but would radically complicate the defense of fleet elements at night, especially when used in combination with more readily visible modern aircraft. (Francillon, *Japanese Aircraft of the Pacific War.*)

Devastator torpedo bombers, which were massacred wholesale during the Battle of Midway. Attacks at night were another matter entirely, especially if, whether by design or accident, they included a mix of both slow-poke trainers and modern aircraft. The complexities that this adds to both radar detection and fire control would have been enormous as harried CIC personnel—though aided tremendously by recent system advances that precisely determined air speeds—would have to make instant decisions as to whether or not the approaching aircraft was likely to be of wooden construction and orally transfer that information to gunnery officers in the 5-inch gun turrets.[45]

Thus the standard operating procedure when there was no ability to get "eyes on" a target would ultimately be to use rounds with the modified proximity fuze against bogies that were unambiguously moving at very slow speeds of little better than one hundred miles per hour. Yet even in these cases there were no guarantees since the Japanese had other ultra-slow trainers with similar maximum speeds that contained significant amounts of metal in their constructions, such as the Tachikawa Ki-17 biplane and Kyushu K11W monoplane, against which the modified proximity fuzes theoretically would be less effective because of the increased likelihood of premature bursts. While smaller in number, their radar signatures (including, most important, their air speeds) essentially would be indistinguishable from the wooden aircraft if the radar personnel were in the midst of a fast-moving combat situation. Moreover at least seven other abundantly produced obsolescent or obsolete metal-frame aircraft flew moderately faster than the wood-and-fabric antiques. But while able to achieve speeds ranging to about 145 miles per hour, well beyond that of the all-wood models, they were themselves far slower than even the mothballed combat models of the late 1930s and early 1940s also turned over for use as suiciders.

Under the right circumstances, at least several rounds with the new fuze could be accurately fired at the fleeting ghosts that appeared on ships' radars as they closed on their targets, and combat experience showed that this was often all that was needed to destroy incoming attackers.[46] In the case of the marginally faster aircraft containing the metal framing which might cause the early activation of a special round, their final dive on a ship would frequently find them flying directly into 5-inch round detonations which, even if too distant to cause an immediate kill, might damage the kamikaze, making it difficult to steer, disturb the pilot's aim, or, with a lot of luck, actually send it plunging into the black sea.

The bottom line was that CICs were already being overwhelmed during periods of intense combat, and these air-sea battles could now be expected to occur not only during the day, but at irregular intervals at night as well, while simultaneously presenting radar operators with a vastly more complicated environment to deal with. Attacks on Japanese air bases by the Pacific Fleet's Night Air Group 90, flying from CV(N)-6, the USS *Enterprise*,[47] had proved their worth, but the mass employment of kamikazes and conventional aircraft during Ketsu-Go No. 6 would have far outstripped the ability of even two such air groups, the maximum that could be made available by Olympic, to suppress the hoards. Any efforts by U.S. air elements that dampened down, or completely removed, hostile aircraft from the equation would save lives, but every sailor understood that it would eventually come down to ship against plane and that the odds that he and his buddies would survive to reach "the Golden Gate in '48" were not looking good.

Despite the limitations of a proximity fuze geared to counter the new threat posed by wooden kamikazes, its appearance would have been an important morale booster for these men, and the specially fuzed shells would have indeed knocked down a number of the stealthy Japanese biplanes that otherwise would have killed even more Americans.

★   ★   ★

Stretching across the Pacific, from Hawaii to the Philippines, a massive medical establishment was being constructed for the invasion of Japan with hospital facilities totaling more than 150,000 fixed beds on Oahu, Guam, Luzon, Okinawa, and other islands. This would include 33,250 fixed beds on Kyushu itself with the arrival of sixteen general hospital organizations direct from the United States.[48] The largest conglomerate of military medical complexes outside of wartime Great Britain, centered around Base "X" at Manila, which contained its own port facilities, was under construction at no less than five separate sites in the Philippines and was to be staffed by a mix of Pacific and European theater units. Base M at San Fernando and Base R at Batangas were, respectively, north and south of Base X in Manila, while Base K was located on Leyte and Base S on the island of Cebu.[49]

More than seven thousand standard medical items, from individual medical kits and tongue depressors to x-ray machines and several billion Atabrine tablets to combat malaria, moved in a continuous flow from U.S. ports, yet the highly perishable nature of one commodity—combined with a predicted steep upsurge in need—defied stockpiling. The chief medical officer in MacArthur's headquarters, Brig. Gen. Guy B. Denit, did not believe that all of the whole blood regarded as necessary for the invasion of Japan could possibly be obtained. Denit requested that the Army Medical Corps' leading authority in blood supply matters, Col. Douglas B. Kendrick, be sent to Manila to work out the best possible program for the operation, and an outline plan was duly completed by the end of July 1945.[50]

By this point in the war, the Medical Corps had built up an extensive body of knowledge on how many and what kinds of casualties were likely to be generated during a wide spectrum of combat settings. Kendrick estimated that if the American ground forces were confronted by the projected (and, as it turned out, underestimated) maximum of ten Japanese divisions on Kyushu, field hospitals would need 11,670 pints of blood within the first fifteen days of combat after excluding (1) the estimated number of wounded for whom blood plasma was an adequate substitute or who required no transfusions at all, (2) those whose transfusions started off with plasma then switched to whole blood to prevent shock, and (3) the soldiers and Marines who died before receiving blood.[51]

Deducting the above categories from General Denit's estimate of approximately 394,859 all-causes casualties by X+120 gave Kendrick a figure of 99,948 men needing whole blood transfusions.[52] From this he projected that requisitions would grow to 149,922 pints four months into the operation, or about the time that the front stabilized across the island's mountainous core, and his figures did not include Navy needs, which ran through a completely different supply and acquisition chain. He later stated, "Once the program to supply blood to the Pacific from the mainland had been instituted, there was never a shortage of blood in these areas." Kendrick was confident that "had Operation OLYMPIC been carried out and the estimated 500,000 to 600,000 casualties come to pass, there is little doubt that sufficient blood would have been provided for all their needs."[53]

The blood supply architecture for Operation Olympic was a marvel to behold. Massive in scale, it was built on a structure that had been fine-tuned and enlarged since its establishment in 1944 and followed strict delivery and transportation timetables all the way back to eleven metropolitan hospitals in the United States. Earlier, in the midphase of the Pacific war, a blood bank at Hollandia, New Guinea, and depot at Biak island were supplied by military donors, but these were phased out at the end of 1944 in anticipation of a more dependable whole-blood pipeline to the Zone of the Interior capable of handling far greater quantities. In both systems the key factors dominating all aspects of the intricately planned transit were, first, that whole blood had to be refrigerated or packed in dry ice and, second, that even with the most stringent care, whole blood's shelf life of only twenty-one days made it not just useless after that point but also potentially *dangerous* to those receiving transfusions.[54]

The ball would start rolling for the Olympic blood supply just twelve days before the precious fluid was needed at loading points at Guam. Red Cross workers at the designated stateside hospitals, who had been attempting with some difficulty to regulate the perishable commodity's inflow with the military's fluctuating needs, would send out the word for donors to local civic organizations, labor unions, church congregations, and government organizations—but not to newspapers for open requests until after the invasion was launched. Whole blood harvested from as far away as New York, Philadelphia, Brooklyn, Boston, and Washington would be ice-packed in "Army expendable insulated boxes" and flown to Oakland, where it was inspected at a Navy laboratory then loaded up for the nearly seven-thousand-mile flight to the Navy's huge refrigerated repository on Guam, where it arrived thirty-two to forty-two hours later after four refueling stops.[55]

Specially configured LST(H) hospital ships containing ice-making machines and insulated storerooms called "reefers" were designated as blood distribution centers, with each handling two thousand pints of whole blood. Because the ships' cruising speeds were so slow, it was decided not to load them at Guam but to fly the quickly inspected and resorted blood to Manila for initial loading, then Okinawa for immediate resupply of the combat zone. Experience from the Okinawa campaign demonstrated that the initial shipments of blood drawn from American donors could be expected to reach Okinawa within six days and that the full allotment of blood for the opening assault could have arrived within four to six more days. Three of these "blood distribution centers afloat" were assigned, one each to the 3d, 5th, and 7th Amphibious Forces, would take station off its beachhead, and would be drawn upon as the sole source of whole blood by the corps ashore that it supported.[56] Theoretically the ice-packed blood being ferried ashore by DUKW amphibious trucks on X-day would still have a minimum of five days life in them, and it would be coursing through the veins of wounded soldiers and Marines long before that.[57]

In hindsight one might suggest that the extreme vulnerability of this system should have been obvious, especially in light of delays experienced at Okinawa. One of the ships supporting LST(H)-929, the sole blood distribution center available for the Iceberg landings, was the USS *Achernar* (AKA-53), carrying a highly specialized blood distribution team tasked with maintaining and dispensing stocks at the beachhead. Struck by both a kamikaze and bomb from a conventional aircraft, the *Achernar* was heavily damaged and the team was unable to reach shore until the third day, D+2.[58] Since the Japanese did not oppose the landing on Okinawa's Hagushi beaches, this event was of no particular consequence, and captured airfields allowed direct shipments of whole blood from Guam before the fighting's rapid escalation. A similar delay at any one of the sorely contested lodgments on Kyushu, however, would have led to untold numbers of seriously wounded troops—for whom use of blood plasma was only a stopgap measure—to drift into shock and die.[59] And while even a seemingly minor delay would have a profound effect on the men's ability to survive long enough to be successfully evacuated to one of the fifteen hospital ships (AHs) rotating between the combat area and rear-area hospitals, the situation could become much worse in a flash.

The stationing of a central repository for blood supplies at each of the three Kyushu beachheads was certainly the most efficient way to distribute whole blood to troops ashore, and made perfect organizational sense from the standpoint of how to handle this highly perishable commodity. But as noted earlier, Japanese plans called for the employment of kamikaze aircraft against assault force vessels that were functionally "locked" into place while supporting the landings (see chapter 8). These densely packed masses of shipping were the main focus of the "special attack" aircraft, and unlike at Okinawa, the shipping's close proximity to an extremely large number of Japanese air bases (many completely unknown to U.S. intelligence) and its operation immediately adjacent to a wide, mountainous land mass was going to make it extremely vulnerable.

The sinking of even one LST(H) blood distribution center would have had a catastrophic effect on the wounded ashore since additional blood shipments by sea could only be phased in at specific intervals as it arrived at Okinawa from Manila, and a fourth LST(H) attached to the Reserve Amphibious Force would have been days away from even reaching Kyushu.[60] Emergency responses to the crisis might have included rushing up whatever whole blood was available on Okinawa in the refrigeration compartment of a fast destroyer, or flying in ice-packed crates of the precious fluid from Guam or Manila on PBY Catalina flying boats. Once in the combat zone, transfer to an AKA or APA, now used as a makeshift distribution center, would commence. Some small amount of whole blood may already have been shared by a surviving LST(H) or hospital ship, but this is problematical since their own supplies would have been desperately needed by the men they were supporting both ashore or in their sick bays. All the while these ships would be fully engaged in trying to ensure that they did not fall victim as well. And what of the specialized blood distribution team on the stricken LST(H)? The team's loss would have rendered any rushed shipments practically useless if unaccompanied by knowledgeable personnel.[61]

No matter how the situation is examined, it appears highly unlikely that a disrupted distribution of whole blood to the affected beachhead would have achieved some degree of stabilization until D+2 at the very earliest and could not operate efficiently for some time after that, thus making the early securing of Japanese airfields even more urgent. Tragically such a loss would have had an impact far beyond the sinking of "just another LST," and the odds were in Japan's favor that at least one of the three floating distribution centers would be sunk or put out of commission in the tightly packed assembly areas. Although there is no inkling in the literature that this vulnerability was perceived by the time of the war's early termination, the need to decentralize the distribution might perhaps have been realized early enough to implement a system that, though less efficient, was also less vulnerable to enemy action.

CHAPTER 13

On the Ground

The principal coastal lowland areas, namely, the MIYAZAKI, ARIAKE, and KUSHIKINO PLAINS, are not, as the designation would suggest, flat areas, but consist of badly dissected alluvial terraces and river flats. These terraces and their steep faces, many of which are very near critical landing beaches, are among the most important terrain features of military significance. Their serrated edges are almost cliff-like in most places, varying from 25 to 250 feet above the flat valley floors. Where the terrace surface has broken down and there are no large rivers, the country is a mass of narrow, deep gullies and ravines. . . . The defensive potentialities of these terrace formations are obvious at a glance; almost unlimited opportunities are presented for the construction of cave and underground fortifications and for the emplacement of artillery, and in some cases even automatic weapons, within easy range of the landing beaches themselves. Many of these positions will probably be immune to neutralization by air and naval bombardment.

—U.S. Sixth Army, "G-2 Estimate of the Enemy Situation,"1945[1]

Positions along the coast . . . are used mainly in beach fighting and for firing against landing craft. It is very important to place installations so that they will not be affected by naval gun fire and to scatter, conceal, and cover them. . . . Positions [both along the coast and inland] will take full advantage of the terrain and will be placed so that fighting can be conducted flexibly. For this purpose, a force with a nucleus larger than an ordinary infantry battalion will occupy key positions which are independent of each other. The positions will be organized mainly for antitank warfare and the field of fire will be short. Installations will be underground fortresses capable of coping with close range actions in which flame throwers, gas, etc., are used. . . . Dummy positions and dummy construction works must be set up for purposes of deception and attracting enemy fire.

—"Organization of Fortified Zones," Imperial Japanese Army, 1945[2]

The United States and Japan did not carry out their mutual suicide pact. On August 14, 1945, a stunned Japanese nation heard their emperor's voice for the first time as Hirohito declared "the enemy has begun to employ a new and cruel bomb, the power of which to do damage is indeed incalculable," and warned that continuing the war would "result in an ultimate collapse and obliteration of the Japanese nation."[3] For a time the dying continued almost unabated from the lingering effects of war and Japanese occupation in places far from American eyes, such as China, the Dutch East Indies, and French Indochina. A final flurry of beheadings of captured B-29 crews occurred at the hand of vengeful Japanese guards—one airman was used as a target for archery practice—and Soviet tanks continued to roll across Manchuria.[4] But Japan itself had managed by a hair's breadth to avoid the conflagration on its doorstep.

Although the opposing forces in 1945 obviously harbored different expectations of who would emerge victorious, there was a shared consensus that the road to "victory" was going to be paved with Japanese corpses, "at least" 5 to 10 million of them according to the U.S. War Department estimate,[5] to perhaps as many as 20 million, if a figure being used within Imperial circles became a reality.[6] Meanwhile much effort and political capital had also been expended by the Roosevelt, and then Truman, administrations to establish a maintainable 100,000-men-per-month replacement stream for the invasion of Japan even in the midst of a partial demobilization.[7]

How America's now one-front war would have played out is a subject that purrs a seductive call for counterfactual analysis. And although I, as author, am as vulnerable as any to this enticement, a more worthwhile understanding comes not from speculating on which alternatives are more or less probable, or even plausible, but instead from focusing principally on what the antagonists themselves actually planned to do or were in the process of implementing when Hirohito read the Imperial Rescript of the Termination of the War. American planners understood that in spite of Japan's eroded industrial base, Imperial forces had the time, manpower, and adequate resources to succeed in their objective of creating a defensive structure that would combine the most deadly aspects of the beachhead killing zones experienced at Tarawa with the in-depth, layered underground fortifications so tenaciously held on Okinawa. The result was that each of the invasion sites presented its own Iwo Jima, its own Peleliu, with the additional deadly wrinkle that the island's terrain would allow significant counterattack forces to move in stages to positions relatively close to the beachheads before striking.[8]

The Ketsu-Go No. 6 build-up on Kyushu had begun in earnest in the spring of that year, intensified significantly during the summer, and would have continued with little real interference from U.S. air power for months beyond the point when Japan announced its capitulation in mid-August. But in all fairness to Admiral King, who told President Truman that Kyushu's great size would provide ground forces "with much more room to maneuver," the scale of the Japanese buildup was not yet clear when he said this on June 18, 1945, and it would remain obscure well into the following month when incontrovertible intelligence finally demonstrated that the three-pronged Olympic assault was effectively going to become three frontal attacks.[9]

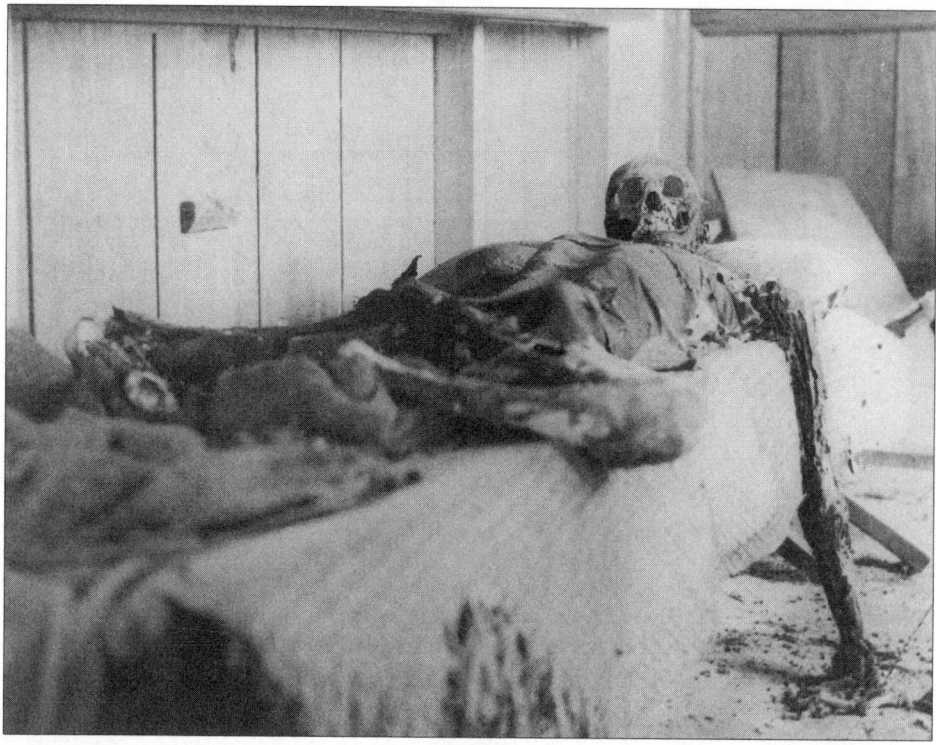

The skeletal remains of an American or Filipino soldier found when members of the 130th Infantry Guerrilla Force (Philippine Army) and an AFPAC Recovered Personnel Field Team entered the Davao Penal Colony in May 1945. Approximately seventy-five unburied bodies in varying stages of decay were found on the evacuated facility, which the Imperial Army had turned into a POW camp. (U.S. Army)

Long before King's statement, however, it was clear to planners that the mountainous terrain, locations of objectives, and sparse road net on southern Kyushu limited the Sixth Army to no more than four widely dispersed invasion sites capable of handling the required minimum of two divisions coming ashore abreast. And even these locations were far from ideal, as they were dominated by various combinations of multiple high ridge lines and rugged hills, with each of them under the direct observation of even more imposing heights further inland.

An astonished Engineering Intelligence Division geologist, William Putnam, working under MacArthur's chief engineer, Maj. Gen. Hugh J. Casey, blurted out the obvious to a planning staff colonel who had asked his opinion of Miyazaki Beach targeted by I Corps. Pointing to the close-set contour lines on a terrain map, he incredulously replied, "That's a cliff, C-L-I-F-F," and stated flatly that anyone sending landing craft ashore there was a "murderer."[10] Likewise, the commander of the 931st Engineer Construction Group (Aviation), Col. John H. Dudley, was initially chagrined to find that his engineers were landing with the second invasion echelon, a delay that could have serious repercussions for troops in desperate need of close air support. A close examination of the operational plans, however, quickly revealed that the second landing force was assigned the exact same objectives as the first. "It was clear to me then," said Dudley. "They expected the first echelon to

Coastal terrain typical of southern Kyushu. This obviously would not be selected as a landing beach, but even the targeted beaches selected had cliffs like these that were already heavily fortified. (U.S. Army)

be wiped out."[11] Long after the war, a comprehensive Marine examination of the opposing forces, terrain, and operational plans came to the conclusion that "V Amphibious Corps would likely have expended itself trying to reach its two primary objectives, Sendai to the north and Kagoshima to the east."[12] Use of the words "trying to reach" instead of "reaching" was not likely by accident.

★   ★   ★

The invasion was scheduled to open on Kyushu's outer islands on October 27, 1945, five days (X-[minus]5) before the main landings and three days after Admiral Turner's bombardment groups had begun their deadly work on X-8. Elements of the 40th Infantry Division were to quickly clear the small islands of Kuchino–Erabu Shima, Kuro Shima, Kusakaki Jima, and Uji Gunto, west and southwest of Kyushu, principally to secure them for air-warning facilities. The following day (X-4) the bulk of the reinforced division would land on the northern-most islands of Koshiki Retto, almost due west of the V Amphibious Corps' targeted beaches, to establish a pair of anchorages where damaged ships could take refuge and serve as a seaplane base. And it would be this large-scale operation at Koshiki Retto that would likely trigger the massive kamikaze and conventional air response by the Japanese, who were wary of launching their attacks against feints designed to draw them out prematurely.[13]

During this period the 158th Regimental Combat Team (RCT) also was to be prepared to land on Tanega Shima, south of Kyushu, if its seizure was found necessary to protect minesweepers clearing a passage between the eastern and western invasion beaches. This operation was not to be launched if the Navy found that it could adequately suppress the suicide speed boats known to be based there (150 were surrendered at war's end) and its garrison, centered around the 109th Independent Mixed Brigade, which received no artillery greater than 4.7 inch (120 mm). Like the IX Corps largely held in reserve, the RCT would be kept available for contingencies or for whatever mission best facilitated the Sixth Army objective of clearing the southern end of Kyushu of Imperial forces, thus permitting the development of Kagoshima Wan and Ariake Wan areas as major bases to support the invasion of the Tokyo area in 1946. As for the Japanese, all major units assigned to Ketsu-Go No. 6 were present on Kyushu at the time of the surrender and, with the exception of a few formations that had yet to move to assigned areas in the south, were all in place.

The main assault was scheduled for X-day, November 1, with the near-simultaneous storming of the Miyazaki and Ariake Bay beaches on the eastern shore and the Kushikino beaches at the base of the island's Satsuma Peninsula. And while the size and scope of the invasion was unprecedented, another aspect of the operation would have also represented a distinct break from the past. Numerous amphibious assaults during the war had experienced significant landing craft losses to hostile fire, such as at Omaha and Juno Beaches at Normandy. In addition assault shipping had received periodic attack (sometimes with spectacularly catastrophic results as when ammunition ships blew up off Okinawa and Sicily), but Kyushu would be the first time that the assembly and fire support areas were subject to massive and sustained aerial assault for days leading up to the landings, and during the assault phase itself. The attempts by suicide craft to get among the assault shipping, some of which would be successful, would further disrupt operations.

At each of the targeted beaches, the attacking corps would go in with two divisions forward and one back following bombardments that, while somewhat less robust than is commonly understood, were to be carried out for more than a week in a torrent that even if it collapsed only a percentage of tunnels and killed few defenders would hopefully leave the survivors in a stunned stupor with little ability to respond effectively. But as noted in the previous chapter, officers of all ranks—Army, Navy, and Marine—were well aware of the recent historical precedents from World War I to the bloody battles only months before on Iwo Jima and Okinawa, prolonged slugfests in which the Americans had virtually the same preponderance of firepower yet suffered nearly 68,000 casualties among their ground troops.

Navy radioman Val Adams Jr., aboard the USS *Rutland*, an attack transport collecting casualties from Iwo Jima, wrote in his diary about the capture of nearby Mt. Suribachi. After watching "thousands and thousands of tons of American red-hot steel blasting almost vainly at its steep slopes," he saw that the Japanese in their "bastion of caves and connecting tunnels" still offered "just as much opposition as if it had never been touched." Adams noted that "possibly no other spot in the world has taken such a pounding," yet the "ceasing of enemy fire from Suribachi" after nine days of extraordinarily bloody fighting came only through "the direct penetration of U.S. Marines."[14] There was nothing that would lead either the Japanese or Americans to believe that things would be any different on Kyushu, only on a much larger scale.

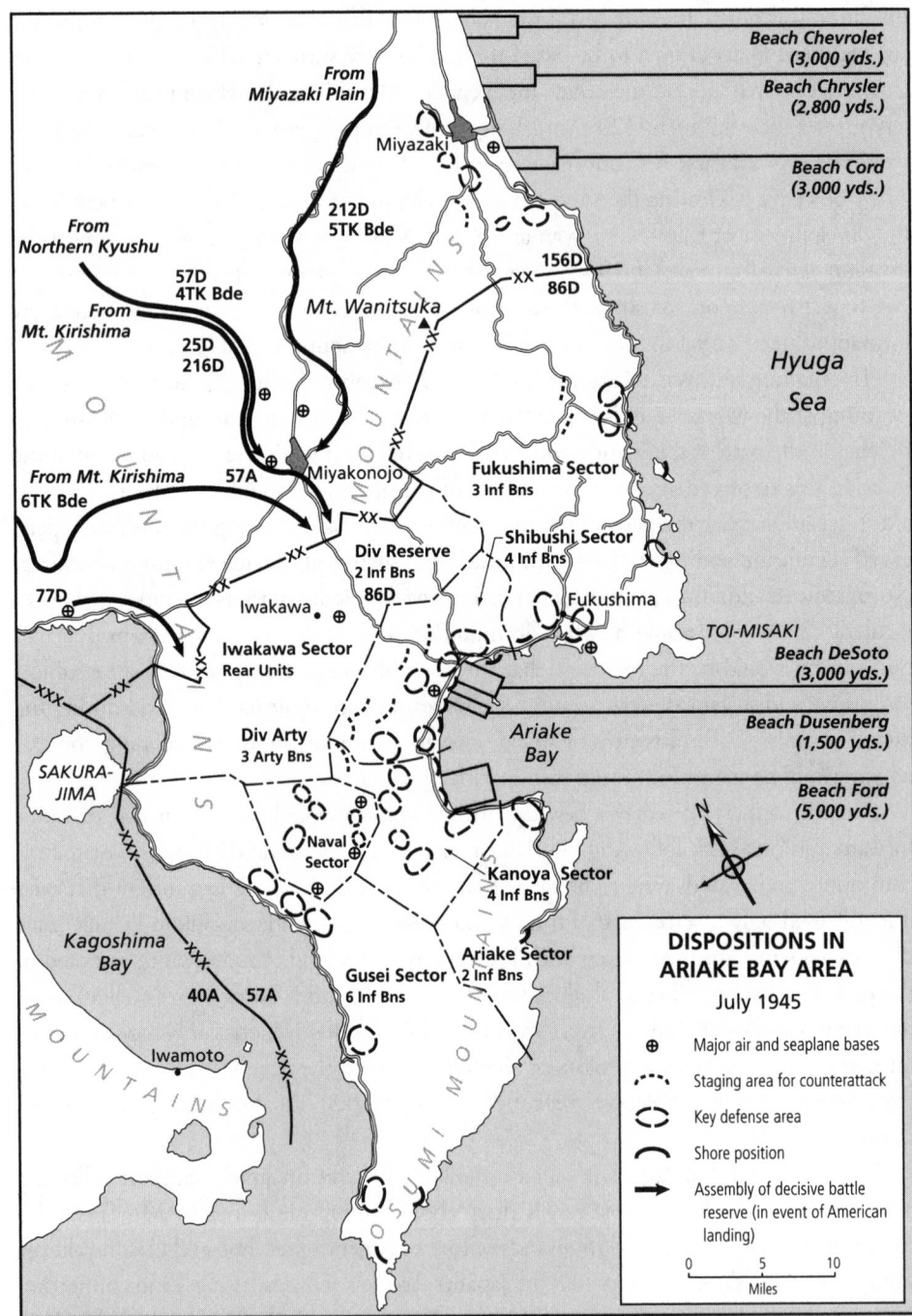

Beach Chevrolet
(3,000 yds.)

Beach Chrysler
(2,800 yds.)

Beach Cord
(3,000 yds.)

*From
Miyazaki Plain*

Miyazaki

212D
5TK Bde

*From
Northern Kyushu*

57D
4TK Bde

*From
Mt. Kirishima*

25D
216D

156D
86D

Mt. Wanitsuka

*Hyuga

Sea*

From Mt. Kirishima   57A
6TK Bde

Miyakonojo

Fukushima Sector
3 Inf Bns

Shibushi Sector
4 Inf Bns

77D

Iwakawa

Div Reserve
2 Inf Bns
86D

Fukushima

TOI-MISAKI

Iwakawa Sector
Rear Units

Beach DeSoto
(3,000 yds.)

Div Arty
3 Arty Bns

*Ariake
Bay*

Beach Dusenberg
(1,500 yds.)

SAKURA-
JIMA

Beach Ford
(5,000 yds.)

N

Naval
Sector

Kanoya Sector
4 Inf Bns

*Kagoshima
Bay*

40A   57A

Gusei Sector
6 Inf Bns

Ariake Sector
2 Inf Bns

**DISPOSITIONS IN
ARIAKE BAY AREA**

July 1945

Iwamoto

⊕   Major air and seaplane bases

⌁   Staging area for counterattack

◌   Key defense area

⌒   Shore position

➤   Assembly of decisive battle
reserve (in event of American
landing)

M O U N T A I N S

O S U M I   M O U N T A I N S

0   5   10
Miles

Map derived from *Reports of General MacArthur* (Tokyo: General Headquarters, Supreme Allied Command, Pacific, 1950), vol. 1, bk. 2, p. 656.

Japanese dispositions in southeast Kyushu and landing beaches.

Beach Chrysler, just north the port of Miyazaki and the mouth of the Honjo River,
represented the extreme right flank of Sixth Army's X-day objectives and, together with
Cord Beach, south of the town, was the target of I Corps and the 7th Amphibious Force,

which would put it ashore. With the 33d Infantry Division (ID) on the right and the 25th ID on its left, I Corps would fight its way directly into an extraordinarily dense defensive zone made up of an equivalent number of Imperial divisions, the 156th Division at Chrysler and the 154th protecting Miyazaki Airfield at Cord. The beachhead would be reinforced by the corps' third division, the 41st ID, on D+2 while the first elements of the Imperial Army's 212st Division just to the north at Tsuno were to reach the front on the same day, and the 5th Independent Tank Brigade from the mobile reserve was well positioned to support the defense if it was not ordered south.

Like the other tank brigades in the mobile reserve, the 5th's training and mission put its 112 tanks and self-propelled guns (twenty-six 37 mm, fifty-six high-velocity 47 mm, twenty-four high-velocity 75 mm, and six 105 mm) solidly into the role of infantry support as a mobile artillery and antitank asset. A Kwantung division from Manchuria, the 25th, was attached to the Fifty-Seventh Army, responsible for the defense of the area, but this association was largely for administrative purposes, and as part of the Sixteenth Area Army's mobile reserve, the division was far more likely to be sent deep into the eastern Osumi Peninsula to defend the Kasano Plain (a generally more vulnerable and strategically vital area than that behind the Miyazaki beaches), which stretched all the way across the peninsula to Kagoshima Bay.

Thirty-five miles to the south—and a world away—at Kasano, the beefed-up XI Corps would assault DeSoto, Dusenberg, and Ford beaches at the base of a deep, ten-mile-wide bay, Ariake Wan, that fronted the plain. Unlike at Miyazaki, where the eighteen coastal defense guns and howitzers were arranged in a string of relatively vulnerable batteries along heights overlooking an open coast, most of the batteries at Ariake were positioned along the mountainous, irregular flanks which stretched for ten miles along its southern shore to Hi Point and some fifteen miles across the north to Toi Point. Complicating matters further, the two large and one small minefields laid across the bay were arranged one-third of the way back between the points jutting out into the Pacific and the targeted beaches, thus making the ships engaged in minesweeping subject to all-around fire from twenty-four coastal cannons, including seven of 150 mm (5.9 inch) and twelve of 240 mm (9.5 inch).

There would be no U.S. Navy version of the "Charge of the Light Brigade" but a systematic and phased reduction of the enemy batteries. Fully six battleships, nearly half of the old battle wagons allotted to shore bombardment, along with two cruiser divisions and quite likely the two battleships freed from operations in Southeast Asia after the British invasion of Malaya, would systematically reduce the Japanese batteries as kamikazes that had broken through the screens of Hellcats and Corsairs tried to crash dive into the ships' bridges. First, the outermost batteries would be pummeled into silence and efforts made to entice the ones further back along the northern and southern shores to expose themselves. In the final stages of the operation the battleships would be moving into the ring of fire within the bay itself to blast at their tormentors.

The possibility existed, however, that the Japanese batteries would not cooperate by offering themselves up for piecemeal destruction and instead use only their smaller 105-mm (4.1-inch) and 120-mm (4.7-inch) guns, in combination with a few of the larger cannons, to slow down the clearing of the minefields. With no possibility of moving back the launching

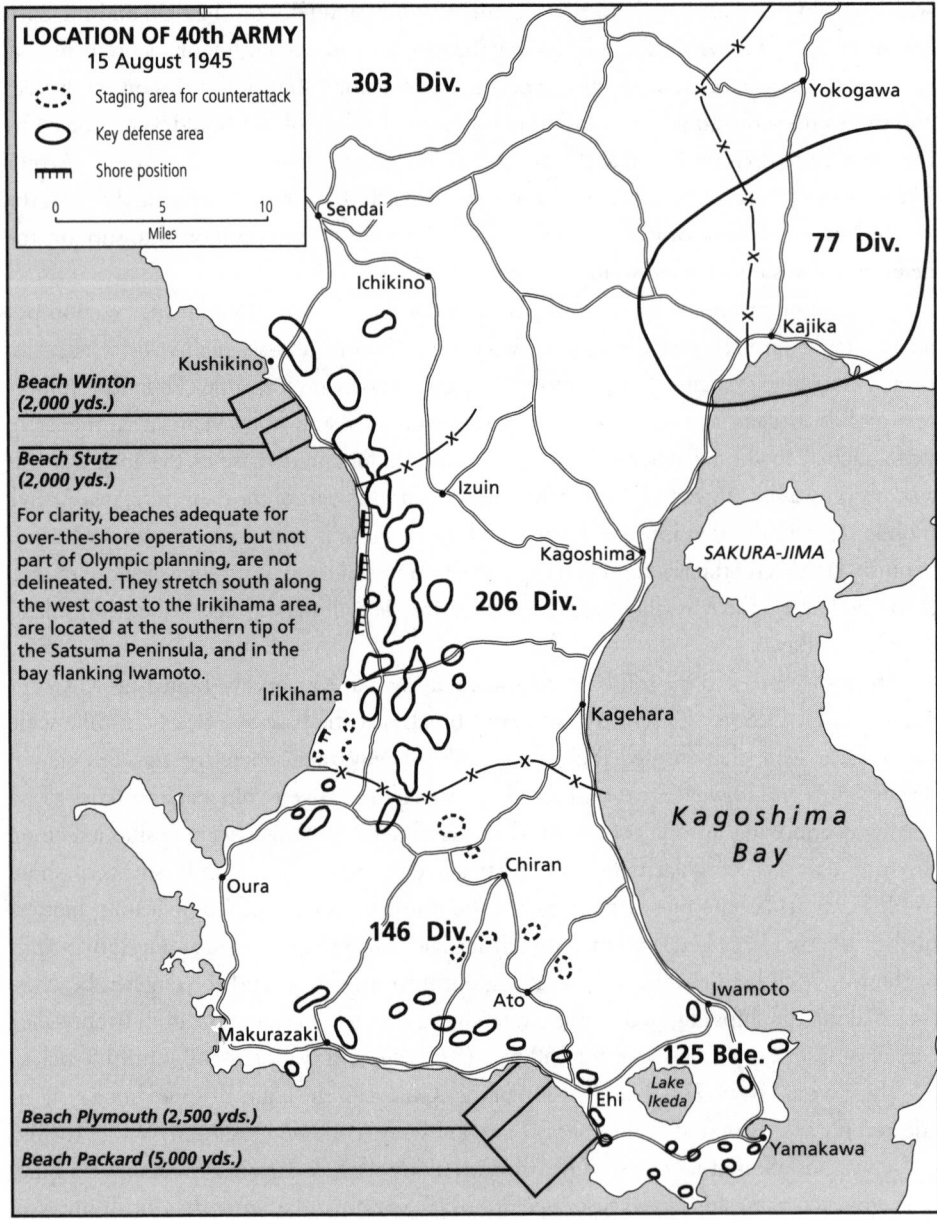

LOCATION OF 40th ARMY
15 August 1945

Staging area for counterattack

Key defense area

Shore position

0   5   10
Miles

303 Div.

Yokogawa

77 Div.

Sendai

Ichikino

Kajika

Kushikino

Beach Winton (2,000 yds.)

Beach Stutz (2,000 yds.)

For clarity, beaches adequate for over-the-shore operations, but not part of Olympic planning, are not delineated. They stretch south along the west coast to the Irikihama area, are located at the southern tip of the Satsuma Peninsula, and in the bay flanking Iwamoto.

Izuin

Kagoshima

SAKURA-JIMA

206 Div.

Irikihama

Kagehara

K a g o s h i m a
B a y

Chiran

Oura

146 Div.

Iwamoto

Ato

125 Bde.

Makurazaki

Lake Ikeda

Ehi

Beach Plymouth (2,500 yds.)

Yamakawa

Beach Packard (5,000 yds.)

Map derived from "Report on Operation 'Olympic' and Japanese Counter-Measures, Part 4, Appendices" British Combined Operations Observers (Pacific), (London: Combined Operations Headquarters, August 1, 1946), app. 12.

Japanese dispositions in southwest Kyushu and landing beaches.

of X-day, and with large, hidden batteries withholding their fire until the packed mass of assault shipping moved into the confined bay (logisticians estimated that the beaches could handle sixty LSTs unloading simultaneously), most of the battleships and cruisers would physically interpose themselves in line-ahead formations between the batteries hidden along the mountainous shores and the assembling invasion force.

It would also be at this stage of the invasion where the position of the batteries, flanking the assembly area and generally well away from the targeted beaches, would expose them to steady assault by heavy bombers with little fear that friendly forces might accidentally be struck. Such attacks, targeting likely sites of hidden guns, would destroy very few of the weapons outright, but might well collapse tunnel entrances, and would certainly degrade the effectiveness of the gun crews through the continual concussive effects of the bombing. Extensive use of smokescreens would have also been a particularly important method of protecting the assembly area in Araike Bay but would have been employed very carefully. Indiscriminate use of smoke to hide ships from the Japanese batteries could have well turned out to be highly disruptive to landing and bombardment operations so would be tightly coordinated by the amphibious force according to the prevailing winds at the time. Its judicious use held great promise, particularly along the force's southern flank, of minimizing the effectiveness of the Japanese batteries.

From the assembly area, flanked by warships engaging coastal artillery to the north and south, and with still more bombarding the invasion beaches to the west including batteries known to be located on Biro Island deep within the bay (all while under persistent air attack), the 3d Amphibious Force would put ashore—in the best order possible under the circumstances—the 43d ID at DeSoto and Dusenberg and the 1st Cavalry Division at Ford. Initially opposing them would be the Japanese 86th Division, backed up by the 89th Independent Mixed Brigade. And while XI Corps would push the Americal Division and 112th RCT ashore as early as X+2, IGHQ was determined to hold the area at all cost. A large portion of the Sixteenth Area Army's mobile reserve of four infantry divisions and three tank brigades (most likely the 25th and 77th divisions and 6th Independent Tank Brigade minus a regiment at Kagoshima) would be sent south in an effort to contain the beachhead in this critically important area if the Americans couldn't be driven into the sea.

Across the island and south of Sendai, the base of the Satsuma Peninsula was so inhospitable to ground movement by an invading army that the Sixteenth Area Army correctly decided that its defenses could wait until the build-ups at Miyazaki and Araike Bay were well underway. Nevertheless, when V Amphibious Corps' 3d Marine Division stormed ashore south of Kushikino at Winton Beach, with the 2d on its right at Stutz, there would be two Imperial divisions to deal with, the 303d astride the beaches and the 206th, located close at hand to the south. The 206th had been positioned closer to Kagoshima on the bay because the peninsula was theoretically more vulnerable to an invading force at this comparatively narrow area. The Sixth Army had, in fact, originally planned for its landings to be further south (although not quite as far south as the Japanese believed the Americans would most likely attack) and only moved the assault an additional ten miles north at the suggestion of the V Amphibious Corps commander.

The 5th Marine Division would join the fight on D+2, shortly before at least one additional Japanese formation, probably the 216th Division (assigned to the Higo Group in central Kyushu for administrative purposes) arrived as part of the mobile reserve. Meanwhile the V Amphibious Force conducting the assault would not only be targeted by large numbers of kamikazes as it was locked into landing operations but also have to contend with night attacks by more than a thousand suicide speedboats, which would emerge from their hideaways along the coast and the gaggle of rocky islands directly to the north.

Four of the pre–Pearl Harbor battleships would support V Amphibious Force operations south of Kushikino (one more than at Miyazaki), in spite of the fact that there was very little coastal artillery defending the area. However, the 5th Fire Support Group was not only tasked with supporting the Marine landings, but also the 40th ID seizing the Koshiki Retto to the west and landings of undetermined size by elements of the IX Corps on beaches Plymouth and Packard near the southwestern tip of the peninsula some ten miles east of Makurazaki. This latter operation was to be carried out on D+3 by the Reserve Amphibious Force putting ashore the corps headquarters and at least one division, the 81st, on Packard. Since the corps' 98th ID was to function as Sixth Army's initial floating reserve to be possibly committed either in its entirety or in RCT slices, it was envisioned that Plymouth Beach to the 81st's left would be stormed by as many elements of the 98th as were available on D+3. The corps' 77th ID, taking over as floating reserve after the commitment of the 98th, was to make an administrative landing here any time after D+5 with whatever elements it still possessed after one or more of its regiments had been carved off to support other beachheads.

The targeted southwestern beaches west of Miyazaki were situated almost at the very base of a jagged ridge line only one to two miles inland that rises an average of 1,300 feet above the surf and ends in a huge, extinct volcano containing the waters of Lake Ikeda. Due south of the volcano and reminiscent of Suribachi on Iwo Jima—only extending well out from the coastline so that it is actually behind the backs of the 81st ID soldiers—is Mt. Kaimon, a 3,000-foot feature rising in a nearly perfect blue cone out of the ocean. Obviously, this was an extremely risky place for a landing, but an assault here had some priceless advantages.

First, neither IGHQ, the Imperial Fortieth Army, nor the commands in between thought this a likely invasion site (although at least one the Fortieth's staff officers considered it a possibility), and they believed that if the area was attacked it would be at beaches along the very tip of the peninsula, or that the Americans would force their way through the minefield guarding the entrance to Kagoshima Bay to strike at the good beaches facing east at Ibusuki. Consequently, the 125th Independent Mixed Brigade responsible for its defense was principally oriented to the south and east, with its four 150-mm (5.9-inch) guns situated to cover both of these areas and the minefields stretching across the bay. Next, the Imperial 146th Division had some forces in the area but they were mostly concentrated well to the west with the mission of denying the small port of Makurazaki to the Americans while the bulk of the division was arrayed to the north along its boundary with the 206th Division.

And finally, with American troops having landed in force at not one or two, but all three, of the anticipated invasion sites, every passing day would reinforce the likelihood to the Japanese that any effort against the southern end of the Satsuma Peninsula would be principally a naval affair aimed at the minefields and Ibusuki. In short the IX Corps strike, planned for the fourth day of the invasion, might well occur after the Japanese concluded that the Americans had "shot their bolt" in terms of assault landings and perhaps shifted a significant portion of the 146th north and even farther away from Plymouth and Packard beaches. The catch? There could be no lengthy preparation from 5th Fire Support Group that might draw Japanese elements south, and whatever portion of the corps landed, it would have to move swiftly to take advantage of the dearth of Imperial troops or face a Pacific version of the Anzio debacle in 1944.[15]

★   ★   ★

At each invasion site, the immediate expansion of captured airfields and establishment of new ones was the top priority. Planners originally envisioned the operation of eleven major airbases on Kyushu to support the softening up of the Kanto Plain before Coronet. Bomb and fuel storage, roads, wharves, and base facilities would be needed to maintain the massive operation, in addition to the U.S. Sixth Army holding the ninety-mile-long stop line one-third of the way up the island. All plans centered on construction of the minimum essential operating facilities, but that minimum grew from eighteen air groups to twenty-five, and then *more than thirty* at twenty-three airbases with some seventy runways.[16] This was all to be based on an island on which there was considerably less terrain information available than what the U.S. planners erroneously believed they knew about Leyte, an island that was originally to be for the Luzon campaign what the Kyushu invasion was to the capture of Honshu's Kanto Plain and Tokyo, a preliminary operation to create a huge staging area.

Today, we can recall MacArthur wading ashore triumphantly in the Philippines. But what President Truman and General Marshall knew only too well was that MacArthur was supposed to have retaken Leyte with four divisions and have eight fighter and bomber groups striking from the island within forty-five days of the initial landings. However, nine divisions and twice as many days into the battle, only a fraction of that air power was operational because terrain conditions were not fully appreciated (and *this* on an island which the United States had occupied for over forty years). The fighting on the ground had simply not gone as planned. The Japanese even briefly isolated Fifth Air Force Headquarters and captured much of the Burauen airfield complex before reinforcements pushed them back into the jungle.[17]

Numerous austere fighter strips on Kyushu would come on line early to support ground operations, but the extensive facilities and thick, extralong runways for Honshu-bound medium and heavy bombers would only start to become available a month and a half into the operation. Most were not projected to be ready until three to three and a half months after the initial landings in spite of a massive engineer effort. Consequently any delays at all in capturing the real estate needed for airbase construction risked a negative and direct effect on Coronet in 1946. Ground operations would have to be pressed to the maximum with as much reliance on tactical maneuver and deception as possible. But the grim reality, now that American forces were moving solidly into the core of Japanese defenses in the Home Islands, was that the ability to accomplish meaningful operational maneuver had radically decreased, and this ground could only be bought through a relentless adherence to grinding attritional warfare dependent on massive firepower and the bravery of Army and Marine infantrymen.

Probably the first Japanese airfield to fall into American hands would be Miyazake, with its three runways ranging in length from 3,900 to 5,050 feet and ample room for expansion. Extending right up to the bluffs overlooking Cord Beach, the airfield's seizure by I Corps'

Highly defensible terraced rice fields, like these on Kyushu, were a common feature of areas that could not be bypassed on the island and, to a lesser degree, the objective area on the Honshu Plain. (U.S. Army)

Sugar Loaf on Okinawa, an unimposing little hill with a total area of not much more than two football fields. Note the size of the two soldiers at the summit. Putting aside the artillery-studded foothills along the Eighth Army's steadily lengthening flank and the ongoing slugfest along the elevated roads and rice paddies, it is useful to note that there were many such terrain features on the Kanto Plain that could not be bypassed easily. In five days of fighting in May 1945, the Japanese defenders here and on two supporting hills behind it inflicted more than three thousand Marine casualties—in spite of lavish tank and artillery support—before they were finally defeated. (National Archives and Records Administration)

25th ID could only be a bloody replay of the 4th and 5th Marine Divisions' fight to wrestle control of Airfield No. 1 on Iwo Jima. And it would remain under indirect fire from artillery in hills ranging far to the rear, and direct fire from two nearby all-around battalion positions, long after the Japanese 125th Division's most forward elements had offered themselves up for destruction along the water's edge.

This to-the-death struggle would be just one of dozens erupting in a giant arc along the coasts of southern Kyushu. The Sixth Army's intelligence staff warned that "because of the terrain and ample forces available to the enemy," the Japanese would be less constrained by circumstances and shortages in material than in the past. They would be able to both defend the beaches *and* erect a defense in depth—instead of having to choose between one or the other—as well as launch coordinated counterattacks:

> The coastal lowlands are ringed with foothills which provide excellent observation over practically all landing beaches in SOUTHERN KYUSHU; the enemy, accordingly, will have good opportunity to oppose our assault echelons with observed artillery fire from artfully concealed battery positions. . . .
>
> The enemy can in this operation revert to his favored doctrine of "annihilating the enemy at the water's edge." The adoption of a strong and active beach defense is a capability to be seriously reckoned with in this operation. . . . The corridors which connect the coastal lowlands with one another and with the inland basins are long, narrow, winding valleys dominated by heights on both sides. These terrain features lend themselves almost ideally to the development of the typical Japanese dug-in defensive systems in depth. Known enemy dispositions and photo interpretation alike suggest that the Japanese are well aware of the potentialities; in the terraced areas and foothills behind the beaches and in the rugged inland areas, like the "SHIMBU" [Line] and BALETE PASS defense lines on LUZON and the "SHURI" [Line] like on OKINAWA.[18]

The significance of this last paragraph would have not escaped the Sixth Army's intelligence customers. For although the Shuri Line was a well-developed position that had ground the U.S. Tenth Army's movement to a virtual halt on Okinawa, the Balete Pass and Shimbu defenses—and, for that matter, those at Breakneck, Corkscrew, and Kilay ridges on Leyte—were virtually ad hoc by comparison, yet Sixth Army soldiers were forced to take each one of them "the hard way," suffering stiff casualties in the process. So while it was plain to see that Imperial divisions were massing at the invasion sites themselves, with little evidence of work on *prepared* defenses in depth, the Sixth Army had seen this before and had no illusion that the Japanese front would burst open once the thin crust, barely five miles wide along the Miyazaki and Kushikino beaches, was penetrated.

The tangled terrain behind these beaches, with their rocky defiles and terraced slopes, required little effort from the throngs of People's Volunteer Corps labor units to make dozens of geographic features into functional clones of Sugar Loaf Hill, a low Okinawan ridge roughly the size of two football fields that the 6th Marine Division was unable to bypass. In spite of lavish tank and artillery support, the Japanese defenders there and on two supporting hills behind it inflicted more than three thousand Marine casualties during five days of fighting before they were finally defeated in May 1945. And behind the Ariake beaches there was no "crust" at all as the entire zone contained one mutually supporting, all-around battalion or company position after another stretching all the way across the Kasano Plain to Kagoshima Bay. Unknown to intelligence officers, there were also a half dozen staging areas, largely underground, strung across the hills north of the plain awaiting the mobile formations that would counterattack XI Corps. Thus the farther that XI at Ariake fought its way west toward the main Japanese airbase complex near the inner bay, the more of these sizable staging areas would be on their right flank.

This flies in the face of what many historians have come to believe about how the Japanese defense would be conducted. The tactical dispositions and intent of Imperial forces on Kyushu is an area where understandable confusion has developed owing to the impression garnered from the term "coastal defense division" and the Japanese determination, clearly expressed in Ketsu-Go, to drive the invaders into the sea. When combined these tend to lead one to the false conclusion that the Imperial troops were going to seemingly offer themselves up in killing fields erected from the full range of American air, ground, and naval weapons.

The plentiful, and dead earnest, exhortations to relentlessly storm the beachheads has tended to obscure the fact that approximately 90 percent of Japanese defensive construction work was finished by the time of the surrender. This included the staging areas near Araike, less extensive ones at threatened areas to the north, underground and cave fortifications along the targeted beaches, inland hills, and ridges up to roughly five miles inland, with most of the uncompleted projects in the Fortieth Army zone to the west. Moreover, the coastal defense divisions tasked with delaying the establishment of American lodgments and movement inland only placed one-fifth to one-third of their men in the well-sheltered positions along the beaches (depending on the nature of the terrain), with the balance ensconced in all-around battalions and company positions to their rear.

In the case of the Fortieth Army, its commander, Nakazawa Mitsuo, understood quite well that he would likely lose the mobile 77th Division under his care to Major General Nishihara Kanji's Fifty-Seventh Army and the battle on the Kasano Plain. Postwar interrogations revealed that massive counterattacks were not in the cards in his western zone of operations: "The Commanding General, Fortieth Army, considered that he would have insufficient troops with which to defeat the enemy at the water's edge. He therefore intended to fight only a delaying battle in the beachhead area, and then to retire to prepared positions in the hills."[19] There was not even a pretext of using one of his coastal defense divisions, the 146th, to defend against a beach assault. Instead he ordered it into a series of all-around defensive positions stretching ten miles *across* the Satsuma Peninsula to the line of mountains guarding Kagoshima Bay.

These dispositions, and the fact that suitable landing beaches stopped short of the division's sector, demonstrate that in spite of the Ketsu-Go's widely publicized intent, Nakazawa was not planning to use this formation to counterattack an enemy lodgment. Instead the 146th was placed as a barrier to American movement into the southern peninsula and thus prolong the denial of the bay's use by the U.S. Navy in much the same way as MacArthur's forces in the Bataan Peninsula prevented Japanese use of Manila harbor for three full months—exactly the type of situation that the IX Corps landing near Mt. Kaimon was designed to prevent.

Despite the Imperial Fortieth Army's bowing out of the Mutsu No. 1, C defense plan, certainly with the concurrence of higher headquarters, U.S. Sixth Army intelligence analysts were nevertheless two-thirds right when warning that the Olympic beaches would be heavily counterattacked after Japanese mobile reserves completed a series of night movements to avoid U.S. air attacks. They were also correct in their estimation that because of the manner in which the night movements and daytime concealments must be conducted, these assaults could start as early as X+3 to X+5. And while their August 1 analysis, "G-2 Estimate of the Enemy Situation, OPERATION OLYMPIC," did not reflect the most recent Japanese deployments both to the beachhead areas and into the mobile reserve (being outdated by from approximately ten days to a month on numerous particulars because of the vagaries of intelligence collection, analysis, and dissemination), it displayed the prescience and insight of an intelligence staff that had been fighting the Japanese with only brief interludes since 1942 on New Guinea.

In combination with the Intelligence section's "Japanese Plans for the Defense of Kyushu," released after an extensive examination of the island's defenses and interrogations of Imperial officers of all ranks, a chillingly clear-eyed picture emerges of what the Sixth Army would have confronted as Operation Olympic smashed headlong into the Ketsu-Go operation's Mutsu-Go No. 1. Highlights of these "before" and "after" documents are reproduced as Appendixes A and B in this volume and can be compared with the Japanese plans excerpted from the "Homeland Operations Record" in chapter 7 and elsewhere in this book.

CHAPTER 14

Unexamined Factors

We did not believe that the entire people would be completely annihilated through fighting to the finish. Even if a crucial battle were fought in the homeland and the Imperial Forces were confined to the mountainous regions, the number of Japanese killed by enemy forces would be small. Despite the constant victories of Japanese troops in the China Incident, relatively few Chinese were killed. Almost all the strategic points in China were occupied, but the Chungking Government could not be defeated. [But] even if the whole [Japanese] race were all but wiped out, its determination to preserve the national polity would be forever recorded in the annals of history.

—LIEUTENANT COLONEL MASAHIKO TAKESHITA, brother-in-law of
War Minister Anami and a staff officer in the War Ministry, 1945[1]

Without speculating on the bloody course that battles unfought might have taken, or Marshall's consideration on August 13, 1945, that WMDs be employed on Kyushu to counter the massive Japanese build-up, we will presume that (unlike at Leyte, Luzon, Peleliu, Iwo Jima, and Okinawa) operations on Kyushu would have gone largely as planned. Beachheads would be consolidated, inland objectives seized, air base construction begun, corps link-ups made, and anchorages safely established in Kagoshima and Ariake bays—all having been accomplished in a timely manner. Upon reaching a defensible line running diagonally from above Sendai on the west to the Tsuno area somewhat farther north on the opposite coast, the Sixth Army would have functionally secured southern Kyushu as a base to launch Coronet the following year.[2] This stop line, however, would leave the Sixth Army with a distinctly shallow defense of the burgeoning infrastructure in the south, and it was originally envisioned that further unspecified operations to enhance and protect the area would be launched. MacArthur's headquarters later showed what it had in mind.

Taking the string of mountains occupying most of the central and western part of this line (east to west: Eboshi, the twin giants of Karakuni and Takochihono, then Omori, then Usuzu) would eliminate easy Japanese observation of the American activities throughout much of the region but would leave Imperial forces dangerously close to vital U.S. facilities. A drive to push north to the next line of heights, roughly eight miles distant in the west below Akune to as much as fourteen miles in the east below Nobeoka, was apparently considered as the optimal stop line for Olympic.[3] Attainment of this objective would mark the Sixth Army's transition from the strategic offensive-tactical offensive to the strategic offensive-tactical *defensive* by approximately D+120 if all went well.

From the standpoint of casualty generation, it was believed by Sixth Army planners that the highest losses during Olympic would come not during the first thirty or so days of consolidating and linking the beachheads while blocking reinforcements from the north but would instead be suffered as U.S. forces fought their way into the mountains and faced yet more Imperial divisions during the latter months of offensive operations.[4] After this point in the campaign (whenever that might have been), monthly casualties *from all causes* for a ground force the size of Olympic's in a hostile environment could conceivably drop back to an average of five to ten thousand among the front line troops and soldiers involved in intensive logistic and construction activities.

The British term for this, adopted at least informally by American planners, is "normal wastage." What is "normal" depends on the amount of such things as enemy activity, both coordinated and in the form of harassment by the very large number of Japanese stragglers that would invariably have been left behind American lines; loading accidents; drownings; sickness and disease; active patrolling along the stop line; plane crashes; and myriad other causes. For example, a similarly sized organization, the Third Army in Bavaria and Czechoslovakia's Sudetenland, saw approximately seventy soldiers killed and five hundred wounded during a single week in July 1945 from the improper handling of German firearms.[5] Offensive operations by either side, even those only limited in nature to "straighten out" portions of the line or gain dominant heights, can quickly send numbers soaring as was demonstrated time and time again during the latter two years of the Korean War on nearly identical terrain.

Two "mobile" Imperial formations which have not figured into the narrative thus far are the 57th Division from Manchuria and the 4th Independent Tank Brigade. Attached to the Fifty-Sixth Army in northern Kyushu at the time of the surrender, they were scheduled to have deployed closer to central Kyushu long before Olympic was launched in order to more easily fulfill their Ketsu-Go roles as part of the mobile reserve. In spite of Ketsu-Go's directive to commit all mobile reserve formations to immediate counterattacks, the movement of these units directly against a beachhead could well have been held up when the Sixteenth Area Army governing its commitment saw that literally all three Mutsu No. 1 invasion sites were being assaulted simultaneously (see chapter 7). Such a development, in combination with the formations' unavoidably slow movement south, would have likely prompted their commitment to Higo Group in central Kyushu to block a feared American lunge toward the more populous, industrialized north. If so, the 57th Division commander would have either assumed control, from the 216th's commander, of the Higo Group responsibility for coordinating the defense of central Kyushu, or more likely, the force's mission would be simply overtaken by events.

The "events" in question would be the Fifty-Seventh Army and a portion of the Fortieth Army falling back along the very narrow coastal plains astride the Ykushu Mountain mass. Although U.S. plans called for a drive north in order to form a defensive line roughly a third of the way up the island, Sixteenth Area Army planned to have its southern forces withdraw *even farther*, to the region of Mt. Aso, if the Americans were not quickly driven into the sea in the opening weeks of the invasion.

This withdrawal to the north is yet another aspect of the Sixteenth Area Army's plan for the prolonged defense of Kyushu that is at odds with the common perception of Japanese operations during the invasion. The area army had already granted its field army in the west, the Fortieth, great flexibility in how the Mutsu No. 1, C defense plan was to carried out and was even willing to let it forgo Ketsu-Go's principal tactic, the immediate and massive coun-terattack, against a Satsuma Peninsula beachhead. Instead, as described earlier, the Fortieth Army would take advantage of the marvelous terrain in its zone to engage the Yankee devils in the same type of warfare that had proven so effective on Okinawa and Iwo Jima earlier that year, both opposite the beachhead and in a defense line barring American movement into the southern peninsula. The withdrawal north would only include surviving elements of the Fortieth and Fifty-Seventh Armies as most of their troops would indeed fight it out in the south, and continued operations would entail the absorption of Higo Group forma-tions into these armies to buy time for further development of the northern defenses by the Fifty-Sixth Army.

Much to the disgust of some within IGHQ in Tokyo, who thought the Sixteenth Area Army's plans "absurd"[6] but had been unable to get them countermanded, the Sixteenth Area Army under Lieutenant General Yokoyama Isamu[7] desired to conduct rear-guard activities relatively near the Mt. Aso redoubt in order to let the Americans, rather than his own men, deal with the long, highly vulnerable supply lines up the coasts. This was not an insignificant matter. The mountains at the center of the island, a fifty-mile-wide massif stretching from the East China Sea to the Philippine Sea, are an infiltrator's dream. Whether it was from sudden rushes by spear-wielding, rag-tag People's Volunteers covered by some regular-army machine gunners or the aerial/artillery spotting by the Alamo Scouts and depredations of the 9th Ranger Infantry Battalion, whoever had to depend on land resupply along the narrow coastal roads was going to be in for a good deal of trouble.

The problem for Lt. Gen. Walter Krueger's Sixth Army was what to do if Yokoyama did not cooperate with American plans by sending his forces regiment by regiment, brigade by brigade, division by division, south to batter themselves against defenses amply supported by artillery and tactical air power. Communications and photo intelligence would quickly reveal that a massive redoubt was being formed at faraway Mt. Aso, and while it would present a useful place to employ the heavy bomber units which had run out of strategic targets, air operations could only slow, not stop, the redoubt's development. But why should this be a concern of the Sixth Army, which already had spent much of the war effectively leapfrogging Japanese concentrations that it would then leave to their own devices?

In the Southwest Pacific theater, Imperial forces were cut off from logistic support and even each other. This would not be the story on Kyushu, a Home Island with a population of roughly 10 million in 1945, and the Sixteenth Area Army had every intention of using the mountains and resource-rich north as a base for "protracted warfare."[8] Excluding the population within the Olympic target area, the sole preoccupations of the more than 7 million civilians still under Imperial control would be their own survival and the defeat of the Americans. As for the civilians in the south, the only official evacuees would be those living near the coasts who would be sent no farther than the Kirishima area, itself a key target of invasion forces.[9] Would the people of southern Kyushu be as compliant to U.S. Army directives as the Okinawans?

The answer is a qualified yes, at least initially, because both the expected food shortages and the shock of invasion would enforce a degree of submissiveness. However, as life began to return to "normal" behind U.S. lines and the routines of the occupation force became better understood, the developing familiarity with the daily pattern of U.S. operations behind the lines and likelihood that isolated Japanese soldiers and fragments of units would "find each other" might invite the stirrings of armed resistance six months or so later, much as it had among Filipinos about a year after the Japanese takeover of their country. In this context the unhindered development of a redoubt could well allow it to become a dangerous center, and symbol, of resistance for Japanese in both occupied and unoccupied Kyushu. That Yokoyama had something like this in mind is clear. And anticipating that the major urban areas such as Sasebo, Fukuoka, Kumamoto, Nagasaki, and Kokura would be heavily bombed (the latter two were indeed slated for nuclear attack), construction was begun on an underground ordnance and ammunition factory complex in the mountains outside Hida,[10] halfway between the large coastal cities and Mt. Aso, which was actually located at the proposed northern redoubt's southern extremity.

Krueger had no crystal ball to look into the distant future, but he and his field commanders had been on the offensive for literally years and would desire to continue. Moreover, orders to the army, its corps, and divisions included "the conduct of such additional overland and amphibious operations on KYUSHU and in the INLAND SEA as may be directed subsequently" and there were sound military reasons for Sixth Army to stay "in contact" with the enemy.[11] After consolidating along the string of heights from Akune to Nobeoka, the farthest line north on any document from MacArthur's headquarters, there would be a natural desire to push aside the Japanese rear guards along the coastal roads.

But Krueger and his staff were an extremely savvy bunch. The long coastal roads, properly baited, could well be death traps waiting to be sprung by forces of unknown composition and size lurking in the mountains. A handful of miserable, single-lane roads winding through the interior could be put to better use by the Japanese than the Americans, and any drive north would almost immediately become two separate and distinct operations much as would occur with disastrous results a few years hence in 1950 for the road-bound U.S. 2d and 7th Infantry Divisions on opposite sides of northern Korea. No activity at all might be detected by air reconnaissance (as, again, would later be the case in Korea), and any that did appear might either be a deception to encourage the Americans to move cautiously or a genuine threat.

The situation would require a very soldier-intensive solution—pushing units up into the mountains along the entire line as Gen. Matthew B. Ridgway would later do in Korea—so that the Sixth Army could see what was real and what was not. And that is exactly what would be done, because unlike the first set of senior American commanders in the Korean War, whose principal combat experience was derived from mechanized warfare in Europe (and were quickly, if delicately, transferred out when Ridgway took command in 1951),[12] the long-serving Sixth Army commanders, who had just battled their way to the stop line, would have, from brutal experience, known better than to initiate "daring" drives to keep on the heels of a "defeated" enemy when there was no adequate way to monitor what was on their mountainous flanks.

The Sixth Army's preferred method for dealing with problems of terrain and distance such as that on Kyushu was to use "MacArthur's Navy," the U.S. Seventh Fleet, to launch amphibious "end runs." But with the insatiable needs of Coronet sucking up nearly all assault assets before the seasonal spring rains of 1946 forced a slowdown in offensive operations, there would have been insufficient shipping for anything more than resupply efforts along the east coast. This was particularly true because an amphibious effort along the west coast would require far too many assets to adequately protect it from sea-borne raids and suicide attacks from the many Japanese-controlled islands all along the route, while a full-scale "right hook" in the east would require not only a robust bombardment group, owing to the Japanese batteries on both shores of the Hayasui Channel (the narrows of the Bungo Strait), but also a sustained commitment by swarms of minesweepers.[13]

One of the half-dozen potential post-Coronet operations considered for the period after the assault shipping had been freed up and before the summer monsoons set in, was a six-division operation launched against northwest Kyushu with the intent of cutting the island off from Honshu. And the target area just happened to be where Mongol hordes had twice met disaster in the thirteenth century, on either side of Fukuoka.[14] But there was no chance of this full-blood, two-corps invasion on the opposite side of the redoubt occurring before July 1946—if at all.[15] The badly bloodied Sixth Army would have little recourse but to settle into a defensive posture in which the width of the island, terrain, and number of combat divisions available would limit it to a troop ratio, or density, along its front that was not only less than that achieved at Okinawa, but also less than the painful struggle up Italy's Apennine Mountains or, later, during either the mobile or stalemate phases in Korea.

Provisions existed within the Downfall strategic plan to siphon off "elements earmarked for CORONET . . . at the rate of three (3) divisions per month," with no stated cap, for Olympic, but this was only if the timely establishment of the staging area for offensive operations against the Tokyo area was at risk. There was no thought to make them available to simply expand the Sixth Army's hold beyond the south no matter what might have been brewing beyond artillery range.[16] Likewise, the original Ketsu-Go plan, which allowed for two divisions on Honshu to be sent to Kyushu if called upon,[17] was eventually expanded to as many as five from throughout the Fifteenth Area Army's zone.[18] There was even a move afoot by some unspecified officers within IGHQ to sell the idea that the Thirty-Sixth Army be sent to Kyushu.

Unlike the other Imperial "armies," which were generally equivalent in size to an American corps, the Thirty-Sixth was what one might call a "robust" organization.[19] Originally activated as a typical, three-division army at the time of the Marianas invasion for the defense of the Tokyo area, it was beefed up and became the mobile reserve of the Twelfth Area Army under Ketsu-Go No. 3.[20] Advocates for its movement south from the Kanto Plain argued that even if it was impractical to send the army immediately to Kyushu, it should be sent below the rail bottlenecks most easily blocked by American air power so that the Thirty-Sixth's two armored and six infantry divisions could be positioned along the principal road-rail system stretching from Kyoto through Hiroshima in order to facilitate easy access to the railroad tunnels running under the Kanmon Strait and innumerable small ports, coves, and inlets. From these sites, wooden craft, largely immune to the variety of U.S. mines used in Operation Starvation, could easily ferry men and supplies across the strait in the dead of night if the Thirty-Sixth Army was ordered to Kyushu.[21]

This plan does not appear to have been taken seriously as it receives no mention in either the *Reports of General MacArthur* volume compiled from Japanese Demobilization Bureau records or the "Homeland Operations Record" in either its early separate volumes produced by the First and Second General Army staffs and General Defense Command or the combined, revised edition. The complex and very time-consuming move was never authorized even though some senior staff officers strongly advocated the change, nor was the shifting of a portion of the Thirty-Sixth's divisions. Colonel Hattori Takushiro, who headed the Operations Section of IGHQ's Army Section, later told Alvin Coox of the U.S. Eighth Army's Japanese Research Division that the plan to move divisions out of the Tokyo area had been formulated because "IGHQ deemed it imperative to inflict a staggering blow against at least the first wave of elite enemy invaders. . . . Hence victory on Kyushu must be sought at any cost."[22]

Coox, however, displayed skepticism that agreement within IGHQ attained such unanimity, and Richard B. Frank's examination of officer interviews conducted immediately after the war brings to light that there was, in fact, opposition within Hattori's former staff (Hattori had been given command of a regiment during the Army's massive expansion and reorganization).[23] Moving the Thirty-Sixth Army would not only undercut Tokyo's defenses but also severely disrupt rail transportation at the precise time that the principal focus of the build-up was scheduled to shift from Ketsu-Go No. 6 to Ketsu-Go No. 3 on the Kanto Plain. Imperial Headquarters' ultimate response to the proposal was to delay any decision until it was too late to implement the move rather than just say no.[24] The crux of the matter was that even though the proponents' arguments made strategic sense, such a massive rail movement—forced into a compressed period of time—could not be hidden from U.S. aerial reconnaissance now operating with distressing regularity out of Okinawa. Thus the large-scale shifting of men and equipment hundreds of miles away from the Kanto Plain and Imperial capital could well prompt the American's own shift of offensive operations to that very area.

The proposal to fundamentally change the deployment of forces within Ketsu-Go is mentioned here because even though it was neither implemented nor accepted in principal, it is sometimes held up as an example of the Japanese government's stated intent to stake everything in the initial American invasion on the Home Islands. In this regard some historians have fallen just as prey to the militarist's call for "*a* decisive battle" on Kyushu as the targets of their exhortations in 1945, not realizing that this is not the same thing as "*the* decisive battle." To the Japanese the term "decisive battle" doesn't necessarily imply the finality that it does to a Westerner. A decisive battle *may* decide the course of a war, but it is most specifically decisive in terms of a campaign. This is why the four Sho operations, such as Sho-Go No. 2 for the region including Okinawa, and Sho-Go No. 1 covering the Philippines (and for that matter, even the earlier fighting on Guadalcanal) were all referred to as decisive battle*s*, plural.[25] Likewise, the expected initial U.S. invasion operation was specifically characterized as "the first decisive battle in KYUSHU to establish a foundation for a victorious battle" at Kanto.[26]

The proposal to move the Thirty-Sixth Army is also emblematic of the same divided opinion within the Japanese military that enabled the Sixteenth Area Army on Kyushu to settle upon forming a redoubt in the north *well before* it had a chance to discover firsthand that division-sized Banzai charges into the face of American artillery and naval guns were less than productive. The loathing among some within IGHQ over the willingness within the chain of command to allow such a "defeatist" defensive strategy was palpable long after the war.[27] But in fact the planning and construction of redoubts to carry on the war into 1947 was first authorized in 1944 by no less than Army Minister Sugiyama Hajime who would later be named field marshal to command the First General Army (army group) protecting Tokyo and all of northeastern Japan. The series of massive underground complexes within three mountains near Matsushiro in Honshu's Nagano Prefecture was to serve as a refuge for the Emperor, and center for both the government and IGHQ's headquarters in the event of an invasion of Honshu.[28] In addition, the area was also to serve as a staging base for troops flowing toward the Kanto Plain from other parts of Japan and as a center for guerrilla activities.[29]

Across the Sea of Japan, the growing threat of Soviet invasion and movement of the last high-quality divisions to Japan necessitated that yet another redoubt be formed. After the dismantling of the once-powerful Kwantung Army, it was rebuilt principally with newly mobilized units that were not only unable to fulfill the Kwantung's previous offensive mission, but would clearly court disaster if they attempted to hold Manchuria's far-flung frontiers. Consequently their new mission called for units along the periphery to conduct delaying actions as they and forces in the interior withdrew into a mountain redoubt straddling the Korea-Manchuria border and centered on Tunghua.[30] Thus it was planned that in the event of a Soviet invasion, most of Manchuria would pass into Soviet hands as the Red Army laboriously struggled, vulnerable to local counterattacks, through the wicked terrain, only to find that the main Kwantung Army massed along the eastern flank of the road and rail net leading to the strategic Dairen Peninsula and Port Arthur.

Viewed within the context of the Nagano and Tunghua redoubts, General Yokoyama's plans for one manned by the Sixteenth Area Army at Mt. Aso were not at all contrary to the thinking of the military leaders who were in positions of ultimate authority, and there was no chance of undermining Yokoyama, or the plans of his Fortieth Army commander on the Satsuma Peninsula, at an intermediate headquarters either. The Sixteenth on Kyushu, like all other formations in southwestern Japan, was under the command of Field Marshal Hata Shunroku's Second General Army at nearby Hiroshima, and although some eighty officers and other headquarters personnel of Hata's staff died during the atomic attack along with the 59th Army commander and staff, the Central Military District commander and staff, and most of the newly formed 224th Division (Hata was in Tokyo), surviving Second General Army officers recounted the strongly held divergent opinions in the "Homeland Operations Record":

> There were two schools of thought regarding the conduct of the defense of the Second General Army's zone of responsibility. One group of the staff felt strongly that the best method would be to fight delaying actions which would husband the strength and resources of the Japanese and would, at the same time, be costly to the enemy. . . . The other school of thought insisted that there was no alternative to a drastic initial action with the objective of crushing any invasion attempt at a single blow. This group held that a defense based on an attempt to balance Japanese strength with that of the enemy (i.e. a holding or delaying operation which attempted to weaken the enemy by gradual attrition) would be fatal to the defense of Japan. Such a defense, they claimed, would enable the enemy to establish bases and accomplish a build-up of manpower and material in southern Kyushu or Shikoku.
>
> The final decision was in the nature of a compromise. Every effort would be made to build up troop strength and defenses to permit aggressive action in the earliest stages of the invasion, but the final decision as to the type of defense to be conducted would not be made until the time of the actual attack. Certain areas where landings might logically be anticipated, such as southern Kyushu and southern shore of Shikoku, would be prepared for positive and aggressive action immediately. . . . All other sections of the Second General Army's coast line would be prepared to conduct delaying actions until sufficient strength could be built up to permit changing to the offensive. Delaying actions, it was emphasized, would be strong and continuous.[31]

The Second General Army's decision to allow its formations considerable flexibility in the conduct of the defense may not have been seen as much of a compromise by those advocating strict adherence to the offensive precepts of Ketsu-Go. This having been said, however, it must be noted that Hata pressed repeatedly, if unsuccessfully, for any divisions he could get from the reserve at Kanto,[32] but the Japanese leadership was just as loath as MacArthur's headquarters to allow the fighting in Kyushu to siphon men and material away from what both sides believed would likely be the climactic battles around Tokyo. Once battle was joined, the U.S. Sixth Army and Imperial Sixteenth Area Army would quickly become orphans, left to fight it out largely with the units already on hand. And this would only change if higher headquarters in either Manila or Hiroshima perceived that the U.S. complex of staging areas in the south, or alternately, the island's rich resources in the north, were at risk.

One significant by-product of the Japanese decision to stick doggedly to the regional priorities of Ketsu-Go as well as their decentralized command and mobilization schemes (see chapter 7) was that they rendered the U.S. strategic, and even operational, deception plans for Olympic largely irrelevant.[33] Code named Pastel, they were patterned after the very successful Bodyguard operations conducted against the Nazis before, and even well after, the Normandy invasion. Through a series of ruses, disinformation, and feints, very substantial German forces were held in check far from France, in Norway and the Balkans, and a well-equipped army north of the invasion area was kept out of the fight until it was too late to intervene effectively.[34]

Deceptions of this type proved to be particularly useful in Europe, with its extensive road and rail nets, but were ineffective against the Japanese at this point in the war. Pastel's planners assumed a strategic mobility that the Japanese no longer possessed for higher formations—divisions and the corps-sized Imperial armies—and were made even less effective by the U.S. air campaign against the Home Islands, which would have essentially frozen those formations into place. Distant movements could only be conducted division by division, in a dispersed manner, and only at a pace that a soldier's own feet could carry him.[35] The Japanese themselves had realized that this would occur and successfully completed major troop movements to Kyushu early in the year (see chapter 3). Moreover, their system of defense call-up and training during 1945 was reoriented toward raising, training, and fielding combat divisions regionally in order to minimize lengthy overland movements.[36] With major population centers on Kyushu and elsewhere within easy marching distance of threatened areas, Imperial forces could actually achieve a high degree of success in this effort.

Interestingly, the effectiveness of the U.S. naval blockade also rendered the Pastel deception operations targeting Formosa and the Shanghai area unnecessary as Japanese shipping could no longer transit the East China Sea to reinforce the Home Islands. In addition the extensive American efforts to play on Japanese fear of airborne operations also were of no avail. Although the Japanese took the threat seriously, even without Pastel, the IGHQ decision to use positional forces in rear areas and People's Volunteer Corps to confirm and contain American paratroopers meant that the dispositions of ground forces would be unaffected unless Airborne operations actually occurred, and MacArthur had no plans to effect such operations.[37]

★　★　★

Whether the U.S. Sixth Army fought its way to a line running generally northeast from Akune to Nobeoka or opted for a shorter front, still starting below Akune but running more easterly through Mt. Omori to the original east coast objective of Tsuno, at some point it would come to a stop. But not the war on Kyushu. After a pause, a sort of collective breather by both sides, Japanese forces, irrespective of earlier losses in the island's south, would be able to go on the tactical offensive. The Sixth Army's preponderance of artillery and air power would have only a limited ability to offset its thin ground force's numerical disadvantage against a foe operating on his home ground and who would only grow more numerous over time. And while there has long been a great deal of fascination in, and focus on, Japan's schemes for a plethora of suicide weapons, the real danger in the type of tactical setting faced on Kyushu would come from a comparatively small number of well-armed regulars directing and supporting a willing population armed with spears, swords, and cheaply produced firearms.[38]

Attainment of a line in the mountains, far enough removed from the staging areas to ensure their relative security from artillery fire and ground attack, would mark the Sixth Army's transition from the strategic offensive-tactical offensive to the strategic offensive-tactical defensive, a setting in which even the badly mauled Japanese forces would have a much greater ability to call the shots. The Imperial Sixteenth Area Army would be able to draw on the labor and cannon fodder of the People's Volunteer Corps for support in hill fighting that had far less in common with the recent struggle in the mountains of central Italy than that of Korea. Terms such as "MLR," for main line of resistance, and "outpost line," which would become a part of the Korean War lexicon in 1952, might well have been introduced to the American public in 1946 because Krueger's Sixth Army would not simply hunker down in a purely defensive mode.

A series of heavily fortified outposts, built for all-around defense, would be established one to three miles forward of the MLR but well within the range of divisional and corps artillery. Depending on the terrain and accessibility to the MLR, they would be manned by anything from a platoon to a company, and be the jump-off points for the aggressive patrolling that was expected to capture prisoners, determine Japanese dispositions, and help blunt attacks on the main line.

It was also a certainty that small teams of Alamo Scouts would work their way forward in stages during the dead of night or be quietly landed far up the coasts to maneuver into positions from which they could monitor Japanese movement along the scattering of trails and roads that zigzagged through the great mass of the Kyushu Mountains forward of the American lines. Missions of this type would involve infiltrations much farther inland than the Alamo Scouts' usual practice of taking prisoners near the coast for intelligence purposes after being landed by PT boat or submarine.[39] And as with South Korean infiltration teams in the days before the deep helicopter insertions and extractions of the Vietnam War, these intelligence efforts could realistically be described as suicide missions.

As for the Japanese, specially trained Izumi (Spring) Military Intelligence personnel were formed to conduct similar operations as "stay behind" agents after the invasion, while still others had earlier formed the Kirishima unit at Nichinan in the Miyazaki Prefecture in January 1945 to organize and train guerrilla bands for activities behind U.S. lines. (One particularly challenging aspect of these agents' training was countering the deeply ingrained tradition of performing ritual *hara kiri*, or engaging in suicidal combat when apparently defeated, with the idea that it was their duty to survive and continue fighting.)[40] A second Kirishima Unit was ordered established in the Mt. Aso area in June.[41] In addition whole units of the People's Volunteer Corps, and even some of the most recently mobilized Army formations, were issued no rifles whatsoever, and although the situation was not as dire within the Kestsu-Go No. 3 and No. 6 areas, rifles were distributed sparingly even in southern Kyushu. As noted earlier, this did not duly alarm the regular officers who would train and lead its units even though there were only 2,468,665 rifles and 186,680 automatic weapons available in the Home Islands to turn over to U.S. military government authorities at the close of hostilities.[42]

The apparent lack of concern among Japanese commanders in the summer of 1945, when it became clear that the Americans would not strike Kyushu immediately after their Okinawa victory, was derived from their understanding that an invasion of southern Kyushu could now not take place until the fall, and an assault on the Tokyo area itself would not likely begin for a full nine or ten months. In the meantime, rifles and automatic weapons of adequate quality could be manufactured very easily in small, decentralized armories As an example, production was already flying on the simple Type 89 grenade launcher—really a personal mortar—in the summer of 1945 because it had become apparent that the weapon, nicknamed "knee mortar," had been responsible for a high percentage of the American casualties on Iwo Jima and Okinawa. Some 28,428 were available at wars' end, and production of their ballistic grenades had far surpassed individual weapons needs as 51 million, or 1,794 per barrel, were turned over to the Americans.[43]

Imperial officers at all levels of command were also very comfortable with the idea of hand-to-hand combat. Those assigned to the People's Volunteer Corps would not have been timid about using civilians in whatever fashion best suited tactical needs and well understood that there was a great deal of utility in less sophisticated weapons such as swords and spears in the close-in hill fighting generated by Japanese forces infiltrating thinly held, comparatively isolated Sixth Army positions at night.

Like the Indians in the American West and the Moros in the Philippines, the Japanese on Kyushu could not actually hope to "win" against U.S. forces (a Japanese win in this campaign being defined as their preventing the U.S. lodgment from properly supporting the critically important operations around Tokyo). But until the war came to a close, the Japanese Sixteenth Area Army would have the ability to inflict casualties more or less at will—up to the time that they received orders to cease—in much the same way that the Chinese Communists did for the last twenty months of the Korean War. U.S. planners assumed that American forces would achieve victory in the Tokyo area by the end of 1946, although some thought the war could drag into 1947, and meanwhile the U.S. Sixth Army, outnumbered and limited to fighting a defensive campaign in the mountains, would just have to persevere in fighting that had more in common with the trench warfare of their fathers than what they had experienced in New Guinea and the Philippines.

Would Japan's poorly trained and ill-equipped citizen soldiers have been up to the task ahead of them? Arens writes:

> At Iwo Jima the 22,000 defenders were a hodgepodge of airmen, unhappy sailors serving as infantrymen, and ill-trained, "second string" Army units. After his first inspection of the island's defenses and the men who would man them, General Kuribayashi [Tadamichi], the Commanding General, told his aide, "These are no soldiers, just poor recruits who don't know anything. Their officers are superannuated fools. We cannot fight the Americans with them." But fight they did, going up against the Third, Fourth, and Fifth Marine Divisions and inflicting more casualties than they received.[44]

CHAPTER 15

A "Target-Rich Environment"

The Japs are asking for an invasion, and they are going to get it. Japan will eventually be a nation without cities—a nomadic people.

—VICE ADM. ARTHUR RADFORD, August 4, 1945[1]

The shattering of the hundred million like a beautiful jewel.

—A common expression of *ichioku gyokusa* (die together gloriously as a nation) in 1945[2]

The limited and cautiously optimistic assessments of Olympic's prospects during May and June 1945 were severely complicated by the intelligence estimates at July's end, and the situation was even more dangerous than was perceived at that time. War plans called for the initial landings on the Home Islands to be conducted approximately 90 days hence. But as we shall see, the invasion of Kyushu would actually have not been able to take place for anywhere from 120 to 135 days—a potentially disastrous occurrence for the successful outcome of stated U.S. war aims.

Beyond the fact that the Imperial Army was in somewhat better shape than is commonly understood today, and that the Japanese had correctly deduced the landing beaches and even the approximate times of both invasion operations, a variety of tactical matters are worth considering. For example, although the Japanese had never perfected central control and massed fire of their artillery,[3] this fact would be largely irrelevant to the type of defense that was being organized on Kyushu. The months that the Imperial Sixteenth Area Army had to wait for the American landings were not going to be spent with its soldiers and the

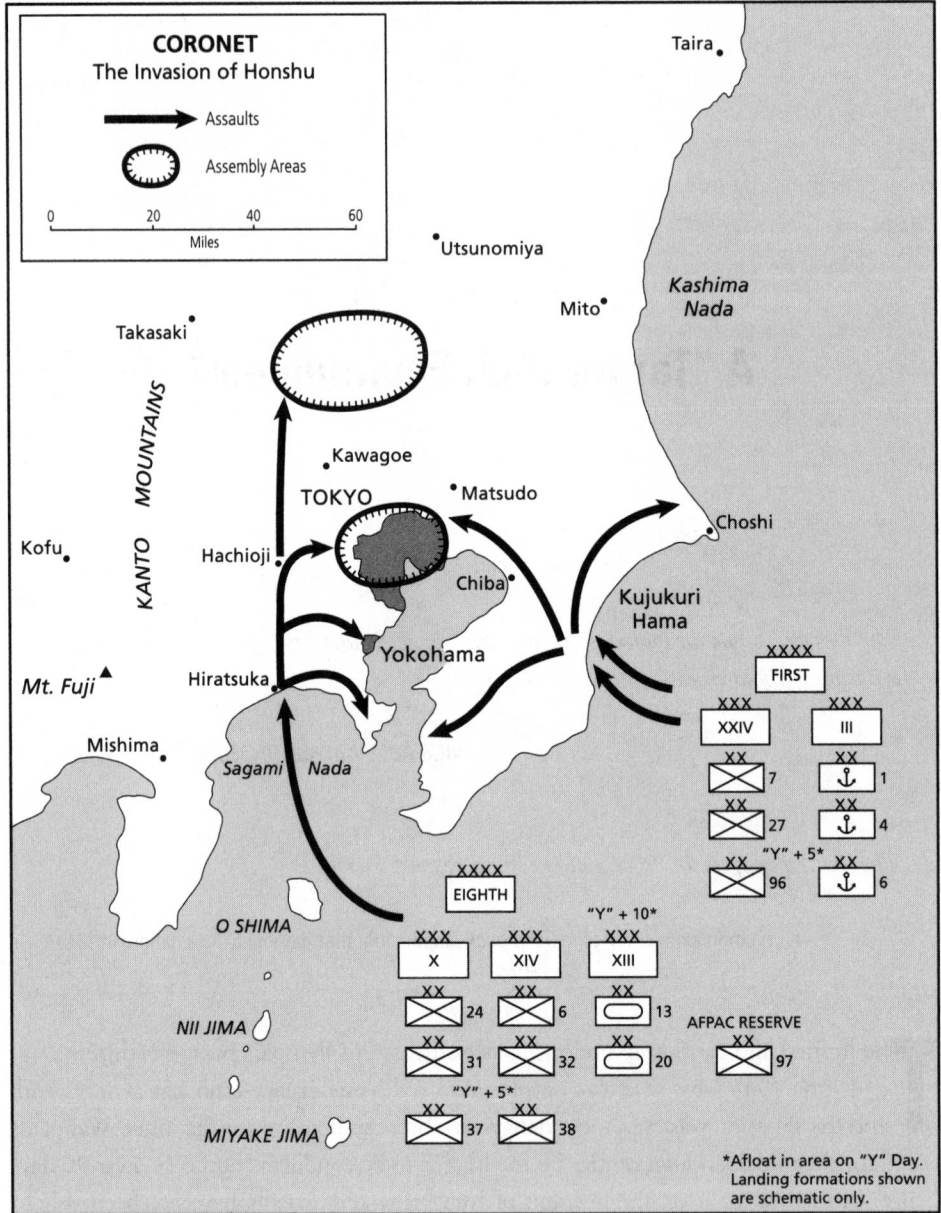

The assault plan for Operation Coronet.

island's massive civilian population sitting idly, and their ability to dig in and preregister their artillery cannot be casually dismissed.

To borrow a phrase from a later Asian war, each Kyushu invasion area was going to be a "target-rich environment" where artillery was going to methodically do its work on a large number of soldiers and Marines whose luck had run out. On Okinawa the U.S. Tenth Army commander was killed by artillery fire when the campaign was ostensibly in the mopping-up phase, and from World War I to the 1995 fighting in Grosny, where shells killed a Russian two-star general,[4] there is ample evidence of artillery living up to its deadly reputation.

It has also been stated that U.S. ground troops didn't really need to worry about Japanese cave defenses since combat experience in the Pacific, and tests run in the U.S., proved the effectiveness of self-propelled 8-inch and 155-mm howitzer against caves and bunkers as well as their vulnerability to direct fire from tanks.[5] That the Japanese were also well aware of this and were arranging defensive positions accordingly from lessons learned on Okinawa and the Philippines was not a fact that was treated lightly in the Pacific as the Japanese had repeatedly demonstrated that they could, with the right terrain, construct strongpoints, such as Item Pocket on Okinawa, which could not be bypassed and had to be reduced without benefit of *any* direct-fire weapons since no tanks—let alone lumbering self-propelled guns—could work their way in for an appropriate shot.[6] Indeed, an I Corps intelligence officer who examined the terrain after the war found that the extensive rice fields "are held in by many stone terraces ranging in height from four to six feet [thus] precluding the off road movement by any type of military vehicle."[7]

Similarly, on the Japanese ability to defend against U.S. tanks, Army and Marine armor veterans of the Pacific war would be amazed to learn from some historians that they had little to fear during the invasion. After all, Japan's obsolescent 47-mm antitank guns supposedly "could penetrate the M-4 Sherman's armor only in vulnerable spots at very close range" and their older 37-mm gun was said to be completely ineffective against the Sherman tank.[8] In fact, the Japanese, through hard experience, had become quite adept at tank killing. During two actions in particular on Okinawa, they managed to knock out twenty-two and thirty Shermans respectively. In one of these fights, Fujio Takeda managed to stop four tanks with six four-hundred-yard shots from his supposedly worthless 47-mm gun.[9] As for the 37-mm gun, its use would depend on the terrain. Along likely axes of attack in valleys containing extensive rice fields, they would be positioned to fire into the highly vulnerable bellies of tanks rearing up high in the air as they began to cross the rice paddy dikes. In areas with irregular ground and vegetation, their fire would not be intended to actually destroy tanks but to immobilize them by blasting at tracks and wheels at very short ranges so that the tanks would become easier prey for the infantry suicide teams that had proven so effective on Okinawa.

Points like these and the overconfidence of later historians in the ability of naval gunfire to pulverize Japanese defenses may appear rather nitpicky, but they assume great importance when it is realized that the November 1, 1945, target date for the invasion of Kyushu was going to get pushed back as much as forty-five days, giving the Japanese perhaps four and a half months from the flashing red light of General Willoughby's July 29 intelligence estimate to prepare their defenses.

★   ★   ★

The Joint Chiefs originally set the date for the invasion of Kyushu, Operation Olympic, as X-day, December 1, 1945, and for Honshu, Operation Coronet, as Y-day, March 1, 1946. To lessen casualties and the chance of a stalemate, the launch of Coronet would await the

Japanese illustration of a "flanking gun emplacement" overlooking Sagami Bay south of Tokyo. This is one of the earlier coastal artillery positions, built into the cliffs much like similar emplacements built into the British fortress at Gibraltar. Later portals were left rough, to both conserve concrete and lessen their visibility. Tunnels were also angled to give better protection from the direct fire of naval guns. (Wartime painting by Junkichi Mukai, U.S. Army)

arrival of two armored divisions from Europe. Attached to the Eighth Army, their mission was to sweep up Honshu's Kanto Plain from the southernmost beachhead at Sagami Bay and cut off Tokyo before the seasonal spring rains, followed by the summer monsoons, turned it into vast pools of rice, muck, and water crisscrossed by elevated roads and dominated by rugged, well-defended foothills. East of Tokyo lay two more invasion sites assigned to the First Army, beaches at Kujukuri and, to the north, Kashima, which would not be assaulted from the sea but be used as a principal landing area for follow-on forces after the area was secured by U.S. forces.

Long before the British experienced the tragedy of trying to push XXX Corps' 50,000 men up a single road through the Dutch lowlands to Arnhem, an event popularized through the book and movie *A Bridge Too Far*, U.S. planners were well aware of the costs that would be incurred if the Kanto Plain was not secured for mobile warfare and airfield construction prior to the wet season.[10] Intensive hydrological and weather studies begun as early as 1943 made it clear that an invasion in early March 1946 offered the best mix of weather conditions for amphibious, mechanized ground, and tactical air operations, with the difficulty of obtaining objectives becoming more acute as the months progressed.[11]

Weather in the Kanto Plain is always unpredictable that time of the year. Indeed, the Tokyo area after the war experienced "sub-Arctic" conditions on the original March 1, 1946, invasion date, and the beginning of several days of snowfall.[12] March, as the "transitional period between the dry winter months and wet summer months," could well be "very dry or very wet," was thought not likely to present serious obstacles to tactical operations.[13] April was a question mark—literally. In a staff study widely disseminated by MacArthur's Intelligence Section, a very conspicuous question mark occupied one, and only one, of the 492 slots on the table-filled fold-out containing weather data.[14] Under the category "Rice Fields Flooded," Willoughby's meteorological and geographical specialists refused to hazard either a yes or no answer as the extremely well documented history of April weather in the Tokyo region demonstrated that there was too much seasonal variation in rainfall to accurately predict the condition of the rice fields.

Thus, with good luck, tolerably free movement across the Kanto Plain *might* be possible well into April. Unfortunately this assumed that the snow run-off from the mountains would not be too severe and that even during a "dry" March the Japanese would not flood the fields while waiting for the weather to lend its divine assistance sometime in April. Although subsequent postwar prisoner interrogations did not reveal any plans to systematically deluge low-lying areas, a quick thrust up the Kanto Plain would not have been as speedy as Army planners desired.

First, none of the vehicle bridges on the Kanto Plain (and there were more than five thousand in the Tokyo area alone) were capable of taking vehicles weighing over twelve tons.[15] Every tank, every self-propelled gun, and prime mover would have to cross structures specifically erected for the event. Next, logistical considerations and the sequence of follow-up units would require that armored divisions not even land until Y+10.[16] This would provide time for the defenders to observe that the U.S. infantry's generic tank support was severely hampered by already flooded rice fields or drained fields (which are almost never truly dry) and, shall we say, *suggest* ways to make things worse for the invaders.

The danger was recognized by MacArthur's intelligence shop, which carefully outlined for commanders and their staffs the areas most susceptible to defensive flooding while leavening their analyses with hopeful observations that the gooey belts at some locations were "narrow, mostly 100 to 200 yards wide" and "very narrow, from 50 to 300 yards wide." Other areas that defied an upbeat assessment would be simply described along the lines of "a 5-to 6-mile belt of large rice fields." The soldiers reading the intelligence group's study needed no elaboration of the terrain's tactical significance to understand the statement: "During late spring, summer, and early fall, movement is, in general, restricted to roads, dikes, and embankments by floods and wet rice fields."[17] Likewise the full-color chart "Effect of Rice Land, Natural, and Artificial Flooding on Cross-Country Movement" from the same document (simplified for clarity on page 173), was also guaranteed to have made chills run up the back of any soldier looking at it.[18]

The principal effect of these materials was to reinforce, in clear, unambiguous terms, that the Kanto Plain must be seized by Y+45, or better yet, by as close to Y+30 as possible. A late start or loss of momentum on Honshu would leave American forces to fight their way up flood plains that were only dry during certain times of the year, but could be suddenly

Even when rice paddies are as ostensibly "dry" as this still very wet one is, they present formidable barriers, and the sodden nature of most dikes and paddy floors do not lend themselves to the effective operation of devices such as the hedgerow cutters used in Normandy. The paddies would have to be taken in a tedious, set-piece manner, and the armored divisions fighting up the main road north past Tokyo would find themselves limited to a one-tank front, as happened to British XXX Corps, when it was delayed reaching Arnhem by minimal German forces in the Dutch lowlands. (Major John L. Aratan, courtesy *Marine Corps Gazette*)

Some rice fields stretched almost unbroken for dozens of miles up Kyushu's valleys, rendering them impassable to vehicles of any kind. On the Kanto Plain, repeated, irregular bands of the fields were seldom less than the length of a football field across and could be as much as half a dozen miles deep. Extreme care would have to be taken to ensure that American units did not blunder their way into se-ductively dry stretches of terrain that could well be kill zones, and commanders at all levels would have to battle trench foot among the troops as diligently as they did the Japanese. (U.S. Army)

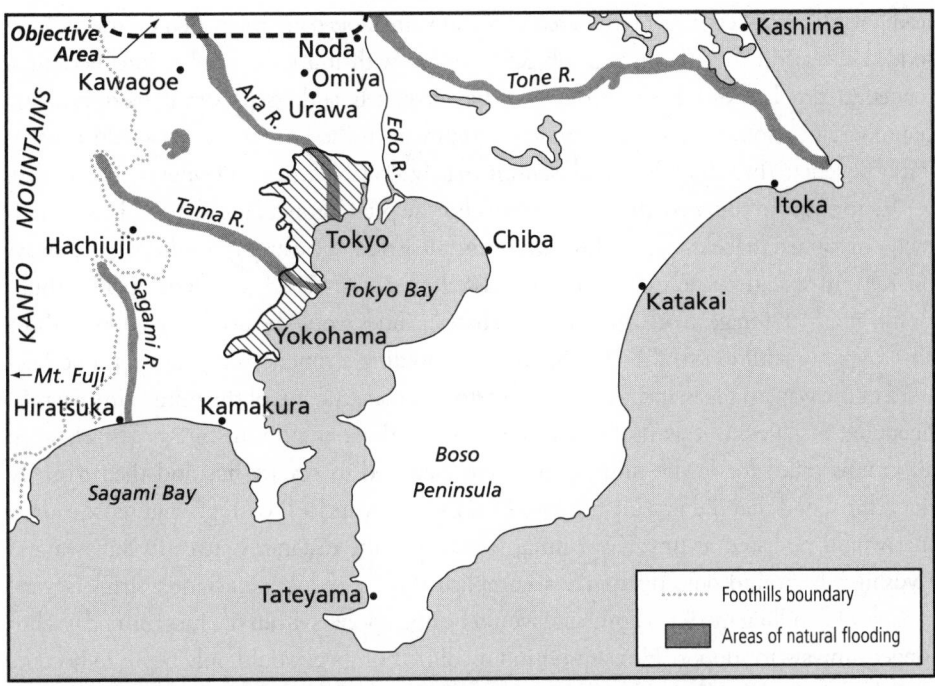

Maps derived from "Staff Study Operations, CORONET," General Headquarters, AFPAC,
August 15, 1945, Enclosure 5, "Effect of Rice Land, Natural, and Artificial Flooding on Cross-Country Movement."

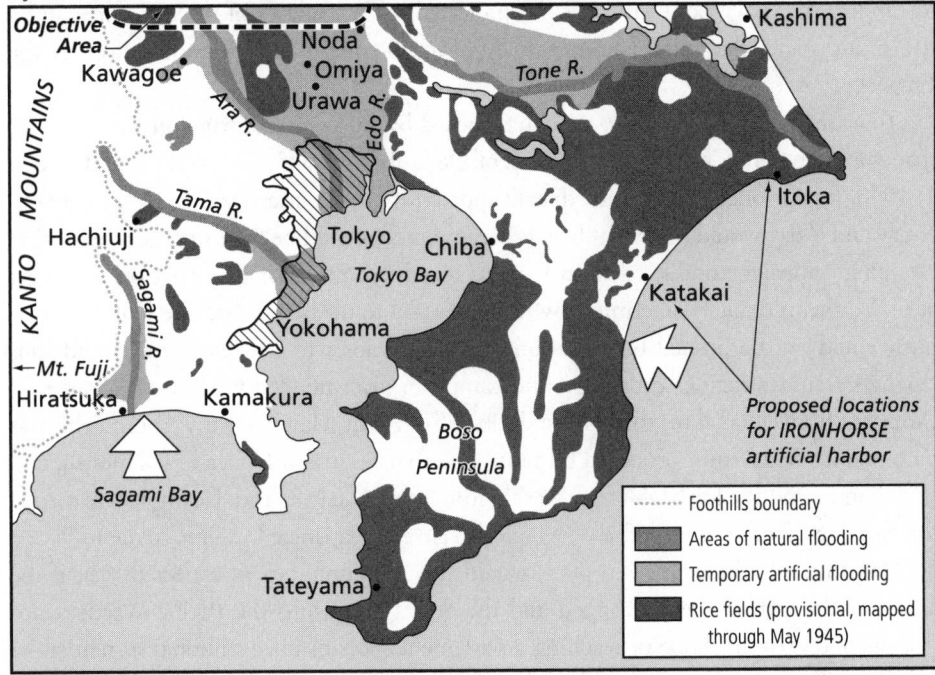

Effect of rice land, natural, and artificial flooding on cross-country movement on the Kanto Plain.

inundated by the Japanese. If the timetable slipped for either Olympic or Coronet, American soldiers and Marines on Honshu would risk fighting in terrain similar to that later encountered in Vietnam—minus the helicopters to fly over the mess—where all movement was readily visible from even low terrain features and vulnerable convoys moved on roads above sodden rice paddies.[19] This was a subject pregnant with immense implications because a maneuver problem of this scale could not be adequately addressed even if every bridging pontoon and associated piece of engineer equipment in the U.S. inventory could miraculously be sent to the Kanto Plain and be immediately available when and where it was needed.

Factoring into this were the requirements for the pre-Coronet air offensive. It was originally envisioned that eleven airfields with twenty-five new or heavily reconditioned runways on Kyushu would be necessary for the massed air power slated to soften up Honshu.[20] Bomb and fuel storage, roads, wharves, and base facilities would be needed to support those air groups, in addition to the U.S. Sixth Army holding a ninety-mile-long stop line one-third of the way up the island. All plans centered on construction of the minimum essential operating facilities. But as outlined in chapter 13, those minimums grew. The eighteen air groups called for in the initial plans were increased to twenty-five and then to more than thirty, and that did not include two P-47D groups and a P-61 night fighter squadron that would be based at tiny Kikai Jima, which split the distance between Okinawa and Kyushu.[21] If ground objectives were accomplished on schedule, ten fighter strips (several capable of handling medium bombers) would be operational within the first thirty days, but longer runways to support Honshu-bound medium bombers would only begin to become available a month and a half into the operation. Most of the runways and infrastructure to support the heavy bombers were not projected to be ready until three to three and a half months after the initial landings on Kyushu, in spite of an enormous effort by the Engineers.[22]

The constraints on the air campaign imposed by the base construction were so clear that when the Joint Chiefs set target dates of December 1, 1945, for Olympic and March 1, 1946, for Coronet, it was immediately apparent that the three-month period between X-day and Y-day would not be sufficient because there would be little time for the tactical bombing campaign conducted from Kyushu to achieve the desired impact on the target area. Weather ultimately determined which operation to reschedule because Coronet obviously could not be pushed back without moving it closer to the rainy season and thus risking serious restrictions on the ground campaign from flooded fields as well as the air campaign from cloud cover that almost doubles from early March to early April.[23] This was a no-brainer. MacArthur proposed bumping the Kyushu invasion ahead by a month, and both Nimitz and the Joint Chiefs in Washington immediately agreed. Olympic was moved forward one month to November 1, which also gave the Japanese less time to dig in.[24]

Unfortunately these best-laid plans would not have unfolded as expected even if the atom bombs had not been dropped and the Soviet entry into the Pacific War had not frustrated Tokyo's last hope of reaching a settlement short of unconditional surrender—a Versailles-like outcome unacceptable to Truman and his contemporaries because it was seen as an incomplete victory that could well require the next generation to refight the war. Olympic could not be carried out on November 1, 1945, or any time at all that month, and the end result of a delay in assaulting Kyushu would have been even more costly campaigns on both Kyushu and Honshu than were predicted. This would have been precipitated by something that the defenders could likely not achieve on their own but a low pressure trough sitting along the Asian littoral would—knock the delicate U.S. timetable completely off balance.

★   ★   ★

The divine wind, or kamikaze, of a powerful typhoon destroyed a foreign invasion fleet off Japan in 1274 and again in 1281. It was for these storms that Japanese suicide missions were named.[25] On October 9, 1945, a similar typhoon named Louise, packing 140-mile-per-hour winds, struck the U.S. staging area on Okinawa, which would have been expanded to capacity by that time if the war had not ended in August yet was still crammed with aircraft and assault shipping. There was enough time to fly most aircraft out of harm's way to bases on Luzon, but 12 ships were sunk, 222 grounded, and 32 very heavily damaged as eighty-three men were lost and more than one hundred severely injured. Fully four-fifths of all the military structures on Okinawa were destroyed or rendered unusable with vast amounts of the carefully assembled war stocks suffering the same fate. U.S. analysts at the scene matter-of-factly reported that the storm would have caused up to a forty-five-day delay in the invasion of Kyushu.[26]

The point that goes begging, however, is that while these postwar reports from the Pacific were correct in themselves, they understandably stayed within the purview of their authors' orders or responsibility and did not make note of the critical significance of such a delay if the war had continued. Simply stated, a forty-five-day postponement would have entailed launching Olympic well past the initial, and unacceptable, target date of December 1, retarding the completion of base construction on Kyushu and, consequently, forcing the Honshu invasion to be pushed back as far as mid-April 1946.

If there had been no atom bombs and Tokyo had attempted to hold out for an extended time (a possibility that even bombing and blockade advocates in Washington granted), the Japanese would have immediately appreciated the impact of the storm in the waters around Okinawa. Moreover, they would know exactly what it meant for the follow-up invasion of Honshu, which they had predicted as accurately as the invasion of Kyushu. But even with the storm delay plus friction of combat on Kyushu, the Coronet schedule would have propelled U.S. engineers to perform virtual miracles to make up for lost time and implement Y-day as early in April as possible. Unfortunately the divine winds packed a one-two punch.

From March 27 to April 7, 1946, yet another typhoon raged in the Pacific. On April 3 Barbara struck Luzon, where it inflicted only moderate damage—ripping roofs off of Base M warehouses at Lingayen Gulf, grounding an Army tugboat, and sinking a ship in Manila Bay, where waves briefly reached an unusual thirty-five feet in the harbor—before pounding toward Taiwan. Coming more than six months after the war, it was of no particular concern. The *Los Angeles Times* gave it several short paragraphs on the bottom of page 2 and didn't even mention the storm's name.[27] But if Japan had held out, this typhoon would have had profound effects on the world we live in today.

Barbara would have been the closest-watched weather cell in history. If the delayed invasion of Honshu was not already in the process of being launched, the typhoon's long, lumbering approach to the Philippines would allow First and Eighth Army soldiers (many of whom would have lived in tents instead of barracks because it was expected that they would have moved north a month earlier) to make the best preparations they could under the circumstances. Ships and craft that could not be sent south would be secured and likely ride out the storm with minimal losses. However, if Coronet was in the midst of its execution from the twenty-five-day window Y-15 to Y+10, chaos would ensue because the storm's track and intensity could only be guessed at within the parameters of the limited data available.

Would slow, shallow-draft landing craft be caught at sea or in the Philippines, where loading operations would be put on hold? If they were already on their way to Japan, how many would be able to reach the Koshiki Retto anchorage and Kyushu's sheltered bays or get back to Luzon? And what about the breakwater caissons for Ironhorse, the massive artificial harbor to be assembled east of Tokyo? The 1945 construction of the harbor's prefabricated components carried a priority second only to the atom bomb, and the first packages of this precious towed cargo would have begun arriving in the western Pacific at this time. They could not be allowed to fall victim to this and other seasonal storms and be scattered across the Philippine Sea.

Whatever stage of deployment U.S. forces were in during those first days of April, a delay of some sort—certainly no less than a week and perhaps much, much more—was going to occur. A delay that the two U.S. field armies invading Honshu could ill afford and that Japanese militarists would see as yet another sign that they were right after all. And while much of the land around Tokyo today contains built-up areas not there during the war and deceptively smooth terrain, thanks to the delays over which the United States had absolutely no control, any soldier or Marine treading this same flat, dry "tank country" in 1946 would, in reality, have been up to their calves in muck and rice shoots by the time the invasion actually took place.

★   ★   ★

Maintenance of the initial two American field armies in central Houshu would require that a minimum of 40,000 long tons of supplies arrive and be processed each and every day to support an initial 1,069,000 ground and air personnel, with far more men on the way.[28] Naval planners originally assumed that early access could be obtained to the sheltered waters of Tokyo Bay and that Yokohama's extensive port facilities, which were likely to be at least partially demolished, could be rehabilitated quickly thanks to lessons learned in the European and Mediterranean theaters. What the Navy discovered upon entering Manila's harbor in January 1945 quickly disabused them of this notion.

The Salvage and Rescue Group, Luzon Attack Force, found that the Japanese had done "a thoroughly professional job blocking [Manila] harbor and rendering the port useless" through the sinking of "an estimated 750 ships, barges, and assorted craft." This was the largest number of wrecks encountered during any operation of the war. In addition the Japanese inserted suicide squads of machine gunners and snipers on the half-submerged wrecks to prolong salvage operations. Unlike the Germans and Italians, who generally holed their blockships with a small charge which allowed them to sink slowly and frequently drift to less effective positions for plugging shipping channels, the Japanese "blew up the ships' magazines with the crews still on board." This method allowed ships to sink "immediately" and thus be "positioned precisely."[29]

The four blockships at the harbor entrance presented the toughest problem as their hulls were well submerged but close enough to the surface to block the passage of even moderately sized vessels and were so badly damaged that compressed air could not be used to restore buoyancy. Rough ocean seas at the entrance to Manila Bay made it impossible to keep cofferdams in place, and Navy salvers were unable to jury rig heavy-lift barges and craft like those the British had used so effectively at places such as Cherbourg and the Schelde Estuary (a failing that was particularly lamented by salvage specialists from the European theater flown in to join those already on hand). The harbor was eventually opened by blowing the masts and superstructures clear off the ships, laboriously pulling the underwater hulks over until they were capsized on the bottom of the bay, then pumping them full of air after some patching so that they rose with the bubble of air to be towed, belly-up, away from the channel.[30]

This situation was rightly seen as a harbinger of things to come. To help answer the coming challenge in Tokyo Bay, the U.S. Navy produced seven "unique" salvage ships, in two classes, principally for Operations Coronet, although some might have been available for Olympic. Similar in capability to the much-admired British lift craft, they were blue-water ships; four ARS(D) salvage ships with LSM-type hulls whose construction was prompted specifically from what the Navy had found in Manila Harbor, and three big ARS(T) salvage tender ships ordered converted from LST hulls before the end of 1944.[31] These ships and dozens of other specialist salvage vessels for refloating, repairing, and towing the casualties of war and the elements, would make up a task group of salvers that was larger than the navies of most nations today, and it was expected that they (and Army Engineers tasked with building at least seven floating Liberty ship berths) would have the waters of Tokyo Bay ready to handle all of the invasion's supply needs before the summer 1946 typhoon season. But how were the First, Eighth, and then Tenth, Armies to be supplied while the salvers were going about the tedious and dangerous business of clearing the wrecks from the port areas and Uraga Strait connecting them to the Pacific?

An artificial harbor was to be erected in the vicinity of Kujukuri, east of Tokyo, to serve the exposed anchorages there and at the Kashima beachhead to the north. Code named Ironhorse, it was intended to handle as much cargo as the pair of Mulberry harbors assembled at Normandy—12,000 deadweight tons per day.[32] The Mulberrys, however, had never been able to achieve this rate of discharge principally because of traffic jams and the fact that one had been partially destroyed during a gale that pounded the English Channel shortly after D-day. The U.S. Navy had learned from this disastrous experience and designed the seaward flanks of the $50 million harbor[33] (which held a production priority "above all military and naval programs except the Manhattan project") to be protected by overlapping barriers of blockships along its ocean flanks, with the dozen or so sunken vessels in the deepest water further reinforced by having their cargo holds filled with rock and sand.[34] As shipping was destroyed or rendered useless by enemy action, it was to be towed by

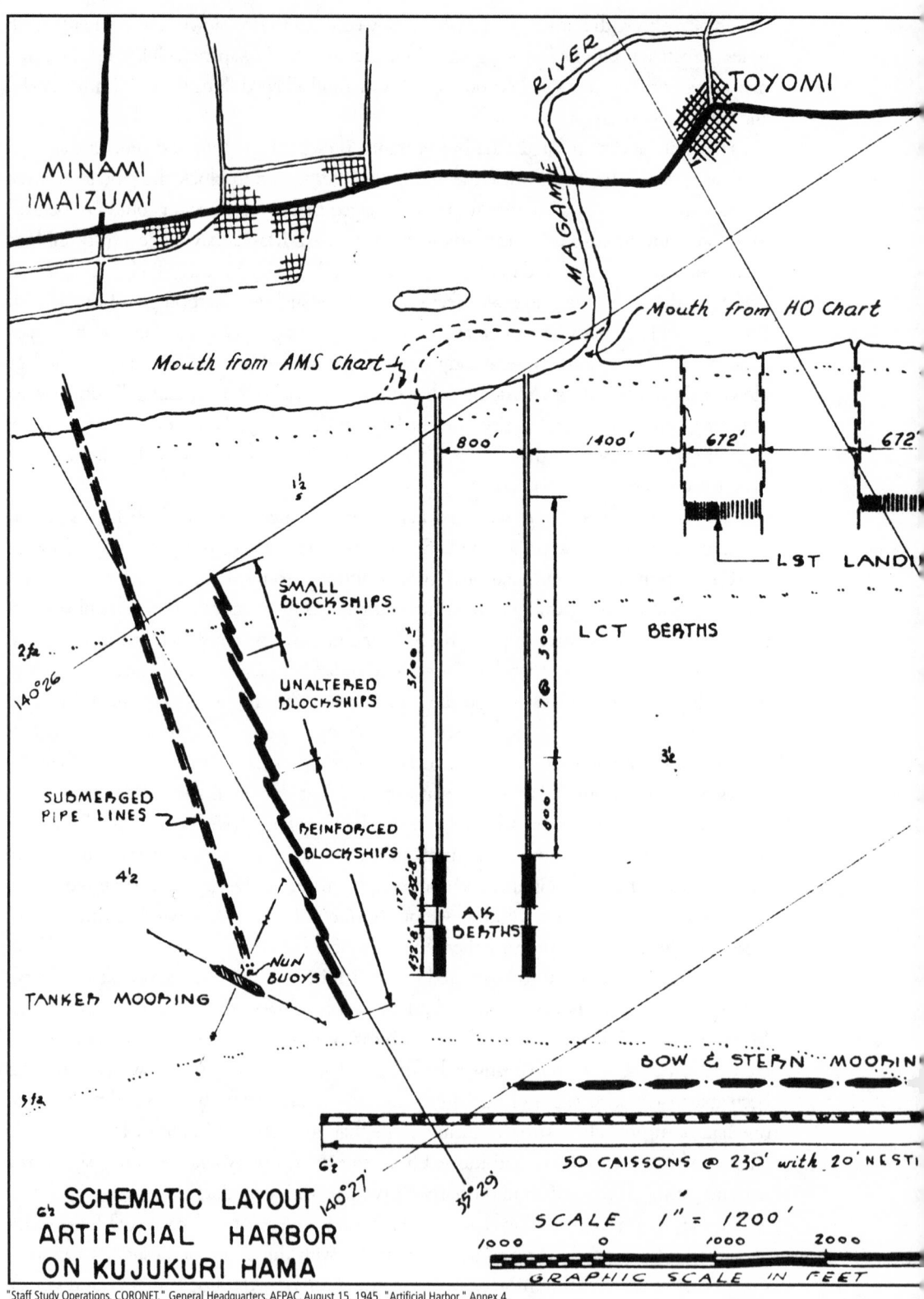

The schematic layout for the Ironhorse artificial harbor, Operation Coronet.

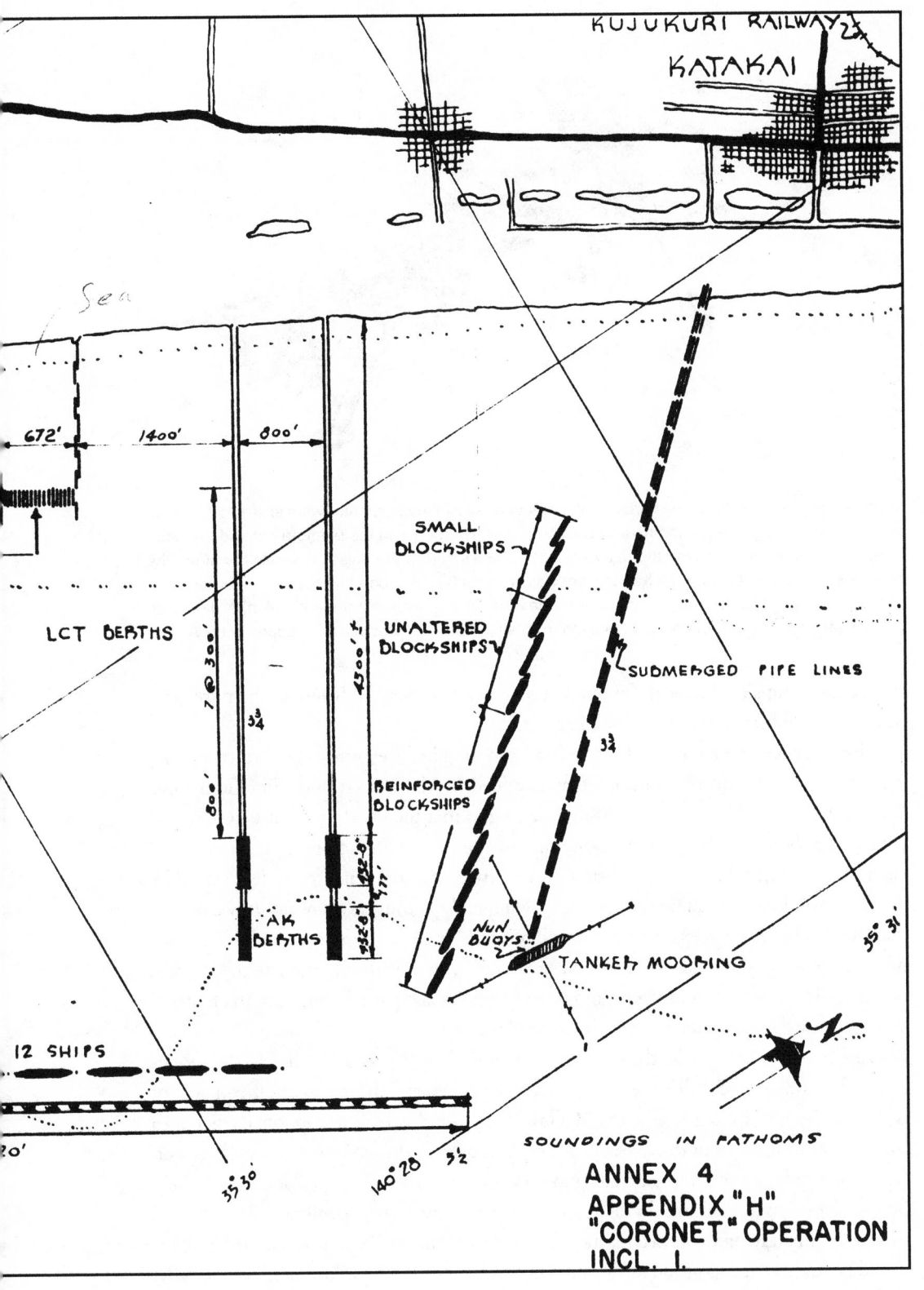

KUJUKURI RAILWAY

KATAKAI

Sea

672' 1400' 800'

LCT BERTHS

7 @ 300'

3¾

800'

4300' ±

SMALL
BLOCKSHIPS

UNALTERED
BLOCKSHIPS

SUBMERGED PIPE LINES

3¾

REINFORCED
BLOCKSHIPS

1920'-9"
4177'

AK
BERTHS

NUN
BUOYS

TANKER MOORING

35 31'

12 SHIPS

20'

35 30'

140 20'   5½

SOUNDINGS IN FATHOMS

ANNEX 4
APPENDIX "H"
"CORONET" OPERATION
INCL. 1.

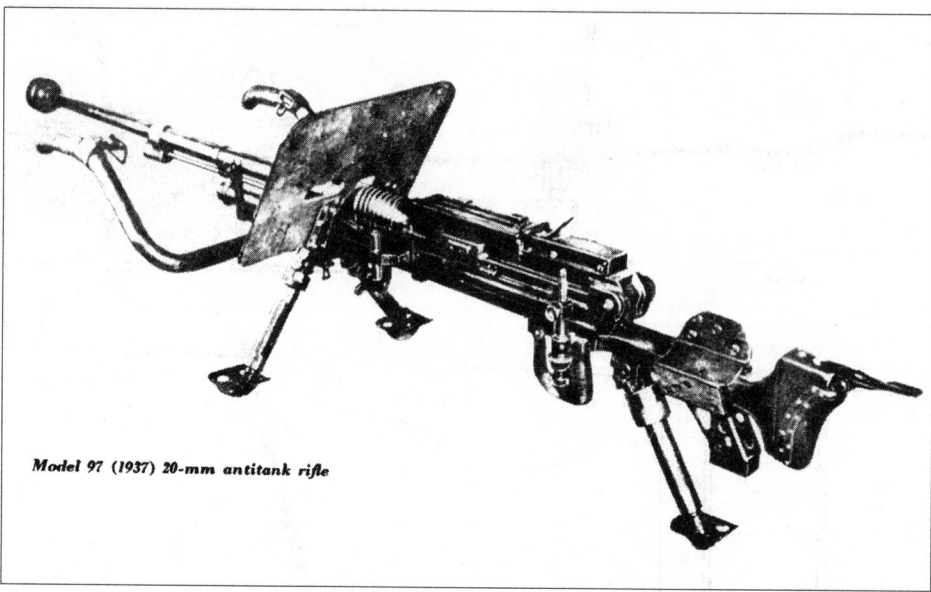

Model 97 (1937) 20-mm antitank rifle

Much has been written about the various antitank weapons Japanese infantry were to employ, such as hollow-charge rifle grenades, the usually suicidal satchel charges, and the plethora of hand-operated hollow-charge mines. However, the real killer of U.S. tanks during the invasion, especially along the countless rice paddy dikes on the Kanto Plain, was going to be a weapon that the Japanese had been unable to put to good use thus far in the war: the Mark 97 20-mm rapid-fire antitank rifle. Japanese defense planners realized this and entered into a crash program to produce the weapon. (U.S. Army)

the salvage groups to the blockship lines and sunk whereever the Ironhorse harbormaster believed would best enhance the flank barriers.

The outer breakwater, located 6,500 feet from low-tide line, was to be formed by fifty 230-foot steel and concrete caissons manufactured by the Barrett and Hilp Company's Belair Shipyard, each with a deep, 20-foot nesting so that the interlocking structure would parallel the shore for 10,520 feet. Even without the support of adjoining caissons, naval engineers estimated that caissons open to the sea (with internal water levels determined by the tides) would immediately protect the growing harbor from waves of up to twelve feet. Each unit would contain its own pumps, and once the seacocks were closed and the caissons filled to the brim with water, twenty-foot waves could be withstood. The painstaking task of filling the caissons with dredged sand would begin as soon as possible with the material automatically displacing the sea water as its level rose.

This last operation could theoretically be wrapped up by Y+42 if the weather cooperated, but this would still have it completed long before June when the frequency of typhoons rises precipitously, and would allow even an individual, unsupported caisson to stand fast against waves of thirty feet or more. Throughout the entire process, each caisson would be the home of an antiaircraft gun crew as well as a barrage balloon unit to help protect the shipping and irreplaceable pierheads from low-flying kamikazes. The caissons used at Normandy had also been armed, but it was highly likely that those off Kujukuri would be somewhat "up-gunned" from the individual 20-mm Oerlikons and few 40-MM Bofors used on Phoenix caissons and that their weapons would be tied into a centralized fire control system. It would not be at all surprising if in addition to twin or quad Bofors along the breakwater, a small number of dual-purpose 5-inch guns were mounted near the entrances on either end of the port.

Within the breakwaters the Ironhorse harbor would have four, two-lane causeways extending approximately 4,300 feet from shore to massive pierheads capable of docking as many as sixteen Liberty-size cargo ships and transports simultaneously. A variety of piers and other facilities would be built within the sheltered waters. The most important of these were berths for LCTs and other landing craft that would be situated along the innermost causeways and three sets of LST berths able to comfortably handle four ships apiece (and up to seven in a pinch) extending out from the beach. Submerged pipelines would run along both sides of the harbor to a terminus and tanker moorings placed outside the lines of blockships in case of a catastrophic accident or successful Japanese attack on an oil tanker. The tankers would bring the number of full-sized ships capable of being handled simultaneously to eighteen, with moorings along the outer breakwater for a dozen more waiting their turn to unload.

Like the caissons all these component pieces were being manufactured in San Francisco Bay and were to be painstakingly towed across the Pacific to a staging area near Guam with assembly scheduled to begin as early as Y+2.[35] Neither of the armored divisions from Europe would use the Ironhorse harbor since their equipment would be disgorged from LSTs along the partially protected beaches of Sigami Bay to the southwest. Navy planners for Coronet believed that, as at Normandy,[36] most of the men and material would be landed directly on the Kujukuri and Kashima beachheads. But with these two lodgments fully exposed to the open ocean, Ironhorse would provide a refuge for vulnerable landing craft during typhoons and allow the continued resupply of the First Army when the frequently heavy seas hampered, and even prevented, resupply across the beach. Continuing model studies were expected to provide reliable data "for possible improvement in form or alignment" of the various breakwater elements.

★   ★   ★

By July 1945 Navy planners had whittled the possible site for Ironhorse down to the two fishing villages on the Kujukuri beachhead, Iioka at its northeastern extremity and Katakai a little over 22 miles to the southwest (16.5 miles today because of urban sprawl and incorporation into the town of Kujukuri). Katakai seemed to be the better of the two due to its slightly gentler wave action and good access to both lateral and interior road and rail lines. At some point before the close of hostilities, however, Iioka was chosen because "highland sheltered it from the north and northeasterly winds which prevail during March and April," and unlike Katakai, which "is exposed to the full sweep of the Pacific Ocean," Iioka's offshore waters were provided with a degree of protection by the Choshi Peninsula. Steep escarpments to the north and east of Iioka, while limiting inland clearance from the port, were duly noted but not thought to be a serious problem. Yet as would happen so many times after Japan's surrender, close inspection of the terrain by occupation troops revealed dangerous secrets that could not be known until there were "boots on the ground." Said one

British observer: "The site . . . is commanded by a long ridge of 250-foot hills and it was only after examination on the spot that we discovered how thoroughly the Japanese, who are expert tunnellers, had honeycombed the hills . . . with caves, underground storerooms, concealed gun emplacements and so on. The Iioka 'Mulberry' would certainly not have been erected or used without enemy interference."[37]

Accounts like this can be found by the hundreds in the literature from servicemen appalled at what they found in the Home Islands. They take on added significance when one remembers that the Japanese capitulation and the end of defensive preparations came respectively four and eight long months before the storm-delayed assault landings of Olympic and Coronet. Any soldier will tell you that there is never "enough" time to prepare for an invasion, but from a purely technical standpoint, eight months is practically an eternity for willing troops and civilian workers toiling by the millions to excavate, strengthen, and stock underground fortifications in anticipation of the coming of the Yankee devils. And the Japanese had no shortage of excellent defensive terrain to work with.

Highly defensible terraced rice fields, discussed earlier, were a common feature on both Kyushu and Honshu and usually could not be easily bypassed because of the nature of their locations. As for the rice paddies stretching for miles along valley floors, even when ostensibly dry, they present formidable barriers to tracked movement and cannot be traversed by wheeled vehicles. Moreover, the sodden nature of most dikes and paddy floors did not lend themselves to effective operation of devices like the hedgerow cutters in Normandy. The rice paddies would have to be seized in a never-ending series of tedious, set-piece struggles through use of tactics similar to those employed in France before the appearance of the hedgerow cutter.[38] Meanwhile the armored elements fighting up the roads north past Tokyo in the west, and toward the capital in the east, would frequently find themselves limited to a one-tank front as happened to the British when they were delayed reaching Arnhem by minimal German forces in the Dutch lowlands. Attempts at flanking movements would be impossible or slowed to a crawl by a deadly combination of terrain and weapons such as the much-maligned 37-mm antitank gun and one that had long since gone out of fashion in Western armies—the antitank rifle.

Many are familiar with the various personal antitank weapons Japanese infantry planned to employ, such as hollow-charge rifle grenades plus the usually suicidal satchel charges and plethora of hand-operated hollow-charge mines. However, when used in the proper tactical setting, traditional if "obsolescent" direct-fire weapons would become deadly tank-killers during the invasion, especially on the Kanto Plain. Of the two mentioned, the Type 97 20-mm semi- or full-automatic antitank rifle[39] had thus far seen little use against the American armor, although it had performed well against landing craft. Even the comparatively thin frontal protection of the M-4 Sherman was too thick for such a weapon, but in the paddy fields it was a different story. At short range from expertly camouflaged positions, even a mediocre rifleman firing semi-automatic to improve accuracy would be able to pump from two to a half-dozen 20-mm rounds into the half-inch belly armor of a Sherman as it reared up high over a dike. Passing beneath the driver and coaxial gunner, the rounds would smash into turret personnel, engine compartment, and stored ammunition with catastrophic results. Only a single round from a 37-mm gun was required to achieve the same effect.

A mountain village in central Honshu with terrain typical of the approaches to the Nagano redoubt and portions of the Olympic invasion area. With dwellings packed from hillside to hillside and extensive paddy areas usually extending from both ends, and sometimes to the next village, such urban/agricultural pockets were a significant hindrance to military movements and highly vulnerable to quickly spreading fires, even during light combat. (U.S. Army)

The number of antitank rifles per division fluctuated according to its actual structure, but eighteen was generally the bottom figure. More robust formations, such as the Kwantung divisions sent to the Home Islands and other Inner Defense Zone locations, fielded eight Type 97s per rifle company, some seventy-two per division. Likewise the number of antitank guns ranged between twenty-two and forty, most of which were the more tactically flexible 47 mm.[40] Nevertheless, large numbers of the 37 mm existed in artillery parks. With Japan's extensive preparations to use obsolete and obsolescent weapons in clever and unexpected ways to help repel the barbarian invaders, it is certain that the Imperial Army would recognize that the dike structure presented unique opportunities for the effective employment of both antitank weapons. Close coordination among American infantrymen and tankers could well keep losses from reaching intolerable levels, but there would be no quick armored thrusts on the Kanto Plain before the rainy season.

★   ★   ★

If there is one thing clear about the various operational schemes for the movement of U.S. mechanized forces out of the Sagami lodgment (hashed over in plans formulated as far back as the summer of 1944), it is that all of them appear to have been produced by planners who seemed blissfully unaware that a wall of mountains, the Kanto Sanchi, and their rugged foothills stretched north along the American's left flank for the full distance of the planned forty-mile drive north. Mt. Fuji at its southern extremity is the feature's most famous peak,

American ships ride peacefully at anchor (but with a portion of their guns still manned) below Mount Fuji during the opening stages of the U.S. occupation of Japan, September 1945. This same area near the entrance of Tokyo Bay was to be the scene of the Eighth Army assault against the Tokyo Plain in the spring of 1946. (U.S. Army)

and the mountain line comes complete with its own moat, the steep-banked Sagami River, which "forms a barrier to maneuver through or against the western foothills[']" last nineteen miles to the ocean. Broad expanses of the river's lower regions could also be flooded to depths that would impede vehicular traffic, but even without assistance from the Imperial Japanese Army, "this river is deep and in [the] wet season floods to 1 mile wide."[41]

MacArthur's intelligence section duly noted that "on the other hand, [the Sagami River] also offers some protection to the west flank of a northward movement," so perhaps the lack of interest was a byproduct of the military truism that a given piece of terrain may affect an enemy's offensive operations just as much as it affects yours.[42] Or perhaps it was a simple assumption that the Eighth Army's assault would be conducted with such speed and violence that the mountains would be essentially irrelevant to the ground offensive. They weren't.

There is no doubt that the lower Sagami was an effective block to Japanese ground operations launched from the foothills, but the principal threat from this area would have come not from Japanese infantry, but from artillery.[43] Exclusive of the divisional artillery belonging to the mobile and coastal defense formations would be long-range guns placed well back into the foothills in positions where their relatively flat trajectories would be unhampered by the intervening heights. A network of roads weaves its way through the foothills, and while most were little better than trails by American standards, they were more than adequate for Japanese needs principally because they had designed their artillery to be extremely compact and horse-mobile. Although Japanese cannons were judged to be "not as rugged as those of comparable calibers in other armies," they were perfect for the killing job at hand and received rave reviews in a War Department intelligence guide distributed all the way down to platoon level: "Japanese artillery weapons exhibit the outstanding characteristic of lightness, in some cases without the sacrifice of range"—pleasant reading indeed for a grunt or jarhead hitting the beach near Tokyo.[44]

The entire expanse of the invasion area can be readily observed from anywhere along the foothills and mountains to their rear, with a clear view all the way to Tokyo Bay. U.S. forces could maintain reasonably effective smoke screens over the lodgment since the northern breeze averages a workable six miles per hour that time of year,[45] but with nearly all vehicular movement confined by terrain to known, preregistered target areas, Japanese artillery would have literally been shooting fish in a barrel as American engineers and transportation elements struggled to clear blasted wrecks from the congested single-lane roads and restricted staging areas. The cannons that would inflict the most damage were the Type 92 105-mm gun (maximum range 11.3 miles) and the Type 89 150-mm gun (maximum range 12.4 miles), a model that was broken down into two maneuverable loads for travel and is often compared to the U.S. 155-mm "Long Tom." A third weapon, similar to the German 88-mm and American 90-mm guns, was the dual-purpose Type 88 75-mm gun (maximum range nearly 8.6 miles), which prior to the Luzon–Iwo Jima–Okinawa battles of 1945 was the Japanese artillery piece most frequently encountered by U.S. soldiers and Marines.[46]

If well emplaced—and there is no reason to believe that the Japanese would suddenly forget all they knew about field craft—these guns would be extraordinarily difficult to target and destroy by either air attack or counterbattery fire as the sky over the foothills would be far too "hot" for effective use of artillery spotting aircraft against the carefully camouflaged and protected guns. The long-range weapons themselves would not be diverted from their task by ground operations aimed at silencing them because, in terms of artillery, a variety of much shorter range howitzers and mountain guns were available to defend the line of foothills to their front. The dearth of American forces available for such an infantry-intensive task would be felt almost immediately, as a brutal series of hill fights to the west was not anticipated by planners but would be thrust upon the Americans. Moreover, as U.S. forces clawed their way deeper into the Kanto Plain, more and more of their left flank would be exposed to artillery in these foothills.

To get at these guns, additional divisions would have to be pushed into the ever-lengthening hill mass on the left flank to conduct fighting similar to that of Italy two years earlier and Korea five years in the future. At some point before Coronet, this certainly would be realized by planners, but as of August 1945 it had not yet been anticipated, and consequently no significant amount of troops had been allocated to this critical mission, which would require a large and growing manpower commitment. Illustrative of this is the absence of the U.S. 10th Mountain Division, a Category II division from Europe, from the initial surge of redeployed formations from the United States to one of the three field armies tasked with destroying organized Japanese resistance on Honshu. The 10th returned from the Mediterranean in August (see chapter 4) and was sent to Camp Carson, Colorado, so that its veterans could, after the obligatory thirty-days leave, resharpen their mountaineering skills at the Mountain Warfare Training Center. Following this, it would be among the very last ETO divisions to ship out for the Pacific, with, perhaps, the idea in mind that the 10th would principally be used to mop up sporadic resistance from fanatical Japanese units holed up in the mountains.[47]

How much long range artillery would the Japanese have emplaced along the ever-lengthening and relatively open flank of the U.S. advance? We don't know. Vast amounts of military and war-related documents were burned in the two weeks between Hirohito's surrender broadcast and the signing on the deck of the battleship *Missouri*. After the war Japanese officers didn't volunteer the details of their operational plans, only the broad outlines, and U.S. interrogators didn't ask. But it would have taken surprisingly few weapons to severely disrupt the thoroughly plotted roads and easily predicted U.S. concentrations.[48] Americans today, familiar with the legendary Ho Chi Minh trail of the Vietnam War, may wish to consider the implications during Coronet of a "Tojo Trail" network extending down to the invasion area from the Nagano redoubt and staging area on the opposite side of the mountains from the U.S. Eighth Army on the Kanto Plain.

CHAPTER 16

Half a Million Purple Hearts

To King, Leahy, Nimitz, and naval officers in general, it had always seemed that the defeat of Japan could be accomplished by sea and air power alone, without the necessity of actual invasion of the Japanese Home Islands by ground troops. In 1942, 1943, and 1944, while the attention of most of the Allied political and military leaders was concentrated on Europe, and while the war against Japan was left largely to King to manage with what forces he could muster, the Pacific war had proceeded largely upon this assumption.

—FLEET ADMIRAL ERNEST J. KING and CDR. WALTER MUIR WHITEHILL, *Fleet Admiral King*[1]

The U.S. Navy found itself in quite a bind by early 1945, and the myopia displayed in the preceding quote, that the war in the Pacific "was left largely to [me] to manage," is at least part of the reason why. Putting aside for the moment the not-insubstantial role of Gen. Douglas MacArthur on the course of events, the need for a swift victory against Japan after the defeat of Germany had been expressed as early as the Casablanca (Anfa) Conference in January 1943, codified at the Quebec Conference (Quadrant) later that year in August, and reaffirmed at the end of 1943 during the Cairo Conference (Sextant). As time moved along and planning progressed, the war leaders and senior staffs of Great Britain and the United States moved away from the conviction that an invasion of the Home Islands "may well not be found necessary" if "blockade and bombardment" proved to be war winners.[2] They still believed such measures to be "inherent in all offensive operations" but that the agreed objective of forcing Japan's capitulation within as little as twelve months after victory in Europe had pushed a third facet of war termination, destruction of Japan's army, to the forefront.

Strenuous objections to this by some members of the Army Air Force staff were trumped by the basic fact that there was no way that they could guarantee success within the parameters of the "twelve-month victory assumption."[3] The JCS, King included, proposed to the Combined Chiefs of Staff that "operations against Japan following [an invasion of] Formosa should envisage an invasion into the industrial heart of Japan. While it may be possible to defeat Japan by sustained aerial bombardment and the destruction of her sea and air forces, this would probably involve an unacceptable delay."[4] Upon the acceptance of the American view by the British chiefs in July 1944, Army logistic and manpower staffs were now able to plan accordingly for the Army ground and air forces' complex redeployment from Europe and the mammoth series of campaigns that would be unleashed under the codename Downfall.

Meanwhile the Joint Planning Staff finalized a blueprint for the invasion, which was adopted by the JCS at the end of June as JCS 924, "Operations Against Japan Subsequent to Formosa," a document that "articulated the JCS consensus on an invasion of Kyushu"[5] and warned that taking the Home Islands "might cost us half a million American lives and many times that number wounded."[6] Subsequently the September 1944 conference at Quebec (Octagon) involved a considerable amount of planning for the end game, and at Yalta (Argonaut), Marshall and King reported that the U.S. military was ready to proceed with the invasions of Kyushu and Honshu, the dates dependent on the close of hostilities in Europe.[7]

Admiral King had attended each of these international conferences and been intimately involved in the U.S. planning process as the agreed-upon invasion and redeployment time-tables were fleshed out. Although he pressed the other American chiefs, both directly and indirectly, for a scheme of operations that would have ultimately promoted "blockade and bombardment" over a direct invasion, he was continually frustrated by the indefinite nature of such a policy in much the same way as its advocates within the air staff.[8] This was only reinforced by the lack of Japanese response to the terrible carnage of the March 9–10 Tokyo firebomb raid, which, said Marshall, "seemingly had no effect whatsoever."[9] The Joint Intelligence Committee summed up the prevailing view when it noted that "under the full impact of air-sea blockade combined with strategic bombing, Japan's 'will' to continue the war can be broken." However: "It does not follow that such air-sea blockades and air attacks upon Japan Proper, without actual invasion of the home islands, will force unconditional surrender within a reasonable length of time. On this point there is a wide divergence of informed opinion. . . . Estimates with regard to the time element vary from a few months to a great many years."[10]

But while Navy personnel on the myriad joint staffs, including King himself, were party to the long-standing strategic objective of not risking that the war drag on for an indefinite period of time (and were deeply involved in working toward that objective), there always lurked the underlying assumption that the Allies would ultimately turn to blockade and bombardment because of the sheer costs of redeployment and invasion. Remarkably this belief persisted well after the Yalta Conference in early February 1945. It was not until mid-March, when the Army was visibly going full bore to reorganize its forces world wide for Downfall and the Japanese had brushed off the Tokyo firebombing, that the ranking soldier on the JWPC, Brigadier General Bessell, could write, "It seems at last to be acknowledged that the ultimate defeat of Japan will require the invasion of Japan proper and the defeat of her ground forces there."[11]

The Navy's belated acknowledgment accelerated numerous current initiatives and prompted the go-ahead on others, such as the conversions of LSMs into ARS(D) salvage lift ships, but came a little too late for them to fulfill (without Army help) one of its vital needs for the invasion—sustaining morale.

★   ★   ★

The U.S. Navy displayed no interest in the Purple Heart after it was brought back into use through the efforts of Douglas MacArthur, then Army chief of staff, in 1932. Within six months after Pearl Harbor, however, the Navy had changed its tune. Army commanders were issuing the decoration to naval and Marine Corps personnel serving with its units, an occurrence that would only increase in frequency. Some sailors and Marines receiving a medal for wounds suffered in combat, while others did not, was a guaranteed morale killer, and the Navy began to petition for its own authority to award the Purple Heart "on the same basis as the Army."[12]

An executive order signed by Roosevelt in December 1942 authorized that the decoration be issued to Navy, Marine, and Coast Guard personnel with wording that opened eligibility not just to combat casualties of the current war, but all previous military actions as well. Soon, and as it had within the Army, the medal became extremely highly prized as its award criteria was rightly seen as being far less subject to the whims of commanders than other decorations, plus it proclaimed for all to see that its recipients had shed blood, or made the ultimate sacrifice, for their country.

Arrangements were made with the Treasury Department's Bureau of the Mint to handle all contracting and ensure quality control of the new Navy medal, with the U.S. Mint in Philadelphia tasked with overseeing everything from the bidding process, through the final assembly and shipping of decorations.[13] The Army Quartermaster Corps, meanwhile, continued its longtime practice of performing all the procurement functions itself through its Philadelphia Quartermaster Depot. The fact that both services' decorations were being procured through government sources in the same city was completely a coincidence but would facilitate increased coordination between the two bodies as the war progressed.

Using Army specifications and samples as a guide, an initial Navy order of 135,000 Purple Hearts was contracted in February 1943 and finally completed exactly one year later after many delays.[14] Schedule problems, however, were not at all confined to the Navy's medals. Enormous technical difficulties plus the fever pitch of production involving dozens of other decorations—all requiring scarce precious metals and extremely high levels of craftsmanship from equally scarce, highly specialized workers—conspired to push the Army's Purple Heart behind schedule as well.[15]

The two manufacturers who produced the decoration's pendants were forced to experiment with different types of inserts for the "toned bronze" core element depicting George Washington affixed to purple heart-shaped centers of fired enamel (cloisonne), painted enamel, or synthetic resin (plastic).[16] The decision in 1943 to settle on the use of molded plastic for the heart essentially solved all the most vexing problems, which included the central elements coming loose or popping out completely. Production was stabilized, but early delays in the December 30, 1941, and July 1, 1942, Army contracts for 525,000 decorations had been so severe that by the advent of the "casualty surge" in the summer of 1944, Purple Heart deliveries to the Army were 110,000 copies behind schedule.[17]

Although the Army continued to order Purple Hearts in such great quantities that it was forced, in an effort to shorten production time, to drop the engraving of individual serial numbers starting with the contracts awarded in 1943 (the highest contracted number being 600,000),[18] the Navy that year was hopeful that "they will not require more than the 135,000 already ordered."[19] As far as the Navy was concerned, it was in no hurry to receive even the items called for in the as-yet-unfilled order. A representative of the Bureau of Naval Personnel felt that the service was "pretty well stocked for the time being" and stated that other than as possible replacements for damaged items, "he didn't think the Navy would require any additional medals during the remainder of the fiscal year."[20]

The Army's situation, however, was completely different, and the contractor handling a portion of its Purple Heart production as well as all of the Navy's (Rex Manufacturing Company) was so swamped by "a large order of Purple Hearts received from the United States Army"[21] of the decoration's unnumbered "Type III" variety,[22] that they approached the Philadelphia Mint for help. Mint superintendent Edwin H. Dressel found that the firm, which had already produced hundreds of thousands of the medal for the Army alone, was now in a situation where "their equipment and personnel is inadequate to meet the requirements."[23] Rex was unable to strike a deal with the Philadelphia Mint but was thankful that they were not under the gun to maintain regular deliveries of the Navy's minutely different variation of the medal and could thus schedule fabrication of its pendant around higher priority Army decorations.

The Navy's now-year-old order was finally filled in February 1944, and contracts were signed for an additional 25,000 medals seven months later in early October. This was done purely as a contingency, and the Navy stressed—orally and in writing—that "this order for Purple Hearts is not pressing" in September, before the contract was let, as well as on several occasions extending into December.[24] The Navy's Board of Medals and Awards even considered canceling the October Purple Heart order altogether,[25] and numerous other awards, such as Unit Commendations Bars, the Distinguished Flying Cross, and Bronze Star, were placed on a higher priority. It was not until the Navy's realization that "blockade and bombardment" was a dead issue and that American forces were indeed going to invade Japan[26] that the acquisition of Purple Hearts became overnight a matter of great urgency.

The Navy was now face to face with the fact that, barring a change in national war objectives, six Marine divisions were going to fight and claw their way ashore while much of the Pacific Fleet was locked dangerously close to the Home Islands during Operations Coronet and Olympic. Although not one medal had been delivered on the October 9, 1944, order,[27] the Navy quickly got together new paperwork and, on March 23, 1945, placed an order for 25,000 more Purple Hearts while making it clear, up and down the chain of command, that this was now the top-priority item.[28] Almost immediately the Navy staff concluded that not enough of the decoration had been ordered, and the Philadelphia Mint received a phone call on March 28 to request yet another 25,000 (with a promise that the paperwork would soon follow).[29] Additional urgency was added to the situation because Navy and Marine losses had mounted precipitously, and unexpectedly, in recent months.

Seizing Peleliu cost 7,368 Marine dead, missing, wounded, and died of wounds, with Navy casualties (principally among medical corpsmen and doctors) totaling an even 700. Equally unexpected were the stiff losses from kamikaze operations and surface actions in the Philippines. All of this drew heavily on the dwindling supply of Purple Hearts even as Navy personnel back in Washington put the decoration's production on the back burner and seriously contemplated turning off the gas. Come the staggering loss of 28,666 men on Iwo Jima and continued fleet actions (989 dead and wounded on the aircraft carrier USS *Franklin*, for example, from a conventional air strike), the Navy suddenly discovered that it had exhausted its reserves of the decoration. Undoubtedly, small consignments of the medal were held throughout the fleet by appropriate command and logistic elements, but the Navy Warehouse in Arlington, Virginia, had run dry.

There are symbols aplenty to denote brave deeds, good conduct, service in a theater of operations, marksmanship, and innumerable other worthwhile accomplishments. But the nature of the Purple Heart puts it in a class by itself, and the medal's absence—or worse yet, sporadic, uneven distribution—would not only have a profoundly adverse affect on morale but also had the potential of generating severe political repercussions at home. The Treasury Department's director of the Mint, Nellie Tayloe Ross, openly feared that she might "be held up on the floor of Congress as one whose organization has fallen down on a job that means so much to the fighting forces."[30]

Although the Purple Heart was by far the most politically sensitive decoration, the steep increase in fighting had pushed up the demand for the full range of combat-related awards. The Navy was pressing hard for decorations that could be made available to Iwo Jima casualties (or to the families of the dead), which, in the case of the Purple Heart, would undoubtedly have been available if the October 1944 order had been fulfilled. Inexplicably the Navy was slow to upgrade the production of the decoration from its AA-3 priority (the War Department maintained the Army's at AA-1 due in no small part to Marshall's absolute insistence that awards be issued immediately),[31] thus it was not until April that the Mint could wave "top priority" in front of suppliers.[32] And although there was ample documentation that it was the sea service that had bounced the Purple Heart back in the production line-up,[33] Tayloe Ross, as bureaucrats are wont to do, passed the heat down to her subordinates: "We are failing to meet the great responsibility that has been placed upon us to provide for these fighting heroes the awards for valour [*sic*] which the Government has determined they shall have. Think of the 20,000 heroes at Iwo Jima, due to receive Purple Hearts which we are unable to supply."[34]

Production was, in truth, just barely eking along, but it was not for lack of willingness at the Philadelphia Mint. All Army planning had been governed by the expectation that U.S. forces would fight it out with Imperial field armies on Japanese soil, and Purple Heart orders (obviously among a vast number of corresponding decisions and acquisitions) reflected that expectation. As an institution the Army had regularly dealt with mass death, and casualties running into the high five and even six figures for individual battles and campaigns; consequently it had started its acquisitions process far earlier than the Navy, which had held fast to the idea of only conducting a blockade. The result, when combined with limited resources, was that the Army had effectively sucked up nearly all of the commercial medals production capacity beyond the confines of the Mint building at 16th and Spring Garden Streets in Philadelphia.

By the time the realization "Oh my God, we're actually going in"[35] hit the Navy Department in March 1945, resulting in back-to-back Purple Heart orders being placed with the Mint, neither supplies nor specialized manpower could be obtained in a timely manner. The situation relating to the decoration's distinctive ribbon that month is an excellent case in point as the Navy's acquisition of approximately 6,300 yards turned out to be a task fraught with delays and complications including a general unwillingness of contractors to bid on the comparatively small amounts needed for its medals.[36] But within the same month that the pair of Mint contracts amounting to 50,000 additional Navy Purple Hearts were issued (and found impossible to execute), Army quartermasters were confident that their earlier orders would be filled and that they would shortly receive a stunning 125,000 yards of the white-edged, pansy-purple ribbon and even promised that "every effort will be made by this Depot to increase the above quantities."[37]

The number of Purple Hearts actually produced for the war effort totaled approximately 1,531,000 medals.[38] Treasury Department officials, who were almost as well versed in the minutia of the Army's contracting as the Quartermaster Corps, collected casualty data and kept a wary eye on activities in Congress, where a range of manpower-related proposals were being hotly debated under the watchful eye of the Senate's presiding officer, Vice President Harry S. Truman (see chapter 2). A bill to provide all mothers and wives of servicemen who had died in the war with a medal, proposed by Senator Joseph O'Mahoney of Wyoming, was particularly worrisome. It not only would have duplicated the Purple Heart's function and resulted in a large number of families eligible to receive two of the proposed medals but also would have made the Mint responsible for production that ultimately "will run into the hundreds of thousands of medals, perhaps millions" at a time when it could not even cover the Navy's existing orders.[39]

As late as April 9, two months after the launch of the Iwo Jima battle, there had been no Purple Heart deliveries whatsoever to the Navy, although Rex Manufacturing had finally acquired the resources to begin fabrication of the medal's pendants.[40] By May 14, one and a half months into the brutal Okinawa campaign, the Philadelphia Mint had received enough pendants and other materials to complete the final assembly of 5,275 decorations from the October order of the previous year.[41] But while Army personnel in Okinawan field hospitals were receiving their Purple Hearts, wounded Marines in the cots next to them were not. The Navy had finally had enough, and the Bureau of Personnel, white hat in hand, went to their Army brethren and asked if they could please "borrow" 60,000 Purple Hearts.[42] Stock transfers between the Philadelphia Quartermaster Depot and the Navy's Arlington Warehouse were quickly initiated, and Treasury Department officials immediately perceived that a useful opportunity was presenting itself to the Mint.

Treasury floated the idea that, with the U.S. Army galloping to the Navy's rescue with commercially produced medals, perhaps the Mint's Purple Heart's production priority could be suspended, thus allowing other backlogged decorations to be pushed ahead while simultaneously relieving the Mint of some of its burden. The Navy, already badly burned over the medal, was noncommittal from the start, but Treasury officials were confident enough that the Navy would jump at the chance to get other needed items earlier, that the Bureau of the Mint's acting director, Leland Howard, drafted a letter to Philadelphia Mint supervisor Dressel instructing him to "slow down production of the Purple Hearts, and concentrate on the Air Medal and Bronze Star."[43] The Navy, however, said "no thanks," and Howard's letter was later found in the archives with a large "X" scratched across the text, obviously placed after the Navy refusal.[44]

The 60,000 loaned Army decorations would finally allow awards to be issued for Iwo Jima, and recent naval operations, plus the even more costly Okinawa battles then raging on land and sea would soon consume nearly all of the Army's largess. With Operation Olympic less than six months in the future, it was past time to follow the Army's lead on acquiring medals. The Rex Manufacturing Company had reached the point where it could now ship an average of 1,500 Purple Heart pendants per day to the Philadelphia Mint for final assembly, and the Navy was in no mood to see those shipments stop.[45]

CHAPTER 17

"Punishment from Heaven"

It was evident to us that the [Japanese] army was still largely in control and they were preparing to fight to the bitter end just as they had done on all of the islands up to and including Okinawa where I think we had to kill 120,000 of them.

Therefore it was the opinion of the Chiefs of Staff at that time that only a tremendous pressure on Japan itself had any hope of terminating the army dictation . . . that nothing less than a terrific shock would produce a surrender, particularly a surrender that was carried throughout the Japanese interests from Burma, China, Indonesia down in New Guinea where we had left them behind, and of course further north.

Our great struggle there was to precipitate that general surrender so that we would not be involved with various hold-out commands in various parts of the Far East. Therefore our own conclusion, that of the Chiefs of Staff, was that we had to either invade Japan [or] bring this to a conclusion with shock action . . . the atomic bomb.

—GEORGE C. MARSHALL in congressional testimony, 1951[1]

Col. I. Ridgway Trimble, at the Office of the Chief Surgeon, U.S. Army Forces, Western Pacific was concerned.[2] Trimble had served as General Denit's eyes and ears on all matters relating to surgical matters and patient care throughout MacArthur's advance across New Guinea jungles and into the Philippines. He was now helping to coordinate the unprecedented build-up of the medical infrastructure needed to support the twin invasions of Japan, and feared that there might not be enough doctors available for Operation Coronet. During consultations in Washington Trimble learned that due to "Congressional pressure," some 350 European theater medical officers had been prematurely discharged in spite of the fact that they had not accrued as many service points as those in the Pacific. He quickly fired off a letter to Denit appraising him of the situation in the hope that Denit's boss, MacArthur, might be able to do something to stop the hemorrhage of physicians.[3]

Detailed medical planning for Coronet had not yet begun as Denit's command was fully engaged in working toward Olympic, but the scale of the Kanto Plain effort can be gauged from Trimble's list of medical units to arrive in the western Pacific from August 1945 through the spring of 1946 with or without their full complement of medical officers:

August	5	evacuation hospitals
	10	1,000-bed general hospitals
	3	250-bed station hospitals
	1	auxiliary surgical group
September	6	evacuation hospitals
	1	convalescent hospital
	16	clearing companies
	5	collecting companies
	16	ambulance companies
	41	1,000-bed general hospitals
	5	750-bed station hospitals
	16	500-bed station hospitals
October	9	evacuation hospitals
	10	1,000-bed general hospitals
	1	medical professional group
	4	500-bed station hospitals
November	5	evacuation hospitals
	1	500-bed station hospital
"later"	41	1,000-bed general hospitals[4]

These units, representing 117,000 new beds, would augment the 16,250 Sixth Army general and station hospital beds principally on Luzon, and sixteen of these new general hospitals would be fully functional on Luzon and Okinawa in time for the invasion of Kyushu, with the balance to be folded into the First and Eighth Armies for operations on Honshu.[5] Trimble also assured Denit that he had made it a point to stress "the importance of sending personnel in advance of the T/O [table of organization] hospitals to which they are attached."[6] Meanwhile stateside Army hospitals were also gearing up for the invasion of Japan.

In addition to the early demobilization of European theater doctors prompted by "Congressional pressure," recently passed legislation had "in effect dictated the replacement training program which the Army now had to follow" by mandating that the training of eighteen-year-old inductees be increased from fifteen weeks to six months before they could be sent overseas (see chapters 1 and 2).[7] This had not yet affected combat operations since the initial delays entailed in fielding the very youngest soldiers would generally fall between Okinawa and the invasion of Kyushu at a time when the only serious fighting involved several divisions reducing the organized Japanese resistance in northern Luzon.

The legislation did, however, "introduce an element of inflexibility into their disposition" at a time when "any accurate forecast of combat requirements was particularly difficult," even without trying to factor in the rapid and ongoing Japanese reinforcement of the Olympic invasion areas which had only become apparent in July.[8]

June and July 1945 had also seen the surge of incoming casualties to stateside hospitals—long expected by the U.S. Army Medical Corps—peak at more than 300,000. Although many hospital wards were filled to capacity, the surgeon general's office had previously managed to keep the number of available beds well ahead of the casualty flow from overseas theaters. Now they looked forward to freeing up the crammed wards by November—almost half of the beds occupied during the early summer peak—through an aggressive policy of furloughs and discharges. It was projected that the downward trend in occupied beds, accentuated by a temporary drop during the Christmas season, would continue. These freed-up beds, however, were not going to be turned over for the use of civilian dependents, as was policy, but were instead to be retained until after Japan's surrender.[9] Until that time there was one more casualty surge for which Maj. Gen. Norman Kirk, the Army's surgeon general, had to plan, and incoming wounded would continue to be dispersed to whatever facilities had openings instead of to hospitals near their homes.[10]

How many casualties were expected in stateside hospitals? Based on earlier casualty data and force-on-force assumptions, the Army was still working with its estimate of "approximately" 720,000 for the number of replacements needed for "dead and evacuated wounded" through December 31, 1946, which included Army Air Force but not Navy and Marine Corps losses.[11] This and other figures, the planned sequence of operations, and experience gained thus far in the war in caring for the wounded led the Army Medical Corps to conclude that approximately 330,000 of these men would be hospitalized in the "Zone of the Interior" (continental United States) on June 30, 1946.[12] The Army Medical Corps had earlier estimated that casualties incurred by the summer of 1945 (all theaters) would make up roughly 50,000 of that number, with perhaps 5,000 more occupied by stateside personnel and those from noncombat theaters. This means that in addition to having facilities to properly handle the influx of casualties, the Army was expecting something on the order of 275,000 cases *serious enough* to require hospitalization in the United States from Operation Olympic and the opening months of Coronet.

Midway through the year-long casualty surge that began in June 1944, the War Department quietly dropped the release of the Army's skyrocketing monthly casualty figures after, just several months earlier, narrowing the criteria for what was released in order to make casualties appear lower than they in fact were (see chapter 2). The War Department then reverted to the practice followed during the first years after Pearl Harbor, where limited casualty figures were periodically released after individual battles instead of on a systematic, monthly basis. Nevertheless it was impossible for Americans to not perceive the enormity of the growing losses, even if they were not stated explicitly. The United States was now suffering the kind of attrition that had been commonplace among the war's other belligerents for several years.[13]

Scrupulously accurate casualty data was made available after the war for anyone among the public interested in obtaining it, but the numbers did not reflect the intensity of the ongoing manpower crisis that the War Department had managed with extreme care for both military and political reasons. In addition to the often-repeated combat losses (which are themselves low), fully 1,225,230 of the soldiers who entered Army hospitals during the war were for nonbattle injuries in combat zones; diseases contracted overseas; and combat-related psychiatric breakdowns, did not recover sufficiently to be returned to duty and were discharged from the Service.[14]

With battle-related casualties and "accidental" deaths from all services topping one and a quarter million by the summer of 1945,[15] and a roughly equal number of discharged soldiers—their health at least temporarily broken by "noncombat" injuries, disease, or psychosis—it was extremely rare for a family to have not suffered either a direct, personal loss, or not know those who did.

One loss category that did not make its appearance even in the voluminous postwar Medical Corps studies was the number of families with multiple deaths. The reason for the omission was less likely some sort of attempt to obscure the losses than to have been the nature of the Army's record-keeping system. The Army did not collect information on families, only individuals soldiers, and the raw data itself, if examined for familial connections, would have lent itself to potentially severe undercounts (although area-specific institutional knowledge on this subject at local draft boards would have been high in the immediate postwar period). Still, in answer to a White House query, the Army "estimate[d] that more than seven thousand families have lost two or more sons in the war," while cautioning that "exact figures are unobtainable"[16]

This data was generated through statistical analysis likely buttressed by both anecdotal accounts and, possibly, empirical evidence gathered by a small number of draft boards. It was never released through the War Department's public information channels, even though the estimate was readily enough available that when an Illinois senator requested a condolence letter from the president to Mr. And Mrs. Raymond Sherman of Aurora, Illinois, it was inserted into the department's speedy verification that all three of their sons, Homer, Robert, and Donald, had been killed in action. Truman's secretaries, Matthew Connelly and William Hassett, were thoroughly opposed to sending the Shermans a letter, and Senator Scott Lucas was informed that "there have been so many instances of this nature that it would be impossible for the President to single out one family for recognition."[17]

The presidential secretaries' instincts paralleled the Army response on such matters, exemplified by the following statement in a letter (approved and signed by Marshall) to a grieving mother who had already lost two sons in 1943, well before the year-long casualty surge that began in June 1944. The mother wanted her remaining son pulled from overseas duty, but was informed that the "numbers are so great and the individual cases so numerous that special authorizations would be impracticable, with so much delay, complication, and investigation that the general movements would be seriously interfered with."[18]

General Marshall considered it his duty to be made aware of personnel matters addressed to his attention (see chapter 2). He examined all drafted responses that went over his signature, and sometimes dealt with such matters personally, as he did in this instance. Upon learning of the family's plight in January 1944, the chief of staff originally felt that "this appears to be a particularly bad case" and he asked the advice of one of his closest assis-

WAR DEPARTMENT PAMPHLET NO. 21–31

Two down and One to go —

This War Department pamphlet distributed to Army and Army Air Force personnel in May and June 1945 explained the points system and why the military might of Imperial Japan must be "completely crushed." Although General Hideki Tojo, at right, had been removed as prime minister and army minister nearly a year earlier because of the fall of Saipan, he remained the public face of Imperial Japan to Americans and was included with Adolf Hitler and Benito Mussolini in the cover illustration by Arthur Szyk. (War Department)

tants, Col. H. Merrill Pasco. The colonel strongly recommended against his boss giving the remaining son any preferential treatment and drafted the response that, in effect, became the Army's policy on such matters until passage of a law in 1948 that contained a "surviving son or brother" provision: "While I can understand why you will find it difficult to appreciate the real necessity for our policy, it is nevertheless quite necessary to the earliest success of our armies that we leave to the various authorities, concerned in a necessarily elaborate system, freedom in the assignment of men for overseas duty without reference to personal circumstances."[19]

Within months Marshall would lose his stepson of thirteen years, 2d Lt. Allen Tupper Brown—the closest to Marshall of his two male stepchildren—to a German sniper near Anzio, Italy.[20] Senior officers in the United States and overseas theaters knew of his family's loss, and many civilian officials in Washington must have known as well, but the general kept his grief a private affair that made neither the newspapers operating under wartime censorship guidelines, nor most of the biographies that would appear in the coming decades. Later that year, as the monthly casualty figures, principally due to fighting in the European theater, climbed inexorably higher, Marshall reiterated to his fellow World War I veterans something to which they could all agree: "War is the most terrible tragedy of the human race and it should not be prolonged an hour longer than is absolutely necessary."[21]

Throughout this period Stimson made similar comments in his diary, in closed meetings, and publicly before congressional committees. In a classified February 1945 briefing for the Senate Military Affairs Committee, he told its members that it was "not the time to think of when the war was going to stop" calling that kind of thinking the "worst psychology in the world." He forcefully maintained:

> Our forces are locked with the enemy in an all-out contest. When that has happened, there can be no falling back. There can be no changes of mind. Every last weapon must be poured into the battle against the final moment when we break down our enemy. The moment has arrived which Marshal Foch said came in every battle, "*Tout le monde à la bataille*"— Everybody get into the fight. . . . Mind you, our basic plans are based upon momentum— momentum for a short war. Momentum to save precious lives which would inevitably be lost in a long war.[22]

By the summer of 1945, however, pressure was building among some quarters of the press and the public to soften "unconditional surrender" demands in the hope that the Japanese might be enticed to throw in the towel if they were assured that their emperor could remain on the throne. Stimson and his colleagues, who were listening in on Japanese communications thanks to U.S. code breakers, knew better yet could not use the intelligence success to defend their continuing tough stance. Meanwhile war weariness was clearly growing in the aftermath of victory in Europe, and though not yet of much significance, it could result in untold consequences if the fighting dragged on too long. As Stimson said, the "country will not be satisfied unless every effort is made to shorten the war."[23]

The Joint Chiefs view of the danger was enunciated most clearly by Marshall,[24] who personally rewrote a key portion of the State-War-Navy Coordinating Committee document explaining the rational for neither dropping nor modifying the unconditional surrender demand (Marshall's deletions are lined out and his additions are underlined):

> 3. If Japan should make a public peace proposal while we are redeploying men from the European Theater to the Pacific Oceans ~~Areas~~, it might have considerable effect on the American people. War weariness in the United States ~~may demand the return home of those~~

~~who have already fought long and well in the European war regardless of the effect of such return on the prosecution of the Japanese ware. It may be politically and psychologically difficult to refuse a Japanese offer which prevents and actual invasion of the home islands with the incident saving of American casualties.~~ might then lead to some public demand for acceptance of a Japanese offer designed to prevent both invasion of the home islands and our prosecution of the war to a point which would destroy Japanese capacity to start a new war. A demand for unconditional surrender now would tend (a) to keep before the American public the national importance of rendering Japan impotent to commit further aggression and (b) to reduce the psychological injury to our effort to win the war which might be the result of any tempting Japanese offer for a peace falling short of destruction of Japan's war potential. These advantages would be in addition to the obvious advantages of the proposal in serving as a useful vehicle of our propaganda and in providing a possible foundation for a surrender which would not lead to an inconclusive peace.[25]

JCS members King, Arnold, and Leahy all approved Marshall's suggested modification. The war had to be won—quickly, unambiguously, and completely—no matter what the cost. Ironically the fear of a lengthy war or delayed U.S. invasion was just as real among Japan's military,[26] as their resources were dwindling at an alarming rate and would reach critical proportions by the summer of 1946 (see chapters 7 and 11).[27] Sadly there was no Magic route into the minds of the senior-most Imperial leaders until they were in American captivity after the war.

Several days later, at a meeting of the Maryland Historical Society in nearby Baltimore, Marshall remarked, "In a war, every week of duration adds tremendously, not only to the costs, measured by appropriations, but in casualties measured in lives and mutilation." He went on to say that the "full impact of the war comes more to me, I think, in some respects than it does to anyone in this country. The daily casualty lists are mine. They arrive in a constant stream, a swelling stream, and I can't get away from them."[28]

While willing to see the war through to the bitter end, Stimson nevertheless held out hope that the Japanese might be induced to surrender before the United States and its allies were forced to invade. He made it plain on many occasions that "this is a matter about which I feel strongly"[29] and based his guarded optimism on the belief that "Japan is not a nation composed wholly of mad fanatics of an entirely different mentality than ours."[30] Truman's advisors were in general agreement "that some way should be found of inducing Japan to yield without a fight" and that it was essential that a carefully crafted "new warning" be issued.[31]

Opinion varied on when was the most effective time for it to be issued. Acting Secretary of State Grew and Admiral Leahy, for example, advocated that the warning be made after the Okinawa campaign, which was then reaching its bloody conclusion, but as Stimson noted, that "does not meet with the President's plans in respect to the coming meeting with Churchill and Stalin." Stimson desired to see it issued before Olympic but after the psychological "shock" of nuclear attack: "My only fixed date is the last chance warning . . . must be given before an actual landing of the ground forces on Japan, and fortunately, the plans provide for enough time to bring in the sanctions to our warnings in the shape of heavy ordinary bombing attacks and an attack of S-1 [the atom bomb]."[32]

Truman's ultimatum that Japan faced "prompt and utter destruction" if it did not agree to terms of the Potsdam Declaration (Appendix C) did not follow, but preceded, the nuclear strikes against Japan's cities and was originally dismissed as empty rhetoric by most of the country's leaders. The president's new secretary of state, Jimmy Byrnes, later stated that the warning had been "phrased so that the threat of utter destruction if Japan resisted was offset with the hope of a just, though stern, peace if she surrendered."[33]

However, those such as Foreign Minister Togo Shigenori, who pointed out that the terms, though harsh, were terms nonetheless—something that had not been offered to Nazi Germany—had their arguments turned against them as the issuance of terms was seen as a sign of American weakness. Said Prime Minister Suzuki at the August 3 cabinet meeting, "Precisely at a time like this, if we hold firm, then they will yield to us."[34]

Even after two cities had been destroyed in a flash and the Soviet entry into the war dashed the last hopes of a negotiated end to hostilities, the emperor's most senior military advisors counseled emphatically against surrender, maintaining that combat on the Home Islands would decide the issue in Japan's favor. These same leaders, and, most important, War Minister Anami, subsequently acquiesced to the emperor's wishes upon receiving clear, heartfelt direction from Hirohito himself—and after it became apparent that continued use of the atom bomb would deny them the murderous "decisive battle" that held out at least some prospect of a settlement on their own terms. Said Suzuki after the news of the Nagasaki blast was announced during a meeting of the Supreme War Council, "The United States, instead of staging the invasion, will keep on dropping atomic bombs."[35]

To these Japanese leaders, the strategic use of nuclear weapons was the ultimate Yankee expression of "island hopping." When the coup attempt (that all or most of them knew was in the works) was launched by well placed midlevel officers, Anami and the senior military leaders refused to join the die-hard elements. And rather than sit on the sidelines awaiting developments as the Imperial Palace was seized and the killings begun, they moved decisively to block the rebels' attempt to "protect" the emperor, murder the peace advocates in his cabinet, and destroy the yet-to-be-broadcast recordings of the emperor's Imperial Rescript announcing the capitulation.[36] The quick suppression of the coup removed the last obstacle to peace even as Marshall and his staff were formulating a proposal to switch from strategic to tactical use of nuclear weapons—as well as employ poison gas—in order to trump the buildup of Imperial forces on Kyushu (see chapters 10 and 11).

Would Marshall's proposal have met with Truman's approval? The president's growing unease over the use of nuclear weapons against urban targets may have made him more receptive to a change in the longstanding nuclear strategy. As early as August 9, Truman had written of his concern for the plight of innocent civilians and "humanitarian feeling for the women and children in Japan" to a particularly jingoistic senator, then the next day expressed his anguish over "wiping out 100,000 more people," including "all those kids," to cabinet members.[37] Thus when Marshall argued that the bomb's value as a vehicle to "shock" the Japanese leadership and stampede them into an early surrender was now gone—moving the last two cities in the approved nuclear target set, Niigata and Kokura, to the shrinking list of conventional bombing targets—the idea of preserving the atom bombs for tactical use may have met with less resistance than before Hiroshima and Nagasaki. Ironically, however, abandonment of the nuclear strategy inherited from Roosevelt would have likely resulted in the loss of more lives to the new weapon than it saved. A significant percentage of them would have been American.

Although the effects of poison gas were well known and had a profound impact on people who had come of age during World War I,[38] a more complete appreciation of the dangers posed by nuclear radiation was still in the future. Marshall's plans called for most— and if he could convince Stimson and Truman, *all*—of the current and future atom bombs to be dropped on Japanese defense concentrations along or near the beaches.[39] And he was apparently confident that the nuclear bombing of urban targets would indeed be suspended, leaving each of the eight to nine weapons that were likely to be built by X-day on Kyushu available for tactical use. He later described plans for their employment in some detail to his biographer, Forrest Pogue:

> I had gone very carefully into the examinations out in New Mexico as to the after-effects of the bomb. . . . It was decided then that the casualties from the actual fighting would be very much greater than might occur from the after-effects of the bomb action. So there were to be three bombs [to support] each corps that was landing. One or two, but probably one, as a preliminary, then the landing, then another one further inland against the immediate supports, and then the third against any troops that might try to come through the mountains from up on the Inland Sea. That was the rough idea in our minds.[40]

This would have amounted to six nuclear detonations in a triangular zone measuring sixty-five by forty by forty-five miles with up to three more blasts within this area or points to the north. The War Department's official position on radioactivity at this time, as stated in an August 12, 1945, press release, was that "the bomb is detonated in combat, at such height above the ground, as to give the maximum blast effect against structures, and to disseminate the radioactive products as a cloud. . . . Practically all the radioactive products are carried upward in the ascending column of hot air and dispersed harmlessly over a wide area."[41] However, an internal report issued after the July Trinity test of a nuclear device in New Mexico described dangerous "hot spots" roughly twenty miles from ground zero. They included a ten-mile strip of U.S. Highway 380 and an area dubbed "Hot Canyon" along the path of the blast cloud.[42]

The close proximity of Bingham, New Mexico, to one of the areas receiving a heavy dusting of fallout, and the fact that two families near the "Hot Canyon" may have received large doses of radiation, was enough to prompt the Manhattan Project's medical chief to warn that "this site is too small for a repetition of a similar test."[43] Yet in spite of this sensitivity to possible radiation sickness and death, the expectation of dreadful casualties from purely conventional warfare during Olympic was so real that Marshall felt that tactical use of nuclear weapons was fully worth the risk, in spite of the possibility that potentially hideous consequences may have awaited some unknown number of the hundreds of thousands of U.S. soldiers and Marines fighting their way through a nuclear battlefield. In addition there would be tens of thousands more men stirring up the radiated dust during base and airfield construction.

The Imperial Rescript announcing Japan's surrender had cast blame on the American's "new and cruel bomb," which threatened not only the "ultimate collapse and obliteration of the Japanese nation" but also "the destruction of all human civilization."[44] It was duly noted by U.S. intelligence that Radio Tokyo's English-language broadcasts frequently repeated this theme and, in addition to protesting the "inhuman and sadistic" nature of the bombing campaign, stressed that "radioactivity was continuing where the Atomic Bombs had fallen."[45] Exactly how true (or not) this was seemed less important to American intelligence analysts and their customers than the fact that Magic intercepts were simultaneously decoding the new foreign minister's instructions to diplomats: "I think we should make every effort to exploit the atomic bomb question in our propaganda."[46]

While statements designed to garner political and diplomatic advantage would tend to make concurrent assertions of radiation sickness rather suspect, Magic, *over time*, may have provided invasion planners with a more clear picture of the lingering effects of radiation and prompted a switch to massive use of carpet bombing by B-29s in place of a tightly packed set of nuclear detonations. Months before Olympic the big bombers were already beginning to run out of "profitable" strategic targets.[47] Conventional use of massed B-29s in the areas likely to be transited by American troops, with atom bombs principally used against Japanese troop concentrations in the interior, would have undoubtedly reduced radiation poisoning among U.S. forces, but the emperor's surrender broadcast effectively ended any need for Marshall and his staff to pursue the initiative, let alone study the best means of employing atom bombs tactically.

The move toward tactical use would have spared some Japanese citizens (who might now be victims of conventional strikes) but would doom others. American planners estimated that of the 2.2 million people in the minimum Olympic target area who were unlikely to flee north with the retreating Imperial Army or to have been killed in the preinvasion bombardments, perhaps as many as 180,000 would be moved to internment camps.[48] If as originally planned the nuclear detonations were concentrated in the south instead of against troop concentrations along the northern approaches, many of the people in these camps would have been living near, or functionally on, the various blast sites, and even those who remained in the countryside would all be at the mercy of prevailing winds. In that case it is not unreasonable to suggest that several million Japanese, and Americans, would be directly affected by nuclear fallout or residual blast radiation on Kyushu, southern Shikoku, and aboard ships on the Philippine Sea.[49] Atomic attacks at locations to the north, however, would have only lessened, not prevented, radiation casualties among U.S. personnel and Japanese outside the blast areas.

★   ★   ★

At a time when Imperial leaders who had no knowledge of the U.S. nuclear program were contemplating the "sacrifice" of 20 million Japanese in the Home Islands to achieve some chimerical "victory" over the Americans,[50] and the war's invisible cost was rising to roughly

400,000 people per month from Indonesia through Manchuria,[51] Prime Minister Suzuki insisted on adding a story from his youth to an otherwise bellicose address before Japan's legislature, the Diet. The italicized text in the passage below was removed by an aide, reinserted by the old admiral, and generated such strident protests that the Suzuki cabinet nearly collapsed—and likely would have if General Anami, the most powerful man in the government, had added his voice to the uproar:

> Once in 1918 I navigated to the western coast of the United States as commander of the training squadron. When I was invited to a welcome reception at San Francisco I delivered an address concerning a war between Japan and the United States . . . I said that there was no cause for a war between the two countries, and that if there ever were a war, it would be much prolonged and would invite a very foolish result. I said that the Pacific Ocean is a blessing given by Heaven for the intercourse of Japan and the United States, and if the ocean were ever used for transporting troops *both countries would receive punishment from heaven.*[52]

Lives in untold numbers were spared by the Japanese capitulation. The war's sudden— and unexpected—conclusion in August 1945 has largely masked the fact that both sides were rushing headlong toward a disastrous confrontation in the Home Islands in which WMDs were to be employed in, as MacArthur's intelligence chief, Charles Willoughby, succinctly put it, "a hard and bitter struggle with no quarter asked or given."[53]

G-2 Estimate of Enemy Situation on Kyushu, U.S. Sixth Army, August 1, 1945

Note: This abridgment of "G-2 Estimate of the Enemy Situation, OPERATION OLYMPIC, 1 August 1945" consists of twenty-four of the document's fifty-two pages. Inconsistencies in the original typescript indicate that it was typed for mimeograph reproduction by at least two persons, and the formatting of the subsections in its latter half have been made to conform to that of the first for clarity. Use of angle brackets around a numeral (<1>) denotes page breaks.

HEADQUARTERS SIXTH ARMY

Office of the Assistant Chief of Staff, G-2
APO 442

1 August 1945

G-2 Estimate of the Enemy Situation
with respect to
Olympic Operation
(Southern Kyushu)

1. SUMMARY OF THE ENEMY SITUATION:

a.   <u>General Trend</u>: By midsummer of 1945 there was little that JAPAN could look backward to with pride or forward to with hope. The crescendo of Allied advance had grown apace, and with portentous results. The sequel to OKINAWA could only be an attack upon some part of the Inner Zone and presumably would be an invasion of the homeland. JAPAN acknowledged that. The key phrase in her own discussions of the war had now become "The decisive battle for the defense of the homeland."

JAPAN had to acknowledge also that for such defense she was, in some respects, in a bad way. Her resources, now that her sea reach had for all substantial purposes been cut off at SHANGHAI, were the resources of the Inner Zone, that is, of Occupied CHINA, MANCHURIA, KOREA, and the home islands. These resources were, as she had always maintained, considerable, but transportation from the continent and from KOREA had become costly because of the Allied surface, submarine, and aerial blockade. Even within the pale of the homeland islands transportation by rail, road, and waterways was suffering from aerial bombardment of communication centers and Superfort mining of strategic harbors and straits. Some 140 square miles of densely industrial concentrations and five major and numerous smaller cities had already been destroyed by the B-29s. Allied task forces plying hard by the coasts of HONSHU and HOKKAIDO taunted the shabby remnant of the Imperial Fleet by shelling selected industrial targets at will. Airfields, airfield installations, and aircraft on HONSHU, SHIKOKU, and KYUSHU were being regularly attacked by Allied land and carrier based planes. All this and more JAPAN had to acknowledge.

Nevertheless, she deliberately girded herself for homeland defense. In KYUSHU particularly, closest of the home islands to the newest Allied bases and naturally vulnerable to invasion, JAPAN with unprecedented speed took steps to meet the anticipated threat. By 1 July, as many combat divisions were estimated to have been disposed in SOUTHERN KYUSHU alone as earlier estimates had computed would be allotted to the whole of KYUSHU by target date. Here especially and in the homeland generally JAPAN intensified defensive construction, busied herself to maintain industrial production at high levels and to keep communications operative. She guarded her precious aircraft jealously, camouflaging and dispersing them, and committing as few as possible. She tightened governmental controls, at the same time making provision for local autonomy in anticipated emergencies. She organized her civilian strength under the Volunteer Corps for maintaining production, repairing damage to communications, and actual fighting in local defense. <1>

This JAPAN did while she considered the chances for success against the anticipated invasion. She hoped for war-weariness in the UNITED STATES. She hoped for Russian disturbance of the Allied political poise. She figured that this time the numerical superiority would be hers: the Allies, she maintained, could not possibly land so many troops in one place as she could oppose to them. She made much of what she believed were her logistic advantages over her enemy. In point of equipment, her still considerable air force, perhaps now almost wholly committed to the method of Kamikaze, offered the most substantial hope. Although she admitted that superiority of equipment still lay with the Allies, she protested once more that this would be outweighed by the spiritual superiority of "100,000,000 Japanese fighting for the Emperor and impelled by the spirit of the Special Attack Forces." These considerations, she hoped, would this time make the difference.

b. Enemy Activity in Forward Areas:

    (1) Ground:

        (a) Command structure: Enemy forces in SOUTHERN KYUSHU are believed to be under the immediate tactical command of one, and possibly two, Armies (Corps), while those in NORTHERN KYUSHU are thought to be under another Army (Corps). Exact boundaries between these armies are unknown; it can be supposed logically that the boundary between the northern Army and the southern Army (or Armies) lies along the central mountain range, or roughly the line MINAMATA-NOBEOKA. If there be in fact two Armies in SOUTHERN KYUSHU, the boundary dividing these may lie approximately along the line KAGOSHIMA WAN–KAJIKI–HITOYOSHI. (See Map Enclosure #1 and #2 for dispositions and tentative command boundaries.)

        These Armies (Corps) are in turn under command of the 16th Area Army believed to have been activated from the former Western District (administrative) Army, whose headquarters was at FUKUOKA. The zone assigned to this Area Army probably comprises KYUSHU and its off-lying islands, possibly including the Northern RYUKYUS.

        (b) Identifications. dispositions. and estimated strengths of principal enemy forces in SOUTHERN KYUSHU are shown in attached Order of Battle Annex #1. As of 21 July 1945, there were an estimated total of 196,000 troops comprising the following:

Mobile Combat Troops   121,000
(including an estimated 5 infantry divisions,
3 brigades, 2 replacement infantry regiments,
and miscellaneous artillery)

Base Defense   17,000
(including principally naval ground troops
and AA units)

Service Troops   58,000
(including principally shipping units and
some air-ground personnel)   _____

Total estimated enemy strength in KYUSHU   196,000*
south of the line MINAMATA-NOBEOKA
as of 21 July 1945

*This total does not include an estimated 25,000 flight and administrative personnel of the
Army and Navy Air Force, the bulk of which will presumably withdraw prior to X-day.

Tentative area breakdown and dispositions of the above enemy forces are illustrated on
Map Enclosure #1 and are summarized as follows:
   <2>

[Note: The detailed estimate of unit dispositions has been removed for clarity.]

SENDAI–KAGOSHIMA–SATSUMA PENINSULA
. . .
Total for area   46,000
<3>

MIYAKONOJO–KANOYA–OSUMI PENINSULA
. . . .
Total for area   42,000

NOBEOKA–MIYAZAKI PLAIN
. . . .
Total for area   65,000
<4>

KOBAYASHI-HITOYOSHI
. . . .
Total for area   27,000

AKUNE-MINAMATA-MIYANOJO
. . . .
Total for area   16,000

   (c)   Offlying islands: From the Order of Battle standpoint, the enemy
         situation on the various islands lying off SOUTHERN KYUSHU
         is obscure, with the exception of TANEGA-SHIMA where there are

an estimated 6,000 troops, of which 4,000 are classified as combat. Interpretation of photographs taken 13 May 1945 indicates the presence of a few AA guns and a radar installation on SHIMO KOSHIKI SHIMA, as well as some military barracks on the southern extremity of the island. KAMI and SHIMO KOSHIKI would be logical locations for assault demolition (suicide) boat units; photographs reveal unidentified small craft in the area. On the basis of the present scanty information, and particularly in view of the fact that late photographic interpretation is not available, it is considered impracticable to venture an estimate of enemy strength on KAMI and SHIMO KOSHIKI.

As further information on the above and other islands off SOUTHERN KYUSHU becomes available, it will be disseminated to interested headquarters.

(d)   Civilian combat strength: The augmentation to an indeterminate extent of regular Japanese Army, Naval, and Air Force strength by combatant civilian personnel is indicated by current enemy preparations for KYUSHU defense and by Allied experience in the RYUKYUS. It is probable that such combatant civilians will be organized as members either of the Home Defense Units or of the People's Volunteer Corps.

The normal function of the Home Defense Units is to supply the Army with common labor. Members of these units are conscripted from able-bodied men between the ages of 17 and 45 by village officials upon receipt, from the prefectural seat, of the Army's labor needs. At first, the units are organized into companies and given a modicum of training. <5> Food, clothing, and equipment are issued by the Army but are described as inferior to what is given the regular troops. The units lose their company identity upon becoming attached to Army battalions or airfield construction units. Although their sole function ordinarily is to provide labor, these units, according to current indications, are being prepared for lookout, liaison and guerrilla warfare duties, and are subject to being immediately incorporated into the regular Army as reinforcements.

The People's Volunteer Corps in its broadest sense includes all Japanese civilians; however, the productively useful of these are the men between the ages of 15 and 60 and the women between the ages of 17 and 40. Their normal and present function is war work in the broad sense: food and munitions production, transportation and communications work, and the like. As part of the general defense program, however, members have recently been given a "Manual for Combat" designed to prepare them for the emergency of Allied invasion. In it they are instructed to train for combat during off-hours at their places of work, to persist as long as possible under the pressure of attack in the work of production and transportation, to aid in the construction of defenses, to repair communications and airfield facilities, and to relieve regular Army units of rear area duties. Indications are that, when there is military need, some of the members will be activated into fighting units or Voluntary Combat Corps; at such time they will receive distinguishing insignia and fixed pay and rations, and they will fight single-handedly, as guerrilla forces, or in cooperation with regular Army units.

On OKINAWA it was inferred from the fact that comparatively few able-bodied men between the ages of 17 and 45 were found among the bypassed civilians, that a considerable number had become absorbed into the Japanese armed forces. On little IE-SHIMA such combatant civilians, aggressively taking part in suicide charges, infiltration raids, and cave and tunnel defense, constituted almost half of the 5,000 enemy opposed to the Allies. It is estimated on the basis of military manpower statistics issued by MIS, WDGS, as of April 1945 that of the 400,000 males between the ages of 17 and 44 in SOUTHERN KYUSHU not then in the military forces, some 300,000 were fit for military service, and hence are now available for civilian combat duty. What portion of these are likely to find their way into combatant service cannot now be estimated. Experience on OKINAWA gives only a token indication. It has been estimated that about one-eighth of the total population served in full or semi-military capacity. It may be assumed that similar ratios would apply in the homeland.

(e)   Military activity and defensive construction: At this time aerial photography of SOUTHERN KYUSHU is too limited in point of areas covered and frequency of coverage to serve as the basis for a full description of the nature and scope of enemy activity and defensive construction on the island. Consequently, although it must be assumed that such activity and defensive preparations are keeping pace with the known enemy troop reinforcement of the area, an adequate account of these developments must await ampler photographic coverage.

Some indication of the thrust and extent of enemy defensive preparations can, however, be suggested here on the basis of partial and merely preliminary photographic coverage, visual air sightings, and a numbered few PW interrogation reports. The defensive installations and activities thus arrived at are graphically shown in

"Consolidated Report #1," prepared jointly by ComPhibsPac and G-2 Sixth Army as of 25 July 1945, and are summarized below.

Apparently the primary enemy concern as thus indicated is for his vulnerable coastal areas, permanent Army, Naval, and Air Force installations and for the routes of communication connecting these with <6> each other and with NORTHERN KYUSHU. So, for example, most of the 23 airfields in SOUTHERN KYUSHU are comparatively densely protected by automatic weapons ranging from heavy AA and DP guns to light MGs. Current indications are that some 875 such automatic weapons have been emplaced for the defense of these fields. The most heavily protected of the fields are the KANOYA–KANOYA EAST–KUSHIRA fields of the OSUMI interior, the MIYAZAKI-MIYAKONOJO fields to the north, and the KAGOSHIMA Naval installations of the northern SATSUMA PENINSULA. It will be remembered that enemy AA guns not destroyed by Allied aerial and ground attack tend to find their way in time to improvised use in a ground role.

The following, described in an order proceeding along the coast from HOSOSHIMA POINT south and west to MAKURAZAKI are some of the representative defensive developments in SOUTHERN KYUSHU. Small trenches observed near the summit of the hill mass rising from the valley of the SHIOMA-GAWA at HOSOSHIMA POINT suggest that this high ground may have been put to its naturally inviting use for gun emplace-ments commanding the beach to the south. Photographic interpre-tation and visual reconnaissance indicate that the HOSOSHIMA-TOMITAKA sector has many large communications (radar, range finding, and air warning) facilities. A heavy artillery position is located just south of TOMITAKA field on a spur at an elevation of 650 feet. Recent photographs show an increase in the number of AA positions at NITTAGAHARA field, and twelve automatic weapons pits on the beach fronting it. Stock piles of lumber are lying about in the vicinity; in late May, 56 box cars and two tank cars were observed on a rail siding in the vicinity of the NITTAGAHARA drome; what are tentatively interpreted to be Baka-revetments have been detected in the hangar area.

There are partially concealed beach defenses east of the HIPPO main-line railroad and north of the mouth of the OYODO-GAWA. The MIYAZAKI airdrome itself has but 8 AA and 20 MGs protecting it, but the beach fronting the drome has been partially prepared for defense. Several bunkers, some 12 automatic weapons pits, and two DP gun positions have been detected here; moreover, firing trenches, weapons pits, and foxholes surround the drome area.

Farther south, at the point of TOZAKI-HANA, unidentified defensive installations and barracks-type buildings have been observed. It deserves notice that the small and land-locked beach immediately north of ABARATSU, a town well served by secondary roads inland, has been prepared for defense by communications trenches, tank traps, and pillboxes in the area behind the beach. In the general area of TOI and TOI-MISAKI, at the northeastern head of ARIAKE-WAN, possible trenches, some AA weapons pits, two occupied DP gun positions, and unidentified camouflaged buildings can be detected. Obviously the elevated terrain inland from both the northern and southern heads of ARIAKE-WAN is naturally accommodating to the emplacement of concealed heavy gun positions. None of these, however, has become apparent to date, nor have any defenses been observed along the ARIAKE beach. Inland, however, in the greater KANOYA area, the Japanese according to present indications have been more active defensively than in any other sector of SOUTHERN KYUSHU. Some 360 AAA guns are believed available for defense of the three fields. There are 25 caves and 125 tunnels in the vicinity of the airfields, large underground storage areas between TABUCHI and SHISHIMA, and much logging in the vicinity of URA. To the south, in the extreme southern portion of OSUMI PENINSULA, look-out posts and coastal defense installations were reported by PWs to be extant in 1942. The same sources indicated that the area just south of ISASHIKI was a restricted area and that on this point of the peninsula coastal guns have been emplaced for which ammunition is hauled from KANOYA. The good western peninsular coastal road confirms the possibility of such defensive installations in this commanding sector. <7>

Moderate barge and coastal vessel traffic is periodically observed in KAGOSHIMA-WAN. The entrance to the bay has the protection of the apparently carefully defended seaplane base at IBUSUKI, PWs indicated that here also coastal guns and built-in defense positions have been emplaced. Four tunnels built into the hill parallel the railroad and have rail spurs leading into them. Earth spoils and log piles confirm the further development of underground storage activity already in evidence. PWs also report gasoline storage and ammunition dumps in the vicinity southeast of IKEDA-KO, a report confirmed at least by the presence of dead-end roads terminating there. At ONO-TAKE northwest of LAKE IKEDA three caves can be seen.

It seems certain that later and periodically repeated photographic coverage will disclose similar defensive activity in the areas of the MAKURAZAKI and SHIBUSHI beaches and, indeed, much more elaborately developed defenses of the SOUTHERN KYUSHU inland generally. That it is reported above, accordingly, must be regarded merely as a preliminary and tentative survey.

(2)   Air: Available to the enemy in SOUTHERN KYUSHU before Allied aerial attacks had begun were a total of 23 airfields and seaplane bases of all types. These were classified as follows:

Name	Class*	U/C	Army	Navy
BYU	HLG	X		
CHIRAN	HLG		X	
IBUSUKI	SS			X
IWAKAWA	MLG	X		
IZUMI	MLG			X
KAGOSHIMA	ASS		X	
KAGOSHIMA	MAD	X		
KANOYA	MAD		X	X
KANOYA EAST	MAD			X
KARASEHARA	HAD		X	
KOKUBU	FAD			X
KORIMOTO	HAD	X		
KUSHIRA	MAD			X
MIYAKONOJO	MAD		X	X
MIYAKONOJO NORTH	MAD		X	

Name	Class*	U/C	Army	Navy
MIYAZAKI	MAD			X
NITTAGAHARA	MAD		X	
RONCHI	MAD			X
SADOHARA	HAD		X	
SAKITA	ASS			X
SHIBUSHI	MAD	X		
TOJIMBARA	FLG	X		
TOMITAKA	FAD		X	X

*HAD—Heavy bomber airfield   HLG—Heavy bomber landing ground
 MAD—Medium bomber airfield   MLG—Medium bomber landing ground
 FAD—Fighter airfield   FLG—Fighter landing ground
 ASS—Auxiliary seaplane station   SS—Seaplane station

Enemy aircraft on these fields have decreased in number as the frequency and force of Allied raids increased. Total combat planes of all types on SOUTHERN KYUSHU fields as of 15 July were estimated to be 300. Of these 200 were bombers, 45 were fighters, and 55 were reconnaissance planes and other types.

> (3) Naval: As in the PHILIPPINES and OKINAWA, the enemy is placing great reliance upon small craft for defense against amphibious landings on KYUSHU. It is probable that many secluded and concealed <8> points along the SOUTHERN KYUSHU coast, the enemy has set up bases for PT-type craft, assault demolition boats, and possibly other suicide naval weapons such as midget submarines and one-man torpedoes. Shore-emplaced torpedoes and ground-launched rockets may also be included in the arsenals of such anti-invasion bases, Their specific locations are unknown; low-level oblique photography and visual reconnaissance may later reveal their presence. Logical locations would include ARIAKE-WAN, KAGOSHIMA-WAN, the coast south of the MIYAZAKI area, and islands lying off KYUSHU.

The enemy is believed to have mined ARIAKE-WAN, and the waters off MIYAZAKI.

c. Movements, Concentrations, and Establishments in Rear Areas:

> (1) Ground:
>> (a) Identifications, dispositions, and estimated strengths of principal enemy forces in NORTHERN KYUSHU (north of the line MINAMATA-NOBEOKA) are shown in attached Order of Battle Annex #1. As of 21 July 1945, there was an estimated total of 225,000 troops in this area, comprising the following:

Mobile Combat Troops	92,000
(including an estimated 2 infantry divisions,	
1 complete depot division, 1 depot division (-2 regiments),	
1 brigade, 1 tank regiment, 2 tank regt repl units, and SNLPs)	
Base Defense	57,000
(including fortress troops, naval ground troops,	
and large concentrations of AA units)	
Service Troops	76,000
(including principally air-ground,	
shipping, and depots)	——
Total estimated enemy strength in KYUSHU	
north of the line MINAMATA-NOBEOKA as	
of 21 July 1945	225,000**

**This total does not include an estimated 20,000 flight and administrative personnel of the Army and Navy Air Force.

Tentative area breakdown and dispositions of the above enemy forces are illustrated on Map Enclosure #2 and are summarized as follows:
<9>

[Note: The detailed estimate of unit movements and dispositions has been removed for clarity.]:

NORTHEAST KYUSHU (OITA KEN)

. . . .

Total for area   28,000

NORTH CENTRAL KYUSHU
(KUMAMOTO PLAIN)

. . . .

Total for area   53,000
<10>

NORTH AND NORTHWEST KYUSHU
(NAGASAKI< SAGA< AND FUKUOKA KEN)

. . . .

Total for area   144,000

(b)   Unlocated units: Several units are definitely known to be in KYUSHU, but exact locations are undetermined. Notable among these are the following:

32nd Ind Tank Bn	630
13th Med Arty Regt	1,650
54th Med Arty Regt	1,650

It is believed that there are possibly many additional units equipped with assault-demolition (suicide) craft, both of the Army (GYORO battalions) and Navy (SHINYO units), not specifically accounted for in any of the above tabulations. Such units are probably located principally along the SOUTH KYUSHU coastline and on the off-lying islands, particularly those lying astride potential convoy routes.

Although there is no direct evidence, it is also believed that rocket battalions and numerous independent mortar units are located in the SOUTHERN KYUSHU area.

(2) <u>Air</u>: Besides those in SOUTHERN KYUSHU, 120 known airfields and seaplane bases of all types, ranging from unclassified fields to heavy bomber airdromes, are available to the enemy within a 600-mile radius of KAGOSHIMA (See Map Enclosure #3). As of 15 July it was estimated that there were 5,000 enemy combat planes of all types within range of intervention, of which approximately 2,800 were fighters, 1,200 were bombers, and 1,000 were reconnaissance planes and other types. In addition, the enemy has an unknown number of training planes of all types, a majority of which can be used in combat, at least for suicide crashes. Some estimates of the number of these training planes range as high as 4,000–5,000.

(3) <u>Naval</u>: Except for a few submarines on patrol or on supply runs in outlying regions, and except for 2 cruisers and 2 destroyers last reported at SINGAPORE, what is left of the Japanese fleet is currently based in home waters. It consists of the following:

Type	**Number**	**Number Operational**
Battleships	3	1
Converted Battleships	2	2
Aircraft Carriers (CV)	4	4 <11>
Escort Carriers (CVE)	3	2
Aircraft Carriers (CVL)	3	2
Heavy Cruisers	2	2
Light Cruisers	2	2
Destroyers	40	37
Destroyer Escorts	8	8
Submarines	60	32

Three of the CVs listed above as operational are under heavy camouflage and are therefore not believed to be immediately available for action. Most of the operational fleet units are currently located at four principal home naval bases. Five or six carriers, two heavy cruisers, and numerous destroyers, submarines and escort vessels were recently under construction in Japanese shipyards; this work has now been suspended for the most part, at least on the heavy units. It can be assumed that further heavy air attacks will probably cause the suspension of the remainder of the building program and the destruction of a substantial portion of the above listed vessels.

The Japanese are known to possess an ample number of small craft for troop and supply movement. As of 1 February 1945, it was estimated that they had in the homeland a total of 3,170 vessels of 100 to 1,000 gross tons, and about 9,500 full-powered and auxiliary craft of less than 100 gross tons. It must be concluded that the enemy will have available in the protected waters adjacent to NORTHERN KYUSHU an adequate supply of small craft for almost any desired scale of troop and supply movement, whether inter-island or along the coast of KYUSHU.

d. <u>Terrain and Weather as They Affect the Enemy</u>:

    (1)   Weather: See Annex #2, "Climatological and Oceanographic Study of SOUTHERN KYUSHU for Period September to February."

    (2)   Terrain: See Annex #3, "Tactical Study of the Terrain, SOUTHERN KYUSHU," with Appendices #1 and #2.

2. CONCLUSIONS

a. <u>Enemy Capabilities</u>:

    (1)   Reinforcement of SOUTHERN KYUSHU prior to X-day: Invasion of the RYUKYUS in April convinced the Japanese that an assault on SOUTHERN KYUSHU would in all likelihood follow soon afterwards. Apparently acting upon an estimate of the situation that the attack might come in mid-summer, the Japanese have spared no effort to build up the mobile combat potential in SOUTHERN KYUSHU to a level, as of 21 July, of an estimated 5 divisions, 3 brigades, and 2 replacement regiments of the 6th Depot Division—the equivalent of about 7 divisions in all. Granted an unexpected respite of several months before the blow actually falls, the enemy presumably will seize the opportunity to strengthen his position to a still greater degree.

        Although our ever increasing aerial offensive can be expected to hamper the execution of the enemy's movements and redispositions, it cannot, in view of the long period of time intervening and the wide choice of means available to the enemy along interior lines of communication, prevent such movements from being carried out prior to X-day. Complete interdiction of the KAMMON TUNNEL and of the KYUSHU railroad and provincial highway system, even if attainable, would mean from a practical standpoint only that the enemy would be compelled to resort to the use of barges and small craft, with which he is plentifully supplied, for inter-island and coastal movement, to the use of detours around <12> obstacles and to travel on the secondary roads of KYUSHU.

        An additional increment of 3 to 4 divisions in the SOUTHERN KYUSHU garrison prior to X-day must be considered as well within the enemy's capabilities. The additions could come from any one or a combination of the following sources: a) Side-slipping one or more of the divisions presently estimated in NORTHERN KYUSHU, replacing them with divisions brought in from MANCHURIA, KOREA, HONSHU, SHIKOKU, or HOKKAIDO; b) direct movement to SOUTHERN KYUSHU of divisions from one or more of these rear areas; c) activation of divisions from either or both of the depot divisions (6th and 56th) presently on KYUSHU; d) enlarging one or more of the estimated brigades in SOUTHERN KYUSHU to divisional status; or e) the formation of provisional combat organizations from surplus Naval, base and service troops, possibly augmented by local conscription.

The conclusion is that by X-day the Japanese could easily have raised the currently estimated 7 combat divisions or division-equivalents in SOUTHERN KYUSHU to 10 or 11 divisions, together with appropriate base and service units. It is believed that depot stocks built up in NORTHERN KYUSHU are sufficient to equip these troops initially and to maintain them for an extended period of time in the objective area. Based on present dispositions and upon the strong probability of further reinforcement to a grand total of 10 divisions or division-equivalents, X-day dispositions will probably be approximately as follows:

MIYAZAKI PLAIN	3 divisions
MIYAKONOJO-ARIAKE	1 division
ARIAKE HARBOR–KANOYA area	1 division
Head of KOGOSHIMA–WAN–KOKUBU area	1 division (initially in army reserve)
KUSHIKINO PLAIN–OKUCHI–MIYANOJO area	1 1/2 divisions (initially in army reserve)
MAKURAZAKI–Southern SATSUMA PENINSULA	1/2 division

(2) Ground defense:

(a) General considerations:

1. Tactics: In estimating the enemy's probable ground reaction to an invasion of SOUTHERN KYUSHU, late trends in Japanese tactical doctrine as promulgated in captured field manuals* and as exemplified in recent campaigns (notably OKINAWA and LUZON) should be given careful consideration. Principal tenets of current enemy defensive doctrine appear to be briefly as follows:

a. In recent campaigns, reliance on strong defenses in the beach areas has been almost wholly abandoned. Beach organization has been directed towards harassing a landing as much as possible, principally by artillery fire, without irrevocably committing the main force to position defense or counterattack in the beach area. Due, however, to the numerical strength and terrain advantages the enemy will possess in SOUTHERN KYUSHU, it is believed highly probable that he will revert to his long-favored doctrine of "annihilating the enemy at the water's edge" and that a very strong and ferocious defense will be interposed at the beaches. (See below, Paragraph 2 a (2) (b), pages 18–21.)

* See particularly "Manual for Defense Against Landings," published by Japanese General Staff Headquarters, Oct 1944, translated by ATIS as Enemy Publication No. 384, dated 2 June 1945; and "Land Defense Doctrine," OGASAWARA Group Hq, 1 Dec 1944, captured on OKINAWA, translated by CINCPAC-CINCPOA as Translations—Interrogations #32, Bulletin 147–145, 16 June 1945. <13>

b. The Japanese have adopted a policy of all-around defense in depth, utilizing rugged ground in the interior of the island under attack. Whenever possible, the rugged area is chosen in the vicinity of beaches on which the attacker is likely to attempt a landing or in the vicinity of key objectives, so that artillery emplaced in such terrain will, in addition to supporting the MLR, be in position to interdict access to harbor and beach areas, airfields, and other key objectives. The rugged inland terrain is thoroughly organized, principally by means of underground positions, in a series of centers of resistance, each of which is usually manned by a unit of battalion size. In the defense of an organized area, the Japanese retire from position to position when they are in immediate danger of being isolated. The majority die in place when there are no further rearward positions to which they can retreat; however, when the Japanese find themselves in such a predicament, or when command control has broken down, the "banzai charge" is sometimes launched.

c. The trend has been away from large-scale counter attacks launched against the beachhead soon after the landing. Instead, the Japanese emphasize smaller counterattacks launched from strongpoints or from their immediate vicinity. They attempt to time such attacks to hit the attacking troops when they are most vulnerable. There has been an increase in the percentage of the defending force held in reserve, but such reserves generally have been used ineffectively. Most counter-attacks have been on a relatively small scale, but a few exceptions—such as that on OKINAWA in early May—indicate that larger ones can be mounted when the Japanese consider them justified. It is highly probable that an invasion of KYUSHU will be regarded by the Japanese as dictating the necessity of a large-scale counterattack, possibly early.

d.   The Japanese have been intent lately on improving their now almost orthodox defensive battle tactics of cave and tunnel warfare. Most of these improvements as outlined in captured documents and partially borne out in PHILIPPINE and RYUKYU practice, aim at better firepower protection of the vicinity of the cave mouths. This is effected in a number of ways: the caves are so sited as to be mutually supporting; carefully concealed open emplacements of weapons cover the mouths when the cave-emplaced weapons have been neutralized; mortar fire is laid on the entrance area from defiladed positions, and artillery fire is registered on the same area at longer range than formerly; and dummy positions are set up to waste opposing fire power. Besides, Jap soldiers show less disposition to remain in or retreat into the caves until disaster strikes; instead they contend for the position in hand-to-hand combat and grenade duels. Moreover, caves are sited on reverse slopes, thus prolonging command of the hilltops and making progress down the slopes difficult. Cave embrasures are made small, and discovery and neutralization become correspondingly difficult. Protective devices, largely field expedients, are encouraged against napalm and flame-thrower attacks.

e.   The defensive value of towns and cities has been stressed. The Japanese can be expected to make maximum use of town warfare. The Battle for MANILA has set the pattern for what the enemy can be expected to do in the defense of Japanese towns and cities.*

   *See "Jap Defense of Cities as Exemplified by the Battle for MANILA," a report by XIV Corps published by AC of S, G-2, Hq 6th Army. <14>

f.   As above indicated, the principal role of artillery is defined as being primarily to support the defense at the MLR (i.e., in the hills inland from the beaches), with the secondary mission of firing at landing craft and beachhead positions. Most of the artillery is emplaced within and to the rear of the MLR, only limited quantities being deployed at beach positions. Fire is directed to be withheld until the landing operations are actually initiated, so as to avoid pinpointing and destruction by opposing naval gunfire and aerial bombing. A far greater use has been made of artillery in recent operations than formerly, apparently because more guns have been available and not because of any fundamental change in the doctrine governing their use. Massed fire, in the modern sense of the term, has not been employed except in a few rare instances (e.g., OKINAWA) and the theory of massed fire is only partially appreciated in higher enemy echelons. A more effective use of artillery in the defense of SOUTHERN KYUSHU than has yet been common could be achieved by the organization of an artillery command such as was employed at OKINAWA. It will be recalled that there the 5th Artillery Command, essentially a corps artillery headquarters, coordinated the massing of the enemy's artillery for a major counterattack on 4–5 May, during which a preparatory barrage of 12,000–14,000 rounds was laid down in a 24-hour period on a corps front.

g. The enemy continues to place great reliance upon numerous varieties of suicide infiltration and raiding tactics. These run the gamut from the "close quarter" suicide attacks upon tanks, employing lunge mines, explosive charges and anti-tank mines, to the "penetration" attacks directed at artillery positions, supply dumps, headquarters, and other rear installations. These infiltration tactics will probably be exploited to the utmost; and it can be expected that in addition to the regular combat troops the "People's Volunteer Corps" and "Home Defense Units" will be widely utilized for such suicide missions.

h. The employment of counterlanding units to attack Allied beachheads from the sea has never attained the success the Japanese expected, but such units will doubtless continue to be used as long as access to the sea exists. There are at least two known amphibious brigades in JAPAN. It is entirely possible that one or both of thorn will be moved to KYUSHU before X day. The mission of these units, as the name implies, is to make amphibious landings. On the defensive, the Japanese will presumably attempt to use them as counter-landing forces; their T/O and T/E provides for a complement of barges equivalent to that of a sea transport unit of a streamlined division.

2. Weapons: Profiting greatly from German designs and technical assistance, the Japanese have developed numerous new weapons, some of which have come to light during recent campaigns; others will probably be unveiled for the first time when the homeland is assaulted. In addition to these now

weapons and devices, the Japanese will probably continue to improvise unusual modes of employment of their older types of weapons. Principal trends to be noted in connection with enemy ordnance are:

a.   Rockets and guided missiles, designed for use not only against the very heavy bombers and amphibious assault forces, but also against ground targets, will probably be extensively employed. Addition of the suicide factor—the piloted bomb—renders these weapons still more potent. Besides the so-called "baka" bomb launched from mother aircraft, there is evidence of a new type of jet-propelled suicide airplane launched from ramps or catapults; an installation at KANOYA airfield is suggestive of the presence of such a weapon. Rocket types likely to be employed are the already familiar 200-mm and 447-mm "spin stabilized" varieties encountered on LUZON. The Japanese have also developed rocket motors by which aerial bombs can <15> be launched from ground installations.

b.   Concentrations of coastal defense guns, protected from aerial obser-vation and attack, representing the reinforcement of portal fixed defenses by surplus naval weapons, may have been installed in the SOUTHERN KYUSHU area. It can be expected that as in the past guns moved from deactivated or damaged naval vessels will be utilized in this manner. Specific evidence of such activity in SOUTHERN KYUSHU is, however, lacking.

c.   Anti-aircraft artillery, including probably a newly developed 88-mm gun will be extensively employed in a ground defense role. In this connection, it will be noted that as of 15 July 1945, it was estimated there were 240 heavy, 585 medium, and 50 light AA pieces active in SOUTHERN KYUSHU. All of these which escape damage from preliminary air and naval bombardment will probably be incorpo-rated into the enemy's ground defense system. In addition, automatic weapons recovered from wrecked aircraft may be similarly utilized in considerable numbers.

d.   Mines and demolition charges of various kinds, many employing the hollow charge principle, will undoubtedly be given widespread use. Minefields actuated by remote control will be encountered in increasing numbers. Use of depth charges and aerial bombs as improvised land mines can be expected. All manner of booby traps will undoubtedly be exploited to the utmost.

e. Increased emphasis on anti-tank weapons, including bazooka-type rocket launchers and high velocity guns, possibly adaptations of similar German weapons, must be expected. Various types of suicide anti-tank weapons such as the lunge mine and shoulder pack mine will be employed in this operation.

f. New and improved tanks, with heavier armor and more powerful weapons, including some armed with flame throwers, may possibly be encountered in KYUSHU. Two improved models of the Type 97 medium tank are supposed to be under development, as well as a Type 4, allegedly superior to the latest German Mark IV, and able to engage the Sherman tank on equal terms. The Type 4 is said to weigh 30 tons, with a maximum armor thickness of 75-mm, and armed with a Type 99 long 75-mm tank gun. The extent to which these items are in production is unknown; however, tank units encountered in KYUSHU may be at least partially equipped with these new vehicles. Allied forces will probably encounter also some self-propelled artillery similar in type to that used on LUZON; 15-cm and 75-mm self-propelled guns were encountered here, and PWs and documents indicate a third type mounting a 10-cm gun.

g. Resort to gas or bacterial warfare must be regarded as an unlikely enemy capability.

3. <u>State of preparation</u>: As elsewhere stated, the enemy, in anticipation of early Allied landings in SOUTHERN KYUSHU, began moving major combat units to this area on a large scale in April. As of 21 July, the presence of mobile combat troops equivalent to about 7 divisions and a total of approximately 75,000 base and service troops is estimated.

It can be assumed that under coordinating direction of the probable SOUTHERN KYUSHU Army (Corps) Headquarters, intensive preparations for defense were initiated by these troops promptly upon arrival in the objective area. These preparations undoubtedly included construction of gun emplacements, underground defensive systems, establishment of bivouac and supply areas, and the all-around organization of critical <16> areas for defense. A plentiful supply of labor is assured by the mobilization of the civilian population. The relatively long time intervening until X-day gives the enemy ample time to complete these preparations. A very high degree of organization of the ground chosen by the Japanese for defense can therefore be assumed.

4. Morale: The largest single important consideration in estimating the state of enemy morale for the defense of KYUSHU is the obvious fact that for the Japanese their "homeland" will be invaded. Inasmuch as the enemy has, even in the defense of island outposts where, comparatively speaking, far less was at stake, proved to be a vigorous and determined defender, it must be assumed that his fighting spirit in this homeland "kessen" [battle] will be unusually high. Moreover, his currently demonstrated ability to withstand sustained Allied aerial pounding is itself an indication of a tough will-to-defend. Until good evidence points to the contrary therefore, it seems most justified to assume that the defenders of KYUSHU, both military and civilian, fighting as they suppose for the Emperor and their own homes, spurred by intense national feeling and continuous propaganda, misinformed about the international state of affairs, and confident of their numerical and spiritual superiority, are facing invasion with high morale.

5. Role of civilian defense units: As stated in Paragraph 1 b (1) (d), the Japanese are exerting maximum effort to mobilize the civilian population to assist in repelling invasion of the homeland. The steps taken in this direction are known to include the SOUTHERN KYUSHU area. As indicated in the paragraph above referred to, it is estimated that a maximum of some 300,000 civilians are available to the enemy in SOUTHERN KYUSHU for "civilian combatant" service. That percentage of these will actually become active in combatant functions of one kind or another cannot now be significantly determined. It is obvious that the principal function and value of these auxiliaries will lie in their use as rear area labor and service troops. It can be expected that they will be used extensively as carriers, trench-diggers, truck drivers, road and bridge repair gangs, and the like. Functioning in this capacity they will naturally release considerable numbers of those trained troops who would normally perform such service functions.

    To some of these Volunteer Corps civilians, sufficient training will probably be given by X-day to develop limited combat value for merely local defense. The enemy is believed to possess a sufficient supply of obsolete small arms (principally 6.5 rifles and machine guns), hand grenades, and possibly anti-tank and lunge mines to equip a considerable number of these troops. Enemy sources indicate that the most scantily equipped will have bamboo spears and clubs. At best, it seems reasonable to conclude, such civilian personnel will be only lightly armed, widely dispersed in small groups, and relatively immobile. Their effectiveness against well-armed troops will be relatively low even in defense and virtually nil in offense. However, inasmuch as eliminating them will require the expenditure of time and means, such civilian auxiliaries will have considerable nuisance value, particularly in rear areas. They will enable the Japanese to fight short local delaying actions (e.g., at the beaches) without sacrificing trained troops. They will require the commitment of additional forces to guarding lines of communications and to security missions. Eventually, they can afford the enemy a means of ready replacement by which the deterioration of combat divisions may be partially retarded. <17>

b.   Probable conduct of the defense:

    (1)   In general:

        (a)   Beach defense: Current enemy dispositions strongly imply the probability of a determined defense at the beaches. The terrain would emphatically favor the adoption of such a course of action. The principal coastal lowland areas, namely, the MIYAZAKI, ARIAKE, and KUSHIKINO PLAINS, are not, as the designation would suggest, flat areas, but consist of badly dissected alluvial terraces and river flats. These terraces and their steep faces, many of which are very near critical landing beaches, are among the most important terrain features of military significance. Their serrated edges are almost cliff-like in most places, varying from 25 to 250 feet above the flat valley floors. Where the terrace surface has broken down and there are no large rivers, the country is a tines of narrow, deep gullies and ravines, the highest points and ridges of which are at or below the elevation of the terrace top. The defensive potentialities of these terrace formations are obvious at a glance; almost unlimited opportunities are presented for the construction of cave and underground fortifications and for the emplacement of artillery, and in some cases even automatic weapons, within easy range of the landing beaches themselves. Many of these positions will probably be immune to neutralization by air raid naval bombardment.

        Moreover, the coastal lowlands are ringed with foothills which provide excellent observation over practically all landing beaches in SOUTHERN KYUSHU; the enemy, accordingly, will have good opportunity to oppose our assault echelons with observed artillery fire from artfully concealed battery positions.

    It must therefore be concluded that because of the terrain and the ample forces available to the enemy, he can in this operation revert to his favored doctrine of "annihilating the enemy at the water's edge" The adoption of a strong and active beach defense is a capability to be seriously reckoned with in this operation.

        (b)   Inland defense: Except for the three main lowland areas facing the sea, SOUTHERN KYUSHU is a complex jumble of low, rugged mountains and upland plateaus varying in elevation from 1,500 to

2,500 feet (with a few peaks rising to 3,500–5,500 feet), interspersed with small basins, notable among which are the MIYAKONOJO and HITOYOSHI BASINS. The corridors connect the coastal lowlands with one another and with the inland basins are long, narrow, winding valleys dominated by heights on both sides.

These terrain features lend themselves almost ideally to the development of the typical Japanese dug-in defensive systems in depth. Known enemy dispositions and photo interpretation alike suggest that the Japanese are well aware of the potentialities; in the terraced areas and foothills behind the beaches and in the rugged inland areas. Allied forces can expect to encounter a whole series of organized positions like the "SHIMBU" and BALETE PASS defense lines on LUZON and the "SHURI" line on OKINAWA. (See Enclosure Map #1, and "Consolidated Report No. 1," prepared jointly by ComPhibsPac and G-2 Sixth Army, 25 July 1945.)

(2) <u>Specific critical areas</u>:

(a) <u>MIYAZAKI PLAIN</u>: An estimated two divisions are believed to be spread from TOMITAKA to TOZAKI-HANA. Probably the bulk of their strength is dug in on the high ground to the rear of the coastal plain, but for the reasons above cited it is likely that a part of their strength, considerably augmented by home defense and base and service troops, will be deployed for beach defense. Massing of the two divisions or counterattack would probably require a minimum of 3–4 days. Movement of an estimated division (probably in corps or army reserve) from the <18> KOBAYASHI area to the MIYAZAKI PLAIN would require a minimum of 3–5 nights. It is therefore estimated that during the 24 to 48 hours subsequent to the Allied landing the Japanese can oppose our forces in the MIYAZAKI PLAIN with the equivalent of one division, building up to 3 divisions, plus an unknown but appreciable number of home defense and base and service troops, during the period X plus 3 to X plus 5. It must be remembered that these are optimum figures; intensive air interdiction of the restricted routes of approach should considerably retard the development of this strength.

The above capability is predicted upon the present enemy strength and dispositions; if, as elsewhere indicated, another division is brought to SOUTHERN KYUSHU and placed in reserve in the MIYAKONOJO BASIN area, the above capability must be correspondingly enlarged.

The enemy will naturally devote much effort to the defense of air bases. He perhaps intends to attempt the interdiction of the use of MIYAZAKI airfield by artillery emplaced on the dominating terrain to the southwest; such artillery would likewise be within range of the adjacent section of landing beach. SADOHARA airfield is constructed on a terrace top and therefore is eminently suitable for close-in perimeter defense from underground positions; the only improved avenues of approach are roads which follow ravines or cuts to the top surface of the terrace. Special emphasis will probably be placed upon the defense and/or demolition of the critical railroad and highway bridges across the OYODO RIVER.

From identifications already obtained, it seems probable that heavy concentrations of artillery weapons will be emplaced in the hills surrounding the MAYAZAKI PLAIN, and particularly on the dominating ground astride the narrow corridors traversed by the highway and railroad line from MIYAZAKI to MIYAKONOJO. It is considered very likely that these corridor approaches will be strongly defended in depth.

(b)   ARIAKE–WAN–KANOYA area: Allied troops landing in this area will probably initially be opposed by elements of the 86th Division. It is believed that the bulk of the division will initially be disposed for position defense in depth; its massing for counterattack would probably require at least 2–3 days. There is at present no known major combat unit either in the KOBUKU or MIYAKONOJO areas; if additional divisions are brought to SOUTHERN KYUSHU prior to X-day, it is quite possible one of them will be disposed in the MIYAKONOJO area, and another in the KOKUBU area. Time and space factors suggest that movement of the division from MIYAKONOJO would require a minimum of 2–3 nights, while that from KOKUBU would take 3–5 nights.

If enemy dispositions on X-day are substantially the same as at present, Allied forces in the ARIAKE area can be opposed by one division, augmented by home guard and base and service troops, within a period of 48–72 hours after landing. If reserve divisions are by X-day located in the MIYAKONOJO and KOKUBU areas, and if the enemy decides to commit them on the ARIAKE beachhead rather than KUSHIKINO or MIYAZAKI, the opposing forces could be built up to the extent of three divisions, plus base and service troops, by X plus 4 or X plus 5. Again, however, optimum conditions are assumed; aerial interdiction of the routes of approach may and probably will appreciably hamper the assembling of this strength in the objective area.

The distinctive terrain feature of the ARIAKE-WAN area is the hills overlooking and dominating the bay area from northeast and southwest; it is very probable that artillery and coast defense guns <19> have been emplaced in these hills under heavy concealment, in defiladed positions masked from naval gunfire. The enemy may take unusual precautions to withhold fire of these weapons until the landing phase of the operation actually begins; at IWO JIMA, it was only the fact that the Japanese confused the minesweeping craft with landing craft that permitted such positions to be discovered and neutralized prior to H-hour.

Resembling the situation on the MIYAZAKI PLAIN, there are at the head of ARIAKE-WAN terraced formations rising from 20–30 feet high in the south to 150–200 feet high behind SHIBUSHI. These terraces vary in distance from 100 yards to 1,000 yards in rear of the beach. Their utilization for underground positions is a high probability.

As elsewhere pointed out, there is considerable evidence of development of underground positions in the vicinity of KANOYA air base; this air base is built on one of the characteristic terrace blocks; and it is eminently adaptable to a dug-in perimeter defense, as well as to interdiction by artillery fire from nearby heights.

SHIBUSHI air strip also occupies a terrace top; there is a sheer face of about 100–125 feet between the seaward end of the strip and the narrow coastal plain. The faces of the terrace and the dissecting gullies around the borders of the terrace offer innumerable opportunities for cave warfare.

It can be expected that the narrow valley corridor leading from ARIAKE to MIYAKONOJO will be organized for strong defense in depth.

(c)   MAKURAZAKI area: The critical terrain feature of this area is the high and precipitous hills immediately behind the narrow beach; the key objectives, BYU and CHIRAN airfields, are located on a plateau and are 2 and 7 miles inland, respectively, from the south coast. The topography of this area is such that it can be stoutly defended with minimum forces. It is believed that a brigade, with an estimated strength of about 4,500, is disposed in the southern portion of the SATSUMA PENINSULA (west of KAGOSHIMA-WAN). Reserves are available in the KAGOSHIMA area to reinforce the MAZURAZAKI area on a substantial scale; the enemy's decision to do so, however, would probably be tempered by the more serious threat in the KUSHIKINO area.

(d)   KUSHIKINO area; On the basis of present dispositions, landing forces in this area will initially be opposed by one division; a minimum of 24–48 hours would presumably be required to assemble it in position to counterattack, If another division is deployed in this general area prior to X-day, as is considered quite possible, the enemy could during the period X plus 3 to X plus 5 build up a force equivalent to two divisions, augmented by home defense and base and service troops, on the Allied beachhead. If there is still another division in reserve in the KOKUBU area, and the enemy decides to commit it to the KUSHIKINO PLAIN, the above capability must be correspondingly enlarged. Again, it must be remembered that the above time-and-space factors are computed on an optimum basis; air interdiction should play a large part in retarding the development of enemy strength.

In point of terrain, the KUSHIKINO PLAIN displays in marked degree the same features noted in connection with the other critical landing areas. There are terraces at varying distances from the beach, except in the northern portion, where there are low rolling hills whose spurs approach the beach rather closely. It is obvious that the main defenses in this area will be anchored on the high terrain in rear of the beaches, and bordering the narrow corridors through low rugged hills connecting the plain area with MAKURAZAKI and the KAGOSHIMA lowlands. The terrace formations, and to some extent the scattered sand dunes <20> along the southern portion of the KUSHIKINO beaches, offer opportunities for dug-in beach defenses which the enemy undoubtedly will not overlook.

C. *[Note: Designated "c" in the original.]* <u>Reinforcement from Rear Bases</u>: Once the enemy becomes aware of the scope, direction, and probable objectives of the Allied amphibious attack, and the battle has been joined, there is little doubt that he will make a major and protracted effort to push reinforcements to SOUTHERN KYUSHU, in pursuance of the general objectives of delaying and if possible preventing our consolidation of the area, and of exacting as heavy a toll of casualties as possible. Manpower is by far the enemy's cheapest and most plentiful military asset; he will expend it on a lavish scale.

The Japanese possess ample reserves in rear areas. Making allowance for requirements of local defense of main installations, it is probable 3 divisions or division-equivalents will be available in NORTHERN KYUSHU on X-day for reinforcement purposes. Moreover, higher headquarters indicate that a sufficient number of divisions are in western HONSHU, in KOREA, and in western SHIKOKU to enable the enemy to reinforce the KYUSHU garrison practically on a scale of his own choosing, without unduly jeopardizing local security or long range strategic requirements for the defense of HONSHU.

Movement of enemy reserves to NORTHERN KYUSHU will present no insurmountable obstacles. Even assuming that the KAMMON TUNNEL connecting SHIMONOSEKI and MOJI is interdicted, the enemy will still possess a sufficient supply of small craft to move, over an extended period of time and taking advantage of darkness and periods of low visibility, almost any desired number of troops across the narrow waters separating the northern tip of KYUSHU from its southern, western, and eastern neighbors.

The critical factor limiting all enemy reinforcement efforts after X-day, will probably be the crippling effect of Allied air attacks on KYUSHU communications, assembly areas, and water transport, and specifically the aerial and naval interdiction of the transportation bottle-necks leading from NORTHERN to SOUTHERN KYUSHU. The two main arteries connecting the northern and southern portions of the island—the east and west coastal highways and railroad system—are peculiarly vulnerable to interdiction because of their numerous defiles, cuts, tunnels and bridges. Assuming, as seems permissible, that large-scale use of these main lines of communication can be denied the enemy, he will be compelled to resort to laborious bypassing and detouring by land and by water, and to the time-consuming use of secondary and tertiary inland roads and trails traversing the central mountain range. <21>

In their general pattern, therefore, the enemy's attempts to move reinforcements in KYUSHU from the north should not differ greatly from previous such attempts where (as on LEYTE, for example), because the Allies held firm control of the highway outlets and corridor exits, the enemy was compelled to avail himself of poorly developed and inadequate mountain routes. It is therefore believed that the enemy will be reduced to the expedient of pushing his reinforcements to the south by a species of infiltration—slowly, furtively and piece-meal—a few along the blockaded coastal routes, a few by coastal small craft movement, but most of them through the trans-island mountain roads and trails. Accordingly, there is little likelihood that divisions or even regiments can be moved as a unit, which means that either these fresh troops will be committed piece-meal as and when they arrive in the objective area, or that they will be tediously gathered in assembly areas south of the mountain range.

Due to this anticipated partial isolation of the battle-field, no precise time-and-space tables can be formulated for the expected rate of Japanese reinforcement from NORTHERN KYUSHU. Hazarding a guess based on previous campaigns, and particularly LEYTE where the Japanese were confronted by a similar problem though of taller scope, it seems highly improbable that they will be able to funnel more than a division or division-equivalent from NORTHERN KYUSHU to the objective area during each period of 10 days, beginning about X plus 7 or X plus 10. Actual performance may fall far short even of this rate; past experience in the SWPA has demonstrated that the Japanese seen incapable of reacting quickly in the movement of their reserves, due not alone to Allied countermeasures but also due to defective staff work, inadequate communications and poor transportation facilities.

Where and how these reinforcements from rear areas will be employed cannot be predicted at this time. Some will almost certainly be deployed to protect the southern exits of the trans-island communication system, including such critical road and rail junctions as SASHIKI, HITOYOSHI, TARAGI, AND TOMITAKA. The employment of the bulk of the reinforcements will naturally depend upon the tactical situation when they debouch from the central mountain range. It is conceivable that the Japanese may seek to build up a strong central reserve in some remote inland area south of the central range, in order to launch a "grand offensive" at an appropriate moment; such, at least; was the strategy allegedly underlying the defense of LEYTE and LUZON. It is probable, however, that as in the precedents mentioned, the enemy will find the situation so pressing as to be obliged to commit his reinforcements piece-meal in order to bolster the defense in critically threatened sectors.

(3)   Naval capabilities: The Imperial Navy which in 1942 had complete domination of the PACIFIC OCEAN almost within its grasp finds itself in mid-1945 rapidly approaching total ineffectiveness. The last important offensive gesture was, characteristically enough, a "banzai" attack aimed at OKINAWA in early April, which cost the Japanese their last modern battleship, the formidable 45,000-ton YAMATO, and several of its escorts. Remaining major units, including 3 battleships, 2 converted battleships (the hermaphrodites ISE and HYUGA), 4 carriers, and 3 light carriers, have either been rendered inoperational by Allied air attacks, have sought temporary refuge by taking on heavy camouflage in home naval bases, or are undergoing repairs and alterations.

Higher headquarters estimates that, with reference to an operation against SOUTHERN KYUSHU, the sole remaining capabilities of the Japanese high seas fleet are to attempt a repetition of the YAMATO attack with the units remaining operational—an attack which would probably prove equally abortive and suicidal; or, to attempt to retain the semblance of a fleet in being by retiring to relatively safer anchorages in the SEA OF JAPAN and the YELLOW SEA. It is entirely possible that the remnants of the Japanese surface fleet will be smashed by air attack prior to X day and thus be totally deprived of the capability of effective intervention in this operation.

The enemy submarine force, however, will remain a serious threat to Allied operations against JAPAN. Although the offensive use of submarines by the Japanese has been singularly unsuccessful during earlier phases of the war, it is probable that offensive submarine activity will reach its highest and perhaps its most effective level when an invasion force approaches the homeland. The enemy has approximately 50 submarines concentrated mainly in EMPIRE waters; and this number may be slightly increased by the recall of those now engaged in patrol and on supply missions in distant waters.

Strong emphasis is being placed upon the development of one-man torpedoes, possibly to be launched from submarines, destroyers, and <22> shore installations. These devices may make their appearance in SOUTHERN KYUSHU bases; these bases may possibly be equipped to handle also midget subs and the assault demolition boats mentioned below.

The Japanese have placed strong reliance upon small suicide ("Q") craft, properly called assault demolition boats. In LUZON waters there were an estimated 1,000 such craft operated by the Army's GYORO ("Fishing") units, and approximately 200 similar boats operated by the Navy's Shinyo units, principally at CORREGIDOR and in the MANILA BAY area. At OKINAWA an estimated 600–700 were encountered. Although the number of successful attacks made by these suicide craft has been far from commensurate with their large numbers, there is reason to believe that the Japanese will continue to rely heavily upon them in the defense of KYUSHU. Judging from photographic evidence of small boat concentrations, it is entirely plausible that bases are being set up at undisclosed points along the SOUTHERN KYUSHU coastline, the greatly indented nature of which offers excellent opportunities for concealment and surprise employment. The Army and Navy assault demolition boats, as well as PT and anti-PT type craft known to have been developed by the enemy, must be reckoned with as a definite threat to attacking amphibious forces along convoy routes and in the crowded anchorages of the objective areas. The advisability of intensive and systematic search for and destruction of these craft and their bases by Allied air and naval forces during the preparatory phases of this operation is clearly indicated.

Suicide swimmers armed with demolitions will probably constitute a minor nuisance threat to Allied amphibious craft. There are indications that the waters of ARIAKE-WAN, KAGOSHIMA-WAN, and off MIYAZAKI have been mined by the Japanese.

(4)   Air reaction: The Japanese recognize that they possess in the suicide crash technique their most effective aerial weapon against Allied invasion forces. Beginning with the invasion of LEYTE and continuing through the landings in the RYUKYUS, an increasingly growing percentage of all offensive sorties executed by the Japanese Army and Navy Air Forces has been of the suicide variety. One estimate states that 20% of the enemy air attacks at OKINAWA were of this type; others range as high as 50%. It can confidently be predicted that the vast majority, perhaps as high as 85% or 90%, of the aerial attacks launched against a landing on SOUTHERN KYUSHU will follow "Kamikaze" tactics. Indeed, the Japanese have publicly announced that a great part of the members of both Army and Navy Air Forces are being inducted into the Kamikaze Corps. The training program in several areas of the EMPIRE, notably CHINA, has been suspended, and the trainees have been formed into suicide squadrons.

The question is, how many airplanes will the enemy have available shortly before X-day for suicide and conventional air attacks? To this, no definitive answer can presently be given. Although lying within the realm of the strategic, and therefore beyond the purview of this headquarters, a brief consideration of the principal factors involved is of interest to ground force commanders and staffs.

As of 20 July 1945, it was estimated that on airbases in KYUSHU and in those portions of SHIKOKU, HONSHU, KOREA, and CHINA lying within a 600-mile radius of KYUSHU, the enemy had 1,500 combat planes, of which roughly 65% were fighters and 20% bombers. The enemy was on the same date estimated to have 3,500 additional combat planes on bases beyond the 600-mile radius of KAGOSHIMA, but capable of intervention in this operation. Current monthly production is estimated by MID as approximately 1,500 in combat types, principally fighters. In addition, the enemy is estimated to possess some 4,000–5,000 miscellaneous training planes of varying degrees of effectiveness, in the same area; many hundreds of these types, including even bi-planes, were committed as suicide planes during the air battles over OKINAWA. <23>

Three imponderables confront anyone attempting to predict the probable weight of the Japanese air reaction to the KYUSHU operation. First, the extent to which the enemy will attempt the air defense of the EMPIRE in order to minimize strategic bombing damage by the B-29s and the carrier forces, Obviously, the Japanese are confronted with a bitter dilemma in this matter. They must choose one of these alternatives. They can commit substantial forces of first-line fighters to repel the B-29 and carrier attacks in an effort to mitigate the damage to industrial JAPAN, in which case they court early destruction of their first-line combat strength; or they can deliberately husband their air strength for the anticipated amphibious assault on the homeland, meanwhile refusing air combat and accepting inevitably heavy damage to their cities, industrial plants, communications, and air facilities to the extent that a trend is discernible from recent reaction to Allied air operations over the homeland, as to which of these choices the enemy will elect, the solution appears to be a compromise: intermittent interception of our strategic bombers by limited numbers of high-performance fighters and rocket planes, coupled with a policy of hoarding a hidden and dispersed reserve of first line planes, all manner of training planes, and baka-type missiles, for use by the suicide corps in attempting to repel the amphibious assault.

A second imponderable factor concerns the magnitude and success of the efforts which the enemy has made and undoubtedly will continue to make to disperse and conceal his aircraft plants, his planes, and his necessary air facilities. The MID report above quoted asserts that 47% of the June plane production in JAPAN was produced by plants as yet undiscovered or unbombed by our air forces. Many of these are undoubtedly underground as was the case in GERMANY during the final months. It is known, moreover, that in anticipation of early amphibious assaults on JAPAN, strong measures are being taken to disperse and conceal aircraft and to accumulate stores of avgas, ammunition, and base ordnance in critical areas. There have been repeated if vague references in captured documents and PW interrogations to the existence of concealed underground hangars and storage warehouses in which planes are being hoarded at various points in JAPAN. Speakers on Radio TOKYO have made the same claim, although undoubtedly exaggerated. It must be conceded that some degree of success will be gained in these dispersal and concealment projects, and that the Japanese will probably succeed in establishing a reservoir of some air power to be released at the proper moment.

The third unknown factor in weighing the probable air reaction to the invasion of KYUSHU is the extent to which the Japanese will decide to retain their then existing air potential to meet the later amphibious assault against the industrial heart of JAPAN. If the air force is committed all-out in defense of KYUSHU, the Japanese thereby accept the risk of leaving the vital TOKYO area undefended or inadequately defended by air. Higher headquarters believes that the enemy will be unwilling to accept such a risk, and therefore tentatively estimates that a reserve of 2,000–2,500 aircraft (which may have to be reduced because of intervening losses) will be retained for the later eventuality. There is, however, some support for the belief that the Japanese may as a last throw of dice deliberately choose to fight the decisive air battle for the homeland at KYUSHU, on the theory that if this air battle were lost there would be no chance of winning the later one over HONSHU. A similar line of reasoning, though with less at stake, impelled the enemy high command to the decision to hurl the entire PHILIPPINE air force, reinforced from the homeland, into the battle for LEYTE, leaving little more than token airpower available for the defense of LUZON.

As to the nature of the enemy's probable aerial reaction, therefore, it has been pointed out that:

(a)   As a result of the Allied counter air force neutralization program, the enemy air force will be driven off SOUTHERN KYUSHU long before X-day, except for concealed suicide planes; <24>

(b)   many of the excellent airfields in NORTHERN KYUSHU will probably still be serviceable for staging purposes, and possibly also for limited basing of planes;

(c)   the bulk of remaining enemy air strength will on X-day still probably be assembled at bases within a 600-mile radius of Allied beachheads and can stage its attacks through NORTHERN KYUSHU, from bases in southwestern HONSHU, SHIKOKU, northern KOREA, and possibly NORTH CHINA;

(d)   the enemy can be expected to make intense and violent air attacks, chiefly of the suicide kind, beginning when the bombardment and amphibious forces approach the objective area;

(e)   dawn, dusk, and moonlit nights will probably continue to be the favored time for such attacks;

(f)   the prime target will of course be Allied naval craft and amphibious forces, with ground positions and advanced air bases in the objective area as secondary targets;

(g)   the longevity of the enemy's major effort will be governed by the proportion of his then available air strength the enemy feels must be retained at all costs for the protection of HONSHU; or, if the enemy decides not to withhold any such reserve, by the depletion of his forces;

(h)   at all events:, the major air effort will be brought to an end when Allied land-based air strength is firmly established on SOUTHERN KYUSHU and has begun wide-scale short-range air attacks against critical air base and industrial targets in HONSHU, KOREA, and SHIKOKU; and

(i) offensive air action against SOUTHERN KYUSHU will at that time probably deteriorate into the familiar pattern of sporadic raiding, principally during hours of darkness.

An especially critical period will probably be that between the voluntary and/or enforced retirement of carrier groups and the firm establishment of land-based aircraft in SOUTHERN KYUSHU, if there is any appreciable time lag between these two phases.

Suicide-piloted rocket-planes of the Baka type, launched from mother aircraft, and ground-launched missiles of the same type, may be extensively employed. The Japanese are known to have shown interest in ground-launched V-weapons similar to the German jet-propelled V-1. There is even some suggestion from photographic interpreters that naval vessels, including even carriers, may be under modification as launching platforms for these projectiles. An aerial threat of decidedly less importance but still deserving of consideration and constant vigilance is posed by the possible employment of parachute troops or crash-landing planes filled with suicide demolition experts, directed against our air bases, communication centers, and other rear installations. The 1st Raiding Brigade, a unit similar to the 2nd Raiding Brigade elements of which executed the paratroop attack on LEYTE on 6–7 December 1944, is believed to have been recently stationed in the MIYAZAKI area of eastern KYUSHU. The possibility exists that this unit, or one similarly organized, may be poised at a rear air base for the purpose of executing a dramatic vertical attack at an auspicious target, possibly in conjunction (as was done at OKINAWA) with a "grand offensive" participated in by the air force, ground units, and counterlanding units. <25>

b. Relative Probabilities:

(1) Reinforcement of SOUTHERN KYUSHU prior to X-day): Despite the fact that enemy reinforcement of SOUTHERN KYUSHU has as of 1 August already brought his strength in this area up an estimated total of the equivalent of about 7 divisions, it is possible, particularly because of the respite of several months before the blow actually falls, that he will further reinforce the area by an additional 3 or 4 divisions by X-day.

(2) Ground defense:

(a) General considerations:

1. Tactics: Enemy defensive battle tactics will most probably include: a) A return to a policy of "annihilation of the enemy

at the water's edge" both by means of artillery and mortar fire from concealed positions in defilade and by direct infantry assault; b) defense in depth behind the beach areas from thoroughly organized, inter-connected and principally underground positions, set up as a series of centers of resistance, manned by units of battalion size, and supported at flank and rear by artillery and mortar fire; c) successive counterattacks, some of them possibly on a large scale from previously prepared strong points, against beachhead positions; d) improved cave and tunnel warfare conducted from mountainous, hilly or terraced terrain well inland from the beaches; e) determined and protracted building-to-building defense of cities; and f) the use of artillery from elevated ground inland, very probably in better coordination with infantry action and in greater mass than heretofore.

2. <u>Weapons</u>: It is likely that the enemy will improvise new and improved modes of employing his old weapons and bring out for the first time newly devised ones. These changes probably will include: concentrations of coastal defense guns, including those from deactivated naval vessels; anti-aircraft artillery, including the newly devised 88-mm gun; various types of mines, minefields, and demolition changes; numerous anti-tank weapons, including bazooka-type launchers and high velocity guns; new tanks, equipped with better weapons and heavier armor than heretofore, some probably with flame throwers; and, though this continues unlikely, gas and bacteriological warfare.

3. <u>State of preparation</u>: It must be assumed from the pace with which the enemy has set about reinforcing his SOUTHERN KYUSHU garrison, that a corresponding effort is going into the construction of gun emplacements, underground defensive systems, establishment of bivouac and supply areas, and the all-around organization of critical areas for defense, and that such effort will continue on the ground chosen by the Japanese for determined defense.

4. <u>Morale</u>: The spirited morale the enemy has exhibited at the outset of his defense of even island outposts, where far less was at stake than there is in KYUSHU, and the systematic intensification in the rallying by the Japanese government of

the KYUSHU population for the expected attack, make it very probable that morale of enemy troops and civilians in SOUTHERN KYUSHU will at the time of the invasion be high.

5.   Role of civilian defense units: Of the 300,000 extra-military, able-bodied men estimated to be available to the enemy for defense purposes, be it by organization under Home Defense Units or the Volunteer Corps, an indeterminate number can be expected to abandon under pressure their normal function of relieving regular Army units of rear area duties, maintaining communications, and building defenses to become combatant or semi-combatant groups. Poorly trained and meagerly equipped, such elements, <26> it is believed, could be effective only in a defensive role.

(b)   Probable conduct of the defense:

(1)   In general:

(a)   Beach defense: The alluvial terraces behind the beaches fronting the MIYAZAKI, ARIAKE, and KUSHIKINO PLAINS and the hills embracing the PLAINS lend themselves to the construction of underground fortifications flanked and backed up by artillery emplacements, and strongly indicate that the enemy will counter landing forces with well-organized and determined beach defense.

(b)   Inland defense: Terrain considerations, particularly the mass of low rugged mountains and upland plateaus behind the three main coastal plains and the narrow corridors dominated by heights interconnecting the coastal plains with each other and with the interior basins, make it probable that a series of organized dug-in defensive systems will be set up and defended by the enemy to her access to the interior.

(2)   Specific critical areas:

(a)   MIYAZAKI PLAIN: Predicated upon present enemy strength and dispositions and ignoring the effects of Allied aerial disruption of enemy movement, it is estimated that the Japanese can oppose the equivalent of 1 division to Allied forces 24–48 hours after the landing, and that this enemy force could be built up to a total of 3 divisions, plus home defense and base and service troops, during the period X plus 3 to X plus 5. The enemy will probably make maximum use of advantageous defensive terrain to defend strongly the MIYAZAKI and SADOHARA airfields, the critical rail and road bridges over the OYODO RIVER, the hill-backed plain itself, and particularly the narrow corridor approaches to the MIYAKONOJO BASIN.

(b) ARIAKE-WAN-KANOYA area: Predicated upon present enemy strength and dispositions and ignoring the effects of Allied disruption of enemy movement, it is estimated that the Japanese can oppose the equivalent of 1 division, augmented by home defense and base and service troops, to Allied forces 46–72 hours after landing. If reserve divisions are by X-day located in the MIYAKONOJO and KOKUBU areas, and if these are committed to the ARIAKE beachhead rather than to KUSHIKINO or MIYAZAKI, the enemy force opposing the landing could by X plus 4 or X plus 5 be built up to a total of 3 divisions, plus home defense and base and service troops. The hills dominating ARIAKE BAY will probably be utilized for artillery and coast defense guns. The site of SHIBUSHI field lends itself to effective close-in defense. The terraces behind ARIAKE BEACH will probably be well defended from underground fortification systems. Such systems are already being prepared for the defense of the invaluable KANOYA air base area. It must be supposed that the valley corridor from the ARIAKE area to MIYAKONOJO will be organized for strong defense in depth.

(c) MAKURAZAKI area: Terrain in the MAKURAZAKI area is such that it can be stoutly defended with a minimum of forces. Whether more than the brigade of 4,500 strength now estimated to be in the area will be committed to this defense and thus to protecting the BYU and CHIRAN fields inland, will probably depend upon whether the enemy supposes some of his reserves in the KAGOSHIMA area are not needed for the defense of the KUSHIKINO PLAIN.

(d) KUSHIKINO area: Predicated upon present enemy strength and dispositions and ignoring the effects of Allied aerial disruption of enemy movement, it is estimated that the Japanese can oppose <27> the equivalent of 1 division to Allied forces 24–48 hours after the landing. Should another division be deployed in the area before X-day, as is likely, the enemy could during the period X plus 3 to X plus 5 build up a force equivalent to 2 divisions. It is probable that the main defense will be anchored on the high terrain in rear of the beaches and bordering the narrow corridors connecting the area with the MAKURAZAKI and KAGOSHIMA lowlands, and that, where terrace formations are available, dug-in beach defenses will be encountered.

(e)   *[Note: Designated "c" in the original.]* <u>Reinforcement from rear bases</u>: Inasmuch as manpower is by far the enemy's most plentiful asset, it is probable that, once he becomes aware of the scope and objectives of the Allied attack, he will draw on this potential for reinforcement to the extent of perhaps 3 divisions. The crippling effect of Allied aerial attacks on KYUSHU communications, assembly areas and water transport, and specifically of bottle-necks in the route from NORTHERN to SOUTHERN KYUSHU, will make it necessary for these reinforcing elements to enter the objective area piece-meal. For this reason, it is hardly probable that more than a division or its equivalent can be added to the forces in SOUTHERN KYUSHU during each period of 10 days beginning about X plus 7 or X plus 10, and actual performance may fall far short of even so much effective reinforcement. Such accretions in troop strength may be employed to protect the southern exits of the trans-island communications system, be used to build up in a suitable centrally located area a reservoir of troops for purposes of a "grand offensive," or be committed piece-meal in progressive efforts to bolster sagging sectors.

(3)   <u>Naval capabilities</u>: It is estimated that the sole remaining capabilities of the remnant Japanese Fleet, provided that even in this remnant status it is still extant on X-day, are to attempt swift sorties against Allied amphibious forces upon their approach to KYUSHU or to retire in the capacity of a "fleet in being" to comparatively safer anchorages in the SEA OF JAPAN or the YELLOW SEA. The enemy submarine force, however, still estimated to comprise a maximum of some 60 units, remains a considerable threat, and may be expected to reach its highest peak of activity as the Allied invasion force approaches the mainland. Besides, one-man torpedoes, whether launched from shore installations or from Naval craft, and "midget submarines" are being greatly emphasized in current reports and will probably be put into action against Allied units. Far from negligible, too, is the Japanese reliance on suicide assault demolition boats; these, as well as PT boats and anti-PT boats, can be well concealed along the irregular SOUTHERN KYUSHU coastline, and it may be expected that quantities of these will attempt attacks against approaching convoys and crowded anchorages.

(4)   <u>Air reaction</u>: To the extent that a trend is discernible from recent enemy reaction to Allied air operations over the homeland, it seems he is electing

a compromise between the alternative of husbanding his still considerable aircraft at the cost of unimpeded destruction of his cities and industrial concentrations and that of intercepting Allied attack intermittently, while at the same time building up and maintaining a hidden and dispersed reserve. The magnitude and degree of success of the Japanese effort to conceal aircraft plants, planes, and facilities cannot be precisely determined now, but there is evidence to indicate that the enemy is partially succeeding in establishing a reservoir of air power beyond the currently estimated total of 5,000 combat type planes for release at the proper moment. What part of this total aircraft strength (less interim losses) will be committed to intervention in the Allied amphibious approach to KYUSHU and what part, if any, will be retained for the protection of HONSHU is not yet clear. The possibility must be reckoned with that the enemy will commit substantially his whole force to the effort of destroying the Allied assault on KYUSHU. It seems indubitable, therefore, that heavy aerial attacks, chiefly of the suicide kind, will be made against the Allied invading amphibious <28> forces, air bases, beachheads, and ground positions, and that such attacks will be sustained until the enemy feels he must save the remainder of his air power for HONSHU defense. Moreover, this main line of enemy action will very probably be supplemented by baka-type planes, ground launched V-weapons, and by parachute troops and crash-landing planes.

F[rederick]. W. Hein,
Colonel, G.S.C. ,
Actg AC of S, G-2.
[Acting Assistant Chief of Staff, Intelligence]

<29>

. . . .

ANNEX #3

TACTICAL STUDY OF THE TERRAIN, SOUTHERN KYUSHU

. . . .

GENERAL TOPOGRAPHY OF THE AREA:

. . . .

<1 [44]>

. . . .

c. General Nature of the Terrain: Peculiar to the overall nature of the terrain is a notable absence of tropical swamps and extensive valleys. In place of the swamps, rice fields when flooded are effective hindrances to movement although foot troops and some types of tracked vehicles should without much difficulty be able to negotiate the fields while wet. Wheeled vehicles will find movement confined almost entirely to existing roads.

True coastal plains are lacking. Open level areas are located on terraces and plateaus which have been dissected into blocks varying in size from one to two miles square. Fronting these terraced areas, the most important feature of military significance is the escarpment. These escarpments are frequently very nearly vertical, covered with scrub, grass or small trees, and offer innumerable opportunities for the development of cave and other underground positions. Where a stream has cut into a terrace, the valley walls have very steep sides while the floors are narrow and generally level.

Wide valleys favorable for the conduct of military operations, such as the CENTRAL PLAIN of LUZON, are lacking. Valleys through the mountains are narrow, have steep sides, are generally wooded, follow tortuous courses through narrow defiles, and are flanked by commanding heights. Natural corridors are practically nonexistent.

Rivers are generally short they are swift in their upper reaches and flow in shallow channels across flat floors near their mouths.

MILITARY ASPECTS OF THE TERRAIN: The physiographic regions of SOUTHERN KYUSHU, shown on the Terrain Diagram of Appendix #1, are the following:

Mountains:
Central Mountains
Eastern Highlands
Osumi-hanto
Satsuma-hanto
Southern Volcanic Uplands and Lowlands

Lowlands:
Hitoyoshi Basin
Miyazaki Coastal Plain
Ariake-Wan-Miyakonojo Lowland
Kokubu Lowland
Kagoshima Lowland
Makurazaki Coastal Lowland
Kushikino Lowland
Sendai-Gawa Lowland
Izumi Lowland

Certain characteristics of military importance repeat themselves so frequently in the two major terrain groups that a generalized discussion of them is presented here rather than a detailed description of each area. Detailed descriptions are adequately presented in the various references cited above.

a. Avenues of Approach: Routes of approach to the lowlands bordering the coasts are generally clear, with the obvious exception of the two areas bordering KAGOSHIMA-WAN and the SENDAI-GAWA and IZUMI LOWLANDS. Interior approaches from one lowland region to another pass through mountainous country and through narrow, winding valleys commanded by high side <3 [46]> walls and narrow defiles. Access from NORTHERN KYUSHU is greatly hampered by the rugged barrier of the CENTRAL MOUNTAINS which is breached by few passes or streams.

b. Obstacles: Appendix 2 indicates the restrictions imposed by slope upon movement. Topographic limitations to movement are immediately evident. Very close conformity exists between the physiographic regions and the areas of low slope.

Natural and artificial barriers to movement exist in abundance. Natural barriers in addition to the steep slopes and ruggedness of the mountain areas consist of terraces and plateau blocks fronted by almost vertical slopes and cliffs. These relatively level surfaces have been dissected into smaller units by small streams which have cut valleys with steep sides and narrow, level floors into the edges, creating a serrated front. These small valleys are of sufficient depth and width to restrict lateral movement perpendicular to the streams. Low discontinuous hills which are remnants of heavily dissected former terraces, e.g., on the MIYAZAKI COASTAL PLAIN, present obstacles which would necessitate movement around them. Artificial obstacles are present in the intensely cultivated areas in two forms: those associated with rice culture in the form of irrigation canals and dikes around the paddies; and the terraced lower slops of hillsides upon which either dry crops or irrigated rice are grown.

c. Concealment and Cover: On lowland areas and the level terrain surfaces, limited concealment is confined to tree bordered roads, occasional areas of reclaimed land along beaches where pines have been planted to hold the sand, occasional orchards, and, in built-up areas, to whatever buildings may be standing. Full concealment is available only in the forested mountainous areas. Partial cover is limited to dikes around rice paddies, dikes confining streams to their channels, and occasional irregularities in the ground surface. Complete topographic cover is available only in the mountains and to a limited extent in the small valleys which cut the borders of the terraces.

d. Observation: Observation from hill and mountain borders of lowland areas is obstructed but slightly by the forests.

e. Fields of fire: Fields of fire should be generally good in the lowland areas for all weapons. The controlling factor affecting fire control from lowland into mountain areas, or from one terrace level to another within the lowland areas, will be the masked areas created by the mountains or terrace faces. Defiladed positions for artillery on the lowlands will be limited to isolated heavily dissected hills or to the valleys cutting the fronts of the terraces.

4. <u>CRITICAL TERRAIN FEATURES</u>: The most important terrain features which will affect ground operations are the cliff-like terrace fronts, the commanding heights surrounding all lowland areas, and the rugged mountains full of tortuous narrow defiles and lacking natural corridors. These features are ideal for the construction of extensive underground installations. Besides the possibilities for suitable under-ground positions in cliff-faces, there is the obvious advantage to the defender of being above the area in which the attacker must maneuver. Numerous possible objective areas are situated atop a terrace or plateau block completely surrounded by steep cliff-like slopes whose natural routes of approach through small valleys leading to the surface are commanded by the heights and sheer walls. SADOHARA and SHIBUSHI airfields are examples of this situation.

5. <u>TACTICAL EFFECT OF THE TERRAIN</u>: Because of the frequency of terraces and the enclosing mountain areas, the terrain is ideal for defensive use. Peninsular arms bordering logical approaches to objective areas are so related to the lowland areas that coastal defense positions can be constructed which can be <4 [47]> masked from naval gunfire and protected to some extent from aerial bombing by the rugged terrain. Field artillery emplacements can be similarly installed to command the lowland areas and have a fair amount of protection from counter-battery fire. The broken nature of the terrain indicates that large-scale armored actions will be difficult to undertake for both the defender and the attacker due to the frequency with which the level areas are cut by small, deep valleys and also to the narrow defiles in rugged terrain which will canalize all movement from one lowland area to another. The level terraced areas appear to offer possibilities for vertical envelopment as a means of reinforcement. Terrain suitable for the establishment of supply bases appear excellent in the lowland areas, and along the hilly margins of the lowlands where such bases would have protection from the spurs of the hills.

<u>KOSHIKI-RETTO</u>

The KOSHIKI-RETTO are a group of three main and several lesser islands lying 14–30 miles off the southwest coast of KYUSHU, west of the KUSHIKINO LOWLAND. The chain trends southwest-northeast for approximately 20 miles and consists of partially drowned volcanic peaks with rugged terrain and steep slopes. The west coast is steep—to while the eastern slopes are more gradual. Numerous small, discontinuous lowlands occupy small bayheads. Lack of developed communications, rugged terrain, terraced lower slopes along the east coast where some agriculture is carried on, dense forest on the upper slopes—these all militate against wheeled or tracked vehicular movement. The terrace banks offer slight concealment and cover. Wooded areas provide good concealment. Several small bayhead beaches appear favorable for amphibious landings. The study prepared by Amphibious Forces Pacific discusses in detail 19 possible landing beaches.

<5 [48]>

APPENDIX B

G-2 Analysis of Japanese Plans for the Defense of Kyushu, U.S. Sixth Army, December 31, 1945

Note: This abridgment of "Japanese Plans for the Defense of Kyushu" consists of eighteen of the document's forty-eight pages. The material in this document was supplied by the former members of the 2d General Army, Sixteenth Area Army, and major field commands on Kyushu. Some of the data and interpretations differ subtly from that presented in the "Homeland Operations Record" (chapter 7), which was also produced under occupation directives. See also chapter 13. Use of angle brackets around a numeral (<1>) denotes page breaks.

HEADQUARTERS SIXTH ARMY

Office of the Assistant Chief of Staff, G-2
APO 442

31 December 1945

THE JAPANESE PLANS FOR THE DEFENSE OF KYUSHU

By the end of July 1945, sufficient information was available for the G-2 to make a preliminary estimate of the enemy strength in KYUSHU. In the Sixth Army G-2 estimate for the OLYMPIC operation, dated 1 August 1945, it was estimated that 421,000 Japanese troops were on KYUSHU, comprising nine divisions (or division-equivalents), plus a large number of base and service troops, and naval personnel. Subsequent information, obtained prior to the end of the war, including new identifications and estimated reinforcements, raised the estimated total to 680,000, including fourteen divisions (or equivalents). This figure was reached just prior to the end of the war.

Information secured since the occupation of JAPAN reveals that the overall total strength on KYUSHU of Japanese units of all services and types as of the final day of hostilities totaled approximately 735,000, including fourteen divisions and seven independent mixed brigades. However, this total includes units on the islands off-lying KYUSHU which were not included in the Sixth Army estimate of the situation. Strength on these islands totaled approximately 25,000 and included three independent mixed brigades. Thus, the Sixth Army, 1 August, estimate was based on information procured in May, June, and July, and full allowance was made for large scale reinforcement, while the projected (but never published) revised estimate with complete information was 96% accurate. The discrepancy in 1 August estimate was largely caused by the underestimation of naval ground troops, whose number was greatly swelled by recruits undergoing boot training and by crews from ships which had been immobilized by allied attacks, and from troop units in transit.

The Japanese expected our invasion of the home islands, they expected it to be made during or after October 1945, they expected it to be made in southern KYUSHU, and that our landings would be made on the beaches of MIYAZAKI, ARIAKE-WAN and SATSUMA PENINSULA. Their available combat forces had been deployed according to those expectations, with reserves being strengthened when hostilities ceased.

Allied convoys approaching KYUSHU would have received mass suicide attacks by every available plane in the KYUSHU area. Transports would have been the main targets of these attacks, and the Japanese expected to destroy 10% in this manner. Offshore, the landing forces would have been hit by large numbers of small suicide craft and submarines, and the Japanese expected to destroy 60 transports by these means.

Once a landing or landings were made, a decisive stand would have been initiated. Placing much stress on artillery, and having three tank brigades, one independent tank company, one independent regiment and four self-propelled gun battalions to support division troops in their operations, the Japanese forces planned to make a final stand near the beaches and units were instructed to remain in place until annihilated. Heavy counter-offensives in the beach areas were planned and little preparation was made for defense in depth.

H[orton]. V. WHITE,
Colonel, G.S.C.,
AC of S, G-2
[Assistant Chief of Staff, Intelligence]

<1>

I. INFORMATION AS PREPARED BY MEMBERS OF THE STAFF OF THE JAPANESE SECOND GENERAL ARMY:

The following information on the defense of KYUSHU was obtained as the result of a directive sent to the Japanese Second Demobilization Headquarters (formerly the Japanese Second General Army). [*Note: The title Second Demobilization Headquarters should not be confused with Second Demobilization Bureau, which refers to the former Naval General Staff.*] The Japanese Second Demobilization Headquarters was directed to submit accurate and complete information on the nature and extent of the Japanese preparations for the defense of KYUSHU at the time of the surrender, such information to be obtained exhaustively from all sources, including when necessary the memory of subordinate unit commanders and staff officers. Slight changes have been made in the grammar and wording of the Japanese answers in order to make a clearer text. No changes were made to content.

GENERAL:

1. Q. Were Allied landings on KYUSHU anticipated? If so, when, where and in what strength?

    A. The landing of the Allied Forces on KYUSHU was anticipated. Allied strength was estimated at 300,000 and three areas in southern KYUSHU (namely the MIYAZAKI, ARIAKE BAY and SATSUMA PENINSULA areas, where landing would be enforced either simultaneously or in succession) were designated as points of landing, the time of which was predicted to be during Autumn (October) or later.

2. Q. What intelligence of Allied intents did the Japanese High Command possess? Specifically what was known and what was the source of this knowledge? Prisoners of war? Captured documents? Special operatives? Aerial reconnaissance and photography?

    A. Various strategic information for judging Allied intents were controlled by the Imperial Headquarters, and from this information deductions were made an d issued to armies under direct control. The Second General Army directed its efforts towards gaining intelligence of the military tactics involved in the minute details of the landing points, dates and strength of the Allied Forces based on the strategic deductions of the Imperial Headquarters. The methods for gaining this intelligence were: movement of controlled planes (reconnaissance and photography); observation of frequency and directions of U. S. bombing and reconnaissance within army area in the form of statistics; and study of movement of task forces and of the development of international affairs, especially that of American public opinion (through radio reception). The main points of issue in the handling of information were: The problem whether the Allied Forces would conduct operations on the CHINA coast prior to their landing on the home islands, or whether SAISHU-TO and Southern KOREA would be used as intermediary battle points when the home islands were attacked directly. However, mainly due to the progress of the PHILIPPINE and OKINAWA campaigns, the conclusion as mentioned before, that the southern part of KYUSHU would be the first landing area, was reached.

3. Q. Was it supposed that the Allied landings on KYUSHU were to constitute the main effort against the Japanese homeland or to be preliminary to larger efforts elsewhere?

    A. The Allied landings on KYUSHU were reasoned as preliminary tactics to the main operations against the KANTO area.

4. Q. Was it supposed that the Allied landings on KYUSHU would precede, follow, or occur simultaneously with landings on the CHINA coast?

    A. The landings on KYUSHU were judged as taking place prior to the operations on the CHINA coast. Judging from the landing dates and reserve strength of the Allied Forces, it was thought impossible for the CHINA and Japanese HOME ISLAND operations to be conducted simultaneously, while the American strategic situation apparently lacked the need for conducting operations in CHINA, only resorting to <1> said tactics for political effects.

5. Q. At what time, if at all, was it anticipated that FORMOSA would be by-passed?

    A. Operations against TAIWAN (FORMOSA) were thought very improbable after the OKINAWA operations.

6. Q. Did the operations of Admiral Halsey's Task Force at all disturb the belief of the High Command that KYUSHU would be the first homeland island to be attacked?

    A. The operations of Admiral Halsey's Task Force did not the least disturb the conviction that Southern KYSUHU would receive the first attack of the home islands group.

JAPANESE TROOP STRENGTH, IDENTITY AND DISPOSITIONS:

7. Q. What was the identity, history, strength and disposition of the KYUSHU garrisons prior to the arrival of reinforcements sent in because of the anticipated imminence of invasion?

A.

16 Army (area army)	Controlled all army units in KYUSHU from FUKUOKA.
56 Army (corps)	Controlled units in northern KYUSHU from IIZUKA.
145 Div	(17,685 persons) Organized summer 1944; in charge of defense in area between KOKURA and FUKUOKA.
57 Army (corps)	Directed units in southern KYUSHU from TAKARABE.
86 Div	(20,614 persons) Organized summer 1944; in charge of defense of entire ARIAKE BAY area.
156 Div	(17,429 persons) Organized summer 1944; in charge of defense of MITAZAKI area.
98 IMB[*]	(5,638 persons) Organized from engineering units of UCHIGAURA FORTIFICATION, ARIAKE BAY, and given to defense of OSUMI PENINSULA.
TANEGASHIMA GARRISON	Composed of three infantry battalions for defense of TANEGASHIMA
ISLAND	
KURUME DIVISIONAL HEADQUARTERS KUMAMOTO DIVISIONAL HEADQUARTERS	Both organized about February 1945, from remaining divisions at KURUME and KUMAMOTO. Units engaged mainly in instruction, training, and recruitment.

IKI FORTIFICATION	
TAUSHIMA FORTIFICATION	
SHIMONOSEKI FORTIFICATION	
HOYO FORTIFICATION	
NAGASAKI FORTIFICATION	Each ordered to reorganize formerfortification units into battle array
107 IMB	Defense of GOTO, NAGASAKI PREFECTURE; headquarters at FUKUE-DHO.

[*IMB: Independent Mixed Brigade]

<2>

WESTERN TAKATOKI GROUP	(21,425 persons) In charge of air raid defense of entire KYUSHU area; headquarters at KOKURA.

8. Q. What was the identity, history, strength and disposition of troop reinforcements brought into KYUSHU between 1 May 1945 and 12 August 1945?

A.

(A) Reinforcements under 56 Army (corps) (Northern KYUSHU)

57 Div	(20,429 persons) Unit transferred from MANCHURIA primarily for defense of FUKUOKA area, later interchanging with 351 Div after the latter's formation, and concentrating as reserves for area army strategy.
351 Div	(12,215 persons) Newly organized in June 1945, interchanging defense duty with 57 Div (mentioned above). Headquarters at FUKUMA, FUKUOKA PREFECTURE.

312 Div

(12,227 persons) Organized
simultaneously with 351 Div, and
undertook defense of KARATSU,
IMARI area. Headquarters
at AICHI-CHO, SAGA
PREFECTURE.

4 ITB[*]

(3,103 persons) Newly organized,
and under direct army control.
Headquarters at FUKUMA-CHO,
FUKUOKA PREFECTURE.

6th ARTILLERY HEADQUARTERS

(119 persons) Newly organized.
Located at HARA-NACHI,
MIIKE-GUN, RUKUOKA
PREFECTURE.

(B) Reinforcements under 57 Army (corps). 57 Army formerly controlled
the entire area of southern KYUSHU, but after the imminence of Allied
invasion, the area east of OSUMI PENINSULA (inclusive) of southern
KYUSHU was designated.

25 Div

(25,804 persons) Unit transferred
from MANCHURIA,
concentrated near KOBAYASHI,
MIYAZAKI PREFECTURE, and
trained as reserves for
defense of southern KYUSHU.

154 Div

(17,341 persons) Newly organized
unit, garrisoned north of 156
DIV on coast of MIYAZAKI
PREFECTURE. Headquarters
at TSUMA-CHO, MIYAZAKI
PREFECTURE.

212 Div

(21,351 persons) Newly
organized as an attacking force,
and concentrated in northern
plains area of MIYAZAKI
PREFECTURE. Part of the unit
was stationed north of 156 Div
on the MIYAZAKI coastline.

Headquarters at TONO-CHO,
MIYAZAKI PREFECTURE.

109 IMB

(6,888 persons) Reorganized from
TANEGASHIMA GARRISON.
Reinforced to total one artillery and
six Infantry battalions.

5 ITB

Newly organized to meet
decisive battle in 6 ITB southern
KYUSHU. 5 ITB (3,108 persons)
was located at HONJO-CHO,
NIYAZAKI PREFECTURE. 6
ITB (3,784 persons) was located
at KIRISHIMA, KAGOSHIMA
PREFECTURE.

[*ITB: Independent Tank Brigade]
<3>

FIRST ARTILLERY HEADQUARTERS

(117 persons) Newly organized,
and located at TSOUMACHI,
MIYAZAKI PREFECTURE.

THIRD ENGINEERING HEADQUARTERS

(167 persons) Newly organized,
and located at TAKARABE-CHO,
MIYAZAKI PREFECTURE.

(C) Reinforcements under 40 Army (corps). The 40th Army headquarters was
newly transferred from FORMOSA and given command of the western
half of southern KYUSHU. Headquarters located at IJUIN-CHO,
KAGOSHIMA PREFECTURE.

46 Div

[No personnel figure given.]
Withdrew from 57th Army,
retaining former status, and entered
jurisdiction of 40 Army.

77 Div

(15,640 persons) Newly transferred
from HOKKAIDO, and first
placed in the area between
KUSHIKINO and IZUMI.

	Later interchanged garrisons with 303 Div, after the latter's formation, and concentrated near KAJIKI and KAGOSHIMA PREFECTURE as strategic reserves. Headquarters formerly at SENDAI.
206 Div	(21,354 persons) Newly organized as decisive battle corps, and entrenched for the main part on the western coast of SATSUMA PENINSULA. Headquarters at IZAKU-MACHI.
303 Div	(12,213 persons) Newly organized, and interchanged garrisons with 77 Div. Headquarters at SENDAI city.
125 IMB	(6,826 persons) Newly organized, and encamped on coast at entrance to KAGOSHIMA BAY, SATSUMA PENINSULA. Headquarters at IKEDA.
FOURTH ARTILLERY HEADQUARTERS	(117 persons) Newly organized.

(D) THE CHIKUGO GROUP. Invested strategic office to the former KURUME DIVISION, and was placed in charge of entire NAGASAKI PREFECTURE and parts of SAGA FUKUOKA and OITA PREFECTURES.

118 IMB	(7,104 persons) Reorganized from former HOYO FORTIFICATION, forming a mixed brigade.
122 IMB	(6,884 persons) Reorganized from former NAGASAKI FORTIFICATION, forming a mixed brigade.

(E) THE HIGO GROUP. Invested strategic office to the former KUMAMOTO DIVISION, and was <4> in charge of entire KUMATO PREFECTURE and part of OITA PREFECTURE.

216 Div	(21,736 persons) Newly organized as decisive battle force. During training in vicinity at KUMAMOTO, held as reserves by area army. Headquarters at UDO-CHO. [The 216th Division commander also commanded Higo Group.]
126 IMB	(6,213 persons) Newly organized. Ordered to guard AMAKUSA ISLAND.
11th ENGINEERING HEADQUARTERS	(103 persons) Newly organized, and situated at NAGASU-CHO, KUMAMOTO PREFECTURE.

(F) 4 AA Div. (21,415 persons) Reorganized from former SEIBU ANTI-AIRCRAFT GROUP. Headquarters at TSUKUSHI, FUKUOKA PREFECTURE.

(G) THIRD COMMUNICATION HEADQUARTERS. (2,388 persons) Newly organized under direct control of area army.

9. Q. What was the identity, history, strength and disposition of Japanese troops of all services on KYUSHU at the time of the surrender? In southern KYUSHU?

   A. (See annex A, with attached map.)

10. Q. Had the reinforcement of KYUSHU troop strength been completed at the time of surrender, or was further reinforcement contemplated? Of southern KYUSHU troop strength?

   A. At the time of surrender, scheduled plans for enlarging strength in the KYUSHU area were completed, especially in southern KYUSHU area, where it was quickly accomplished. After that, strengthening of reserves was planned.

11. Q. Precisely what use would have been made of Home Defense Units and of
         Peoples' Volunteer Corps in the event of Allied landing? Would the Peoples'
         Volunteer Corps have been organized into Combat Corps?

     A. (a) The Peoples' Volunteer Corps would have been appointed for traffic,
              communication, supply, transportation and other rear area duties. (At
              the time of Allied landing Home Defense Units did not exist.)

         (b) When the Allied landing date became more imminent, the Peoples' Volunteer
              Corps would have been organized into Combat Corps.

AIR DEFENSE:

*[Note: This material is covered in chapter 8, but the former Second General Army
personnel providing answers to U.S. Sixth Army Intelligence also revealed that the
number of Imperial Japanese Army kamikazes specifically based on Kyushu was eight
hundred. Army suicide aircraft based in Shikoku and southern Honshu, aircraft slated
for conventional missions, or matters pertaining to the larger air arm of the Imperial
Japanese Navy were not addressed authoritvely and are not included. Other naval matters
are adequately covered below.]*

. . . .

<5>

. . . .

NAVAL DEFENSE:

19. Q. Which waters off KYUSHU were mined? How and to what extent? <6>
         Which waters off KYUSHU were earmarked for future mining?

     A. The mined waters off KYUSHU are shown in the attached sheet, and these
         are all completed. (See ANNEX B). Future plans were to lay thousands of
         small mines along the coasts of KAGOSHIMA and MIYAZAKI against
         Allied amphibious forces.

20. Q. Were any Fleet units available for and intended for intervention in the Allied
         amphibious movement to KYUSHU? If so, what kind (carriers, cruisers,
         destroyers, submarines), how many, and how were they to be employed?

     A. We had intended to interdict the Allied amphibious movement to KYUSHU,
         but no powerful fleet units were available. The tactics of our fleet for this
         purpose were as follows:

Type	Number	How to be employed
Destroyer	12	Carrying suicide torpedoes to attack transports off the landing coast.
Submarine	40	(a) Patrolling the waters east and south of KYUSHU by low speed submarines.
		(b) Attacking the convoys by high speed submarines.
		(c) Attacking the reinforcement at sea by large submarines.

21. Q. Were any small PT-type craft, assault demolition boats, midget submarines, or 1-man "human" torpedoes to be committed to the defense of KYUSHU? If so, where were the principal concentrations of these, how and, with expectations of what kind of success were, these to be used?

A. Small boats to be committed to the defense of KYUSHU were as follows:

Type	Number	How to be employed
PT-type craft	none	
Type	Number	How to be employed
Assault demolition boat	1,000	Attacking transports by concentrating on the several coasts of MIYAKI
Midget submarine	30	and KAGOSHIMA Prefectures.
Human torpedo	50	
Small submarine	100	Attacking transports by running out of BUNGO STRAIT.

The expectation of success was to sink about 60 transports.

22. Q. Were amphibious brigades available and intended for counter-landings? How many? Where and when were the counter-landings to be made?

     A. We had neither counter-landing intentions nor amphibious brigades.

23. Q. Had any ramps or catapults been set up for launching jet-propelled suicide planes or aerial bombs against Allied amphibious units?

     A. (a) We had been selecting 10 places for the catapults of jet-propelled suicide planes in the northern district of KYUSHU and YAMAGUCHI PREFECTURE, but the construction had not yet begun.

<7>

         (b) We have no ramps or launching slopes.

         (c) Aerial bombs were under experiment, and not yet in use.

GROUND DEFENSE:

24. Q. Anti-tank tactics: What anti-tank tactics were contemplated? Armor? Tank traps? Close combat assault? Raiding parties? Ground mines? Shoulder-pack mines? Lunge mines? Bazooka-type launchers?

     A. Anti-tank tactics: The main anti-tank tactics were close combat assault with various types of portable explosives (torpedo), while anti-tank armor, gunfire, tank traps and bazooka type launchers, etc., were expected to render secondary effect.

25. Q. Armor: How many armored units were available in KYUSHU for commitment to its defenses? In southern KYUSHU? How many tanks, and of what types were available? In which areas would the tanks have been committed? In coordinated attack or in piecemeal fashion?

     A. Armor:

         (a) Tank units for the KYUSHU operations consisted of three brigades (4ITB, 5ITB, 6ITB), one regiment (46th ITR), one independent company and four self-mobile gun battalions.

         (b) There were 275 tanks in southern KYUSHU (standard number), and composed for the main part of average-sized tanks, while light tanks and self-mobile guns were included.

(c)   The areas used by tanks in southern KYUSHU were scheduled mainly in the MIYAZAKI and ARIAKE BAY areas. Strategy lay in direct cooperation with the infantry.

26.   Q.   Chemicals: Was any type of chemical warfare projected? Why not? Was any type of chemical warfare expected from the Allies? What preventative measures were taken?

A.   Chemical warfare:

(a)   We did not anticipate active chemical warfare to any degree.

(b)   The reason why we could not use chemical warfare was that world confidence would have been lost and the great disparity between the capacity of American and Japanese chemical industry put us in a situation which we could not hope to contest.

(c)   We did not expect Allied chemical warfare, but in the final stages of the war, that is in the case where Allied forces would have been defeated at their first landing in the KYUSHU area, we judged that the Allied forces might have resorted to chemical warfare tactics.

(d)   The army was well equipped against gas attack by the Allies with masks, suits, antiseptics, etc., in quantities, while the civilian population as a whole was hardly provided for, with no means of counteracting any large-scale warfare.

27.   Q.   Artillery: What role would the use of artillery have played in the defense of KYUSHU? Would more emphasis have been placed on it than in previous operations? Would it have been used, against Allied amphibious units at any points? Where?

A.   Artillery:

(a)   The principle object in defending KYUSHU was to defeat the Allied landing forces near the shorelines. Therefore, in order to accomplish this purpose, we put great stress on artillery. According to the military experience gained in fighting on islands of the Pacific, especially that on the PHILIPPINE and OKINAWA islands, the use of superior artillery was absolutely necessary in order to crush the establishment of beach heads.

<8>

(b)   We did not plan to use general artillery against Allied amphibious units.

28.   Q.   <u>Coastal Guns</u>: Where were the greatest concentrations of coastal guns located? Would these have withheld their fire in the interest of concealing their positions until Allied units concentrated in landing areas or would they have fired on the first vessel to come within range? Had the guns of any dismantled ships been emplaced to assume a coastal defense role?

      A.   Coastal guns:

           (a)   Areas where the most guns were situated on seashores for shooting landing units, men-of-war, and ships were the coast of MIYAZAKI and the front of ARIAKE BAY.

           (b)   Coastal guns were directed towards concentrations of Allied landing forces and at ships coming within firing range, greater stress being laid on the former. These gun positions were disposed to provide maximum defilade from naval gunfire, while protection from aerial attack was gained by concealment. The main object was to provide flanking fire on the landing beaches.

           (c)   Guns from battleships were converted for coastal defense (none on ordinary ships).

29.   Q.   <u>Anti-aircraft</u>: What was the total number of AA actually emplaced on KYUSHU by 1 August? Was it planned that some of these were to be committed in a ground defense role?

      A.   Anti-aircraft guns:

           (a)   All anti-aircraft guns in KYUSHU up to 1 August numbered 410.

           (b)   The total number of Army anti-aircraft artillery was so little that there was no plan designed for utilization in land defense. However, should the AA entrenchment area turn into a battlefield, it would naturally participate in ground warfare. Moreover, quite a number of naval high-angle anti-aircraft guns were used for coastal defense purposes in KYUSHU.

30.   Q.   <u>Mines</u>: Where had ground mines already been laid? Which further areas had been earmarked for mining, and under what circumstances would these

have been mined? What kinds of mines were used, and how were they to be controlled?

A.   Mines:

Mines wore not used either on a great scale or systematically for ground defense for the reasons given below. However, each unit carried mines on a small local scale (mainly for killing and wounding men and horses and as an anti-tank weapon). There are three types of mines.

> (a)   The use of mines on a large systematic scale would have been rendered powerless beforehand by the overwhelming superiority of battleship and aerial bombardment of the Allied forces.

> (b)   Due to lack of gunpowder and iron it was more profitable to produce portable blasting powder instead of mines.

TACTICS:

31.   Q.   a.   Which of the following beach areas were considered most vulnerable to attack and which were best defended: (1) MIYAZAKI, (2). ARIAKE, (3) MAZURAZAKI, (4) KAGOSHIMA and (5) KUSHIKINO?

A.   The MIYAZAKI coast, the front of ARIAKE BAY and the coastal area between KUSHIKINO and MAKURAZKI were given equal consideration as mutual points of operation. However, the degree of defense at the date of surrender, owing to the time element, showed the ARIAKE BAY front to be first and the MIYAZAKI coast second in degree of readiness. (In the first part of October, the three district areas were scheduled to be <9> fortified to an equal degree.

Q.   b.   Was Allied entrance into KAGOSHIMA-WAN considered possible? Probable?

A.   The possibility of Allied invasion into KAGOSHIMA BAY were perceived.

Q.   c.   Would a strong defense have been made on the beaches? If so, in what strength, with what tactics, and supported by what kind of fixed installations?

A.   Powerful defense was established directly near coastal areas. One third to one fifth of the whole coastal defense strength was stationed along the beaches. The beach defenses were uniformly strong; where natural terrain features were advantageous for defense less troops were stationed, but poor defensive terrain was defended with greater strength. The principal fighting method and object of coastal stationed units was to persistently destroy the establishment of beach heads (airfields), and to enforce continuous counter-attacks in wave formation to attain the same. For this purpose fighting units would take their stand even to utter annihilation. Camps were basically established underground or in caves. Weapons were set up for last-ditch defense against allied fire and bombardment.

Q. d. How would the defense in the plains areas of southern KYUSHU have been conducted? With what type of support from the rugged interiors? How and around what installations was the defense of these plains areas to be organized?

A. The defense of plains area in southern KYUSHU was primarily to resist airborne troops (parachuters). There were no systematic plans for large scale coordinated defense of the plains. Fortifications on coast lines were stressed while areas behind were given to attack-proof fortification necessary for the concentration, deployment and fighting of strategic reserve units. (These fortifications were to protect the units from aerial and naval bombardment, also having tunnels to facilitate counterattacks). At the time of surrender, part of these fortifications had been completed.

Q. e. Would large scale counterattacks have been launched to drive the Allies off the island, or would these attacks have been small scale harassing and raiding attacks?

A. Large scale counterattack and transition to the offensive against Allied landing were contemplated.

Q. f. Would the strategy on southern KYUSHU have been designed to achieve delay or annihilation?

A. The action in southern KYUSHU was for the purpose of thorough annihilation.

Q. g. What use would have been made of cave and tunnel warfare? Where? How conducted? What preparations for such warfare had been completed at the time of surrender?

A. Cave and tunnel establishments were apportioned to bases for counterattack and offensive against Allied gunfire and bombardment, and meant to exist indefinitely. Consequently these establishments were at all points where

Allied troops were expected to land. At the time of surrender, granting difference in district areas, sixty to ninety percent of these establishments had been
completed.

Q. h. Would any KYUSHU cities have been strongly held in house-to-house
        defense?

A. In KYUSHU, no cities were prepared for house-to-house warfare.

Q. i. Would the southern KYUSHU forces have been committed to defend
        to the death, in place, or had arrangements been made for their possible
        retreat?

A. All units in southern KYUSHU were given orders to defend to the death
    <10> and retreat was not recognized as a possibility.

Q. j. What were the locations and strength of the main tactical reserves for
        defense of southern KYUSHU? If called upon, how much time would
        have been required to commit them to action?

A. Strategic reserve strength for southern KYUSHU operations were as follows:

Primary:	216 D	(vicinity of KUMAMOTO)
	25 D	(vicinity of KOBAYASHI, MIYAZAKI PREFECTURE)
	77 D	(vicinity of KAGOSHIMA)
	212 D	(plains of northern MIYAZAKI)
Secondary:	57 D	(southern area of FUKUOKA PREFECTURE)
	145 D	(northern KYUSHU)
Third:	231 D	(YAMAGUCHI CITY)
	230 D	(NEU, HINO-GUN, TOTTORI PREFECTURE)
	225 D	(TATSUND, HYOGO PREFECTURE)

According to developments, the following were held in reserve:

	205 D	(OKATOYO-MURA, NAGAOKA-GUN, KOCHI PREFECTURE)
	11 D	(KOCHI CITY)

(The reserve strategic strength immediately available amounted to the above 11 divisions, but the transfer of from three to five divisions from the KANTO area was expected

according to the Imperial Headquarters reserve strategy). The participation in warfare of the above strategic reserve forces would be enforced from those units in southern KYUSHU approximately within a week; in ten days in central KYUSHU and within two weeks in northern KYUSHU. (Concentration and maneuvers would be obviously conducted by marching under enemy aerial bombardment). (See annex C).

32.   Q.   <u>Communications</u>: To what extent had Allied bombing impeded railroad and highway communications on KYUSHU by 1 August? Was it assumed that communications between northern and southern KYUSHU would be effectively cut off by Allied aerial bombardment, prior to the Allied invasion? Had supplies been stored accordingly? Was the use of bypasses, secondary routes, or over-water communications contemplated? Could reserves have been brought down from the north to the south?

      A.   (a)   Land transportation status in KYUSHU up to about 1 August was as follows: Due to Allied aerial bombardment, railroads in southern KYUSHU were almost entirely blocked both day and night while road transportation was greatly reduced during the day. In central and northern KYUSHU, both road and railroad systems were only partly damaged from these raids.

           (b)   We were convinced that the transportation between northern and southern KYUSHU would be fully intercepted due to aerial bombardment prior to the Allied landings.

           (c)) The plans for and actual work on building new roads joining northern and southern KYUSHU, together with regulation of sea transportation, were in progress.

<11>

           (d)) It was anticipated that the shifting of northern KYUSHU reserves to the south was probable.

HOSPITALS AND SUPPLY:

33.   Q.   a   In considering an Allied invasion of southern KYUSHU what in general was the supply situation of the Japanese troops in southern KYUSHU? All of KYUSHU?

      A.   (A)   Supply situation in southern and entire KYUSHU:

                 (1)   In KYUSHU various Army supply depots which had been established in peacetime (under the direct control of the Minister

of War), were reinforced in July of this year for field operations, and organized under the Commander of the Western Army Area Headquarters. The said commander not only placed branch depots and agencies at different requisite points, but divided sections of supply depots other than ordnance, forming temporary field freight depots in each army area for the purposes of troop and supply concentration.

(2)   In southern KYUSHU, branch ordnance supply depots and field freight depots were established at TAKARABE (57th Army), and KAGOSHIMA (40th Army), besides agencies and stationary groups at requisite points. Field freight depots had been posted since peacetime in various areas, temporarily formed from controlled agencies of supply depots, and were not fully organized at the time of surrender. Agencies and stationary groups remained at their former posts and engaged in concentration and supply.

. . . .

.   (B)   Status of concentration of military supplies in entire KYUSHU:

(a)   Ammunition: The projected amount (i.e., planned amount) of ammunition was for 12 division battles, of which 8 were scheduled for shore operations and 4 for reserve (a division battle is considered as 30 days of normal operations. The supply of ammunition for a division battle would be that amount equivalent to approximately enough for 10 days continuous battle, or the equivalent of 10 units of fire). Should circumstances necessitate the expectation of other operations in KYUSHU, enough ammunition for 8 division battles was to be transferred from HONSHU. Ammunition for coastal operations had been distributed to each Army and stored near the shore lines. Reserves were placed for the main part in southern KYUSHU.

Plans for the distribution of ammunition in KYUSHU is as of the attached list (See Annex D).

<12>

(b)   Fuel: Projected amount of fuel for concentration was approximately 8,000 kilo-litres. The reserve amount was approximately 20,000 kilo-litres from Imperial Headquarters, to be retained in KYUSHU.

    (c)   Provisions: One month's provisions for 2 million men and 80,000 horses were concentrated, while reserves for further operations in KYUSHU, namely, one month's provisions for 1 million men and 110,000 horses were to be diverted from HONSHU.

    (d)   Medical supplies: The projected amount was one month's supply for 6 million troops; of which enough for 4 million were supplied to each Army (corps) for coastal warfare, while supplies for 2 million were retained as reserves.

    (e)   Veterinary supplies: The projected amount was one month's supply for 350,000 head, of which 200,000 were distributed to each Army (corps) for coastal warfare and 150,000 kept as reserves.

(C)   Main ammunition concentrations in southern KYUSHU:

Concentration of ammunition in southern KYUSHU had priority from a strategic point of view, forming from 60 to 70 percent of the entire KYUSHU stock. Two-thirds of the munitions supply to each army (40th Army and 57th Army) were distributed to front line divisions and consequently dispersed among shore encampments, one-third being kept in reserve.

Operational reserve ammunition for the area army in southern KYUSHU was stored at HITOYOSHI and TAKARABE; enough for 2 division battles. Reserve supplies were to be used for offensive operations, while defense of landing areas would utilize the amount distributed to each division.

Q. b.   What quantity of artillery, mortar, and small arms ammunition was available to the combat units charged with the defense of the landing beaches at (a) KUSHIKINO, (b) ARIAKE-WAN, (c) MIYAZAKI, and (d) SATSUMA PENINSULA? For how many days sustained combat?

A. (1)   For the defensive battles at the landing coast, plans were to use ammunition concentrated along the coast besides that equipped for the unit (ammunition equipped for the unit means that ammunition which is a component part of the unit equipment). The quantity was as follows:

Ammunition equipped for units for 0.2 battle

Concentrated ammunition
Vicinity of KUSHIKINO	0.5 division-battle.
Vicinity of ARIAKE-WAN	0.8 division-battle.
SATSUMA PENINSULA	0.9 division-battle.
Vicinity of MIYAZAKI	1.4 division-battle.

Each division was to have enough for 0.6 to 0.9 battles, including that equipped for the unit. The detailed quantity is unknown due to lack of records.

   (2)   The concentrated ammunition was supposedly the amount possible for the continuation of coastal defense battle for approximately one month; <13> but through past experience, after taking into consideration the difficulty of supplement and the consumption of the concentrated ammunition in combat, it was decided that it was only enough for a battle duration of 2 weeks.

Q.   c.   Where were the main ammunition dumps in southern KYUSHU? What method of transport was available to move the ammunition to the units engaged in battle?

A.   (1)   The principal ammunition concentration points in southern KYUSHU were the vicinities of TAKARABE, HONJO, TSUMA, MATSUYAMA, KAWABE, SENDAI, HITOYOSHI, and KOBAYASHI.

   (2)   The transportation of ammunition to the first line units was scheduled as follows:

      a.   To units engaged in combat, the principal means of transportation was by shoulder pack. Consequently, civilian combat corps and volunteer troops were to be used as supplying units.

      b.   To divisions supply points, transportation would have been carried out at night on animal backs and by shoulder packs.

      c.   It was judged that motor vehicle transportation was possible only in the rear zone and during the night.

Q.   d.   Were plans made to disperse supply dumps dug-in in the areas considered as possible battle fields? How much of this storage of supplies in the planned battle field areas had already been carried out by 15 August 1945?

A.   All concentration of ordnance and ammunition in underground storage protected by fortifications from bombardment and battleship firing were 70 percent completed at the time of the ending of the war.

Q.   e.   Was it planned to bring additional supplies from northern KYUSHU, or possibly HONSHU, to the troops engaged in battle in southern KYUSHU or were these troops to depend entirely on supplies previously stored in their battle areas?

A.   All munitions necessary to carry out operations in southern KYUSHU were planned to be transferred from both northern KYUSHU and HONSHU. However, in KYUSHU great portions of the Seibu Army (16th Area Army) munition allotments were distributed to southern KYUSHU, with a view to minimizing the transfer of munitions after commencement of operations. The supplies to be transferred from HONSHU were mainly ammunition for 8 division battles and provisions for a strength of 1,000,000 men for one month.

Q.   f.   How long was it believed that the Japanese forces could continue effective resistance in KYUSHU from a supply standpoint?

A.   The probable lengths of time for continued operation in KYUSHU viewed from the standpoint of replenishment of ordnance and ammunition were judged as follows:

   (a)   In event of possible replenishment from HONSHU—3 months.

   (b)   In the case of impossibility of replenishment from HONSHU—2 months.

   (c)   The continuation of protracted warfare was judged possible by maintenance of northern KYUSHU mountain areas. For that reason a synthetic underground factory for ordnance and ammunition was under construction on the vicinity of HIDA [HITA].

Q.   g.   What was the main line or route of supply and evacuation for southern KYUSHU?
A.   The main line or route of supply and evacuation for <14> southern KYUSHU is shown on the attached map (See annex E).

Q.   f.   [*sic*] What was the capacity of hospital units for caring for wounded in southern KYUSHU? What was the plan for evacuation of wounded, and to what places?

A.   The plans were that all military hospitals in KYUSHU, with a capacity of approximately 63,500 patients, were to receive the wounded soldiers of southern KYUSHU. All patients accommodated before commencement of operations were to be transferred to HONSHU. The arrangements were as follows:

Hospitals in southern KYUSHU and their accommodation capacity:

ARIAKE BAY DISTRICT	1,000 patients
MIYAZAKI DISTRICT	2,000 patients
SATSUMA PENINSULA	1,000 patients
HITOYOSHI, YOKOGAWA DISTRICT	4,000 patients

In addition to the above:

1 commissary hospital in the MIYAZAKI district (accommodation capacity approximately 1,000 patients)
2 commissary hospitals (location in southern KYUSHU undecided) (accommodation capacity of approximately 1,000 patients)

Furthermore, the above accommodations being insufficient, it was planned for ordinary hospitals to be utilized as occasion demanded.

In view of the inevitable operations in JAPAN proper, the wounded were to receive field medical treatment In as far as possible except in those serious cases where evacuation was required, strict caution was taken against decrease of strength in front lines.

Due to the above circumstances, and the regular transportation units being extremely limited, transit of patients was to be entrusted to civilian combat corps and volunteer troops. Also thorough utility was planned for the return cars.

Accommodations for patients were located as follows:

Vicinity of the front lines:
ARIAKE BAY DISTRICT   KLNOYA, IYAKONOJO
MIYAZAKI DISTRICT   NOJIRI, SUGIYASU, TORAKI
SATSUMA PENINSULA   CHIKAKU, GUNZAN, KAWATO, ISHIKI

Rear area: KOBAYASHI, YOSHIMATSU, YOKOGAWA, OGUCHI, HITOYOSHI

<15>

II. NOTES FROM AN INTERVIEW BY V AMPHIBIOUS CORPS AND ALLIED OFFICERS OF THE COMMANDING GENERALS AND STAFF OFFICERS OF THE JAPANESE 40TH AND 57TH ARMIES:

40TH ARMY:

The 40th Army was responsible for the ground defense of southeastern KYUSHU. The Japanese estimate of the situation was that enemy landings in force could be expected any time after 1 October 1945 in the areas of KUSHIKINO, ARIAKE-WAN, and MIYAZAKI. It was also considered possible that landings might take place on the southern coast of the SATSUMA PENINSULA, particularly on the beaches immediately to the west of LAKE IKEDA. In view of this estimate, 40th Army located the 303rd, 206th and l46th Divisions on the coast, with general instructions to defeat the enemy in the beach-head area; and in view of the expected threat to the southern tip of the SATSUMA PENINSULA, the 125th

Independent Mixed Brigade was located in this area, and it was placed under the command of the 146th Division.

The 77th Division was held in general reserve and located centrally at the head of KAGOSHIMA-WAN. If further reinforcement of the troops in southern KYUSHU was required during the course of the battle, it was possible that 16th Area Army would send the 216th Division from the KUMAMOTO area south to support either 40th or 57th Army. If the main battle developed in the MIYAZAKI and/or ARIAKE-WAN area, 16th Area Army might transfer the 77th Division to the command of the 57th Army. However, if the 77th Division and the 206th Division were sent to support the 57th Army in the east, the Commanding General, 40th Army, considered that he would have insufficient troops with which to defeat the enemy at the water's edge. He therefore intended to fight only a delaying battle in the beachhead area, and then to retire to prepared positions in the hills.

For battle purposes, headquarters of major formations would be located as follows:

Hq 40th Army (Adv)	IJUIN
Hq 303rd Division	SENDAI
Hq 206th Division	BONO
Hq 146th Division	KAWANABE
Hq l25th IMB	IKEDA

The initial intention was to prevent the enemy from obtaining a proper footing ashore. This was to be done by the coastal divisions inflicting the maximum amount of damage on the enemy in the vicinity of the beaches themselves. After the initial assault had been held by the coastal divisions, the strongest possible counter-attack was to be delivered by reserve forces concentrated for the purpose.

It was intended to prevent enemy shipping from entering KAGOSHIMA-WAN. The Japanese considered that entrance to KAGOSHIMA-WAN might be attempted either by enemy ships forcing an entry through the minefield covering the entrance, or initially taking the LAKE IKEDA area by a landing from the south and then capturing the guns covering the straits.

303RD DIVISION: Within the area assigned to it, this division was to hold the following three areas in strength: (1) KUSHIKINO, (2) mouth of SENDAI RIVER and (3) AKUNE. Three battalions of the division were to be ready to move south at short notice under orders of 40th Army as immediate reinforcements to 206th Division. The division's responsibilities in respect to KURANOSHATO STRAIT were to provide coast watchers for the approach of enemy shipping, and guns to cover the straits to ensure that enemy small craft did not get through. These responsibilities were shortly taken over by the Navy.

206TH DIVISION: Assigned the KAMINOKAWA-KAMINOYAMA beach front area, the division was to hold the enemy within the beach-head area until a strong counter-attack could be developed. Reference is also made to the possibility of transferring this division to the MIYAZAKI area if the main battle developed there. In the event of the 206th Division being <16> withdrawn, it was intended to divide its area between 303rd Division moving farther south and 146th Division moving north.

146TH DIVISION: This division was to be employed in a purely holding role, and particular emphasis was placed on defense of the KASEDA area and the south coast of SATSUMA PENINSULA. The 125th IMB was to obstruct the entry of the enemy into the mouth of KAGOSHIMA-WAN, and oppose any enemy forces landing in the KAIMONDAKI area.

77TH DIVISION: It was expected that this division would be employed in making a strong counter-attack in support of the 206th division in the area of IZAKU. Prior to 1 October, they were to be employed in training and repairing defenses.

No general directive had been issued to the coastal divisions regarding the tactics to be employed in bench defense. However, the defense depended mainly on localities, prepared for all-around defense, sited in depth and mutually supporting, as far as ground would permit. The main localities were of approximately battalion strength; other localities of approximately company strength. In addition to those defended localities, the various battalions had forward elements in foxholes and trenches at the back of the beach, to act as look-outs, to send information back to the main localities and to provide suicidal opposition to the initial landing. The majority of these forward positions were apparently sited on forward slopes with good fields of fire onto the assault beaches.

If available, land mines were to be employed in beach defenses, but there seemed little likelihood of supplies forthcoming. No plan existed for the employment of under-water obstacles on the beaches.

The main tank strength was to be concentrated in the area of LAKE IKEDA, and was to be employed in a non-mobile role, the tanks being dug in and used purely as anti-tank artillery. The second regiment of the 6th Tank Brigade was under command of the 57th Army and was located at KIRISHIMA. The 13th ITB consisted of not more than 10 light tanks and was located to the north of LAKE IKEDA.

Artillery would be located in rear areas, covering the Japanese between defended localities and with ability to fire on the beaches. It was intended that 4th Artillery Headquarters would work in close cooperation with the 206th Division and would thereupon be located in the vicinity of IZAKU. The 9th Independent Field Artillery Regiment, equipped with 75-mm guns, was to be allotted to divisions as required. The 28th Field Medium Artillery Regiment, equipped with twenty-four 150-mm guns, was to be allotted half to the 206th Division (and located in the area of IZAKU) and half to the 146th Division (and located in the area of TSUZIKAZE). No allotment of the 20th Field Medium Artillery Regiment had been made, as the guns had not been received, but the regiment would probably have been allotted to the 206th Division. The 44th Independent Medium Artillery Regiment, consisting of four 150-mm guns, was under the command of the 125th IMB, and located in the area of IWAMOTO, to fire against ships entering KAGOSHIMA-WAN.

The 40th Army had under its direct control the 35th and 36th Suicide Boat Squadrons, which consisted of suicide craft of the shinyo type, manned by army personnel. The 35th Company was based on TANIYAMA and the 36th on ICHIKINO. From the latter base, it was intended to move the craft by road to the SENDAI RIVER and on down to KAGOSHIMA-WAN. None of the boats allotted had as yet arrived, and no final decision had been reached as to how they would be employed. It was practically certain that they would be used only at night, and in attack against enemy transports.

Little information was gained of the various anti-aircraft units. The 21st Mortar Battalion was located in KAGOSHIMA to provide AA defense for the city. Other AA units located at BANSEI, CHIRAN, SENDAI, etc., were manned by naval and air force personnel and there appeared to be no overall anti-aircraft control or link-up of these various units

<17>

Questions regarding the coordination of the three services for the defense of KYUSHU revealed the usual almost complete lack of knowledge of the organizations and plans of the other services. As far as the 40th Army was concerned, everything had to come through Hq 16th Area Army, and there appeared to be no coordination with the Navy or air force on the lower levels.

When the landings took place, civilians were to evacuate the forward areas and were to be organized for employment in company supplies, repairing roads, etc., in the rear areas.

57TH ARMY: At the time of invasion, it was intended that the major formations of the 57th Army should occupy the following general areas:

212 Division	Northern MIYAZAKI coast
154 Division	Central MIYAZAKI coast
156 Division	Southern MIYAZAKI coast
86 Division	Area of SHIBUSHI and coastline of ARIAKE-WAN
25 Division	Area of KOBAYASHI PLAIN
98 IMB	East coast area–KAGOSHIMA BAY
109 MB	TANEGA-SHIMA
5 Tank Brigade	Area of central MIYAZAKI plain
1 Regt 6 Tank Bde	KIRISHIMA (in support of 86 Div)

For the initial battle, it was intended that the headquarters of the 57th Army and its units would be located as follows:

Hq 57th Army	AYAMCHI
Hq 212 Division	undecided
Hq 154 Division	TSUMA
Hq 156 Division	HONJO
Hq 25 Division	KOBAYASHI

Hq 86 Division	MATSUYAMA
Hq 98 IMB	OIRA
Hq 109 IMB	NOMA
Hq 5 Tank Bde	MORNINAGA

The Japanese plans for the defense of southern KYUSHU were based on the assumption that the American landings in strength would take place simultaneously in the areas of MIYAZAKI, ARIAKE-WAN and KUSHIKINO. In addition, it appeared from the 40th Army plans, that considerable importance was attached to the possibility of a landing in the MAKURASAKI area. In the light of this overall plan, 57th Army had placed its main strength in the MIYAZAKI PLAIN area.

Of the three divisions located on the coast line of MIYAZAKI, it was intended that the 154th and 156th Divisions should remain in position, wherever the landing was made, and should maintain a purely static defense. The 212th Division in the north was, if necessary, to be employed in a mobile role and was to be used to move initially to support the 154th and 156th Divisions. In addition, it might possibly be employed even further south if the main battle developed in the area of ARIAKE-WAN. It was anticipated that the 212th Division would be able to counter-attack in support of the 154th and 156th Divisions within 48 hours of the landing.

Farther back, in the KOBAYASHI area, the 25th Division was held centrally in general mobile reserve, prepared to move to any area where the resistance required strengthening. It was anticipated, however, that it would probably be committed to the defense of the MIYAZAKI Plain and in such circumstances, it would have under its command the 5th Tank Brigade. It was apparently not intended to commit the tank brigade piecemeal, but to employ it at maximum strength in a strong counter-attack in conjunction with the 25th Division. It was expected that this strong counterattack would probably be delivered within 4–7 days of the landing. At the conclusion of this counter-attack, the 5th Tank Brigade would revert to the control of the 57th Army.

<18>

The 5th Tank Brigade was to consist of a headquarters and two regiments, each of approximately 50 tanks and self-propelled guns. The total for the whole regiment was estimated as follows:

Medium tanks	56
Light tanks	26
S. P. guns (150-mm)	6
S. P. guns (75-mm)	<u>24</u>
	112

57th Army had not received any allotments of heavy tanks mounting 75-mm guns, and the Commanding General considered that no such tanks were located anywhere in

KYUSHU. Tactically, it was intended to use the medium and light tanks, as far as possible, as mobile units in a tank-versus-tank role. The self-propelled guns were to be used mainly in previously selected and prepared positions as anti-tank weapons, although the 150mm guns might also be used as normal supporting artillery.

In addition to the reserve provided by the 25th Division and 5th Tank Brigade, the 77th Division, initially under the command of the 40th Army, might also be switched to the command of the 57th Army if conditions required it. The Commanding General, 57th Army, further explained that the tactic of quick and weighty counter-attack was being insisted on in the light of the experience gained during the LEYTE Campaign, where the Japanese reserve had not come up quickly enough to the counter attack.

Divisions allotted to coastal defense were committed to a policy of annihilation of the invader within the beach-head area. No general directives as to how such a defense should be conducted had been issued either by the 57th Army or by any higher command. This statement that no detailed tactics for beach defense had been laid down by higher authority agreed with the information obtained from the 40th Army. The only instructions given to divisions were that the coastline was to be held by a defense at the water's edge and that there was to be no retreat under any circumstance.

The tactical disposition of the 156th Division is a good example of a typical coastline division disposed tactically for the defense of its area. The system of defense is almost identical with that employed by the divisions of the 40th Army on the west coast. The 156th Division consisted of four regiments, and of those, the 453rd, 454th and 455th were to be located on the coast itself, while the 456th was to be held in the rear, immediately behind the 453rd. Within each regimental area on the coast, the first line of resistance which the invaders would meet would be a thin screen of infantry dug-in among the dunes at the back of the beach in foxholes and tunnels. It was hoped that a percentage of those troops would survive the preliminary bombardment and offer a certain amount of suicide resistance to the first wave of invading forces, and also send back some information to the defended localities behind. Behind the line of dunes, positions were prepared for all-around defense, from which considerable resistance could be offered. The kernel of the defense, however, was still farther back in completely prepared positions, almost invariably selected on high ground. Such positions were to be occupied by the equivalent of a battalion group strength and were to be defended to the very end.

The following were quoted as comprising a typical battalion locality:

Infantry Battalion (approximately 1000 rifles)
Two 70-mm battalion guns
Twelve HMB [heavy machine guns]
Thirty-one LMG [light machine guns]
Two 75-mm guns (allotted by regiment)
Four anti-tank guns (37-mm)
A proportionate number of mortars [approximately thirty-six to forty-nine]

The Commanding General considered that the 57th Army was definitely deficient in artillery, which was allotted in small numbers to divisions and regiments. Artillery was so placed that it could range on the <19> beaches and provide supporting fire to the infantry within the gaps left by the defended localities. It appeared that the Japanese had no method of centralizing control of artillery fire with sufficient flexibility to mass the fire of all artillery on a specific target. They were unable to shift all the fire from one target to another on a wide front.

No land mines had been laid in the area, although it was intended to use them to the maximum if supplies were forthcoming. There appeared to be no intention of erecting under-water obstacles on the beaches. No preparations had been made for blowing bridges.

It was intended that all forward troops should hold three months' food; artillery—500 rounds per gun dumped at the gun position; small arms ammunition "enough for one major engagement." The re-supply situation was very vague.

The employment of airborne troops by the Americans was also regarded as possible, and to meet this threat, the 1st Special (Adv) Tank Unit was located in the area of MIYAKONOJO. The unit was equipped with 27 light tanks and was intended to move rapidly to any area in the vicinity where airborne troops were dropped. In addition, poles were to be erected and plane-traps (10 meters wide, 6 deep and 40 long) were to be dug in MIYAKONOJO PLAIN to prevent plane and glider landings.

The 31st and 32nd Suicide Boat Units, each consisting of 150 craft of the shinyo type manned by army personnel, and located at ABURATSU and ONESHIME respectively, were under the direct orders of the 57th Army. These army craft were apparently quite separate from the navy, and were intended to be employed close inshore, whereas the navy was to attack farther out to sea. The 57th Army claimed to be aware to a large extent of the naval plan and that a degree of coordination between the two services had been achieved. It was intended to employ the army boat units only at night, and that attack would be delivered by companies of 33 or so craft, and not in complete units. The main objects of attack would be the transports and the LSTs.

The degree of coordination achieved with the Air Force was practically non-existent. In order for close air support of the ground forces, the demand would have to be submitted through army channels to the 16th Area Army, who would pass it to the 6th Air Army Headquarters, who would pass the order all the way down the chain of air command.

. . . .

<20>

Proclamation Defining Terms for Japanese Surrender Issued at Potsdam, July 26, 1945 (Potsdam Declaration)

(1) We—the President of the United States, the President of the National Government of the Republic of China, and the Prime Minister of Great Britain, representing the hundreds of millions of our countrymen, have conferred and agree that Japan shall be given an opportunity to end this war.

(2) The prodigious land, sea and air forces of the United States, the British Empire and of China, many times reinforced by their armies and air fleets from the west, are poised to strike the final blows upon Japan. This military power is sustained and inspired by the determination of all the Allied Nations to prosecute the war against Japan until she ceases to resist.

(3) The result of the futile and senseless German resistance to the might of the aroused free peoples of the world stands forth in awful clarity as an example to the people of Japan. The might that now converges on Japan is immeasurably greater than that which, when applied to the resisting Nazis, necessarily laid waste to the lands, the industry and the method of life of the whole German people. The full application of our military power, backed by our resolve, will mean the inevitable and complete destruction of the Japanese armed forces and just as inevitably the utter devastation of the Japanese homeland.

(4) The time has come for Japan to decide whether she will continue to be controlled by those self-willed militaristic advisers whose unintelligent calculations have brought the Empire of Japan to the threshold of annihilation, or whether she will follow the path of reason.

(5)   Following are our terms. We will not deviate from them. There are no alternatives. We shall brook no delay.

(6)   There must be eliminated for all time the authority and influence of those who have deceived and misled the people of Japan into embarking on world conquest, for we insist that a new order of peace, security and justice will be impossible until irresponsible militarism is driven from the world.

(7)   Until such a new order is established and until there is convincing proof that Japan's war-making power is destroyed, points in Japanese territory to be designated by the Allies shall be occupied to secure the achievement of the basic objectives we are here setting forth.

(8)   The terms of the Cairo Declaration shall be carried out and Japanese sovereignty shall be limited to the islands of Honshu, Hokkaido, Kyushu, Shikoku and such minor islands as we determine.

(9)   The Japanese military forces, after being completely disarmed, shall be permitted to return to their homes with the opportunity to lead peaceful and productive lives.

(10)   We do not intend that the Japanese shall be enslaved as a race or destroyed as a nation, but stern justice shall be meted out to all war criminals, including those who have visited cruelties upon our prisoners. The Japanese Government shall remove all obstacles to the revival and strengthening of democratic tendencies among the Japanese people. Freedom of speech, of religion, and of thought, as well as respect for the fundamental human rights shall be established.

(11)   Japan shall be permitted to maintain such industries as will sustain her economy and permit the exaction of just reparations in kind, but not those which would enable her to re-arm for war. To this end, access to, as distinguished from control of, raw materials shall be permitted. Eventual Japanese participation in world trade relations shall be permitted.

(12)   The occupying forces of the Allies shall be withdrawn from Japan as soon as these objectives have been accomplished and there has been established in accordance with the freely expressed will of the Japanese people a peacefully inclined and responsible government.

(13)   We call upon the government of Japan to proclaim now the unconditional surrender of all Japanese armed forces, and to provide proper and adequate assurances of their good faith in such action. The alternative for Japan is prompt and utter destruction.

APPENDIX D

Extract from a Letter
Written by James Michener,
October 20, 1995

The following is from an October 20, 1995, letter to Martin Allday by fellow veteran James Michener. Author Michener had been asked to sign a petition criticizing the bombing of Hiroshima and Nagasaki and had been approached to speak out against the use of the atom bomb in 1945. He declined. However, fearful of the reaction from the literary and Hollywood circles he moved in to his views on President Truman's atom bomb decision, Michener also asked Allday not to make the letter public until after his death.

Dear Martin,

. . . In the summer of 1945 I was stationed on Espiritu Santo close to a big Army field hospital manned by a complete stateside hospital staff from Nebraska and Colorado. I had close relations with the doctors, so I was privy to their thinking about the forthcoming invasion of Japan. They had been alerted to prepare for moving onto the beaches of Kyushu when we invaded there and they were prepared to expect vast numbers of casualties when the Japanese home front defense forces started their suicide attacks.

More important, I was on my own very close to an Army division that was stationed temporarily in a swampy wooded section on our island. They were a disheartened unit for the Japanese had knocked them about a bit in the action on Saipan; their assignment to our swamp was a kind of punishment for their ineffective conduct on Saipan. Now they were informed unofficially that they would be among the first units to hit the beach in our invasion of Kyushu, and they were terrified. In long talks with me, they said that they expected 70 or 80 percent casualties, and they could think of no way to avoid the impending disaster.

So it was with knowledge of what the doctors anticipated and what the Army men felt was inescapable that I approached the days of early August, and I, too, became a bit shaky because the rumor was that I might be attached to the Army unit because of my expertise in keeping airplanes properly fitted and in the sky. Then came the astounding news that a bomb of a new type had been dropped on Hiroshima, a second one on Nagasaki, and that the Japanese emperor himself had called upon his people to surrender peacefully and await the Allied peace-keeping forces to land and establish the changes required by the recent turn of events.

How did we react? With a gigantic sigh of relief, not exultation because of our victory, but a deep gut-wrenching sigh of deliverance. We had stared into the mouth of Armageddon and suddenly the confrontation was no longer necessary. We had escaped those deadly beaches of Kyushu.

I cannot recall who was the more relieved, the doctors who could foresee the wounded and the dying, or the G.I. grunts who would have done the dying, or the men like me who had sensed the great tragedy that loomed. All I know is that we said prayers of deliverance and kept our mouths shut when arguments began as to whether the bombs needed to be dropped or not. And I have maintained that silence to this moment, when I wanted to have the reactions of the men understood who had figured to be on the first waves in.

Let's put it simply. Never once in those first days nor in the long reconsiderations later could I possibly have criticized Truman for having dropped that first bomb. True, I see now that the second bomb on Nagasaki might have been redundant and I would have been just as happy if it had not been dropped. And I can understand how some historians can argue that Japan might have surrendered without the Hiroshima bomb, but the evidence from many nations involved at that moment testify to the contrary. From my experience on Saipan and Okinawa, when I saw how violently the Japanese soldiers defended their caves to the death, I am satisfied that they would have done the same on Kyushu. Also, because I was in aviation and could study battle reports about the effectiveness of airplane bombing, especially with those super-deadly firebombs that ate up the oxygen supply of a great city, I was well aware that the deaths from the fire bombing of Tokyo in early 1945 far exceeded the deaths of Hiroshima.

So I have been able to take refuge in the terrible, time-tested truism that war is war, and if you are unlucky enough to become engaged in one, you better not lose it. The doctrine, cruel and thoughtless as it may sound, governs my thought, my evaluations and my behavior. I could never publicly turn my back on that belief, so I have refused opportunities to testify against the United States in the Hiroshima matter. I know that if I went public with my views I would be condemned and ridiculed, but I stood there on the lip of the pulsating volcano, and I know that I was terrified at what might happen and damned relieved when the invasion became unnecessary. I accept the military estimates that at least 1 million lives were saved, and mine could have been one of them.

Sincerely,
James Michener

Notes

Chapter 1. The Maximum "Bloodletting and Delay"

1. Maj. Mark P. Arens, Marine Corps Intelligence Activity, USMCR, *V [Marine] Amphibious Corps Planning for Operation Olympic and the Role of Intelligence in Support of Planning* (Quantico, Va.: Marine Corps Command and Staff College, 1996), 81.

2. Col. Takushiro Hattori, *The Complete History of the Greater East Asia War* (Tokyo: Headquarters, 500th Military Intelligence Group, 1954), 4:289–90, translated from Hattori's *Daitoa Senso zenshi* (Tokyo: Masu Shobo, 1953), 4 vols. Colonel Hattori headed the Operations Section of Imperial General Headquarter's Army Section and served as secretary to War Minister Anami Korechita during the later war years then worked after the surrender as a translator and analyst for G2, General Headquarters, U.S. Far East Command, where he coordinated the efforts of twenty-three Japanese general and field grade officers in the production of "Japanese Special Study on Manchuria"

(hereafter cited as JSSM), vol. 1, "Japanese Operational Planning Against the USSR," the four-book vol. 3, "Strategic Study of Manchuria: Military Typography and Geography," and other volumes in JSSM.

3. Lt. William M. Rigdon, USN, *Log of the President's Trip to the Berlin Conference, 6 July 1945 to 7 August 1945* (Washington, D.C.: White House, 1945), 51, Harry S. Truman Library and Museum, Independence, Mo. (hereafter cited as HSTL). Following an earlier gunnery exercise aboard the *Augusta*, Truman wrote that he found it "most interesting" and that "I'd still rather fire a battery than run a country." See Truman diary entry, July 9, 1945, in Robert H. Ferrell, *Off the Record: The Private Papers of Harry S. Truman* (New York: Harper & Row, 1980), 49. The term "pom-pom" was derived from the sound made by the original rapid-firing Vickers 2-pounder (40-mm) antiaircraft gun, and subsequent weapons of this type, such as the Bofors used on the USS *Augusta*, inherited the nickname.

4. Untitled field notes to "Operations Report of Battery D, 129th F. A. From Morning

of Sept. 26, 1918, To: Evening of Oct. 3, 1918," and the first of three drafts produced by Truman while still in France of account covering D Battery operations during the Muese-Argonne offensive, both in Family Business and Personal Affairs—Military File WWI, Box 30, folder "Military Service— Longhand Notes by HST Regarding." Also Harry S. Truman to Bess Wallace, November 23, 1918, in Correspondence from Harry S. Truman to Bess Wallace Truman, 1921–1959, Family Business and Personal Affairs—Family Correspondence File, Correspondence from Harry S. Truman to Bess Wallace, 1910–1919, Box 5, HSTL.

5. Harry S. Truman to Bess Truman, July 18, 1945, in Robert H. Ferrell, ed., *Dear Bess: The Letters from Harry to Bess Truman 1910–1959* (New York: W. W. Norton, 1983), 519.

6. Jeff Nichols, *Liberators: The Story of the 20th Armored Division in World War II* (Mountain City, Tenn.: 20th Armored Division Association, 2006), 94; Shelby L. Stanton, *World War II Order of Battle: U.S. Army (Ground Force Units)* (Mechanicsburg, Pa.: Stackpole Books, 2006), 214, 217–18; and Rigdon, *Log of the President's Trip* iv, 49–50. The USS *John Ericsson* was the former Swedish luxury liner MS *Kungsholm*.

7. The finely tuned Point Discharge Plan, or "points system," was structured in such a way that public demand for a return of troops after VE-day might be satisfied but the Army would still retain a sizable core of veterans for the upcoming series of campaigns in Japan, which were expected to last at least through 1946.

8. Stanton, *World War II Order of Battle* 81, 88. See also Capt. Harry H. Ransom, "Redeployment in the AAF," *Air Force* 28, no. 7 (July 1945): 4–6, which notes that the thirty-day leave was not included in the annual leave or furlough time already allotted to soldiers and airmen.

9. Rigdon, *Log of the President's Trip* iv, 4, 7–12; and Stanton, *World War II Order of Battle* 77, 79, 131, 159. Like those of the 44th Infantry Division aboard the *Queen Elizabeth*, soldiers returning to the U.S. aboard the *Queen Mary, Aquitania, Mauretania, Nieuw Amsterdam*, and *Ile de France* (collectively known as the "Monsters") first transited to Britain, where they boarded the liners. The *Aquitania* and others of this group were to begin the movement of redeployed troops to the Pacific from West Coast ports and British troops to the Far East in the fall of 1945. See Stephen Harding, *Great Liners at War* (St. Paul, Minn.: MBI, 1997), 96, 112–17, 138–39; and Robert W. Coakley and Richard M. Leighton, *Global Logistics and Strategy, 1943–1945*, United States Army in World War II series (hereafter cited as USAWWII series) (Washington, D.C.: Center of Military History, United States Army, 1948), 540–41, 544, 588–89, 612–13.

10. D. M. Giangreco, "Spinning the Casualties: Media Strategies during the Roosevelt Administration," *Passport* 35 (December 2004): 22–30.

11. Department of the Army, "Army Battle Casualties and Nonbattle Deaths in World War II, Final Report, 7 December 1941–31 December 1946," Office of the Adjutant General, Washington, D.C. 1987, 6; and *Diaries of Henry Lewis Stimson*, January 11, 1945, microfilm ed., Reel 9, Henry Lewis Stimson Papers, Yale University Library, New Haven, Conn., from microfilm at HSTL.

12. As an example, see Gerhard L. Weinberg's comprehensive *A World at Arms: A Global History of World War II*, 2nd ed. (New York: Cambridge University Press, 2005), 894–95.

13. The number of Merchant Marine personnel who were killed in action, died of wounds, and died while prisoners of war during World War II is approximately 9,521, or 1 in every 26, as opposed to the next closest group, the U.S. Marines, which suffered 1 in every 34 to these three categories, and the Army (including the Army Air Force), which stood at 1 in 48. Data supplied by U.S. Maritime Service Veterans, Berkeley, Calif.

14. Gen. George C. Marshall to Lt. Gen. Jacob L. Devers, January 18, 1944, memorandum, in Larry I. Bland and Sharon Ritenour Stevens, eds., *The Papers of George Catlett Marshall*, vol. 4, "*Aggressive and Determined Leadership,*" *June 1, 1943–December 31, 1944* (Baltimore: Johns Hopkins University Press, 1996) (hereafter cited as *Marhall*, followed by volume number), 235–36; *Selective Service and Victory: The 4th Report of the Director of Selective Service, July 1, 1944 to December 31, 1945* (Washington, D.C.: GPO, 1946), 590; and Lt. Gen. Lewis B. Hershey, prepared by Lt. Col. Irving W. Hart, *Outline of Historical Background of Selective Service: From Biblical Days to June 30, 1965* (Washington, D.C.: U.S. Selective Service System, 1966), 52; Some 9,920,436 of the 12,435,500 were inducted into the Army through the Selective Service, while the balance entered through voluntary enlistments before the practice was terminated by executive order in December 1942.

15. Department of the Army "Army Battle Casualties," 118.

16. Frank A. Resiter, ed., *Medical Department, United States Army: Medical Statistics in World War II* (Washington, D.C.: Office of the Surgeon General, Department of the Army, 1975), 13–14, 43.

17. Capt. Louis H. Roddis, MD, USN, "Naval and Marine Corps Casualties in the Wars of the United States," *Military Surgeon* 99 (October 1946): 305–10; and Department of the Army, "Army Battle Casualties," 5. Nonbattle deaths are frequently included in battle casualty tabulations because, unlike other categories of nonbattle casualties, dead personnel are irrevocably removed from the manpower pool, while a percentage of those in other categories returned to full duty status or were able to serve in a reduced capacity within the United States and thus free healthy personnel for overseas duty. The total number of POWs (all armed services and both those who survived and died during captivity) was 128,589. See William Paul Skelton III, MD, *American Ex-Prisoners of War*, in the Veteran's Health Initiative series (Washington, D.C.: Department of Veteran's Affairs, 2002), 5, 11.

18. *Selective Service and Victory*, 593.

19. Maurice Matloff, "The 90-division Gamble," in *Command Decisions*, USAWWII series (Washington, D.C.: Center of Military History, United States Army, 1960), 365–81, esp. 376; and Maj. William R. Keast, "Provision of Enlisted Replacements," Study No. 7, Historical Section, Army Ground Forces, Washington, D.C., 1946, 23–24.

20. Stanton, *World War II Order of Battle*, 3–4.

21. Ibid., 4. See also Bell I. Wiley, "Effects of Overseas Requirements on Training, 1944–45," in *The Procurement and Training of Ground Combat Troops*, by Robert R. Palmer, Bell I. Wiley, and William R. Keast, USAWWII series (Washington, D.C.: Center of Military History, United States Army, 1948), 470–93, esp. 472–74, as well as Robert R. Palmer and William R. Keast, "The Provision of Enlisted Replacements," expanded from Study No. 7, Army Ground Forces, in the same volume, 165–239.

22. Hattori, *Complete History of the Greater East Asia War* 4:175.

23. For example, Matloff notes in "90-division Gamble," 370, that in February 1943, one U.S. House and five Senate probes of U.S. Army or military-industrial manpower were underway. All of these congressional initiatives received at least some degree of coverage in the Washington and New York press.

24. William L. Shirer, *The Rise and Fall of the Third Reich: A History of Nazi Germany* (New York: Simon and Schuster, 1960), 895.

25. Sadao Asada, *From Mahan to Pearl Harbor: The Imperial Japanese Navy and the United States* (Annapolis: Naval Institute Press, 2006), 182–84.

26. In addition to newspapers of the day, see also John D. Chappell's *Before the Bomb: How America Approached the End of the Pacific War* (Lexington: University Press of Kentucky, 1997).

27. See Wayne S. Cole, *Charles A. Lindbergh and the Battle against American Intervention in World War II* (New York: Harcourt Brace Jovanovich, 1974); Justus D. Doenecke, *Storm on the Horizon: The Challenge to American Intervention, 1939–1941* (Lanham, Md.: Rowman and Littlefield, 2000); Manfred Jonas, *Isolationism in America, 1935–1941* (Ithaca, N.Y.: Cornell University Press, 1966); and Garet Garrett, *Defend America First: The Antiwar Editorials of the Saturday Evening Post, 1939–1942* (Caldwell, Idaho: Caxton Press, 2003).

28. Hattori, *Complete History of the Greater East Asia War* 4:297.

29. "Casualties," *Yank* 3 (February 2, 1945): 17.

30. Hattori, *Complete History of the Greater East Asia War* 4:4–5; Japanese Monograph No. 17, "Homeland Operations Record," U.S. Army Forces Far East, Military History Section, Tokyo, 1959, distributed by the Office of the Chief of Military History,
Washington, D.C. (hereafter cited as Japanese Monograph No. 17, "Homeland Operations"), 103–104; and Alvin D. Coox, *Japan: The Final Agony* (New York: Ballantine Books, 1970), 81. Translations courtesy Edward J. Drea, January 19, 2006.

31. Coox, *Final Agony,* 88.

32. Ibid., 10–11.

Chapter 2. Spinning the Casualties

1. "Roosevelt Urges Work-or-Fight Bill to Back Offensives," *New York Times,* January 18, 1945, 1; and "Letters [from General Marshall and Admiral King] on the Pressing Manpower Problem," 13.

2. James Jones, *WWII: A Chronicle of Soldiering* (New York: Ballantine, 1975), 230.

3. Even before the advent of the casualty surge, the U.S. Army struggled to keep combat units up to strength, and Secretary of State Henry L. Stimson was convinced that there was insufficient Army manpower available for the American field armies that would conduct the final drive into Nazi Germany. Events during the Germans' Ardennes counteroffensive of December 1945 would prove him right. See Henry L. Stimson diary entries of May 10 and 16, 1944, in Bland and Stevens, *Marshall* 4:450–51. Also see Marshall's "Memorandum for the President—Subject: Strength of the Army," in Bland and Stevens, *Marshall* 4:556–60.

4. Although casualty-related data was produced or examined by an extremely wide variety of staff elements, particularly as it related to manpower questions, this was done to meet the needs of individual staff elements and their own chains of command. Consequently, the output from these groups is often narrowly focused, based on assumptions held by the individual staff element and its

chain of command, and communicated in a military shorthand. The great utility derived from *Yank*'s publication of casualty data (though limited in scope) is its presentation of what soldiers were being officially told over a period of several years through a single, popular, mass-circulation Army organ.

5. "Our Casualties," *Yank* 2 (July 23, 1943): 11.

6. A useful synthesis of these works is found in Mary Ellen Condon-Rall and Albert E. Cowdry, *The Medical Department: Medical Service in the War against Japan*, USAWWII series (Washington, D.C.: Center of Military History, United States Army, 1998), 302–11.

7. Ibid., 130–41.

8. Col. Ronald F. Bellamy and Col. Craig H. Lewellyn (Ret.), "Preventable Casualties: Rommel's Flaw, Slim's Edge," *Army*, May 1990, 52–56.

9. Dr. Michael E. DeBakey (Colonel, Ret.) and Capt. Gilbert W. Beebe (Ret.), *Battle Casualties: Incidence, Mortality and Logistic Considerations* (Springfield, Ill.: Charles C. Thomas, 1952), 14; see also 31.

10. See chapter 1, note 16 for a breakdown of this figure; Re. siter, *Medical Statistics in World War II*, 13–14, 43.

11. The Allied deception campaign aimed at Nazi Germany, Operation Bodyguard, and specifically its Fortitude South component, was geared to creating the impression that the Allies had considerably larger forces massing in England than they in fact did. While it is true that the Allies were leading the German intelligence agencies around by the nose at this point in the war, they had to presume that the Abwehr and other agencies had some very smart number crunchers within their ranks. A detailed analysis of the casualty figures in conjunction with demographic information, shipping data, and so on might have severely complicated the invasion of France if it led the Germans to reassess the manpower actually available to the United States. See Anthony Cave Brown, *Bodyguard of Lies*, 2 vols. (New York: Harper & Row, 1975), 1:511; 2:532–33, 549, 559–60, 691–92; and Charles G. Cruickshank, *Deception in World War II* (New York: Oxford University Press, 1979), 87–88, 177–185. For a useful summary of deception operations during this period, see Maj. James R. Koch, "Operation Fortitude: The Backbone of Deception," *Military Review* 72 (March 1992): 66–77.

12. "Casualty Lists," *Yank* 2 (June 2, 1944): 17.

13. "They Could Have Been Worse," *Yank* 2 (July 23, 1943): 17.

14. "Army Separations," *Yank* 3 (June 23, 1944): 17.

15. "Total Army Losses," *Yank* 3 (August 25, 1944): 17.

16. Department of the Army, "Army Battle Casualties," 6.

17. "Total Army Losses," *Yank* 3 (September 29, 1944): 17. See also Department of the Army, "Army Battle Casualties," 6.

18. The finely tuned "points system" was structured in such a way that public demand for a return of troops after VE-day might be satisfied but the Army would still retain a sizable core of veterans for the upcoming series of campaigns in Japan, which were expected to last at least through 1946.

19. Bland and Stevens, *Marshall* 4:285–89, 308–11. In addition, the Army anticipated that any system for discharging soldiers while retaining others could well precipitate a significant amount of dissatisfaction among those who were not released. To minimize morale problems among the pool of troops to be retained, the Army conducted extensive surveying among enlisted personnel to determine what combination of discharge criteria would meet with the most favor while not culling too many veterans from

the future fighting in the Pacific. The War Department maintained that the plan adopted received ratings of 21 percent "Very Good" and 49 percent "Fairly Good," with only 8 percent judging it "Not Good at All." Not surprisingly, "Ground troops, Combat veterans" unlikely to have enough points for early discharge made up nearly half of those in the latter category and 27 percent "Not So Good." See "The Point Discharge Plan in Operation," *What the Soldier Thinks* 16 (September 1945): 8–12 (distributed down to company commander level); and "Point System Fixed to Send Veterans Back: Length, Toughness of Service to Be Factors in Release," Associated Press, May 10, 1945.

20. Bland and Stevens, *Marshall* 4:285–89, 308–11; and "The Finest Soldier," in Larry I. Bland and Sharon Ritenour Stevens, eds., *The Papers of George Catlett Marshall*, vol. 5, *"The Finest Soldier," January 1, 1945– January 7, 1947* (Baltimore: Johns Hopkins University Press, 2003) (hereafter cited as *Marhall*, followed by volume number), 225, in a speech before the Maryland Historical Society.

21. "Army Casualties," *Yank* 3 (November 17, 1944): 17; and "Army Losses," *Yank* 3 (December 1, 1944): 17.

22. "Army Casualties" and "Transfers to AGF [Army Ground Forces]," *Yank* 3 (January 12, 1945): 17.

23. "Casualties," *Yank* 3 (February 2, 1945): 17.

24. Department of the Army, "Army Battle Casualties," 6. This information was made available soon after the war, but other data, such as the loss by at least seven thousand families of two or more sons serving in the U.S. Army, was never released, even within the numerous comprehensive Army Medical Department analyses produced over the following twenty years. Apparently such data did not fit the criteria of the published

works. The information on multiple deaths per family was outlined in a 1947 War Department memorandum to a member of President Truman's White House staff and was discovered in 1998 at the Harry S. Truman Library and Museum. See D. M. Giangreco and Kathryn Moore, *Dear Harry . . . Truman's Mailroom, 1945–1953: The Truman Administration Through Correspondence with "Everyday Americans"* (Mechanicsburg, Pa.: Stackpole Books, 1999), 100–102.

25. Robert R. Palmer, Bell I. Wiley, and William R. Keast, *The Procurement and Training of Ground Combat Troops*, USAWWII series (Washington, D.C.: Center of Military History, United States Army, 1948), 230–31.

26. Dr. Arthur G. Volz, Bammental, Germany, to author, November 2004.

27. December 9, 1944, address in Bland and Stevens, *Marshall* 4:690–92.

28. Ibid. 5:75.

29. Ibid. 5:77. See also text to note 23 regarding press coverage.

30. For example, see U.S. House of Representatives, *Hearings Before the Subcommittee on Appropriations on the Military Establishment Appropriations Bill for 1946*, 79th Cong., 1st sess., May 25, 1945 (Washington, D.C.: GPO, 1945), 1–18. Marshall and Stimson testified separately before Congress. Both went off the record when they discussed this highly charged manpower question. Only many years later did references to what was discussed surface in other congressional testimony. In addition to his off-the-record remarks before the House Appropriations Committee in which he discussed, among other matters, the "inadvisability of war of attrition," Marshall testified before the House Military Affairs Committee and discussed "the terrific losses which we would sustain when we invaded

Japan." See the transcript of Charles E. Bohlen's testimony before the Senate Foreign Relations Committee on March 2, 1953, in Charles E. Bohlen, *Witness to History: 1929–1969* (New York: W. W. Norton, 1973), 317.

31. "Casualties," *Yank* 3 (March 9, 1945): 17.

32. "Army Full Strength," *Yank* 2 (April 28, 1944): 17.

33. Mattie E. Treadwell, *The Women's Army Corps*, USAWWII series (Washington, D.C.: Center of Military History, United States Army, 1954), 686.

34. *Selective Service and Victory*, 53–59, 70–71, 85–88.

35. *Diaries of Henry Lewis Stimson*, January 4, 1945.

36. *Selective Service and Victory*, 112.

37. *Diaries of Henry Lewis Stimson*, January 11, 1945.

38. *Selective Service and Victory*, 595.

39. "Roosevelt Urges Work-or-Fight Bill," 1; and "Letters on the Pressing Manpower Problem," 13.

40. D. M. Giangreco, "'A Score of Bloody Okinawas and Iwo Jimas': President Truman and Casualty Estimates for the Invasion of Japan," *Pacific Historical Review* 72 (February 2003): 93–132, esp. 104–5; and D. M. Giangreco, "Casualty Projections for the U.S. Invasions of Japan, 1945–1946: Planning and Policy Implications," *Journal of Military History* 61 (July 1997): 521–81, esp. 537–38.

41. Frank McNaughton and Walter Hehmeyer, *Harry Truman: President* (New York: McGraw-Hill, 1948), 3.

42. "Palmer Warns Nips Set for Murderous Combat," *Los Angeles Times*, May 8, 1945, sec. 2, p. 1. This article was published alongside "New Casualty List Released," which named seventy-eight dead, missing, and wounded from the Los Angeles area.

43. "Palmer Warns No Easy Way Open to Beat Japs," *Los Angeles Times*, May 17, 1945, sec. 1, p. 5.

44. "The Jap War," *Yank* 3 (June 8, 1945): 1.

Chapter 3. The First Army and Kwantung Redeployments

1. Alvin D. Coox, "The Myth of the Kwantung Army," *Marine Corps Gazette* (July 1958): 36–43.

2. Saburo Hayashi and Alvin D. Coox, *Kogun: The Japanese Army in the Pacific War* (Quantico, Va.: Marine Corps Association, 1959), 59–61.

3. *Reports of General MacArthur* (Tokyo: General Headquarters, Supreme Allied Command, Pacific, 1950) (hereafter cited as *Reports*), vol. 2, bk. 1, pp. 200–204, 272–73.

4. Coox, "Myth of the Kwantung Army," 37; and Philip A. Crowl, *Campaign in the Marianas*, USAWWII series (Washington, D.C.: Center of Military History, United States Army, 1960), 264–65, 356–60.

5. Hayashi and Coox, *Kogun*, 76–77, 105–6.

6. Edward J. Drea, *Nomonhan: Japanese-Soviet Tactical Combat, 1939*, Leavenworth Papers No. 2 (Fort Leavenworth, Kans.: Combat Studies Institute, 1981), 13; Jacob W. Kipp and General Makhmut Akhmetevich Gareev, "'To Break the Back of Japan': Soviet-American Cooperation for the Manchurian Offensive of August 1945," paper presented at the annual meeting of the Society for Military History, Pennsylvania State University, April 16, 1999; and Department of Defense, "The Entry of the Soviet Union into the War Against Japan: Military Plans, 1941–1945," Washington, D.C., 1955, 24, where Stalin at the Teheran Conference is quoted as saying, "Our forces now in the East are more or less satisfactory for defense.

However, they must be increased about three-fold for purposes of offensive operations. This condition will not take place until Germany has been forced to capitulate."

7. Hayashi and Coox, *Kogun*, 76–79.

8. Ibid., 109, 113–15.

9. Hattori, *Complete History of the Greater East Asia War* 4:209–17.

10. Ibid. 4:113; and Richard Fuller, *Shokan: Hirohito's Samurai, Leaders of the Japanese Armed Forces, 1926–1945* (London: Arms and Armour Press, 1992), 143.

11. *Reports*, vol. 2, bk. 2, pp. 522–27.

12. Hattori, *Complete History of the Greater East Asia War* 4:217.

13. Ibid.; and Drea, *Nomonhan*, 86.

14. Rear Adm. Samuel Eliot Morison, USN, *History of United States Naval Operations in World War II* (hereafter cited as *USNOWWII*), vol. 12, *Leyte, June 1944–January 1945* (Boston: Little Brown, 1958), 300–06, 339–49, 354–60, 366–68, 380–85; and M. Hamlin Cannon, *Leyte: The Return to the Philippines*, USAWWII series (Washington, D.C.: Center of Military History, United States Army, 1954), 8–9. See also Samuel Eliot Morison, *The Two-Ocean War: A Short History of the United States Navy in the Second World War* (Boston: Little Brown, 1958), 422–23.

15. Hattori, *Complete History of the Greater East Asia War* 4:217.

16. E. B. Potter, *Nimitz* (Annapolis: Naval Institute Press, 1976), 385.

17. "'Magic'—Far East Summary," No. 338, February 21, 1945, 2–4, Combined Arms Research Library, Fort Leavenworth, Kans. (hereafter cited as CARL).

18. Hattori, *Complete History of the Greater East Asia War* 4:43–44.

19. JSSM, vol. 1, "Japanese Operational Planning Against the USSR," ed. Takushiro Hattori, Military History Section, Headquarters, Army Forces Far East, Tokyo, 1955, 163.

20. Coox, *Final Agony*, 17.

21. Ibid., 11.

22. David M. Glantz, *August Storm: The Soviet 1945 Strategic Offensive in Manchuria*, Leavenworth Papers No. 7 (Fort Leavenworth, Kans.: Combat Studies Institute, 1983), 1–3; and Kipp and Gareev, "To Break the Back of Japan."

23. Hayashi and Coox, *Kogun*, 155–57; and *Reports*, vol. 2, bk. 2: 619–22.

24. Richard B. Frank, *Downfall: The End of the Imperial Japanese Empire* (New York: Random House, 1999), 200–201. See also *Reports*, vol. 1, suppl., 117–18, which notes that at the time of the surrender, the Japanese forces in the home islands (excluding naval and air elements) stood at fifty-nine divisions plus thirty-six independent brigades and forty-five regiments.

25. Coox, *Final Agony*, 67.

26. Alvin D. Coox, "Japanese Military Intelligence in the Pacific: Its Non-Revolutionary Nature," in *The Intelligence Revolution: A Historical Perspective*, ed. Walter Theodore Hitchcock (Washington, D.C.: U.S. Air Force Academy—Office of Air Force History, 1991), 200; and Edward J. Drea, *MacArthur's ULTRA: Codebreaking and the War against Japan, 1942–1945* (Lawrence: University Press of Kansas, 1992), 202–25.

27. Hayashi and Coox, *Kogun*, 146, 156; and *Reports*, vol. 2, bk. 2, p. 621n.

28. See translation of "Explanatory Data to Estimate of Situation for Spring of 1946," IGHQ Army Department, July 1, 1945, in *War in Asia and the Pacific, 1937–1945* (hereafter cited as *WAP*), vol. 12, *Defense of the Homeland and End of the War*, ed. Donald S. Detwiler and Charles B. Burdick (New York: Garland, 1980), 3, 21–22.

29. Hayashi and Coox, *Kogun*, 148, 171–73; Hattori, *Complete History of the Greater East Asia War* 4:218–21; and JSSM 1:163.

30. Coakley and Leighton, *Global Logistics and Strategy*, 536–38. For a detailed treatment of this subject see Michael Coles, "Ernest King and the British Pacific Fleet: The Conference at Quebec, 1944 ('Octagon')," *Journal of Military History*, 61 (January 2001), 105–29. It is also touched on in Nicholas Evan Sarantakes, "One Last Crusade: The British Pacific Fleet and its Impact on the Anglo-American Alliance," *English Historical Review*, 121 (no. 491, April 2006): 429–66, esp. 439–41.

31. John Winton, *The Forgotten Fleet: The British Navy in the Pacific, 1944–1945* (New York: Coward-McCann, 1970), 18, 32–37, 46–49, 108–69; Nicholas Evan Sarantakes, "One Last Crusade: The British Pacific Fleet and its Impact on the Anglo-American Alliance," *English Historical Review* 121, no. 491 (April 2006): esp. 434–42, 451–58; Thomas Hall, "'Mere Drops in the Ocean': The Politics and Planning of the Contribution of the British Commonwealth to the Final Defeat of Japan, 1944–45," *Diplomacy & Statecraft* 16 (March 2005): 93–115, esp. 101, 107–8; and H. P. Willmott, *Grave of a Dozen Schemes: British Naval Planning and the War Against Japan, 1943–1945* (Annapolis: Naval Institute Press, 1996), 1.

32. Winton, *Forgotten Fleet*, 396–403; and "The Second World War 1939–1945" on the Royal Navy/ Ministry of Defense web site, http://www.royal-navy.mod.uk/server.php?show=nav.3862/ (accessed February 24, 2006). This excludes, however, the extremely large number of small ships used as escorts for the Atlantic convoys by the British and Canadians that were quickly retired or returned to civilian owners after the end of hostilities in Europe. See also Sarantakes, "One Last Crusade."

33. Henry Probert, *The Forgotten Air Force: The Royal Air Force in the War Against Japan, 1941–1945* (London: Brassey's, 1995), 291–95; Probert, *Bomber Harris: His Life and Times* (London: Greenhill Books, 2001), 315–16; and Brereton Greenhous, Stephen J. Harris, William C. Johnston, and William G. P. Rawling, *The Crucible of War, 1939–1945*, vol. 3, in *The Official History of the Royal Canadian Air Force* (Toronto: University of Toronto Press and Department of National Defense, 1994), 106–24. See also Nicholas Evan Sarantakes, "The Royal Air Force on Okinawa: The Diplomacy of a Coalition on the Verge of Victory," *Diplomatic History*, 27 (no. 4, September 2003): 479–502, esp. 498–99.

34. Coakley and Leighton, *Global Logistics and Strategy*, 572–73.

35. Probert, *Forgotten Air Force*, 291–95.

36. Field Marshall Lord Alanbrooke, *War Diaries: 1939-1945*, ed. Alex Danchev and Daniel Todman (Phoenix, Ariz.: Phoenix Press, 2001), 526; and Thomas B. Allen and Norman Polmar, *Code-Name Downfall: The Secret Plan to Invade Japan—And Why Truman Dropped the Bomb* (New York: Simon & Schuster, 1995), 142–43.

37. Coakley and Leighton, *Global Logistics and Strategy*, 588, 666–67; and Alanbrooke, *War Diaries*, 706–7. See also Hall, "Mere Drops in the Ocean," 99–103.

38. Coakley and Leighton, *Global Logistics and Strategy*, 664–70.

39. "Winston Churchill memorandum of conversation," July 18, 1945, *Documents on British Policies Overseas*, 3 vols. (London: Her Majesty's Stationery Office, 1984), 1:291.

40. Winston Churchill, *The Second World War*, vol. 6, *Triumph and Tragedy* (Boston: Houghton Mifflin, 1953), 592–93.

41. Coakley and Leighton, *Global Logistics and Strategy*, 664.

42. *Documents Relating to New Zealand's Participation in the Second World War, 1939–1945*, vol. 3, in *Official History of New Zealand in the Second World War, 1939–45 (OHNZSSW)* (Wellington, NZ: War History Branch, Department of Internal Affairs, 1949), 468–96; Peter Bates, *Japan and the British Commonwealth Occupation Force, 1946–52* (London: Brassey's, 1993), 5; and Allen and Polmar, *Code-Name Downfall*, 143, 316.

43. Hall, "Mere Drops in the Ocean," 103–4; Probert, *Bomber Harris*, 353; and Tom McCarthy, "True Loyals: A History of the 7th Battalion, the Loyal Regiment (North Lancashire) / 92nd (Loyals) Light Anti-Aircraft Regiment, Royal Artillery," http://www.geocities.com/lightackack/index.html/ (accessed August 2007).

44. Bland and Stevens, *Marshall* 4:294–95; and "AHQ Report No. 16: The Canadian Army Pacific Force, 1944–1945, July 15, 1947," Directorate of History and Heritage, National Defence Headquarters, Ottawa, 37, 42. However, a Canadian proposal that they supply an armored instead of an infantry division was rejected because "General MacArthur would prefer such a unit and it would receive much more gainful employment."

45. "AHQ Report No. 16," 30.

46. Ibid., 37–43, 69–73. See also "AHQ Report No. 63: Manpower Problems of the Canadian Army in the Second World War," Directorate of History and Heritage, National Defence Headquarters, Ottawa, 290.

47. "AHQ Report No. 63," 99–104.

48. Ibid., 33–38.

49. Bates, *Japan and the British Commonwealth Occupation Force*, 12–13.

50. D. M. Horner, *High Command: Australia and Allied Strategy, 1939–1945* (Sydney: Allen & Unwin, 1982), 399–410; Gavin Long, *Australia in the War of 1939–1945*, ser. 1 (Army), vol. 7, *The Final Campaigns* (Canberra: Australian War Memorial, 1963), 52, 55–59, 66–69; and D. Clayton James, *The Years of MacArthur*, vol. 2, *1942–1945* (Boston: Houghton Mifflin, 1975), 703–8. See also John Robertson and John McCarthy, eds., *Australian War Strategy, 1939–1945, A Documentary History* (St. Lucia: University of Queensland Press, 1985), 403–14.

51. Horner, *High Command*, 418.

52. Long, *Final Campaigns*, 549.

53. Ibid.

54. Bates, *Japan and the British Commonwealth Occupation Force*, 11–19, 68–69.

55. *Reports* 1:369–87; James, *Years of MacArthur* 2:702–14, 731–63 and Long, *Final Campaigns*, 41–51, 56–70.

56. Long, *Final Campaigns*, 548.

57. Horner, *High Command*, 416.

58. Ibid., 404; and Long, *Final Campaigns*, 52.

59. *Reports* 1:427; and Horner, *High Command*, 418.

60. Long, *Final Campaigns*, 52; Horner, *High Command*, 404; and *OHNZSSW* 3:493–95.

61. David M. Glantz, *The Soviet 1945 Strategic Offensive in Manchuria, 1945: August Storm* (London: Frank Cass, 2003); and David M. Glantz, *Soviet Operational and Tactical Combat in Manchuria, 1945: "August Storm"* (London: Frank Cass, 2003). Earlier, and less comprehensive, versions of these works are *August Storm: The Soviet 1945 Strategic Offensive in Manchuria*, Leavenworth Papers No. 7 (Fort Leavenworth, Kansas: Combat Studies Institute, 1983), and *August Storm: Soviet Tactical and Operational Combat in*

Manchuria, 1945 (Leavenworth Papers No.
8). Also see his "Soviet Invasion of Japan,"
Military History Quarterly 9, no. 4 (Spring
1995): 96–97.

62. Glantz, *Soviet 1945 Strategic Offensive*, 301.

63. JCS 1417, "Operations Following Invasion
of Kanto Plain (Broad Plans)," July 10, 1945,
Enclosure B, Appendix F, 63–72, Records of
the Joint Chiefs of Staff, CARL.

64. Glantz, *Soviet 1945 Strategic Offensive*,
403–15; and Richard A. Russell, *Project
Hula: Secret Soviet-American Cooperation
in the War Against Japan*, No. 4 in the
U.S. Navy in the Modern World Series
(Washington, D.C.: Naval Historical Center,
Department of the Navy, 1997), 32–34,
39–40. The Soviets had obtained thirty
LCI(L)s through Lend-Lease that were given
DS (landing ship) designations which appear
as DC in translations of some operations
orders. The LCIs slated to take part in the
invasion of Hokkaido were LCI(L) 584
(DS-38), LCI(L) 586 (DS-37), LCI(L) 590
(DS-34), LCI(L) 592 (DS-39), LCI(L) 593
(DS-31), and LCI(L) 675 (DS-42). See
also Prezmyslaw Budzbon, *The Soviet Navy
at War* (London: Arms and Armour Press,
1989.

Chapter 4. The Pacific Build-up and Berlin Decision

1. *Diaries of Henry Lewis Stimson*, January 11,
1945.

2. Coakley and Leighton, *Global Logistics and
Strategy*, 539–41, 584–85.

3. *Reports* 1:394.

4. Fleet Admiral Ernest J. King, *U.S. Navy
at War, 1941–1945: Official Reports to
the Secretary of the Navy* (Washington,
D.C.: Navy Department, 1946), 218;
and Headquarters Marine Corps Strength

Figures, Reference Branch files, Marine
Corps History Division, Quantico, Va.

5. JCS 1190/8, "Planned Deployment of
Strategic Very Heavy Bomber Groups,"
June 9, 1945," 99–101, Records of the Joint
Chiefs of Staff, CARL. Unlike the Twentieth
Air Force in the Marianas and Eighth Air
Force on Okinawa, the Far East Air Forces'
principal offensive arm, the Fifth Air Force
(also on Okinawa) would remain under
AFPAC's control and eventually deploy
forward to Kyushu.

6. Henry L. Stimson, "The Decision to Use
the Atomic Bomb," *Harper's Magazine* 194
(February 1947): 102.

7. Earl F. Ziemke, *The U.S. Army in the
Occupation of Germany, 1944–1946*, 328;
Coakley and Leighton, *Global Logistics and
Strategy*, 594–95.

8. Bland and Stevens, *Marshall* 5:188–89;
Coakley and Leighton, *Global Logistics
and Strategy*, 614; Karl C. Dod, *The Corps
of Engineers: The War Against Japan*,
USAWWII series (Washington, D.C.:
Center of Military History, United States
Army, 1966), 547. See also *Engineers in
Theater Operations*, vol. 1, in *Engineers of the
Southwest Pacific, 1941–1945* (hereafter *ESP*,
vol. 1) (Tokyo: Office of the Chief Engineer,
General Headquarters, Army Forces, Pacific,
1950), 277, 305.

9. Keast, "Provision of Enlisted Replacements,"
30.

10. *Reports* 1:394.

11. Department of the Army, "Army Battle
Casualties," 32.

12. Charles B. MacDonald, *The Last Offensive*,
USAWWII series (Washington, D.C.: Center
of Military History, United States Army,
1984), 340–41, 407–9, 440–41.

13. MacDonald, *Last Offensive*, 399, See also
John Toland, *The Last 100 Days* (New York:
Random House, 1965), 391–92.

14. Forrest C. Pogue, *The Supreme Command*, USAWWII series (Washington, D.C.: Center of Military History, United States Army, 1989), 441–47. See also Martin Blumenson, "The Problem of Berlin," *Army*, August 1998, 35–42.

15. Carl Von Clausewitz, *On War*, trans. O. J. Matthijs Jolles (New York: Random House, 1943), 21.

16. Pogue, *Supreme Command*, 445–46; and James M. Gavin, *On to Berlin: Battles of an Airborne Commander, 1943–1946* (New York: Bantam Books, 1978), 303, 335.

17. Stanton, *World War II Order of Battle*, 170–71.

18. Pogue, *Supreme Command*, 446.

19. Gavin, *On to Berlin*, 303–4.

20. Coakley and Leighton, *Global Logistics and Strategy*, 585, 588.

21. Stanton, *World War II Order of Battle* (see individual division synopses and the chart on page 603).

22. Gavin, *On to Berlin*, 303, 334–35.

23. Omar N. Bradley, *A Soldier's Story* (New York: Henry Holt, 1951), 535–36; and Pogue, *Supreme Command*, 445.

24. Hugh M. Cole and Forest C. Pogue once stated succinctly that "SHAEF, acting as the representative of the British and American Chiefs of Staff, had to deal with five American, two British, and one French army," and thus, "in order to understand the action of the higher headquarters, it is essential to go beyond the army level." *Military Affairs* 12 (Spring 1948): 57.

25. Marshall relates that he "was forced to speak quite frankly" during the Combined Chiefs of Staff Executive session in Malta, February 1, 1945, about his "deep concern" over "pressures of the Prime Minister [on Eisenhower] and the fact of the proximity of the British chiefs of staff." Interestingly, the subject was actually brought up by Brooke, who said that he and the other British chiefs "were very much worried by the influence on General Eisenhower by General Bradley and . . . . General Patton." Marshall responded: "Well, Brooke, they are not nearly as much worried as the American chiefs of staff are worried about the immediate pressures and influence of Mr. Churchill on General Eisenhower. The President practically never sees Eisenhower, never writes to him—that is at my advice because he is an *Allied* commander." Marshall pointed out that Brooke and Churchill "were seeing him every week, and not going through the Combined Chiefs of Staff" while the Americans "were playing according to the rules." Said Marshall, "We had a terrible meeting." See Forrest C. Pogue, *George C. Marshall Interviews and Reminiscences for Forrest C. Pogue*, 3rd ed. (Lexington, Va.: George C. Marshall Foundation, 1996), 541 (interview of November 19, 1956); and interview with Marshall by Dr. Sidney T. Matthews et al., Office of the Chief of Military History, Pentagon, July 25, 1949, pt. 2, Reel 322, George C. Marshall Library, Lexington, Va. (hereafter cited as GCML).

26. MacDonald, *Last Offensive*, 407–9, 440–43.

27. Pogue, *Supreme Command*, 391–93; Coakley and Leighton, *Global Logistics and Strategy*, 548.

28. Gavin, *On to Berlin*, 335.

29. V. M. Andronikov, P. D. Burikov, V. V. Gurkin, A. I. Kruglov, E. I. Rodionov, and M. V. Filimoshin, *Grief sekretnosti snyat: Poteri Vooryzhennykh Sil SSSR v voynakh, boevykh deystviyakh konfliktakah: Statisticheskoe issledovanie* (Moscow: Voyenizdat, 1993), 219–20. See also Donald E. Shepardson, "The Fall of Berlin and Rise of a Myth," *Journal of Military History* (January 1998); Georgi K. Zhukov, trans. by Theodore Shabad, ed. by Harrison E. Salisbury, *Marshal Zhukov's Greatest Battles*

(New York: Harper & Row, 1969); and Cornelius Ryan, *The Last Battle* (New York: Simon & Schuster, 1966).

30. Department of the Army, "Army Battle Casualties," 32; Edward Steere and Thayer M. Boardman, *Final Disposition of World War II Dead, 1945–1951* (Washington, D.C.: Office of the Quartermaster General, 1957), 271.

31. Dod, *Corps of Engineers*, 678.

32. *ESP* 1:316; and Dod, *Corps of Engineers*, 684.

33. David H. Grover, *U.S. Army Ships and Watercraft of World War II* (Annapolis: Naval Institute Press, 1987), 55–58, 238, 250–51.

34. Coakley and Leighton, *Global Logistics and Strategy*, 565–570.

35. Ibid., 455–80, 604–20; Joseph Bykofsky and Harold Larson, *The Transportation Corps: Overseas Operations*, USAWWII series (Washington, D.C.: Center of Military History, United States Army, 1957), 497–508, 523–27.

36. *ESP* 1:298–317. Also see John W. Huston, ed., *American Airpower Comes of Age: General Henry H. "Hap" Arnold's World War II Diaries* (Maxwell Air Force Base, Ala.: Air University Press, 2002), 2:339–40, 356. During an inspection of bomber bases in the Pacific, Army Air Forces chief, Henry H. Arnold was appalled at the lack of progress. He wrote that during a June 22, 1945, conference on Guam he bluntly told Nimitz, the new Tenth Army commander Joseph W. Stilwell, and other senior officers that "(a) There would be a backlog of 1,000,000 tons of shipping on Okinawa by September; (b) There would not be sufficient bombs to carry out program for destruction of Japanese industry, pre-invasion bombing, and support of invading army; (c) The docks would not be completed to permit

unloading of supplies; (d) There were Seabees and Engineer battalions awaiting shipment to Okinawa." He wrote that "Nimitz's staff assured me that everything I said had been taken care of; Engineers and Seabees were being sent as rapidly as they were available, etc." Less than three weeks later, on July 11, Far East Air Force commander, Lt. Gen. George Kenney wrote Arnold, "Thanks to your intercession with Admiral Nimitz, the arrival of engineer units into Okinawa has been speeded up tremendously."

37. Field Order 74, Annex 3a, Troop List, Sixth Army Troops, July 28, 1945, Headquarters Sixth Army.

38. Chauncey E. Sanders, "Redeployment and Demobilization," in *The Army Air Forces in World War II* (hereafter cited as *AAFWWII*), vol. 7, *Services Around the World*, ed. Wesley Frank Craven and James Lea Cate (Chicago: University of Chicago Press, 1954), 564.

39. Ibid., 565–66.

40. Frank Futrell and James Taylor, "Reorganization for Victory," 701, in *AAFWWII*, vol. 5, *The Pacific: Matterhorn to Nagasaki, June 1944 to August 1945*, ed. Wesley Frank Craven and James Lea Cate (Chicago: University of Chicago Press, 1953).

41. Sanders, "Redeployment and Demobilization," 565.

42. Ibid., 565–66.

Chapter 5. "Not a Recipe for Victory"

1. Bland and Stevens, *Marshall* 5:220–27, especially 223, from a Marshall-edited transcript made by the Maryland Historical Society. It was published as "Some Lessons of History," *Maryland Historical Magazine* 40 (September 1945): 175–84.

2. Divisional information in this and the following two paragraphs is distilled principally from Stanton, *World War II Order of Battle*, 71–185; "Order of Battle, U.S. Army Forces in the Pacific (as of 14 August 1945)," in *Biennial Report of the Chief of Staff of the United States Army, July 1, 1943, to June 30, 1945, to the Secretary of War* (Washington, D.C.: GPO, 1945), 87; and "The Operation Requirements," in "Staff Study Operations, CORONET," General Headquarters, AFPAC, August 15, 1945, Annex 3b (4) (hereafter cited as "Staff Study Operations, CORONET").

3. "Staff Study Operations, CORONET," Annex 3b (4).

4. Marshall to MacArthur, May 28, 1945, memorandum, War Department transmission WAR-89587, May 29, 1945, GCML.

5. Larry Bland to author, memorandums, including March 17, 2006, "Forrest Pogue, General Marshall's authorized biographer, on two separate occasions told the editors of the *Papers of George Catlett Marshall* that the general had *not* kept a 'little black book' that listed individual officers he had known and recorded his opinions of their capabilities, and that he, Pogue, was sorry that early in his writing of the biography he had repeated the myth." When Bland was asked if Pogue had accidentally created the myth when speaking metaphorically, he replied that the black book was "not a metaphor; it was presumed real." Bland noted that "when Pogue repeated [the myth], it gained authority," and said, "The myth *may* have existed during World War II; its chief exponent after the war was James Van Fleet, who needed to explain why he was still a colonel at D-Day when his peers were two-stars and why he rose so rapidly thereafter." A plausible story exists that Marshall had for a time confused Van Fleet with another officer of somewhat lesser abilities.

6. Bland and Stevens, *Marshall* 5:256–57.

7. *Register of Graduates and Former Cadets of the United States Military Academy* (West Point, N.Y.: Association of Graduates, 1992), 243, 249. See also Jeffrey J. Clarke and Robert Ross Smith, *Riviera to the Rhine*, USAWWII series (Washington, D.C.: Center of Military History, United States Army, 1993), 38–39.

8. James, *Years of MacArthur* 2:736–37.

9. Maj. Gen. Bruce Jacobs, "Tensions Between the Army National Guard and the Regular Army," *Military Review*, October 1993, 5–17.

10. Bland and Stevens, *Marshall* 5:133–34.

11. Col. Robert S. Allen, *Lucky Forward: The History of Patton's Third U.S. Army* (New York: Vanguard Press, 1947), 27, 51, 394. During a spring 1999 conversation with Larry Bland, the *Papers of George Catlett Marshall* editor mentioned that his predecessor Forrest Pogue (who served as Third Army's combat historian during the war) had been told by his First Army colleague, Hugh M. Cole, that the First and Ninth Army commanders and staffs had been "fully focused" on their own theater. This had apparently been stated with a note of disapproval directed at Patton and his staff, but the fact that there was official and ongoing interest in Pacific operations at Third Army does not mean that this organization was somehow less focused on defeating the Germans.

12. James, *Years of MacArthur* 2:735–36.

13. *Diaries of Henry Lewis Stimson*, May 11, 1944; and Bland and Stevens, *Marshall* 4:447–50.

14. Bland, *Marshall Interviews*, 591.

15. Pogue, *Supreme Command*, 441–47; see also Blumenson, "Problem of Berlin," 35–42.

16. *Diaries of Henry Lewis Stimson*, January 5, 11, 1945.

17. Bland and Stevens, *Marshall* 5:20–21; and Bland to author, January 10, 2006, memorandum.

18. Stanton, *World War II Order of Battle,* 158–59, 173–74. See also William S. Triplet, *In the Philippines and Okinawa: A Memoir,* ed. Robert H. Ferrell (Columbia: University of Missouri Press, 2001). According to Ferrell in a March 27, 2006, telephone conversation, the inability of the 86th Infantry Division to engage in any meaningful training or retraining, as well as lax discipline standards during this extended period, contributed heavily to the formation's "miserable" performance even as a garrison force. In the event that the war continued, however, the 86th would have received considerable sharpening before commitment to combat the following year on Honshu.

19. One intriguing piece of intelligence on the U.S. order of battle did come from an American prisoner of war captured on Okinawa: The "3, 4, 5 [Marine] Divisions have withdrawn from Iwo Jima." The prisoner was likely a Marine, and the fact that no U.S. prisoners were freed on Okinawa or could be evacuated to Japan indicates that he was executed after his interrogation. See "Explanatory Data to Estimate of Situation for Spring of 1946," 35.

20. "Estimate of Situation for Spring of 1946," in *WAP* 12:7.

21. Doc. 16172 B, "An Estimate of American Strength Facing Japan," May 1945, in "Full Translation of a Report on the 'Japanese Defense Strategy and Tactics,'" produced by the Ministry of the First Demobilization (formerly the Army Ministry) and received by Allied Translator and Interpreter Section, Military Intelligence Section, General Headquarters Supreme Commander for the Allied Powers, Tokyo, April 5, 1946, n.p., CARL (hereafter cited as "Japanese Defense Strategy and Tactics").

22. "Explanatory Data to Estimate of Situation for Spring of 1946."

23. Matloff, "90-division Gamble," 370.

24. *Selective Service and Victory,* 592–93. During the eleven months of 1943 for which complete data is available, Selective Service calls for the Army were 2,364,693, which garnered only 2,079,585 inductions. This resulted in a shortfall of 285,108 soldiers for 1943. Draft calls excluded men previously granted agricultural, industrial, and other deferments, and the number of those ordered to report to their draft boards far exceeded the calls. For example, in December 1943, 344,767 men were ordered to report for examination to meet all-service calls of 314,413. Some 193,979 were inducted, and the 150,788 rejected represented the ninth highest monthly rejection total that year.

25. Matloff, "90-division Gamble," 373; and Stanton, *World War II Order of Battle,* 603.

26. See chapter 2, note 11.

27. The *Yank* "Message Center," which contained the prominent "Should Patch Exchange" notices, was also a conduit for nuggets of unit disinformation. It was discontinued after the August 4, 1944, edition and launch of Operation Cobra in France.

28. Arthur E. Du Bois, "The Heraldry of Heroism," in *Insignia and Decorations of the U.S. Armed Forces, Revised Edition* (Washington, D.C.: National Geographic Society, December 1, 1944). Heraldic data accompanying the various wartime *National Geographic* publications—and specifically this special edition—must be closely checked before reuse because even legitimate emblems sometimes had disinformation inserted into their associated data for reasons that are today unknown. For example, a random examination of the 1945 reprint's page 87

displays 1943 approval dates for the 63d Infantry Division patch on March 27, and the 75th Infantry Division patch on January 16, even though both were still months away from their activations on June 15 and April 15 respectively. The earlier dates are unlikely to be simple errors and may have been submitted to *National Geographic* in order to lend credence to other disinformation, or to imply that the formations had received more training than they, in fact, had to that point. Concern over more readily apparent "errors" led to the publisher's release of the following statement after the war: "Concerned for the National Geographic Society's reputation for accuracy and objectivity, Society President Gilbert H. Grosvenor reviewed the procedures that went into producing the book. He concluded that the Society had merely reproduced material provided by the Heraldic Section of the War Department."

29.   Matloff, "90-division Gamble," 375–79.

30.   Stanton, *World War II Order of Battle*, 603; and D. M. Giangreco and Kathryn Moore, *Eyewitness D-DAY: Firsthand Accounts from the Landing at Normandy to the Liberation of Paris*, 2nd ed. (New York: Union Square Press, 2005), 25–25, 222; see also 82, 95, 201.

31.   Brown, *Bodyguard of Lies* 2:8, 19–20, 822, 867–68.

32.   "Table Showing Locations of American Divisions," in "Estimate of Situation for Spring of 1946," n.p.; and "Location Chart of the Divisions of the United States Army middle of June," in "Japanese Defense Strategy and Tactics," n.p.

33.   In a March 15, 2006, phone interview, Shelby Stanton noted that when conducting research for his *World War II Order of Battle: U.S. Army (Ground Force Units)*, he came across SHAFE and War Department documents that indicated post-Fortitude use of

Phantom divisions to mask the weakness of the U.S. thrusts toward the Nazi Redoubt in Bavaria and Austria. The references were found in Records of the Historical Division of the U.S. Members of the Combined Chiefs of Staff (Established February 9, 1942 Past End of War), RG 218.2, NARA. In the chaotic final days of the Reich, such efforts, if even perceived by the Germans, had little or no effect on their tactical operations as a spearhead of the U.S. 10th Armored Division was cut off from April 8–11 at Crailsheim and very badly mauled (including having C-47 cargo planes flying in supplies strafed and bombed by German aircraft), while a task force of the 4th Armored Division was cut off and destroyed near Hammelburg. See MacDonald, *Last Offensive*, 415–19; and Toland, *Last 100 Days*, 291–302.

34.   Hattori, *Complete History of the Greater East Asia War* 4:185–89. Also see "General Plans," in "Japanese Defense Strategy and Tactics," n.p.

35.   Alvin D Coox, "Needless Fear: The Compromise of U.S. Plans to Invade Japan in 1945," *Journal of Military History* 64 (April 2000): 431. In this article published shortly after Dr. Coox passed away, he examined the very real fear in the summer of 1945 that Japanese intelligence operatives had penetrated the "dangerously sloppy" security set-up in General MacArthur's Manila headquarters and stolen the invasion plans thus precipitating the August 9, 1945, orders to change the operation's code name from Olympic to Majestic. Coox concluded (436–37) that "the substance of the U.S. invasion plans somehow survived unscathed, and that the Japanese did not profit from the several security breaches which we have uncovered." See also Craven and Cate, *AAFWWII* 5:686n.

36. Coox, "Japanese Military Intelligence," 200;
and Drea, *MacArthur's ULTRA*, 202–25.
See also Edward J. Drea, "Previews of Hell:
Intelligence, the Bomb, and the Invasion of
Japan," *Military History Quarterly* 7 (Spring
1995): 74–81, which was published with
extensive endnotes in Edward J. Drea, *In
the Service of the Emperor: Essays on the
Imperial Japanese Army* (Lincoln: University
of Nebraska Press, 1998) as chapter 11,
"Intelligence Forecasting for the Invasion
of Japan: Previews of Hell," 154–68.
Also available in Robert James Maddox,
ed., *Hiroshima in History: The Myths of
Revisionism* (Columbia: University of
Missouri Press, 2007), 59–75.
37. Coox, "Japanese Military Intelligence," 200.
38. Giangreco, "Casualty Projections," 521–81,
esp. 552.
39. "Amendment No. 1 to G-2 Estimate of the
Enemy Situation with Respect to Kyushu,"
G-2, AFPAC, July 29, 1945, CARL (a
transcription error in *Reports* 1:414 changed
"recipe" to "receipt" and is repeated in some
works). In hindsight, one could argue that
the trend of the buildup should have been
clear by President Truman's June 18 meeting
with the JCS and service secretaries, but
allowing for the lag time in both the formulation and dissemination of the intelligence
information, the troop-strength figures available to the individual JCS members would
have been anywhere from about five days to
two weeks old at the time of the meeting,
and most important, the scale of the buildup
was not yet apparent. Once the matter of
Japanese reinforcements had been flagged as
an area of great concern (as it almost certainly
was by July), extraction, analysis, and
dissemination of the information could be
accomplished within a two-day cycle or even
less. Willoughby's analysis in Manila came at

roughly the same time that similar conclusions were being reached in Washington.
40. Ibid.
41. Maj. Gen. Charles A. Willoughby,
"Occupation of Japan and Japanese
Reaction," *Military Review* 26 (June 1946):
esp. 3–4.
42. Drea, *In the Service of the Emperor*, esp. 219.
Communications intelligence garnered from
military transmissions was code named Ultra
while Japanese Foreign Ministry transmissions, which passed on large amounts of
military data, was code named Magic (Drea,
In the Service of the Emperor, 128). Drea
warns, however, that while the "'Magic'—
Diplomatic Summary" published daily by
the War Department was derived purely
from Foreign Ministry traffic, about early
1945, the two sets of intelligence began to be
intermixed in "'Magic'—Far East Summary,"
"'Magic'—European Summary," and other
War Department intelligence products, as
well as those originating in MacArthur's
headquarters (letter to author, November
21, 2006). The designation "Ultra" above
"Top Secret" on the covers of the "Magic"
summaries referred to their inclusion within
the highest level of security classification,
"Ultra," which was higher than "Most Secret"
and was, ironically, derived from the original
use of Ultra intelligence by the British early
in the war.

Chapter 6. The Decision

1. Harvey H. Bundy, August 29, 1960, in
Columbia Oral History Project (New York:
Butler Library, Columbia University), 269,
in John Bonnett, "Jekyll and Hyde: Henry L.
Stimson, "*Mentalité*, and the Decision to Use
the Atomic bomb on Japan," *War in History*
4 (April 1997): 204.

2. Director William J. Donovan, Office of Strategic Services, to the Joint Chiefs of Staff, in JCS 1452/1, "Operational Plans for OSS Activities in Pacific Ocean Areas," July 18, 1945, Appendix B, 22, Records of the Joint Chiefs of Staff, CARL.

3. An analysis outlining this trend (and excluded Navy losses) was published by Col. Michael E. DeBakey, MD, USA, and Capt. Gilbert W. Beebe in *Health*, May 31, 1945, Box 613, Monthly Progress Reports, Office of the Commanding General, RG 160, Records of Army Service Forces, NARA. *Health* was a classified Army publication distributed to senior military planners by the U.S. Army Surgeon General's Office. The analysis was further disseminated to President Truman and top administration officials through subsequent reports in June and July of 1945 including the June 18, 1945, meeting between the president, the JCS, and service secretaries. For what was shown President Truman, see JCS 1388/4, "Details of the Campaign Against Japan," July 11, 1945, Records of the Joint Chiefs of Staff, CARL; Marshall's remarks and extracts of the president's meeting with the JCS, Stimson, and Forrestal in "Joint Chiefs of Staff Corrigendum to JCS 1388," June 18, 1945, pt. 1, 1942–1943: The Pacific Theater, Reel 2, Records of the Joint Chiefs of Staff, CARL. An analysis of this material can be found in D. M. Giangreco, "Casualty Projections for the U.S. Invasions of Japan, 1945–1946: Planning and Policy Implications," *Journal of Military History* 61 (1997): 521–81, esp. 553–60.

4. The final total of Army and Army Air Force casualties stands at 945,515 (Department of the Army, "Army Battle Casualties," 118), but while this figure includes nonbattle deaths and POWs who died in captivity, it does not include categories which drained the Army of manpower and were closely monitored by senior leaders, such as nonbattle injuries in combat zones (e.g., loading accidents), losses due to disease and combat-related psychiatric breakdowns, and 111,426 Army and Army Air Force prisoners of war who survived their captivities and were counted as casualties during the war. Although Navy and Marine Corps battle casualties were only 159,495 to 162,668 (depending on how one constructs the numbers), Roddis, "Naval and Marine Corps Casualties," 305–10, notes that these figures were more than eight times the number of killed and wounded among our naval personnel in all the other wars of the United States combined. An additional 12,000-plus Merchant Marine and Coast Guard battle casualties, primarily from German submarines, were not included in Roddis's study but do not alter his basic point. The 12,000 figure includes dead and missing but not combat injuries (burns, wounds, etc.), and there were an additional 30,442 Navy and Marine nonbattle deaths. Nonbattle deaths are frequently included in battle casualty tabulations because, unlike other categories of nonbattle casualties, dead personnel are irrevocably removed from the manpower pool, while a percentage of those in other categories returned to full duty status or were able to serve in a reduced capacity within the United States and thus free healthy personnel for overseas duty.

5. JPS 476, "Operations Against Japan Subsequent to Formosa," June 6, 1944, and JCS 924, "Operations Against Japan Subsequent to Formosa," June 30, 1944, ABC [American-British Conversations] 381 Japan (8-27-42), sec. 7, Box 353, RG 165, NARA. These records are also in Geographic File 1942–1945, CCS [Combined Chiefs of Staff] 381 Pacific Ocean Area (6-10-43),

sec. 5, Box 683, Records of the United States Joint Chiefs of Staff, RG 218, NARA.

6. Henry I. Shaw Jr., Bernard C. Natly, and Edwin T. Turnbladh, *Central Pacific Drive: History of U.S. Marine Corps Operations in World War II* (Washington, D.C.: Historical Branch, U.S. Marine Corps, 1966), 346.

7. The Central Intelligence Agency's former deputy director for intelligence, Douglas J. MacEachin, explains that JCS 924 "incorporat[ed] various modifications [and] articulated the JCS consensus on an invasion of Kyushu." *The Final Months of the War with Japan: Signals Intelligence, Invasion Planning, and the A-Bomb Decision* (Washington, D.C.: Central Intelligence Agency Center for the Study of Intelligence, 1998), 1–2.

8. JCS 924/2, "Operations against Japan Subsequent to Formosa," August 30, 1944, 120, Records of the Joint Chiefs of Staff, CARL.

9. For example, the OPD estimated that an invasion of Formosa would cost 88,600 American casualties, including approximately 16,000 dead, which George C. Marshall rounded out to "approximately 90,000 casualties" in a September 1, 1944, memorandum to Joint Strategic Survey chief Lt. Gen. Stanley C. Embick, in Bland and Stevens, *Marshall* 4:567–69.

10. For an analysis of the lead time required to draft, process, train, and ship soldiers overseas in preparation for combat operations, see Giangreco, "Casualty Projections," 564–69.

11. Palmer, Wiley, and Keast, *Procurement and Training of Ground Combat Troops*, 216–25.

12. Willoughby, "Occupation of Japan," 3–4. See also Giangreco, "Casualty Projections," 549, 574–77.

13. *Selective Service and Victory*, 53–59, 70–71, 85–88. The Army's finely tuned program was structured in such a way that public demands might be placated while still allowing the Army to retain a sizable core of veterans for the upcoming campaigns on the Japanese home islands.

14. Truman also continued to do his daily business out of the Senate Office Building, Room 240, where his small staff labored, and not in either the relatively lavish Vice President's Office in the Capital or his assigned space in the West Wing of the White House.

15. Francis B. Kish, "Citizen-Soldier Harry S. Truman, 1884–1972," *Military Review*, February 1973, 30–44.

16. Harry Truman to Bess Truman, February 11, 1937, in Ferrell, *Dear Bess*, 391.

17. David McCullough, *Truman* (New York: Simon & Schuster, 1992), 229.

18. Kish, "Citizen-Soldier Harry S. Truman."

19. Alfred Steinberg, *The Man from Missouri: The Life and Times of Harry S. Truman* (New York: G. P. Putnam's Sons, 1962), 190.

20. Gen. Harry H. Vaughan, Oral History Interview, Alexandria, Va., January 14 and 16, 1963, 81–82, HSTL; and McCullough, *Truman*, 335.

21. This quotation is from the cover story of a particularly widely disseminated and read article, "How Long Will We Have to Fight the Jap War?" *Yank* 4 (June 8, 1945): 2. *Yank*'s circulation at the time was 2.6 million per edition. For a useful look at the political context in which this U.S. Army's "information campaign" was made, see John W. Dower, *War Without Mercy: Race and Power in the Pacific War* (New York: Pantheon Books, 1986), esp. 15–32.

22. JIC [Joint Intelligence Committee] 266/1, "Defeat of Japan by Blockade and Bomb," April 18, 1945; JWPC 263/4, "An Outline Plan for Invasion of Kanto (Tokyo) Plain," May 5, 1945; JWPC 264/1, "Strategic Positions Selected for Occupation Upon Japanese Withdrawal, Collapse, or

Surr[ender]," May 16, 1945; JWPC 264/2, "Forces Required for Occupation of Strategic Positions in Japan Proper," May 16, 1945; and JCS 1331/3, "Directive for Op[eratio]n 'Olympic,' Kyushu," May 25, 1945. JWPC and JIC papers may be found in RG 319, NARA.

23. *New York Times*, January 18, 1945, p. 1.

24. Samuel Halpern to Barton J. Bernstein, July 16, 1990, in *The Enola Gay Debate* (Arlington, Va.: Air Force Association, 1995), chap. 10, n.p.

25. "Strategic Bombing Symposium on the Atomic Bombing of Japan" question and answer session, Smithsonian Institution, Air and Space Museum, July 12, 1990; Gen. Andrew J. Goodpaster, former superintendent of the U.S. Military Academy, telephone interview with author, May 7, 1997. See also Giangreco, "Casualty Projections," 537–38. During a spring 2001 conversation between the author and *Papers of George Catlett Marshall* editor Larry Bland, as well as e-mail exchanges in early December 2003 and January 12, 2005, Bland insisted that Stimson, who was deeply concerned with the "limitations of America's manpower pool," would have been familiar with the Saipan ratio used by Marshall when making quick estimates for his own purposes. Bland speculated that while "Stimson may have been influenced by other senior members of Marshall's staff, who were convinced of the superiority of American arms, industry, and technology" and their ability to lessen American casualties, such "confidence may have eroded substantially as the Okinawa Campaign ground on."

26. "Summary of Redeployment Forecast," March 14, 1945, p. 6, Demobilization Branch, Plans and Operations Division, Army Service Forces, CARL. For an examination of how the three principal types of casualty estimates—medical, strategic, and logistical—are formulated, connected, and used, see the brief explanation in Giangreco, "Score of Bloody Okinawas," 93–132, esp. 97–101, 117–20 (also in Maddox, *Hiroshima in History*, 76–115, esp. 80–84, 98–102) or the more lengthy treatment in Giangreco, "Casualty Projections," 521–81, esp. 530–43.

27. The expectation that Imperial Japan would execute its prisoners was based on its actions during its decade-long war in China, the Bataan Death March and outrages in Southeast Asia, its lack of cooperation with Swiss government intermediaries and the International Red Cross, and the capture of Japanese documents and photos in New Guinea (see Col. R. H. Lee to Brig. Gen. Thomas D. White, May 23, 1943, memorandums, and Stimson to Marshall, October 8, 1943, in Stimson "Safe File" Japan [After 7/41], Box 8, Records of the Secretary of War, RG 107, NARA (hereafter cited as Stimson "Safe File"), all of which predated the Imperial War Ministry's August 1, 1944, policy statement on the "final disposition" of Allied POWs, popularly known as the "Kill All Order" (see Skelton, *American Ex-Prisoners of War*, 5, 11–13, and 25). Before Japan's formal surrender it provided details on the 103,855 Allied prisoners still alive and under its control in the home islands and Asian mainland (*MacArthur in Japan: The Occupation: Military Phase*, vol. 1, suppl., p. 97, from *Reports*). Of these, 32,624 were American military personnel in Japan itself (*MacArthur in Japan: The Occupation: Military Phase* 1:102–8), in addition to 1,307 at Hoten, Manchuria, and 22 senior U.S. officers at Hsian, Manchuria (Findings of the World War II Working Group, Joint U.S.-Russia Commission on POW/MIA under "Mukden Rescue and

Evacuation," http://www.us-japandialogue-onpows.org/.

28. Halpern to Bernstein, August 27, 1990, in *Enola Gay Debate*.

29. Robert H. Ferrell, from panel discussion following "What Did They Know and When Did They Know It? Intelligence Assumptions Before the Invasion of Japan," at the annual meeting of the Society for Military History, Pennsylvania State University, April 16, 1999. Ferrell's paper from this conference, "Intelligence Assessments and Assumptions: The View from Washington," is available in slightly modified form in his *Harry S. Truman and the Cold War Revisionists* (Columbia: University of Missouri Press, 2006) as chapter 2, "The Bomb—The View from Washington," 37–43.

30. William LaVarre to Ivan D. Yeaton, January 10, 1978, Box 4, folder "Increment," Papers of Ivan D. Yeaton, Hoover Institution Library, Stanford, Calif., copies from Herbert Hoover Presidential Library, West Branch, Iowa (hereafter cited as HL).

31. Ibid.

32. Ibid.

33. See Matloff, "90-division Gamble," 370.

34. See Ferrell, "What Did They Know"; Miller to Ferrell, August 3, 1999; Ferrell to author, August 7, 1999; and Miller to author, October 8, 1999. John Callan O'Laughlin's relationship with Marshall—and their mutual friend Gen. John J. Pershing—is presented in Larry I. Bland and Sharon Ritenour Stevens, eds., *The Papers of George Catlett Marshall*, vol. 1, *"The Soldierly Spirit," December 1880–June 1939* (Baltimore: Johns Hopkins University Press, 1981) (hereafter cited as *Marshall*, followed by the volume number), 475, 520–21; and Larry I. Bland and Sharon Ritenour Stevens, eds., *The Papers of George Catlett Marshall*, vol. 2, *"We Cannot Delay," July 1,*

1939–December 6, 1941 (Baltimore: Johns Hopkins University Press, 1986) (hereafter cited as *Marshall*, followed by the volume number), 153–54, 277–78, 287–88, 287.

35. Ferrell to author, August 7, 1999. See also Ferrell, *Harry S. Truman and the Cold War Revisionists*, 42–43.

36. "Palmer Warns No Easy Way to Beat Japs," *Los Angeles Times*, May 17, 1945, p 5. Also see "Palmer Warns Nips Set for Murderous Combat," *Los Angeles Times*, May 8, 1945, sec. 2, p. 1. The latter article was placed next to "New Casualty List Released" with the names and home addresses of seventy-eight Los Angeles area servicemen wounded or killed in action.

37. Ferrell, "What Did They Know." See also Ferrell, *Harry S. Truman*, 41–42.

38. McNaughton and Hehmeyer, *Harry Truman*, 3.

39. "Japanese Military Manpower," *Military Research Bulletin*, no. 13, April 25, 1945, 5–9. In the final analysis, the upwardly revised estimate was short by nearly half a million, and the total number of Japanese armed forces personnel demobilized by the U.S. military government after the surrender was 6,465,435, some 916,828 of them on Kyushu, in *Reports*, vol. 1, suppl., p. 266. See also "Japanese Military Manpower Potential for 1945," *Military Research Bulletin*, no. 18, July 4, 1945, 1–4; and "The Japanese System of Defense Call-up," *Military Research Bulletin*, no. 19, July 18, 1945, 1–3.

40. The new information on Japanese manpower trends was not yet widely disseminated—even within higher headquarters' organizations. Military intelligence analysts would have been among the very first personnel working the revised figures against the Saipan ratio plus other ratios developed from more recent operations.

41. "U.S. Tenth Army Action Report, Ryukyus, 26 March to 30 June 1945," vol. 1, chap. 11, sec. 1, p. 12, call no. N11432, CARL; Thomas M. Huber, *Japan's Battle for Okinawa, April–June 1945* (Fort Leavenworth, Kans.: Combat Studies Institute, U.S. Army Command and General Staff College, 1990), 119–20. See also Giangreco, "Casualty Projections," 539–40.

42. From a summary of a March 26, 1996, telephone interview with George L. McColm, U.S. Navy (Ret.), examined and approved by McColm on April 17, 1996. McColm was a highly respected agricultural specialist before the war, dubbed by Secretary of Agriculture Henry Wallace the "Weather Bookmaker." His studies were used as the basis for Office of Strategic Services (OSS) theater map "Crop Growing Season Climate Map of the Japanese Home Islands of Honshu-Shikoku-Kyushu" as early as 1942. He served as chief of agriculture on the JCS working group planning for the invasion and occupation of Japan.

43. "Stimson, Henry L., 1945–1950" and "Truman, Harry S., 1945," Post Presidential Individual File, Hoover Papers, HL; President's Secretary's Files (hereafter cited as PSF), HSTL. See also Timothy Walch and Dwight M. Miller, eds., *Herbert Hoover and Harry S. Truman: A Documentary History* (Worland, Wyo.: High Plains, 1992), 34–37.

44. Giangreco and Moore, *Dear Harry*, 34, 141–44, 400–406, 416–21, 432–33.

45. Ibid., 43–53, esp. 50–53. For a more detailed account of Hoover's meeting with Truman and the effort to get Hoover's memorandums past the "Roosevelt holdovers," see Giangreco, "Score of Bloody Okinawas," 93–132, esp. 110–14.

46. In addition to Bernstein's "A Postwar Myth: 500,000 Lives Saved," *Bulletin of the Atomic Scientists*, June–July 1986, 38–40, where the author of the memorandum is referred to as "a layman" instead of by name or former occupation, other examples include Frank, *Downfall*, 133, and Gar Alperovitz, *The Decision to Use the Atomic Bomb and the Architecture of an American Myth* (New York: Knopf, 1995), 43–45, 350–51, 520.

47. Barton J. Bernstein to the author, telephone call, February 2, 1996.

48. Ferrell, "What Did They Know." See also Ferrell, *Harry S. Truman*, 41–42.

49. The original copy of Hoover's "Memorandum on Ending the Japanese War" (May 30, 1945, memorandum 4 of 4) with Truman's notation, the White House retypes/carbon copies of this document, and the subsequent exchange of memorandums among Truman, Grew, Cordell Hull, Stimson, and Vinson, are under "State Dept., WWII" in Box 43 of the White House Confidential File, HSTL. The memorandum had been modified substantially in form, but not content, from the document Hoover sent to Stimson after their May 13, 1945, meeting. Both versions of the memorandum are well known, with the May 30, 1945, version frequently cited. After locating the original annotated copy and subsequent exchange between Truman and his senior civilian advisers, I supplied copies to numerous scholars, such as Robert Ferrell and Robert Newman, as well as various institutions.

50. Grew to Rosenman, June 16, 1945, Stimson "Safe File." The lack of a cover letter for the carbon copy of Grew's memorandum to Rosenman in Stimson's possession suggests that memorandum 4 was also personally discussed by Stimson and Grew.

51. *Diaries of Henry Lewis Stimson*, June 11, 1945; and Grew to Rosenman, Stimson "Safe File."

52. Grew to Rosenman, Stimson "Safe File."

53. Daily Sheets, May 28, 1945, Truman's Appointments File, PSF, HSTL; and Joseph C. Grew, *Turbulent Era: A Diplomatic Record of Forty Years, 1904–1945*, 2 vols. (Boston: Houghton Mifflin, 1952), 2:1429.

54. Daily Sheets, June 13, 1945, Truman's Appointments File, PSF, Truman Library.

55. Leahy to JCS members Marshall, Henry H. Arnold, and Ernest J. King; Secretary of War Stimson; and Secretary of the Navy James Forrestal, Memo SM-2141, June 14, 1945, in Department of Defense, "Entry of the Soviet Union," 76.

56. Truman diary, June 17, 1945, HSTL, in Ferrell, *Off the Record*, 46–47.

57. For the full text of the July 2, 1945, memorandum, see Stimson, "Decision to Use the Atomic Bomb," 97–107. First, second, and final drafts in Stimson "Safe File."

58. "Joint Chiefs of Staff Corrigendum to JCS 1388"; JCS 1388, "Details of the Campaign Against Japan," June 16, 1945, Records of the Joint Chiefs of Staff, CARL. For the text and a detailed analysis of the June 18, 1945, meeting and exchange between Generals Marshall and MacArthur beforehand, see Giangreco, "Casualty Projections," 544–61, 578–80. For an analysis of the Pentagon staff work on Hoover's memorandum 4 and the June 18 meeting, see Giangreco, "Score of Bloody Okinawas," 113–21.

59. Giangreco, "Casualty Projections," 554–58.

60. The figure of sixty-three thousand was ultimately adopted by the National Air and Space Museum at the insistence of Barton Bernstein as the total number of casualties expected by the U.S. military during the invasion of Japan. Use of this artificially low figure further inflamed veterans' passions during the *Enola Gay* controversy and contributed directly to Harwit's dismissal. See Martin Harwit, *An Exhibit Denied: Lobbying the History of the Enola Gay* (New York: Copernicus/Springer-Verlag, 1996), 345–46, 380; Robert P. Newman, *Enola Gay and the Court of History* (New York: Peter Lang, 2004), 133; and John T. Correll, *The Smithsonian and the Enola Gay* (Arlington, Va.: Aerospace Education Foundation, 2004), 20–21. See also Charles T. O'Reilly and William A. Rooney, *The Enola Gay and the Smithsonian Institution* (Jefferson, N.C.: McFarland, 2005), 129–30; and Correll, "The Activists and the Enola Gay," *Air Force Magazine*, September 1995, 18.

61. Diary entry, June 18, 1945, William D. Leahy Diaries, 1897–1956, microfilm edition, Reel 4, interlibrary loan, Naval War College, Newport, R.I., to CARL. See also William D. Leahy, *I Was There: The Personal Story of the Chief of Staff to Presidents Roosevelt and Truman Based on His Notes and Diaries Made at the Time* (New York: Whittlesey House, 1950), 384.

62. Michael Kort, "Casualty Projections for the Invasion of Japan, Phantom Estimates, and the Math of Barton Bernstein," *Passport*, December 2003, 4–12.

63. Ibid.; and Newman, *Enola Gay*, 105–33.

64. Marshall's figure of 766,700 differs only slightly from that of MacArthur's headquarters, which gave 766,986 as the number of men to be landed within a month and a half of the invasion in "Staff Study, 'Olympic,' Operations in Southern Kyushu," May 28, 1945, Appendix B, Annex 4, Commander in Chief, Army Forces, Pacific, call nos. N11619 and N11619-B, CARL.

65. For Leahy's frequent accompaniment of Truman, see George M. Elsey to author, March 30, 1997. Elsey was then the "watch officer" for the White House Map Room,

where the progress of the war was graphically charted and updated daily. He noted the close attention paid to growing Japanese troop strength and remembers "Admiral Leahy discussing the invasion plans with the President in the Map Room prior to our departure for Potsdam." Elsey emphasized "the concern they both had as to the size of the Japanese forces available to oppose us" and that during the course of many conversations with Truman that fateful summer, Truman made it very clear he "was deeply worried about the casualties that would inevitably be incurred in an invasion." See also Elsey's lengthy introduction to "Blueprints for Victory," *National Geographic* 187 (May 1995): 55–77, for information on their visits to the White House Map Room; and George M. Elsey, *An Unplanned Life: A Memoir by George McKee Elsey* (Columbia: University of Missouri Press, 2005), 80–82, 89, 99.

66. "Joint Chiefs of Staff Corrigendum to JCS 1388," 4–5.

Chapter 7. Japanese Defense Plans

1. Morison, *Two-Ocean War*, 556.

2. Hattori, *Complete History of the Greater East Asia War* 4:135.

3. "Estimate of Situation for Spring of 1946"; and "Estimate Concerning the Allied Force Plans for the Invasion Operation of the Japanese Homeland," in "Japanese Defense Strategy and Tactics," n.p.

4. "Estimate of Situation for Spring of 1946," 22; Hayashi and Coox, *Kogun*, 176.

5. "Estimate of Situation for Spring of 1946," 18.

6. Ibid., 19. The original "Estimate of Situation for Spring of 1946" and *Defense Strategy and Tactics* were completed and issued approximately two weeks apart on, respectively,

July 1 and mid June 1945, and significant portions of both documents contain text that appears to differ only slightly. Although most variations could well be the result of multiple U.S. translators preparing the documents, a close examination displays differences not likely to stem from the translations. For example, the passage cited here from "Estimate of Situation for Spring of 1946" notes that the president was addressing Congress but doesn't say when, while text in *Defense Strategy and Tactics* gives the date but doesn't mention Congress.

7. Brig. Gen. Lauris Norstad, Assistant Chief, U.S. Strategic Air Force, Plans (operations section) from his deputy for operations, November 4, 1944, memorandum, Col. Cecil E. Combs in James Lea Cate and James C. Olson, memorandum, in Craven and Cate, *AAFWWII* 5:662.

8. *Defense Strategy and Tactics*, under subhead "Estimate on the number of American troops to be used for the invasion of Japan," n.p.; and Hayashi and Coox, *Kogun*, 157–58.

9. *Reports*, vol. 2, bk. 2, p. 657; and June 6, 1945, speech by the chief of the Imperial Navy General Staff, Toyota Soemu, in Hattori, *Complete History of the Greater East Asia War* 4:135. Also see Hattori, *Complete History of the Greater East Asia War* 4:153, 295; Coox, *Final Agony*, 81; and Drea, *In the Service of the Emperor*, 199.

10. Shikoku was seen as a potential target for smaller-scale U.S. landings, which could both serve as a feint to draw some forces away from Kyushu and provide the establishment of U.S. air bases that would be closer to Tokyo, yet well situated to help protect the main invasion across the Bungo Strait at Kyushu. Japanese Monograph No. 17, "Homeland Operations," 101. Additional analysis in *Reports*, vol. 2, bk. 2, p. 648.

11. Hayashi and Coox, *Kogun*, 177–78.

12. Japanese Monograph No. 17, "Homeland Operations," vol. 1, "General Defense Command," by former staff officers of the General Defense Command, Major General Yoshihide Kato, Colonel Shigeru Nishioka, Lieutenant Colonel Yoshito Ogata, and Major Yoshikiyo Ichinomiya; Japanese Manuscript No. 18, "Homeland Operations Record," vol. 2, "First General Army," by former staff officers of the First General Army, Lieutenant Colonel Tooru Itagaki and Lieutenant Colonel Ken Arai; Japanese Manuscript No. 19, "Homeland Operations Record," vol. 3, "Second General Army," by former staff officers of the Second General Army, Colonel Kumao Imoto, Lieutenant Colonel Masakatsu Hashimoto, and Major Tosaku Hirano; Japanese Manuscript No. 20, "Homeland Operations Record," vol. 4, "Sixteenth Area Army Records," by former staff officer of the Sixteenth Area Army, Major Yasunobu Haba. Japanese Manuscripts 17–20 are superseded by Japanese Monograph No. 17, "Homeland Operations."

13. Japanese Monograph No. 17, "Homeland Operations," iii–v; see also note 10 above.

14. Ibid., 40–41.

15. Ibid., 42.

16. Ibid., 47–48.

17. *Reports*, vol. 2, bk. 2, p. 605.

18. Hayashi and Coox, *Kogun*, 156.

19. Hattori, *Complete History of the Greater East Asia War* 4:280.

20. Hayashi and Coox, *Kogun*, 157; and Japanese Monograph No. 17, "Homeland Operations," 56.

21. Japanese Monograph No. 17, "Homeland Operations," 62–63.

22. Ibid., 44, 64.

23. Ibid., 45, 65.

24. Ibid., 71.

25. Ibid., 66–67.

26. Ibid., 90–94.

27. Hattori, *Complete History of the Greater East Asia War* 4:145.

28. Hayashi and Coox, *Kogun*, 152–53. See also Leon V. Sigal, *Fighting to a Finish: The Politics of War Termination in the United States and Japan* (Ithaca, N.Y.: Cornell University Press, 1988), 70.

29. Japanese Monograph No. 17, "Homeland Operations," 67. For more on *Sei-Go*, see Japanese Monograph No. 157, "Homeland Air Defense Operations Record," United States Army Forces, Far East, Tokyo, June 1952, 81, 125–26; and Japanese Monograph No. 23, "Air Defense of the Homeland, 1944–1945," United States Army Forces, Far East, Tokyo, 68–69.

30. *Reports*, vol. 2, bk. 2, pp. 604–5.

31. Ibid.; Japanese Monograph No. 17, "Homeland Operations," 82; *Defense Strategy and Tactics*, "Appended Chart No 1, Chart for the concentration in Operation KETSU 3," n.p; and *Defense Strategy and Tactics*, "The Employment of Strength," n.p.

32. Japanese Monograph No. 17, "Homeland Operations," 75.

33. Ibid., 77–78.

34. Ibid., 75–77.

35. Ibid., 80.

36. Hayashi and Coox, *Kogun*, 156; and Drea, *In the Service of the Emperor*, 146.

37. Japanese Monograph No. 17, "Homeland Operations," 77–78, 110–13.

38. Ibid., 79–80, 117, 119.

39. Drea, *In the Service of the Emperor*, 146–47.

40. Japanese Monograph No. 17, "Homeland Operations," 117–18.

41. Ibid., 126.

42. Ibid., 126–27.

43. *Reports*, vol. 2, bk. 2, p. 655.

44. Japanese Monograph No. 17, "Homeland Operations," 129–32.

45. Ibid., 129–30.

46. *Reports*, vol. 2, bk. 2, pp. 653–54.

Chapter 8. "Victory Might Be Salvaged"

1. Interrogation of Inoguchi, Rikibei, Captain, IJN, 10th Air Fleet by Myron Lieberman, G-2, Historical Section, USAFFE, March 7, 1947, CARL.

2. Rikibei Inoguchi and Tadashi Nakajima with Roger Pineau, *The Divine Wind: Japan's Kamikaze Force in World War II* (Annapolis: U.S. Naval Institute Press, 1958), 26–27.

3. Ibid., 61–62; and Saburo Sakai with Martin Caidin and Fred Saito, *Samurai!* (New York: Bantam Books, 1978), 294–95.

4. The name *Shimpu* harkened back to the original "Divine Wind," which destroyed a Mongol invasion force sailing for Japan in 1281. American forces, however, immediately adopted the word "kamikaze," because even though it means essentially the same thing, "kamikaze" also carries pejorative overtones of foolish or reckless behavior. Similarly, the Ohka (Cherry Blossom) piloted rocket used in suicide attacks was dubbed Baka, for "fool" (noun) or "crazy" (adjective). In both cases the American appellations stuck.

5. Morison, *Leyte*, 12:339–49, 354–60, 366–68, 380–85.

6. Cannon, *Leyte*, 365–67; and Stanley L. Falk, *Decision at Leyte* (New York: W. W. Norton, 1966), 55–61, 314–15.

7. Ibid., 306–8.

8. Lt. Cdr. Buford Roland, USNR, and Lt. William B. Boyd, USNR, *U.S. Navy Bureau of Ordnance in World War II* (Washington, D.C.: U.S. Navy Dept., 1955), 234, 245–46.

9. Samuel Eliot Morison, *USNOWWII*, vol. 14, *Victory in the Pacific, 1945* (Boston: Little, Brown, 1960), 101, 133, 186–91; plus James Belote and William Belote, *Typhoon*

of Steel: The Battle for Okinawa (New York: Harper & Row, 1970), 91–94, 143–45.

10. Morison, *USNOWWII* 14:282, 389–92.

11. This figure was rounded to 10,500 in *Reports* 1:419 and has almost uniformly appeared as such in subsequent works.

12. "Army-Navy Central Agreement Concerning the *Ketsu-Go* Air Operation," in Hattori, *Complete History of the Greater East Asia War* 4:164. For the impact that the formation of Special Attack Units had on readiness in the conventional force, see Japanese Monograph No. 157, "Homeland Air Defense Operations Record," 14, 31–32, 46, 80–81, 122–26, 160.

13. See René J. Francillon, *Japanese Aircraft of the Pacific War* (Annapolis: Naval Institute Press, 1988), 241–43, for details on the Nakajima Ki-115 Tsurugi (Sabre). Technical data outlined by Francillon is accurate and well presented in this invaluable reference, but the author was unaware that the Japanese Army decision to build the purpose-built suicide aircraft—on the heels of highly successful Kamikaze operations in the Philippines—preceded the IGHQ decision to convert all flight training units into combat units by six months and thus assumed incorrectly that the Ki-115 was ordered produced because there was a shortage of training aircraft available as suicide missions. The conversion of the training units many months after the decision to produce the Ki-115 was in part because of the persistent technical problems associated with its construction. Only 105 of this model were completed by war's end.

14. Francillon, *Japanese Aircraft*, 404–7, 443–45, 488. The Mitsubishi J8M Shusui (Sword Stroke) was modeled on Germany's bat-shaped Messerschmitt Me163 rocket-powered fighter, while the Nakajima Kikka (Orange Blossom) and Nakajima Ki-201 Karyu (Fire Dragon) were based on the

Messerschmitt Me262 twin-jet fighter. Seven J8Ms were produced before Japan's surrender along with approximately fifty to sixty similarly shaped gliders for pilot training. Likewise, two prototypes of the Kikki were produced, and eighteen more were in various stages of production before being abandoned. No Ki-201s were completed and, oddly, no airframe number was assigned to the Kikki, even though its flight testing had actually begun.

15. Joint study conducted by the General Air Army and Combined Fleet, in Hattori, *Complete History of the Greater East Asia War* 4:171–74.

16. Hattori, *Complete History of the Greater East Asia War* 4:191.

17. "United States Strategic Bombing Survey, Pacific," No. 72, vol. 2, "Interrogations of Japanese Officials," Naval Analysis Division, USSBS, Tokyo, 1946 (hereafter cited as "USSBS—Interrogations," followed by name), 551. Inoguchi's interrogators, Lt. Cdr. J. A. Field Jr. and Lt. Cdr. R. P. Aikin noted that he was a "difficult witness" who "attempted continually to take charge of the interview and to return to the discussion of his favorite subject, the philosophy of Kamikaze."

18. Interrogation of Inoguchi, Rikibei, Captain, IJN, March 7, 1947, CARL.

19. "USSBS—Interrogations," Capt. Mitsuo Fuchida, 1:24. Capt. Mitsuo Fuchida commanded an air group during operations at Pearl Harbor, Darwin, Ceylon, and Midway, where he was badly wounded.

20. "USSBS—Interrogations," Capt. Rikibei Inoguchi, 1:64; "USSBS—Interrogations," Cdr. Yoshimori Terai, 2:533; "Japanese Air Power, United States Strategic Bombing Survey, Pacific," No. 62 , Military Analysis Division, Tokyo,1946 (hereafter cited as

"Japanese Air Power"), 28–29, 33, 35, 40; and Frank, *Downfall*, 208–9.

21. Frank, *Downfall*, 208.

22. "'Magic'—Far East Summary," No. 501, August 3, 1945, 2, CARL.

23. "Japanese Air Power," 24–25, 42.

24. "Outline of Preparations for the *Ketsu-Go* Operation," in Japanese Monograph No. 17, "Homeland Operations," October 1945, 226.

25. Hattori, *Complete History of the Greater East Asia War* 4:159–60, 173–74, 191. Interestingly, misinterpretations or mistranslations of a Japanese summary of planned operations produced under American auspices immediately after the war by the First Demobilization Bureau (Japanese Army) were made in the 1950 *Reports* 1:419, 430. It states that the "bulk of the air fleet of 10,500 planes [*sic;* the number represents only kamikazes, not the total air fleet], mostly of the small, special-attack type, would be launched against warships and transports in the crucial invasion area. Japanese plans called for these planes to be completely expended within a ten-day period." In fact, the Japanese did plan to utilize their entire force of kamikazes and conventional aircraft *available in Kyushu and Shikoku,* as well as a significant number of conventional aircraft in southern Honshu, but the Intelligence personnel producing *Reports* mistakenly took this to mean that all aircraft throughout Japan would be "expended"—a physical and logistical impossibility that was not part of Japanese defense plans but subsequently has been uncritically repeated in a wide variety of works, including, this author is embarrassed to say, some of his own. Further complicating the historiography of kamikaze operations is that some researchers have represented numbers from documents discussing the operations of one service or the other as

representing both the Imperial Navy and Imperial Army.

26. Although this was apparently confirmed by USSBS investigators immediately after the war and subsequently repeated without question in many works, an analysis by Manny Horowitz of data supplied by Japanese firms and published in open Japanese government sources demonstrated that USSBS conclusions regarding crude oil and synthetic oil production and refining were "both unsubstantiated and incorrect." See Manny Horowitz, "Were There Strategic Oil Targets in Japan in 1945?" *Air Power History* 51 (Spring 2004): 26–35.

27. "Oil in Japan's War: Report of the Oil and Chemical Division, United States Strategic Bombing Survey, Pacific," No. 51, Oil and Chemical Division, USSBS, Tokyo, 1946 (hereafter cited as "Oil in Japan's War"), 40–41.

28. Hattori, *Complete History of the Greater East Asia War* 4:6.

29. Ibid.; and "'Magic'—Far East Summary," No. 322, February 5, 1945, 2–3; and No. 324, February 7, 1945, 4–6, CARL.

30. "Interrogations of Japanese Officials (Fukudome)." Also see "Oil in Japan's War," 54, 57, where the forty thousand tons of fuel, refined and ready for use, is characterized as "a final dribble as a few isolated tankers managed to reach port." The "dribble" is detailed in "Oil in Japan's War," appendix, 19, as 761,000 barrels, of which 440,000 were aviation fuel.

31. "'Magic'—Far East Summary": No. 322, February 5, 1945, 2–3; No. 324, February 7, 1945, 4–6; No. 325, February 8, 1945, 3–4, 6; No. 327, February 10, 1945, 2–3; No. 339, February 22, 1945, 5–6; No. 348, March 3, 1945, 3–4; No. 350, March 5, 1945, 3–6; No. 352, March 7, 1945, 1–3; No. 369, Naval Section, March 7, 1945,

N2–N3; No. 353, March 8, 1945, 5; No. 354, March 9, 1945, 3; No. 372, Naval Section, March 10, 1945, N2; No. 359, March 14, 1945, 8–9; No. 364, March 19, 1945, 6–7; No. 366, March 21, 1945, 5–6; No. 367, March 22, 1945, 3; No. 368, March 23, 1945, 1–3; and No. 369, March 24, 1945, 3–4, all in CARL. A cursory examination of the February and March summaries quickly reveals that there was more interest in the location and possible transfer to the home islands of combatant elements of the Japanese Fleet in Singapore than in the movement of tankers and cargo ships.

32. "Oil in Japan's War," 68, 88–89.

33. Ibid., appendix, 25. Other totals (combined services and civilian in barrels) included 365,000 barrels of motor gasoline, 173,000 barrels of diesel fuel, 813,000 barrels of fuel oil, and 328,000 barrels of lubricating oil.

34. Navy sortie totals in Inoguchi and Nakajima with Pineau, *Divine Wind*, 160, 233–34. Army totals courtesy Edward J. Drea, who compiled them from Jiro Kimata, *Rikugun koku senshi* (*Operational History of the Army Air Force*) (Tokyo: Keizai Oraisha, 1982), 281.

35. "Oil in Japan's War," appendix, 23.

36. Ibid.

37. Commissioning dates on many of the last *Essex*-class carriers bear some scrutiny because all had their construction times lengthened to varying degrees after the early end of hostilities. If the fighting had continued, they would have kept apace with the late-war trends which demonstrated that a ship of this class was now taking an average of only eight months to be commissioned after its launching. On average, it took a further seven months for an *Essex* carrier to complete its shakedown cruise, postconstruction modifications, air wing training, and movement to the combat zone. See Gareth L. Pawlowski,

Flat-Tops and Fledglings: A History of American Aircraft Carriers (New York: Castle Books, 1971) under individual ship names; *Conway's All the World's Fighting Ships, 1922–1946* (London: Conway Maritime Press, 1980), 102–6; and Alan Ravan, *Essex-Class Carriers* (Annapolis: United States Naval Institute, 1988), 8–9.

38.　An eleventh ship badly damaged at Okinawa, HMS *Illustrious*, almost certainly would have made it back in time for Operation Coronet, but repairs became a low priority after the early end to the war and she did not rejoin the fleet until the summer of 1946. Like the U.S. light fleet carriers, those of the British Pacific Fleet regularly operated with far more aircraft than their official compliments which were more closely adhered to in the Atlantic. For representative operational figures, see Winton, *Forgotten Fleet*, 81–82, 113–14, 308–9; and for standard complements, see *Conway's All the World's Fighting Ships*, 19–20, 22. See Winton, *Forgotten Fleet*, chap. 10, for an examination of Royal Navy commitments for the fall of 1945. The arrival of four Royal Navy light carriers would have allowed the British Pacific Fleet to carry out the planned reorganization of its carrier force into two balanced carrier groups containing a mix of CVs and CVLs, and they were to be employed as such during Olympic. See "Joint Staff Study, OLYMPIC, Naval and Amphibious Operations," CINCPAC, June 18, 1945 (this and later dates hereafter cited as "Joint Staff Study, OLYMPIC," Appendix B, "Air Forces," 21–39, esp. 30.

39.　Morison, *USNOWWII* 14:53–54; and Pawlowski, *Flat-Tops and Fledglings*, 37–40.

40.　The June 5, 1945, typhoon wrenched 130 feet of bow off of a heavy cruiser, heavily damaged thirty-two other ships, including one escort and two fleet carriers that lost great lengths of their flight decks and resulted

in the loss of 142 aircraft jettisoned, blown overboard, or irreparably damaged. An earlier typhoon on December 18, 1944, had capsized three destroyers and heavily mauled seven other ships with nearly eight hundred lives lost in addition to 186 planes. Totals from Potter, *Nimitz*, 423, 456.

41.　"Joint Staff Study, OLYMPIC," Appendix B, "Air Forces," 29–32, and Annex 1, "Operations of the Fast Carrier Task Forces." See also "Report on Operation 'OLYMPIC' and Japanese Counter-Measures," pt. 4, "Appendices by the British Combined Operations Observers (Pacific)," Combined Operations Headquarters, August 1, 1946, (hereafter cited as "Report on Operation OLYMPIC"), 89–93.

42.　Edward P. Stafford, *The Big E: The Story of the USS Enterprise* (New York: Random House, 1963), 420, 431–32, 451–52, 460–64.

43.　The virtually rebuilt USS *Franklin* was decommissioned in February 1947, reclassified CVA-13 in 1952, reclassified as CVS-13 a year later, and then as AVT-8 in 1959 while a part of the Reserve Fleet. She was stricken from the Naval Vessel Register in October 1964 and sold for scrapping in July 1966.

44.　See note 37 above.

45.　JCS 1388/4, "Details of the Campaign Against Japan," 33.

46.　"Joint Staff Study, OLYMPIC," Annex 1 to Appendix C; and "Staff Study, Operations, OLYMPIC," General Headquarters USAFP, April 23, 1945, 13 and map 8.

47.　"Joint Staff Study, OLYMPIC," Annex 1 to Appendix C; and "Joint Staff Study, OLYMPIC." After completing operations against German forces in the central and eastern Mediterranean, a squadron of British light carriers arrived in the Pacific during the summer of 1945, and a squadron of escort carriers would make their appearance after supporting the British Fourteenth Army's invasion of Malaya, Operation Zipper. See Winton, *Forgotten Fleet*, 360, 375; and Charles W. Koburger Jr., *Naval Warfare in the Eastern Mediterranean, 1940–1945* (Westport, Conn.: Praeger, 1993), 116–17.

48. See CINCPAC map "Appendix 35, Provisional Layout of Fighter Defense" in "Report on Operation OLYMPIC," pt. 4, August 1, 1946.

49. Bemis M. Frank and Henry I. Shaw Jr., *History of U.S. Marine Corps Operations in World War II*, vol. 5, *Victory and Occupation* (Washington, D.C.: Historical Branch, U.S. Marine Corps, 1968), 187, 671; and Robert Sherrod, *History of Marine Corps Aviation in World War II* (Bonita, Calif.: Presidio Press, 1980), 385–86.

50. "Joint Staff Study, OLYMPIC," 35–36; and "Report on Operation OLYMPIC," 13 and map 8.

51. "Report on Operation OLYMPIC," 13 and map 8; "Report on Operation OLYMPIC." The first PB-1W airborne early warning aircraft (ungunned B-17Gs with an APS-20 air search radar in a large dome beneath the fuselage) were not delivered to the Navy until April 1946.

52. JCS 1388/4, "Details of the Campaign Against Japan."

53. Stafford, *Big E*, 459, 466.

54. Kamikaze's made particularly effective use of the mountainous islands of Aka Shima and Zamami Shima during their approach to the U.S. Navy's Kerama Retto anchorage. See Lt. Cdr. Arnold S. Lott, USN (Ret.), *Brave Ship, Brave Men* (New York: Bobbs-Merrill, 1964), 225.

55. From Jack Moore interview in D. M. Giangreco, "The Truth About Kamikazes," *Naval History* 11 (May–June 1997): 28.

56. "COMINCH P-0011, Anti-Suicide Action Summary," August 31, 1945, 20, Naval Historical Center, Washington Naval Yard, Washington, D.C. (hereafter cited as NHC). See also Robert F. Wallace, *From Dam Neck to Okinawa: A Memoir of Antiaircraft Training in World War II* (Washington, D.C.: Naval Historical Center, Department of the Navy, 2001), esp. 9–11, 18, 27–28, 32–35.

57. Roland and Boyd, *U.S. Navy Bureau of Ordnance*, 242, 245–47, 566.

58. Ibid., 268. The lack of specificity in "Nakajima-type fighter planes" likely indicates that the testing involved two or three readily available types, the Ki-44 Shoki "Tojo," Ki-84 Hayate "Frank," and possibly the older Ki-43 Hayabusa "Oscar," which remained in production throughout the war.

59. This seemingly radical proposal came about because even though the Pacific Fleet had progressively strengthened the antiaircraft defense at the most vulnerable picket stations throughout the Okinawa campaign, its efforts often proved insufficient. For example, on May 3, 1945, more than a month into operations, Radar Picket Station No. 10 was made up of a pair of destroyers, *Little* (DD-803) and *Aaron Ward* (DM-34), supported by LCM(R)-195, as well as three "coffin bearer" LCSs for additional fire support and the inevitable rescue operations. During an hour-long assault by twenty-five aircraft at sundown, two "suiciders" hit *Little*, breaking it in half, and another struck LSMR-195, blowing it up. The *Aaron Ward* shot down four but was struck by six kamikazes and two 500-pound bombs, which left her dead in the water, badly holed, and the entire ship aft of the forward superstructure smashed almost flat (Lott, *Brave Ship, Brave Men*, 162–92).

60. "Anti-Suicide Action Summary," 21. Also see Confidential Information Bulletin No. 29, "Anti-Aircraft Action Summary, World War

II," COMINCH, October 1945, for an overview of gun, ammunition, and fire-control development.

61. Inoguchi and Nakajima with Pineau, *Divine Wind*, 90–94.

62. Report of the *Fletcher*-class destroyer USS *Kimberly*, DD-521, March 25, 1945, excerpted in Richard O'Neill's *Suicide Squads: Axis and Allied Special Attack Weapons of World War II, Their Development and Their Missions* (New York: Ballantine, 1984), 164–65.

63. Terry Griswold and D. M. Giangreco, *DELTA: America's Elite Counterterrorist Force* (Osceola, Wisc.: MBI, 1992), 88. The continued success of the Iraqis at hitting Israeli and Saudi population centers during the 1991 Gulf War necessitated that a full squadron of F-15Es essentially be pulled from the air campaign and assigned the task of eliminating mobile Scuds. Other air assets were soon added as the equivalent of three squadrons became tied up by the effort and the number of sorties by Scud-hunting intelligence and refueling and strike aircraft sometimes climbed to more than three hundred in a twenty-four-hour period. Although a severe drain on U.S. resources for meager tactical results, this heavy and prolonged commitment did serve a larger political purpose since these operations were instrumental in convincing the Israelis to call off two planned raids into western Iraq that could have had a disastrous effect on public opinion within several Arab countries in the coalition opposing Iraq and severely hampered the war effort. For the effective use of inexpensive ground decoys in modern combat operations, see Timothy L. Thomas, "Kosovo and the Current Myth of Information Superiority," *Parameters* 30 (Spring 2000): 13–29; and David A. Fulghum, "Pentagon Dissecting

Kosovo Combat Data," *Aviation Week and Space Technology* 151 (July 26, 1999): 68–69.

64. Hattori gives the number of Japanese airfields on the home islands, including those under construction and 95 concealed airfields, at 325. Figures from the July 13, 1945, "Central Agreement Concerning Air Attacks" between the Japanese Army and Navy, in Hattori, *Complete History of the Greater East Asia War* 4:165.

65. Hattori, *Complete History of the Greater East Asia War* 4:234. Hattori states that the blow destroyed fifty-eight Navy and two Army aircraft on the ground. Smoke and decoys prevented an accurate U.S. assessment, and Morison calls it "indeterminate" in Morison, *USNOWWII* 14:100.

66. "Oil in Japan's War," 87–89; and Hattori, *Complete History of the Greater East Asia War* 4:165.

67. See Inoguchi and Nakajima with Pineau, *Divine Wind*, 85–87, for an examination of high-grade decoy production and their employment at an austere facility. The quality of dummy aircraft varied considerably from location to location, but even simple constructions of straw and fabric were effective since pilots under fire in speeding fighters had little time to closely examine aircraft on the ground.

68. Kenneth P. Werrell, *Blankets of Fire: U.S. Bombers over Japan during World War II* (Washington, D.C.: Smithsonian Institution Press, 1996), 207, 322; Edward Jablonski, *Airwar*: vol. 2, bk. 2, *Wings of Fire* (Garden City, N.Y.: Doubleday, 1971), 167; and "Homeland Air Defense Operations Record," 122–26, 160, which discusses the 11th and 12th Air Divisions' "complicated command system" necessitated by the appearance of special attack units within the organizations and the great difficulties they faced in performing their air defense mission in the

face of taskings that curtailed such operations in order to build up and plan for the
expected invasion. See also *Homeland Air
Defense Operations Record*, 14, 31–32, 46,
80–81.

69. Hattori, *Complete History of the Greater East
    Asia War* 4:191. Transports had always been
    a high priority for suicide aircraft but did not
    become the main focus of Japanese planning
    until the spring and summer of 1945. See
    "USSBS—Interrogations," Adm. Soemu
    Toyoda, 2:318, and Vice Adm. Shigeru
    Fukudome, 2:504.

70. King, *U.S Navy at War*, 188–89; and
    MacArthur to Marshall, copied to King in
    transmission WAR-45369, then King to
    Nimitz in transmission C-31897, August 9,
    1945, CINCPAC Command Summary, bk.
    7, 3508–10, NHC; War Department trans-
    mission WAR-45369, August 7, 1945, is
    also available through MacArthur Memorial
    Archive, Norfolk, Va. (hereafter cited as
    MMA) and National Archives Collection,
    X1297, GCML.

71. A useful window to the thinking of some
    senior members of Nimitz's staff can be
    found in "Joint Staff Study, OLYMPIC,"
    5, produced under the direction of Adm.
    Forrest Sherman, deputy chief of staff,
    COMINCH. Updated through at least July
    8, 1945, it echoes the intelligence reports
    referred to in this comment and states that
    attacks by U.S. forces "will have served to
    reduce the enemy air force to a relatively
    low state" by the projected November 1
    invasion. However, the assessment in "Staff
    Study, Operations, CORONET," General
    Headquarters USAFP, August 15, 1945,
    demonstrates a more realistic appraisal of
    Japanese plans for employment of kamikaze
    aircraft.

72. See CINCPAC map "Appendix 36, Radar
    Build Up" in "Report on Operation
    OLYMPIC," pt. 4.

73. "Army-Navy Central Agreement Concerning
    the *Ketsu-Go* Air Operation," in Hattori,
    Complete History of the Greater East Asia War
    4:164. For the impact that the formation of
    Special Attack Units had on the conventional
    force, see Japanese Monograph No. 157,
    "Homeland Air Defense Operations Record,"
    14, 31–32, 46, 80–81, 122–26, 160.

74. In addition to the systematic code breaking
    of Japanese radio transmissions by U.S.
    cryptologists, other communications intel-
    ligence focusing on the quantity and types
    of Japanese transmission was routinely
    performed. See Drea, *MacArthur's ULTRA;*
    and Rear Adm. Edwin T. Layton, USN
    (Ret.), Capt. Roger Pineau, USNR (Ret.),
    and John Costello, *And I Was There: Pearl
    Harbor and Midway—Breaking the Secrets*
    (New York: William Morrow, 1985).

75. Maj. Thomas E. Griffith Jr., USAF, Strategic
    Attack of National Electrical Systems
    (Maxwell Air Force Base, Ala.: Air University
    Press, 1994), 22–23, 27; and "United States
    Strategic Bombing Survey No. 41, Electric
    Power Industry of Japan," 5–6, 17.

76. John C. Reilly Jr., *United States Navy
    Destroyers of World War II* (Poole, Dorset,
    UK: Blandford Press, 1983), 114–16.

77. In a June 24, 2006, letter to the author,
    Capt. Lefteris "Lefty" Lavrakas, USN (Ret.),
    notes, "On the USS *Eberle* (DD-430) during
    42–44 period, we went with no radar/CIC
    until we received early search and fire control
    and installed rudiments of a combat informa-
    tion center which included, initially at least,
    the CO and XO/navigator on the bridge.
    Probably the biggest problem to commu-
    nication/coordination among ships was the
    lack of effective communication systems.
    . . . Later, with *Aaron Ward* (DM-34) at

Okinawa picket station no. 10, CIC had improved greatly and [ours] was a fairly efficient, well-manned unit which maintained in close touch with gun control. As you are well aware, however, the heavy number of attacking planes rendered CICs only partially effective in getting the job done—reporting all planes in sufficient time to shoot them down." Captain Lavrakas (then a lieutenant) served as the assistant gunnery officer in the *Aaron Ward*'s Main Director, controlling its 5-inch and 40-mm guns. Also see Lott, *Brave Ship, Brave Men*, 162–92.

78. The lack of discharge facilities, which was the principal factor behind the "shipping crisis" of late 1944 in which cargo ships had to anchor for prolonged periods while waiting to unload, had alleviated somewhat thanks to a massive effort to construct port and logistical facilities in the Philippines but threatened a resurgence during the invasion of Japan, particularly during Operation Coronet. Part of the answer to this dilemma was the secret construction in San Francisco, California, of prefabricated components for a massive artificial harbor, code named Ironhorse, to be assembled near Tokyo. This project, examined in chapter 15, carried a priority second only to the Manhattan Project, which developed the atom bomb. See Ray S. Cline, *Washington Command Post: The Operations Division*, USAWWII series (Washington, D.C.: Center of Military History, United States Army, 1951), 347; "Artificial Harbor," in "Staff Study Operations, CORONET," Annex 4, Appendix H; and additional details in Martin Halliwell's "The Projected Assault on Japan," *Royal United Service Institution Journal* (*RUSI*), August 1947, 348–51.

79. As with Operation Iceberg, the invasion of Okinawa in 1945, Coronet in 1946 had to be launched early enough in the year to ensure that flight operations would not be disrupted by the summer monsoon season.

80. U.S. estimates in May 1945 that 6,700 aircraft could be made available in stages grew to only 7,200 by the time of the surrender. After the war, occupation authorities discovered that the number of military aircraft actually available in the home islands was over 12,700. See *Reports*, vol. 1, suppl., 136; and Hattori, *Complete History of the Greater East Asia War* 4:174. Even in the unlikely event that Japan's fanciful production goal of producing an additional 4,000 aircraft could be met, it would be virtually impossible to provide an appropriate number of new pilots for the custom-built kamikazes because of the greatly reduced training program. Plans were being implemented, however, to provide the flight time needed by the plentiful number of experienced pilots to maintain proficiency by using Japan's strategic depth—Manchuria and Korea—for this purpose. The Soviet invasion of Manchuria eliminated roughly a third of the air bases that were to take part in this program. See also note 20 above.

81. In fact, the figures displaying the divergence were not only split between two different volumes of his *Reports*, vol. 1, suppl., 136, and 1:405, but the disparity was softened by using larger figures from a postwar Japanese summary that included their projected aircraft availability by the end of September. Some historians also ignore this fifty-five-hundred-aircraft miscalculation between the estimated and real numbers. For example, John Ray Skates in *The Invasion of Japan: Alternative to the Bomb* (Columbia: University of South Carolina Press, 1994), 109, characterizes U.S. and Japanese figures as "roughly consistent" by making an apples-and-oranges comparison between U.S. assessments of what the Japanese could eventually field with Japanese status reports

of the number of machines available near the war's end. Such glib comparisons ignore the grim reality that the Japanese figures represented only a snapshot gained through Magic intercepts months before Olympic was to be launched and nearly nine months before the target date for Coronet. A highly useful account of the fluctuating American intelligence picture in the spring and summer of 1945 can be found in Frank, *Downfall*, 206–11.

82. Inoguchi and Nakajima with Pineau, *Divine Wind*, 160, 233. These are Imperial Japanese Navy figures only.

83. The Sixth Air Army flew 848 kamikaze and escort missions, and the rounded figure of 500 represents an estimated loss rate generally comparable to that of the Navy. Army sortie total courtesy Drea from Kimata, *Rikugun koku senshi*, 281. The combined totals for operational flights and losses from Inoguchi (Navy) and Kimata (Army) total 2,657 sorties with approximately 1,430 lost or expended. Somewhat larger figures in both categories, of 6,526 and 2,007 respectively, can be compiled from Hattori, *Complete History of the Greater East Asia War* 4:123–31, but Hattori's totals, likely originating at IGHQ, Tokyo, represent the full range of administrative activities and reconnaissance flights, and, judging by the size of the figure, includes aircraft destroyed on the ground during U.S. fighter sweeps in the loss category.

84. Morison, *Two-Ocean War*, 556.

Chapter 9. The "Manpower Box"

1. William B. Shockley to Edward L. Bowles, July 21, 1945, "Proposal for Increasing the Scope of Casualties Studies," War Department study, with attached paper, Quincy Wright, "Historical Study of Casualties," Edward L. Bowles Papers, Box 34, Library of Congress (hereafter cited as Bowles Papers).

2. "Japanese Military Manpower," *Military Research Bulletin*, no. 13, April 25, 1945, 5–9. In the final analysis, the upwardly revised estimate of 5 million—an increase of some 1.5 million men—was short by nearly 500,000 in the initial invasion area and yet another 1.5 million overall. The total number of Japanese armed forces personnel demobilized by the U.S. Military Government in Japan proper after the surrender was 6,465,435; see *Reports*, vol. 1, supplement, 266. See also "Japanese Military Manpower Potential for 1945," *Military Research Bulletin*, no. 18, 4 July 1945, 1–4; and "Japanese System of Defense Call-up," 1–3.

3. JCS 924/2, "Operations Against Japan Subsequent to Formosa," August 30, 1944, 120.

4. Reel 115, Item 2656, National Archives Collection, GCML (also available in RG 165, NARA, and Vertical File, HSTL).

5. Ibid.

6. "Daily Summary of Enemy Intelligence," No. 1209, July 26–27, 1945, 8, Military Intelligence Section, General Staff, United States Army Forces, Pacific, CARL.

7. Comment by anonymous instructor in the Department of Combat Support, USACGSC, circa 1985–1986. The department has since changed its name to Department of Logistics and Resource Operations. Also see Coox, "Japanese Military Intelligence," 200; and Drea, *MacArthur's ULTRA*, 202–25.

8. "Amendment No. 1 to G-2 Estimate of the Enemy Situation with Respect to Kyushu"; and *Reports*, vol. 1, suppl., 266. See also Giangreco, "Casualty Projections," 574–77.

9. Giangreco and Moore, *Dear Harry*, 282–90.

10. For a look at the divergence in thinking between the Pentagon's strategic and logistic staffs when conducting long-range planning, see Giangreco "Casualty Projections," 530–33, 535–39.

11. Matloff, "90-division Gamble," 368.

12. See Henry L. Stimson diary entries of May 10 and 16, 1944, in Bland and Stevens, *Marshall* 4:450–51.

13. Palmer, Wiley, and Keast, *Procurement and Training of Ground Combat Troops*, 234–37. See also Shockley, "Proposal for Increasing the Scope of Casualties Studies"; and Wright, "Historical Study of Casualties."

14. Stimson to Truman, July 2, 1945, memorandum, in Stimson, "Decision to Use the Atomic Bomb," 97–107. At the June 18, 1945, meeting with the president, Marshall stated that because of Japan's mountainous terrain, "the problem would be much more difficult than it had been in Germany." "Joint Chiefs of Staff Corrigendum to JCS 1388," 3.

15. Department of the Army, "Army Battle Casualties," summarized in Giangreco, "Casualty Projections," 540. The final total of Army and Army Air Force casualties stands at 945,515, with Navy, Marine Corps, Coast Guard, and Merchant Marine battle casualties standing at a minimum of 201,937. See Giangreco, "Casualty Projections," 540n. But while the Army figure includes nonbattle deaths, it does not include categories that drained the Army of manpower and were closely monitored at the time by senior military and political leaders. Excluding men returned to duty, these included disability discharges due to nonbattle injuries in combat zones (e.g., loading accidents) totaling 50,520; losses due to disease, including 862,356 discharges; and combat-related psychiatric breakdowns accounting for 312,354 discharges. Resiter,

Medical Statistics in World War II, 13–14, 43. In addition, the Department of the Army, "Army Battle Casualties" does not include 128,598 American prisoners of war who survived their captivities and who, along with the 14,059 U.S. POWs who were confirmed to have died, were counted as casualties during the war but are not included in the postwar casualty totals. POW figures from Skelton, *American Ex-Prisoners of War*, 5, 11.

16. Department of the Army, "Army Battle Casualties," 6.

17. *Diaries of Henry Lewis Stimson*, January 9 and 11, 1945.

18. Ibid.

19. Ibid., January 11, 1945.

20. "Roosevelt Urges Work-or-Fight Bill," 1; "Letters on the Pressing Manpower Problem," 13.

21. Palmer, Wiley, and Keast, *Procurement and Training of Ground Combat Troops*, 221–25.

22. "How Long Will We Have to Fight the Jap War?" *Yank* 3 (June 8, 1945): 2.

23. JCS 924/2, "Operations against Japan Subsequent to Formosa," August 30, 1944, 120.

24. Matloff, "90-division Gamble," 371.

25. Herbert Hoover, "Memorandum on Ending the Japanese War," Stimson "Safe File." See also Walch and Miller, *Herbert Hoover and Harry S. Truman*, 34–37.

26. Reel 115, Item 2656, National Archives Collection, GCML (also available in RG 165, NARA, and Vertical File, HSTL).

27. Ferrell, from panel discussion following "What Did They Know." For Ferrell's presentation, see "The Bomb—the View from Washington," in Ferrell, *Harry S. Truman*, 37–43.

28. Increases in Japanese troop strength were also being leaked by a headquarters far removed from Washington—Adm. Chester

A. Nimitz's press organization. One of these articles ("Palmer Warns No Easy Way to Beat Japs," *Los Angeles Times*, May 17, 1945, p. 5) specifically tied an estimate of up to one million American dead to future combat with five to six million Japanese troops. See also Ferrell, *Harry S. Truman*, 42; and McNaughton and Hehmeyer, *Harry Truman*, 3.

29. The original copy of Hoover's "Memorandum on Ending the Japanese War" (May 30, 1945, memorandum 4 of 4) with Truman's notation, the White House retypes/carbon copies of this document, and the subsequent exchange of memorandums among Truman, Grew, Cordell Hull, Stimson, and Vinson are under State Dept., WWII, Box 43, White House Confidential File, HSTL. The memorandum had been modified significantly in form, but not content, from the document Hoover sent to Stimson after their May 13, 1945 meeting. Both versions of the memorandum are well known with the May 30, 1945, version frequently cited.

30. Grew, *Turbulent Era* 2:1429. For the full text of Stimson's July 2, 1945, memorandum to Truman, see Stimson, "Decision to Use the Atomic Bomb," 97–107. First, second, and final drafts in Stimson "Safe File."

31. Leahy to JCS members Marshall, Henry H. Arnold, and Ernest J. King; Secretary of War Stimson; and Secretary of the Navy James Forrestal, Memo SM-2141, June 14, 1945, in Department of Defense, "Entry of the Soviet Union," 76.

32. "Joint Chiefs of Staff Corrigendum to JCS 1388," 4–5.

33. Ibid.

34. Palmer, Wiley, and Keast, *Procurement and Training of Ground Combat Troops*, 234–37.

35. Shockley-Wright report, Bowles Papers. Shockley extrapolated these numbers from

earlier analyses summarized by DeBakey and Beebe in *Health* (a classified Army publication distributed to senior military planners by the U.S. Army Surgeon General's Office) and others compiled by the Military Intelligence Division from field reports. The analysis was further disseminated to Truman and top administration officials through subsequent reports in June and July 1945, including the June 18, 1945, meeting between the president and the JCS and service secretaries.

36. Shockley-Wright report.

37. Palmer, Wiley, and Keast, *Procurement and Training of Ground Combat Troops*, 237.

38. A very lengthy memorandum prepared by Col. (later Brig. Gen.) John Banville for the committee apparently became much of the basis of an Army Ground Forces study on replacements (Keast, "Provision of Enlisted Replacements") and was further absorbed into a the official Army history of the Army Ground Forces in World War II; Palmer, Wiley, and Keast, *Procurement and Training of Ground Combat Troops*. And as for the Shockley-Wright report, it languished deep in Box 34 of the Bowles Papers, and likely elsewhere, for five decades until it was retrieved by Professor Robert Newman.

39. Their position is most succinctly summed up by Kai Bird in his October 9, 1994, *New York Times* article "The Curators Cave In." Said Bird: "No scholar of the war has ever found archival evidence to substantiate claims that Truman expected anything close to a million casualties, or even that such large numbers were conceivable."

40. The question was recast by Barton Bernstein as (italics in original) "fundamentally about what *top* U.S. officials—not lower and middle-level people—believed." Bernstein maintains: "No scholar has been able to find any *high-level* supporting archival documents from the *Truman months* before Hiroshima

that, in unalloyed form, provides even an explicit estimate of 500,000 casualties, let alone a million or more." Barton Bernstein to the editor, *Journal of Military History* 63 (January 1999): 247; and "Truman and the Bomb: Targeting Noncombatants, Using the Bomb, and Defending the 'Decision,'" *Journal of Military History* 62 (July 1998): 552. In a letter to the editor, *Pacific Historical Review* 69 (2000): 352, Bernstein states, "There is no reliable evidence that in mid-1945 [Truman] anticipated 500,000 or a million U.S. casualties."

41. For Leahy's frequent accompaniment of Truman, see George M. Elsey to author, March 30, 1997. See also Elsey's lengthy introduction to "Blueprints for Victory," 55–77, for information on their visits to the White House Map Room. See also Elsey, *Unplanned Life*, 80–82, 89, 99.

42. Memorandum in Stimson, "Decision to use the Atomic Bomb," 102–4.

43. Ibid., 102.

44. D. M. Giangreco, "The Soldier from Independence: Harry S. Truman and the Great War," *Journal of the Royal Artillery* 130 (Autumn 2003): 56–56. Forthcoming in 2009, *The Soldier from Independence: Harry S. Truman, A Military Biography of Harry S. Truman*, vol. 1, *1906–1919* (Minneapolis: Zenith Press, 2009).

45. Perhaps the best account of how Americans felt about the run-up to the invasion of Japan is Chappell's *Before the Bomb*. Although some of Chappell's conclusions echo revisionist themes, by focusing almost exclusively on "the attitudes, opinions, and perceptions on the home front during the final chaotic months of the war" the author fleshes out our knowledge of the environment in which all life-and-death decisions had to be made in 1945. See also Dower, *War Without Mercy*, 111–16, 133–44.

Chapter 10. Mistakes and Misperceptions

1. Anami to Lord Keeper of the Privy Seal Kido Koichi, June 13, 1945, in Frank, *Downfall*, 99. See also Robert J. C. Butow, *Japan's Decision to Surrender* (Stanford, Calif.: Stanford University Press, 1954), 95–96, 114; Anami, August 9, 1945, in Kazutoshi Hando, *Japan's Longest Day* (Tokyo: Kodansha International, 1968), 27.

2. Naval Intelligence analysis of Ultra communications intercepts excerpted in "'Magic'— Diplomatic Summary," No. 1219, July 27, 1945, CARL; and Frank, *Downfall*, 231–32.

3. Palmer, Wiley, and Keast, *Procurement and Training of Ground Combat Troops*, 234–37. See also Keast, "Provision of Enlisted Replacements," sec. 15, 1–3.

4. Coakley and Leighton, *Global Logistics and Strategy*, 839.

5. Anonymous instructors in the Department of Combat Support, USACGSC, c. 1985–86. Despite coming of age during the Vietnam War, the instructors were obviously the recipients of institutional knowledge from the World War II period.

6. Ibid.

7. Condon-Rall and Cowdry, *Medical Department*, 416. Using Okinawa as a model and excluding soldiers sent back to their units after light care, the figure of 394,859 is broken down to 269,859 losses to disease (scrub typhus, dysentery, etc.) and nonbattle injury (drowning, psychiatric breakdowns, etc.), plus 124,935 serious battle casualties, including 24,987 dead, in "Medical Service in the Asiatic and Pacific Theaters," unpublished monograph, chap. 15, p. 18, Center of Military History, Washington, D.C. The expected deaths among previously captured U.S. and other Allied personnel were not a component of these or any other casualty estimates produced for the invasion of Japan

because they were not part of the U.S. force structure.

8. "Amendment No. 1 to G-2 Estimate of the Enemy Situation with Respect to Kyushu."

9. Drea, *MacArthur's ULTRA*, 202–25.

10. Giangreco, "Casualty Projections," 574–77.

11. A preliminary study recycling material from earlier analyses of a northern approach to Japan via the Aleutian and Kurile islands was already underway. See JWPC 397, "Alternatives to OLYMPIC," August 4, 1945.

12. *Diaries of Henry Lewis Stimson*, July 28–August 10, 1945.

13. Bland and Stevens, *Marshall* 5:246–47; *Reports*, vol. 1, bk. 1, p. 440.

14. "Size of the Army," memorandum, distributed to reporters by General Marshall at an August 7, 1945, press conference, in Bland and Stevens, *Marshall* 5:260. This figure was further broken down in an August 10 memorandum to Admiral Leahy, which noted that approximately 330,000 of these men were projected to be hospitalized troops (Box 74, Folder 20, Marshall Papers Collection, GCML). The Army Medical Corps had earlier estimated that casualties incurred *by summer of 1945* (all theaters) would continue to occupy approximately 50,000 beds in June 1946 with approximately 5,000 more occupied by personnel from noncombat theaters and CONUS. This means that the Army, at senior levels, was expecting something on the order of 280,000 cases *serious enough* to require hospitalization in the United States from operations in Japan, and the estimate does not include (1) Navy-Marine personnel; (2) Army patients in "forward" hospitals, including Hawaii, the Philippines, and Australia; (3) Army patients discharged and sent back to their units; (4) patients moved into the Veterans Administration system; or (5) "Killed in Action—Died of Wounds." See also "Casualty Projections," 567.

15. When the atom bomb exploded, it was 8:15 am on Monday, August 6, in Hiroshima, 9:15 am on Tinian, where the bomber was launched, and 7:15 pm on Sunday, August 5, in Washington, D.C.. A report was issued to newsmen at the White House the following morning, and Monday evening papers throughout the country carried the stunning news under banner headlines on August 6, but the story had come too late to make the Late City Edition of the *New York Times*. Instead, the *Times* ran the story in its Tuesday, August 7, editions and made it a point to make it clear to readers that the atom bomb was dropped "about the time that citizens on the Eastern seaboard were sitting down to their Sunday suppers."

16. Selwyn Pepper, interview with author, May 13, 2004, Overland Park, Kans. Major Pepper, the officer giving the briefing, noted that the figure was released with the approval of the chief public relations officer, Brig. Gen. LeGrande A. "Pick" Diller, and "very likely" MacArthur himself. Approximately fifty reporters were present from all major American news organizations as well as some from Britain and Australia. Discussions with reporters centered around the fact that "the Japanese still had their forces intact on Japan and [that] they had armed every civilian with a spear to defend their own homes." Pepper won three Pulitzers before and after the war for his work at the *St. Louis Post-Dispatch* and later held several senior editorial positions at the paper.

17. JCS 924, "Operations Against Japan Subsequent to Formosa," June 30, 1944. The recently approved JCS 1417, "Operations Following Invasion of Kanto Plain (Broad Plans)," and certainly others as well, offered a range of possible invasion sites to consider. However, the act of examining alternate sites is not the same as finding a site that meets

enough of the required criteria to act as a reasonable substitute to Olympic.

18. Barton J. Bernstein states, "The skimpy evidence—a few early August 1945 memos by Hull and Lincoln—does not suggest that these two men were deeply worried. Rather there is some hint that Lincoln sincerely had doubts about the ULTRA reports, that both men believed that Marshall strongly wanted to go ahead with Olympic, and that the two men were seeking to head off pressures from other planners." Barton J. Bernstein, "The Alarming Japanese Buildup on Southern Kyushu, Growing U.S. Fears, and Counterfactual Analysis: Would the Planned November 1945 Invasion Of Southern Kyushu Have Occurred?" *Pacific Historical Review* 68 (1999): 583.

19. Galen Roger Rerras, "We Have Opened the Door to Tokyo: United States Plans To Seize the Kurile Islands, 1943–1945," *Journal of Military History* 61 (1997): 65–91. See also Futrell and Taylor, "Reorganization for Victory," 677; and Brian Garfield, *The Thousand-Mile War: World War II in Alaska and the Aleutians* (Garden City, N.Y.: Doubleday, 1969).

20. This assumes that invasion shipping running parallel to the coast would maintain a distance of at least three hundred miles in order to provide time to locate and intercept marauding Japanese aircraft before turning west toward northern Honshu. The considerably less vulnerable carrier task forces commonly maneuvered from 200 to 250 miles out at sea then closed to within 100 miles when launching strikes. Morison, *USNOWWII* 14:315.

21. JWPC 397, "Alternatives to OLYMPIC," August 4, 1945.

22. Gordon A. Harrison, *Cross-Channel Attack*, USAWWII series (Washington, D.C.: Center of Military History, United States Army, 1951), 36–44, 79.

23. Willoughby, "Occupation of Japan," 3–4. During a spring 1978 conversation with Maj. Gen. John J. Maginnis, USA (Ret.) in Cambridge, Massachusetts, Maginnis related to the author that Willoughby once told him that the size, and "especially the nature" of Japan's preparations, combined with the "inexorable countdown" toward the invasion date, rendered alternative sites "useless." Maginnis said that Willoughby was interested in using B-29s tactically as well as poison gas to "up the ante" on Kyushu's defenders.

24. The general dearth of population in the Aomori Prefecture would work to the advantage of a Sixth Army landing in the Ominato–Mutsu Bay area, but its extreme distance from U.S. air bases on Okinawa and Iwo Jima meant that an invasion there would have to be supported almost exclusively from carriers operating in gale-swept northern waters. The area had also not been thoroughly examined to see if it would make an appropriate base from which to launch an assault toward Tokyo, and it was too far removed from the Tsushima Straits to act as barrier against Japanese reinforcements being sent from Korea and China to Japan.

25. CINCPAC Command Summary, bk. 7, pp. 3508–10, NHC. War Department transmission WAR-45369, August 7, 1945, is also available through MMA and National Archives Collection, X1297, GCML.

26. CINCPAC Command Summary, bk. 7, pp. 3508–10, August 9, 1945, NHC. While messages pertaining to routine operational matters were passed directly between MacArthur's and Nimitz's headquarters, all messages related to war strategy were routed through the opposite theater commander's superior in Washington as per strict interser-

vice protocol, and were functionally written as much for the opposite superior's eyes as for the adjacent theater commander.

27. Said Drea: "MacArthur consistently dismissed ULTRA evidence that failed to accord with his preconceived strategic vision. . . . MacArthur thought in strategic terms and was willing to take calculated risks to achieve higher goals. Likewise he was willing to ignore intelligence that contradicted that strategic appreciation to which he was committed. Paradoxically, such steadfast-ness of purpose is essential for a successful commander. ULTRA was normally ambig-uous, and to use it effectively, a commander had to be straightforward and clear about his plans and objectives" (Drea, *MacArthur's ULTRA*, 230).

28. CINCPAC Command Summary, bk. 7, p. 3510. Even though all of these messages were sent "Eyes Only," which meant that they, and any copies, were not to be filed with routine message traffic but, instead, were subject to a higher level of security, some later observers have attached additional, and frequently conspiratorial, meaning to the term. For example, Bernstein, not understanding how message traffic was handled and routed, finds significance in King not personally instructing Nimitz to insert the classifica-tion into a message, and thinks that King is allowing a series of supposedly back-channel communications to be seen by MacArthur and thus, Bernstein supposes, "produce a near crisis" when MacArthur saw them (see below).

In fact, when the initial message in an exchange was tagged "Eyes Only," all subsequent messages in the exchange simply repeated the classification. Bernstein appar-ently did not realize, first, that all parties' headquarters had been receiving the commu-nications from the start (see note 25 above),

and, second, that the classification has to do with how the message is handled and filed. As a result Bernstein perceives dark motives behind Admiral King's request that Nimitz send comments on MacArthur's reply to both him and MacArthur, mistaking routine message traffic for an attempt by King to goad MacArthur into a confrontation over supposed Navy opposition to invading Japan.

Having Nimitz put MacArthur specifi-cally on an "information line" as was done here ensures that the message was seen by MacArthur personally in case the exchange of messages was only being reviewed by his chief of staff, Lt. Gen. Richard K. Sutherland. (It is noteworthy that intra-Army communications were handled slightly differently and had their own problems in this regard. For example, earlier that summer General Marshall, when soliciting MacArthur's opinion of possible casualties during Olympic ahead of a hastily called meeting with the president, quickly recognized that his questions had been routed to either Sutherland or MacArthur's G-3, Gen. Stephen J. Chamberlain. This forced Marshall to shoot back a request for clarification, but this time, instead of from "Washington" to Headquarters AFPAC and signed "Marshall," it was from "General Marshall" to "General MacArthur (Personal)." See Giangreco, "Casualty Projections," 545-50.)

King did not direct that Nimitz put MacArthur on the addressee line—the "action line" requiring a response—and the search by some for hidden meaning to King's order requires one to believe that King was engaging in subtleties not characteristic of his well-documented dealings with the Navy's sister service and his subordinates. Bernstein maintains, however, that "King's decision not to restrict Nimitz's reply to an 'eyes only to King' message is significant. Sending a copy of Nimitz's message to MacArthur, if Nimitz's assessment was negative (as would have seemed likely), could produce a bureaucratic conflict in the Pacific and difficulty in Washington."

Bernstein, after stating that King had "suppressed" Nimitz's message from several months earlier expressing reservations about Olympic, then proposed that King "seemed to be triggering events that were likely to produce a near crisis" (Bernstein, "Alarming Japanese Buildup," 587–88). Unfortunately, Frank (*Downfall*, 276) apparently examined copies of the exchange that did not include the transmissions' addressee and information lines which led him to similarly miss that all parties were being kept abreast of their exchange, as per interservice protocol, and that King wisely wished to ensure that Nimitz's response would be read by MacArthur, not just his chief of staff.

29. King, *U.S. Navy at War*, 188–89.

30. Brown, *Bodyguard of Lies* 1:43–49, 61, 220; and Capt. F. W. Winterbotham, *The Ultra Secret* (New York: Harper & Row, 1974), 82–84, whose accounts are convincingly debunked by R. V. Jones, *The Wizard War: British Scientific Intelligence, 1939–1945* (New York: Coward, McCann, & Geoghegan, 1978), 146–52; and N. E. Evans, "Air Intelligence and the Coventry Raid," *Journal of the Royal United Services Institute* 121 (September 1976): 66–73.

31. See note 26 above. To a certain degree this was also relevant to officers across the senior command structure.

32. "Joint Staff Study, OLYMPIC," 5, produced under the direction of Adm. Forrest Sherman, Deputy Chief of Staff, COMINCH. Updated through at least July 8, 1945.

33. King, *U.S. Navy at War*, 188. Interestingly, misinterpretations of how the message traffic among King, Nimitz, Marshall, and MacArthur was addressed and distributed

has led some scholars to speculate that King intended to force a change in Pacific war strategy and pursue a course far different from what he states here, in that the invasion would be put off indefinitely. See notes 25 and 27 above. Similarly, Nimitz's lack of response to King's query of August 9, 1945, led Frank (*Downfall*, 356–57) to speculate that "Admiral Nimitz [was] poised to announce to Army and civilian officials that he no longer supported an invasion of Japan." When Larry Bland, the editor of the *Papers of George Catlett Marshall*, was asked to comment on the notion that the Navy and Admiral King were operating as an independent power center willing and able to make or break presidential decisions by withdrawing or granting "support," he responded (August 3, 2005): "I find it hard to believe that even Ernie King would risk the wrath of both HST [Truman] and Marshall on an issue of such importance. . . . Marshall had the experience of Okinawa and Iwo and other places where the Japanese wouldn't surrender on his side, while King could only *assert* that naval blockade alone would win. . . . If King went along with Marshall's plans, the Navy might gripe; but if King convinced HST to risk everything on a blockade, and surrender didn't happen quickly, he risked a major catastrophe in Congress and the press. Which one would you choose?"

34. JWPC 398/1, "Plan for the Invasion of Northern Honshu (Alternative to Invasion of Southern Kyushu)," August 9, 1945.

35. William Manchester, *American Caesar: Douglas MacArthur, 1880–1964* (Boston: Little, Brown, 1978), 160.

36. Interestingly, the record depth of 209 centimeters (6.9 feet) of ground snow was recorded earlier that same year in January 1945 (International Relations Section,

Aomori City Office, http://www.city.aomori.
aomori.jp/english/engd01.html/).

37. "Weather in the Tohoku Region, Aomori
City," from *Chronological Scientific Tables,
National Astronomical Observatory of Japan*
(Tokyo: Maruzen, 1988), n.p.

38. *Foreign Relations of the United States,
Diplomatic Papers, 1945*, vol. 6, *The British
Commonwealth, The Far East* (Washington,
D.C.: GPO, 1969), 627, 631–32; Marc
Gallicchio, "After Nagasaki: General
Marshall's Plan for Tactical Nuclear Weapons
in Japan," *Prologue* 23 (Winter 1991):
396–404, esp. 397–98; Kort, "Casualty
Projections," 68–72, and 324–26; Morison,
USNOWWII 14:282; Craven and Cate, in
AAFWWII 5:732; and Bland and Stevens,
Marshall 5:266–69.

39. Sadao Asada, "The Shock of the Atomic
Bomb and Japan's Decision to Surrender—A
Reconsideration," *Pacific Historical Review*
67 (November 1998). This article is also
available in Maddox, *Hiroshima in History*,
24–58. See also Butow, *Japan's Decision to
Surrender*, 160–205; and Tristan Grunow, "A
Reexamination of the 'Shock of Hiroshima':
The Japanese Bomb Projects and the
Surrender Decision," *Journal of East Asian
Relations* 12 (Fall–Winter 2003): 155–89.
Grunow argues convincingly that the early
refusal of Japanese scientists to admit that
the nuclear weapons were being used against
Japan further delayed the surrender.

40. Bland and Stevens, *Marshall* 5:271.

41. Josette H. Williams, "The Information War
in the Pacific, 1945," *Studies in Intelligence*
(unclassified edition) 46, no. 3 (Summer
2002).

42. Although he had not yet been formally
briefed on the matter, Truman would have
at least been aware of the Japanese buildup
in general terms if by no other means than
through his regular visits to the White House
Map Room and the *White House Summary*
produced daily by the Current Section of
the War Department. Map Room watch
officer George M. Elsey notes that the details
of the buildup were so freshly acquired that
he and the Map Room staff, as yet, had
"no comprehension of how massive it was"
(Elsey to author, December 1, 2006). Thus
while they were cleared to see the "Magic"
summaries, the Map Room staff was in the
same boat as everyone else in that they also
had to deal with a flood of other incoming
data as well as the irregular delays that came
with the dissemination of intelligence materials. The president had no personal meetings
with General Marshall between July 25 at
the Potsdam Conference (where the atom
bomb and future operations were discussed
with Lord Louis Mountbatten) and Japan's
capitulation.

43. Larry Bland, telephone conversation with
author, c. November 7, 2005.

44. Although Truman and his most senior
military and civilian advisors proceeded with
invasion plans while fully cognizant that
casualties for the duration of the war could
well match those suffered by the United
States during the fighting against Germany
(see chapters 6 and 9), the extensive
Ketsu-Go No. 6 reinforcement on Kyushu
threatened to both delay base construction
on Kyushu and sap resources needed for
Operation Coronet on Honshu. Frank carefully notes that "the Japanese buildup on
Kyushu was sufficient to threaten to make
the cost of invasion unacceptable" (*Downfall*,
343), but Bernstein speculates that the
United States might have given up its war
aims, and the title of his article in the *Pacific
Historical Review* (68 [November 1999]:
561–609) is self-explanatory: "The Alarming
Japanese Buildup on Southern Kyushu,
Growing U.S. Fears, and Counterfactual

Analysis: Would the Planned November 1945 Invasion Of Southern Kyushu Have Occurred?" Robert James Maddox wrote in response (69 [May 2000]: 349–50): "Whereas before [Bernstein] had claimed that the mid-June [casualty] estimates were so low as to raise 'troubling questions' about using the bombs, his new bag is that they were so high as to have appalled Truman. Therefore, Bernstein asserts without any evidence (he lards his prose instead with 'probably,' 'most probably,' and the like), that the Japanese troop buildup on Kyushu eventually would have caused Truman either to switch the site of the invasion or to have given up American war aims by canceling it altogether. The latter provides the ultimate low casualty figure Bernstein has been searching for all these years: Zero."

45. The carefully considered target set of Hiroshima, Niigata, Kokura, and Nagasaki had been developed by Secretary Stimson's "Interim Committee" in conjunction with other agencies and approved by Stimson with Truman's concurrence while at the Potsdam Conference. See Vincent C. Jones, *Manhattan: The Army and the Atomic Bomb*, USAWWII series (Washington, D.C.: Center of Military History, United States Army, 1985), 534. After the first atom bomb was dropped, seemingly "everyone was trying to get into the act" as senior military leaders, including Nimitz and Spaatz, made recommendations of a half-dozen other cities for the third bomb's target (Bland telephone conversation with author; and Frank, *Downfall*, 303).

46. *Army and Navy Journal* publisher John Callan O'Laughlin in letter to Herbert Hoover, August 11, 1945, Post Presidential Individual File, HL; courtesy Maddox and Gary Clifford. Also see chapter 6, note 34.

47. Cate and Olson, in Craven and Cate, *AAFWWII* 5:638, 827 fn114.

48. Anthony Eden, *The Reckoning: The Memoirs of Anthony Eden, Earl of Avon* (Boston: Houghton Mifflin, 1965), 613–14.

49. Gallicchio, "After Nagasaki," 398–400.

50. Bonnett, "Jekyll and Hyde," 174–212, esp. 192–93, 196–97; and Robert P. Newman, "Hiroshima and the Trashing of Henry Stimson," *New England Quarterly* 71 (March 1998): 5–32, esp. 20–22 (also available in Maddox, *Hiroshima in History*, 146-170). Also, Bland telephone conversation with author.

51. Gallicchio, "After Nagasaki," 400–402.

52. Ibid., 398. Gallicchio notes in a February 14, 2007, letter to the author that his cite for the memorandum from Groves to Handy regarding the shipment of bomb components should have stated that the order was written on August 13, 1945, not August 14 as was given in his note 13. The minor error in the endnote does not change the accuracy of Gallicchio's narrative. See also Bonnett, "Jekyll and Hyde."

53. Skates, *Invasion of Japan*, 94, citing Marshall memorandum to Admiral King in "U.S. Chemical Warfare Policy," June 14, 1945, OPD 385 TS, RG q65, NARA.

54. Bland and Stevens, *Marshall* 5:206.

55. Skates, *Invasion of Japan*, 95, citing USAFPAC to TAG, July 6, 1945, File No. AG 381 TS, OPD 385 TS, sec. 1, Cases 5–14, 17 February 1945–13 August 1945, RG 165; and Memo for the Secretary, Joint Chiefs of Staff, August 13, 1945, in "Availability and Production of Chemical Munitions," August 9, 1945, OPD 385 TS, RG 165, both in NARA.

56. Drea, *In the Service of the Emperor*, 154–68; Pogue, *Marshall Interviews*, 425; Robert James Maddox, *Weapons for Victory: The Hiroshima Decision Fifty Years Later*

(Columbia: University of Missouri Press, 1995), 82–85; and Harvey H. Bundy, August 29, 1960, in Bonnett, "Jekyll and Hyde," 204.

57. Japanese Monograph No. 17, "Homeland Operations," 90, 133.

58. *Reports* 1:427–30; *Reports*, vol. 1, suppl., pp. 117–18, 427–30; *Reports* vol. 2, bk. 2, pp. 657–68 (esp. fn. 163); Japanese Monograph No. 17, "Homeland Operations," 80–86; Hattori, *Complete History of the Greater East Asia War* 4:195–98; "Explanatory Data to Estimate of Situation for Spring of 1946," 18–44; *Defense Strategy and Tactics*, "Appended Chart No 1, Chart for the concentration in Operation KETSU 3," n.p., and "The Employment of Strength," n.p.; plus Haruko Taya Cook, "Nagano 1945: Hirohito's Secret Hideout," *Military History Quarterly* 10 (Spring 1998): 44–47.

Chapter 11. What Is Defeat?

1. Although the 100 million population figure cited in the epigraph was a staple of both Japanese internal and external propaganda efforts during this period (as in "100 million fiery bullets against the enemy"), the population within the Home Islands was closer to 70 million at wars' end with 6,614,200 ethnic Japanese (3,163,200 of them civilians) eligible for repatriation from its lost overseas territories (*Reports*, vol. 1, suppl., p. 148). The balance of the 100 million figure is made up of approximately 23 million Koreans, 5 million Formosans (Taiwanese), and other groups, such as Okinawans. Japan's 1940 census of the empire fixed its population at 105,226,101 (*The 1943 World Almanac and Book of Facts*, New York: New York World-Telegram, 196–98).

2. Paul Fussell, *Thank God for the Atom Bomb and Other Essays* (New York: Summit Books, 1988), 27. In the original quote from the "Fifth Air Force Weekly Intelligence Review," No. 86, Col. Harry F. Cunningham placed the words "There are no civilians in Japan" in all capital letters. See Craven and Cate, *AAFWWII* 5:696–97.

3. Figure from the USSBS's "The Effects of Atomic Bombs on Health and Medical Services in Hiroshima and Nagasaki," No. 13, in Jones, *Manhattan*, 547. Frank notes (*Downfall*, 285–87) that the Japanese Economic Stabilization Board report of April 1949, based on a November 1945 accounting by the Police Department of the Hiroshima Prefecture, lists the number of people killed at Hiroshima at 78,150, and that, much later, a questionable accounting of bombing survivors subtracted from a conjectural population estimate at the time of the bombing produced an estimate of over 200,000 deaths for Hiroshima.

4. *Reports*, vol. 2, bk. 1, p. 33; and Hattori, *Complete History of the Greater East Asia War* 2:1, citing *Konoye Ayamaro Ko Shuki* (*Memoirs of Prince Ayamaro Konoye*), 30. Some translations replace "but I have utterly no confidence for the second or third year" with "after that, I have no expectation of success."

5. Giangreco and Moore, *Eyewitness D-DAY*, 252.

6. These figures are drawn principally from Michael Clodfelter, *Warfare and Armed Conflicts: A Statistical Reference to Casualties and Other Figures, 1618–1991*, vol. 2, *1900–1991* (Jefferson, N.C.: McFarland, 1992), 2:956, and I am indebted to Werner Gruhl, author of *Imperial Japan's World War Two, 1931–1945* (Piscataway, N.J.: Transaction Publishers, Rutgers University, 2006), for assistance in researching this subject. See

also Donald Niewyk Francis Nicosia, *The Columbia Guide to the Holocaust* (New York: Columbia University Press, 2000), 45–52. Although Holocaust victims west of the post-1939 Soviet border in Eastern Europe are included in these figures, they do not incorporate two significant categories. First is the approximately 2 million Soviet Holocaust victims, perhaps a third of whom were exterminated early in the war by Einsatzkommanda (action squads) after they were overrun by German forces instead of being shipped to concentration camps in Poland, where most internees subsequently died. The second is made up of the roughly 50 percent of the nearly 2.2 million German deaths, principally by starvation, exposure, and mob action, among the 10.7 million civilians ejected from eastern Germany and other locations in the East that occurred in the immediate postwar period. Inclusion of the postwar German deaths and extermination of Soviet Holocaust victims who survived into 1944–45 could likely raise the civilian death toll during, and immediately after, the collapse of the Nazi regime by approximately 2 million people.

7. Shockley-Wright report, Bowles Papers.

8. Allen and Polmar, *Code-Name Downfall*, 173–19; Jeffery K. Smart, "History of Chemical and Biological Warfare: An American Perspective," in *Medical Aspects of Chemical and Biological Warfare*, ed. Frederick R. Sidell et al. (Washington, D.C.: Office of the Surgeon General, United States Army, 1997), 35–46; and Frederic J. Brown, *Chemical Warfare: A Study in Restraints* (Princeton, N.J.: Princeton University Press, 1968), 262–65.

9. George W. Merck to Gen. George C. Marshall, "Sub: Destruction of Crops by 'LN' Chemicals," March 8, 1945, memo-

randum, ABC 475.92 (February 2, 1944), sec. 1-B, RG 165, NARA.

10. "Report by the Joint Staff Planners and Joint Logistics Committee on Policy on Use of Chemical Agents for the Destruction of Japanese Food Crops," sec. 1-B, RG 165, NARA.

11. From notes taken by Lt. George L. McColm, USNR, during a February 1945 briefing at the Civil Affairs Staging Area (CASA), Monterey, California, by Col. William A. Hartman on the "U.S. Basic Policy for Invasion and Occupation of Japan," Papers of George L. McColm, HSTL.

12. Interview with George L. McColm, U.S. Navy (Ret.), March 18, 1995, 19–20, Admiral Nimitz Foundation and University of North Texas Oral History Collection, Fredericksburg, Tex. See also George L. McColm, Oral History Interview, May 20–21, 1991, 75–79, HSTL; and *Civil Affairs Handbook, JAPAN, Section 7: Agriculture*, Army Service Forces Manual M354-7, Department of the Army Pamphlet 8-3153, Army Service Forces, Washington, D.C., April 1, 1944, 50, 151–54. The principal benefit to tactical planners of dry fields was increased vehicle mobility, and agricultural planners were also tasked with examining the load-bearing capacity of the soil.

13. "Assumptions and Policies for Civil Affairs Projects," February 7, 1945, in ASF-P-SL-2, "Logistic Study for Projected Operations, Kyushu" *History History of Planning Division, ASF*, vol. 7, Appendix 9-R, Planning Division, Office of Director of Plans and Operations, Army Service Forces, 33, CARL. Japanese concerns regarding a partial evacuation of southern Kyushu, ncluding care of refeguees is briefly outlined

in Hattori, *Complete History of the Greater East Asia War* 4:194.

14. "Assumptions and Policies for Civil Affairs Projects," July 1945, in ASF-P-SL-1, "Ligistic Study for Projected Operations, Honshu (Tokyo Plains)" *History of Planning Division, ASF*, vol. 6, Appendix 9-A to 9-Q, Planning Division, Office of Director of Plans and Operations, Army Service Forces, 36, CARL.

15. McColm, telephone interview.

16. Michael Kort, *The Columbia Guide to Hiroshima and the Bomb* (New York: Columbia University Press, 2007), 411n15; and Maddox, *Weapons for Victory*, 84–85.

17. McColm, telephone interview.

18. "Final Report Covering Air-Raid Protection and Allied Subjects in Japan, United States Strategic Bombing Survey, Pacific," No. 62, Civilian Defense Division, Tokyo, 1947, 171.

19. Cate and Olson, in Craven and Cate, *AAFWWII* 5:662–74; and Morison, *USNOWWII* 14:291–93. See also JIC 266/1, "Defeat of Japan by Blockade and Bomb," April 18, 1945, in Cline, *Washington Command Post*, 343.

20. Vice Adm. Arthur W. Radford, commander, Task Group 38.4, to reporters aboard the USS *Yorktown*, early August 1945, in Dower, *War Without Mercy*, 55.

21. *Civil Affairs Handbook, JAPAN, Section 7: Agriculture*, 85–109.

22. "USSBS Summary Report, Pacific War," No. 1, Office of the Chairman, USSBS, Washington, D.C., 1946.

23. Cate and Olson, in Craven and Cate, *AAFWWII* 5:743.

24. McColm telephone interview; and Theodore Cohen, *Remaking Japan: The American Occupation as New Deal*, English ed., ed. Herbert Passin (New York: Free Press, 1987), 141; see also 137–46. In 1946 Cohen was the chief of the Occupation Authority's Labor Division, where he helped push through important labor reforms.

25. Maurice Matloff, *Strategic Planning for Coalition Warfare, 1943–1944*, USAWWII series (Washington, D.C.: Center of Military History, United States Army, 1959), 488.

26. *History of the Medical Department of the United States Navy in World War II*, 2 vols. (Washington, D.C.: Department of the Navy, 1953), 1:174. This document explains that the "Saipan operation, as the midphase of the offensive against the Japanese, lends itself well to a portrayal of amphibious medical service, afloat and ashore. There was both furious resistance on the beachhead reminiscent of Tarawa, and prolonged fighting over rugged terrain that gave the Medical Department an opportunity to establish itself fully on shore."

27. Shaw, Natly, and Turnbladh, *Central Pacific Drive*, 345; plus Allen and Polmar, *Code-Name Downfall*, 167.

28. Crowl, *Campaign in the Marianas*, 264–65.

29. Maj. Carl W. Hoffman, USMC, *The Seizure of Tinian* (Washington, D.C.: Historical Branch G-3 Division, Headquarters USMC, 1951), 141.

30. Allen and Polmar, *Code-Name Downfall*.

31. W. Robert Moore, "South from Saipan," *National Geographic* 87 (April 1945): 441–74.

32. Repeated American requests that civilians be allowed to leave, radioed in the clear and on Japanese frequencies, were ignored by naval commanders (*Reports*, vol. 1, bk. 1, p. 275). A partial list of body counts (five hundred to seven thousand dead) from the February massacres, by location, compiled by the Philippine government's 1951 Quirino Presidential Committee of Secretary of Economic Coordination, Salvador Araneta, can be found in Richard Connaughton, John

Pimlott, and Duncan Anderson, *The Battle for Manila* (London: Bloomsbury, 1995), 174–75; see also 15, 110–11, 107–38, 144–55, 168–69, 195–96; Robert R. Smith, *Triumph in the Philippines*, USAWWII series (Washington, D.C.: Center of Military History, United States Army, 1991), 264; and "Japanese Defense of Cities as Exemplified by the Battle for Manila, A Report by XIV Corps," Assistant Chief of Staff, G-2, Headquarters, Sixth Army, Manila, July 1, 1945, 16–17, 26, CARL.

33. Condon-Rall and Cowdry, *Medical Department*, 408–10; Roy E. Appleman, James M. Burns, Russell A. Gugeler, and John Stevens, *Okinawa: The Last Battle*, USAWWII series (Washington, D.C.: Center of Military History, United States Army, 1948), 415–19. See also Belote and Belote, *Typhoon of Steel*, 310; plus Hayashi and Coox, *Kogun*, 215.

34. Condon-Rall and Cowdry, *Medical Department*.

35. Joseph D. Harrington, *Yankee Samurai: The Secret Role of Nisei in America's Pacific Victory* (Detroit: Petigrew Enterprises, 1979), 221–23, 225–27, 231–34, 240–41; also Belote and Belote, *Typhoon of Steel*, 315–17.

36. Belote and Belote, *Typhoon of Steel*, 279–80, 303, 315; and Harrington, *Yankee Samurai*, 245.

37. Condon-Rall and Cowdry, *Medical Department*, 409.

38. Belote and Belote, *Typhoon of Steel*, 279; and Col. Hiromichi Yahara, *The Battle for Okinawa* (New York: John Wiley & Sons, 1995), 99–101, 105–6, 135–38, 199–200. Leaflets also instructed civilians to travel in groups and gather along the closest points to them on the coastal highways, and the Japanese command on Okinawa also instructed them to seek refuge in the Chinen area which it correctly perceived to be off the U.S. Tenth Army's axis of advance.

39. Dower, *War Without Mercy*, 240–50, 256–61.

40. Asada, "Shock of the Atomic Bomb," 505–8, esp. quote from *Diary of Marquis Kido*, 507; Robert P. Newman, *Truman and the Hiroshima Cult* (Lansing: Michigan State University Press, 1995), quoting Prime Minister Suzuki Kantaro and Chief Cabinet Secretary Sakomizu Hisatsume, 48–49; and John W. Dower quoting Emperor Hirohito's surrender broadcast, *Embracing Defeat: Japan in the Wake of World War II* (New York: W. W. Norton, 1999), 36. See also Grunow, "Reexamination." Ferrell writes, in *Harry S. Truman and the Bomb: A Documentary History* (Worland, Wyo.: High Plains, 1996), 37–39, that "as the war was coming to an end the Americans, British, and Soviets were publicly stating that they would arraign war criminals, but Tokyo officials deluded themselves into believing it would be possible to bargain to save the people involved; they had in mind an arrangement that would put the matter delicately, in terms of preserving the imperial institution, so that Japanese authorities rather than the Allies would hold war-crimes trials."

41. Hattori, *Complete History of the Greater East Asia War* 4:194; *Reports*, vol. 2, bk. 2, p. 619; and Coox, *Final Agony*, 78.

42. "Estimate of Situation for Spring of 1946," 18–19.

43. Kengo Tominaga, ed., *Gendaishi shiryo* (*Documents on Contemporary History*), vol. 5, *Taiheiyo senso* (*Pacific War*) (Tokyo: Misuzu shobo, 1975), 756, in Asada, "Shock of the Atom Bomb," esp. 491–94. Asada notes that there are forty-five volumes in *Gendaishi shiryo*, of which five are on the Pacific war.

44. Butow, *Japan's Decision to Surrender*, 99.

45. Saburo Ienaga, *The Pacific War* (New York: Pantheon Books, 1978), 150.

46. From a summary under "Separate Volume 1B Part II, Outline of the Concentration Plan for the Homeland Operation," in "Japanese Defense Strategy and Tactics," n.p. See also *Reports*, vol. 2, bk. 2, pp. 609, 612; Coox, *Final Agony*, 71; Frank, *Downfall*, 188–90; Allen and Polmar, *Code-Name Downfall*, 167–68.

47. Hattori, *Complete History of the Greater East Asia War* 4:282–85, 486–94.

48. Coox, *Final Agony*, 93.

49. Stephen C. Mercado, *The Shadow Warriors of Nakano: A History of the Imperial Japanese Army's Elite Intelligence School* (Washington, D.C.: Brassey's, 2002), 125–27, 150–61.

50. Coox, *Final Agony*, 57.

51. Ibid., 88–89.

52. Edward J. Drea to author, December 13, 2006. Quote from Drea's presentation at the Admiral Nimitz Museum Conference, March 1995, appears in his *In the Service of the Emperor* as chapter 10, "Japanese Preparations for the Defense of the Homeland," 147.

53. Shockley-Wright report, Bowles Papers.

54. Statement at an August 13, 1945, meeting with Army Chief of Staff, General Umeza Yoshijiro; Chief of Naval General Staff, Admiral Toyoda Soemu; and Foreign Minister Togo Shigenori in Butow, *Japan's Decision to Surrender*, 204–5. Lord Keeper of the Privy Seal Marquis Kido Koichi also used the figure of twenty million when speaking to an interrogator for the Tokyo War Crimes Trials, but he characterized the figure as representing "casualties" instead of deaths. See Robert P. Newman, "The Trashing of Henry Stimson," in Maddox, *Hiroshima in History*, 152. For Emperor Hirohito's private views on what was most critical for Japan's

survival see John W. Dower, *Embracing Defeat:* see p. 297, 289–90.

55. "Joint Chiefs of Staff Corrigendum to JCS 1388," 5.

Chapter 12. The Amphibious Operation

1. "Essentials for the Directing of Surface and Submarine Special Attack Operations," in "Japanese Defense Strategy and Tactics," n.p.

2. Samuel Eliot Morison, *USNOWWII*, vol. 13, *The Liberation of the Philippines: Luzon, Mindanao, the Visayas* (Boston: Little, Brown, 1959), 139.

3. Samuel Eliot Morison, *USNOWWII*, vol. 11, *The Invasion of France and Germany, 1944–1945* (Boston: Little, Brown, 1957), 101. These figures include airborne elements, Army Air Force personnel, Navy shore parties engaged in logistic operations, and likely their British equivalents as well. At least two of the soldiers who came ashore on D-day were women, Iris Bower and Molly Giles of the Princess Mary's RAF Nursing Service assigned to the British Number 50 Mobile Field Hospital (Giangreco and Moore, *Eyewitness D-DAY*, 16, 70, 170–72, 209–10. The frequency of Japanese banzai charges, which sometimes reached deep into rear areas as at Attu and Guam where field hospitals was overrun and Okinawa, effectively guaranteed that no women would take part in Operation Olympic until, perhaps, its later stages.

4. "Operation 'OLYMPIC' Amphibious and Heavy Cargo Shipping Requirements, X-Day to X+15," in "Staff Study, Operations, 'OLYMPIC,'" Appendix B, Annex 4, Basic Logistic Plan, n.p., General Headquarters, Army Forces, Pacific, May 28, 1944. In addition to the nine divisions, one regi-

mental combat team, and support elements assaulting Kyushu, this figure includes the 40th Infantry Division securing the outer islands before X-day but excludes three divisions of IX Corps which would not land until four or more days later, the 158th Regimental Combat Team which was available for a number of contingencies, or follow-on divisions.

5. Morison, *USNOWWII* 11:77. Morison also notes that these ships carried another 5,333 landing craft. Also see Giangreco and Moore, *Eyewitness D-DAY*, 43–51, 60–66, 72, 111–24.

6. Extrapolated from King, *U.S. Navy at War*, 196–97; JCS 1388/4, "Details of the Campaign Against Japan," 33; and Vice Adm. George Carroll Dyer, USN, *The Amphibians Came to Conquer: The Story of Admiral Richmond Kelly Turner* (Washington, D.C.: U.S. Navy Dept., 1972), 1105 (assault shipping figure for Olympic from 1109).

7. Dyer, *Amphibians Came to Conquer.*

8. Grover, *U.S. Army Ships and Watercraft*, xi–xv, 3–6, 50, 55–58, 238, 250–51; and *Reports* 1:181–83. See also *ESP*, vol. 2, *Organization Troops and Training* (Tokyo: Office of the Chief Engineer, General Headquarters, Army Forces, Pacific, 1953), 73–88; and *ESP* 1:199–200, 205–6, 223.

9. *Reports*, vol. 2, bk. 2, pp. 653–54.

10. JCS 1388/4, "Details of the Campaign Against Japan," 33.

11. Skates, *Invasion of Japan*, 129.

12. Battle casualties amounting to 28,666 on Iwo Jima are detailed in Morison, *USNOWWII* 14:69. Battle casualties on Okinawa stand at 39,262, with figures frequently stated for ground force "losses" running from 65,631 to 72,000, when including the addition of 26,211 to 33,096 nonbattle casualties. "U.S. Tenth Army Action Report, Ryukyus, 26

March to 30 June 1945," vol. 1, chap. 11, sec. 1, p. 12; and "G-1 Periodic Reports," No. 13, 1–3, in Huber, *Japan's Battle for Okinawa*, 119–20. Insight into what most military personnel mean by the word "lost" is essential to understanding minutes of mid- and senior-level meetings as well as oral history interviews conducted after the war. In general the term "lost" represents the total number of men deducted from a unit's "effectives" or the men unavailable or incapable of performing their duties for any of several reasons: casualties severe enough to be evacuated, troops missing or captured, and the dead. Men temporarily assigned to other duties or wounded but able to return to their unit after a modest amount of medical care do not figure in but nevertheless can have a severe effect on a unit's present-for-duty strength.

13. Winton, *Forgotten Fleet*, 389.

14. "Joint Staff Study, OLYMPIC," 40–41, Annex 3 to Appendix C; and K. Jack Bauer and Alvin D. Coox, "OLYMPIC vs KETSU-GO," *Marine Corps Gazette* 49 (August 1965): 32–44.

15. Winton, *Forgotten Fleet*, 367, 396.

16. Morison, *USNOWWII* 14:31.

17. Ibid. 14:20–52, 62–66 provides a superb glimpse at how fire support during amphibious assaults was conducted during the later stages of the Pacific War.

18. Ibid. 14:40.

19. Ibid. 14:69. Morison also notes that there were 2,798 Navy casualties, including 881 dead and missing, among the large number of landed medical personnel, Seabees, gunfire support ships, and so on, as well as 37 Army casualties.

20. Cate and Olson, in Craven and Cate, *AAFWWII* 5:653–58, 674–75.

21. *Reports*, vol. 2, bk. 2, p. 572, abridged in O'Neill, *Suicide Squads*, 84, where he notes

that the *Renraku-tei* were also referred to as *maru-ni* (capacious boat); he uses this term throughout his text. See also O'Neill, *Suicide Squads*, 84, 97–101.

22. "'Magic'—Far East Summary": No. 518, August 3, 1945, 3, 5–6; No. 520, August 5, 1945, 1; and No. 521, August 6, 1945, 1–3, all in CARL.

23. *Reports*, vol. 1, suppl., p. 145. In addition to the 2,412 suicide craft, some 393 midget submarines and 177 Kaiten human torpedoes were surrendered to U.S. occupation forces. Also, while most of the existing suicide boats slated for use in Ketsu-Go No. 6 were based in either southern Kyushu or the large number of islands northwest of the V Corps invasion zone, the midget submarines and human torpedoes earmarked for Ketsu-Go No. 6 were principally stationed in southeastern Kyushu and along Inland Sea harbors from the Hiroshima area through points east—all within reach of the Olympic beaches ("Report on Operation OLYMPIC," Appendix 5, n.p.).

24. "Report on Operation OLYMPIC," Appendix 5, n.p.

25. O'Neill, *Suicide Squads*, 84, 97–101; and "Report on Operation OLYMPIC," 6–10.

26. "Report on Operation OLYMPIC," Annex D, 64–65. Because of the ease of constructing realistic looking decoys and false clues to fake basing areas, strikes would generally be conducted against sites where the presence of real boats was considered to be confirmed or highly probable. It was realized, of course, that a group of decoys, apparently "carelessly camouflaged," could be made to more readily appear genuine by the simple addition of one or two moving targets.

27. Capt. Lefteris Lavrakas, USN (Ret.), to author, January 6, 2007. The destroyer USS *Eberle* broke up an attack by German E-boats against the transport anchorage at Naples, Italy, on the night of April 19–20, 1944, sinking one and damaging three others so badly that they were subsequently beached. Aboard the high-speed transport USS *Horace A. Bass*, APD-124, as the naval component commander for special operations along Korea's eastern seaboard in 1951–1952, Lavrakas oversaw many small-boat night operations involving LCVPs, river gunboats (PRs), and rubber rafts where "at night the only sign of approaching SMG [Special Mission Group] boats towed by personnel carriers with muffled engines were phosphorescent wakes on the surface." Also see John B. Dwyer, "Korean War: CIA-Sponsored Secret Naval Raids," *Military History*, December 2002.

28. Morison, *USNOWWII* 14:124–25. Robert N. Colwell, in "Intelligence and the Okinawa Battle," *Naval War College Review* 38, no. 2 (Spring 1985): 86–87, places the number at approximately three hundred boats.

29. O'Neill, *Suicide Squads*, 103–4, 107–11; and Morison, *USNOWWII* 13:138–40, 202.

30. O'Neill, *Suicide Squads*, 103–4; and Morison, *USNOWWII* 13:139. A bow or stern approach is also the preferred method of modern-day "Somali pirates" of the East African coast and in the Gulf of Aden.

31. This "inability to engage" by ships' guns sited well above the waves was the principal reason for the extensive conversion of landing craft to gunboats after the series of engagements off Luzon.

32. For an account of the difficulty in moving a small craft through an invasion anchorage and locating specific ships for scheduled delivery of supplies while under aerial attack and with smokescreens being discharged, see Brig. Gen. Douglas B. Kendrick, *Memoirs of a Twentieth-Century Army Surgeon*, ed. Julie Riley Bush (Manhattan, Kans.: Sunflower University Press, 1992), 100.

33. "Japanese Air Power," 24–25, 42.

34. Morison, *USNOWWII* 14:279–80. The aircraft that attacked these ships were most likely the Yokosuka K5Y2 or Y3 Intermediate Trainer, code named Willow by the Allies, or the Yokosuka K4Y1 Training Seaplane. Other Japanese biplanes either had a centerline float with smaller floats attached to the wings or twin floats like these Yokosuka models but with significantly more radar-friendly metal incorporated into their bodies. See Francillon, *Japanese Aircraft*, 446–48, 494.

35. In the case of the USS *Prichett* (frequently misspelled as "Pritchett"), every gun on the *Fletcher*-class destroyer that could bear on the slow-moving aircraft was firing as it approached in level flight from port. The biplane was engaged by the time that it reached five thousand yards out but still managed to strike and stove in the side of the ship. Although this action is noted in the *Prichett*'s Presidential Unit Citation and discussed in the August 3, 1945, "'Magic'—Far East Summary,'" it has largely escaped examination because the kamikaze strike is not listed in the table "United States Ships Sunk or Badly Damaged by Enemy Action in the Iwo Jima and Okinawa Operations, 17 February–30 July 1945," Morison, *USNOWWII*, vol. 14, Appendix 2. Morison may have felt that the damage sustained was not severe enough for the ship to be listed. Similarly, the August 9, 1945, suicide strike on the USS *Borie*, which killed forty-eight men and wounded sixty-six, is not listed because it took place after July 30 and off the coast of Honshu.

36. "'Magic'—Far East Summary," No. 369, tab A, A4–A7, CARL. Material in this and the following paragraph from analysts' comments to an intercepted message from the German embassy's air attaché in Tokyo, Col. Wolfgang von Gronau.

37. "Army-Navy Central Agreement Concerning the *Ketsu-Go* Air Operation," in Hattori, *Complete History of the Greater East Asia War* 4:164. See also Francillon, *Japanese Aircraft*.

38. Another dangerous all-wooded plane manufactured in quantity was the Kokusai Ki-76, code named Stella by the Allies, which was modeled after the German Fieseler Fi156 Storch. The Ki-76 was used principally as an artillery spotter and utility aircraft by the Imperial Army and an antisubmarine patrol plane by the Navy.

39. In the U.S. stealth programs of the 1970s and 1980s, industry and Air Force personnel used the term "junk" and "hanging junk" when referring to highly radar reflective ordnance mounted on aircraft. See D. M. Giangreco, *Stealth Fighter Pilot* (Osceola, Wisc.: MBI, 1993).

40. Morison, *USNOWWII* 14:279–80. See also Wallace, *From Dam Neck to Okinawa*, 45.

41. Roland and Boyd, *U.S. Navy Bureau of Ordnance*, 271–87, esp. 284–87.

42. The dueling Navy official histories are Roland and Boyd, *U.S. Navy Bureau of Ordnance*; and Morison, *USNOWWII*, vol. 14.

43. Morison, *USNOWWII* 14:260–81.

44. Roland and Boyd, *U.S. Navy Bureau of Ordnance*, 285–86.

45. Fire-control radar fed a target's range, heading, air speed, and other data into an analogue computer that arrived at a fire-control solution then instantly transmitted the information and corrections on a moving target directly to the gun for automatic firing (guns could also be directed and fired locally). Under normal circumstances, 5-inch rounds with a standard proximity fuze were used as a matter of course against aerial targets but were found to be ineffective against aircraft of

wooden construction. Since the transmitted fire-control data was not actually seen by the gunnery officers in the 5-inch gun turrets, they would have to be notified orally by the CIC if it was judged that the nature of the target required that a differently fused round be fired.

46. Wallace, *From Dam Neck to Okinawa*, 27–28.

47. Stafford, *Big E*, 422–35, 451–53, 458–64, esp. 460–62.

48. Condon-Rall and Cowdry, *Medical Department*, 415; and *Field Order 74*.

49. Condon-Rall and Cowdry, *Medical Department*, 418–24; Brig. Gen. Douglas B. Kendrick, "Blood Program in World War II," in *Medical Department, United States Army* (Washington, D.C.: Office of the Surgeon General, Department of the Army, 1964), 635, 638–40; and Charles M. Wiltse, *Medical Supply in World War II* (Washington, D.C.: Office of the Surgeon General, Department of the Army, 1968), 538, 543–48.

50. Kendrick, "Blood Program," 639. See also Wiltse, *Medical Supply*, ix.

51. Ibid., 635, 638–40.

52. Ibid., 640; See also Condon-Rall and Cowdry, *Medical Department*, 416.

53. Kendrick, "Blood Program," 640. At the time Kendrick wrote these words, in the early 1960s, he was the chief of Walter Reed Hospital's Division of Surgical Physiology.

54. Ibid., xv, 599, 605, 632–33, 636.

55. Ibid., 599–602, 638, 640. Brooklyn was frequently referenced as a municipality separate from New York (in this case, referring to Manhattan), and the New York City borough was displayed in many period reference works as the fifth largest city in the United States.

56. Ibid., 639–40. Kendrick, in his *Memoirs*, 100, further notes that whole blood, apparently moving through the Navy's supply pipeline, was sent forward from the Ulithi anchorage for use off Okinawa.

57. Kendrick, *Memoirs*, 627–28.

58. Ibid., 628; and Morison, *USNOWWII* 14:175.

59. Kendrick, "Blood Program," 635–36.

60. Wiltse, *Medical Supply*, 537.

61. Kendrick, "Blood Program," 605.

Chapter 13. On the Ground

1. "G-2 Estimate of the Enemy Situation, OPERATION OLYMPIC, 1 August 1945," Office of the Assistant Chief of Staff, G-2, Headquarters, Sixth Army, August 1, 1945.

2. Japanese Monograph No. 17, "Homeland Operations," 159–60.

3. From Stanley Weintraub, *The Last Great Victory* (New York: Penguin Books, 1995), 594–95. The obscurely traditional Imperial diction used in crafting the proclamation of the deified emperor lent itself to variable and subtle translation differences, and inconsequential differences exist between the translation of the August 14, 1945, Imperial Rescript of the Termination of the War in Weintraub and that in Butow, *Japan's Decision to Surrender*, 248. Both differ noticeably, however, from the version published in *Reports*, vol. 2, bk. 2, pp. 727–28. For example, where the Weintraub and Butow texts say "ultimate collapse and obliteration of the Japanese nation," the former Imperial staff officers, working under U.S. jurisdiction in the Japanese Demobilization Bureau, viewed the *Rescript*'s meaning somewhat differently, and instead of using the words "Japanese nation," they

translated it into English as "obliteration of the race."

4. Timothy Lang Francis, "'To Dispose of the Prisoners': The Japanese Executions of American Aircrew at Fukuoka, Japan during 1945," *Pacific Historical Review* 66, no. 4 (November 1997): 484–86.

5. Shockley-Wright report, Bowles Papers.

6. Vice Chief of the Naval General Staff Onishi Tikijiro, in Butow, *Japan's Decision to Surrender*, 204–5; and Lord Keeper of the Privy Seal Marquis Kido Koichi, in Newman, "Trashing of Henry Stimson," 152.

7. Giangreco, "Score of Bloody Okinawas," 93–132, esp. 100–102. See also Giangreco, "Spinning the Casualties," 22–30.

8. See chapter 7.

9. "Joint Chiefs of Staff Corrigendum to JCS 1388," 4.

10. Allen and Polmar, *Code-Name Downfall*, 234.

11. Weintraub, *Last Great Victory*, 229. In Dudley's previous assignment with the Manhattan Project, he had been a key figure in the site selection for the Los Alamos National Laboratory, New Mexico, and he later retired as a brigadier general.

12. Arens, *V [Marine] Amphibious Corps Planning*, 81.

13. Unless cited otherwise, the possible course of **planned U.S. operations** outlined in this paragraph through the balance of the chapter is distilled and combined from Arens, *V [Marine] Amphibious Corps Planning*; Jack Bauer and Alvin D. Coox, "OLYMPIC vs KETSU-GO," *Marine Corps Gazette* 49 (August 1965): 23; Maj. Edmund J. Winslett, I Corps, "The Defenses of Southern Kyushu," presented at the Military History institute, Army War College, Carlisle Barracks, Pennsylvania, June 3, 1946; "Joint Staff Study, OLYMPIC," May 1945; "Staff Study, Operations, OLYMPIC," General Headquarters USAFP, April 23, 1945; "'Downfall' Strategic Plan for Operations in the Japanese Archipelago," General Headquarters USAFP, May 28, 1945; "Report on Operation OLYMPIC"; Field Order 74, "'DOWNFALL' Strategic Plan for Operations in the Japanese Archipelago," General Headquarters USAFP, May 28, 1945; "IX Corps Field Order Number 1, Operation Olympic," Headquarters IX Corps, August 12, 1945; "IX Corps Administrative Order Number 1, Operation Olympic, To Accompany Field Order No. 1," Headquarters IX Corps, August 12, 1945; *ESP*, vol. 1; *Amphibian Engineer Operations*, vol. 4, in *ESP* (Tokyo: 1949); and *Reports*, vol. 1.

Japanese capabilities and plans are distilled and combined from Arens, *V [Marine] Amphibious Corps Planning*; Bauer and Coox, "OLYMPIC vs KETSU-GO"; "Japanese Plans for the Defense of Kyushu," Office of the Assistant Chief of Staff, G-2, Headquarters, Sixth Army, December 31, 1945; "G-2 Estimate of the Enemy Situation, OPERATION OLYMPIC, 1 August 1945," Office of the Assistant Chief of Staff, G-2, Headquarters, Sixth Army, August 1, 1945; Hattori, *Complete History of the Greater East Asia War*; Drea, *In the Service of the Emperor*; "Japanese Defense Strategy and Tactics"; "'Magic'—Far East Summary," Nos. 499–508 (including Naval Sections Nos. 518–525), August 1–10, 1945, CARL; Japanese Monograph No. 17, "Homeland Operations"; Japanese Monograph No. 157, "Homeland Air Defense Operations Record"; *Reports*, vol. 2, bk. 2, *Japanese Operations in the Southwest Pacific Area* (Tokyo: SACP, 1950); and *Soldier's Guide to the Japanese Army*, Special Series No. 27 (Washington, D.C.: Military Intelligence Service, War Department, November 1945).

Direct quotes, references to works outside of this subject area, and data derived from earlier campaigns retain individual citations.

14. Val Adams Jr. with Jim Adams, "Conductive to Fright Itself," *Naval History* 21 (February 2007): 38–41.

15. See Martin Blumenson, *Anzio: The Gamble that Failed*, 2nd ed. (New York: Cooper Square Press, 2001); and Carlo D'Este, *Fatal Decision: Anzio and the Battle for Rome* (New York: HarperCollins, 1991).

16. ASF-P-SL-2, "Operations Against Kyushu," December 18, 1944, 5, in "History of Planning Division, ASF," Planning Division, Army Service Forces, Washington, D.C., 1946, vol. 7, Appendix 9-R, 16; *ESP* 1:319–320; and Dod, *Corps of Engineers*, 672–73. The thirty groups did not include two P-47D groups that would be based at Kikai Jima.

17. Cannon, *Leyte*, 8–9, 306. See also Morison, *Two-Ocean War*, 422–23.

18. "G-2 Estimate of the Enemy Situation," 18.

19. "Japanese Plans for the Defense of Kyushu," 16. For the Imperial 146th Division's dispositions, see "Report on Operation OLYMPIC," pt. 4, Appendix 12, 1.

Chapter 14. Unexamined Factors

1. Hayashi and Coox, *Kogun*, 218.

2. "DOWNFALL" Strategic Plan for Operations in the Japanese Archipelago, General Headquarters USAFP, May 28, 1945, 1–4, 8.

3. *Reports* 1:411, 413.

4. For example, a Sixth Army analysis of strictly battlefield casualties by Brigadier General Denit arrived at a projected 22,576 through X+30, 33,330 the following month, and a monthly average of 34,514 until the front stabilized around X+120 (Maj.

Warren W. DaBoll, chapter 15, "From Olympic to Blacklist," in the unpublished manuscript "Medical Service in the Asiatic and Pacific Theaters," c. 1968, Center of Military History, Washington, D.C.). See also Kendrick, "Blood Program," 640; and Condon-Rall and Cowdry, *Medical Department*, 416.

5. Bland and Stevens, *Marshall* 5:254.

6. Coox, *Final Agony*, 87.

7. Implicated in the vivisection of eight downed American fliers, Yokoyama Isamu was convicted of Atrocities Committed against Captured Airmen in 1948, sentenced to death, and died in prison in 1952. See Ikuhiko Hata, ed., *Sekai senso hanzai jiten* (*Encyclopedia of War Crimes in Modern History*) (Tokyo: Bungei Shunju, 2002), 185–86; and Ikuhiko Hata, ed., *Nihon Riku-Kaigun Sogo Jiten* (*A Comprehensive Encyclopedia on the Japanese Army and Navy*) (Tokyo: Tokyo University Press, 1991), 155. See also Francis, "To Dispose of the Prisoners," 483–84; and Fuller, *Shokan*, 241.

8. "Japanese Plans for the Defense of Kyushu," 14. See also "Outline for the Concentration Plan for the Homeland Operation," B. Internal Resistance and C. The Home Guard, in "Japanese Defense Strategy and Tactics," n.p.

9. Hattori, *Complete History of the Greater East Asia War* 4:194.

10. "Japanese Plans for the Defense of Kyushu," 14. Modern references spell the city's name Hita.

11. "'DOWNFALL' Strategic Plan for Operations in the Japanese Archipelago," General Headquarters USAFP, May 28, 1945, 8; IX Corps Field Order Number 1, Operation Olympic (Headquarters IX Corps, August 12, 1945), 2.

12. See excerpts from General Ridgway's May 9, 1984, address and lengthy question-and-

answer session at the U.S. Army Command
and General Staff College in Giangreco, *War
in Korea, 1950–1953* (New York: Random
House/Presidio Press, 2001), 175–76, also
163–72.

13. "Report on Operation OLYMPIC," pt, 1, p.
22, Appendix 13, n.p.

14. JCS 1417, "Operations Following Invasion
of Kanto Plain (Broad Plans)," 14–26.

15. Ibid., 23–24; and "Effect of Weather on
Operations, Tokyo Plain," in "Staff Study
Operations, CORONET," Enclosure 5.

16. "'DOWNFALL' Strategic Plan for
Operations in the Japanese Archipelago," 4.

17. Japanese Monograph No. 17, "Homeland
Operations," 129–31.

18. "Japanese Plans for the Defense of Kyushu,"
11. See also Japanese Monograph No. 17,
"Homeland Operations," 121.

19. Japanese Monograph No. 17, "Homeland
Operations," 239–40; *Reports*, vol. 2, bk. 2,
pp. 662–63.

20. Japanese Monograph No. 17, "Homeland
Operations," 25; and *Reports*, vol. 2, bk. 2,
pp. 662–63.

21. Hattori, *Complete History of the Greater East
Asia War* 4:189. See also Yasuo Wakuda,
"Wartime Railways and Transport Policies,"
Japan Railway & Transport Review,
November 1996, 32–35; "Bridges and
Tunnels Linking the Japanese Archipelago"
(unbylined), *Japan Railway & Transport
Review*, June 1994, 42–45. See also Cate
and Olson, in Craven and Cate, *AAFWWII*
5:662–72; and Frederick M. Sallagar,
"Lessons from an Aerial Mining Campaign
(Operation 'Starvation')," R-1322-PR,
United States Air Force Project Rand, Santa
Monica, Calif., April 1974, 31–50.

22. Coox, *Final Agony*, 86–87.

23. Ibid.; and Frank, *Downfall*, 167, 397.

24. Alvin D. Coox, discussion with author, c.
1998.

25. Hayashi and Coox, *Kogun*, 115.

26. "Defense Strategy and Tactics," 1A
Separate Volume No. 1, n.p.; and
Japanese Monograph No. 17, "Homeland
Operations," 62–64. See also chapter 10,
note 58.

27. Hayashi and Coox, *Kogun*, 87. This point
was further reinforced by Coox in a February
1999 telephone conversation with the author.
Elements of the government making up the
"peace faction" were also dismissive of the
redoubt strategy, and three-time premier
Prince Konoye Fumimaro explained to
USSBS investigators that "their [the Army's]
idea of fighting on was fighting from every
little hole or rock in the mountains." See
Newman, "Trashing of Henry Stimson,"
in Maddox, *Hiroshima in History*, 151.
Regarding the efforts of the peace faction,
some historians have made much of Emperor
Hirohito's request that the Soviets accept
Prince Konoye as a special envoy to discuss
ways in which the war might be "quickly
terminated." But far from a coherent plea to
the Soviets to help negotiate a surrender, the
proposals were hopelessly vague and viewed
by both Washington and Moscow as little
more than a stalling tactic to prevent Soviet
military intervention, an intervention that
Tokyo had known was coming ever since the
Soviets' recent cancellation of their Neutrality
Pact with Japan. The subsequent exchange of
diplomatic communications between foreign
minister Togo and Sato Naotake, ambassador
to the Soviet Union, has been characterized
by authors such as Gar Alperovitz and, most
recently, Tsuyoshi Hasegawa, as evidence that
Japan was on the brink of calling it quits.
American officials reading the intercepted
messages, however, could not help noticing
that the defeatist ideas of the ambassador
received nothing more than a stinging rebuke
from Tokyo. Moreover, it was the fanatical

Japanese militarists who were fully in control of the decision-making process until the combined shocks of the of the atom bombs in August 1945 and Soviet entry into the war stampeded Japan's leaders into an early capitulation.

28. Cook, "Nagano 1945," 44–47; Hattori, *Complete History of the Greater East Asia War* 4:198; Hayashi and Coox, *Kogun*, 157; Drea, *In the Service of the Emperor*, 206, 208; Allen and Polmar, *Code-Name Downfall*, 253–54; *Reports*, vol. 2, bk. 2, p. 664 n163; and Coox, *Final Agony*, 77, 87.

29. *Reports*, vol. 2, bk. 2, pp. 604–5, 657–68 (esp. fn. 163); Japanese Monograph No. 17, "Homeland Operations," 82–85; Hattori, *Complete History of the Greater East Asia War* 4:195–98; "Explanatory Data to Estimate of Situation for Spring of 1946," 18–44; "Defense Strategy and Tactics, Appended Chart No. 1, Chart for the concentration in Operation KETSU 3," n.p., and "The Employment of Strength," n.p.; and Mercado, *Shadow Warriors of Nakano*; 125–27, 153–56.

30. Glantz, *August Storm*, 34–38; Edward J. Drea, "Missing Intentions: Japanese Intelligence and the Soviet Invasion of Manchuria," *Military Affairs* 48 (April 1984): 66–73, esp. 66–67; Hattori, *Complete History of the Greater East Asia War* 4:212–14; Hayashi and Coox, *Kogun*, 172–75; and Coox discussion with author.

31. Japanese Monograph No. 17, "Homeland Operations," 84, 103–5, 139–40. The Second General Army officers working on their segment of this document were under the direction of Col. Imoto Kumao, who had considerable experience in dealing with American offensive operations. Imoto's service as a staff officer with the Eighth Area Army during the fighting on New Guinea and the Solomon Islands is recounted in

Imoto Chūsa nisshi (*Diary of Lieutenant Colonel Imoto Kumao*). His *Sakusen nisshi de tsuzuru Daitoa senso* (*The Greater Asian War as Narrated by Operational Journals*) was published in 1979 and reappeared in 1998 through Fuyo Shobo, Tokyo, as *Daitoa senso sakusen nisshi* (*Operational History of the Great East Asian War*).

32. Frank, *Downfall*, 167.

33. Thomas M. Huber, *Pastel: Deception in the Invasion of Japan* (Fort Leavenworth, Kans.: Combat Studies Institute, 1988).

34. Brown, *Bodyguard of Lies*, vol. 2, esp. 900 and 904 in epilogue; Cruickshank, *Deception in World War II*, 87–88, 177–185; and Koch, "Operation Fortitude," 66–77.

35. *Reports*, vol. 2, bk. 2, pp. 604–5; Japanese Monograph No. 17, "Homeland Operations," 82; and "Defense Strategy and Tactics, Appended Chart No. 1, Chart for the Concentration in Operation KETSU 3," n.p., and "The Employment of Strength," n.p. It was envisioned that the first of the divisions reinforcing the Tokyo area from beyond the Kanto Plain could not arrive at the Nagano staging area until at least ten days after receiving their marching orders and that the most distant divisions could take up to thirty days.

36. "Japanese System of Defense Call-up," 1–3; and "Amendment No. 1 to G-2 Estimate of Enemy Situation with Respect to Kyushu."

37. Japanese Monograph No. 17, "Homeland Operations," 210–11; and "Defense Strategy and Tactics," "Outline of Concentration Plan for Homeland Operation," n.p.

38. D. M. Giangreco, letters to the editor, *Journal of American History* 84 (June 1997): 322–23.

39. For an informative look at Alamo Scout practices and procedures, see Lance O. Zedric, *Silent Warriors of World War II: The Alamo*

Scouts Behind Japanese Lines (Ventura, Calif.: Pathfinder, 1995).

40. Hiroo Onoda, "Kono michi" ("My Path"), *Tokyo Shimbun* (March 4 and 6, 1995), 1, in Mercado, *Shadow Warriors of Nakano*, 94–95; also see 10–14.

41. Mercado, *Shadow Warriors of Nakano*, 150–54; see also 125–27, 142–42, and 161–63.

42. *Reports*, vol. 1, suppl., pp. 136–38, 142.

43. Ibid., 136. Could this figure be a typo? Even if an extra zero was inadvertently added and the true number of rounds was "just" 5.1 million, this quantity of mortar bombs per tub would still have to be judged as more than ample for the upcoming operation.

44. Arens, *V [Marine] Amphibious Corps Planning*, 81; and Kuribayashi quote from Bill D. Ross, *Iwo Jima: Legacy of Valor* (New York: Vanguard Press, 1985), 62.

Chapter 15. A "Target-Rich Environment"

1. Vice Adm. Arthur Radford while commanding a carrier task force off Japan in Dower, *Embracing Defeat*, 55.

2. Haruko Taya Cook and Theodore F. Cook, "A Lost War in Living Memory: Japan's Second World War," *European Review* 11, no. 4 (2003): 573–93.

3. Skates, *Invasion of Japan*, 121.

4. Lt. Gen. Simon Bolivar Buckner Jr., June 18, 1945, and Maj. Gen. Viktor Vorobyov, January 7, 1995.

5. Skates, *Invasion of Japan*, 89.

6. Appleman et al., *Okinawa*, 208–19. See also Belote and Belote, *Typhoon of Steel*, 204–6, 211, 214.

7. Winslett, "Defenses of Southern Kyushu," 5.

8. Skates, *Invasion of Japan*, 114.

9. Belote and Belote, *Typhoon of Steel*, 199.

10. Cornelius Ryan, *A Bridge Too Far* (New York: Simon and Schuster, 1974). See also Charles B. MacDonald, *The Seigfried Line Campaign*, USAWWII series (Washington, D.C.: Center of Military History, United States Army, 1984), 119–248.

11. "Effect of Weather on Operations, Tokyo Plain," in "Staff Study Operations, CORONET." In addition to this enclosure, Enclosure 5A (not listed in the "Staff Study" contents), provides an excellent, four-page "Summary of Weather Conditions, Tokyo Area—March." Also, Harold A. Winters with Gerald E. Galloway Jr., William J. Reynolds, and David W. Rhyne, *Battling the Elements: Weather and Terrain in the Conduct of War* (Baltimore: Johns Hopkins University Press, 1998) should be read by anyone seriously interested in what the authors refer to as the "potent and omnipresent synergy between the environment, or physical geography, and battle."

12. Halliwell, "Projected Assault on Japan," 348–51.

13. "Summary of Weather Conditions, Tokyo Area–March," in "Staff Study Operations, CORONET," Enclosure 5A, 1.

14. "Effect of Weather on Operations, Tokyo Plain," in "Staff Study Operations, CORONET."

15. "Terrain and Weather," sec. 1 in "Staff Study Operations, CORONET," 1, 4–5.

16. "Staff Study Operations, CORONET," Annex 3b (4).

17. "Terrain and Weather," in "Staff Study Operations, CORONET," 3, 9–13.

18. "Effect of Rice Land, Natural, and Artificial Flooding on Cross-Country Movement," in "Staff Study Operations, CORONET," Enclosure 5.

19. "Terrain and Weather," in "Staff Study Operations, CORONET," 2–3.

20. ASF-P-SL-2, "Operations Against Kyushu," December 18, 1944, 5, in "History of Planning Division, ASF," Planning Division, Army Service Forces, Washington, D.C., 1946, vol. 7, Appendix 9-R, 16; *ESP* 1:319–20; Dod, *Corps of Engineers*, 672–73. In this latter work, which presents much valuable information and analysis, the fact that plans originally called for the construction of eleven airfields, is inadvertently combined with later data after the proposed number of air groups operating from Kyushu had been expanded and the number of airfields and runways had grown to twenty-three and seventy, respectively.

21. JCS 1190/8, "Planned Deployment of Strategic Heavy Bomber Groups," Appendix B, 95–98, Appendix C, annex, 100, and Appendix D, 101; and Hattori, *Complete History of the Greater East Asia War* 4:43. Kikai Jima sat across a highly defensible channel from an entire Japanese brigade on Amami Oshima. The island, itself, was almost completely undefended and would have been invaded before the end of August 1945. Including the substantial, artillery-heavy garrison, some 26,666 personnel would be jammed onto the island.

22. See "Report on Operation OLYMPIC," pt. 4, CINCPAC table "Appendix 43, Air Base Development." See also "Staff Study, Operations, CORONET," Annex 4, Appendix C.

23. "G-2 Estimate of the Enemy Situation with Respect to an Operation Against the Tokyo (Kwanto) Plain of Honshu," General Headquarters USAFP, G-2 General Staff, May 31, 1945, sec. I-2, 1.

24. *Reports* 1:399.

25. A fine account of the storms and their effect on tactical operations can be found in Winters Galloway, Reynolds, and Rhyne, *Battling the Elements*, 9–14.

26. Samuel Eliot Morison, *USNOWWII*, vol. 15, *Supplement and General Index* (Boston: Little, Brown, 1962), 14–17; *Reports*, vol. 1, suppl., 270; *ESP* 1:306, 332; "Memorandum for Chief, Strategic Policy Section, S&P Group, OPD [Strategy and Policy Group, Operations Division, War Dept.]," April 30, 1946, from Col. R[iley] F. Ennis in Marshall Foundation National Archives Project: OPD (ABC) 471.6 Atom (17 Aug. 45), sec. 7, Folder 6, 1–3, 6, esp. 2, NARA; and Capt. Charles A. Bartholomew, USN, *Mud, Muscle and Miracles: Marine Salvage in the United States Navy* (Washington, D.C.: Department of the Navy, 1990), 191.

27. "Typhoon Lashes at Philippines," *Los Angeles Times*, April 4, 1946, A-2; Joint Typhoon Warning Center data courtesy Unisys Corporation, Unisys Way, Blue Bell, Pa., and on the web at http://weather.unisys.com/hurricane/index.html/.

28. Dod, *Corps of Engineers*, 674, 677–78. One long ton equals 2,240 pounds.

29. Bartholomew, *Mud, Muscle and Miracles*, 174–79.

30. Ibid. This was the same method the British had used to clear the Royal Navy's Scapa Flow base of scuttled German ships after World War I.

31. Ibid., 449–52.

32. Unless otherwise noted, all data on the Ironhorse artificial harbor are from "Staff Study Operations, CORONET," Appendix H, Annex 4, 1–10, from a summary of logistic support given to CINCAFPAC on July 16, 1945, and CINCPAC on July 21, 1945.

33. Halliwell, "Projected Assault on Japan," 350.

34. Cline, *Washington Command Post*, 347.

35. Halliwell, "Projected Assault on Japan," 350.

36. Morison, *USNOWWII* 11:178–79; Harrison, *Cross-Channel Attack*, 426; and Roland G. Ruppenthal, *Logistical Support of*

the Armies, USAWWII series (Washington, D.C.: Center of Military History, United States Army, 1959), 2:58–60.

37. Halliwell, "Projected Assault on Japan," 350.

38. See Michael D. Doubler, *Busting the Bocage: American Combined Arms Operations in France 6 June–31 July 1944* (Fort Leavenworth, Kans.: Combat Studies Institute, 1988), 29–51.

39. *Soldier's Guide to the Japanese Army*, Special Series No. 27 (Washington, D.C.: Military Intelligence Service, War Dept., November 1945), 87–91. The Type 97 fired both armor-piercing shot and high-explosive shell from seven-round magazines and was found capable of piercing thirty millimeters of case-hardened armor at 370 yards.

40. Ibid., 87–93, 131–37.

41. "Terrain and Weather," in "Staff Study Operations, CORONET," 12–13. One writer who observed the ground in modern times (and apparently in the dry tourist season as opposed to when conditions approximated that of the invasion) disagrees with USAFP's intelligence assessment and refers to the Sagami Valley as "a flat, now industrialized, but then agricultural plain that runs north like a highway into western Tokyo. . . . This valley provides a natural corridor suitable for high speed mobile forces." (See Skates, *Invasion of Japan*, 200.)

42. "Staff Study Operations, CORONET," 13.

43. There are no similar obstacles north of where the Sagami's turbulent waters curve west into the mountains. It was from points running approximately thirty miles north from this bend, then northeast across the broad, twenty-five-mile-wide flood plain to the Ashio Mountains that counterattacks and infiltrations would be launched from staging areas in Nagano Prefecture, where,

more recently, the 1998 Winter Olympics were held.

44. *Soldier's Guide*, 101. Many units were able to distribute this booklet down to squad leaders, with additional copies circulated among the enlisted men.

45. "Effect of Weather on Operations, Tokyo Plain," in "Staff Study Operations, CORONET."

46. *Soldier's Guide*, 101, 106–7. The dual-purpose Type 88 75-mm gun is erroneously listed in this publication as having a maximum range of nearly seventeen miles.

47. Another formation reconstituting in the United States, the 6th Infantry Division (Canadian Army), as well as the Pacific-bound U.S. 69th, 78th, 91st, and 100th Infantry Divisions still in Europe, had received no specific assignments by the end of the war. The overseas divisions receiving movement alerts in August would also go into the general reserve for Coronet after returning to the United States but were not likely to be committed until well after the "Mountaineer" and Canadian divisions had left for Japan.

48. Cdr. John T. Kuehn, USN (Ret.), USACGSC, to author, August 28, 2007, memorandum: "During postwar discussions with their U.S. Seventh Fleet colleagues, officers of the Japan Maritime Self Defence Force Fleet Air Force and Army General Staff, expressed that during the postwar period, the issue of rebuilding the Japanese roads along more Western lines had been considered and rejected. In particular, it was common knowledge among the General Staff officers that their wartime planners had realized the incredible hindrance to mobility that the chaotic road infrastructure on the Kanto Plain would have provided—in concert with the terrain and the high

urbanization—to an invasion force. Once Japan became a Cold War ally of the United States, this long-held position became well ensconced as a self-defense measure against Soviet mechanized forces. In other words, the Japanese decided that they had more to gain by *not* creating a highly linear road infrastructure in the 'New Japan' than by Westernizing it." Development of the transportation infrastructure would center around a rail system inherently unfriendly to any invading army.

Chapter 16. Half a Million Purple Hearts

1. Fleet Admiral Ernest J. King and Cdr. Walter Muir Whitehill, *Fleet Admiral King: A Naval Record* (New York: W. W. Norton, 1952), 598.
2. Cline, *Washington Command Post*, 336–38.
3. Ibid., 337.
4. Ibid., 338–39. Marshall personally briefed the proposal to representatives of the British Chiefs of Staff in Washington on July 14, 1944. See also Futrell and Taylor, "Reorganization for Victory," 676–77; plus Coakley and Leighton, *Global Logistics and Strategy*, 415–16, 561–65.
5. MacEachin, *Final Months of the War with Japan*, 1–2. Members of the Joint Planning Staff are commonly referred to as "Joint Staff Planners."
6. JCS 924/2, "Operations Against Japan Subsequent to Formosa," August 30, 1944, 120. This grim prognosis was made in the midst of the Mariana Islands battles. See "Saipan ratio" in chapter 6.
7. Cline, *Washington Command Post*, 340.
8. Ibid., 338–40.
9. Pogue, *Marshall Interviews*, 423. See also Marshall's May 11, 1951, congressional testimony on the effect that the lack of a Japanese response to the Tokyo firebombing had on

decisions made by the JCS in U.S. Senate, *Military Situation in the Far East: Hearings before the Committee on Armed Services and the Committee on Foreign Relations, United States Senate*, 82nd Cong., 1st sess. (Washington, D.C.: GPO, 1951), pt. 1, pp. 563–64.
10. JIC 266/1, "Defeat of Japan by Blockade and Bomb," April 18, 1945, in Cline, *Washington Command Post*, 343.
11. Brig. Gen. William W. Bessell Jr. to Brig. Gen. Frank F. Everest, USAAF, March 16, 1945, memorandum, in Cline, *Washington Command Post*, 342.
12. Testimony of Cdr. (later Rear Adm.) Herbert G. Hopwood before the House of Representatives Committee on Naval Affairs, May 26, 1942, in Frederic L. Borch III and C. F. Brown, *The Purple Heart: A History of America's Oldest Military Decoration* (Tempe, Ariz.: Borch & Westlake, 1996), 81.
13. Ibid., 56–57, 81–83; and Stan Sirmans, "The Navy's World War II Purple Hearts," *Medal Collector* 42, no. 5 (May 1991): 29–36. (This journal's title was changed later to *Journal of the Orders and Medals Society of America*.)
14. Sirmans, "Navy's World War II Purple Hearts."
15. Ibid.; Borch and Brown, *Purple Heart*, 45–59, 224–25; D. M. Giangreco and Kathryn Moore, "Half a Million Purple Hearts," *American Heritage* 51 (Dec. 2000), 81–83. Also see "Too Many Purple Hearts?" *American Heritage* 52 (May 2001): 6–7. RG 92 (Records of the Office of the Quartermaster General, Philadelphia Quartermaster Depot at NARA, Mid-Atlantic Region, Philadelphia) and RG 104 (Records of the U.S. Mint, NARA, College Park, Md.) are wonderful sources for individuals interested in researching this subject, although acquiring an understanding

of government procurement practices is recommended before tackling this material.

16. The firms were Rex Manufacturing Company of New Rochelle, New York (300,000 complete decorations) and the Robbins Company of Attleboro, Massachusetts (225,000 complete decorations), with Rex also responsible for the key element of the Navy decoration (135,000 pendants). A variety of other firms were also involved in the manufacture of presentations cases ("coffin boxes"), ribbon bars, and subcomponents.

17. "Delinquencies as of 30 June 1944" from Army Service Forces, Office of the Quartermaster General, Washington, D.C., to Commanding General, Philadelphia Quartermaster Depot, July 26, 1944, memorandum, folder "Miscellaneous—Purchase File, From 2 June 1944 to 11 August 1944," Box 85, Records of the Office of the Quartermaster General, Philadelphia Quartermaster Depot, RG 92, NARA, Mid-Atlantic Region, Philadelphia (hereafter cited as PQD, RG 92, MAR).

18. The numbering apparently continued beyond that called for in the contract specifications as a Robbins-produced medal, serial number 601,677, is known to exist. The names of servicemen killed or died of wounds continued to be added to medals given to the families who received the medal posthumously. See Frederic L. Borch III, "The 'First' Purple Hearts: A Study of Naming and Numbering on Purple Hearts Manufactured Prior to World War II," 19–15, in *Journal of the Orders and Medals Society of America* 56, no. 1 (January–February 2005): 2–19.

19. "Memorandum for the Files," October 7, 1943, to Edwin H. Dressel, Superintendent, U.S. Mint, Philadelphia, on phone call from Mr. Wilkins, Bureau of Naval Personnel, folder "Navy—Medals, Purple Heart, 1942–

1945," Box 3, Correspondence Concerning U.S. Government Medals, 1917–1950, Records of the U.S. Mint, RG 104, NARA (hereafter cited as RUSM, RG 104, CP).

20. Ibid.

21. Edwin H. Dressel to Director of the Mint Nellie Tayloe Ross, October 7, 1943, Treasury Department, RUSM, RG 104, CP.

22. For a technical description of the various types and subtypes of the Purple Heart medal and ribbon bars, see Borch and Brown, *Purple Heart*, 43–57.

23. Ibid.

24. September 10, 1944, Treasury Department interoffice communication, folder "Medals—General—June 1945–Dec. 1947 File #2," Box 2; and Tayloe Ross to Edwin H. Dressel, December 7, 1944, folder "Medals—General—1925–1945 File #1," Box 2, both in General Subject Files on Medals, 1918–1978, RUSM, RG 104, CP.

25. "Purple Hearts" from E. F. Wilkins to Tayloe Ross in reference to letter of same date (note 24 above), December 7, 1944, memorandum, folder "Navy—Medals, Purple Heart, 1942–1945," Box 3, Correspondence Concerning U.S. Government Medals, 1917–1950, RUSM, RG 104, CP. Care should be taken in examining RG 92 and RG 104 to not confuse E. F. Wilkins from the Treasury Department's Bureau of the Mint, who is frequently referred to as simply "Mrs. Wilkins" in documents, with "Mr. Wilkins" from the Bureau of Naval Personnel, who also appears regularly with no identifying references beyond his name.

26. Brig. Gen. William W. Bessell Jr. to Brig. Gen. Frank F. Everest, USAAF, March 16, 1945, memorandum, in Cline, *Washington Command Post*, 342.

27. "Status of Medal Deliveries" from Edwin H. Dressel to Tayloe Ross, April 9, 1945, memorandum, folder "Medals—General—

1925–1945 File #1," Box 2, General Subject Files on Medals, 1918–1978, RUSM, RG 104, CP.

28. Dr. Leland Howard, Acting Director of the Mint, to Edwin H. Dressel, March 23, 1945, folder "Navy—Medals, Purple Heart, 1942–1945," Box 3, Correspondence Concerning U.S. Government Medals, 1917–1950, RUSM, RG 104, CP.

29. Dr. Leland Howard, Acting Director of the Mint, to Edwin H. Dressel, April 3, 1945, folder "Navy—Medals, Purple Heart, 1942–1945," Box 3, Correspondence Concerning U.S. Government Medals, 1917–1950, RUSM, RG 104, CP.

30. Tayloe Ross to Edwin H. Dressel, April 10, 1945, folder "Navy—Medals, Purple Heart, 1942–1945," Box 3, Correspondence Concerning U.S. Government Medals, 1917–1950, RUSM, RG 104, CP.

31. Pogue, *Marshall Interviews*, 490–91. Said Marshall, "It was very harmful to morale" to make a soldier "wait maybe six months" for his decoration, but "if you decorated a man then and there, he got it and everybody else reacted to the spirit of the occasion."

32. Howard to Dressel, April 3, 1945; also in folder "Medals—General—1925–1945 File #1," Box 2, in General Subject Files on Medals, 1918–1978, RUSM, RG 104, CP. According to the War Production Board's *Regulations Applicable to the Operation of the Priorities System*, AA-3 is a rating for priority civilian goods while AA-1 is a war rating, and the second highest that can be designated by one of the armed services.

33. One unsigned Treasury Department memorandum explained that "25,000 Purple Hearts were ordered by the Navy in September [*sic*; October 9, 1944], but were not urgent at that time" and went on to list the "additional orders . . . which were urgent" (folder "Navy—Medals, Purple Heart, 1942–1945," Box 3, Correspondence Concerning U.S. Government Medals, 1917–1950, RUSM, RG 104, CP). They were the Air Medal, Bronze Star, Legion of Merit, Navy–Marine Corps Medal, Silver Star, and Distinguished Flying Cross.

34. Ross to Dressel, April 10, 1945.

35. Humorous characterization by an anonymous instructor in the Department of Combat Support, USACGSC, 1985–1986 (I guess you just had to be there). The department has since changed its name to Department of Logistics and Resource Operations.

36. Dressel to Tayloe Ross and other subsidiary memorandums, April 5, April 6, and April 13,1945, folder "Navy—Medals, Purple Heart, 1942–1945," Box 3, Correspondence Concerning U.S. Government Medals, 1917–1950, RUSM, RG 104, CP. The Mint was attempting, as part of the same contract, to acquire forty-nine hundred yards of ribbon for five other decorations. See also Dressel to Tayloe Ross, March 13, 1945, and other memorandums, folder "Medals—General—1925–1945 File #1," Box 2, General Subject Files on Medals, 1918–1978, RUSM, RG 104, CP.

37. "Ribbons, Decoration" from Capt. Malcolm D. McMeekan, Philadelphia Quartermaster Depot, to Capt. Chas. A. Janss, Office of the Quartermaster General, Washington, D.C., March 6, 1945, memorandum, folder "Miscellaneous—Purchase File, From 2 June 1944 to 11 August 1944," Box 85, Records of the Office of the Quartermaster General, Philadelphia Quartermaster Depot, PQD, RG 92, MAR.

38. This figure is twenty-five thousand larger than the one given in Giangreco and Moore, "Half a Million Purple Hearts," because the authors had failed to include a very early Army wartime order to the Robbins

Company on December 30, 1941, for that number of decorations. However, one critic of President Truman's A-bomb decision, Barton J. Bernstein, stated, "To my knowledge, and despite my own efforts, no one has found WWII records on any 1944–1945 Purple Heart procurement, in the National Archives or elsewhere." Bernstein filed a Freedom of Information Act (FOIA) request for information on World War II production with the Defense Supply Center Philadelphia, the successor organization to the Philadelphia Quartermaster Depot, but because the organization had turned over its records through 1950 to NARA some decades earlier, they had nothing of significance to release. Bernstein also found no "mention of any such procurement" in a number of unnamed archive collections yet failed to examine NARA holdings. And rather than consult the *Journal of the Orders and Medals Society of America*, earlier titled the *Medal Collector*, which has run many comprehensive articles on aspects of Purple Heart production and the decoration's history, he fatuously suggested that a "chemical test of the Purple Hearts might be able to date them." See Barton J. Bernstein, "Reconsidering 'Invasion Most Costly': Popular History Scholarship, Publishing Standards, and the Claim of High U.S. Casualty Estimates to Help Legitimize the Atomic Bombings," *Peace and Change* 24 (1999): 220–47, esp. 244–45.

39. Mrs. E. F. Wilkins, Bureau of the Mint, to Dr. Leland Howard, Acting Director of the Mint, March 26, 1945, memorandum, folder "Navy—Medals, Purple Heart, 1942–1945," Box 3, Correspondence Concerning U.S. Government Medals, 1917–1950, RUSM, RG 104, CP.

40. Dressel to Tayloe Ross, "Status of Medal Deliveries," April 9, 1945, memorandum,

folder "Medals—General—1925–1945 File #1," Box 2, General Subject Files on Medals, 1918–1978, RUSM, RG 104, CP.

41. "Recapitulation" (wording in this document such as "probably completed" indicates that this document was generated within the Treasury Department's Bureau of the Mint and not the Philadelphia Mint), May 14, 1945, memorandum, folder "Navy—Medals, Purple Heart, 1942–1945," Box 3, Correspondence Concerning U.S. Government Medals, 1917–1950, RUSM, RG 104, CP.

42. Treasury Department memorandum for the files by E. F. Wilkins, May 19, 1945, folder "Navy—Medals, Purple Heart, 1942–1945," Box 3, Correspondence Concerning U.S. Government Medals, 1917–1950, RUSM, RG 104, CP.

43. Howard to Dressel (unsent with large manuscript "X" crossing out the text), May 18, 1945, folder "Navy—Medals, Purple Heart, 1942–1945," Box 3, Correspondence Concerning U.S. Government Medals, 1917–1950, RUSM, RG 104, CP.

44. Tayloe Ross to Navy Department, Board of Medals and Awards, May 21, 1945; Dressel to Tayloe Ross, May 21, 1945; and Tayloe Ross to Dressel, May 22, 1945, all in Box 3, Correspondence Concerning U.S. Government Medals, 1917–1950, RUSM, RG 104, CP.

45. Arthur Rosenburg, Rex Manufacturing Company, to Tayloe Ross, May 24, 1945, RUSM, RG 104, CP. The Navy subsequently made arrangements to borrow 4,500 Air Medals and 9,000 Bronze Stars as well (Treasury Department memorandum for the files by Wilkins, May 19, 1945). Later that year the Navy obtained "5,000 excess Purple Heart cases from the Quartermaster Depot." See Tayloe Ross to Dressel, December 4, 1945; and Tayloe Ross to Dressel, December

11, 1945, folder "Army, Purple Heart 1941,"
Box 3, in General Subject Files on Medals,
1918–1978, RUSM, RG 104, CP.

Chapter 17. "Punishment from Heaven"

1. U.S. Senate, testimony of Secretary of
    Defense George C. Marshall, *Military
    Situation in the Far East: Hearings before
    the Committee on Armed Services and the
    Committee on Foreign Relations, United
    States Senate*, 82nd Cong., 1st sess., May 11,
    1951 (Washington, D.C.: GPO, 1951), pt.
    1, pp. 563–64.
2. The U.S. Army Southwest Pacific Area's
    (SWPA) was absorbed into the newly
    formed U.S. Army Forces Western Pacific
    (AFWESPAC).
3. Col. I. Ridgway Trimble, "Southwest Pacific
    Area: August 1944 through January 1946,"
    in Col. John Boyd Coates Jr., ed., *Surgery
    in World War II: Activities of Surgical
    Consultants*, vol. 2, in *Medical Department,
    United States Army* (Washington, D.C.:
    Office of the Surgeon General, Department
    of the Army, 1975), 744–45.
4. Ibid.
5. "Base 1" Medical, 6–7; "Base 2" Medical, 21;
    and "Base 3" Medical, 29–30, all in "Field
    Order 74."
6. Trimble, "Southwest Pacific Area," 745.
7. Palmer, Wiley, and Keast, *Procurement and
    Training of Ground Combat Troops*, 224–25.
8. Ibid.
9. Clarence McKitterick Smith, *The
    Medical Department: Hospitalization and
    Evacuation, Zone of Interior*, USAWWII
    series (Washington, D.C.: Center of Military
    History, United States Army, 1956),
    200–213. See also "Wednesday, June 20,
    1945, to Sunday, June 24, 1945," *Diaries of
    Henry Lewis Stimson*.

10. "Casualties," *Yank* 3 (February 2, 1945):
    17. Prior to 1945, efforts were made to try
    to place patients as close to their homes, but
    this became impractical during the casualty
    surge beginning June 1944. In January 1945
    civil and official media outlets were informed
    that "the number of returned sick and
    wounded is now so large that the Medical
    Department can no longer make it a policy
    to send patients to hospitals nearest their
    home towns."
11. "Summary of Redeployment Forecast,"
    March 14, 1945, p. 6, Demobilization
    Branch, Plans and Operations Division,
    Army Service Forces, call no. N8864, CARL.
12. August 10, 1945, Marshall to Leahy
    (unsent), 2–3, Box 74, Folder 20; and August
    7, 1945, "Size of the Army," Box 86, Folder
    25, distributed and briefed to reporters by
    Marshall as "not to be quoted" at his press
    conference of this date. Both from Marshall
    Papers Collection, GCML. Estimate does
    not include (a) Navy-Marine patients;
    (b) Army patients in "forward" hospitals
    including Hawaii, Okinawa, the Philippines,
    and Australia; (c) Army patients discharged
    and sent back to their units; (d) patients
    discharged from the Army and moved into
    the Veterans Administration system; or (e)
    Killed in Action—Died of Wounds. See also
    "Casualty Projections," 567.
13. Monthly combat casualties among just the
    Army and Army Air Force were averaging
    some sixty-five thousand during the casualty
    surge, with November, December, and
    January figures standing at seventy-two thou-
    sand, eighty-eight thousand, and seventy-
    nine thousand respectively in postwar tabula-
    tions. See Department of the Army, "Army
    Battle Casualties," 6.
14. See chapter 1 for a breakdown of this figure.
    Resiter, *Medical Statistics in World War II*,
    13–14, 43.

15. See chapter 1 for a breakdown of this figure. Roddis, "Naval and Marine Corps Casualties," 305–10; Department of the Army, "Army Battle Casualties," 5; and Skelton, *American Ex-Prisoners of War*, 5, 11.

16. Lt. Col. R. [Raymond] B. Marlin to Presidential Secretary William D. Hassett, July 26, 1946, folder "Miscellaneous," Box 801, White House Official File 190, HSTL. See also Giangreco and Moore, *Dear Harry*, 100–102.

17. Exchange of memorandums between Hassett and presidential secretary Matthew J. Connelly, July 22–July 30, 1946, including correspondence of Senator Scott W. Lucas, July 22, 1946, in Giangreco and Moore, *Dear Harry*, 100–102. The language in Marlin's memorandum leaves the impression that the estimate of seven thousand families included all the armed services. However such wording is commonly used even when referring to Army personnel alone. The War Department data Marlin had available to him included only the Army and Army Air Force and not the Navy, Marines, Coast Guard, and Merchant Marine. Consequently, the figure is actually larger than the estimate Hassett had before him.

18. Marshall (authored by Col. H. Merrill Pasco) to Mrs. George A. Moran, February 4, 1944, Box 34, Folder 37, Papers of George C. Marshall, GCML.

19. Ibid.; and Mrs. George A. Moran to Marshall, re: disposition of Cpl. George M. Moran, 26th Infantry Division, January 19, 1944; undated exchange of memorandums between Marshall and Col. H. Merrill Pasco, February 4, 1944, Box 34, Folder 37, Papers of George C. Marshall, GCML. With great effort and persistence, a sole surviving son could be extricated from combat as occurred when 101st Airborne Division chaplain, Capt. Francis L. Sampson, succeeded in having a Sgt. Frederick (Fritz) Niland in the division reassigned to stateside duty, according to 101st Division and family lore, against the soldier's wishes. The movie *Saving Private Ryan* was loosely (very loosely) based on this event. See Francis L. Sampson, *Look Out Below: A Story of the Airborne by a Paratrooper Padre* (Washington, D.C.: Catholic University of America Press, 1958), 78–79. Sampson was captured during the Germans' Ardennes counterattack and later rose to the Army's chief of chaplains as a major general.

20. Throughout the war Marshall had worked diligently to ensure that his sons were allowed absolutely no advantages due to their relation to him as when Clifton, who joined the anti-aircraft artillery, tried to use a badly injured foot as a means to maneuver his way to a stateside hospital from where he might then obtain a transfer to a Pacific-bound unit. By 1944 it was clear that the German Luftwaffe was no longer an offensive threat, and Clifton wanted to get to a theater where the anti-aircraft combat was still hot. Papa Marshall slammed the brakes on the scheme as soon as he got wind of it. The end of the war saw Clifton S. Brown, now a major, sidelined to the United States due to a bad flare-up of his burn injury, and he was released from Walter Reed Army Hospital in March 1946, in Bland and Stevens, *Marshall* 4:468, 569–70; Kathryn Tupper Marshall, *Together: Annals of an Army Wife* (New York: Tupper & Love, 1946), 3, 195–96, 200–203, 268–68; and Stanton, *World War II Order of Battle*, 429 (see 44th Antiaircraft Artillery Brigade).

21. September 18, 1944, speech before the American Legion, in Bland and Stevens, *Marshall* 4:592.

22. "Notes Used by the Secretary of War at Hearing in Executive Session before the Senate Military Affairs Committee re the

Bailey-May Bill, February 6, 1945," in *Diaries of Henry Lewis Stimson*, February 6, 1945.

23. Recounting meeting with Forrestal and Grew, *Diaries of Henry Lewis Stimson*, June 26, 1945.

24. An insightful and comprehensive look at the military's view of civilian war weariness, both institutionally and during this period, can be found in Michael D. Pearlman, *Warmaking and American Democracy: The Struggle over Military Strategy, 1700 to the Present* (Lawrence: University of Kansas Press, 1999), 239–79. See Chappell, *Before the Bomb*, for a fine account of the American public's attitudes in the spring and summer of 1945. The complex management of limited manpower assets for competing industrial-military needs during the final year of the war is examined in Keith E. Eiler, *Mobilizing America: Robert P. Patterson and the War Effort, 1940–1945* (Ithaca, N.Y.: Cornell University Press, 1997), 405–40.

25. Bland and Stevens, *Marshall* 5:211–12. Amendment to Paragraphy 3 on pages 7 and 8 of J.C.S. 1340/1, Proposed by General marshall. Leahy returned his copy of the document with the handwritten note: "I prefer action after the capture of Okinawa." The demand for Japan's "unconditional surrender" would both lead and close the Potsdam Declaration but was pointedly directed at "the Japanese armed forces" instead of the Japanese government itself. The distinction was immediately recognized by many in Japan's ruling circles but discarded by the dominant militarists among them.

26. Hattori, *Complete History of the Greater East Asia War* 4:194; *Reports*, vol. 2, bk. 2, p. 619; and Coox, *Final Agony*, 78.

27. Cohen, *Remaking Japan*, 137–46, esp. 141; and McColm telephone interview.

28. Bland and Stevens, *Marshall* 5:220–27, esp. 223, from a Marshall-edited transcript made by the Maryland Historical Society. It was published as "Some Lessons of History."

29. *Diaries of Henry Lewis Stimson*, June 26, 1945.

30. Ibid., July 2, 1945.

31. Ibid., June 19, 1945.

32. Ibid.

33. James F. Byrnes, *Speaking Frankly* (New York: Harper & Brothers, 1947), 207.

34. Herbert P. Bix, *Hirohito and the Making of Modern Japan* (New York: HarperCollins, 2000), 496–516, esp. 503; and Asada, "Shock of the Atomic Bomb," 477–512. This article is also available in Maddox, *Hiroshima in History*, 24–58. See also Butow, *Japan's Decision to Surrender*, 160–205; Hando, *Japan's Longest Day*, 12–18; plus Lawrence Freedman and Saki Dockrill, "Hiroshima: A Strategy of Shock," in *The Second World War in Asia and the Pacific* (New York: St. Martin's Press, 1994).

35. Tominaga, *Taiheiyo senso*, 756, in Asada, "Shock of the Atom Bomb," esp. 491–94.

36. The earliest comprehensive account of the Japanese decision to surrender and attempted coup d'etat is contained in *Reports*, vol. 2, bk. 2, pp. 669–759, constructed from postwar interrogations and interviews. Copiously documented, it has served as the basis of innumerable subsequent narratives although it is seldom unambiguously credited. A rich, but not excessively detailed, account of the coup attempt can be found in Weintraub, *Last Great Victory*, 567–603; and a brief, insightful analysis in Frank's *Downfall* (308–21) picks up on Kazutoshi Hando's theme (*Japan's Longest Day*, 191–212) that the coup was "not the fleeting dream of a few young officers but a plan in which some central figures in the Army were participants." Hando's Pacific War Research Society

account of the events of August 14, 1945, in *Japan's Longest Day*, was originally published in Japanese in 1965 and recently released in an English-language paperback edition (Kodansha, 2002).

37. Giangreco and Moore, *Dear Harry*, 294–95; and John Blum, ed., *The Price of Vision: the Diary of Henry A. Wallace, 1942–1946* (Boston: Houghton Mifflin, 1973), 473–74.

38. John Ellis van Courtland Moon, "Chemical Weapons and Deterrence: The World War II Experience," *International Security* 8 (Spring 1984): 3–35. See also John Ellis van Courtland Moon, "United States Chemical Warfare Policy in World War II: A Captive of Coalition Policy?" *Journal of Military History* 60 (July 1996): 495–511; and John Ellis van Courtland Moon, "Project SPHINX: The Question of the Use of Gas in the Planned Invasion of Japan," *Journal of Strategic Studies* 12 (September 1989): 303–23.

39. Gallicchio, "After Nagasaki," 400–402; John R. Sutherland, "The Story General Marshall Told Me," *U.S. News and World Report*, November 2, 1959, 53.

40. Pogue, *Marshall Interviews*, 420–25, esp. 424.

41. Leslie R. Groves, *Now It Can Be Told: The Story of the Manhattan Project* (New York: Harper and Brothers, 1962), 351–52.

42. Col. Stafford L. Warren to Maj. Gen. Leslie R. Groves, July 21, 1945, memorandum, with copy to J. Robert Oppenheimer, "Report on Test II at Trinity, 16 July 1945," RG 200, National Archives Gift Collection, "Diary of Lt. Gen. Leslie R. Groves," Microfilm Roll 2, NARA. Colonel Warren was chief of the Medical Section, Manhattan District.

43. Ibid.

44. Dower, *Embracing Defeat*, 36–37. See chapter 13, note 3, describing the various translations of the August 14, 1945, Imperial Rescript.

45. "2605," sect. 3, Japanese Propaganda Efforts, Headquarters United States Army Forces Middle Pacific, 1 November 1945, 70–71. The title "2605" is a reference to the year 1945 being the 2,605th year of Japanese history. AFMIDPAC's intelligence summary for 1944 had been titled "2604."

46. Foreign Minister Shigemitsu Mamoru in "'Magic'—Diplomatic Summary," No. 1791, September 15, 1945. See also Bruce Lee, *Marching Orders: The Untold Story of World War II* (New York: Crown, 1995), 547–51.

47. Cate and Olson, in Craven and Cate, *AAFWWII* 5:653–58, 674–75. See also chapter 12.

48. "Logistic Study for Projected Operations: Kyushu," Planning Division, Army Service Forces, March 1945, 33, 35, CARL.

49. A somewhat different situation existed for occupation troops entering Hiroshima and Nagasaki more than a month after the August 6 and 9 detonations. Based on data published shortly after the war on measured patterns of residual radioactivity in the ground zeros and fallout areas, plus lengths of operation in affected areas, estimates were made of the upper limits of the radiation doses that elements of the various American units could theoretically have been exposed to. Measurable contamination levels were low by the time that the 2d Marine, 24th and 41st Divisions arrived, and despite considerable activity in certain areas, the report concluded that there is no basis for assuming that any individual in the occupation units received even the theoretical upper limit doses. The same conclusion was reached for the approximately ten thousand U.S. and Allied POWs processed through Nagasaki for evacuation to hospital ships more than a month after the nuclear blasts. See DNA 5512F, "Radiation Dose Reconstruction U.S. Occupation Forces in Hiroshima and Nagasaki, Japan, 1945–1946," by W.

McRaney and J. McGahan, sponsored by Defense Nuclear Agency (Washington, D.C.: Defense Nuclear Agency, 1980).

50. Vice Chief of the Naval General Staff Onishi Tikijiro to Army Chief of Staff, General Umeza Yoshijiro; Chief of Naval General Staff, Admiral Toyoda Soemu; and Foreign Minister Togo Shigenori, August 13, 1945, in Butow, *Japan's Decision to Surrender*, 204–5. Lord Keeper of the Privy Seal Marquis Kido Koichi also used the twenty million figure when speaking to an interrogator for the Tokyo War Crimes Trials and characterized the figure as representing "casualties" instead of deaths.

51. Newman, *Enola Gay*, 134–48. Newman arrived at this monthly average by extrapolating from the conservative twenty million figure for Chinese deaths from the *Report of the Working Group for Asia and the Far East of the Temporary Sub Commission on the Economic Reconstitution of Devastated Areas* published by the United Nations Economic and Social Council in 1948 (the Chinese government maintains that the figure is closer to thirty million) plus figures for

hard-hit Indonesia and elsewhere. He notes that this is buttressed by recent scholarship such as Seiitsu Tachibana, "The Quest for a Peace Culture: The A-Bomb Survivor's Long Struggle and the New Movement for Redressing Foreign Victims of Japan's War," in *Hiroshima in History and Memory*, ed. Michael J. Hogan (Cambridge: Cambridge University Press, 1996), 184; Toshio Iritani, *Group Psychology of the Japanese in Wartime* (London: Kegan Paul, 1991), 237; and Gavan Daws, *Prisoners of the Japanese* (New York: William Morrow, 1994), 363. An extensive examination of this subject can be found in Gruhl, *Imperial Japan's World War II*. Gruhl is a former chief of the National Aeronautics and Space Administration's Cost and Economic Analysis Branch.

52. Coox, *Final Agony*, 108. See also Leon V. Sigal, *Fighting to a Finish: The Politics of War Termination in the United States and Japan* (Ithaca, N.Y.: Cornell University Press, 1988), 70; and Lester Brooks, *Behind Japan's Surrender: The Secret Struggle that Ended an Empire* (New York: McGraw-Hill, 1968), 31.

53. *Reports* 1:430.

Index

A

Abwehr (German military intelligence), 284n

Adams, Val Jr., 145

aircraft

American, B-17. *See* PB-1W; B-29 Superfortress, xvi, xviii, 16, 53, 79, 88, 108–10, 117, 129, 124, 203, 208, 235, 318; conversion of torpedo and bomber squadrons to fighter squadrons, 82; F-15E Strike Eagle, 310n; F4U Corsair, 147; F6F Hellcat, 147; heavy bombers in support of tactical operations, 130, 151, 158, 174, 203; nightfighters, 82, 134, 137, 174; PBY Catalina, 140; PB-1W airborne early warning aircraft, 309 n51; P-47D Thunderbolt, 174, 333n; P-61 Black Widow, 174; TBD Devastator, 135

British, 23, 81, 133, 307–08 n38; Lancaster, 23; Mosquito, 23, 133

Japanese, *Baka* piloted rocket, 86, 213, 224, 236, 238, 243, 305n; D3A "Val," 87; J2M Raiden "Jack," 88; J8M Shusui (no code name), 305n; *Kikka* (no airframe number or code name), 305n; K11W monoplane trainer (no code name), 137; K4Y1 training seaplane (no code name), 136, 329n; K5Y2 or Y3 intermediate trainer "Willow," 329n; E7K "Alf" reconnaissance seaplane, 136; Ki-17 "Cedar" biplane trainer, 137;

Ki-115 *Tsurugi* (no code name), 305n; Ki-201 *Karyu* (no code name), 305n; Ki-43 *Hayabusa* "Oscar," 309n; Ki-44 *Shoki* "Tojo," 309n; Ki-61 Hein "Tony," 88; Ki-76 "Stella" reconnaissance and liaison aircraft, 330n; Ki-84 *Hayate* "Frank," 309n; *Ohka*. *See* Baka

German, Fi156 Storch, 330n; Me262 twin-jet fighter, 305n; Me163 rocket-powered fighter, 305n

airfield development, American, 23, 36, 83–84, 116, 108–10, 151, 156, 174, 290n, 292n, 303n, 318n; British, 23–24; Japanese, 77, 79, 87–88, 140–41, 310n; Soviet, 27

Air Force (magazine), 5

Akune, 157, 159, 164, 210, 272

Alamo Scouts. *See* United States Army

Alanbrooke, Lord (Alan Francis Brooke, 1st Viscount Alanbrooke), 24, 291n

Amakusa-Shoto, 89

America First movement, 6

Anami Korechita, 45, 64, 69, 102, 156, 201, 204, 280n

Antisubmarine Warfare Operations Research Group, 98

Ardennes Offensive, 7, 13–15, 34, 41–42, 94–95, 289n, 344n

Arens, Mark P., 166

Ariake Bay, 45, 73, 85, 127-28, 141, 145, 147,
       153, 154, 156, 214, 216, 220, 227, 229–30,
       234, 240–41, 249–50, 252, 261–63, 268,
       270–72, 274–75. *See also* Operations
       (Japanese), Mutsu No. 1-B
Army and Navy Journal, 54
Arnhem, 170, 172, 182
Arnold, Henry H., 97, 112, 200, 292n
atom bomb, xi, xvii, 72, 128, 134–36, 147,
       224–25, 335n; Hiroshima, xiii, xvi, xxiii,
       2, 99, 105, 120, 163, 201, 205–06, 315n,
       317n, 323n, Nagasaki, xiii, xxiii, 110–11,
       120, 159, 201, 205–06, 322n; planned
       tactical use, xx, 110–12, 115, 120, 156,
       201–04; as psychological weapon, 97,
       110–12, 136, 194, 200–01, 231n, 358n;
       residual radioactivity, xx, 114, 202–06,
       346n; target set, 159, 201, 322n. *See also*
       Enola Gay, Manhattan Project, and WMDs
       (weapons of mass destruction)
Atomic Bomb Casualty Commission, 98
Atomic Energy Commission's Military
       Application Division, 98
atrocities, 118–19, 142, 223–24n, 294n, 299n,
       324n
Attlee, Clement, 26
       Australia, 18, 24–27, 112, 317n, 317n
Australian Imperial Force, 26; engineers, 35; 1st
       Corps, 25–26
Austria, 31, 42, 295n

B

Barrett & Hilp Company, Belair Shipyard, 177
Beebe, Gilbert W., 98
Beightler, Robert S., 40–41
Berlin, xxi, 8–10, 32–34, 291n
Bernstein, Barton J., 59, 302n, 315n, 319n,
       321–22n, 341–42n
Bessell, William W. Jr., 105, 109, 188
Biak, 138
Bintan (Singapore Strait), 133. *See also* Japan,
       Southern Resource Area
biological weapons, 115–16. *See also* WMDs

Bissell, Clayton L., 54, 57
Black, Percy G., 54
Bland, Larry I., xxi–xxii, 293n, 299n, 320n,
       322n
Borneo, 25. *See also* Japan, Southern Resource
       Area
Bose Peninsula, 66
Bougainville, 8, 26
Bower, Iris, 327n
Bowles, Edward, 98
Bradley, Omar, 32–33, 41, 291n
Brewster, Oswald C., 94
Bricker, John W., 54
British Army, 23–26, 115; Fourteenth Army,
       308n; Number 50 Mobile Field Hospital,
       327n; XXX Corps, 170, 172; 20th Anti-
       Tank Regiment, 24; 3d Infantry Division,
       24, 27; British Commonwealth (incorpo-
       rates British Empire), 23–27, 62, 83. *See
       also*, United Kingdom and South East Asia
       Command
British Commonwealth Occupation Force, 25.
       See also Commonwealth Corps
British East Indies Fleet, 23, 128
British Pacific Fleet, 23, 81–83, 128, 308n. *See
       also* Royal Navy
Bridges, Styles, 54
Brown, Allen Tupper, 199
Bundy, Harvey H., 49
Bungo Strait, 63, 72, 74, 160, 259, 303n
Burauen airfield complex, 151
Burma, 9, 24, 41, 194
Byrnes, James F., 16, 51, 96, 200

C

Camp Cook, Calif., 2, 30, 41
Camp San Luis Obispo, Calif., 30, 41
Canada, 24–25
Canadian armed forces, Canadian Army Pacific
       Force, 25–26; 6th Infantry Division, 25,
       388n; proposal to field an armored division,
       289n; Royal Canadian Air Force, 23; Royal
       Canadian Navy, 23, 288n

Capra, Frank, 10

Casey, Hugh J., 143

casualties, American, 3–4, 8–17, 31–34, 37,
47–48, 49–60, 61–63, 92, 94–101, 103–06,
166, 196–97, 282n, 297n, 302n, 314n,
317n 391n; American, blood supply for,
127, 138–40; American casualty surge
(1944-1945), xiii, 3, 8–15, 49–50, 94–95,
190, 196–97, 283n, 343n; American,
nonbattle, 3–4, 9, 11, 104, 197, 282n, 297n,
314n, 316n, 328n; Asia, closing months
of war, 203, 347n; Berlin (Soviet), 33–34;
British and Commonwealth, 10, 13–14,
24; Chinese, xi, xv, 123, 142, 156, 299,
347n; European civilians, 115, 323–24n;
Formosa (Taiwan), 298n; German, 9,
98–99, 115; Hiroshima, xxiiii, 114, 163,
323n; Iwo Jima, 128, 191, 328n; Japanese,
xv, xxiii, 19, 92, 98–99, 115, 117–20, 122,
123–24, 142, 166, 203, 315n, 323n, 377n;
Manila, 118–19, 325; Marshall on, xiii–iv,
12, 14–16, 50, 58–59, 92–98, 200, 202,
317n, 342n, 343n; Okinawa, xiv–xv, 41,
49, 51–53, 56, 58–59, 61, 75, 91, 96, 99,
119, 128, 145, 152, 153, 194, 326n; Peleliu,
191; psychological, 4, 9, 14, 59, 197, 297n,
313n; Saipan, 50, 118, 325n; "Saipan ratio,"
(incorporating JCS 924), 50–56, 92, 94,
188; "sinister ratio," 48, 51; Stimson on, 52,
57–59, 92–100; Truman on, 14, 56–60,
96-97, 99, 302n. *See also* hospitals

chemical weapons (poison gas), xx, 112, 115,
201–02, 261, 318n. *See also* WMDs

Chamberlain, Stephen J., 319n

Chifley, Joseph B., 26

China, xv, 18–19, 22, 41, 62, 78, 115, 123, 142,
156, 198, 204, 235, 237, 251, 278, 299n,
318n

Choshi Peninsula, 181; Iwo Jima, 128, 191,
328n

Churchill, Winston, x, xiv, 24–26, 32–34, 200,
291n

Collins, J. Lawton, 38

Combined Chiefs of Staff, 24, 32, 188, 291n

Commonwealth Corps, 24–27

Conferences, Cairo, 187; Casablanca, 187;
Potsdam, xiv–xvi, xix, 2, 24–25, 59, 82, 97,
99, 104–05, 110, 112, 127, 302n, 321n,
322n; Quebec (Octagon), 188; Quebec
(Quadrant), 187; Yalta, 21, 34, 188. *See also*
Potsdam Declaration

Commonwealth Corps, 24–25

Connelly, Matthew, 197

Coox, Alvin D., xix, xxi, 18, 19, 46, 123, 161,
295n, 334n

Custer, George Armstrong, 38

Czechoslovakia, 42, 157

D

DeBakey, Michael, xxi–xxii, 98-99, 296–97n

Denit, Guy B., 138, 194–95, 333n

Dewey, Thomas E., 54

Diller, LeGrande A., 317n

"Divine Wind," 76, 87, 175, 305n. *See also*
kamikaze

Donovan, William J., 49

Drea, Edward J., xix, xxi, 46, 123, 296n, 342n

Dressel, Edwin H., 190, 193

Du Bois, Arthur, 44, 294n

Dudley, John H., 143–44

E

East China Sea, 20, 22, 158, 164

East Indies. *See* Japan, Southern Resource Area

Eden, Anthony, 111

Eichelberger, Robert L., 38

Eisenhower, Dwight D., 14, 32–34, 42, 106,
291n

Elsey, George M., xvii, xxi, 302n, 321n

Enola Gay, xiv, xxiii, 53, 58–59, 114, 302n

Erskine, Graves B., 1

F

Ferrell, Robert H., 53–55, 57, 97, 293n, 301n,
326

Formosa (Taiwan), 7, 20, 23, 50, 73, 77–78, 80,
83, 90, 107, 134, 164, 188, 251, 255, 298
Forrestal, James, 58, 97
France, xvi, 3, 4–5, 10, 31, 42, 44, 50, 94, 101,
103, 106, 115, 118, 123, 164, 182, 281n,
284n, 294n, 327n
Frederick, Robert T., 38–39
Freeman, Douglas Southall, 51
Fuchida Mitsuo, 78
Fukuoka, 159–60, 209, 217, 252, 253, 254,
256, 257, 265
Fussell, Paul, xvi, 114

G

Gate Archipelago, 74
Gavin, James M., 38
Germany, xiii–xiv, xvi–xvii, 3, 5, 11, 13–17, 19,
21, 24, 28, 31–34, 36, 42, 45, 50–51, 53,
58, 63, 97, 99–101, 115, 133, 187, 201,
236, 283n, 284n, 287n, 305n, 314n, 321n,
324n; Berlin, xxi, 32-34; East Germany, 34;
National Redoubt, ("Nazi Redoubt"), 31,
295n. *See also* Ardennes Offensive; United
States Army, redeployment from Europe
Giles, Molly, 327n
Gillem, Alvin C., 38
Goto Islands, 74, 253
Great Britain. *See* United Kingdom
Grew, Joseph C., on potential casualties during
Downfall, 57–58, 97, 99, 200, 315n
Grosvenor, Gilbert H., 295n
Guadalcanal, 8, 9, 18, 115, 126, 152
Guam, 19, 118, 138–40, 181, 292n

H

Halifax, Lord Edward, 111
Handy, Thomas J., 42, 57, 93, 95, 322n
Harper's Magazine, 100
Harwit, Martin, xxiii, 59, 302n
Hassett, William, 197, 334n
Hata Shunroku, 163
Hattori Takushiro, 45, 61, 161, 280n
Hershey, Lewis B., 15, 51
Hess, William E., 14

Hida, 159, 270
Hirohito, xi, xvi, 6, 20–22, 76, 110–12, 123,
142–43, 162, 186, 199, 201, 206, 209, 226,
334n; Imperial Rescript, 143, 201–02, 331n;
surrender broadcast, xx, 112, 142, 186, 201,
203
Hiroshima, atomic bombing, xiii, xvi, xxiii, 2, 99,
105, 120, 163, 201, 205–06, 315n, 317n,
322n, 323n; in Ketsu-Go and Olympic
planning, 71, 82, 161, 163; military casualties, 163; total casualties, 323n
Hitler, Adolf, 5–6, 15, 32, 198
Hodges, Courtney H., 38
Hokkaido, 27, 69, 107, 208, 220, 255, 279,
290n
Hollandia, 138
Honshu, 22–24, 38, 41, 47, 64–65, 66, 67, 69,
71–72, 74, 75, 78–80, 85, 90, 93, 103,
105–09, 119, 128, 151, 152, 160, 162,
169–71, 174–76, 182–83, 185, 188, 195,
208, 220, 231–32, 235–37, 243, 258,
267–70, 279, 306n, 318, 321. *See also*
Operations (Japanese), Ketsu-Go
Hoover, Herbert, 53–58, 92–93, 96–97, 99,
301n; Hoover Memo, Truman reaction,
96–99
Hori Eizo, 47
hospitals, 4, 116, 138, 195, 197, 205, 317n;
field-mobile, 9, 98, 119, 138, 140, 192,
327n; general, 36, 138, 140, 195, 205,
317n, 343n; continental US, 7, 13, 138v39,
196, 317n, 343n, 344n; Japanese, 266,
270–71; ships, 139–40, 346n
Howard, Leland, 193
Huebner, Clarence R., 38
Hull, John E., 105, 111–12
Hull, Cordell, 57, 97, 301n

I

Iioka, 181–82
Ikeda, Lake, 150, 214, 256, 271–73
Imperial air forces (Army and Navy), xviii,
64–65, 80–81, 83, 88,107,109, 115, 128,
132, 134, 140, 154, 161, 235, 250, 266–67,

310n; air fleets (Navy), 78, 91, 278, 306n; Air General Army-air armies, 164–65, 67, 69, 277, 313n; conversion of training units to suicide units, xviii, 78–79, 92, 134, 305n; fuel availability, xviii, 22, 79–81, 88, 267, 307n; pilots, xviii, 76–80, 83, 85, 87–90, 115, 132–134, 312n; kamikaze, xviii, 2, 6–7, 20, 22, 75, 76–91, 92, 99, 127, 133–37, 139–40, 144, 147, 149, 175, 180, 191, 208, 235–38, 258, 305n, 306n, 309n, 311n, 312n, 313n, 330n; Sei-Go (unified air defense plan), 69; stealth characteristics of training aircraft, xviii, 133–37, 330n. *See also* aircraft, Japanese

Imperial General Headquarters, xv, xix, 5, 7, 19–22, 42–43, 45, 61–65, 67–71, 75, 77, 80, 93, 109, 112–13, 121, 127, 149–50, 158, 161–62, 164, 280n 305n, 313n; Operations Section (Army), 45, 161, 280

Imperial Japanese Army, 53, 56, 62–63, 184, 211, 317n; deployments-redeployments, 18–22, 28, 70, 120, 162; division types-capabilities, 20, 70–71, 73, 154, 162, 166, 182–83; *Izumi* (Spring) intelligence units, 165; Kirishima special forces units, 165; mobilization, 20, 56, 70–71, 92, 120

numbered formations:

general armies, First General Army, 64–65, 67, 69–71, 162, 303n; Second General Army, 64–67, 69, 71, 161, 163, 250, 258, 303n, 335n

area armies, 64–65, 67; Fifth Area Army, 27, 65; Eighth Area Army, 335n; Eleventh Area Army, 65; Twelfth Area Army, 65–68, 161; Thirteenth Area Army, 65; Fifteenth Area Army, 65, 74–75, 160; Sixteenth Area Army, 65–66, 72–75, 147, 149, 157–59, 162–63, 166, 167, 209, 248, 252–53, 257, 268, 270, 272, 274, 277n; Seventeenth Area Army, 65

armies, Thirty-sixth Army, 161–62; Fortieth Army, 73–74, 150, 154, 158, 163, 255, 267–68, 271–72, 274–76; Fifty-fifth Army, 71; Fifty-sixth Army, 157–58, 74; Fifty-

seventh Army, 74, 147, 154, 158, 255, 267v68, 272–77; Fifty-ninth Army, 71, 163

divisions, 1st Division, 19; 1st Armored Division, 21; 2d Armored Division, 20; 4th Anti Aircraft Division, 257; 6th Depot Division, 229; 8th Division, 19; 9th Division, 20; 10th Division, 19; 11th Division, 21, 265; 12th Division, 20; 14th Division, 19; 20th Division, 19; 23d Division, 20; 24th Division, 19; 25th Division, 21, 74, 75, 147, 49, 254, 265, 274–76; 28th Division, 20; 29th Division, 19; 32d Division, 19; 35th Division, 19; 41st Division, 19; 43d Division, 19; 46th Division, 255; 51st Division, 19; 52d Division, 19; 56th Depot Division, 220; 57th Division, 21, 74, 75, 157–58, 253, 265; 71st Division, 20; 77th Division, 74, 75, 149, 154–56, 265, 272–73, 276; 86th Division, 74, 149, 229, 252, 274–75; 109th Division, 20; 111th Division, 21; 120th Division, 21; 121st Divisions, 21; 125th Division, 151, 271; 145th Division, 252, 265; 146th Division, 74, 150, 154, 271–73; 154th Division, 74, 147, 254, 274–75; 156th Division, 74, 14, 252, 254, 274–76; 205th Division, 265; 206th Division, 149–50, 256, 271–73; 212th Division, 74; 147, 254, 265, 274–75; 216th Division, 74, 75, 149, 158, 257, 265, 272; 220th Division, 21; 221st Division, 21; 224th Division, 163; 225th Division, 265; 230th Division, 265; 231st Division, 265; 303d Division, 74, 149, 256, 271–73; 312th Division, 254; 351st Division, 253–54

regiments and brigades, 147, 4th Independent Tank Brigade, 74, 75, 157, 254; 5th Independent Tank Brigade, 74, 147, 255, 274–76; 6th Independent Tank Brigade, 74, 149, 273–74; 9th Independent Field Artillery Regiment, 273; 13th Medium Artillery Regiment, 217; 20th Medium Artillery Regiment, 273; 28th Medium Artillery Regiment, 273; 44th Independent

Field Artillery Regiment, 273; 54th Medium Artillery Regiment, 217; 98th Independent Mixed Brigade, 74, 149, 252, 274–75; 107th Independent Mixed Brigade, 74, 253; 109th Independent Mixed Brigade, 74, 255, 274–75; 118th Independent Mixed Brigade, 256; 122d Independent Mixed Brigade, 256; 125th Independent Mixed Brigade, 74, 150, 256, 272–73; 126th Independent Mixed Brigade, 257; Chikugo Group, 256; Goto Group, 74, Higo Group, 149, 157–58, 257. *See also* Kwantung Army; special forces; National Volunteer Combat Force (Peoples Volunteer Corps); redoubts

Imperial Japanese Navy, 7, 67–69, 76, 78, 80, 130, 233–34, 258–59. *See also* suicide craft, manned torpedoes, and midget submarines

Imperial Rescript. *See* Hirohito

Imperial War Ministry, 45, 64, 156, 201, 280n, 299n

Indochina, 80, 142. *See also* Japan, Southern Resource Area

Inland Sea, 159, 202, 329n

Inoguchi Rikibei, 76, 78, 306n

internment camps (Kyushu), 203

Ironhorse artificial harbor, 176–82, 311–12n

Ise Bay, 67

"island hopping," xiv, 19–20, 46, 62, 115, 201

Italy, 31, 33, 130, 160, 165, 185, 199, 329n

Iwakawa, 74, 215

Iwo Jima, xiv, 14, 16, 20, 49, 51, 53, 55, 58, 73, 92, 94, 100, 106, 114, 128, 143, 145, 150–51, 156, 158, 166, 185, 191–93, 230, 294, 318n

Izumi (Spring) special forces, 165

Izumi, 215, 244–45, 255

J

Japan, bombing of, xx, xvi, 2, 6, 58, 79, 110–11, 114, 117, 120, 123, 142, 163, 174–75, 187–88, 194, 200–03, 206, 323n; Diet (legislature), 121, 203; flooded rice fields, 171–74, 184, 243–44; food shortages and famines, 116–19, 159; Internal Resistance and Home Guard (National Resistance Program), 100, 114, 120–24, 159, 211, 223, 226–27, 229, 231, 240–41, 258; military manpower, 21, 47, 50, 55–56, 70–71, 92, 287n, 313n; National Volunteer Combat Force ("Peoples Volunteer Corps"), 121–24, 153, 158, 164, 165–66, 208–09, 211, 223, 226–27, 240, 258, 269, 271; perceptions/intelligence gained from American news media, 5–7, 10, 42–45, 120, 124, 199, 201; propaganda efforts, xix, 118–19, 123, 202–03, 236, 250–51; Southern Resource Area, 20, 78–80, 133–34; Supreme War Council, 201; surrender decision, xvi, xix–xx, 110–11, 174–75, 201; terrain, 27, 58, 88–89, 100, 104, 140, 143, 147, 154, 157–60, 162, 165–66, 171–85, 227–33, 240, 243–47; weather, 89–90, 107–10, 160, 170–71, 174–77, 180–81, 320n. *See also* casualties, Japanese; Imperial Japanese Army; Imperial Japanese Navy; Imperial air forces (Army and Navy); and suicide craft, manned torpedoes, and midget submarines

Japanese Demobilization Bureaus (incorporating Homeland Operations Record), 63–64, 155, 161, 163, 248

JCS 924, 50, 54–55, 92, 94, 188, 297n, 317n. *See also* casualties, "Saipan ratio"

Joint Chiefs of Staff, 22, 47, 50, 53, 82, 97, 112, 116, 127, 169, 174, 188, 199–200; June 18, 1945, meeting with President Truman, 58–60, 97, 104, 296n, 297n, 315n. *See also* State–War–Navy Coordinating Committee

Joint Intelligence Committee, 188

Joint Planning Staff, 106, 109, 188, 339n

Joint War Plans Committee, 105–06, 109, 188. *See also* Strategy and Policy Group

Joint Strategic Survey Committee, 50

Jones, James, 8

K

Kagoshima Bay, 74, 147, 150, 153–54, 256, 263, 274

Kikai Jima, 87, 174, 337n

kamikaze. *See* Imperial air forces (Army and Navy)

Kanmon Strait, 161

Kanto Plain. *See* Tokyo Plain

Kanto Sanchi (Mountains), 183

Karafuto, 65

Kasano Plain, 137, 153–54

Kashima, 170, 177, 181

Kashima Sea, 66

Katakai, 181

Kendrick, Douglas B., 138, 329n, 331n

Kenney, George, 292n

Kerama Retto, 89, 309n

Kido Koichi, 327n

"Kill All Order," 299n

King, Ernest J., xiii, 8, 16, 86, 95, 22, 106–09, 143, 187–88, 319–20n, 322n, Marshall-King letter to Congress, xiii–xiv, xvi, 8, 16, 51. *See also* Joint Chiefs of Staff

King, Mackenzie, 25

Kirishima, 159, 165, 255, 273–74

Kirk, Norman, 196

Kokura, 159, 201, 252–53, 322n

Konoye Fumimaro, xvi, 49, 323n, 334n

Korea, 7, 18–19, 21–22, 62, 65, 80, 118, 162, 208, 220, 231, 235, 237, 251, 312n, 318n, 323n

Korean War, 157, 159–60, 165–66, 185, 329n

Koshiki Retto, 128, 144, 150, 176, 246

Krueger, Walter, 37–38, 41, 158–159, 165

Kuchino-Erabu Shima, 144

Kujukuri, 66, 70, 170, 177, 180–81

Kumamoto, 159, 217, 252, 257, 265, 272

Kuril Islands, 27, 65, 316n

Kuro Shima, 144

Kusakaki Jima, 144

Kushikino, 141, 145, 149, 153, 220, 227, 229–31, 240–41, 244, 246, 255, 263, 268, 271–72, 275

Kwajalein, 89

Kwantung Army, 18–22, 28, 70, 75, 120, 147, 162, 182

Kyoto, 64, 129, 161

Kyushu, *See* Operations (Allied), Downfall; Olympic; Operations (Japanese), Ketsu-Go; Ketsu-Go, No. 3 (Kyushu)

Kyushu Mountains, 158, 165

L

LaVarre, William, 54

Lavrakas, Lefteris, 89, 131, 311n, 329

Leahy, William D., 58–59, 99, 187, 200, 302n, 345

Learned, Edmund. P., 97–99

Learned-Smith Committee, 96–99, 102–04

Lee, Robert E., 51

Lee, Willis A., 135

Le Havre, 3, 42

Lend Lease, 24, 27, 290

Leyte, 49, 77, 85, 138, 151, 153, 156, 233, 235, 237–38, 276

Leyte Gulf, Battle of, 7, 21, 77

Lincoln, George A., 93, 105–06, 109, 295, 317

Los Angeles Times, 16, 55, 175, 314n

Lucas, Scott, 197

Luzon, 20, 23, 35, 37–38, 49, 77, 106, 107, 112, 134, 138, 151, 153, 156, 175–76, 185, 195, 220, 224–25, 228, 233–34, 237, 244, 325n

Lingayen Gulf, 175

M

Magic and Ultra communications intelligence, xvi, 80, 89, 102, 105, 116, 200, 203, 296n, 312n, 321n; *"Magic"—Diplomatic Summary*, 102, 296n; *"Magic"—Far East Summary*, 135, 296n, 330n

Malaya, 128, 147, 308n. *See also* Japan, Southern Resource Area

Malone, George, 54

MacArthur, Douglas, xx, 20–21, 24–27, 28, 31–32, 35, 38–41, 45–48, 51, 63, 90, 104–12, 127, 138, 143, 151, 154, 157, 159–61, 163–64, 171, 174, 184, 187, 189, 194–95, 204, 289n, 295n, 302n, 317n, 318–19n, 319–20n

Maddox, Robert James, 321–22n

Manchuria, xx, 7, 18–22, 23, 27, 70, 75,
    120, 142, 147, 157, 162, 203, 208, 220,
    253–54n, 312n. *See also* Kwantung Army
Manhattan Project, 94, 111, 177, 202, 312n.
    See also atom bomb
Manila, 47, 105, 138, 139–40, 154, 175,
    176–77; Battle of Manila, 118–19, 222,
    234, 325n
Manila Bay, 29, 154, 175, 176–77, 234n
Marianas Islands, 6, 8, 10–11, 19, 22, 29, 50, 62,
    76, 79, 88, 108, 114, 126, 161, 290n
Marshall, George C., xiii–xiv, xvi, xix–xxi, 8,
    12, 14, 16, 24–25, 32–33, 37–42, 50–52,
    54, 57–59, 92–98, 100, 104–12, 115, 120,
    151, 188, 194, 197–203, 285–86n, 291n,
    298n, 299n, 317n, 319n, 320n, 321n,
    341n, 343n, 344n; "black book," 38, 293n;
    on atom bomb as psychological weapon, 97,
    110–12, 194, 201; on casualties and size of
    the Army, 12, 14, 41–42, 93, 95, 200, 299n,
    302n, 317n, 343n; on tactical use of atom
    bombs, xx, 110–12, 115, 120, 156, 201–04;
    Marshall-King letter to Congress on need for
    replacements, xiii–xiv, xvi, 8, 16, 51; Truman
    June 18, 1945, meeting with, 58–60, 97,
    104, 296n, 297n, 315n. *See also* Joint Chiefs
    of Staff; WMDs (weapons of mass destruc-
    tion)
Marlin, Raymond B., 343–44n
Maryland Historical Society, 200
Matsushiro, 162
McAuliffe, Anthony C., 38
McColm, George L., 56, 300n
McCormack, James, 98
Merrill's Marauders, 9
Meuse-Argonne Offensive, 1, 51, 100
Michela, Joseph A., 54
Midway, Battle of, 75, 115, 132, 135
Military government-civil affairs, 34, 36, 119,
    224, 116, 300n, 301n, 313n
Miller, Dwight M., 54, 96
Mitscher, Marc, 85
Mongol invasion, 160, 175, 305

Moran, George M., 344n
Morison, Samuel Eliot, 61, 125, 128, 134–35,
    310n, 327n, 328n
mountain warfare, 185–86
Mountbatten, Lord Louis, 321n
Mt. Aso, 158–59, 162, 165
Mt. Kaimon, 150, 154
Mt. Omori, 157, 164
Mt. Suribachi, 145, 150
Mulberry. *See* Ironhorse artificial harbor
Mutsu Bay, 106, 109, 318n
Miyazaki, 45, 67, 72–74, 127–28, 141, 143,
    145–47, 149–50, 165, 210, 213, 215–16,
    220, 227–30, 238, 240–41, 244–45, 250,
    254–55, 258, 261–65, 268, 270–75. *See also*
    Operations (Japanese), Mutsu No. 1-A

N

Nagano Prefecture, 22, 69, 80, 162, 183, 186,
    335n, 338n
Nagasaki, atomic bombing, xiii, xxiii, 110–11,
    120, 159, 201, 205–06, 322n, 346n; in
    Ketsu-Go and Olympic planning, 72, 74,
    159, 217, 253, 256
Nakazawa, Mitsuo, 154
National Air and Space Museum, xiv, xvi, xxiii,
    59, 302n
National Geographic Magazine, 44, 294–95n
National Volunteer Force. *See* Japan, National
    Volunteer Combat Force
New Britain (Rabaul), 9, 26
New Guinea, 5, 9, 18–19, 26, 35, 76, 112, 138,
    155, 166, 194, 299n, 335
New York Times, xiv, xvi, 16, 56, 95, 315n, 317n
News media (American), xiv, xvi, 5–7, 9–12,
    16, 24, 32, 38, 43, 51, 55–56, 95, 101,
    105–06, 120, 124, 199, 202, 314n, 317n,
    320n, 343n. *See also* Japan, monitoring the
    American news media
New Zealand, 24, 26–27; 2d Infantry Division,
    24
Nimitz, Chester A., 16, 29, 55, 106–09, 174,
    187, 292n, 319–20n, 322n

Nishihara Kanji, 154

Nobeoka, 157, 159, 164, 209–10, 216

Normandy, 8, 11, 23, 43–45, 106, 115, 125–26, 130, 145, 164, 172, 177, 180–82, 327n

North Africa, 9

Nuremberg Tribunal, 98

O

Office of Censorship, 5, 12, 199

Office of Strategic Services, 49, 301

Office of War Information, 9, 110

Office of War Mobilization, 3, 16, 51, 96

Office of War Mobilization and Reconversion, 57, 97

Okinawa, 29, 31, 35–36, 37–38, 41, 47, 67, 71, 88, 99–100, 106, 108, 110, 130, 138–40, 161, 174–75, 216, 251

Okinawa, Battle of, xiv–xv, xix, xxiii, 14, 16, 19–20, 23, 24, 37–38, 41, 49, 51–53, 56, 58–60, 61, 63, 65, 69, 71, 73, 75, 77–78, 80–91, 92, 94, 96–97, 104, 106, 114, 118–19, 124, 126–28, 131–32, 139–40, 143, 145, 153, 156, 158–60, 162, 166, 168–169, 185, 192–93, 194–95, 200, 206, 212, 118, 220–23, 234, 235, 238, 251, 261. *See also* casualties, Okinawa

O'Laughlin, John Callan, 54

O'Mahoney, Joseph, 192

Ominato, 106–09, 318n

Onishi Tikijiro, 123

Operations:

Allied:

Arc Light, 130; Avenger, 130; Bodyguard, 164, 184n; Cobra, 118, 138; Coronet, xviii–xix, xxii–xxiii, 23, 25–26, 32–35, 38, 50, 55, 79, 81–83, 85–86, 89–90, 96, 104–05, 110, 116, 124, 127, 151, 156, 160, 169, 171, 174–82, 185–86, 190, 194–96, 312n, 321n, 338n; Downfall, xiii, xvii, xix–xxi, xxiii, 29, 160, 188, 312n; Forager, 3, 118; Fortitude South, 284n; Iceberg, 83, 132, 139, 312n; Majestic, 295n; Olympic, xvii–xviii, xix, xxii, 22, 25, 33, 35, 37–38, 27, 50, 53,

55–56, 59, 61, 74, 78–90, 94–96, 104–09, 112, 116, 121, 124, 125–32, 137–39, 143, 154–55, 157–60, 164, 167, 169, 171, 174–75, 177, 182–83, 190, 193, 195–96, 200, 203, 207, 295n, 302n; Overlord, 3, 106, 115, 118; Pastel, 38, 164; Roundup, 106; Starvation, 161; Zipper 128, 308

Japanese:

Ketsu-Go, xix, xxii, 65, 67, 69, 120–21, 131–32, 137, 154, 157–58, 162–64; Ketsu-Go, No. 3 (Tokyo Plain), xix, 65, 70, 79, 112–13, 161, Ketsu-Go, No. 6 (Kyushu), xix, 66–67, 71, 73, 78–79, 90, 112, 143, 145, 155, 161, 321n, 329n; Ketsu-Go, other regional operations, 65, 67; Mutsu No. 1 (Southern Kyushu), xix, 73, 74, 155, 157; Mutsu No. 1-A (Miyazaki Plain), 74–75; Mutsu No. 1-B (Ariake Bay), 74–75; Mutsu No. 1-C (Satsuma Peninsula), 74–75, 154, 158; Mutsu No. 2 (northern) and No. 3 (central) Kyushu; Mutsu, other local operations, 73–75; Sei-Go (unified air defense plan), 69; Sho Go No. 1 and 2 (Philippines and Okinawa), 65, 162

Osborn, Frederick H., 10

Osumi Peninsula, 67, 72, 210, 213–14, 244, 252, 254. *See also* Mutsu No. 1-B

P

Palmer, Kyle, 16, 55, 286n, 314n

Palau Islands, 19

Panama Canal, 23, 31, 36

Pasco, H. Merrill, 198, 344

Patriotic Citizen's Fighting Corps. *See* Japan, National Volunteer Combat Force

Patton, George S., 32, 41, 44, 95, 110, 291n, 293n

Pearl Harbor, 5–6, 18, 21, 31, 86, 115, 123, 128, 149, 189, 196

Peleliu, 19, 143, 156, 191

Peoples Volunteer Corps. *See* Japan, National Volunteer Combat Force

Philippine Islands, 5–7, 18–20, 22, 30, 35, 38, 42, 62, 64, 76–78, 80, 83, 85, 100, 107, 114, 125, 127, 131–32, 138, 142, 151, 162, 166, 169, 175–76, 191, 194, 303, 216, 222, 236, 251, 261, 293–94n, 305n, 312n, 317n, 325n, 343n. *See also* Manila

Philippine Scouts, 3, 9

Philippine Sea, 19, 158, 176, 203

Pogue, Forrest, 202, 291n, 293n, 341n

Points Discharge System, 3, 12, 15, 51, 96, 198, 281n, 284n, 285n

Poison gas. *See* chemical weapons

Potsdam, 32. *See also* conferences, Potsdam

Potsdam Declaration, xx, 104, 110–11, 200–01, 278 (text), 345n

prisoners of war, American, 4–5, 9–11, 13, 42, 142, 250–51, 279, 282n, 294n, 297n, 299n, 314n, 333n, 346n; German, 115, 234n; Japanese, 47, 165, 171, "Kill All Order," 299n. *See also* atrocities; war criminals

proximity fuze, xviii, 134–37

Purple Heart, xxi, 189–93, 339n, 341–42n; Navy "borrow[s]" Army medals, 192–93; production totals, 341n

Putnam, William, 143

Q

Qui Nhon, 80. *See also* Japan, Southern Resource Area

R

Rabaul, 26

Radford, Arthur, 167

Red Army. *See* Soviet Army

Red Cross, American, 163; International, 323, n27

redoubts, Konoye Fumimaro on, 334n; Nagano (central Honshu), 22, 69, 80, 162, 183, 186, 335n, 338n; National (Bavaria-Austria), 31, 34, 295n, Mt. Aso (northern Kyushu), 158–60, 162, 165; Tunghua (eastern Manchuria-northern Korea), 162

Redeployment. *See* United States Army, redeployment from Europe

Rex Manufacturing Company, 190, 193–93, 339n

Ridgway, Matthew B., 38, 160

Robbins Company, 339n, 340n, 341n

Roosevelt, Franklin D., xvii, 28, 32, 53, 56–57, 94, 189, 201; on raising draft quotas for Downfall, xv, xvii, 12, 51, 52, 95, 142

Rosenman, Samuel L., 57

Ross, Charley, 56

Ross, Nellie Tayloe, 191

Royal Air Force, 23–24

Royal Australian Navy (incorporating Commonwealth naval forces), 23, 27, 288n

Royal Navy, 22–24, 81, 135, 288n, 337; ships, *Illustrious*, 303n; *King George V* class, 128. *See also* British East Indies Fleet; British Pacific Fleet

Rusk, Dean, 98–99

Russia, 9, 10, 18, 49, 80, 169, 208, 299. *See also* Soviet Union

Ryukyu Islands, 67, 209, 211, 219, 222, 235

S

Sakhalin, 27, 65

Sasebo, 73–74, 159

Saipan, 19, 50, 110, 118, 198, 205–06, 325

"Saipan Ratio." *See* casualties, "Saipan ratio"

Sato Naotaki, 116, 334

Satsuma Peninsula, 45, 67, 73–74, 127–28, 145, 149–50, 154, 158, 163, 210, 213, 220, 230, 244, 249, 250, 256, 268, 270–71, 273. *See also* Operations (Japanese), Mutsu No. 1-C

Sea of Japan, 22, 162, 234, 242

Sendai, 105–08, 144, 149, 156, 210, 244–45, 256, 269, 272, 274

Shanghai, 21, 62, 164, 208

Sherman, Forrest, 109, 311n

Sherman, Mr. and Mrs. Raymond, 197

Shikoku, 63, 71, 105–06, 131, 163, 203, 208, 220, 231, 235, 237, 358, 279, 303

Shimokita Peninsula, 67

Shimpu Tokubetsu Kogekitiai (Divine Wind Special Attack Corps). *See* kamikaze

Shockley, William B., 92, 98–99, 115, 123, 315n

Sigami Bay, 181

Singapore. *See also* Japan, Southern Resource Area

Smith, Dan T., 97–99, 102–04

Smith, Howard, 54

Smith, Truman, 54

Snyder, John, 51

Solomon Islands, 35, 76, 115

South East Asia Command, 48

Southwest Pacific Theater, 127, 159

Soviet Union (incorporates Russia), xvi, 2, 9–10, 18, 22, 49, 80, 208, 334n; plans for invasion of Japan, 27; Soviet Army (incorporates Red Army), 18–19, 27, 34, 162, 286n; Soviet Navy, 27, 290–91n; 87th Rifle Corps, 27

Spaatz, Carl A., 29, 110, 322

Sprague, Clifton A. F., 88

Stalin, Joseph, xiv, 2, 19, 33, 200n, 286n

State-War-Navy Coordinating Committee, 199

Stilwell, Joseph W., 38, 41, 292n

Stimson, Henry L., 28, 49; atom bomb and ultimatum on Japan, 104, 110–12, 199–202, 322n; on Army manpower, xiii–xv, xix–xx, 8,12, 14–16, 29, 41–42, 53, 55–59, 92–100, 102–04, 283n, 285n, 299n; Hoover memo and June 18 meeting with President Truman-JCS, 55–59, 92–94, 96–97, 301n; Learned-Smith Committee, 97–99, 102–04

Strategy and Policy Group, 93, 105. *See also* Joint War Plans Committee; Joint Planning Staff

Strong, Kenneth, 33

Sugiyama Hajime, 162

suicide craft, manned torpedoes, and midget submarines, 131–32, 145, 217, 234, 249, 274; *Kaiten* (Those Who Shake the Heavens, manned torpedo), 131, 328n, *Renraku-tei* (liaison boat, Army), 130–32, 274, 277, 328n; *Shinyo* (Sea Quake, suicide craft),

127, 130–32, 217; *Kairyu* (Sea Dragon, midget submarine),130–31, 216, 242, 259, 328–29n

Sumatra, 18, 22. *See also* Japan, Southern Resource Area

Sutherland, Richard K., 319n

Suzuki Kantaro, 123, 201, 203

Sylvania Electric Products, Inc., 135

T

Tague, James R., 81

Tanegashima Island, 74, 252, 255

Taylor, Maxwell D., 38

Tinian, 19, 114, 118, 317n

Togo Shigenori, 201, 327n, 334n

Toi Point, 147

Tojo Hideki, 20–21, 186, 198

Tokyo, xviii, 3, 6, 21, 50, 59, 63, 66–7, 69, 82, 88, 103,105, 108, 111, 115–16, 119, 122–23, 151, 163, 170, 176–77, 182; fire-bombed, 111, 188, 206

Tokyo (Kanto) Plain, 23, 26, 35, 55, 62–72, 93, 96, 99, 106–08, 112–13, 122, 145, 151, 160–63, 166, 170–71, 184–85, 236

Tokyo Bay, 177, 184–85

Toyoda Soemu, 327n

Treaty of Versailles, xvi, 101, 174

Trimble, I. Ridgway, 194–95

Trinity atom bomb test, 202

Truk, 19

Truman, Harry S., xii–xvii, xix–xxiii, 1–2, 4, 15–16, 24, 47–48, 49–52, 53–59, 62, 82, 85, 92, 110–12, 124, 127, 142–43, 151, 174, 200–04, 205–06, 296n, 297n, 302n, 315–16n, 320n, 321–22n; commands artillery regiments, 51; Hoover memo and June 18 meeting with service secretaries-JCS, 53–59, 92–101, 104, 301n; as senator and vice president, 15–16, 51–52, 192, 298n; World War I, 1, 51, 100–01

"Truman-Grew-Hull-Stimson-Vinson exchange," 57–58

Tsugaru Strait, 67

Tsuno, 147, 156, 164

Tunghua, 162. *See also* redoubts

Turner, Richmond Kelly, 85, 126, 144

typhoons, 175–81; *Barbara* (Luzon 1946),
    175–76; *Louise* (Okinawa 1945),175;
    Philippine Sea (1944), 308n; Philippine Sea
    (1945), 82, 308n

U

Uji Gunto, 144

Ultra. *See* Magic and Ultra communications
    intelligence

Umeza Yoshijiro, 327n

United States, public support/opinion, x, xiii,
    xv, 3, 5–7, 8-16, 28, 43, 51–53, 95–96, 98,
    103, 105, 195–200, 250, 298n. *See also*
    Combined Chiefs of Staff; Joint Chiefs of
    Staff; War Department

United Kingdom (incorporates Great Britain),
    xvi, 2, 10, 14, 22, 24, 26, 44, 56, 101, 109,
    138, 187, 278, 281n. *See also* British Army;
    Royal Air Force; Royal Navy

Ulithi Atol, 77, 81, 85–86, 331n

United States Army:

Army Air Forces. *See* United States Army Air
    Forces

Army Forces in the Pacific (AFPAC) (also
    referenced as "Manila"), 47, 105, 138, 163,
    295n, 296n

Army Ground Forces (AGF), 12–13, 41, 94–95,
    97–99, 102–04

Army Medical Corps, 10, 29, 98, 138, 196, 317n

Army Service Forces (ASF), 12–13, 29, 35, 53,
    103, 115–16, 118

Army Specialized Training Program (ASTP), 6,
    12, 25, 103

Army Quartermaster Corps (incorporating
    Philadelphia Quartermaster Depot), 189,
    192, 342n; Quartermaster General, 44

Bureau of Public Relations, 9

Engineering Intelligence Division, 143

Engineer support, 31, 35, 143, 174–75, 177,
    180, 185, 292n, 336n

Heraldic Section, Army Quartermaster General,
    44, 295

manpower needs, 2–5, 14–16, 29–31, 37–42,
    52–53, 92–99, 102–05

National Guard, 35, 41

Operations Division, 57, 92, 97–98

Phantom and unactivated "ghost" divisions,
    43–45, 295n

redeployment from Europe, xxi, 8, 28–36,
    38–42, 103–04, 185–86, 188, 199.

redeployment categories (divisions), 31–33, 185.
    See also Points Discharge System

roll-up from Southwest Pacific, 35

Special Services Division, Army Service Forces,
    10

Training and staging bases, 30. *See also* hospitals

United States Army formations:

armies and army groups, First Army, xiv, 31–32,
    38, 40, 53, 170, 175, 181, 293n; Third
    Army, 32–33, 41, 157, 293n; Sixth Army,
    xix, 35, 37, 40, 45, 75, 104, 116, 126, 141,
    143–55, 156–66, 174, 195, 207, 248, 258,
    318n, 333n; Seventh Army, 39; Eighth
    Army, 31, 38, 40, 152, 161, 170, 175, 184,
    186; Ninth Army, 32–33, 293n; Tenth
    Army, 26, 31, 37–38, 40–41, 61, 119, 153,
    168, 292n, 328n; Twelfth Army Group, 32

corps, I Corps, 40, 143, 146–47, 151; III Corps,
    38, 40; V Corps, 38, 40, 329n; VII Corps,
    38, 40; IX Corps, 40, 145, 150, 154, 327n;
    X Corps, 40; XIV Corps, 40, 222; XI Corps,
    40, 147, 149, 154; XIII Corps ("A" Corps),
    38, 40; XVIII Airborne Corps, 38, 40; XXIV
    Corps, 38, 40, 119; "lettered" corps (B, C,
    D, E), 38, 40

divisions, 1st Cavalry Division, 37, 40, 149;
    2d Infantry Division, 2, 30; 4th Infantry
    Division, xxii, 2, 40; 5th Infantry Division,
    3, 30, 40; 7th Infantry Division, 40,
    159; 8th Infantry Division, 30, 40; 10th
    Mountain Division, 30, 185–86; 11th
    Airborne Division, 30; 24th Infantry
    Division, 40, 346n; 25th Infantry Division,

8, 37, 40, 146; 28th Infantry Division, 30, 40; 32d Infantry Division, 9, 40; 33d Infantry Division, 40, 146; 35th Infantry Division, ix, 30, 40, 100–01; 37th Infantry Division, 40–41; 40th Infantry Division, 40, 144, 150, 327n; 41st Infantry Division, 40, 147, 346n; 43d Infantry Division, 37, 40, 149; 44th Infantry Division, 3, 30, 40, 281n; 45th Infantry Division, 39; 63d Infantry Division, 294n; 69th Infantry Division, 5, 30, 338n; 75th Infantry Division, 294n; 77th Infantry Division, 37, 40, 150; 78th Infantry Division, 30, 338n; 81st Infantry Division, 40, 150; 82d Airborne Division, 38; 86th Infantry Division, 30, 40–42, 74, 95, 293–94n; 87th Infantry Division, 2, 30, 40; 91st Infantry Division, 30, 40, 338n; 95th Infantry Division, 30, 33, 40; 96th Infantry Division, 38, 40; 97th Infantry Division, 30, 40–42, 95; 98th Infantry Division, 37, 40, 150; 100th Infantry Division, 30, 338n; 104th Infantry Division, 30, 40; Americal Division, 37, 40, 149; Philippine Division, 5; Seventh Army Airborne Division (Provisional), 39; 4th Armored Division, 295n; 10th Armored Division, 295n; 13th Armored Division, 30, 40; 20th Armored Division, 2, 30, 40

regiments, 112th Regimental Combat Team, 40, 149; 158th Regimental Combat Team, 40, 144. 327n; 379th Field Artillery Regiment, 51; 381st Artillery Regiment, 51; Merrill's Marauders (5307th Composite Unit [provisional]), 9

battalions and specialized units, Alamo Scouts, 158, 165; 9th Ranger Infantry Battalion, 158; 931st Engineer Construction Group (Aviation), 143

United States Army Air Forces, xviii, xxi, 3–4, 12-13, 23, 29, 34, 36, 43, 53, 83, 87, 95, 97–8, 107–09, 117, 129–30, 134, 151, 161, 187–88, 196; Fifth Air Force, 36, 83, 114, 134, 151, 290n; Eighth Air Force, 23, 36, 290n; Fifteenth Air Force, 36; Twentieth Air Force, 290n; redeployment to Pacific, 36; US Army Far East Air Forces, 290n; US Army Strategic Air Forces, 29. *See also* aircraft, American

United States Congress, manpower issues and Selective Service, 4, 10, 12, 14–16, 51-54, 56, 63, 98, 103, 191–92, 194–96, 320n; Hoover testimony, 96; Marshall-King letter to Congress on need for replacements, xiii–xiv, 16; Marshal testimony 194, 285–86n; Stimson testimony, 199, 285–86n, Truman's June 3, 1945, message to Congress, 62; Truman as senator and as vice president observing floor fights over changes in Selective service legislation, 15–16, 51–52, 192, 298n

United States Marine Corps, 1, 3–4, 9, 16, 28–29, 37–38, 52-53, 83, 95, 115, 118–19, 128, 134, 138–39, 144–45, 149–53, 166, 168–69, 171, 176, 189, 190–92, 196, 202; III Amphibious Corps, 40; V Amphibious Corps, 40, 144, 149, 271; 1st Marine Division, 40; 2d Marine Division, 40; 3d Marine Division, 1, 40, 149, 294n; 4th Marine Division, 40, 294n; 5th Marine Division, 40, 145, 151, 294n; 6th Marine Division, 40, 153; casualties, 4, 128, 191. *See also* United States Navy, Pacific Fleet Amphibious Force

United States Merchant Marine, 3–4, 282n, 297, 314

United States Mint (Philadelphia), 189–93

United States Navy, xiii, xviii, 8, 16, 20, 23, 28–29, 35, 42, 52–53, 55, 58, 61, 76—91, 95, 97, 109–10, 119, 127–40, 154, 160, 176–82, 187–93, 196, 199, 242, 258; Bureau of Ordnance, 86, 135; casualties, 4, 128; Fifth Fleet, 82–83, 89; Seventh Fleet, 127, 160, 338n; Task Force 58, 85, 88, 135

Pacific Fleet Amphibious Force, Task Force (TF) 51, 85, 126, 144; III Amphibious Force, (incorporating 3dth Fire Support Group), 126, 128, 149; V Amphibious Force, (incorporating 5th Fire Support Group), 126, 128, 149–50; VII Amphibious Force, (incorporating 7th Fire Support Group), 126, 128, 139, 146; Reserve Amphibious Force ("Reserve Afloat"), 127, 140

Ships, craft, and attached foreign vessels, *Aaron Ward*, 309, 311; *Achernar*, 139; *Antietam*, 81; *Aquitania*, 29, 281n; *Augusta*, 123, 280n; *Bon Homme Richard*, 81; *Borie*, 330n; *Boxer*, 81; *Bunker Hill*, 82, 85; *Callaghan*, 134–33; *Cassin Young*, 133–34; *Eberle*, 131, 311n, ; *Essex*, 82; *Essex* class, 81–82, 307n; *Enterprise*, 82, 85, 137; *Franklin*, 76–77, 82, 191, 308n; *Hornet*, 82; *Horace A. Bass*, 329n; *Ile de France*, 29, 281n; *Independence* class, 82; *Intrepid*, 82; *John Ericsson*, 2, 281n; *Kimberly*, 87; *Lake Champlain*, 81–82; *Langley*, 82; LCI(G)-365, 132; LCI(M)-974, 132; LCM(R)-195, 309n; LCS(L)-7, 132; LCS(L)-26, 132; LCS(L)-49, 132; Liberty and Victory ships, 35, 55, 90, 177, 181; *Little*, 309n; LST 610, 132; LST 925, 132; LST(H)-929, 139; LST-1028, 132; *Mauretania*, 29, 281n; *Midway*, 81-82; *Midway* class, 82; *Missouri*, 31, 186; *Nieuw Amsterdam*, 29, 281n; PC-1129, 132; *Porterfield*, 132; *Prichett*, 133, 330n; *Princeton*, 82; *Queen Elizabeth*, ; *Queen Mary*, 3, 29, 281n; *Randolph*, 85; *Roosevelt*, 81-82; *Rutland*, 145; *St. Lo*, 77; *Saipan* class, 82; *Saratoga*, 81–82; *Shangri-La*, 81; *Tarawa*, 82; *Wadleigh*, 85; *War Hawk*, 135; and *Wasp*, 82

Salvage and Rescue Group, Luzon Attack Force, 176

United States Selective Service, viii, xiv, 4–7, 15–16, 50–53, 95–96, 98, 103–04, 197, 282n, 294n, 298; Legislation to draft women nurses, 6, 15, 51

United States Strategic Bombing Survey, 78–79, 117, 130, 306n, 310n, 323n, 334n

V

Van Fleet, James A., 38, 294n

Versailles Treaty, xvi, 101, 174

Vietnam, xvi, 119, 130, 165, 173, 186, 313n

Vinson, Fred M., 57, 97, 301n, 315n

Vischer, Peter, 54

W

Wainwright, Jonathan, 7

Wallace, Henry, 301n

war criminals, 279, 326n, 327n, 333n, 347n

War Department, xv, xvii, 3, 9, 11–15, 33, 41–42, 44, 50–51, 109, 115, 142, 185, 191, 196–98, 285n, 296n, 318n; organization, xiv, 109

White, Horton V., 45

Whitehill, Walter Muir, 187

Willoughby, Charles A., 47–48, 51, 90, 104, 106, 169, 171, 204; "sinister ratio," 48, 51

WMDs (weapons of mass destruction), xx, 111–12, 115–16, 156, 204

World War I, xvi, 51, 100–01, 145, 168, 199, 202

Wright, Quincy, 98–99

Y

Yamamoto Isoroku, 6, 115

Yank, 5, 9v10, 13–15, 44, 283–84n, 294n, 298n

Yeaton, Ivan D., 54

Yellow Sea, 28, 78, 234, 242

Yokoyama Isamu, 75, 158–59, 162–63, 333n

Yonai Mitsumasa, 69

Z

Zone of the Interior, 139, 196

About the Author

D. M. Giangreco served as an editor at *Military Review* at the U.S. Army Command and General Staff College for twenty years. He has lectured widely on national security matters. An award-winning author of eleven books on military and sociopolitical subjects, he has also written extensively for various national and international publications and news agencies. Mr. Giangreco was awarded the Society for Military History's 1998 Moncado Prize for his article "Casualty Projections for the US Invasions of Japan, 1945-1946: Planning and Policy Implications." He also won the Gerard Gilbert Award (1988 France and Colonies Philatelic Society) for his book *Roosevelt, de Gaulle, and the Posts: Franco-American War Relations Viewed Through their Effects on the French Postal System, 1942–1944,* and his article "The Truth about Kamikazes" was the principal nomination of U.S. Naval Institute, Annapolis, for the Association of Naval Aviation's award for Best Article of 1997 on Naval Aviation. Mr. Giangreco's work has been translated into French, German, Spanish, Russian (pirated), Japanese, and Chinese. Some of his most recent books are *Dear Harry,* on the correspondence of "everyday Americans" with the Truman White House (2000), *Artillery in Korea: Massing Fires and Reinventing the Wheel* (2003), *Eyewitness D-Day* (2004), and *Eyewitness Vietnam* (2006).